BUSINESS DATA COMMUNICATIONS

THIRD EDITION

David A. Stamper

The Benjamin/Cummings Publishing Company, Inc.

Redwood City, California • Menlo Park, California
Reading, Massachusetts • New York • Don Mills, Ontario • Wokingham, U.K.
Amsterdam • Bonn • Sydney • Singapore • Tokyo • Madrid • San Juan

Sponsoring Editor: Michelle Baxter
Assistant Editor: Lisa Weber
Production Coordinator: Eleanor Renner Brown
Text Design: Victoria Vandeventer
Cover Design: Victoria Vandeventer
Illustrations: Ben Turner Graphics
Copy Editor: Anna Huff
Composition: Beacon Graphics Corporation

The basic text of this book was designed using the Modular Design System, as developed by Wendy Earl and Design Office Bruce Kortebein.

Many of the names used by manufacturers and sellers to distinguish their products are claimed as trademarks. Where those names appear in this book, and Benjamin/Cummings was aware of a trademark claim, the symbol for trademark (™) or registered trademark (®) appears after the name.

Library of Congress Cataloging-in-Publication Data

Stamper, David A.
    Business data communications / David A. Stamper. -- 3rd ed.
        p.   cm.
    Includes bibliographical references and index.
    ISBN 0-8053-7720-4
    1. Data transmission systems.   2. Computer networks.   I. Title.
TK5105.S734   1991
004.6--dc20   91-27105
                                                                            CIP

ISBN 0-8053-7720-4

2 3 4 5 6 7 8 9 10 HA 95 94 93 92

The Benjamin/Cummings Publishing Company, Inc.
390 Bridge Parkway
Redwood City, California 94065

To Virginia

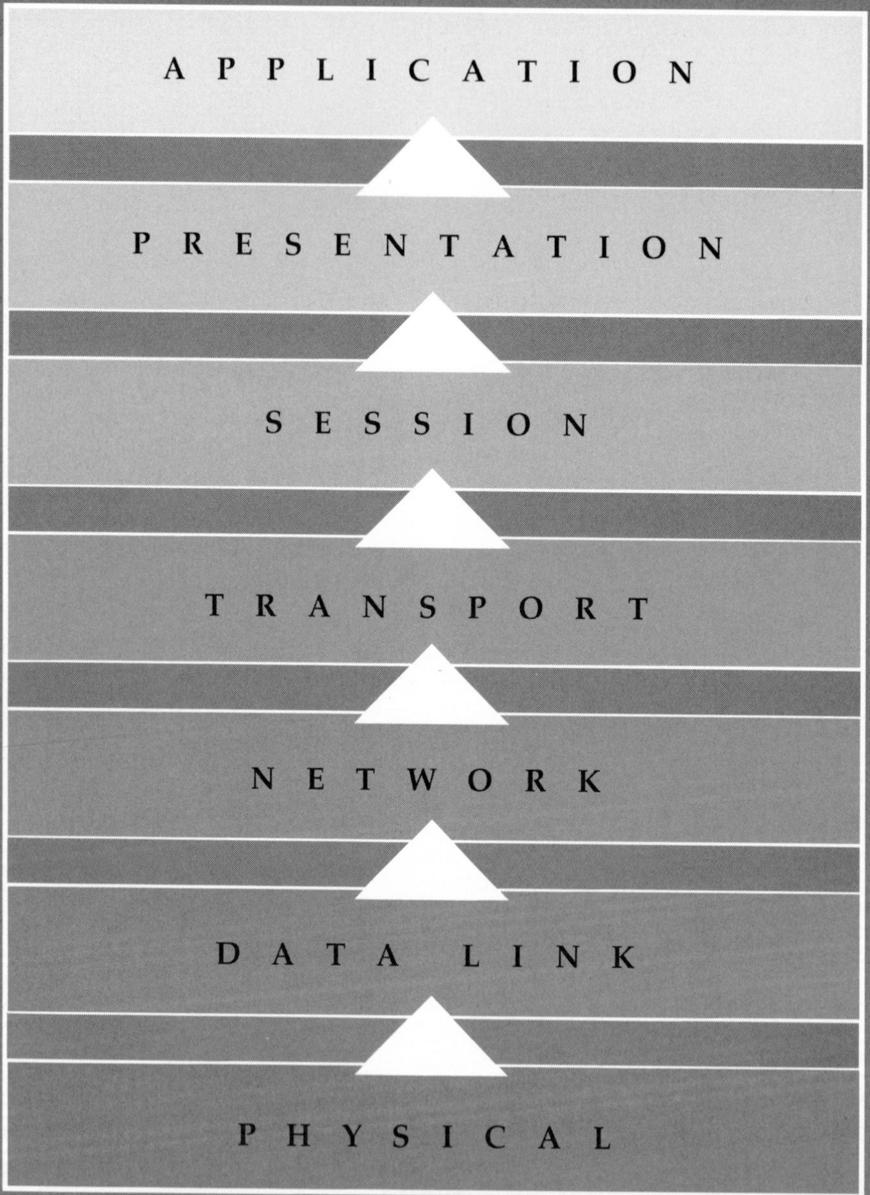
APPLICATION
PRESENTATION
SESSION
TRANSPORT
NETWORK
DATA LINK
PHYSICAL

Preface

Business Data Communications is designed for an introductory course in data communications, a required course within the Information Systems curriculum. Previous editions have been used at over 200 universities, colleges and community colleges. The text provides a balanced approach, emphasizing both the technical aspects of data communications and related managerial issues.

This third edition retains the fundamental structure and organization of previous editions: the chapters are arranged to follow the seven layer model for Open Systems Interconnection from the bottom up. In addition, when appropriate, differences between U.S. and international standards and usages and their unique associated problems are covered. Finally, recognizing that changes and developments in the computer industry since the publication of the previous edition render selected topics outdated, we have accommodated the need for currency by expanding and extensively updating topics in the area of local area network connectivity, management and telecommunications.

NEW AND EXPANDED IN THIS EDITION

Emphasis on Local Area Networks

Advances in microcomputers and data communications have given rise to a computing environment that is larger than the sum of its parts: the microcomputer Local Area Network (LAN). Chapter 8 explores general LAN technology. Chapter 9 is devoted to microcomputer LANs with a focus on LAN interconnections.

Reorganization and Expansion of Network Management Topics

Today's networks are comprised of equipment from a variety of vendors and are complicated by the emergence of networks of different types, such as LANs and Wide Area Networks (WANs). As the complexity of

v

network management increases, industry standards for network management are evolving to accommodate today's configurations. We introduce the basic terminology, configuration and operation of networks in Chapter 7; at the recommendation of reviewers, the packet distribution network material has been moved to augment the WAN coverage in Chapter 10. Meanwhile, new hardware and network management systems continue to be introduced. Chapter 11 explores these topics in detail, and has been moved forward to provide a solid grouping of chapters on networks.

In addition, new or updated material includes:

- Telecommunication topics, including telephone company operation and the services such companies provide
- Enhanced details regarding digital data transmission
- New examples and explanations of the ISO Reference Model
- Expanded coverage of Integrated Services Digital Network (ISDN)
- Extended Key Terms and Acronyms Glossaries

Reorganization of Appendices

Supplements that previously appeared at the end of Chapters 6, 7 and 10 have become appendices. Each appendix now contains additional in-depth explanations and a business implementation. For example, the Asynchronous Data Link Protocol appendix explores the implementation of asynchronous transmission, its advantages and disadvantages and describes typical implementations. This rearrangement makes this book suitable for use in both a short overview course as well as in a more detailed introductory data communications presentation.

PEDAGOGY AND LEARNING AIDS

Chapter Introductions, Summary, Review Questions, Exercises, Key Terms, Bibliography

New to this edition are two sets of end-of-chapter questions. Review Questions stimulate discussion and reflection on key points in the chapter. Exercises provide specific research topics or situational problem-solving to augment chapter material. Each chapter concludes with a bibliography. Over 300 key terms are indicated in italics throughout each chapter and are defined in the glossary.

 ### Case Study

This icon identifies a realistic case study based on the fictional Syncrasy Corporation, which appears in eight chapters to illustrate data communications applications. The case study chronicles a vigorous young company as it grows and diversifies; and provides a business context for students to apply the different technologies described in the text to the changing communications needs of a realistic situation.

SOFTWARE

The full version of **Saber Menu System for DOS,** a LAN administration package by Saber Software, is available free to adopters of *Business Data Communications,* third edition. Laboratory exercises and business applications may be built around this software to provide students with hands-on exposure to one of the best data communications software packages. System requirements: 320K RAM and DOS 2.1 or higher. Please contact your sales representative for a demonstration of this software and a description of other terminal emulator demo software available with this text.

SUPPLEMENTS

Instructor's Guide

The accompanying Instructor's Guide contains over 200 Transparency Masters to illustrate key figures and concepts from the text, as well as the following features for each chapter in the text:

- Over 635 multiple choice and fill-in test questions and answers
- Objectives and Teaching Suggestions
- Answers to selected Review Questions and Exercises

Casebook to Accompany Business Data Communications

The six realistic cases in the Casebook help test analytical skills by relating data communications concepts to real-life business applications. The cases are designed to provide flexibility with respect to both focus and solutions. The new case for the third edition presents LAN management at the fictional Courtney Chemical Company. The other five cases explore the following topics:

Case 1	LANs and LAN Alternatives
Case 2	Network Interconnection
Case 3	Distributed Computing
Case 4	International Networks
Case 5	Network Configuration

For more information about the third edition of *Business Data Communications* and its supplements or to request the software described above, please contact your Benjamin/Cummings Sales and Marketing Representative, or call the publisher directly at 800-950-BOOK.

ACKNOWLEDGEMENTS

I am grateful to the numerous individuals who contributed to the third edition of this textbook. I wish to thank the reviewers of the third edition, who were instrumental in providing suggestions and constructive criticisms for improving the text as we built on the foundation laid by the first and second editions. These people gave willingly of their time, and the third edition of *Business Data Communications* is much improved as a result of their contributions:

Warren Benson	*University of Nebraska at Omaha*
Robert A. Fleck, Jr.	*Columbus College*
Jon E. Juarez	*Dona Ana Branch Community College*
Akhil Kumar	*Cornell University*
James McBriar	*Milwaukee Area Technical College*
Lawrence Palecek	*Charles County Community College*
R. Waldo Roth	*Taylor College*
James Van Speybroeck	*St. Ambrose University*
Maureen Thommes	*Bemidji State University*
James R. Walters	*Pikes Peak Community College*
David C. Yen	*Miami University*

Much appreciation goes to the editorial and production departments of Benjamin/Cummings Publishing. In particular, I wish to thank Michelle Baxter, editor; Eleanor Renner Brown, production coordinator; and Lisa Weber, assistant editor, for their ideas, assistance and support.

Last, but not least, I wish to thank all of you—faculty, students and business professionals alike—who have used this book. I have received many suggestions for improvements from you both formally and informally and your comments are sincerely appreciated.

David A. Stamper

Research Participants

THIRD EDITION

CONTENT SURVEY

Warren Benson
University of Nebraska

Thomas Case
Georgia Southern University

Jan Guynes
University of Texas, Arlington

Carol Hicks
Georgia State University

Lawrence Palecek
Charles County Community College

Jerry Van Os
Westminster College of Salt Lake City

Bill Winter
Mary Baldwin College

David C. Yen
Miami University

TECHNOLOGY SURVEY

Dick Belanstegui
University of Nevada, Reno

Patrick Bobbie
University of West Florida

Dale Brutlag
Concordia University

Rich Christoph
James Madison University

Roger Clery
Roosevelt University

James Decker
Washburn University

Virginia Gibson
University of Maine

Bruce McLaren
Indiana State University

Frank Mighetto
City University

George Pacheco
Babson College

Steve Richards
University of Alabama, Huntsville

Bill Ross
DeVry Institute of Technology

Steven Zeoli
Marist College

Brief Contents

Detailed Contents

**PART III   DATA LINK PROTOCOLS:
THE DATA LINK LAYER   207**

**PART IV   NETWORKS AND SYSTEMS SOFTWARE:
THE NETWORK, TRANSPORT,
AND SESSION LAYERS 239**

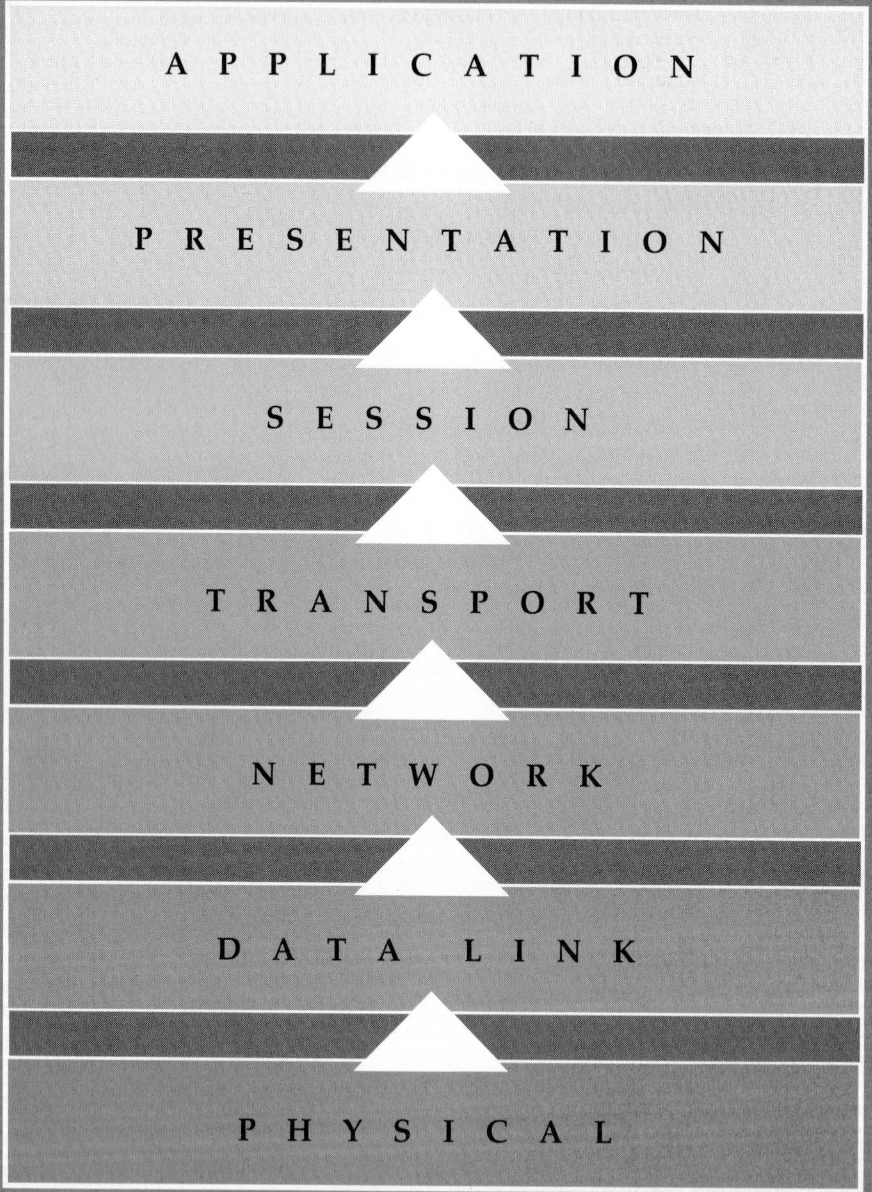
APPLICATION
PRESENTATION
SESSION
TRANSPORT
NETWORK
DATA LINK
PHYSICAL

INTRODUCTION: OVERVIEW AND HISTORY

Introduction to Data Communications

INTRODUCTION

This book provides an overview of *data communications,* a field so extensive that entire books are devoted to each chapter topic presented here. This text will familiarize you with the terminology and capabilities of data communications systems, and your mastery of this material will enable you to participate in decisions about alternative configurations of data communications components.

A data-processing system may be viewed as an integration of subsystems that aid in solving business or scientific problems. Common subsystems include the operating system, database management system, languages, applications, and data communications. Each subsystem is implemented as a combination of software and/or hardware. This text discusses the data communications subsystem along with its *interfaces* with the other subsystems. In this chapter you learn about:

The history of data communications

The essential features of communication

Characteristics of several types of data communications applications

1

Requirements of online systems

The basics of data communications networks

Telecommunications Versus Data Communications

What is meant in this text by the term *data communications*? Although the terms *telecommunications* and *data communications* have become almost synonymous in some circles, there is a distinction between them. James Martin (1972, p. 654) gives a broad definition of *telecommunications*:

> Any process that permits the passage from a sender to one or more receivers of information of any nature delivered in any easy to use form (printed copy, fixed or moving pictures, visible or audible signals, etc.) by any electromagnetic system (electrical transmission by wire, radio, optical transmission, guided waves, etc.). Includes telegraphy, telephony, video-telephony, data transmission, etc.

This definition is too broad for the scope of this book, which presents only that portion of telecommunications involving the transmission of data to and from computers and components of computer systems. Data com-

Figure 1-1   A Simple Data Communications System

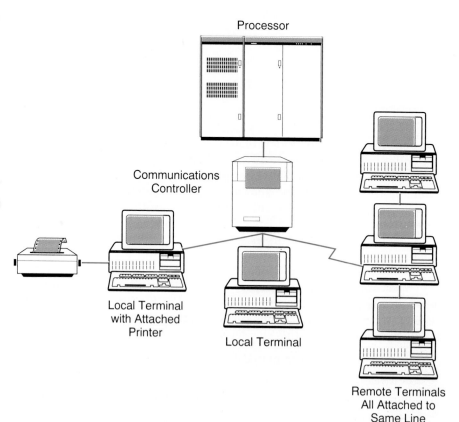

Processor

Communications Controller

Local Terminal with Attached Printer

Local Terminal

Remote Terminals All Attached to Same Line

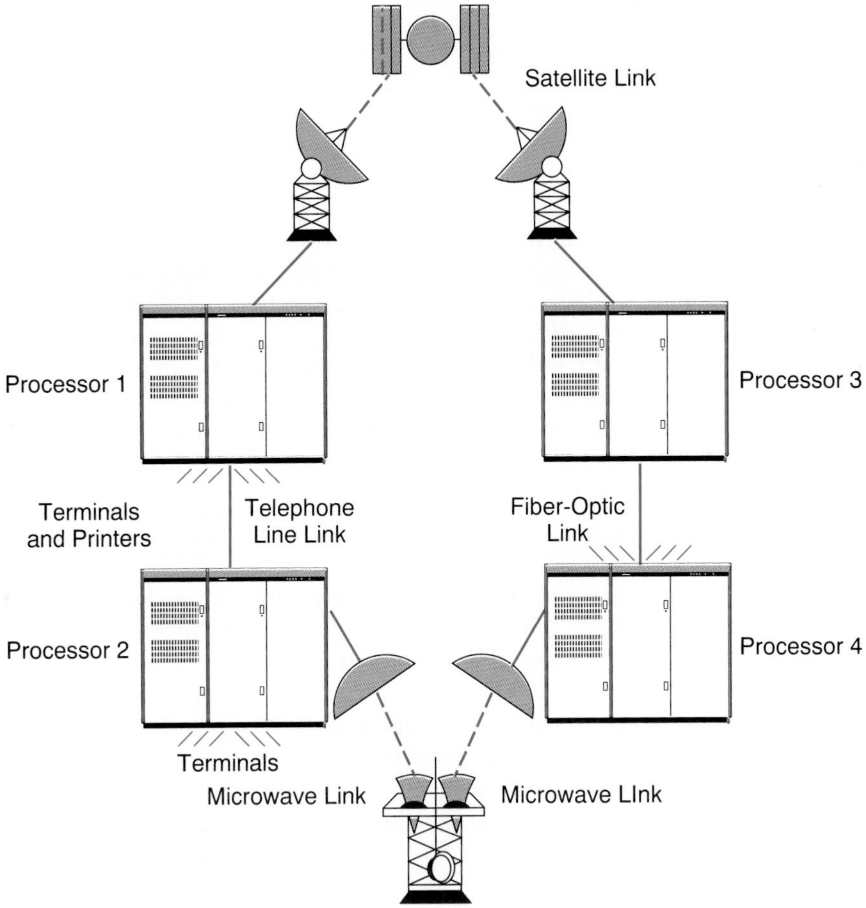

Figure 1-2 An Expanded Data Communications System

munications thus can be defined as that part of telecommunications that relates to computer systems: the electronic transmission of computer-readable data. This definition excludes the transmission of data to directly attached peripherals such as disk or tape drives and printers.

System Complexity

Data communications systems may be simple or complex. A simple system might be composed of a processor and some terminals, all located within a single building. Figure 1-1 illustrates the hardware components of such a system, which are the terminals, processor, and user-provided wiring. A more elaborate system might consist of many processors and terminals in multiple locations, all connected via communications lines leased from a common carrier (such as a telephone company) and via microwave and satellite transmission. Figure 1-2 depicts a system that meets this description. These two figures indicate the variety and complexity of communications systems. The illustrated components are discussed in detail in later chapters.

HISTORY OF THE COMMUNICATIONS INDUSTRY

The history of data communications differs significantly from that of other computer technologies, such as languages, hardware, database management, and applications. Because data communications is a joint venture between the communications industry and the computer industry, development has been a combined effort. And because the telephone companies have been the primary source of long-distance communication circuits, this history begins with the state of telephone companies at the start of the computer era.

Early Communications Networks

At the beginning of the computer era, the communications industry was already well established. Telephone and telegraph companies had developed a network of communications facilities throughout the industrialized world. In the United States and many other countries, telephone companies had been given exclusive rights to install lines and to provide services in specific geographical areas, with government agencies exercising control over tariffs and the services provided. This situation appeared to benefit both the telephone companies and consumers. The goal of the system was to provide affordable service. However, some users paid less than the actual cost of service while others paid more, due to the following pricing structure.

Every individual was to have access to telephone service at a reasonable cost. Service was to be provided to all geographical areas, regardless of remoteness or population density. Small, remote towns were to have the same type of service as large metropolitan communities, at about the same rates. If the total cost of installing lines and switching equipment in a small town had actually been borne entirely by users in that town, the cost of service would have been prohibitive to most residents. Therefore, losses incurred in such a town were offset by profits from other geographical areas. The three major sources of profit in the United States were the major metropolitan areas, businesses, and long-distance service. The large metropolitan areas were profitable because of economies of scale and density of installations. Business rates were much higher than rates for individuals because the value received was ostensibly greater (since the telephone was being used to generate income) and because businesses ostensibly could afford to pay more. Finally, long-distance tariffs were set high to subsidize those portions of the system operating at a loss. The service thus provided was generally good and prices were reasonable for each class of user. (Note that two of these profitable segments—business and long distance—also pertain to data communications.)

In addition to having exclusive rights to transmission facilities, the telephone companies in the United States and numerous other countries had exclusive rights to attach any equipment to the telephone networks. This gave them a monopoly on the equipment needed to transmit and receive data, such as modems. (A modem changes a computer signal from digital to analog format for transmission along a *medium* such as telephone lines, and another modem converts the signal back to digital format at the receiving end. See Chapter 2 for more on modems.) These exclusive rights allowed telephone companies to turn the sale or lease of such equipment to profit, which is what U.S. telephone companies did.

System Growth

In the United States, telephone companies were viewed as "natural" monopolies, meaning that it was considered wasteful to have two or more telephone companies servicing the same location. The "price" attached to the monopoly was that telephone companies like AT&T were prohibited from involvement in certain business segments, for example, the computer industry. Partly because of this monopoly on equipment, as well as the special status given providers of data transmission facilities, the growth of data communications was somewhat slower than that of other computer-related technologies. The development of databases, languages, operating systems, and hardware components was strong from the 1950s through the early 1970s, but large-scale expansion of data communications systems really did not occur until the 1970s. The growth experienced then was primarily the result of three developments:

Large-scale integration of circuits reduced the cost and size of terminals and communications equipment

Development of software systems made the establishment of data communications *networks* relatively easy

Competition among providers of transmission facilities reduced the cost for data circuits

Without these developments, data communications systems would have been financially unfeasible for many computer users.

Consider the transmission costs in 1968 and 1973, just before and just after competition appeared. In 1968, American Telephone and Telegraph Company (AT&T) charged an average of $315 for 100 miles of leased telephone line. In 1973, the average cost of the same line was as low as $85. A simple teletypewriter terminal (TTY) that sold for $2595 in 1971 could be replaced in 1975 for $750, and the 1975 terminal had more features than the older model. In July 1971, an International Business Machines (IBM) model 3270 terminal cost $71,000 (with a lease price of $1900 per month). In early 1988, the equivalent terminal listed for under $5000!

HISTORY OF DATA COMMUNICATIONS

The development of the first electronic computer is variously attributed to Howard Aiken, IBM, and Harvard University, for the MARK I; to John Atanasoff and Clifford Berry at Iowa State University, for the ABC (Atanasoff, Berry computer); or to John Mauchly and J. Presper Eckert at the University of Pennsylvania, for the ENIAC (electronic numerical integrator and calculator). Work on each machine started before 1940 and all three were fully operational by the early to mid-1940s. Other computer and sophisticated calculator projects were undertaken in parallel with these efforts, and some machines were actually operational sooner. A chronological list of the development of data communications is shown in Figure 1-3.

Figure 1-3 History of Data Communications

1939—ABC computer operational

1940—Data communications performed using COMPLEX computer

1944—MARK I computer operational

1946—ENIAC computer operational

1948—Hush-a-Phone case begins

1951—First commercial computer installed, the UNIVAC I

1953—First private commercial computer installed, UNIVAC at General Electric Corporation

1954—IBM introduces remote job entry (RJE)

1956—Hush-a-Phone decision in favor of Hush-a-Phone Company

1958—First U.S. communications satellite sent into orbit
Start of SAGE radar early warning system

1959—FCC approves private microwave communications networks

1963—First geosynchronous orbiting satellite, SYNCOM II
MCI files with FCC to provide communications services

1964—SABRE airline reservation system completed
Packet switching network concept proposed by the Rand Corporation

1966—Carterphone case begins

1967—IBM's binary synchronous (BISYNC or BSC) protocol announced

1968—Carterphone case concludes in favor of Carter Electronics

1969—ARPANET, first packet switching network, begins operation

1972—Ethernet local area network specifications formulated
IBM's synchronous data link control (SDLC) protocol announced

1974—IBM announces its systems network architecture (SNA)

1975—General Telephone and Electronics' Telenet public packet distribution network (PDN) becomes operational

1976—Personal computers introduced

1981—IBM PC introduced

The Role of Computers

Data communications was present at the beginning of the computer era, long before there were any operating systems, high-level languages, assemblers, or databases. In 1940, data was transmitted remotely from three sites to a Bell Laboratory computer in New York City. This computer, called the COMPLEX computer, had been developed to perform complex calculations for the U.S. military. Later that year, Bell Lab publicly demonstrated this communications capability by transmitting data via a modified teletypewriter circuit from Dartmouth University in Hanover, New Hampshire, to a computer in New York City.

In 1951 the first commercial computer, a UNIVAC I, was sold to the U.S. Bureau of the Census; the first private commercial computer was installed in 1953 at the General Electric Research Park in Louisville, Kentucky. Just one year later, IBM introduced *remote job entry* (RJE) communications. RJE involves input from a remote location, and optional remote output, via a data transceiver, a device that transmits and receives card images remotely. One RJE application is depicted in Figure 1-4.

Equipment Attached to Telephone Networks

A 1948 court case not specifically related to data communications eventually had a significant impact on that industry: the *Hush-a-Phone case*. Recall that telephone companies in the United States had a legal monopoly over all equipment attached to their networks, to keep anyone from attaching devices that might interfere with or destroy signals and equipment in the network. The Hush-a-Phone Company developed and marketed a passive device (no electrical or magnetic components) that could be installed over the transmitting telephone handset to block out background noise and provide more privacy; AT&T threatened to suspend service for users and distributors of the device. Hush-a-Phone appealed to the Federal Communications Commission (FCC). After several hearings, the FCC decided for AT&T. In 1956, however, an appeals court overturned the FCC ruling and decided in favor of the Hush-a-Phone Company, holding that no harm to the AT&T network would result from use of such a device. This precedent opened the door for other companies to attach equipment to the telephone networks. The telephone regulations as modified by this decision stated that the telephone company would not prohibit a customer from using

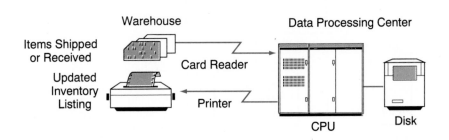

Figure 1-4 Remote Job Entry

a device that served his or her convenience so long as the devices did not injure the telephone system, involve direct electrical connection to the system, provide a recording device on the line, or connect the telephone company line with any other communication device.

Satellites and Microwave Transmission

The first U.S. communications satellite was launched in 1958. That year also saw the beginning of one of the first major data communications networks, the *Semi-Automatic Ground Environment* (*SAGE*) radar early warning systems, installed by the U.S. Department of Defense to provide early warning and fire control in the event of nuclear attack. Work continued on the SAGE project until 1961, when it consisted of more than 1.5 million miles of communication lines. The SAGE configuration is given in Figures 1-5 and 1-6.

The door to greater competition for communications circuits opened further when the FCC approved private microwave communications networks in 1959. This allowed a business to set up its own microwave transmission network if the network was used only for that company's data. The owner of such a network was prohibited from selling or leasing transmission facilities to other companies or to individuals. Having much the same impact as the Hush-a-Phone case, this decision helped set the stage for competition in areas that previously were the exclusive domain of the telephone and telegraph companies.

Figure 1-5 The SAGE Early Warning System

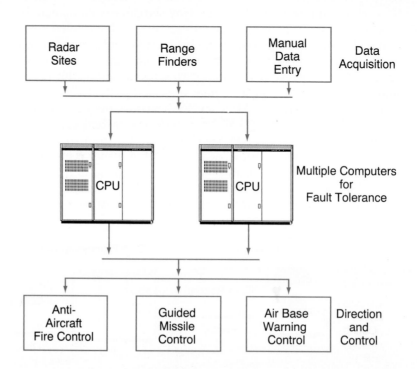

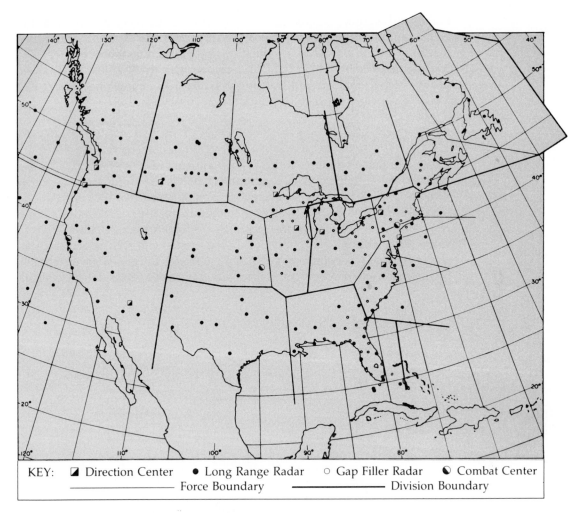

Figure 1-6 The SAGE Radar Environment

The first *geosynchronous* orbiting satellite, SYNCOM II, was launched in 1963. In geosynchronous orbit, which requires an altitude of approximately 22,300 miles, a satellite maintains a fixed position relative to the earth. A geosynchronous orbit ensures that a satellite remains permanently stationed over one point on the planet and hence is continuously available for communication between all points in its range, for instance, between North America and Europe.

Also in 1963, Microwave Communications Incorporated (MCI) filed with the FCC to provide microwave communications services between Chicago and St. Louis, their goal being to sell data transmission circuits to private industry. AT&T objected to MCI's petition because MCI could operate at much lower overhead than AT&T, since MCI—unlike AT&T—would not have to serve the lower volume markets, such as Montana, Wyoming,

Idaho, and Kansas. Despite AT&T's objections, MCI received approval for the communications link in 1970. Since then, MCI has expanded into other major metropolitan areas. It added an individual telephone service (Execunet) in 1975, by which date MCI had service to 24 cities. This era of heavy competition for data transmission circuits in the United States has led to lower rates for data communications users.

Transaction Networks

Two major data communications events occurred in 1964. The first was the completion of the ten-year development of the *Semi-Automatic Business Research Environment (SABRE)* network, a joint venture of IBM and American Airlines. The SABRE system, depicted in Figure 1-7, handles airline reservations. It was one of the first major *online transaction processing* systems. With online transaction processing, a business transaction such as reserving a seat on an airplane, placing an order for goods, or withdrawing money from a bank account is recorded in the business database at the

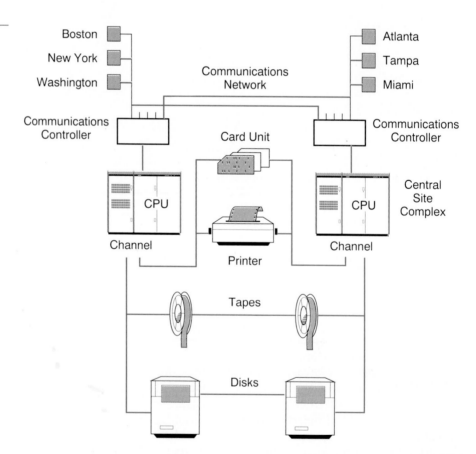

Figure 1-7 An Airline Reservation System

time the transaction occurs, rather than being recorded at a later time (as in a *batch* system). A modern airline would be unable to compete successfully without an online reservations system, due to the problems inherent in making reservations manually. Online transaction processing has grown considerably since the introduction of SABRE.

The second milestone of 1964 was not a new system but a new concept. The Rand Corporation introduced the idea of a packet switching network, or *packet distribution network (PDN)*. A PDN divides a user's message into specific-size packets, or units of transmission. These message packets are transmitted to the receiving station, where they are reassembled into the message. In 1969, the Advanced Research Projects Agency (ARPA) of the U.S. Department of Defense established the first two links in a packet switching network known as ARPANET, which has since been expanded to over 100 sites. Other packet switching networks have been developed throughout the world. PDNs can be either public or private. Public PDNs allow companies to subscribe to their packet switching service, and the utility company providing the PDN service is responsible for providing and operating the network. This is particularly helpful for companies that need to communicate with geographically distributed sites, because the utility company provides the necessary communication links and users are charged according to the number of data packets transmitted. In 1975, the Telenet system, owned by General Telephone and Electronics (GTE), became operational. Telenet is a packet distribution network. Figure 1-8 shows some of the cities connected by Telenet. PDNs are discussed in more detail in Chapter 10.

Another court case that helped open data communications to competition occurred in 1966: the *Carterphone case*. Carter Electronics Company had been marketing a radio telephone system that allowed for communication between a moving vehicle and a base station via radio-wave transmission. Because the original Carterphone was unable to forward a mobile call to another location, the company introduced a device that could pass on the radio transmission through a telephone network. AT&T objected to attaching the Carterphone to its network on the grounds of potential harm to the network and violation of the FCC prohibition against connecting an outsider's communications device to AT&T's telephone line. The 1968 ruling was in favor of Carter Electronics. As an outgrowth of the decision, it became legal for any device to be attached to the telephone network provided the telephone companies were allowed to install a protective device between the "foreign" equipment and the network. This provision later was changed to allow connection of FCC-approved equipment without any protective devices, which made it legal to attach other manufacturers' communications equipment to the network and led to improved products at lower prices. As another side effect of the Carterphone decision, individuals were allowed to purchase and install their own telephone sets.

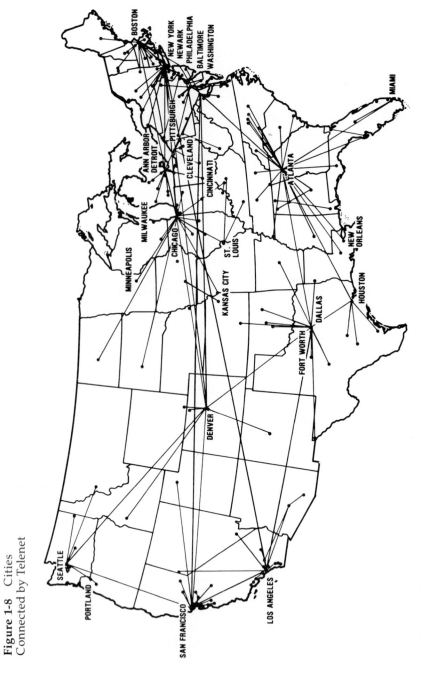

Figure 1-8 Cities
Connected by Telenet

12

Local Area Networks

A *local area network* (*LAN*) is a communications network whose components are all located within several kilometers of each other. Major uses of LANs include exchange of data at high speed between computers within a local area, factory or production control, *office automation*, and financial system. The original specifications for Ethernet, one of the most publicized LANs, were published by the Xerox Corporation in 1972. Later, Digital Equipment Corporation (DEC) and Intel joined Xerox in developing Ethernet further. LANs and Ethernet are discussed in greater detail in Chapters 8 and 9.

Data Link Protocols

A *data link protocol* governs the flow of data between sending and receiving stations. The original data communications *protocols* were borrowed from the telegraph and telephone industries. In 1967, IBM introduced the binary synchronous (BISYNC or BSC) protocol for use in remote job entry applications, and it was later expanded for use in other applications. In 1972, IBM introduced the synchronous data link control (SDLC) protocol, which has become the prototype for many current data link protocols. Data link protocols are discussed in more detail in Chapter 6.

System Network Architecture

In 1974, IBM introduced its system network architecture (SNA). Its significance is twofold. First, since IBM has long dominated the computer industry, SNA has become a de facto industry standard. Second, since all communications networks on IBM systems are meant eventually to conform to SNA, other manufacturers participating in networks using IBM equipment probably will have to provide some type of interconnection to SNA (until IBM implements industry-wide standards that are starting to emerge). SNA is discussed in Chapter 10.

Digital Communications

At the beginning of the data communications age, most transmission facilities were analog. This meant that digital data stored by computers had to be transformed to analog format for transmission and then back to digital format at the receiving end. Because the communications facilities were not designed for the transmission of computer data, the speed of transmission was somewhat limited. The computer age has brought about a change from analog to digital transmission facilities, resulting in higher transmission speeds and lower error rates. Digital and analog transmission are discussed in Chapters 2 and 3.

Microcomputers

Microcomputers were introduced in the 1970s and proliferated in the 1980s. A wide variety of microcomputer software and hardware, coupled with increased processing and storage capacity and low costs, have made microcomputers an important element in data communications networks. In many installations they have replaced terminals. Moreover, the introduction of local area networks with microcomputers as workstations has created many changes in the ways offices process data. Microcomputers are discussed further in Chapters 4, 8, and 10.

ESSENTIAL FEATURES OF COMMUNICATION

Data communication has several important features. Communication of any type requires a *message*, a *sender*, a *receiver*, and a *medium*. In addition, the message should be understandable and there should be some means of error detection. Figure 1-9 illustrates the sender, receiver, medium, and message in a telephone connection.

Message

For two entities to communicate, there must be a message, which can assume several forms and be of varying length. Data communications message types include a file, a request, a response, status, control, and correspondence. These are illustrated in Figure 1-10. Let us briefly look at each of them.

A File. With remote job entry (RJE), one of the first applications of data communications, messages were transmitted from a remote location to a

Figure 1-9 The Essential Features of Communication

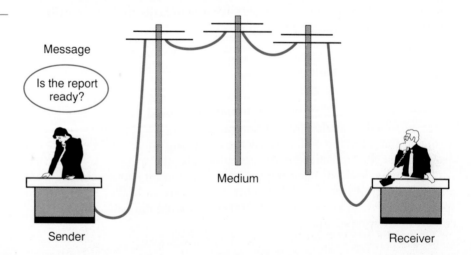

Message

Is the report ready?

Medium

Sender

Receiver

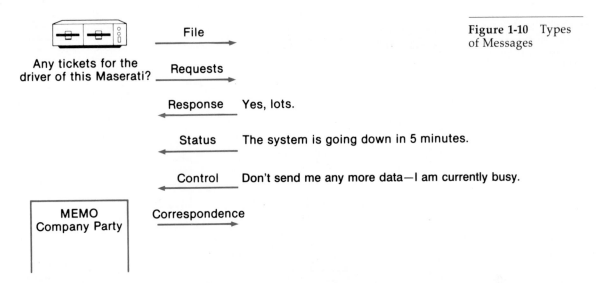

Figure 1-10 Types of Messages

processor. The message was the entire card file. In computer networks where several processors are connected, it is not unusual for complete or partial files to be transferred between processing units.

A Request.   In online transaction processing, a user may request that the computer processor(s) take some type of action, such as display information, update the database, or "logon" or "logoff."

A Response.   A request ordinarily receives a return message, or response. For an information inquiry, the response is either the information requested or an error message saying why the data was not returned (for instance, security violation, information not on file, or hardware failure). For a database update transaction, the response could be either an explicit message that the action was performed, an error message, or an implicit acknowledgment that the transaction has been performed successfully, such as progressing to the next transaction.

Status.   A status message, which can be sent to either all users or only selected users, reveals the functional status of the system. For example, if the system must be halted for scheduled maintenance, a status message might be broadcast to all users to enable them to bring their work to an orderly halt.

Control.   Control messages are transmitted between system components. For instance, an automatic teller machine (ATM) might indicate to the controlling computer that it is out of cash; a printer might indicate that its buffer (information storage area) is full and cannot receive additional data; or the message that a new processor has been added to the network might be routed to all other processors, thus updating routing tables. (*Network*

Figure 1-11   A
Network Showing
a Network Routing
Table

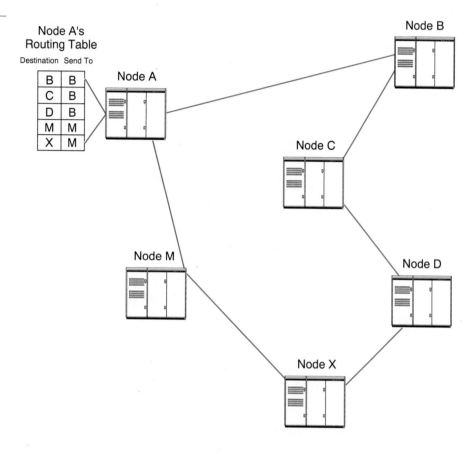

routing tables are used to determine a communications path between a sender and a receiver.) A small network is illustrated in Figure 1-11. A possible routing table for one of the computers, Node A, is also shown.

Correspondence.   Correspondence involves messages sent from user to user. Such messages include those sent on electronic mail systems, where memos and correspondence may be routed between employees of a company. Some systems transmit document images, provide bulletin-board message posting, or enable telephone-like *interactive* communication.

Sender

The sender is the transmitter of the message—either a person or a machine. Frequently the sender is a computer or terminal with enough intelligence to originate a message or response without human intervention. The sender can also be a system user, sensor, badge reader, or other input device.

Receiver

Receivers include computers, terminals, remote printers, people, and devices such as drill presses, furnaces, and air conditioners. A message and a sender can exist without a receiver; however, without a receiver, no communication takes place. For example, signals have been beamed into space in an attempt to contact other intelligent life forms, but until these signals are received, no communication has occurred. In a computer system, a message could be sent to all terminals saying that a new system feature is available, but if all terminals happen to be turned off at that time, no communication will have occurred.

Medium

Messages are carried from sender to receiver through some medium of communication. For instance, in oral communication, sound waves are transmitted through air (the medium). Data communications uses several media to transmit data, including wires, radio waves, and light pulses. Media are discussed in Chapter 2.

Understandability

Even if all the components discussed above are present, if the message is not understood correctly, then accurate communication has not taken place. In human communication the most obvious obstacle is language differences, for which a translator or interpreter may be necessary. Computer systems have similar obstacles to communication. For instance, data can be represented by any of several different codes, the two most common being the American Standard Code for Information Interchange (ASCII) and the Extended Binary Coded Decimal Interchange Code (EBCDIC). Sometimes it is necessary to translate from one code to another to be sure that data is interpreted correctly.

Error Detection

In human communication, receivers can frequently detect errors because humans can reason and interpret. Grammatical errors, misspellings, and even some misstatements can usually be corrected by a human receiver. (For example, if a teacher mistakenly gives the distance between the earth and the sun as 93 million light years rather than 93 million miles, we would probably realize the error and, presumably, even correct it.) But computer networks don't reason. And even when a human computer operator realizes that a received message is erroneous, that operator may be unable to correct the error. When the receiver is a piece of hardware, incapable of reasoning and unable to detect or correct errors, it becomes necessary to employ special schemes for determining if an original message has been distorted during transmission. All such schemes involve transmitting additional information along with the data, which increases the chances of detecting errors without eliminating the possibility that the received data actually may be erroneous. Error detection is discussed in Chapter 3.

DATA COMMUNICATIONS APPLICATIONS

There are several broad classes of data communications applications: *inquiry/response*, *interactive*, *batch*, *data entry*, *distributed*, and *sensor-based*. Note that the classes are not mutually exclusive; some transactions may fall into more than one class.

Inquiry/Response Applications

In this type of application, inputs generally have only a few characters and output responses have many. Inquiry/response applications involve requests to display information. For example, a police inquiry might consist of a driver's license number and the response could be several thousand characters of information detailing the driver's name, address, driving record, and so on. In a hospital application, a nurse might enter the nurse's station number (relatively few characters) and the output would likely consist of several thousand characters giving each patient's name, status, medical requirements, and so on.

Interactive Applications

The interactive type of application is characterized by relatively short inputs and outputs. The computer system prompts the user for an input, eliciting a short response. Since the sender and receiver are essentially conversing with each other, this application is sometimes referred to as *conversational*. Interactive applications are frequently used for online transaction processing with terminals that cannot accept an entire screenful of information. Applications in which the user's response dictates the next prompt, such as certain computerized games, are also interactive. Figure 1-12 shows an interactive session used to add a name and address to a file. Prompts are italicized.

Batch Applications

Batch applications, including RJE, are characterized by large data transfers in two directions. For instance, information from a batch of inventory cards might be transferred from a warehouse to a remote computer center, and in return the warehouse would receive an updated inventory list. In some batch applications, large amounts of data flow in one direction only

```
ENTER LAST NAME:           JOHNSON
ENTER FIRST NAME:          RALPH
ENTER MIDDLE INITIAL:      F
ENTER STREET ADDRESS:      123 MAIN STREET
ENTER CITY:                SYDNEY
ENTER STATE:               COLORADO
ENTER ZIP CODE:            80201
```

Figure 1-12 Inter-
active Data Entry

(this actually resembles data entry—see the next section). When a sales representative records sales on a portable computer terminal but waits until the end of the workday to transmit the entire day's orders, a large amount of data flows in one direction and little or no data flows in the other direction.

Data Entry Applications

Data entry applications consist of lengthy inputs with short responses. For example, in a credit authorization system in Australia, input for a "batch" of receipts consists of credit card number, merchant number, and charge amount, plus the batch total. The system then calculates its own batch total and compares it with the input total; if the figures agree, the only response is a prompt to continue entering the next batch.

Distributed Applications

Distributed applications are characterized not so much by input and output size as by whether data or processing or both are distributed among several processing units. Thus, requests as well as data flow between several system components, with possibly some parallelism in data access and processing. Order entry is an example of this type of processing. When an order for an item is entered, the system tries to determine if the item is in stock in any of its several regionally located warehouses. Since each warehouse has a computer system and maintains its local inventory, the system inquires into these remote databases to find a location with enough stock to fill the order. The system then updates the inventory at the location(s) from which the order is to be filled, updates the invoicing and accounts receivable at the accounting location, and supplies the ordering location with a shipment date and other relevant data.

Office automation systems are a special case of distributed systems, with both data and processing distributed among several different components. Applications include word processing, communications between members of the corporation via electronic mail, spreadsheet analysis, graphics, and facsimile generation for presentations, reports, and contracts.

Sensor-Based Applications

Sensor-based applications involve special data collection devices for such uses as controlling temperature in buildings, monitoring and maintaining patient condition in hospitals, and controlling a manufacturing process. The processor receives data from the sensors and, if necessary, takes control action.

Combined Applications

The typical computer in a network of large systems supports more than one type of activity. It might have a batch processing requirement and one or more types of data communications applications. One task in designing a data communications system is to balance the workload to assure effective and efficient use. Effective use means minimizing idle time for system components. For example, it is not effective to have a data communications line idle for long periods and then have many users attempting to use it at once. Efficient use means using the components in an optimal manner. Efficient uses of a data communications line include compressing the data before transmitting it or eliminating sources of data errors. These goals can be reached through good design and management.

Often, good management requires that tradeoffs be made. If batch jobs must run concurrently with data communications applications, a manager may configure a computer system so batch applications do not run as efficiently as possible so that transaction-oriented applications are optimized.

REQUIREMENTS OF AN ONLINE SYSTEM

Although data communications applications are diverse, most have certain basic requirements: *performance, consistency, flexibility, availability, reliability, recovery,* and *security.*

Performance

System performance can be measured in several ways. Two very common measures are response time and transaction rate (or throughput). Response time is the interval between entering a message and getting the response. Some define the measurement interval as being from the end of the entry to the appearance of the first response character; others define it as the interval from the end of the entry to receipt of the final response character. The difference between the two can be significant. For example, if the speed of the communications circuit is 30 characters per second and the response consists of 1200 characters, the response time by the first definition is 40 seconds less than that by the second definition. Response time has two major components: the time required for data transmission and the time required for processing. (Each component has subcomponents.) This text deals only with data transmission time.

Response times are quoted for transactions of a given type. For example, in a hospital application there are response times for each of the following transactions:

patient admission

patient discharge

patient look-up

room occupants

In addition to each transaction having a response time, one transaction type may have different response times in different systems. This happens because of hardware differences or because the transactions are implemented in different ways. For example, Figure 1-13 illustrates the work Transaction A may do to admit a patient at one hospital and Figure 1-14 shows the work a patient admission transaction, Transaction B, does at another hospital. The work accomplished by these two transactions is different; therefore, their response times differ. When comparing or evaluating transaction response times, you also need to evaluate the work done by those transactions.

Transaction rate, or throughput, is the amount of work performed by the system per unit of time. It may appear that fast response time and high throughput are equivalent. Actually, the opposite is sometimes true. For example, transactions in which customers are involved need quick re-

Obtain vacant room list header from memory location

Read vacant room record

Read patient record

Update vacant room list header in memory from room record

Rewrite room record linked to patient record

Rewrite patient record

Figure 1-13 Activities for Transaction A

Obtain vacant room header from memory

Read vacant room record

Read patient record

Update vacant room header from room record

Rewrite room record linked to patient record

Read related charge record for room

Write charge record for patient

Read standard patient issue record

Write patient charge record for issue of supplies

Rewrite patient record

Figure 1-14 Activities for Transaction B

sponse time. Optimizing the speed of such transactions might slow down other processing activity, such as batch reporting. Thus, although response time in customer transactions might be reduced, the total amount of work accomplished may decline. In a truly successful system, both response time and throughput are optimal.

Consistency

A consistent system is one that works predictably both with respect to the people who use the system and with respect to response times. Inconsistent response time is extremely annoying to system users and in fact is sometimes worse than a slow but consistent response time. Of course, complete consistency is difficult to achieve because of occasional periods of heavy processing. One common system design objective is for the response time of most transactions of a given type—for example, 95%—to be lower than a certain threshold—for example, 3 seconds. It would be quite disconcerting if 50% of these transactions took 3 seconds, 20% took 10 seconds, 15% took 30 seconds, 10% took 1 minute, and 5% took over a minute. Such inconsistency is not only frustrating, but it also limits the effectiveness of the system.

Flexibility

One thing typical of online systems is that they change. For instance, users might want to alter the types of transactions available, change the data format, expand an application, or add new applications. Both growth and change must be accommodated with minimal impact on existing applications and users. The ability to increase processing power, terminals, communication circuits, and database capacity is critical to the long-term success of a system, and the network implementation ought to accommodate such changes. One of the best ways to ensure this is to use industry-standard network architectures and protocols. This method also helps when adding or upgrading nodes and gives users a wider variety of options from which to choose. There are two general types of standards: official standards, produced by recognized standards organizations, and de facto standards, which arise from widespread use but are not officially sanctioned.

Availability

An online system must be continuously available to the user community during the workday. In some cases this means 24 hours a day, every day of the year. In certain applications the unavailability of the online system can result in significant financial loss to a business. For example, an airline might be unable to sell seats on a flight if the reservation system is down, or it may overbook a flight, which will cause extra work for the employees and possible penalty payments to travelers for their inconvenience. Availability is discussed in more detail in Chapter 11.

Reliability

Reliability is an important system attribute. It is a measure of the frequency of system failure and in some ways combines consistency and availability. A system failure is any event that prohibits users from processing transactions. This includes any hardware breakdown, such as a processor failure in a system that is not fault tolerant, as well as an application or system software failure or the failure of the medium (such as a faulty data communications line). *Mean time between failure (MTBF)* is a measure of the average time until a given component may be expected to fail, and *mean time to repair (MTTR)* is the average time required to fix a failed component. Both figures are important in determining the frequency of failure and the time required to return the system to successful operation. Reliability is discussed in more detail in Chapter 11.

One way to improve the reliability of data communications systems is *fault tolerance*, which is the ability to continue processing despite component failure. In a fault-tolerant system, single points of failure do not cause system failure because every component in the system has a backup component that takes over if a failure occurs. Fault-tolerant data communications systems are formed by combining fault-tolerant hardware (available from several vendors, including Tandem Computers and Stratus Computers) with fault-tolerant software and two or more distinct communications paths to each network node.

Recovery

All systems, even those built for continuous operation, can fail. In some cases it may not be the system that fails but either the source of power or the people who operate the system. Regardless of the cause, the system must be able to recover to a consistent point—a point where the database has no partially updated transactions, no transactions have been processed twice, and no transactions have been lost. System users should also be advised of the state of all work they had in progress at the time of failure, to keep them from submitting a duplicate transaction or failing to reenter a transaction not received before the failure.

Security

Security has become increasingly important as the microcomputer has made computer networks accessible to almost everyone (as is evident from the recent reports about computer hobbyists "invading" computer systems across the country). Furthermore, as more businesses use data communications, the number of accessible computer systems continues to grow, thus making a vast amount of sensitive information available, including financial data and classified military information. Unfortunately, security has not always received a high priority in system and network design, so making up for these deficiencies is a necessity in the development of future systems and in enhancing existing ones. Systems security is discussed in more detail in Chapter 13.

INTRODUCTION TO COMMUNICATIONS NETWORKS

This section discusses two definitions of computer networks and some functions common to them. The functions described are the bases for later chapters.

Computer Networks

What exactly is a *computer network*? First, a computer network can be defined as a single computer, called a *host*, together with communications circuits, communications equipment, and terminals (see Figure 1-1). A network can also be defined as two or more computers connected via a communications medium, together with associated communications links, terminals, and communications equipment (see Figure 1-2). In this case the host computers are referred to as *nodes*. In Figures 1-1 and 1-2, the communications links are depicted by lines attached to the nodes. These are sample configurations only; actually, a wide variety of configurations is in use, and several viable configurations may exist for one application.

The only difference between these two definitions is the number of computers involved. Also, the second definition can refer to a network of either computers or systems. In general, the term *computer network* refers to the former type of network. This definition also includes such major data communications networks as an airline reservation system with miles of communication lines, a large central processor, and over 1000 terminals, many of which contain some degree of processing power and can participate in the processing of transactions.

Data Communications Applications and Configurations

We ignore, for now, the distinction between the two definitions and present several different applications and configurations of computer equipment.

Company X.   This company provides a service to trucking companies that enables their drivers to cash script at truck stops throughout the country. The advantages are that drivers do not need to carry large amounts of cash for long trips, truck stop owners are guaranteed against losses from bad checks, and the trucking companies need not provide significant cash advances to their drivers. The communications network consists of approximately 50 terminals located in the same building as the host computer in Company X's office. Truck stop employees can telephone data entry personnel on a toll-free number to receive authorization to pay the driver (or advice to call the police). The total amount of money allocated to the driver is updated after each transaction. All links between computer and terminals are local and are controlled by Company X, rather than being leased or purchased from a common carrier such as a telephone company. The Company X configuration is depicted in Figure 1-15. The figure also illustrates a component called a controller, which is used to manage data communications lines, transmit and receive data, and provide error checking and recovery functions.

Company Y. This service company is involved in the automated preparation of tax returns. Its clients are accounting firms who contract to use Company Y's computer facilities and software. Depending on the size of the accounting firm, clients may choose to have a private, dedicated communications link to the host computer, or they can share a communications link with other users. Clients who share a telephone link compete with each other for access to the available telephone lines. Suppose 50 lines are shared by 150 clients and each client typically uses the connection fewer than 2 hours per day. In this case, because of time zone differences, the workday is 12 hours long and the average use of the facility is 50% (300 hours of the 600 available connection hours). Ordinarily, there will not be much competition for these shared lines. But just before the April 15th income tax filing deadline, clients may dramatically increase their use of the system, so availability of the communications links might become a problem. For a client that needs a line more than 2 hours per day, it is probably more economical to use a dedicated line. The Company Y configuration is depicted in Figure 1-16.

Company Z. This multinational company manufactures and markets computer systems. Every large sales office has a demonstration computer, and all of these computers as well as the computers in the software devel-

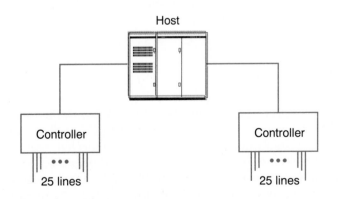

Figure 1-15 The Company X Configuration

Figure 1-16   The
Company Y
Configuration

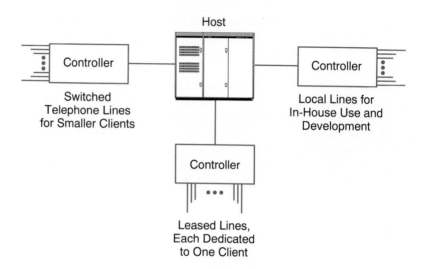

opment facility, home office, and manufacturing plants are linked in one large network, consisting of over 200 nodes and about 3000 terminals. In addition to long-distance telephone lines and local, private lines, Company Z uses several newer transmission facilities: fiber optics, to link computers located within 1 kilometer of each other; satellite communications, for long-distance, high-volume transmissions between manufacturing plants and divisional offices; and packet switching networks (these types of media are all discussed in Chapter 2). The Company Z configuration is represented in Figure 1-2.

These three companies have greatly different network configurations, yet each network is effective and cost efficient for the business that uses it. Both Company X and Company Y could have installed a network similar to that of Company Z, with terminals at client locations and computers in the larger clients' offices; unfortunately, by doing so they would have to charge considerably more for their services and thus would lose their competitive edge.

Clearly, many alternatives are available to a system designer, and any of numerous configurations can probably solve the communications requirements. A few such alternatives might be highly cost effective, some may be only mediocre, and a few might drive the company into bankruptcy. It is important to realize that several "right" approaches usually exist.

Hierarchy of Functions

Regardless of the scope of a network and the equipment and media used, all networks share common functions. To contend with the growing number of different computer networks being developed, and in the belief that these diverse systems eventually need to be connected, the *International Standards Organization (ISO)* has identified and stratified the functions that every network must fulfill. This definition makes it easier to develop interfaces among these different networks.

The ISO recommendation is called the *reference model for open systems interconnection (OSI)*, or the ISO OSI recommendation. The reference model does more than describe network interconnections; it also defines a network architecture. Many ISO standards have been established and more are being formulated. When the standards process is completed, network developers will have an alternative to corporate architectures like IBM's systems network architecture (SNA). Details of this reference model are found in the chapters on networks (Part IV), but since the OSI model is used as a road map for the development of this text, a brief description is provided here. This discussion also provides an overview of communications systems.

OSI Functional Layers

The OSI recommendation identifies the seven functional layers shown in Figure 1-17: *application, presentation, session, transport, network, data link,* and *physical*. The goal of a data communications network is to exchange data between applications or between users. The information to be transferred must be formatted, packaged, routed, and delivered. The receiver must then unpackage and possibly reformat the information. These are essentially the functions performed by the seven layers.

Figure 1-18 depicts the layers in two different processors. The information from the application layer in Processor 1 moves down through the layers in its node until it reaches the physical layer, which transmits the data to the physical layer in Processor 2. The data then works its way up through the layers in Processor 2 until it reaches the application layer.

Each layer in the sending processor performs work for, or acts on behalf of, its peer layer in the receiving processor. Thus, presentation layers support presentation layers, session layers support other session layers, and so on. Between the different layers are interfaces through which data passes. These interfaces are flexible so designers can implement various communications protocols and still follow the ISO OSI reference model. The following sections briefly describe the function of each layer.

Application. The *application layer* is functionally defined by the user. Sometimes application programs must communicate with each other. The content and format of the data being exchanged are dictated by the needs of the organization. The application determines which data is to be transmitted, the message or record format for the data, and the transaction codes that identify the data to the receiver. Suppose an order entry transaction started on a sales node needs to pass product shipping information to a warehouse node. In this application, the message contains the ship-to address, part identifiers, quantities to be shipped, and a message code showing the action to be taken by the receiving application.

Presentation. The *presentation layer* formats the data it receives from the application layer. Thus, if certain data preparation functions are common

Figure 1-17 The
Seven OSI Functional
Layers

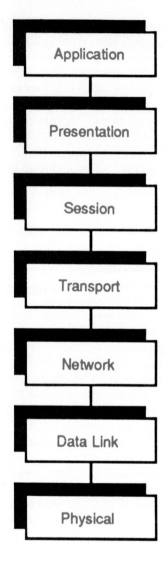

to several applications, they can be resolved by the presentation services
rather than being embedded in each application. The types of functions
performed at the presentation level are encryption, compression, terminal
screen formatting, and conversion from one transmission code to another
(such as EBCDIC to ASCII).

Session.   The *session layer* establishes the connection between applications,
enforces the rules for carrying on the dialogue, and tries to reestablish
the connection if a failure occurs. The dialogue rules specify both the
order in which the applications are allowed to communicate and the pacing of information so as not to overload the recipient. If an application is
sending data to a printer with a limited buffer size, the agreed-upon dia-

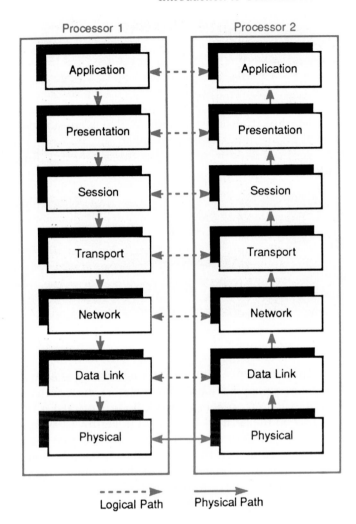

Processor 1   Processor 2

Application ◄ - - - ► Application

Presentation ◄ - - - ► Presentation

Session ◄ - - - ► Session

Transport ◄ - - - ► Transport

Network ◄ - - - ► Network

Data Link ◄ - - - ► Data Link

Physical ◄———► Physical

- - - - ► Logical Path   ———► Physical Path

Figure 1-18 OSI Peer Layer Communication

logue may be to send a buffer-size block to the printer, wait for the printer to signal that its buffer has been emptied, and then send the next block of data. The session layer must control this flow to avoid buffer overflow at the printer.

Transport. The *transport layer* is the first layer concerned with the world external to its processor. It generates the address of the end user and ensures that all blocks or packets of data have been received, that there are no duplicate blocks, and that blocks have not been lost in transmission.

Network. The *network layer* does end-to-end routing of packets or blocks of information, collects billing and accounting information, and routes messages.

Data Link.   The *data link layer* must establish and control the physical path of communication to the next node. This includes error detection and correction, defining the beginning and end of the data field, resolving competing requests for a shared communications link (deciding who can use the circuit and when), and ensuring that all forms of data can be sent across the circuit. The last point may sound trivial, but as Chapter 6 illustrates, some data link transmission systems that were not designed for transmission of binary fields must accomplish this in a rather awkward way. The conventions used to accomplish these data link functions are known as protocols.

Physical.   The *physical layer* specifies the electrical connections between the transmission medium and the computer system. It describes how many wires are used to carry the signals, which wires carry specific signals, the size and shape of the connectors or adapters between the transmission medium and the communications circuit, the speed at which data is transmitted, and whether data (represented by voltages on a line, modification of radio waves, or light pulses) is allowed to flow in both directions and, if so, whether the flow can be in both directions simultaneously.

OSI Reference Model Example

Let us look at an example of activities that might occur at each level of the reference model as an application on one network node transmits a message to an application on another network node. Consider a financial application running on the network illustrated in Figure 1-19. Suppose that a bank customer uses an ATM attached to Node A and that the customer's account is located on Node X. A transaction-oriented application on Node A sends a message to Node X requesting that the customer's account record be updated by an application running at Node X. To reach Node X, the message must pass through Node M.

Application Layer.   The application on Node A builds a record with a transaction identifier, the number of the account to be updated, the date and time of the transaction, and the amount to be deducted or added. The transaction identifier tells the message recipient what to do with the record: insert it, update it, and so on. The message is illustrated in Figure 1-20(a). The application then invokes a procedure call to send the message to the recipient.

Presentation Layer.   The application layer formatted each field in the record being transmitted according to its own format rules. The receiving application may have a different set of format conventions. For example, the sending application may view a date in one format while the receiving application uses a different date format. The presentation layer is responsible for translating from one format to another. It can do this by changing to a standard transmission format, which is converted by its peer layer, or it can convert directly to the format expected by the receiving applica-

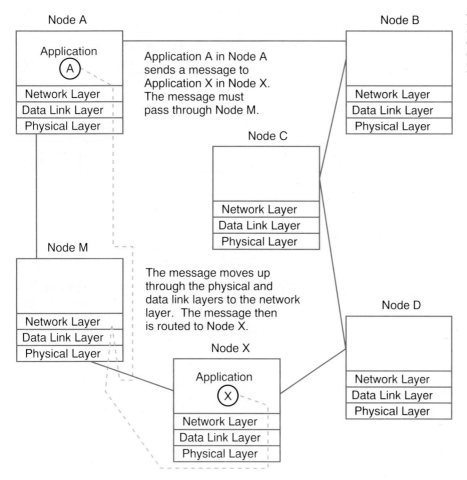

Figure 1-19 Application-to-Application Communication in a Network

tion. The message after such translation has taken place appears in Figure 1-20(b). The presentation layer then sends the message down to the session layer by requesting the establishment of a session.

Session Layer. The session layer's major functions are to set up, and perhaps monitor, a set of dialogue rules by which the two applications communicate and to bring a session to an orderly conclusion. A session dialogue can be one-way (simplex) or bi-directional. In *simplex transmission*, one application sends messages to another but receives no messages in return. Bi-directional sessions can allow messages to flow in both directions simultaneously (*full duplex* mode) or in both directions but in only one direction at a time (*half duplex* mode). Setting up how messages are transferred is called *flow control*. Once the connection has been made, data transfer can occur. The session layer appends an identifier and length indicator at the beginning of the data block, as illustrated in Figure 1-20(c). These two fields are used to identify the function of the message, for example, whether it contains user data as opposed to control functions like session establishment or termination.

Figure 1-20 OSI
Reference Model
Formatting

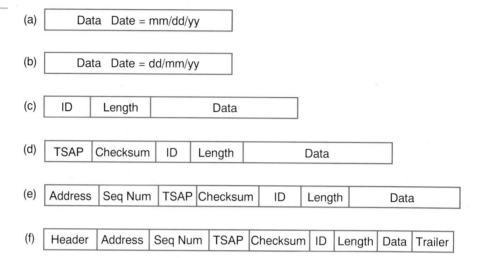

Transport Layer.   The transport layer is the first OSI layer responsible for actually transmitting the data. The higher layers described above are oriented toward the data and application interfaces, not toward data transmission. The transport layer uses an address called a transport service access point (TSAP) to uniquely identify session entities. TSAPs of the source and destination session entity, together with a checksum to detect errors, are appended to the message received from the session layer. A *checksum* is used to help detect transmission errors. It is created by the sender according to some algorithm. The receiver also creates the checksum using the same algorithm. If the sender's checksum and receiver's checksum agree, the data is assumed to be correct. This step is shown in Figure 1-20(d).

Network Layer.   The network layer provides accounting, addressing, and routing functions. Upon receiving a message from the transport layer, the network layer logs the event to the accounting system and then prepares the message for transmission to the next node on the path to the destination (Node M in our example). It looks up the destination address in its network routing table to find the next address along that path. (A routing table for a node in a small network is shown in Figure 1-11.) If the message is lengthy, the network layer divides it into transmission units, appends a transmission sequence number to each unit, and sends the units across the link. This is illustrated in Figure 1-20(e).

Data Link Layer.   The data link layer is responsible for data delineation, error detection, and logical control of the link. Logical link control consists of determining how and when a station can transmit, connecting and disconnecting nodes on the link, and controlling flow between data link entities. Thus, the data link layer facilitates flow control between Nodes A and M and between Nodes M and X. Note that data link flow control is for a link, while session flow control is end-to-end (between source and destination applications). To fulfill its function, the data link layer appends a header and a trailer to the message. The header contains a flag that indicates the beginning of the message, the address of the recipient, message sequence numbers, and the message type (data or control). The trailer contains a checksum for the data link block and a frame-ending flag. Headers and trailers are illustrated in Figure 1-20(f).

Physical Layer. The physical layer does not append anything to the message. It simply accepts the message from the data link layer and translates the bits into signals on the medium.

In our example, the message arrives at Node M and percolates up to the network layer. The network layer services recognize that the message is destined for Node X and send the message down to the data link layer for delivery to the next (and final) node. This is illustrated in Figure 1-19. Our discussion in subsequent chapters starts from the bottom up, beginning with the physical layer (together with hardware components used in configuring a data communications network).

The Software Environment

Before we begin the technical discussion of the data communications system, an explanation of how it supports applications is worthwhile. Therefore, we take a brief look at the application environment of a data communications system. Within the central processing system resides an operating system, together with data communications, database, and application software. This is illustrated in Figure 1-21. These software subsystems perform the following functions.

Application Programs. Application programs are the heart of the system. They are the sole reason for having a computer and associated software and hardware. Application software may be purchased from the computer vendor or a third party or developed locally. There are many varieties of application programs. For example, an inventory system has many programs, each of which performs one or more inventory functions, such as inventory update, inventory listings, printing packing lists, and so on. A banking system consists of many programs that provide functions like creating new accounts, deleting accounts, updating accounts, reporting account statuses, and so on.

To make the development process efficient, programmers should not have to concern themselves with the intricacies of data communication and data storage. Thus, application *support* software, such as the operating system, data communications system, and database system, is used. The purpose of these systems is to allow application developers to concentrate on solving business problems rather than on the specifics of devices such as terminals and disk drives. By isolating applications at this level of detail, a company can also introduce devices into a system with minimal or no impact on existing application programs.

Figure 1-21 An
Applications
Environment

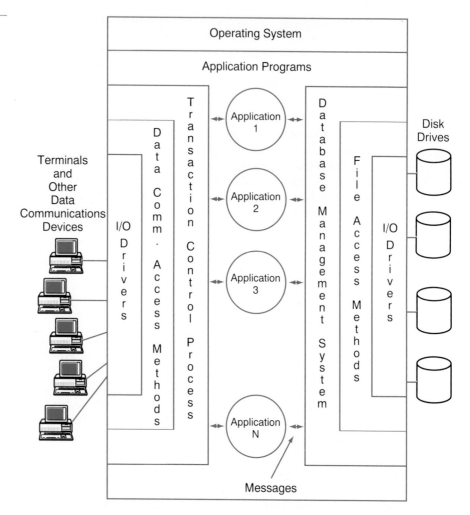

For example, it is typical to have a variety of terminals within a computer network. The way data is displayed on these devices often differs from one terminal to the next. Furthermore, the capabilities supported by the devices may differ. One terminal may have a color display, and another, a monochrome display. Requiring each application to keep track of these differences would place a heavy, unnecessary burden upon the application programmer. The data communications system accommodates device differences and provides a standard interface that allows an application to deal with any type of terminal.

Operating System.   The operating system manages the resources of the computer. It manages memory; controls access to the processor(s); and provides interfaces to users, the input/output (I/O) subsystems, and the file system.

Data Communications.   The data communications subsystem is responsible for interfacing to terminals and other devices that are attached via communications lines. These devices are distinguished from locally attached peripherals such as disk drives, printers, and tape drives. In addition to the function defined above, the data communications system provides a bridge between applications and the devices with which they must communicate. In this capacity, it switches messages between terminals and applications and becomes involved in recovery in the event of a system failure. The data communications component that provides this service is called a *transaction control process* (TCP).

Database Management System (DBMS). The DBMS serves as an interface between the application programs and the data they need to resolve business problems. The functions provided by the DBMS are data definition, data manipulation, and data management and control. Data definition provides the ability to define fields; to combine fields into records; and to define files, data access methods, and associations. Data manipulation allows users to retrieve, insert, delete, and modify data in the database. Data management and control allows the database administrator and operations personnel to start, stop, monitor, and reorganize the database.

Let's look at how these software components work together by tracing a transaction through the system. A *transaction* is a user-defined piece of work that, from the perspective of the database, performs a series of operations that leaves the database in a consistent state. The entire transaction must be completed or the database must be left in the state it was in before the transaction started. For a transaction that transfers money between two accounts, for example, there are three database states: (1) at the start of the transaction, (2) after taking money from one account, and (3) after placing the money in the second account, or the end of the transaction. The database is inconsistent in the second state.

Transaction Processing. For a particular example of a transaction, consider adding a new employee to the database. This process consists of inserting two records into the database, an employee record and a payroll record. The transaction starts at a terminal in the personnel department; the activity is shown in Figure 1-22.

From an opening menu displayed on the terminal, the operator selects an option for adding a new employee. This selection is transmitted to the data communications system, which determines that an employee input form is required. This screen template or input form is transmitted to the terminal, where the operator enters the required information. The terminal access method is responsible for ensuring that the proper control characters are inserted to format the data for the type of terminal being used. The lower levels of the data communications system provide the logic to properly place the data on the communications line, to detect transmission errors, and to provide the proper electrical signals for transmission.

The operator enters the data pertaining to the new employee and transmits it back to the computer, where it is received by the data communications system. The TCP checks the message for transmission errors, logs the message to a transaction log file, and determines the transaction type.

Figure 1-22   User
Interaction

Transaction control process (TCP) displays menu on terminal

User selects "add employee" activity and sends to TCP

TCP responds to terminal with data entry screen

User fills out screen and sends to TCP

TCP checks data for consistency and writes data to transaction log

TCP begins transaction

TCP sends message to application to process transaction

Application formats data and calls DBMS routine to add employee record to database

DBMS processes application request and returns completion status to application

Application formats data and calls DBMS routine to add payroll record to database

DBMS process application request and returns completion status to application

Application sends completion status to TCP

TCP ends transaction

TCP sends completion status to user at terminal

Since this transaction updates the database, the TCP formally begins a transaction for recovery purposes. Recognizing that it is a message for an application, the TCP determines which application should process the transaction and sends it to the proper application.

The application program receives the message—to insert two new records into the database—from the data communications system and begins to process it. It formats the records and makes the DBMS request to insert them.

The DBMS accepts the records and inserts them into the database. Before inserting the records, however, the DBMS logs the record images, both before and after making the changes. These before and after images can be used for recovery if a failure occurs. All necessary associations and access method retrieval capabilities are established as well. Upon successful completion of the record insertions, the DBMS returns a successful completion status to the application program. The application program then responds to the data communications system that the transaction has been successfully processed. The TCP ends the transaction and sends the completion status back to the terminal operator.

Throughout the transaction the operating system is actively involved, transferring control from one software subsystem to another, interfacing with the peripheral devices, and managing memory. Through the interaction of all the software systems, the transaction is completed. The operating system, the data communications system, and the DBMS support the application process in performing its work.

CASE STUDY

To make the discussions more understandable and relevant, examples are cited throughout this book. In addition, a common case study is carried from chapter to chapter, where applicable. This case study is adapted from actual situations.

Syncrasy Corporation is a startup company in Puma Flats, Kansas. The president and two founders decided to capitalize on the boom in the microcomputer marketplace by becoming a mail-order discount outlet for microcomputer hardware, software, and supplies. They have just opened their offices and warehouse and have begun taking orders. All their data processing requirements are met by a microcomputer and there is no need for data communications. As subsequent chapters illustrate, Syncrasy will become a high-growth company whose needs for computing power and data communications change rapidly as they grow and extend the enterprise.

SUMMARY

The data communications industry, somewhat dormant through the 1960s, has experienced tremendous expansion in the 1970s and 1980s, largely as the result of lower prices for both equipment and transmission media. In the 1970s, competition emerged for the provision of data communications circuits and the hardware components that attach to these circuits. The number of applications making use of data communications facilities has continued to grow, with online data processing forming one of the most rapidly growing segments of the industry. This demand for online data processing has given rise to computer systems designed to meet the needs of high performance, expansion, and reliability. The requirements of an online system are shown in Figure 1-23.

Performance	Consistency	Flexibility
Availability	Reliability	Recovery
Security		

Figure 1-23 Online System Requirements

Key Terms

application layer
availability
batch
Carterphone case
checksum
consistency

conversational
data communications
data entry
data link layer
data link protocol
distributed

fault tolerance
flexibility
flow control
full duplex
geosynchronous
half duplex
Hush-a-Phone case
inquiry/response
interactive
interface
International Standards
    Organization (ISO)
local area network (LAN)
mean time between failure (MTBF)
mean time to repair (MTTR)
medium
message
network
network layer
network routing table
node
office automation
online

open systems interconnection (OSI)
packet distribution network (PDN)
performance
physical layer
presentation layer
protocol
receiver
recovery
reliability
remote job entry (RJE)
security
Semi-Automatic Business Research
    Environment (SABRE)
Semi-Automatic Ground
    Environment (SAGE)
sender
sensor-based
session layer
simplex transmission
telecommunications
transaction control process (TCP)
transaction processing
transport layer

Review Questions

1. What is the distinction between telecommunications and data communications?

2. Why did the data communications industry grow so rapidly in the 1970s and 1980s?

3. Explain the significance to the data-processing industry of each of the following:
    a. the Hush-a-Phone decision
    b. the Carterphone decision
    c. MCI

4. Characterize each of the following types of application:
    a. inquiry/response
    b. interactive
    c. batch
    d. data entry
    e. distributed
    f. sensor-based

5. What are the requirements of an online system?

6. What is a fault-tolerant data communications network? How does fault tolerance improve the reliability of a network?

7. List the seven layers of the OSI reference model.

8. List two functions of each layer in the OSI reference model.

Exercises

1. How does the history of data communications differ from that of database development?

2. Investigate in detail two data communications applications. Note specifically the hardware used. Determine the categories of data communications into which the applications fall.

3. Select a specific application of data communications and identify the functions that would be required in the application, presentation, and session layers of the OSI reference model.

4. Discuss the history of telephone companies in the United States or your country as that history relates to the data communications industry.

5. How do U. S. telephone companies differ from their counterparts in Great Britain, France, Germany, Japan, and Australia? In what respects are they the same?

6. How might data communications systems be used in the home?

7. Which components (if any) can be deleted from Figure 1-16? Support your answer.

8. Do all transactions require database services? Give an example to support your answer.

9. In the section on performance (see "Requirements of an Online System"), two different definitions were given for response time. Using each definition, calculate the response time for a response of 1200 characters transmitted over a 30-character per second data communications line.

10. Syncrasy has only one microcomputer and the company does not use data communications. Explain how Syncrasy could use data communications to help run its business. For example, how could Syncrasy use information utilities like CompuServe and Prodigy?

11. Suppose Syncrasy has several microcomputers rather than just one. Can Syncrasy use data communications effectively? Explain your answer.

References

Bell Laboratories. *A History of Engineering and Science in the Bell System, National Service in War and Peace (1925–1975)*. Murray Hill, NJ: Bell Laboratories, 1982.

Brock, Gerald W. *The Telecommunications Industry*. Cambridge, MA: Harvard University Press, 1981.

Kleinfield, Sonny. *The Biggest Company on Earth*. New York: Holt, Rinehart & Winston, 1981.

Martin, James. *Introduction to Teleprocessing*. Englewood Cliffs, NJ: Prentice-Hall, 1972.

Metropolis, N., H. Howlett, and Gian-Carlo Rota, eds. *A History of Computing in the Twentieth Century*. New York: Academic Press, 1980.

Stallings, William. *Handbook of Computer Communications Standards: The Open Systems Interconnection (OSI) Model and OSI-Related Standards*, Volume 1. New York: Macmillan Publishing Company, 1987.

Tanenbaum, Andrew S. *Computer Networks*. Englewood Cliffs, NJ: Prentice-Hall, 1981.

PHYSICAL

II

MEDIA AND HARDWARE: THE PHYSICAL LAYER

Physical Aspects of Data Communications

Conducted Media
Radiated Media
Media Selection Criteria
Signal Representation and Modulation
Case Study

INTRODUCTION

In the first chapter we examined the essential features of communication, one of which was a medium. We also briefly discussed the OSI reference model, including the physical layer. This chapter acquaints you with the various media available for transporting information, the strengths and weaknesses of each medium, and the ways to represent data during its transmission. Specific topics in this chapter include:

Conducted media—wires, coaxial cable, and fiber optic cable

Radiated media—microwave radio, broadcast radio, satellite radio, and infrared transmission

Media selection criteria—cost, speed, availability, expandability, error rates, security, distance, environment, application, and maintenance

Strengths and weaknesses of each medium relative to the selection criteria

How signals are represented in analog and digital formats

The transmission media commonly used in today's data communications networks can be broken down into two major classes: conducted and radiated. *Conducted media* include telephone and telegraph wires, private

43

Figure 2-1 Trans-
mission Media

Conducted Media	**Radiated Media**
Electrical Conductors	Radio Frequency
Wires	Broadcast
Coaxial cable	Microwave
Light Conductors	Satellite
Fiber optics	Light Frequency
	Infrared

wires, *coaxial cables*, and *fiber optics*. *Radiated media* include broadcast radio, *microwave radio*, infrared transmission, and *satellite radio*. These options are listed in Figure 2-1. Each medium, together with its necessary transmission facilities, is discussed below. The discussion focuses on those characteristics that make each medium desirable or undesirable in different situations, including speed, security, distance, susceptibility to error, and cost. These attributes form the basis of the selection criteria discussed later in the chapter.

CONDUCTED MEDIA

Wires

Wires, today's most commonly used data transmission medium, are also the earliest. Much of the terminology and technology regarding this communications medium derive from telephony and telegraphy because, in setting up its own data communications networks, the computer industry used the existing network of telephone and telegraph lines. The advantages of wires are their availability and relatively low cost. Their disadvantages include susceptibility to signal distortion or error and the relatively low transmission rates they provide for long-distance links.

Private Versus Public Lines. Wires employed in data communications are either private or public. *Private lines* are those deployed by the user, and public lines are those provided by a common carrier like a telephone company. In general, public lines are in use where distances are great or the terrain or other environmental factors prohibit the use of private wires.

Transmission Speed and Frequency Range. Theoretically, the maximum transmission speed along wire links is over 10 million bits per second (bps). The speed is a function of the distance spanned, the diameter of the wire, and—for the twisted wire pairs used by the telephone companies—the mutual capacitance of the wires in the pair. Local or private wire links typically operate at speeds up to 80,000 bps and long-distance connections operate at up to 56,000 bps, with speeds of 9600 and 19,200 bps commonly used. Higher speed long-distance circuits are also available for applications with high-volume data transfer requirements. Technology improvements in the mid-1980s have produced very high transmission rates over twisted wire pairs for local area networks (LANs). In 1987 several companies released LAN implementations running at speeds up to 16 million bps over unshielded twisted wires. This enables users to employ existing telephone wires for high-speed local area networks.

Cable Cost, Gauge, and Types. Private cable ranges in cost from 8 cents per foot to over $1 per foot, depending on the shielding, gauge, and number of conducting wires in the cable. The type of wire most commonly used for private lines is stranded copper, of American Wire Gauges 19, 22, 24, 26, and 28. Figure 2-2(a) shows a single conductor wire. Private wires are usually bundled, providing multiple conductors inside one insulating sheath. The number of conducting strands in such a cable varies, with 4, 7, 8, 10, 12, 15, and 25 conductors being the most common. Figure 2-2(c) shows a wire bundle with multiple conductors.

Ordinary telephone wire consists of a twisted pair of wires. Bundles of these wire pairs from telephones in a given area are sheathed together. Each pair of wires is twisted together to minimize signal distortion from adjacent wire pairs in the sheath. Figure 2-2(b) depicts an individual twisted wire pair.

Switched Connections Versus Leased Lines. Data communications over long distances can use either switched or leased line connections. *Switched connections* use the same equipment as a standard voice telephone call. One of the two devices to be connected dials the telephone number of the other device's line. Since the telephone company cannot guarantee exactly which path or switching equipment such a connection will use, the speed and quality of the switched connection is limited by the equipment used to set up the circuit. Because the circuit may be routed in a variety of ways, it is possible that lower quality equipment may be used to establish the call. Most switched connections operate at speeds of 300, 1200, 2400, 4800, 9600, 19,200, or 38,400 bps. Higher speeds are possible, but the potential for error

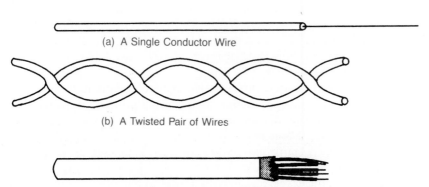

(a) A Single Conductor Wire

(b) A Twisted Pair of Wires

(c) A Shielded Multi-Conductor Wire Bundle

Figure 2-2 Types of Wires

and the cost of the necessary extra equipment currently make such speeds cost prohibitive for most users. This limit on speed is being increased in certain areas as telephone companies implement digital data transmission technology, which allows speeds of up to 56,000 bps with switched connections. In the next chapter you read about digital data transmission.

Because they are more expensive for dedicated use than leased lines are, switched lines are used when the amount of transmitted data is small or when many locations must be contacted for relatively short periods. Two examples are (1) a team of salespersons entering information on their portable terminals and (2) a central host computer for a retail organization that contacts each retail outlet at the close of the business day to collect sales and inventory data. In both these situations the amount of data to be transferred is small, and the number of locations may be large or changeable. Switched lines become more expensive as the connection time increases, and their cost effectiveness may depend on their location, the hour of transmission, and the number of required connections. Chapter 10 discusses an alternative to switched lines—packet distribution networks.

Leased lines are used if the connection time between locations is long enough to cover the cost of leasing or if speeds higher than those available with switched lines must be attained. The cost of a leased line is a function of the distance covered, the transmission speed of the line, and the line's susceptibility to error. *Common carriers* provide a wide variety of options to satisfy diverse needs. For example, a leased line would enable terminals in a sales office in Seattle to communicate with a host computer in San Francisco. For this application the data volume is relatively low and a low transmission speed is adequate but the connection is maintained throughout the day, which makes the leased line cost effective. An application in which a leased line would be used for both economy and speed is when two distant computers—in Chicago and Los Angeles, for example—must exchange high volumes of information in a timely manner. (For now, only the medium of wires is being considered, and alternatives are being ignored.)

Leased telephone lines can be *conditioned* by the telephone companies to provide lower error rates and increased transmission speeds. One example of conditioning is the use of special equipment that equalizes the signal delay for all frequencies. There are five levels of conditioning, C1 through C5, with level C3 not commercially available. Conditioned leased lines typically operate at speeds of up to 64,000 bps. Again, digital data transmission may be considerably faster.

Very high speed connections are also available. Although such high-speed links may utilize other media, such as fiber optics and microwaves, they are included in this discussion of wires because of their association with telephone lines. These high-speed services are designated T-1, T-2, T-3, and T-4 and offer transmission rates of 1.5, 6.3, 46, and 281 million bits per second (Mbps), respectively. T-2 service is not commonly available. More detail about these services may be found in Chapter 3 in the section about common carrier services. The cost of leased lines has continually changed as a result of new technologies and industry competition.

Coaxial Cable

Coaxial cable is primarily used in local area networks or over relatively short distances, generally less than 10 miles (except for uses by common carriers). Most local area networks (LANs) are privately owned and are restricted to a relatively small geographical area such as an office building or complex of buildings. LANs are discussed in more detail in Chapters 8 and 9. Coaxial cable is also used to connect terminals with terminal controller units (see Chapter 5 for information about communications controllers). Data transmission rates of up to 100 Mbps are not uncommon, and the theoretical bit rate is more than 400 Mbps.

Technology. Coaxial cable comes packaged in a variety of ways, but essentially it consists of one or two central data transmission wires surrounded by an insulating layer, a shielding layer, and an outer jacket, as depicted in Figure 2-3. Coaxial cable transmission involves two basic techniques: *baseband* and *broadband*. In *broadband transmission* the data is carried on high-frequency carrier waves; thus, several channels may be transmitted over a single cable. Frequency separation, referred to as *guardbands*, helps keep one signal from interfering with another. Broadband technology allows one medium to be used for a variety of transmission needs. For example, voice, video, and multiple data channels of varying transmission speeds could all exist on one cable.

 Baseband transmission, on the other hand, does not use a carrier wave but sends the data along the channel by voltage fluctuations. Baseband technology cannot transmit multiple channels on one cable, but it is less expensive than broadband because it can use less expensive cable and connectors. Some coaxial cable can be used for either baseband or broadband. The advantages and disadvantages of baseband versus broadband technologies are discussed in Chapter 8, in conjunction with local area networks. Baseband and broadband transmission are illustrated in Figure 2-4.

Cost. The cost of coaxial cable ranges from approximately 30 cents per foot to several dollars per foot. Other major cost items in a coaxial cable

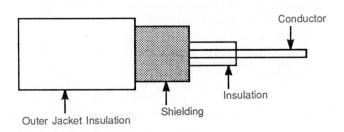

Figure 2-3 A Single Conductor Coaxial Cable

Figure 2-4 Base-
band and Broadband
Transmission

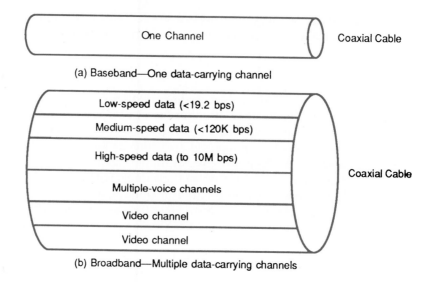

(a) Baseband—One data-carrying channel

(b) Broadband—Multiple data-carrying channels

network are the adapters, controllers, and transceivers that transmit and receive data at high speeds.

Advantages and Disadvantages. The television industry has helped develop coaxial cable technology, including the capabilities to add stations or tap into a line without interrupting existing service. In an environment where workstations are regularly added, moved, or deleted, the ability to alter the equipment configuration without disruption to existing users is significant. However, the ability to tap into the cable without disrupting service is a disadvantage if a high degree of security is required. Coaxial cable shielding provides a high degree of immunity to externally caused signal distortion. In local area networks of less than a half-mile range (the distance varies with specific implementations), signal loss (*attenuation*) is not a concern; for longer distances, however, repeaters that enhance the signals are necessary.

One disadvantage of coaxial cable might also be considered an advantage—security. If a very secure medium is required, with taps being difficult to make and easy to detect, coaxial cable presents a serious problem. Whenever distances are great, attenuation becomes a problem, as does cost—the cost of the greater amount of cable and the repeaters that must be installed to enhance the signals over long distances. The advantages of coaxial cable include its high data transmission rates, its immunity to noise or signal distortion (compared with twisted wire pairs), its capability for adding stations, and its reasonable cost over short distances.

Fiber Optic Cable

Fiber optic cable is a relatively new communications medium used by telephone companies in place of long-distance wires. It is also used by private companies in implementing local data communications networks.

Technology. Although fiber optic cables come in three varieties, each with a different way of guiding the light pulses from source to destination, they all have the same form and characteristics. One or more glass or plastic fibers are woven together to form the core of the cable. This core is surrounded by a glass or plastic layer called the *cladding*. The cladding in turn is covered with plastic or some other material for protection. Figure 2-5 shows a cross-section of a fiber optic cable. All three cable varieties require a light source, with laser and light-emitting diodes (LED) being those most commonly used.

The oldest of the three fiber optic technologies uses *multimode step-index fiber*, in which the reflective walls of the fiber move the light pulses to the receiver. Figure 2-6 illustrates multimode step-index transmission. Multimode *graded-index* fiber acts to refract (bend) the light toward the center of the fiber by variations in the density of the core. Figure 2-7 depicts the movement of light in a multimode graded-index fiber. The third and fastest fiber optic technique is *single mode transmission*. With single mode transmission, light is guided down the center of an extremely narrow core. Single mode transmission is depicted in Figure 2-8. Fiber optic transmis-

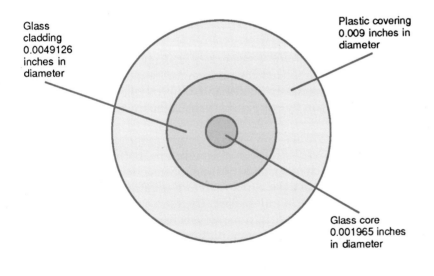

Glass cladding 0.0049126 inches in diameter

Plastic covering 0.009 inches in diameter

Glass core 0.001965 inches in diameter

Figure 2-5 An End View of a Fiber Optic Cable

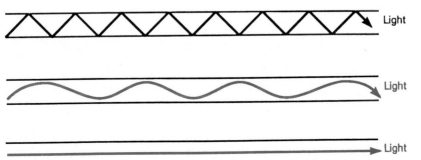

Light

Figure 2-6 Fiber Optic Multimode Step Index

Light

Figure 2-7 Fiber Optic Multimode Graded-Index

Light

Figure 2-8 Fiber Optic Single Mode

sion rates currently available range up to approximately 1 billion bps (Gbps), with speeds over 2 billion bps (2Gbps) possible.

Benefits and Cost.   One of the shortcomings of fiber optics is the inability to add new nodes while other nodes are active. Although it is now relatively easy to splice the fiber optic cable and add new stations, the network or a portion of the network must be down while the splice is being prepared. Fiber optic links for very short distances cost more than wires, but as distance or the required transmission rate increases, fiber optics becomes cost effective. The break-even point generally occurs when the distance is so great that coaxial cable or wires would require expensive signal-enhancing equipment. A significant advantage that fiber optics has over copper wires is its reduced size and weight—about 20 times lighter and five times smaller than equivalent copper wire (either coaxial or twisted pair). Very low error rates and immunity to environmental interference are additional benefits.

RADIATED MEDIA

Microwave Radio

It was MCI's proposal for a *microwave* linkage between Chicago and St. Louis that first stimulated competition for long-distance telephone service. The first commercially implemented digital microwave radio system was installed in Japan by Nippon Electric Company in 1968.

Technology.   Microwave transmission rates range up to 45 Mbps. Because microwave signals travel in a straight line, both transmitter and receiver must be in each other's line of sight (obstructions cannot be between them). The curvature of the earth therefore requires that microwave stations be approximately 30 miles apart. The total *bandwidth* of a microwave channel can be subdivided into many subchannels. The subchannels are used for voice-grade transmission, high-speed data links, or both. Bandwidth, one measure of the carrying capacity of a medium, and other measures of carrying capacity are discussed later in this chapter.

Advantages and Disadvantages.   Microwave transmission offers speed, cost effectiveness, and ease of implementation; however, it has the unfortunate potential for interference from other radio waves. It also is limited by line-of-sight considerations, and commercial transmissions are insecure, since they can be intercepted by anyone with a receiver in the line of transmission. Microwaves can also be affected by environmental conditions. Transmissions at the same or nearly the same frequencies can interfere with each other, and some atmospheric conditions—for example, high humidity—can affect the signal. Figure 2-9 shows a picture of a microwave relay station.

Figure 2-9 A Microwave Relay Station

Broadcast Radio

Broadcast radio employs not only the radio frequencies typical of AM and FM stations, but *short-wave* or short-distance radio frequencies as well, with total frequency range from 500,000 to 108 million cycles per second. Broadcast radio's primary applications are in paging terminals, the devices carried by people (such as doctors) who are on call; for cellular radio telephones; and in wireless local area networks. A good example of radio broadcast for data communications is in the AlohaNet at the University of Hawaii. Broadcast radio was chosen to overcome the difficulty of setting up wire links in the islands, and it proved quite effective when the number of stations was relatively small. As more stations were added, however, contention between broadcasting stations increased, collisions or interference became more frequent, and effective utilization dropped. Furthermore, the medium proved to be susceptible to interference from other radio broadcast sources. The AlohaNet transmission rate was 9600 bps. When broadcast radio is used with local area networks, cables connecting each microcomputer are eliminated. The elimination of cables makes installation and changing of workstations easier and reduces the problems of loose connections that can occur as a result of people walking or pulling on cables.

Satellite Radio

Satellite radio transmission, like microwave radio transmission, transmits data via very-high-frequency (VHF) radio waves; both media require line-of-sight transmission between stations. The primary difference between the two media is station location. Microwave makes use of land-based stations only, whereas satellite uses both land-based stations and orbiting stations. Commercial communication satellites are placed in an equatorial, geosynchronous orbit at an altitude of 22,300 miles. A *geosynchronous* orbit means that the satellite remains stationary relative to a given position on the earth, as illustrated in Figure 2-10. At this altitude, only three satellites are required to have all points on the earth within range, as shown in Figure 2-11.

Technology.   The basic components of satellite transmission are the earth stations, for sending and receiving, and the satellite component called a *transponder.* The transponder functions to receive the transmission from earth (*uplink*), amplify the signal, change the frequency, and transmit the data to a receiving earth station (*downlink*). The uplink frequency differs from the downlink frequency so the weaker incoming signals are not interfered with by the stronger outgoing signals. Thus, satellite frequencies are spoken of in pairs, such as 12/14 gigahertz. The first number represents the downlink frequency and the second, the uplink frequency. *Giga* means one billion, and 1 hertz is one cycle per second. Thus, 12/14 giga-

Figure 2-10   A
Geosynchronous
Satellite Orbit

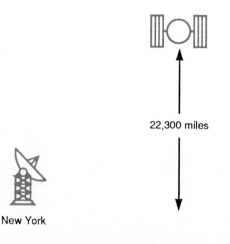

22,300 miles

New York

Los Angeles

Figure 2-11 Satellite
Positioning

22,300 miles
35,880
kilometers

Earth

hertz means a downlink transmission frequency of 12 billion cycles per second and an uplink transmission frequency of 14 billion cycles per second. To avoid interference, communication satellites in space must be separated by an arc of at least 4 degrees, as depicted in Figure 2-12. (This has led to concern, especially among countries presently incapable of launching satellites, that only a limited amount of space is available for these satellites and that the space will be allocated without them obtaining a slot.)

Each transponder has a transmission rate of approximately 50 Mbps, which can be divided into 16 1.5-Mbps channels, 400 64-Kbps channels (Kbps means kilobits per second, or 1000 bits per second), or 600 40-Kbps

Figure 2-12 Satellite Separation

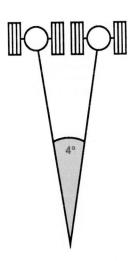

4°

channels. Although this transmission rate is high, there still is a significant delay, since the signals must travel a long distance from source to destination.

Propagation Delay.   The amount of time it takes for a signal to travel from its source to its destination is called *propagation delay*. Since most data communications signals travel at nearly the speed of light, propagation delay on earth is insignificant (about 16 milliseconds for a 3000-mile transcontinental journey). Across the extremely long distances of space, however, propagation delay can be noticeable. In addition to travel time, the delay includes the time required to accept, enhance, and retransmit the signal. Propagation delay becomes significant for applications that have sending times of less than a quarter-second or response time of a half-second or less. Although propagation delay is ordinarily ignored for terrestrial links, satellite transmission system designers must be aware of this factor. Figure 2-13 gives an example of how propagation delay is computed for a transaction in which a remote terminal sends a message to a host computer and receives a reply from it.

Satellite Providers.   There are several providers of transponders for satellite communication, including RCA, Satellite Business Systems (a joint venture started by IBM, Comsat, and Aetna), American Satellite, AT&T, GTE, Western Union, and NASA, as well as broadcast agencies in Canada, Japan, Europe, and the Soviet Union. The number of transponders per satellite is typically between 12 and 24. Providers of satellite time usually lease a whole transponder, but it is also possible to sublease transponder subchannels from another user. Satellites make expansion of a data communications network relatively easy. All that is required is to add earth stations (except when the area being served is outside the area serviced by the satellite(s) being used). Satellite networks can present security problems, however, since transmission can be intercepted by anyone with proper receiving equipment.

Infrared Transmission

Infrared transmission uses electromagnetic radiation of wavelengths between visible light and radio waves. Like microwaves, infrared trans-

Figure 2-13 Satellite Propagation Delay	Remote–satellite input uplink 22,300 miles
	Satellite–host input downlink 22,300
	Host–satellite response uplink 22,300
	Satellite–remote response downlink 22,300
	Total distance 89,200 miles

$$\text{Travel time} = \frac{89{,}200 \text{ miles}}{186{,}000 \text{ miles/second}} = 0.48 \text{ seconds}$$

Frequency (Hz)	Wave Length
10^{16}	X-rays, Gamma rays
10^{15}	Ultraviolet light
	Visible light
10^{14}	Infrared light
10^{13}	
10^{12}	Millimeter waves
10^{11}	Microwaves
10^{10}	UHF television
10^{9}	VHF television
10^{8}	VHF TV (high band)
	FM radio
10^{7}	VHF TV (low band)
10^{6}	Shortwave radio
	AM radio
10^{5}	
10^{4}	
10^{3}	Very low frequency
10^{2}	
10^{1}	

Figure 2-14 Frequency Spectrum Classification

mission is a line-of-sight technology. It is used to provide local area connections between buildings and also is the medium used in some wireless local area networks. Data transmission rates are typically on the order of 100 Kbps or less. This technology, like broadcast radio, is not used extensively in the data communications industry.

Radiated Media Frequencies

The frequencies of various radiated media are given in Figure 2-14.

MEDIA SELECTION CRITERIA

Several factors influence the choice of a medium for a data communications network. These factors are given in Figure 2-15. Since every configuration has its own set of constraints, not all factors apply in every situation; in some situations, there may even be only a single viable alternative. However, system designers must consider each criterion, either im-

Cost	Security
Speed or Capacity	Distance
Availability	Environment
Expandability	Application
Error Rates	Maintenance

Figure 2-15 Media Selection Criteria

plicitly or explicitly. In most situations, the factors may influence one another. For example, a strong correlation often exists between a medium's
application and its required speed, so much so that the application usually
dictates a minimum acceptable transmission speed (although other factors
such as cost and expandability can also pertain).

Cost

A dramatic expansion in the application of data communications began in
the 1970s, influenced strongly by improvements in technology and a lowering of costs. Cost reductions were the result of the improved technology
and the competition among the common carriers providing transmission
services. The technological advances included communications equipment
capable of supporting higher data transmission rates at lower costs, as well
as the commercial availability of fiber optics and satellite transmission.

The costs associated with a given transmission medium include not
only the costs of the medium but also ancillary costs, such as the costs for
additional hardware and software that might be required. A deferred ancillary cost that is important to consider when making an initial selection
is the cost of expansion. For example, an emerging marketing organization located in Houston, Texas, might initially select the specific market
areas of New York City, Chicago, Houston, and Los Angeles. The logical
choice for connecting the remote offices to the host computer in Houston
is to lease a line from a common carrier. As the corporation expands into
other cities, however, a satellite link could be more economical because the
expense of adding new locations might be less than that of leasing more
land lines.

Speed

A tremendous range of transmission speeds is available. Low-speed circuits transmit at rates under 100 bps, and high-speed circuits, at over
100 Mbps. Within a given medium, higher speeds mean higher costs,
though this is not necessarily attributable to the medium itself. Higher
data transmission rates require more sophisticated (expensive) communications equipment. Two factors dictate the required speed of a medium:
response time and *aggregate data rate*. Design goals for an online application
should include the expected response time for each type of transaction.
Aggregate data rate refers to the amount of information that can be transmitted per unit of time. Media speeds are summarized in Figure 2-16.

Response Time.   Response time has two components, *transmission time*
and *processing time*, and each of these can be broken down into subcomponents. Suppose the design objective is a response time of 3 seconds for
95% of one type of transaction. If processing takes 1 second, transmission
must take 2 seconds or less. If the transaction involves the exchange of

Medium	Common Transfer Rates (bps)
Private line	300, 1200, 2400, 4800, 9600, 19,200, 38,400, 56,000, 64,000, 80,000
Switched line	300, 1200, 2400, 4800, 9600, 19,200, 38,400
Leased line	2400, 4800, 9600, 19,200, 56,000, 64,000
T1, T2, T3, T4	1.5M, 6.3M, 46M, 281M
Coaxial cable	1M, 2M, 10M, 50M, 100M (over 400M potential)
Fiber optics	over 2 Gbps
Microwave	to 45M
Broadcast radio	9600 (in AlohaNet)
Satellite	to 50M

Figure 2-16 Media and Their Common Transmission Speeds

500 characters of information, then the speed of the medium must be at least 250 characters per second (500 characters divided by 2 seconds), which represents approximately 2400 bps. (This assumes there is no sharing of the communications link. If the line is shared, allowances must be made for the amount of time that the line might be unavailable to a specific user. Chapters 4 and 5 discuss several ways that one communications line can be shared among several users.)

Aggregate Data Rate.   In other applications, such as bulk data transfers, aggregate data rate may be the factor dictating line speed. Suppose the application just discussed required that the line be available to office personnel during the day for inquiries and updates and that within an hour of closing time a file of 2 million characters had to be transmitted to a host computer. The business day requirements for response time could be satisfied with a 2400-bps channel, but the file transfer would require an aggregate data rate of about 555 characters per second (2 million characters per hour divided by 3600 seconds per hour), which is a 7200 bps channel. (These examples do not allow for any overhead or re-transmissions due to errors.)

Availability

Availability here has two meanings: (1) Is the medium available when it is needed? (2) Is there sufficient carrying capacity to handle the volume of data? An operation that uses a switched telephone line would be at a disadvantage when phone lines are busy, as on certain holidays. For instance, imagine a fast-food chain with stores throughout the United States that maintains a central file of sales and inventory data. Each store's terminals record the daily receipts and foods dispensed. At the end of the business day, the central location dials the phone number of each store's computer, transfers and processes the data collected during the day, and then orders supplies for each restaurant. On Mother's Day, the phone circuits are extremely busy, which interferes with the chain's ability to contact all of its locations. This lack of availability would not be catastrophic for this application, but for a process control or factory control application, lack of availability could produce disastrous results.

Shared Lines.   Shared lines also can create problems of availability. One user may monopolize the line, thus making it unavailable to others. Suppose that two terminals share a line, and one user is attempting interactive queries into a database while the other attempts to copy a lengthy file to an attached printer. The line's capacity may be taken up with the file transfer, making the line unavailable to the other user.

Control Messages.   Some of a line's capacity must be reserved for control messages. For instance, error detection requires additional bits of information to be appended to the data. A long message that must be broken down into segments for transmission requires extra information to delimit the message's beginning, end, and segments. Acknowledging receipt of transmitted data creates additional line congestion. When erroneous messages are received, then the last message, and perhaps several previous messages, must be re-transmitted. Multiple devices per line requires that addresses be appended to messages; in many instances, control sequences need to be transmitted to establish when each device can use the medium and receive data. Finally, idle time may occur on the circuit because there is no data to send or because the state of the circuit is being changed (such as the transition from sending data to receiving, known as *turnaround*). These types of control functions can take up a considerable amount of the carrying capacity of a circuit—as much as 30%, excluding idle time. Figure 2-17 illustrates some of the extra fields appended to a message for transmission and for segmenting a long message.

Expandability

Frequently it becomes necessary to expand the scope of a data communications configuration, either by adding more devices at a given location or by adding new locations. Some media—such as coaxial cable and satellites—make expansion into new locations relatively easy, whereas others—such as leased telephone lines—make expansion more difficult or more costly. It is important that communications networks be designed for the future as well as for immediate needs. Suppose a rapidly growing computer company used private wires to attach terminals for some employees in the head office. The initial applications were extremely successful, and new applications and employees were quickly added. This created a need for more terminals, which required additional communications circuits. The company had to go through the time-consuming and expensive process of stringing additional wires throughout the facility. Had they anticipated their growth correctly, the additional wires could have been installed with the initial set.

Several alternatives are also available in such situations. Instead of supplying additional circuits, the company could have added new hard-

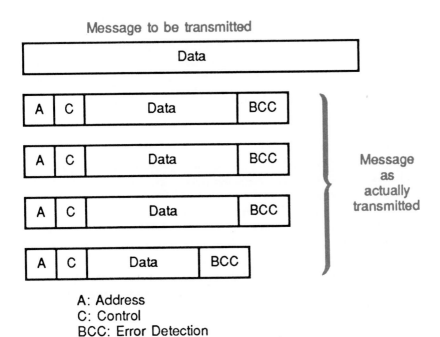

Message to be transmitted

Figure 2-17 Message Transmission

A: Address
C: Control
BCC: Error Detection

ware, such as concentrators, multiplexers, or addressable terminals. Such solutions are the subject of Chapters 4 and 5. Expandability is a problem not just of media availability but also of hardware. When a system has reached its maximum capacity with respect to the available number of devices and communications circuits, a larger machine or additional machines must be added. The airline industry's reservations systems have faced this problem several times as more subscribers were added to the network.

Error Rates

All transmission media are subject to signal distortion, which can produce errors in the data. The propensity for error influences not only the quality of transmission but also its speed. For example, switched telephone lines are subject to noise from switching equipment and other sources, which typically limits the speed to 38,400 bps or less. Such errors pose no problem in voice communication because humans are adept at detecting errors and recovering from them—either a person does not understand what is being said or the context is incorrect. And recovery is simple because a person can usually ask that a message be repeated from a particular point. Computers, on the other hand, do not understand context, and therefore are unable to detect a corrupted data bit. The impact of even one undetected inverted bit can be significant. Suppose that a bank must use data communications to transfer several million dollars to another bank. If just one of the high-order bits in the money field is changed, a difference of several million dollars can result. To detect transmission errors in data communications environments requires that redundant information be included with the transferred data. This technique reduces the efficiency of the link and still cannot ensure absolute accuracy of the data. The common methods for detecting errors are discussed in Chapter 3.

Security

The lack of security in data communications networks was made clear when hackers penetrated several major networks. Personal computers have provided a low-cost capability for entering other systems, and competition among the providers of communications networks and value-added carriers has reduced the cost of long-distance connections. Providing complete security, like providing an error-free medium, is impossible. However, some media—such as fiber optics—are more difficult to penetrate, whereas others—such as coaxial cable, microwave, and satellite—are relatively easy to tap. The medium most vulnerable to the average hacker is switched lines.

Distance

Distance includes not only transmission distance but also the number of locations served. If the distances are short (within one building or complex of buildings), private media such as wires, coaxial cable, or fiber optics may be feasible. With greater distance or number of locations, it usually becomes necessary to obtain media from a common carrier. As the number of locations to be reached becomes very great, or when it is necessary to communicate with remote locations, a broadcast medium such as satellite may be the only viable solution.

Environment

The constraints of environment can eliminate certain types of media. For instance, even when the distance between two buildings to be connected in a data communications network is small enough to make private lines feasible, local ordinances may prohibit the user from installing them. If a locale prohibits the stringing of wire over or under a public street, the user might have to pick a medium other than private wires. Direct satellite links in leased office facilities might be impossible because the lease prohibits installing earth stations on the premises. Private lines that must be strung through areas with considerable electrical or magnetic interference might be impractical because of the potential for inducing error in transmission. Clearly, environment plays a critical role in the selection of a transmission medium.

Application

Certain applications (such as environmental monitoring) employ devices designed to connect to a system in a very specific way and at specific speeds. In such applications, the characteristics of the required equipment may dictate the type of medium and interfaces to be used. Furthermore, as noted above, the particulars of an application help determine other required characteristics of the medium, such as speed, security, and availability. For instance, the most obvious media for a high-speed local area network are twisted wire pairs, coaxial cable, and fiber optics, with the private branch exchange (PBX) telephone system being a lower speed alternative.

Maintenance

Just as all media are subject to error, all are subject to failure. In some cases repair or replacement is simple—a telephone cable severed in an excavation accident can be repaired within several days, and while repairs are being made, an alternate path might be made available. Repair or replacement of a defective satellite, however, is a lengthy process, which is why communications companies frequently have a backup transponder available. Because such failures are infrequent, maintenance concerns do not have a high priority. Nonetheless, system designers must consider the impact of medium failures and their probable duration and must prepare a backup or contingency plan so communications can continue while repairs are being made. Consider a major bank in Australia that depended heavily on its computer center. The bank established multiple computer centers, each serviced by different telecommunications trunk lines. It also made provisions for switching lines from one center to another should the communications links to one of the centers be severed. As a result, no failure at a single point was able to disrupt the bank's ability to process data.

A comparison of the principal data communications media is provided in Figure 2-18. In some instances it is difficult to separate one criterion

	Wires	Coaxial Cable	Fiber Optics	Microwave	Broadcast Radio	Satellite
Availability	Good	Good	Good	Good	Possible contention	Fair to good
Expandability	Fair	Good in local area	Good	Good	Good	Good
Errors	Fair	Good	Good	Fair	Fair	Fair
Security	Fair	Fair	Good	Poor	Poor	Poor
Distance	Good	Poor	Good	Good	Good	Good
Environment	Fair	Good	Good	Fair	Fair	Fair

Figure 2-18 Media Comparison Chart

from another. Consider the expandability of a network that uses wires. Some of the options available involve hardware; one option adds lines. If this last alternative is chosen, there is usually no problem in obtaining the circuit. Unfortunately, the cost may be high, which is why this cell in the chart is assigned a rating of fair. (This chart should be used in conjunction with Figure 2-16, on transmission speeds.)

SIGNAL REPRESENTATION AND MODULATION

Now that we have discussed the various transmission media, it is time to explore how data are stored and transmitted.

Bit Rates, Baud Rates, and Bandwidth

Up to this point, data transmission speed has been discussed exclusively in bits per second. This *bit rate* is the most appropriate unit for systems analysis. However, two other terms also are in common usage: *baud* and *bandwidth*. The *bandwidth* of a channel is the difference between the minimum and maximum frequencies allowed. Thus, a voice-grade channel that can transmit frequencies between 300 and 3400 hertz (Hz) has a bandwidth of 3100 Hz. Bandwidth is a measure of the amount of data that can be transmitted per unit of time and is directly proportional to the maximum data transmission speed of a medium. The higher the bandwidth, the greater the data-carrying capacity.

Baud Rate. The *baud rate* is a measure of the number of discrete signals that can be observed per unit of time. Only in the binary situation is the baud rate exactly the same as the bit rate. Unfortunately, the two terms frequently are used synonymously. But the bit rate is higher than the baud rate when a baud represents more than one bit of information. For example, in the binary amplitude modulation situation, two different signal levels can represent the bits 0 and 1 (as discussed earlier). If the signal changed 1200 times a second, the baud rate would be 1200 and the bit rate would be 1200 bps. Suppose, instead, that four different amplitudes were represented—1, 2, 3, and 4 per unit of time, as in Figure 2-19. Each level could then be used to represent two bits. This technique is referred to as *dibits*. One possible representation is given in Figure 2-20.

Suppose that a signaling rate of 1200 changes per second is maintained. The baud rate remains at 1200, but the bit rate doubles to 2400 bps because each signal represents two bits. Figure 2-21 shows the transmission of the bit pattern 1001001 using dibits (with one bit added to make the number of bits even). Similarly, eight signal levels could represent three bits with each signal, a technique referred to as *tribits*. If 16 different sig-

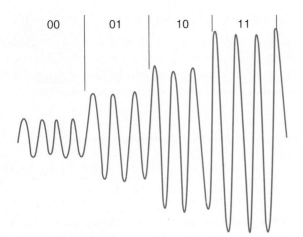

Figure 2-19 Dibits Using Amplitude Modulation

Bit Pattern	Amplitude
00	1
01	2
10	3
11	4

Figure 2-20 One Possible Dibit Representation

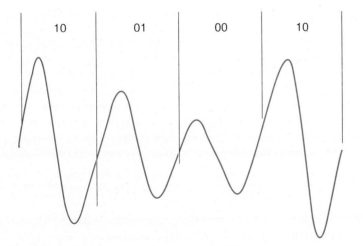

Figure 2-21 Dibits Using Amplitude Modulation

naling levels were used, four bits per signal could be represented, a technique referred to as *quadbits*. Hence, with current technology the bit rate equals the baud rate or a multiple thereof (two, three, or four times the baud rate). *Phase shift keying* (*PSK*) or a derivative is the most common method of achieving dibit and tribit transfer; *quadrature amplitude modulation* (*QAM*) is the most common for quadbit transfer. Later in this chapter you read about how PSK and QAM are implemented.

Digital Versus Analog Representation

All the computers we are considering store data in digital form and transmit this data in *analog* or *digital* form. In *digital form*, data is represented by a series of distinct entities. In data communications equipment this series is almost always a binary digit, or bit — either 0 or 1. *Analog* refers to measurable physical quantities, which in data communications take the form of voltages and variations in the properties of waves. Data is represented in analog form by varying the amplitude (voltage), frequency (hertz), and/or phase of a wave.

Modems

Translation from digital format to analog format and back to digital format is accomplished by a device known as a *data set* or *modem* (an acronym for modulator-demodulator). A modem functions to accept digital data (a string of bits), transform it into an analog signal, and pass the signal along a medium to another modem. The receiving modem translates the analog signal back into digital data. Since the telephone companies' original communications systems transmit information in analog form, these systems must change the data to analog form to meet the requirements of data communications transmission facilities.

Carrier Signals

Figure 2-22 depicts a simple sine wave, which has the potential for carrying information. If the wave continues without change, as depicted, no information can be discerned. Such an unmodulated signal is called a *carrier signal*. The object of a modem is to change (modulate) the characteristics of the carrier wave so a receiver can interpret information. The simple sine wave has several properties that can be altered to represent data: *amplitude* (height), *frequency* (period), and *phase* (relative starting point). Modems alter one or more of these characteristics to represent data.

Amplitude Modulation

The simplest characteristic to visualize is *amplitude modulation (AM)*. Figure 2-23 represents two sine waves superimposed on one another. One curve represents sin *wt* and the other represents 2 sin *wt*. Note that the

Figure 2-22   A
Simple Sine Wave

$y = \sin x$

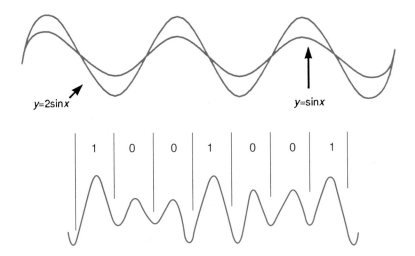

Figure 2-23 Super-imposed Sine Waves

y=2sinx   y=sinx

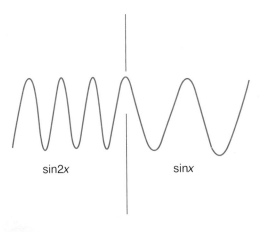

Figure 2-24 Amplitude Modulation

2 sin *wt* curve has twice the amplitude of the sin *wt* curve. (Varying the amplitude of a curve is similar to changing the voltage on a line.) How is this variation used to convey information? Suppose the bit pattern 1001001 is to be transmitted. If a 1 bit is represented by the curve of 2 sin *x*, and a 0 bit, by the curve traced by sin *x*, the bit pattern would be represented by the modulated sine curve depicted in Figure 2-24.

Frequency Modulation

The period, or frequency, of a sine curve is the interval required for the curve to complete one entire cycle. In the simple sine curve the period is 2 pi, where pi is approximately 3.14159. In data transmission, such intervals are only seconds, so the period is the number of seconds required for the wave to complete one cycle. The mathematical function that alters the period is sin *wt*. Figure 2-25 shows the curve of sin 2*x*. When the horizon-

Figure 2-25 The Curve of Sin 2*x*

sin2x   sinx

tal axis represents time, the period is frequency (oscillations) per unit of time. *Hertz* (Hz) is the term used to denote frequency; one hertz is one cycle per second. The human ear can detect sound waves with frequencies between 20 and 20,000 Hz. Telephone systems use the much smaller frequency range between 300 and 3400 Hz, which is satisfactory for carrying voice transmission.

To convey information by *frequency modulation* (FM) is to vary the frequency of the transmission. To transmit the binary pattern 1001001 by frequency modulation on a voice-grade line, a frequency of 1300 Hz can represent the 1 bit and a frequency of 2100 Hz can represent the 0 bit (one of the actual values used by some modems). The signal received must be within 10 Hz of these values to be acceptable, which means the range for a 1 bit is 1290–1310 Hz. These frequency values must be different enough to minimize the possibility of signal distortion altering the values transmitted. Thus, if the 1 bit were represented by 1500 Hz and the 0 bit by 1510 Hz, a decrease of only 10 Hz would change a 0 bit into a 1 bit. Figure 2-26 shows an example of frequency modulation for our selected bit pattern 1001001.

Phase Modulation

A third modulation technique is *phase modulation* (phase shifting). If the simple sine curve is represented by sin *wt*, then a change of phase is represented by sin (*wt* + *n*). Figure 2-27 shows the curve of sin *wt*, Figure 2-28 shows the curve of sin (*wt* + pi), and Figure 2-29 shows the two curves superimposed on one another. Transmitting the bit pattern of 1001001

Figure 2-26   Frequency Modulation

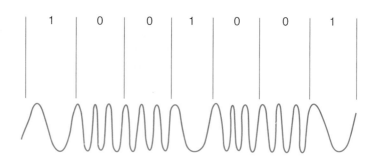

Figure 2-27   The Curve of Sin *wt*

sin*wt*

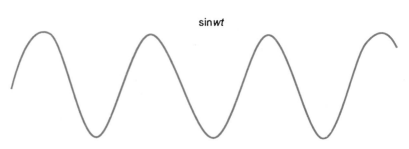

sin*wt*+π

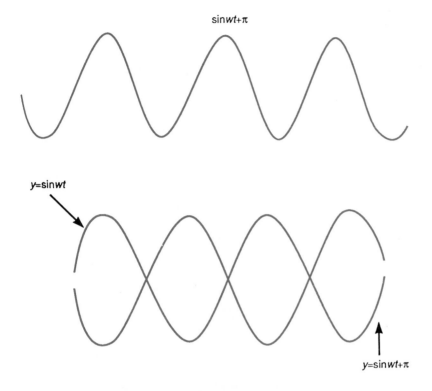

Figure 2-28 The Curve of Sin *wt* + π

y=sin*wt*

y=sin*wt*+π

Figure 2-29 Super-imposed Sine Waves

using phase modulation—where a 1 bit is represented by no phase change and a 0 bit, by a change in phase of pi radians—yields the curve in Figure 2-30.

Phase modulation is often used for high-speed modems because it lends itself well to the implementation of dibits, tribits, and quadbits. Figure 2-31(a) shows eight different angles in a full circle. Suppose each angle is used as a phase shift in phase modulation. Thus, with eight different signals we can represent three bits of information per signal, or tribits. In Figure 2-31(b) the eight angles are combined with two levels (amplitudes) of signal, providing 16 different signals, each of which can

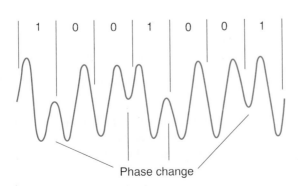

| 1 | 0 | 0 | 1 | 0 | 0 | 1 |

Phase change

Figure 2-30 Phase Modulation

Figure 2-31(a) Phase
Modulation Angles
and Amplitudes

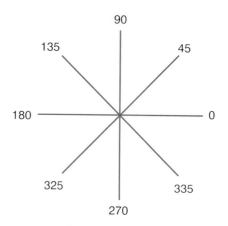

(a) Eight different phase changes,
suitable for tribits

Figure 2-31(b) Phase
Modulation Angles
and Amplitudes

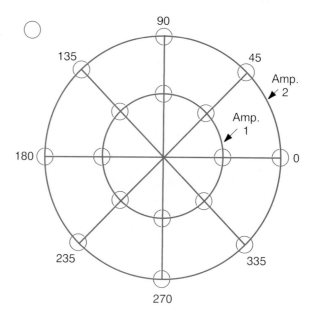

(b) Eight phase changes plus two amplitudes
yields 16 different signals, for quadbits

The 16 different signals are represented by circles

represent four bits. This combination provides a quadbit capability known
as quadrature amplitude modulation (QAM). QAM on a 1200 baud line
can provide transmission of 9600 bps. The most common modulation techniques in data communications are frequency modulation, also known as

frequency shift keying (FSK), and phase modulation, also known as *phase shift keying* (PSK). Also available are a variation known as *differential phase shift keying* (DPSK) and QAM.

Modem Capabilities

When modems are needed to transmit data over communications links, they are always used in pairs. The modems in each such pair must be configured exactly alike. Most modems have a variety of available options; setting these options is sometimes referred to as *strapping*, a term held over from times when the options were set by wiring, as opposed to switches or computer control. Figure 2-32 shows a modem. Some modem capabilities are presented in Figure 2-33, and a terminal-computer connection using modems is illustrated in Figure 2-34. Most modems on the market do not offer all of these capabilities. Some options are explained here; the remainder are discussed in Chapters 3, 5, and 6.

Speed. All modems are designed to operate at a specific speed or range of discrete speeds. The speed of a variable-speed modem can be set via switch(es) on the modem, via program control, or by automatic adjustment to the transmission speed.

Telephone Options. Auto-answer, manual answer, auto-dial, auto-disconnect, automatic redialing, and keyboard dialing all refer to use of switched telephone lines. Most newer modems can react to the ring indicator on the line and automatically answer a call. For a manual-answer

Figure 2-32 A Codex 2680 High-Speed Modem

Photo courtesy of Codex Corporation. The 2680, a high speed, leased line modem is marketed by Codex Corporation of Canton, MA, the largest independent vendor of data communications and network equipment.

Figure 2-33   Some
Modem Capabilities

Speed and variable speed

Auto-answer

Manual answer

Auto-dial

Manual dial

Auto-disconnect

Manual disconnect

Programmable control (e.g., computer-controlled dialing and setting of data rate)

Automatic redial

Keyboard dial

Speaker (to monitor dialing and connection)

Synchronous or asynchronous

Full or half duplex

Reverse channel

Secondary channel

Multiport

Line conditioning capabilities (equalization)

Self-testing mode

Voice-over data

Compatibility with:

    Bell modems

    Hayes modems

    Microcomputer network protocol (MNP)

        MNP 4—error correction

        MNP 5—data compression

    Consultative Committees on International Telegraphy and Telephony (CCITT) standards

    Electronic Industries Association (EIA) standards

    U.S. government standards

modem, someone must help in making the connection. This "inconvenience" actually promotes security. Auto-dialing means the modem can dial a number itself. Many modems can remember frequently called numbers. Each memory location can usually be associated with a code name, making dialing even easier. For example, the code name "school" can be used to represent the telephone number for the school's computer center. The user can then direct the modem to dial school rather than selecting the specific number. With auto-disconnect a modem terminates a call automatically whenever the other party hangs up or a disconnect message is received. Automatic redialing modems automatically redial a call that re-

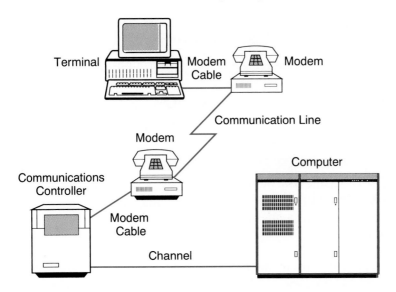

Figure 2-34
Terminal-Computer
Connection Using
Modems

sulted in a busy signal or no connection. Finally, keyboard or programmable dialing means that the number can be dialed using the keyboard of a terminal or via program control.

Self-Testing. Most new modems, and many older models, have some type of self-testing mode. These include a loop-back test, in which the modem's outgoing signal is looped back to itself; memory diagnostic checks; and modem-to-modem test transmissions. These self-tests are quite valuable in isolating problems in the communications equipment.

Voice-Over. Voice-over data capability allows voice communication over the same circuit as the data, either as voice or data or as voice and data simultaneously. This arrangement is beneficial when the data transmission application requires a dedicated circuit to a remote location. Suppose a company requires voice telephone communication between offices already linked by leased lines. Every such call can be dialed, incurring a toll for each, or voice-over data modems can be used, occupying a portion of the line capacity already leased. The only additional costs of voice transmission, then, are the price of the modems and the reduced data capacity on the line.

Compatibility. A variety of modem standards exist, and adherence to widely accepted standards helps establish modem compatibility. One of the references for compatibility is the modems supplied by AT&T; more recently, compatibility with modems manufactured by the Hayes Corporation is often cited. Two other entities involved in modem standards are the *Consultative Committee on International Telegraph and Telephony* (*CCITT*) and Microcom, Inc. Microcom has established or helped to establish a series of standards referred to as *microcomputer network protocols* (*MNP*). Some of the standards to which modems might adhere include:

CCITT V.32, modulation specifications for high-speed modems.

CCITT V.42, error correction.

CCITT V.42bis, data compression. Data compression can significantly increase the apparent speed of a modem.

MNP 1, 2, 3, and 4, error correction.

MNP 5, data compression.

Multiport modems are discussed in Chapter 5; reverse and secondary channels, full and half duplex operations, and conditioning are covered in Chapter 3; synchronous and asynchronous transmission are addressed in Chapter 6.

Cost. The price of modems is much like that of media—constantly changing and, in general, dropping as a result of new technology and competition. The price also varies according to the capabilities offered, with speed being the most influential factor. The chart shown in Figure 2-35 provides basic modem costs. The costs presented are for very basic models; actual costs might be somewhat lower or considerably higher (for additional capabilities).

Short-Haul Modems. For short distances, short-haul modems can be used. These allow for transmission distances up to about 20 miles, at varying speeds. As distance increases, speed decreases. Figure 2-36 presents the relationship between distance and speed with short-haul modems. Strictly speaking, distance is a function of the resistance of the conductor, and speed, a function of the capacitance and resistance of the conductor. For practical purposes, distance and speed are functions of the thickness or gauge of the conductor. Figure 2-36 holds for 22-gauge wire; greater speeds or distances are possible with 19-gauge wire, and lower speeds or distances would result from the use of 26-gauge wire. The advantage of short-haul modems is a significant reduction in cost—tenfold savings or better are possible.

Figure 2-35 Representative Modem Costs

Speed (bps)	Cost
300	$100
1200	$100
2400	$150
4800	$700
9600	$700

Distance (miles)	Maximum Speed (bps)
17	2,400
15	4,800
12	9,600
7	19,200

Figure 2-36 Short-Haul Modems, Speed vs. Distance

Modem Eliminators. For very short distances, *modem eliminators* provide additional savings and very high data transmission rates. Modem eliminators, also referred to as line drivers or null modems, can connect two devices that are in close proximity. A modem eliminator provides clocking and interface functions between two devices. One modem eliminator can replace two modems, as illustrated in Figure 2-37. The spannable distances are covered by interface specifications such as the RS-232-C standard, which recommends a distance of 50 feet for standard wires, or the RS-449 standard, which specifies 200 feet. Although manufacturers usually certify their modem eliminators at these standard distances, longer distances are possible. One use of modem eliminators is high-speed, computer-to-computer communications links. Data transmission rates up to 1 million bps can be supported by modem eliminators.

The previously described modems are connected directly to communications wires. An *acoustic coupler*, such as the one shown in Figure 2-38, allows for data transmission across telephone lines, using the telephone handset to pass the data. Acoustic couplers have a send-and-receive receptacle into which the handset is placed. Transmission rates for acoustic couplers are usually either 300 or 1200 bps. Acoustic couplers are frequently used with portable terminals, some of which even incorporate the acoustic coupler as an integral part of the terminal.

Current Loops. For distances up to 1500 feet, *current loop* technology allows data transmission speeds up to 19,200 bps without any type of modem. The common model is a *20-milliampere current loop*. To transmit data by this technology, the current on the line is switched on and off or the direction of the current is changed. In the first method, the presence of current represents a 1 bit and the absence of current indicates a 0 bit. This technique is referred to as *neutral working*. When current direction is

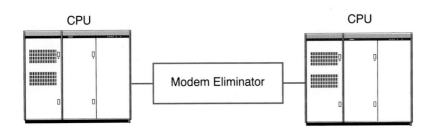

Figure 2-37 A Modem Eliminator

Figure 2-38 An
Acoustic Coupler

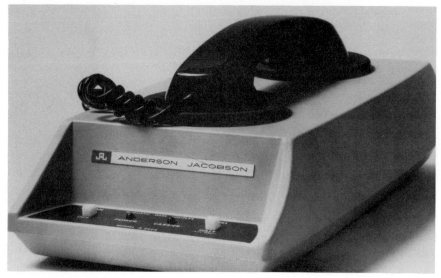

Courtesy Anderson Jacobson, Inc.

switched, current flowing in one direction represents a 1 bit and current in the opposite direction is a 0 bit. This technique is called *polar working*.

Fiber Optic Modems.   Modems are also used for fiber optic transmission at speeds ranging from 1200 bps up to 50 Mbps, with popular intermediate speeds of 56 Kbps, 100 Kbps, 250 Kbps, 1.544 Mbps, 5 Mbps, and 10 Mbps.

CASE STUDY

Business at the Syncrasy Corporation has been progressing. President Ima Overseer and the other two founders report that business has been excellent and expansion is in order. The first phase of expansion will include a larger computer system and two new locations in New York City and Los Angeles. The remote offices will each have ten terminals connected to the host computer in the Puma Flats office, where all inventory, pricing, and customer information is stored. It is expected that sales activity will occur throughout the day in both remote locations. The average order consists of 500 input characters and 100 response characters. The company's objective is to provide 5-second response time for each order; it has been determined that processing time per order averages 2.5 seconds. Thus far, each terminal operator enters 20 orders per hour on the average, with peak loads of 30 transactions per hour. Ms. Overseer wants to know which medium will best serve Syncrasy's immediate needs. Determining this requires some basic calculations, the first of which is to figure the necessary speed of the lines.

Line Speed

Usually a system is configured to meet the peak transaction load; if it can handle the peaks, it can definitely handle the valleys. Although configuring for peak loads is not absolutely necessary, it is undesirable to have the system bog down when it is needed the most. Configuring to the peak workload also provides latitude for expanding work during off-peak periods, including development activities like program compiling and batch operations such as payroll and periodic reports.

Line speed is based on response time and throughput. Syncrasy has decided to use the conservative response time definition, which requires all response characters to be received. It is assumed that two or more terminals might share a communications path (Chapters 4 and 5 discuss how this is done). First the needs of a single terminal are considered. Five hundred input characters and 100 output characters total to 600 characters transmitted per average transaction. The expected response time is 5 seconds, of which 2.5 seconds is communication time (estimated processing time was 2.5 seconds). Thus, one terminal will require a path with a speed of $600/2.5 = 240$ characters per second. Assuming 10 bits per character, a line speed of 2400 bps is required. Since it is inconceivable that a line can operate at 100% capacity, a 4800 bps line is preferable.

Number of Terminals per Line

To determine how many terminals could effectively share a line demands some intuition: A peak rate of 30 transactions per hour per terminal equates to 300 transactions per hour or 5 transactions per minute. This rate is not excessive, and all ten terminals could conceivably use the same 2400-bps line. The only problem would be if two users were to enter data at exactly the same time: One response time would be the expected 5 seconds, whereas the other would be approximately 7 seconds. The logic behind this is provided in Figure 2-39, in which T represents transmission time, P represents processing time, and W represents wait time. Terminal 2 sees a slower response time because it must hold off transmitting until Terminal 1 has sent its data. If the line speed were twice as fast (4800 bps), two concurrent terminals could be handled within the 5-second response time.

If three users enter information at exactly the same time, one of them, of course, will have a lower response time. However, the chances of that happening with ten terminals on a line is slight. Assuming a random arrival rate, the probability of three transactions arriving in a 2-second in-

Terminal 1   `TTTTTTTTTTPPPPPPPPPPPPPPTT`
Terminal 2   `WWWWWWWWWWTTTTTTTTTTPPPPPPPPPPPPPPTT`
              `----1----2----3----4----5----6----7----8`
Time in Seconds

Figure 2-39 Transaction Activity

terval is less than one in a thousand (0.00065) (see Exercise 8). A 4800-bps line should be satisfactory for all ten terminals.

Other Criteria

There are no special environmental, security, expansion, maintenance, or error rate concerns to resolve in this system, and the application issues have already been addressed. The calculations show that a high-speed path is not necessary. Distance is a factor in the remote connections, and transmission facilities should therefore be acquired from a common carrier. Private wires are best for the local terminals in the Puma Flats offices because the offices are free of environmental disturbances and there are no distance problems to overcome. Private wires also are far more cost effective than other solutions, and their speed can be greater than that of leased lines. Fiber optics and coaxial cable are possibilities, but they would be more costly if privately implemented, and such high data transmission rates are not presently required.

SUMMARY

A wide variety of transmission media are available to the network designer, and many networks employ several of them. If the telephone companies' use of fiber optics, microwave, and satellite channels is considered, most long-distance networks are a combination of media. Numerous factors influence the selection of transmission media. Each medium has information-carrying capacity, which varies from a few characters per second to millions of characters per second. The terms *bit rate*, *baud rate*, and *bandwidth* are used to describe a medium's carrying capacity, and these measures are interrelated.

In transmitting information between devices in a computer network, it is frequently necessary to convert a device's digital signals to analog format. There are several ways to do this; frequency modulation, phase modulation, and phase modulation plus amplitude modulation are the most common. The device that translates digital signals to analog signals and then back again is known as a modem or data set. Modems differ greatly in the bit rate provided as well as in the options available.

Key Terms

acoustic coupler	baud rate
amplitude modulation (AM)	bit rate
analog representation	broadband transmission
bandwidth	carrier signal
baseband transmission	coaxial cable

common carrier
conditioned lines
conducted media
Consultative Committee on International
    Telegraph and Telephony (CCITT)
data set
dibit
differential phase shift keying (DPSK)
digital representation
fiber optics
frequency modulation (FM)
frequency shift keying (FSK)
leased line
microcomputer network
    protocols (MNP)
microwave radio

modem
modem eliminator
phase modulation
phase shift keying (PSK)
private line
propagation delay
public line
quadbit
quadrature amplitude
    modulation (QAM)
radiated media
response time
satellite radio
switched connection
tribit
20-milliampere current loop

Review Questions

1. What are the advantages and disadvantages of private lines?

2. Distinguish between switched lines and leased lines.

3. Compare broadband and baseband transmission.

4. Rank wires, coaxial cable, and fiber optics with respect to speed, cost, and resistance to noise. Which is fastest? Which is least expensive? Which is least error prone?

5. Describe the effects of propagation delay on satellite transmission.

6. Describe:
    a. amplitude modulation
    b. frequency modulation
    c. phase modulation

7. Explain how the terms *baud*, *bit rate*, and *bandwidth* are used to describe the speed of a communications link.

8. Describe what a modem does.

9. What are the advantages of current loop transmission?

Exercises

Given the different modes of communication—private lines, switched lines, leased lines, coaxial cable, fiber optics, microwave, and satellite—which would be the most suitable for the following applications (1–7)? Why?

1. A U. S. marketing organization must transmit large amounts of product information, sales data, facsimiles, and electronic mail to 40 cities. Each of the 40 locations has computers and sends volumes of sales data, facsimiles, and electronic mail. Response time is not critical.

2. A manufacturing plant has multiple computers, data-processing workstations, and terminals, all spread throughout six buildings. All facilities are located within 1 kilometer of each other and all rights of way are controlled by the company. The data being transmitted includes small files, memos, electronic mail, and online transactions. Response time is critical for the online transactions.

3. A hospital has automated its patient care system. Terminals have been placed in all administrative offices, laboratory facilities, doctors' and nurses' offices, and nursing stations. The online transactions include data entry, inquiries, and short reports. Rapid response time is important.

4. A research corporation is evaluating solar energy systems. It has data collection devices attached to several experimental wind and solar collectors. A large, continuous volume of data is transmitted to the computer center, which is 10 miles from the test grounds. The computer center can be seen from the test grounds.

5. A major fast-food chain has chosen to centralize its inventory and sales data. Each restaurant maintains its sales and inventory data on a small computer located in the store. This computer is attached to point-of-sale terminals that serve as data entry devices. Every time an item is sold, the inventory and sales data on the local computer is updated. Every evening the central office must retrieve the information from each store. The amount of information to be transmitted is approximately 10,000 characters per restaurant.

6. A major car rental agency has decided to regionalize its inventory and reservations system. Approximately 75% of the reservation requests are resolved by the regional center, and the remaining 25% must be forwarded to another regional processing center. The peak amount of data to be transmitted to another center is approximately 10,000 characters per minute. This also means that each regional center will receive approximately 10,000 characters per minute.

7. A research corporation must exchange data between three computers located in different departments within one building. The data is highly sensitive, so security is a major concern. The data consists of text, research results, graphics, and electronic mail. Response time is not critical. A communication speed of 9600 bps would be adequate. The optimum path for private wires would require the wires to pass through research areas with a considerable amount of electrical or magnetic activity.

8. The probability of k random arrivals in an interval of length T is given by the formula

$$P_k(T) = \frac{(LT)^k}{k!} \times e^{-LT} \quad \text{for} \quad K = 0, 1, 2, 3, \ldots$$

where

$P_k(T)$	is the probability that k transactions will arrive in time interval T
k	is the number of arrivals
T	is the time interval being considered
e	is the natural base for logarithms
L	is the average number of transactions per unit of time
$!$	is the factorial function

Thus, if the arrival rate of transactions per second is 0.25, the probability that two transactions will arrive in 5 seconds is given by

$$P_2(5) = \frac{(0.25 \times 5)^2}{2!} \times e^{-(0.25 \times 5)} = \frac{(1.25)^2}{2} \times e^{-1.25} = 0.22$$

Using this formula, verify that the probability of three transactions arriving in a 2-second interval is approximately 0.00065 when the number of transactions arriving per hour is 300.

References

Bellamy, John. *Digital Telephony.* New York: Wiley, 1982.

Digital Equipment Corporation. *Introduction to Local Area Networks.* Digital Equipment Corporation, 1982.

Douglass, Jack L., and Bill Zupko. *More About Modems.* Huntsville, AL: Universal Data Systems, 1983.

Faletra, Robert. "Data Compression, Networks on Modem Maker's Horizon." *PC Week*, October 17, 1988.

Farmer, Robin. "Cost Benefits of Fibre-Optic Systems." *Telecommunications*, July 1983.

Frank, Howard. "Broadband Versus Baseband Local Area Networks." *Telecommunications*, March 1983.

Freeman, Roger L. *Telecommunication Transmission Handbook.* New York: Wiley, 1981.

Glass, L. Brett. "Modern Modem Methods." *Byte*, Volume 14, Number 6, June 1989.

Held, Gilbert. *Data Communication Components.* Rochelle Park, NJ: Hayden Book Co., 1979.

Hewlett-Packard Corporation. *Guidebook to Data Communications.* Santa Clara, CA: Hewlett-Packard, 1977.

Jurenko, John A. *All About Modems.* Huntsville, AL: Universal Data Systems, 1981.

Lowndes, Jay C. "Optical Fiber Threatens Satellite Role in Voice Links." *Aviation Week & Space Technology*, January 31, 1983.

Martin, James. *Telecommunications and the Computer.* Englewood Cliffs, NJ: Prentice-Hall, 1976.

Methvin, Dave. "V.32 Modems: Closer to the Mainstream." *PC Week*, January 29, 1990.

Redmond, Donald L., and Gregory J. Beveridge. *Fiber Optics, Believe It—Or Not.* Mountain Bell Network Engineering, June 22, 1983.

Schmidt, Wolfgang. "Field Trial of Fiber-Optic BIGFON LAN." *Telecommunications*, July 1983.

More Physical Aspects
of Data Communications

Data Flow
Data Codes
Error Sources
Error Prevention
Error Detection
Error Correction
Digital Data Transmission
Interface
Common Carrier Services

INTRODUCTION

This chapter, an extension of Chapter 2, continues the discussion of physical transmission of data and data transmission utilities. Setting up and managing today's communications networks is more complex than ever. More vendors are providing communications services over a wider variety of speeds. Moreover, different forms of communication are increasingly being integrated onto one transmission medium. Thus, the sphere of responsibility for the modern data communications manager is expanding. In addition to selecting communications facilities for data transmission, the communications manager may also be responsible for selecting hardware and software that can meet the corporate needs for data, voice, video, facsimile, and other forms of electronic communication. In this chapter you learn about data transmission facilities and other common communication facilities. The topics discussed include:

Sources of data transmission errors
How transmission errors are detected and corrected

Advantages of digital transmission of data

Various standards for interfacing transmission media and data-processing equipment

How the telephone companies' communications networks operate

DATA FLOW

Every data communications network must have some mechanism of control over the flow of data. This is accomplished at two levels. The first level provides for *contention control*, which determines which stations may transmit, the conditions under which transmission of data is allowed, and the pacing of data transmission. Contention control is discussed in subsequent chapters. The other, more basic level of data flow relates to the transmission equipment used—lines, modems, and devices. There are three elementary types of data flow: *simplex*, *half duplex*, and *full duplex*.

Simplex Transmission

Simplex transmissions are those in which data may flow in only one direction, like traffic on a one-way street. Radio and television transmissions, which are illustrated in Figure 3-1(a), are examples. In simplex transmis-

Figure 3-1   Examples of Data Flow

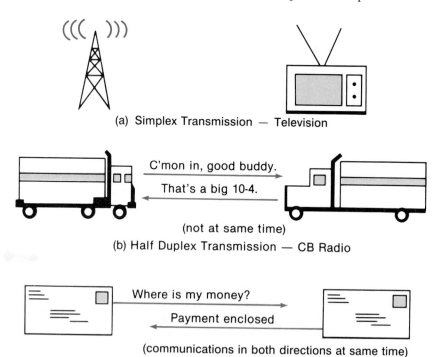

(a) Simplex Transmission — Television

C'mon in, good buddy.

That's a big 10-4.

(not at same time)
(b) Half Duplex Transmission — CB Radio

Where is my money?

Payment enclosed

(communications in both directions at same time)
(c) Full Duplex Transmission — Mail System

sion one station assumes the role of transmitter while the other station is the receiver; these roles may not be reversed. Although this may appear rather limiting, simplex transmission still has numerous applications. Receive-only devices such as keyboards, microcomputer monitors, and optical character recognition (OCR) scanners involve simplex communication. Although communications with printers that are capable of transmitting status information back to the host are not classified as simplex, data collection devices that serve as input devices only do use simplex communication. For instance, in solar energy research installations, heat sensors, solar monitors, and flow meters have been used to monitor the environment and transmit samples of data via a simplex line. A building environmental monitoring system also operates in this mode, sending temperature and humidity readings to a computer that controls the heating and cooling of the building. Simplex lines are less common in business applications than half duplex or full duplex. Simplex lines are used for some printers, for monitoring devices in environment and process-control applications, for transmission of stock exchange data (stock tickers), and for most radio and cable television data transmissions.

Half Duplex Transmission

In *half duplex transmission*, data may travel in both directions, although only in one direction at a time, like traffic on a one-lane bridge. An example, illustrated in Figure 3-1(b), is citizens band (CB) radio, where radio operators on the same frequency may be either sender or receiver but not both at the same time.

Continuous Versus Noncontinuous Carriers. When data flow is controlled by a modem, two half duplex options are available—*continuous carrier* and *noncontinuous carrier*. A carrier signal, which involves a continuous frequency, is the signal that is modulated to represent data. In continuous carrier mode, even though data may only pass in one direction at a time, the carrier signal on which the data is imposed is passed in both directions, as shown in Figure 3-2. Noncontinuous carrier mode allows a carrier signal to be passed in either direction but only in one direction at a time, as shown in Figure 3-3. A transmitter "raises" the carrier signal that is propagated along the medium to the receiver.

Modem Turnaround Time. In noncontinuous carrier mode there is an additional delay in transmitting the data. This delay, referred to as *modem*

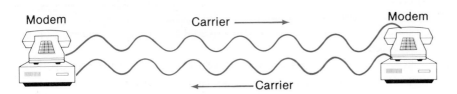

Modem   Carrier ——→   Modem

←———— Carrier

Figure 3-2 Continuous Carrier

Figure 3-3   Noncontinuous Carrier

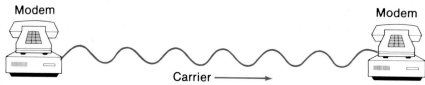

Carrier ⟶

Figure 3-4   Modem Turnaround Time

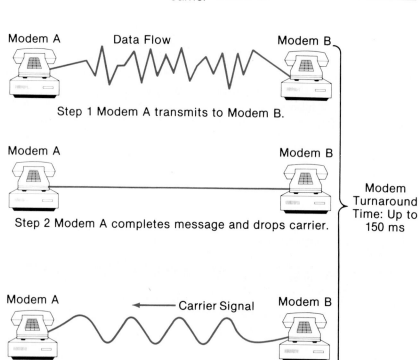

Step 1 Modem A transmits to Modem B.

Step 2 Modem A completes message and drops carrier.

Modem Turnaround Time: Up to 150 ms

Step 3 Modem B recognizes carrier loss and raises carrier in preparation to send message. Modem A recognizes the existence of carrier.

Step 4 Modem B transmits data to Modem A.

turnaround time, is illustrated in Figure 3-4. Modem turnaround time is the period required for the old sender to drop the carrier signal, for the new sender to recognize that the carrier signal has been dropped, and for the new sender to raise the carrier signal that must be detected by the new receiver.

Because modem turnaround time can exceed 100 milliseconds, it has an important impact on total transmission time. Suppose a banking transaction at an automatic teller machine (ATM) requires the following transmissions on a half duplex line with noncontinuous carrier and a transmission speed of 4800 bps.

1. ATM transmits 20 characters to host computer.
2. Host computer transmits 40 characters to ATM.
3. ATM transmits 20 characters to host computer to acknowledge the transaction.
4. Host computer transmits 10 characters to ATM to ready it for the next transaction.

In all, 90 characters are transmitted, with four modem turnarounds. Assuming 10 bits per character and a modem turnaround time of 50 milliseconds, this gives: 10 bits per character × 90 characters = 900 bits transmitted, requiring 900/4800 = 0.19 seconds transmission time; and 4 modem turnarounds × 50 milliseconds per turnaround = 0.20 seconds modem turnaround time. This shows that modem turnaround time can be a significant part of total data transmission time.

Reverse Channel Capability.   To lessen the effect of modem turnaround time, some half duplex modems provide a *reverse channel*. For example, certain communications systems require the receiver to briefly (with a few characters) acknowledge receipt of each data transmission before another can be sent. In other situations, printers pass back brief status signals to indicate their readiness to receive more data. One set of conventions is known as *XON* and *XOFF*: When a terminal or printer wants the host to send more data, it transmits an XON signal, and when it does not want more data transmitted it sends an XOFF signal. If modem turnaround were required for each of these short sequences, then overall turnaround time would be significant. A reverse channel provides a very slow circuit that allows the receiver to send these short messages without forcing a line turnaround. Thus, reverse channel capability is a subcase of continuous carrier mode: There is a carrier in both directions, but the reverse channel has a lower transmission rate than the forward channel. Bell series 202 modems provide a reverse channel capability with a 50 bps carrying capacity, as illustrated in Figure 3-5.

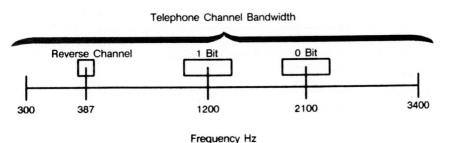

Figure 3-5   Reverse Channel Bell 202 Modem

Full Duplex Transmission

In *full duplex* mode, data can be transmitted in both directions simultaneously, like traffic on a two-way street. An example of data transmission using full duplex capabilities is the postal service: Letters can be transmitted in both directions simultaneously, as illustrated in Figure 3-1(c). Figure 3-6 shows full duplex communication. In full duplex transmission there is no modem turnaround time to consider. Full duplex operations are effected in radio wave transmissions by using two different frequencies, one for each direction. With coaxial cable, full duplex operations require broadband transmission.

DATA CODES

As already mentioned, data is stored in digital computers as sequences of binary digits (bits), each with a value of either 0 or 1. To provide meaning to a sequence of bits, you must set up the number of bits that are grouped to form a data character and create an encoding scheme, or translation table, by which the system translates each group of bits into a character. In the encoding scheme of telegraphy—Morse code—each character is represented as a combination of dots and dashes. Although these could be also interpreted as bits, Morse code is not suitable for data communications because characters are represented by a different number of bits (for example, the letter A is represented by dot-dash and the letter S by dot-dot-dot). Telegraphers distinguish one letter grouping from another by the time delay between characters. Such a scheme is not practical for computer-based systems. As a result, virtually all computer codes use a fixed number of bits per character. The number of bits that makes up the characters also

Figure 3-6 Data Flow Alternatives

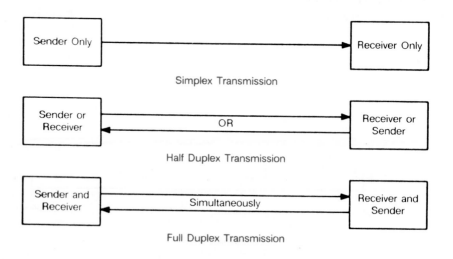

Simplex Transmission

Half Duplex Transmission

Full Duplex Transmission

Coding Scheme	Number of Bits	Characters Representable
BCD	4	16
Baudot	5	32 (62 using Shift key)
BCD	6	64
SBT	6	64
Standard ASCII	7	128
Extended ASCII	8	256
EBCDIC	8	256
Touch-tone telephone		12 frequencies

Figure 3-7 Some Common Data Codes

determines the number of distinct characters that can be represented. Figure 3-7 lists several data encoding schemes as well as the number of bits per character and the number of characters that can be represented by those codes.

BCD

BCD, an acronym for binary coded decimal, exists in both 4-bit and 6-bit versions. The 4-bit code is used for economy in transmission of numeric data. With 4 bits, at most 16 different entities can be represented, so 4-bit BCD is not at all suited to the transmission of alphabetic or punctuation characters. However, for transmitting strings of numeric data, 4-bit BCD uses 3 bits fewer than ASCII and 4 bits fewer than EBCDIC or Extended ASCII, thus increasing the effective line utilization. When used in this manner, 4-bit BCD is normally transmitted in mixed mode with another code, making it the responsibility of the application to determine the context of the data. The 4-bit BCD code is given in Figure 3-8. The 6-bit BCD code is not used extensively because it can represent only 64 different symbols, a rather limited number. Using 6-bit BCD code, one could repre-

Bit Pattern	Numeric Equivalent
0000	0
0001	1
0010	2
0011	3
0100	4
0101	5
0110	6
0111	7
1000	8
1001	9

Figure 3-8 The 4-Bit BCD Code

sent only 26 letters (uppercase or lowercase but not both), 10 numeric digits, and 28 other symbols for punctuation and control. A standard type-writer has 24 special punctuations or use symbols alone.

Baudot

Baudot is a code derived from the telegraph industry, so its primary use in data communications is with telegraph lines or equipment originally de-signed for telegraphy. Its biggest limitation is in the number of repre-sentable characters: With only 5 bits per character, Baudot can represent at most 32 distinct characters, which is inadequate for all 26 letters of the Roman alphabet and the ten numeric digits, let alone uppercase and low-ercase letters and punctuation. Consequently, a technique is needed to ex-tend the limited character set. One additional bit, for instance, would allow a total of 64 characters to be represented. But since Baudot cannot physically be extended to 6 bits, obtaining this additional bit requires up-shift and down-shift modes, like on a typewriter (up-shift produces capi-tal letters and punctuation, down-shift produces lowercase letters and numbers—in this way, 47 typewriter keys create 94 characters). In the Baudot code, the 5 bits transmitted must be interpreted according to whether they are up-shifted (uppercase) or down-shifted (lowercase). The bit pattern 11111 represents down-shift characters and the bit pattern 11011 represents up-shift characters. All characters transmitted after the se-quence 11111 but before the shifted sequence 11011 are treated as down-shift characters. Similarly, all characters transmitted after the sequence 11011 are treated as up-shift (uppercase) characters until the pattern 11111 is recognized. Since two bit patterns are reserved to indicate the shift mode and therefore may not be used to represent transmitted characters, the total number of characters that can be represented is reduced to 30 bit patterns, each of which represents two characters. Figure 3-9 gives the Baudot code. Suppose the message FLIGHT 10 is to be transmitted. This would necessitate the sequence given in Figure 3-10.

Baudot code has an additional shortcoming: It does not follow the standard collating sequence for letters and numbers. The bit pattern 11101, which represents the number 1, is numerically higher than the pattern for the number 9—00011; 11000, the pattern for the letter A, is higher than 10001, the pattern for Z. Although this is not a problem purely from a data communications point of view, it does require additional overhead when used for comparing data field values.

SBT

SBT, an abbreviation for six-bit transcode, was created by IBM primarily for remote job entry communications. It is not used extensively.

ASCII

ASCII is an acronym for American standard code for information inter-change. ASCII and EBCDIC (see next section) are the codes most com-

Bit Pattern	Down-Shift Character	Up-Shift Character
00000	Blank	Blank
00001	T	5
00010	Carriage return	Carriage return
00011	O	9
00100	Space	Space
00101	H	£
00110	N	,
00111	M	.
01000	Line feed	
01001	L	)
01010	R	4
01011	G	&
01100	I	8
01101	P	0
01110	C	:
01111	V	;
10000	E	3
10001	Z	"
10010	D	$
10011	B	?
10100	S	Bell
10101	Y	6
10110	F	!
10111	X	/
11000	A	-
11001	W	2
11010	J	'
11011	Shift down	Shift down
11100	U	7
11101	Q	1
11110	K	(
11111	Shift up	Shift up

Figure 3-9 The Baudot Code

11111	10110	01001	01100	01011	00101	00001	00100	11011	11101	01101
Up-shift	F	L	I	G	H	T	Space	Down-shift	1	0

Figure 3-10 An Example of Baudot Transmission

monly used. ASCII (also known as USASCII) is implemented primarily as a 7-bit code, although an extended 8-bit version also exists. With 7 bits, 128 characters can be represented; with 8 bits, 256 characters are available. As an alternative to the 8-bit code, the 7-bit form can be extended in the same manner as the Baudot code (using the special characters shift out and shift in, with bit patterns of 0001110 and 0001111, respectively). Extending the number of characters provides for additional character sets for graphics and for foreign languages such as Katakana. The 7-bit ASCII code is presented in Figure 3-11.

Figure 3-11   The
USASCII 7-Bit Code

High Order Bits

		000	001	010	011	100	101	110	111
	0000	NUL	DLE	SPACE	0	@	P	`	p
	0001	SOH	DC1	!	1	A	Q	a	q
	0010	STX	DC2	"	2	B	R	b	r
	0011	ETX	DC3	#	3	C	S	c	s
L	0100	EOT	DC4	$	4	D	T	d	t
o	0101	ENQ	NAK	%	5	E	U	e	u
w	0110	ACK	SYN	&	6	F	V	f	v
O	0111	BEL	ETB	'	7	G	W	g	w
r	1000	BS	CAN	(	8	H	X	h	x
d	1001	HT	EM	)	9	I	Y	i	y
e	1010	LF	SUB	*	:	J	Z	j	z
r	1011	VT	ESC	+	;	K	[	k	{
B	1100	FF	FS	,	<	L	\	l	|
i	1101	CR	GS	-	=	M	]	m	}
t	1110	SO	RS	.	>	N	^	n	~
s	1111	SI	US	/	?	O	_	o	DEL

EBCDIC

EBCDIC stands for extended binary-coded decimal interchange code. It utilizes 8 bits to form a character, and, thus, 256 characters can be represented. The EBCDIC code is presented in Figures 3-12(a) and 3-12(b). As Figures 3-11 and 3-12 show, both ASCII and EBCDIC have some codes (for example, ASCII 0000000 and 0000011) with mnemonic names such as NUL and ETX. These special characters, which are discussed in more detail in Chapter 6, are used to provide control information to nodes on the network as well as to represent binary data.

The EBCDIC tables show gaps following the letters i, r, z, I, R, and Z. The gaps represents unassigned bit values. This is a disadvantage relative to the ASCII tables, which have no such gaps. The disadvantage arises because the unassigned bit values fall within the letter sequence. If these values are ever assigned, it may interrupt the collating sequence of the letters. Moreover, the gaps make arithmetic operations on the characters

High Order Bits

Low Order Bits	0000	0001	0010	0011	0100	0101	0110	0111
0000	NUL	DLE	DS		SPACE	@	-	
0001	SOH	DC1	SOS					
0010	STX	DC2	FS	SYN				
0011	ETX	DC3						
0100	PF	RES	BYP	PN				
0101	HT	NL	LF	RS				
0110	LC	BS	ETB	UC				
0111	DEL	IL	ESC	EOT				
1000		CAN						
1001	RLF	EM						\
1010	SMN	CC	SM		¢	!	|	:
1011					.	$	'	#
1100	FF	IFS		DC4	<	*	%	@
1101	CR	IGS	ENQ	NAK	(	)	-	'
1110	SO	IRS	ACK		+	;	>	=
1111	SI	IUS	BEL	SUB	|		?	"

Figure 3-12(a) The EBCDIC 8-Bit Code

more difficult. In ASCII, for instance, we can obtain the numeric value of an ASCII character and manipulate it arithmetically. For example, add 15 to the numeric representation of the letter A and obtain the letter 15 characters down the alphabet from A. Another disadvantage of EBCDIC is that some characters—for example, [and]—have not been defined. Omission of these characters raises problems in programming languages like Pascal and C, which use these symbols.

Touch-Tone Telephone

The *touch-tone telephone code* turns a touch-tone telephone into a data communications terminal. Some banks, for instance, allow customers to pay bills and transfer money between accounts using their touch-tone telephone. Also, many colleges and universities allow students to register for classes using a touch-tone telephone. Each telephone key transmits a signal at a unique frequency that is acceptable to voice-grade lines. Telephone sets have 12 keys, so 12 different frequencies can be transmitted. This

Figure 3-12(b)   The EBCDIC 8-Bit Code

High Order Bits

		1000	1001	1010	1011	1100	1101	1110	1111
	0000					{	}	\	0
	0001	a	j	~		A	J		1
	0010	b	k	s		B	K	S	2
	0011	c	l	t		C	L	T	3
L o w	0100	d	m	u		D	M	U	4
	0101	e	n	v		E	N	V	5
O r d e r	0110	f	o	w		F	O	W	6
	0111	g	p	x		G	P	X	7
B i t s	1000	h	q	y		H	Q	Y	8
	1001	i	r	z		I	R	Z	9
	1010								
	1011								
	1100								
	1101								
	1110								
	1111								

rather limited code set also limits the communications applications of the telephone instrument.

Data Code Size

The transition from 5-bit and 6-bit codes to 7-bit and 8-bit codes became necessary to increase the number of unique code sequences that could be represented. The two most common data communications codes are 7-bit and 8-bit codes, which are able to represent 128 and 256 unique symbols, respectively. Is this a sufficient number of symbols? An 8-bit code can represent the 26-letter Roman alphabet (both uppercase and lowercase), the 10 Arabic numerals (0 through 9), and punctuation, totaling approximately 100 characters and symbols. Additional bit patterns may be required for line control, so perhaps up to 128 characters can be used. What are the rest used for?

For one thing, there may be a need to accommodate other alphabets, such as Greek and Cyrillic (Russian), and their accompanying diacritical marks, such as the tilde, umlaut, and accents. Still, 256 bits can accommodate the Roman alphabet and one other alphabet, with characters left over—until we look at Asian and Middle Eastern languages. The Kanji character set used for written communication in Japan and China, for instance, contains over 30,000 ideograms and symbols. Thus, 256 unique symbols do not really go very far.

In addition to accommodating various alphabets, a data code may need to transmit, store, manipulate, and display graphics information, thus requiring additional characters. Line drawing characters can easily exceed 100 different symbols. Several microcomputers use an extended ASCII code to permit use of business graphics symbols. It is also likely that some of the newer technologies, such as *videotex* (in which text and images are transmitted together), will require a large number of characters. The data communications codes in current use have proved to be inadequate in meeting the communication demands between different cultures and languages, as well as the anticipated demands for extended services such as videotex. Now that the limitations of 8-bit codes are apparent, perhaps an international code using 16 bits will emerge. In Japan this has already been addressed by several standards.

In addition to providing a sufficient number of characters, to be effective a good communications code must provide three other capabilities: It must be standardized, it must be nonsequential, and it must provide for error detection. Being *standardized* means that the bit representations are sanctioned by a recognized standards group. Being *nonsequential* means that the sequence in which characters are detected is immaterial. The Baudot code is sequential, as the up-shift and down-shift characters are critical to the meaning of characters received. If an up-shift or down-shift character is missed in the transmission, the message text following the missed shift character is incorrectly interpreted. An *error detection capability* inherent in the code allows detection of transmission errors. For instance, a parity bit is often appended to 7-bit ASCII to detect errors. Parity is less commonly used with 8-bit codes such as EBCDIC. In the next section we discuss how errors are caused and how they can be detected.

ERROR SOURCES

All data transmissions are subject to error, although some media are more susceptible than others. Contextual recognition of errors is usually impossible in data communications systems. If the data transmitter and receiver are computers, it is virtually impossible for editing routines to determine if one or more bits have been changed; even if data is displayed on a terminal, the operator may be unable to discern all the errors. For example, if a bank teller interrogates a customer's account balance as illustrated in Figure 3-13, it is unlikely that the teller would recognize that a 1-bit error

Figure 3-13   A
Transmission Error

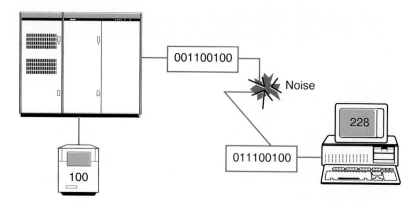

had altered the balance from $100 to $228. There are a number of ways in which errors can be induced during data transmission. The most common are white noise, impulse noise, crosstalk, echo, phase jitter, attenuation, and envelope delay distortion.

White Noise

White noise, also referred to as *thermal noise* and *Gaussian noise*, results from the normal movements of electrons and is present in all transmission media at temperatures above absolute zero. The amount of white noise is directly proportional to the temperature of the medium (hence, the term *thermal noise*). White noise also is distributed randomly throughout a medium (hence, the term *Gaussian noise*). White noise in telephone circuits is sometimes heard as static or hissing on the line. Usually, the magnitude of white noise is not sufficient to create data loss in wire circuits, but it can become significant in radio frequency links such as microwave and satellite. Because white noise is proportional to bandwidth as well as temperature, improperly focused antennas (for example, those directed toward the sun) can create enough disturbance to produce errors. Figure 3-14 illustrates the impact of noise on a data communications signal.

Impulse Noise

Impulse noise is characterized by signal "spikes." In telephone circuits it can be caused by switching equipment or by lightning strikes, and in other situations, by transient electrical impulses such as those occurring on a shop floor. The various pieces of equipment on a shop floor require large amounts of electricity. Moreover, this equipment frequently cycles up and down, drawing more and less power. Setting an electrical charge in motion generates a magnetic field, and magnetic fields can, in turn, affect electrical transmissions. Thus, unshielded data communications wires passing through a shop floor in close proximity to current-carrying wires

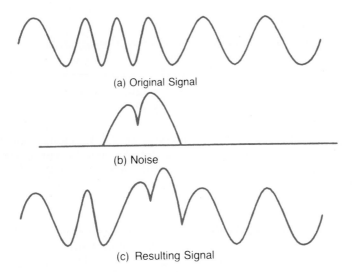

(a) Original Signal

(b) Noise

(c) Resulting Signal

Figure 3-14 The Impact of Noise on a Data Signal

can have their signals affected. Impulse noise, the primary cause of data errors in telephone circuits, is heard as a clicking or crackling sound. It usually is short (several milliseconds), with varying levels of magnitude.

Crosstalk

Crosstalk occurs when signals from one channel distort or interfere with the signals of a different channel. In telephone connections, crosstalk sometimes appears in the form of another party's conversation heard in the background. Crosstalk is also present in radio frequency and multiplexed transmissions (see Chapter 5) when the frequency ranges are too close together. Crosstalk in wire-pair transmission occurs when wire pairs interfere with each other as a result of strong signals, improper shielding, or both. Another common cause of crosstalk is interference between receivers and transmitters when a strong outgoing signal interferes with a weaker incoming signal. Crosstalk is directly proportional to distance, bandwidth, signal strength, and proximity to other transmission channels; it is inversely proportional to shielding or channel separation. Crosstalk is not usually a significant factor in data communications errors.

One special form of crosstalk is *intermodulation noise*, which is the result of two or more signals combining, or "adding together," to produce a signal outside the limits of the communications channel. Suppose one mode of FSK modulation represents a 1 bit as a frequency of 1300 Hz and a 0 bit as a frequency of 2100 Hz with a variation of 10 Hz. Intermodulation noise might result in two acceptable signals, such as 1305 Hz and 2105 Hz, combining to form a signal of 3410 Hz (1305 + 2105 = 3410). This signal is out of the accepted frequency range of voice communication over telephone lines (300–3400 Hz).

Echo

Echo is essentially the reflection or reversal of the signal being transmitted. This is most likely to occur at junctions where wires are interconnected or at the end of a line in a local area network. To minimize this echo effect, telephone companies have installed *echo suppressors* on their networks. The echo suppressor works by allowing the signal to pass in one direction only. In voice transmission, the suppressor continually reverses itself to match the direction of conversation. Obviously this would impede data transmission in full duplex mode, so echo suppressors are disengaged when full duplex transmission is required.

Phase Jitter

Phase jitter is a variation in the phase of a continuous signal from cycle to cycle; it is especially significant when the modulation mode involves phase shifting.

Attenuation

Attenuation is the weakening of a signal as a result of distance and characteristics of the medium. Attenuation can produce a significant number of data errors. For a given gauge of wire and bit rate, a signal can be carried for a certain distance without enhancement. Beyond that distance, however, a signal repeater or amplifier would have to be included to ensure that the receiving station can properly recognize the data.

Envelope Delay Distortion

Envelope delay distortion occurs when signals that have been weakened or subjected to outside interference by transmission over long distances are enhanced by being passed through filters. Passing the signals through a filter delays them a certain amount, depending on the frequency of the signal.

Impact of Data Errors

Figure 3-15 shows the possible effects of impulse noise of various durations, for different line speeds. It is significant that fewer bits are subject to error when transmission is at lower rather than higher speeds. Although the figure applies to any type of noise for the same durations, impulse noise was chosen because it is one of the most common types of noise affecting telephone wires. The most significant thing shown by Figure 3-15 is that the potential number of bit errors increases with both duration of the noise and line speed. While the ideal is to eliminate all errors in data, a goal of fewer than one error per 100,000 bits is considered satisfactory. (Most line media and radio wave transmission systems are designed for fewer than one error per 1 million bits transmitted.)

Line Speed (bps)	Impulse Noise Duration (milliseconds)				
	0.2	0.4	0.6	0.8	1.0
300	0.06	0.12	0.18	0.24	0.30
1200	0.24	0.48	0.72	0.96	1.20
2400	0.48	0.96	1.44	1.92	2.40
4800	0.96	1.92	2.88	3.84	4.80
9600	1.92	3.84	5.76	7.68	9.60
19,200	3.84	7.68	11.52	15.36	19.20

Figure 3-15 Potential Number of Corrupted Data Bits

ERROR PREVENTION

The best method to guard against data errors is to correct their source. Eliminating all noise is impossible, but error prevention techniques can reduce the probability of error corruption in the data. Such techniques include telephone line conditioning, reducing transmission speed, shielding, line drivers, and using better quality equipment.

Telephone Line Conditioning

When a line is leased from a telephone company, *conditioning*—sometimes referred to as equalization—can be included for an additional charge. Two classes of conditioning are available, Class C and Class D, with four commercial levels of Class C conditioning—C1, C2, C4, and C5. Each level of Class C conditioning provides increasingly stringent constraints on the amplitude and phase distortion permitted on the line. For instance, a line with C5 conditioning should be more error-free than a line with C1 conditioning. One useful aspect of Class D conditioning—a relatively new service—is that the telephone company will inspect the circuits available between the desired communication points to select the one with the least amount of noise. Users can also obtain equipment, such as certain modems, that aids in the conditioning of lines.

Lower Transmission Speed

As we just discussed, a bit error is much less likely to occur at lower transmission speeds. Some modems adjust their speed automatically or via program control to accommodate noisy lines. With a high-quality line such a modem will operate at 2400 bps; if the quality of the line deteriorates, the modem has the capability of switching to a lower speed such as 1200 bps.

Shielding

Although additional shielding of leased telephone cables is not a user option, shielding can be provided for private lines to reduce the amount of crosstalk and impulse noise from the environment.

Line Drivers (Repeaters)

Line drivers, or repeaters, can be placed at intervals along a communications line to amplify and forward the signal. Digital signal noise can usually be eliminated, because the signal is being regenerated. For analog signals, however, it is difficult to separate most noise from the signal. Thus, noise that is picked up also will be amplified by the repeaters. The function of repeaters is to restore signals to their full strength and overcome signal loss due to attenuation.

Better Equipment

Since some older mechanical equipment and some older transformers and power supplies are more likely to produce noise than newer equipment (such as electronic switches), replacing older components with better equipment can reduce the amount of noise.

ERROR DETECTION

Unfortunately, the remedies just cited to minimize the number of errors may be impractical from either a cost or a feasibility standpoint. Also, since error elimination is impossible, it is necessary to determine if a transmission error has occurred and, if errors have occurred, to return the data to proper form. Error detection algorithms in data communications networks are based on the transmission of redundant information. In telegraphy, one way to ensure correctness of data is to transmit each character twice. Since even this is not entirely error-proof, it could be taken one or more steps further by sending each character three or more times. However, although this might increase the reliability of the transmission, line utilization drops dramatically. As the error rate approaches zero, so does the effective utilization of the medium. Obviously, some middle-ground approach is required that can detect almost all errors without significantly reducing the data-carrying capacity of the medium.

Parity Check

One of the simplest and most widely used forms of error detection is known as a *parity check* or *vertical redundancy check* (*VRC*). A parity check involves adding a bit—known as the parity bit—to each character during transmission. The parity bit is selected so that the total number of 1 bits in the code representation of each character adds up to either an even number (even parity) or an odd number (odd parity). Each character is checked upon receipt to see if the number of 1 bits is even or odd. Consider the string of characters "DATA COMM" as coded in 7-bit ASCII with odd parity. The representations of these characters plus the parity bit for odd par-

Letter	ASCII	Parity Bit	Transmitted Bits
D	1000100	1	10001001
A	1000001	1	10000011
T	1010100	0	10101000
A	1000001	1	10000011
space	0100000	0	01000000
C	1000011	0	10000110
O	1001111	0	10011110
M	1001101	1	10011011
M	1001101	1	10011011

Figure 3-16 Parity Bit Generation

ity are given in Figure 3-16. It can be seen that the number of 1 bits in each 8-bit sequence (octet) is always odd (either one, three, five, or seven); it is the parity bit that ensures this. If even parity were chosen, the parity bit would be selected so that the number of 1 bits would always be an even number.

Besides even and odd parity, you can have no parity, a parity bit with no parity checking, mark parity, or space parity. If there is no parity bit or if the parity bit is not checked (called *no parity check*), the ability to detect errors using this method is lost (although other methods, to be described later, could be utilized). *Mark parity* means that the parity bit is always transmitted as a 1 bit, and *space parity* means that the parity bit is always transmitted as a 0 bit. Clearly, mark and space parity are ineffective as error detection schemes. If two stations attempting to communicate disagree on the parity scheme, all messages will be seen as being in error and will be rejected.

In the odd parity example in Figure 3-16 each character transmitted consists of eight bits—seven for data and one for parity. Parity enables the user to detect whether one, three, five, or seven bits have been altered in transmission, but it will not catch whether an even number (two, four, six, or eight bits) has been altered. One common error situation involves *burst errors*, or a grouping of errors (recall the possible effect of impulse noise during high transmission rates). The likelihood of detecting errors of this nature with a parity check is approximately 50%. At higher transmission speeds this limitation becomes significant. (A burst error for the duration of two bits does not necessarily result in two bit errors. None, one, or two bits could be affected.)

Longitudinal Redundancy Check (LRC)

We can increase the probability of error detection beyond that provided by parity by making, in addition, a *longitudinal redundancy check* (LRC). With LRC, which is similar to VRC, an additional, redundant character called the *block check character* (BCC) is appended to a block of transmitted characters, typically at the end of the block. The first bit of the BCC serves

Figure 3-17 Longitudinal Redundancy Check (LRC) Generation

Letter	ASCII	Parity Bit	Transmitted Bits
D	1000100	1	10001001
A	1000001	1	10000011
T	1010100	0	10101000
A	1000001	1	10000011
space	0100000	0	01000000
C	1000011	0	10000110
O	1001111	0	10011110
M	1001101	1	10011011
M	1001101	1	10011011
BCC	1000011	0	10000110

as a parity check for all of the first bits of the characters in the block; the second bit of the BCC serves as parity for all of the second bits in the block; and so on. An example of LRC is provided in Figure 3-17. Since an odd parity scheme has been chosen to perform the redundancy check, each column has an odd number of 1 bits.

LRC combined with VRC is still not sufficient to detect all errors (indeed, no scheme is completely dependable). Figure 3-18 presents the same "DATA COMM" message transmission, with errors introduced in rows and columns marked by an asterisk. Although both LRC and VRC appear correct, the data received is not the same as that transmitted. Adding LRC to VRC brings a greater probability of detecting errors in transmission.

Cyclic Redundancy Check (CRC)

A *cyclic redundancy check* (CRC) can detect bit errors better than either VRC or LRC or both. A CRC is computed for a block of transmitted data. The transmitting station generates the CRC and transmits it with the data. The receiving station computes the CRC for the data received and compares it

Figure 3-18 LRC Transmission Errors

Letter	ASCII	Parity Bit	Transmitted Bits
D	**1000100	1	10001001
A	1000001	1	10000011
T	*1100100	0	10101000
A	*1110001	1	10000011
space	0100000	0	01000000
C	1000011	0	10000110
O	1001111	0	10011110
M	1001101	1	10011011
M	1001101	1	10011011
BCC	1000011	0	10000110

to the CRC transmitted by the sender. If the two are equal, then the block is assumed to be error-free. The mathematics behind CRC requires the use of a generating polynomial and is beyond the scope of this book.

If the CRC generator polynomial is chosen with care and is of sufficient degree, over 99% of multiple bit errors can be detected. Several standards exist—CRC-12, CRC-16, and CRC-CCITT—that define both the degree of the generating polynomial and the generating polynomial itself. Since CRC-12 specifies a polynomial of degree 12 and the last two standards specify a polynomial of degree 16, the BCC will have 12 or 16 bits. CRC-16 and CRC-CCITT can:

Detect all single-bit and double-bit errors

Detect all errors in cases in which an odd number of bits are erroneous

Detect two pairs of adjacent errors

Detect all burst errors of 16 bits or fewer

Detect over 99.998% of all burst errors greater than 16 bits

Because of its reliability, CRC is becoming the standard method of error detection for block data transmission (as opposed to transmission of one character at a time). Chapter 6 discusses different data transmission protocols and their associated error detection schemes.

Sequence Checks

When a data communications network is simple enough so that sending and receiving nodes are connected directly, the receiving station receives all transmissions without the intercession of other nodes. However, large communications networks may have one or more intermediate nodes responsible for forwarding a message to its final destination, and one complete message may be divided into a number of transmission blocks. Furthermore, these blocks may not all be routed along the same path and hence could be received out of order. In such a case, it is important to assign sequence numbers to each block so that the ultimate receiver can determine that all blocks have indeed arrived and can put the blocks back into proper sequence.

Message Sequence Numbers. Suppose you send someone one letter per day for five days through the postal system. There is no guarantee that the letters will be received in the order sent. Several might arrive on the same day (and out of order), one might be lost, or all five might arrive at the same time. If the letters are intended to be read in order, you can number them sequentially, such as 1/5, 2/5, 3/5, and so on. This alerts the recipient to the order and allows him or her to detect missing messages. A similar scheme can be used for data communications messages.

One sequencing technique appends a *message sequence number* to each data block transmitted between two stations. If a processor is communicating with two different stations, each link would have its own sequence number. Every time a message is transmitted, the sequence number is sent along with the message. The receiving station compares the received sequence number with a number maintained in its memory. If the message numbers agree, no messages have been lost; if the received message number disagrees with the expected message number, an error condition is created and the receiver requests that the sender retransmit the missing messages.

Packet Sequence Numbers.   In some networks, messages are segmented into smaller transmission groups, or packets. If there are multiple communication paths between sender and receiver, the packet routing strategy may use several of the paths simultaneously to speed delivery of the entire message, in which case the packets could arrive out of order. To ensure that such a message can be reassembled in proper sequence, *packet sequence numbers* are appended to each packet. These sequence numbers also allow for error control.

In any of the situations just discussed, if a data block arrives and an error is detected, or if some of the blocks in a sequence have not been received, the recovery method is to ask the sending station to retransmit the erroneous or lost data. Usually, an acknowledgment is sent for all blocks received correctly; if a block is not positively acknowledged, the transmitter must re-send it. This obligates the transmitting node to retain all transmitted blocks until they have been acknowledged. Being able to request that a message be retransmitted implies that the flow control is either half duplex or full duplex. If an error is detected on a simplex line, the recipient cannot send a request for retransmission. The only recourse in this case is to ignore the message or to use the message as received.

Error Correction Codes

Some error detecting schemes allow the receiving station not only to detect errors but also to correct some of them. Such codes are called *forward error correcting codes*, the most common of which are called *Hamming codes*. As with straight error detection codes, additional, redundant information is transmitted with the data. Error correcting codes are convenient for situations in which single-bit errors occur, but for multiple-bit errors, the amount of redundant information that must be sent is cumbersome. Since the effectiveness of forward error correcting codes is reduced by transmission noise that frequently creates bursts of errors, these codes are not used as commonly as are error detection schemes. Error correcting codes have good applications in other areas, however, such as memory error detection and correction, where the probability of single-bit errors is higher. Some semiconductor memories use a 6-bit Hamming code for each 16 bits of data to allow for single-bit error correction and double-bit error detection.

Miscellaneous Error Detection Techniques

There are several other methods for increasing the probability of detecting data errors.

Check Digits.   *Check digits* or check numbers are one or more characters (often simply the sum of fields being checked) that are appended to the data being transmitted, usually generated by the sending application or device and checked by the receiving application or device.

Hash Totals.   One technique that validates operator input as well as augmenting an error detection scheme involves appending a *hash total*, which is the sum of a group of items. For example, for a batch of credit card authorizations, the sum of all charges can be computed separately or by the input device. Computing separately prior to operator input provides an accuracy check of data entry as well as transmission. The receiving computer sums the number of fields transmitted and compares its total with the transmitted hash total. If the totals agree, it is assumed that there are no errors; if the hash totals do not agree, the data must be retransmitted.

Byte Counts.   A *byte count field* can be added to a message. When an entire block of data is sent at one time (synchronous transmission), the loss of a character would ordinarily be detected either by LRC with VRC or by CRC. When every character is transmitted individually with its own error detection scheme (asynchronous transmission using parity checking), if a character is lost, it can go undetected. Thus, transmitting one or more characters that indicate the total number of characters in the message helps detect transmission errors in which entire characters may be lost.

Character Echoing.   In some systems, especially with asynchronous transmission, the characters transmitted are echoed back to the user as a check. Because of the additional line time required, this technique is less frequently used in synchronous transmissions. Consider an operator at an asynchronous terminal: When a key is struck the character is transmitted to the host computer, which echoes back (re-sends) the received character to the terminal. If the character displayed at the originating terminal is incorrect, the operator backs up the cursor to the character position and enters the correct character. With a high-speed communications line it appears to the operator as if the character is locally displayed as well as being transmitted to the host; with low-speed communicatons links, or when communicating with a busy processor, the echoing may become somewhat apparent. Echoing has the disadvantage of doubling the chances of obtaining an error, since the message must be transmitted twice. The original message may be received correctly, but if the echoed message has been corrupted, the original sender will detect an error.

ERROR CORRECTION

Whenever an error is detected, it must be corrected. If an error correcting code is used, the transmitted data can be corrected by the receiver. However, this is seldom the case in data communications. The most common error correction mechanism is to retransmit the data. In asynchronous transmission, individual characters are retransmitted, whereas in synchronous transmissions, one or more blocks may need to be retransmitted. This type of correction is known as *ARQ*, which stands for automatic request for retransmission or automatic request for repetition.

Message Acknowledgment

The mechanism used to effect retransmission is the positive or negative acknowledgment, often referred to as *ACK* and *NAK*, respectively. When a station receives a message, it computes the number of error detection bit(s) or characters and compares the result with the check number received. If the two are equal, the message is assumed to be error-free and the receiver returns a positive acknowledgment to the sender; if the two are unequal, a negative acknowledgment is returned and the sending station retransmits the message. Of course, the sending station must retain all messages until they have been positively acknowledged.

Retry Limit

In some instances the second message will also be received in error, perhaps due to an error-prone communications link or to faulty hardware or software. To cut down on continual retransmission of messages, a retry limit—typically between 3 and 100—can be set. Thus, a retry limit of five means that a message received in error will be retransmitted five times; if it is not successfully received by the fifth try, the receiving station either disables the link or disables the sending station itself. The objective of a retry limit is to avoid the unproductive work of continually processing corrupted messages. Once the cause of the problem has been corrected, the communications path is reinstated.

DIGITAL DATA TRANSMISSION

All communications media are capable of transmitting information in either digital or analog form; despite the fact that computer data is represented in *digital form*, originally computer data was transmitted mostly in analog form. The primary reason for this is that the providers of communications transmission facilities had established analog facilities for voice transmission. However, advances in digital technology and lower prices for digital transmission electronics are bringing about a change to digital transmission. Within several decades most major metropolitan areas will have made the transition; were it not for the considerable existing investment in analog transmission facilities, the changeover might be even sooner. If telephone companies were to begin today, it is likely that their transmission facilities would be digital rather than analog. There are two primary reasons for this.

Advantages of Digital Transmission

The advantages of digital transmission for data communications are lower error rates, higher transmission rates, elimination of the need to convert from digital format to analog and back to digital, and better security.

Lower Error Rates. Current telephone networks transmit signals over wires or via radio broadcast, continually amplifying the signals to overcome weakening from attenuation. Long-distance transmission demands that the signals be amplified multiple times to overcome attenuation. And since any frequency within the bandwidth is acceptable, it is difficult to filter out introduced noise or distortion, so both are amplified and propagated along with the original signals.

Like analog signals, digital signals also lose strength due to attenuation. In Figure 3-19(a), we see a digital signal as it is originated. Figure 3-19(b) illustrates a possible effect of attenuation on that signal. Since a digital signal represents only two discrete values, it is possible to completely regenerate the signal. Restored to its original state and strength, the data can be forwarded to the next regeneration point or to the final destination without any associated noise. This is accomplished by a digital regenerator. Figure 3-19(c) shows a regenerated signal.

Higher Transmission Rates. Another benefit of digital transmission is increased transmission speed. With digital transmission, switched connections can operate at speeds up to 56 Kbps. The current limit is 38,400 bps for switched circuits and leased lines.

No Digital-Analog Conversion. Theoretically, digital transmission avoids the need for conversion between formats. Unfortunately, not all locations are serviced by digital networks, whose implementation has been restricted thus far to highly populated urban centers. Furthermore, the connection from a given location to the digital transmission and switching equipment is, in many cases, still an analog link. In such instances it is necessary to convert a signal from digital to analog and back to digital for transmission to the message's destination. The device that converts the analog signal to digital is known as a *codec*, an acronym for coder-decoder.

Security. Companies are becoming increasingly concerned about security of data and voice transmissions. One method for protecting these

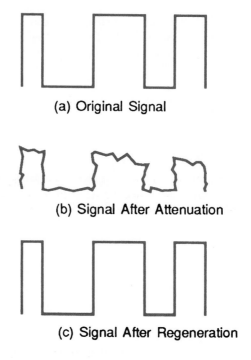

Figure 3-19 Digital
Signal Regeneration

(a) Original Signal

(b) Signal After Attenuation

(c) Signal After Regeneration

transmissions is encryption. You may be familiar with this concept as voice scramblers used on secure telephone lines. Although encryption algorithms exist for both analog and digital formats, digital encryption algorithms are more advanced and hence more secure and difficult to crack. Therefore, digital transmissions have the *potential* of greater security.

Digital Voice Using Pulse Code Modulation

In converting from analog to digital transmission lines, telephone companies are faced with the opposite problem faced by the data communications industry: On a digital line it becomes necessary to transform analog voice patterns into digital representation and then convert the digital patterns back to analog format. This is illustrated in Figure 3-20. A variety of conversion techniques exist, but the most commonly used is known as *pulse code modulation (PCM)*. On a communications wire, PCM is represented as pulses of current. A pulse of 3 volts could represent a 1 bit, and 0 voltage could represent a 0 bit. In some schemes a 1 bit would be represented by a

Figure 3-20 Codec
Converting Analog
and Digital Signals

Analog Signal   Digital Transmission Line

voltage of +1.5, and the 0 bit, by a voltage of −1.5. The first technique is referred to as *unipolar signaling*; the latter is termed *polar signaling*. Both techniques are illustrated in Figures 3-21(a) and 3-21(b), respectively.

Let us briefly look at how analog data is transmitted in digital format. Consider the analog curve in Figure 3-22. (If your voice were played over an oscilloscope, it might look somewhat like this curve.) The curve has a changing amplitude. The objective of transforming analog signals to digital signals is to capture or digitize the changing amplitudes over time. This is accomplished by assigning digital values to the amplitudes represented by the curve. It has been found that for voice communications, 128 different digital values are satisfactory, which means the amplitudes are divided into 128 ranges, allowing each range to be associated with a seven-bit number. To convert the signal to digital format, all that is necessary is to regularly sample the amplitude, determine in which of the 128 different ranges the amplitude lies, and then generate the seven bits that represent that range. Finally, we can add a bit for control or for error checking. The only thing that is undetermined is the sampling rate. For PCM, 8000 samples are taken per second. Thus, each second 64,000 bits are generated and transmitted—seven data bits plus one control bit, for eight

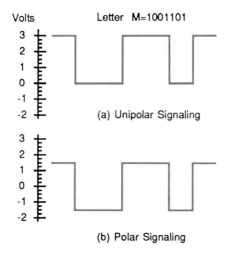

Figure 3-21   Pulse Code Modulation

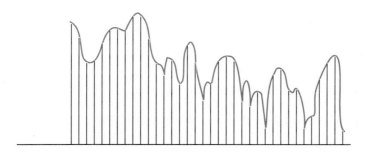

Figure 3-22   Voice Transmission Wave and Associated Pulse Code Modulation Representation

bits per sample and 8000 samples per second. Thus, digitized voice is transmitted at 64,000 bits per second, well below the capacity of telephone wire pairs.

INTERFACE

Once a medium has been selected, it is necessary to connect it to the computer equipment. There are two classes of equipment in data communications: *data communications equipment* (*DCE*) (modems, media, and media-support facilities such as telephone switching equipment, microwave relay stations, and transponders) and *data terminal* (or terminating) *equipment* (*DTE*) (including terminals, computers, concentrators, and multiplexers, all of which are covered in Chapters 4 and 5). The physical interface is the manner in which these two classes of equipment are joined together. Figure 3-23 depicts a data communications linkage with the DCE and DTE components identified.

The interface between DCE and DTE can be divided into four aspects: mechanical, electrical, functional, and procedural. The mechanical portion includes the type of connectors to be used, the number of pin connections in the connectors, and the maximum allowable cable lengths. The electrical characteristics include the allowable line voltages and the representations for the various voltage levels. The functional interface specifies which signals — timing, control, data, or ground leads — are to be carried by each pin in the connector. Figure 3-24 lists the signals assigned to each of the 25 pins in an RS-232-C interface.

Procedural characteristics define how signals are exchanged and delineate the environment necessary to transmit and receive data. For example, one pin or conducting wire in the connector might represent the ability of a terminal to accept a transmission; when the terminal is ready to receive data, a signal will be raised on that lead. When no signal is raised on that circuit, transmission to the terminal is not valid. A procedural interface to transmit from a processor to a terminal is given in Figure 3-25.

Interface Standards

Numerous standards are adhered to in establishing an interface between DCE and DTE. The following brief descriptions familiarize you with these standards and what they generally cover.

RS-232-C. Currently in the United States the predominant interface standard is the Electronic Industries Association (EIA) *RS-232-C standard*, established in October 1969 and reaffirmed in June 1981. RS-232-C encompasses serial binary data interchange at rates up to 20,000 bps and a recommended distance of up to 50 feet; longer distances are possible for

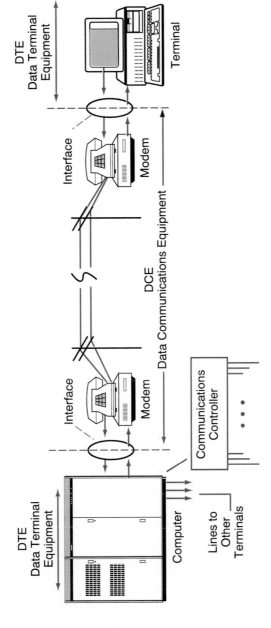

Figure 3-23 DTE and DCE Components

109

Figure 3-24 Inter-
face Connector Pin
Assignments

Pin Number	Circuit	Description
1	AA	Protective Ground
2	BA	Transmitted Data
3	BB	Received Data
4	CA	Request to Send
5	CB	Clear to Send
6	CC	Data Set Ready
7	AB	Signal Ground (Common Return)
8	CF	Received Line Signal Detector
9	—	(Reserved for Modem Testing)
10	—	(Reserved for Modem Testing)
11		Unassigned
12	SCF	Secondary for Pin 8
13	SCB	Secondary Clear to Send
14	SBA	Secondary Transmitted Data
15	DB	Transmission Signal Timing
16	SBB	Secondary Received Data
17	DD	Receiver Signal Timing
18		Unassigned
19	SCA	Secondary Request to Send
20	CD	Data Terminal Ready
21	CG	Signal Quality Detector
22	CE	Ring Indicator
23	CH/CI	Data Signal Rate Selector
24	DA	Transmit Signal Element Timing
25		Unassigned

Figure 3-25 Pro-
cedural Interface
between Processor
and Terminal

1. Processor and terminal raise DTR (data terminal ready) signal to modem.

2. Modems raise DSR (data set ready) signal.

3. Processor raises RTS (request to send) signal.

4. Processor's modem sends a carrier signal.

5. Terminal's modem detects carrier and raises CD (carrier detect) signal to processor's modem.

6. Processor's modem raises CTS (clear to send) signal.

7. Processor sends data on TD (transmit data).

8. Processor's modem modulates data onto the carrier wave.

9. Terminal's modem demodulates data onto RD (received data).

10. Processor lowers RTS signal.

11. Processor's modem drops CTS and carrier wave.

12. Terminal's modem drops CD.

13. Transmission is complete.

shielded wires. (Shielded wire is certified by the manufacturer as capable of spanning 500 feet at 9600 bps.) Because of the speed limitations, RS-232-C has its greatest application in interfacing to wire media, where this bit transmission rate is most common. It covers private, switched, and leased connections, with provisions for auto-answer switched connections. *Serial binary transmission* (or bit serial transmission) is a mode wherein bits are transmitted in single file. This is contrasted with *bit parallel transmission*, wherein bits are transmitted in parallel. Figure 3-26 illustrates the difference between these two techniques.

The RS-232-C standard does not specify size or type of connectors to be used in the interface, although it does define 25 signal leads, three of them unassigned, two reserved for testing, and the remaining 20 used for grounding, data, control, and timing. In the absence of a standard, one connector—a 25-pin connector—has become common in implementing RS-232-C connections. Figure 3-27(a) depicts this type of connector. Despite the fact that 25 signal leads have been specified, actual transmissions typically use fewer. A simple modem interface, for example, can require that only 7 pins be active; yet on occasion, connectors supporting 15, 9, and 7 pins are used to interface with these devices. A 15-pin connector and a 9-pin connector are illustrated in Figures 3-27(b) and 3-27(c). The RS-232-C standard covers all four aspects of the interface: mechanical, electrical, functional, and procedural. This is significant because other interface specifications treat them separately, and thus, two or three standards may be cited that together form the equivalent of what is specified by RS-232-C.

RS-449. Because of the speed and distance constraints of the RS-232-C standard, the EIA *RS-449 standard* was adopted. It provides for a 37-pin

Message to Be Transmitted: LINE
Representation: ASCII

L	1001100
I	1001001
N	1001110
E	1000101

1001100	1001001	1001110	1000101
L	I	N	E

(a) Bit Serial Transmission

```
1 1 1 1
0 0 0 0
0 0 0 0
1 1 1 0
1 0 1 1
0 0 1 0
0 1 0 1
L I N E
```

(b) Bit Parallel Transmission

Figure 3-26 Serial vs. Parallel Transmission

Figure 3-27   Cable
Connectors

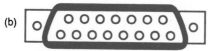

(a) 25-pin connector for RS-232-C or CCITT V.24 interface

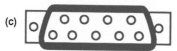

(b) 15-pin connector for RS-232-C or CCITT V.24 interface

(c) 9-pin connector for RS-232-C, RS-449, or CCITT V.24 interface

connection, cable lengths up to 200 feet, and data transmission rates up to 2 million bps. RS-449 equates with the functional and procedural portions of RS-232-C (the electrical and mechanical specifications are covered by RS-422 and RS-423). Because of RS-449's enhanced capabilities over RS-232-C, it should eventually replace RS-232-C as the predominant interface within the United States.

RS-366.   EIA has also adopted an RS-366 standard, which is a 25-pin connection with enhanced capabilities for automatic calling equipment. RS-366 covers interface details such as what signals need to be present when the dial tone is detected, when dialing, and so on. (The electrical portion of the interface is covered by the RS-423 standard.)

ISO and CCITT Standards.   The International Standards Organization (ISO) and the Consultative Committee on International Telegraph and Telephony (CCITT) also have adopted standards that are widely adhered to. The most significant of these international standards for interfaces are briefly described below.

ISO-2110 standard: ISO-2110 is a functional interface standard similar to the functional portion of RS-232-C. It describes which signals will be carried on specific pins.

CCITT V.10 and V.11: CCITT V.10 and V.11 are electrical interfaces similar to those specified by RS-422 and RS-423.

CCITT V.24: The CCITT V.24 standard covers both the functional and the procedural aspects of a 25-pin interface similar to that specified by RS-232-C.

CCITT V.25: The CCITT V.25 standard covers the procedural aspects of establishing and terminating automatic calling unit connections over switched lines.

CCITT V.28: The CCITT V.28 standard covers the electrical interface in a manner similar to that of RS-232-C.

CCITT V.35: The CCITT V.35 standard defines a 34-pin connection for interfaces with speeds of 48,000 bps.

CCITT X.20 and X.21: The CCITT X.20 and X.21 standards cover the interface between DCE and DTE for packet distribution networks (PDNs). (PDNs are discussed in detail in Chapter 10.)

CCITT X.24: The CCITT X.24 standard covers the functional aspects of interface for PDNs.

Other Standards. The U.S. government and U.S. military have their own interface standards. Specifically, MIL-STD-188-114 and U.S. government standards 1020 and 1030 provide for electrical interfaces similar to those of RS-422 and RS-423.

COMMON CARRIER SERVICES

In the past, a marked distinction existed between communications facilities used for voice and video and those used for transmitting data. In today's networks, however, that distinction is less apparent. Today's high-speed transmission facilities are available at low cost. We are able to combine data, voice, and graphic images on one of these high-speed communications links. Thus, the modern data communications manager may be responsible for the entire spectrum of corporate electronic communications. Therefore, knowledge of the basic services and operations of the common carriers is important. A brief summary of major offerings is given below.

Common Carrier Network Organization

First, let us look at the organization of the common carrier communications network. Specifically, we consider how the network was organized in the United States prior to the AT&T divestiture. Some telephone networks outside the United States still are organized along these lines. Next, we examine how the U.S. network is organized after the divestiture.

Pre-Divestiture Organization. Prior to the divestiture, one company, AT&T, dominated the telephone service industry. There were other general service providers, for example, GTE, and competition for long-distance service had begun to appear. The AT&T network is described here. Figure 3-28 illustrates the organization of the AT&T network. Note that there is a hierarchy of switching stations through which a call can be forwarded. A telephone subscriber is connected to a local switching office called a *class 5* office. Class 5 offices are also called *end offices* because they

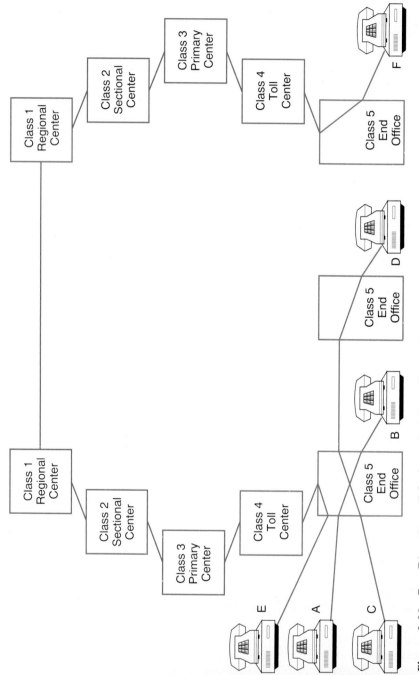

Figure 3-28 Pre- Divestiture Telephone Switching Network

are at the extremities of the telephone switching network. If the subscriber calls another subscriber who is also attached to the same local office, the call is switched through that single end office. This is illustrated in Figure 3-28 by Subscriber A's connection to Subscriber B. It is also possible for Subscriber C to call Subscriber D, whose telephone is connected to another class 5 office in the same general area. C's call goes directly from C's end office to D's end office and then to D's local line. Both of these calls are local calls and will incur no long-distance fee.

If, however, the call is not local, as in Subscriber E's connection to Subscriber F, the call is routed from the class 5 station to a *class 4* station called a *toll center*. This initiates the billing process for the call. From the class 4 station, the call goes to a *class 3* station called a *primary center*. At this point, if the call is destined for a regional high-use area, the class 3 station might route the call directly to the recipient's class 5 local switch. Alternatively, the call is routed up through the *class 2* station, termed a *sectional center*, to a *class 1* station, called a *regional center*. The class 1 station then passes the call to another class 1 station. A class 1 station might then send the call to another class 1 center. Class 1 centers form a backbone transmission network. When the call reaches the class 1 station "closest" to the call's recipient, the connection is switched down through the hierarchy until it reaches the recipient's class 5 end office. At the end office, the call is switched to the recipient's local line.

Post-Divestiture Network.   After the AT&T divestiture in 1984, AT&T was broken up into independent *regional Bell operating companies (RBOCs)* and a separate AT&T company. The divestiture not only ended the regulated monopoly AT&T had enjoyed but also freed AT&T and the RBOCs to enter into business areas formerly denied them, such as the computer industry. RBOCs are responsible for handling subscriber services within their area; one of the functions of AT&T is to provide long-distance services. The divestiture resulted in a revamping of how long-distance calls are handled.

Local calls are handled in much the same way as in the pre-divestiture era. However, the regions served by RBOCs were divided into *local access and transport areas (LATAs)*. A LATA is roughly equivalent to the area serviced by an area code. More generally, a LATA corresponds to a common calling area. Thus, in areas of high population density, for example, the San Francisco Bay area, several area codes may fall within the same LATA. All calls originating and terminating within a LATA are handled exclusively by the RBOC. Any call that crosses a LATA boundary becomes the responsibility of a long-distance carrier, such as AT&T, MCI, or Sprint.

Each telephone subscriber is free to choose a long-distance carrier, and long-distance carriers are required to have equal access to subscribers. To provide equal access, each LATA has a designated inter-exchange *point of presence (POP)*. An inter-LATA call is routed to the POP, where it is accepted by the designated long-distance carrier. The long-distance carrier routes the call to the POP in the recipient's LATA and the call is switched to the recipient's end office and telephone. This is illustrated in Figure 3-29.

Figure 3-29 Post-
Divestiture Long
Distance Switching

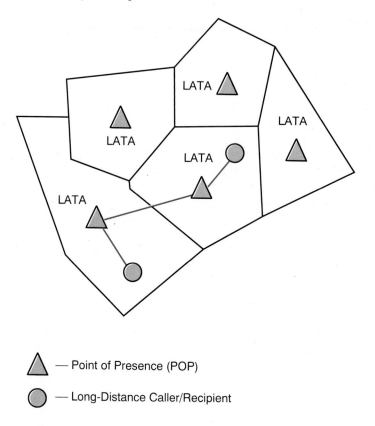

— Point of Presence (POP)

— Long-Distance Caller/Recipient

Available Services

A common carrier typically provides a broad range of services. The primary services are discussed in the following sections.

Switched Lines. Switched lines, as defined in Chapter 2, simply make use of the existing telephone circuits and switching equipment to establish a connection between sender and receiver. This facility is available wherever telephone wires exist.

Leased Telegraph-Grade Lines. Leased telegraph-grade lines provide lower transmission rates than the voice-grade lines described below. They are used for very low transmission rates.

Leased Voice-Grade Lines. Like switched lines, leased lines were discussed in Chapter 2. Leased lines may be conditioned to reduce error rates, which allows higher transmission speeds.

Wide Band Transmission. Wide band transmission allows very high data transmission rates. Transmission rates in this category are in the range of

48 Kbps to 80 Kbps. Most wide band services available today are digital rather than analog.

T-1 Service. *T-1 service*, also referred to as *DS-1 signaling*, provides digital transmission rates of 1.544 Mbps. A T-1 communications link is created by multiplexing (combining) a number of lower speed lines. While the implementation may vary, generally a T-1 circuit is created by multiplexing twenty-four 64-Kbps lines. The product of 24 and 64,000 is 1.536 million. The additional 8000 bits per second are control bits. The 8000 bps derives from the PCM algorithm discussed earlier. A T-1 service that began to appear in the late 1980s is known as fractional T-1 service. Before fractional T-1, high-speed transmission options were 56 or 64 Kbps or 1.544 Mbps with few options in between. Fractional T-1 is intended to fill this void by providing a portion of a T-1 line to customers. With fractional T-1, a customer can obtain transmission lines of 128, 256, and 768 Kbps.

Higher speeds are available with *T-3* and *T-4 services*, also referred to as *DS-3* and *DS-4 signaling*, respectively. T-3 service provides a data rate of 45 Mbps and is derived from multiplexing 672 64-Kbps lines. T-4 service provides transmission at 274 Mbps and is derived from multiplexing 4032 64-Kbps lines. Of these options, T-1 is the most common; however, as the need for speed increases and the rates for T-3 and T-4 services decline, higher speed services like T-3 are likely to become more common. One of the needs for higher data rates may be full motion video. With current technology, T-1 and T-2 speeds are insufficient for full motion video transmission.

WATS. *WATS* is an acronym for *wide area telecommunications* or *telephone service*. Both inbound and outbound services are available. The inbound WATS service is the familiar toll-free 800-prefix numbers. A customer may subscribe to an inbound service, an outbound service, or both. The common carrier charges a flat monthly fee for the service, which provides for a specific number of hours of connect time to designated regions. The cost of the service is based on both the number of hours of connect time and the distance to be covered by the service. When WATS service is used for data transmission, the effect is the same as using switched lines, but the cost of the call differs.

Packet Switching Network Service. This service allows users to establish connections between many locations for a fixed monthly fee plus a cost per packet of data sent. This facility is discussed in more detail in Chapter 10.

Satellite Service. Users may rent satellite transponder time from a number of common carriers. Satellite transmission was described in Chapter 2.

Integrated Services Digital Networks (ISDNs). Increased use of common carrier facilities for data communications has prompted providers of such services to evaluate their networks. One conclusion that has been drawn is the need for one network capable of transmitting data in various forms. These forms could include digital data, voice, facsimile, graphics, and video. The benefits to the user community of this type of network are higher transmission speed and potential cost reductions for communications services resulting from the ability to combine multiple data forms onto one network.

One objective of *ISDNs* is to allow international data exchange. This requires interfaces between a number of national and regional providers of such services. The first mission of the ISDN program has been to define the functions and characteristics of the network and to establish implementation standards. In 1984, the CCITT produced the first of what is likely to become several standards for ISDN implementations. This standard provides for several different types of service.

The ISDN system specifies three basic types of channels designated as B, D, and H types. Within the H-type channel several options are available. These options are shown in Figure 3-30. ISDNs will initially provide two interface structures designated as basic service and primary service. The basic service is designated as $2B_{64} + D_{16}$, which indicates that it consists of two type B channels and one 16-Kbps type D channel, for an aggregate speed of 144 Kbps. The primary service has a different configuration for North America and Japan than for Europe. The North American and Japanese specification is designated as $23B_{64} + D_{64}$, for an aggregate speed of 1.544 Mbps. Note that this is the same speed as the T-1 service. In Europe, the primary service is designated as $30B_{64} + D_{64}$, for an aggregate speed of 2.048 Mbps, equivalent to the European version of T-1 transmission.

As an emerging technology, ISDNs have great potential for data transfer and the integration of different forms of data. All of the uses for ISDNs

Figure 3-30   ISDN Channel Types and Options

ISDN Channel Types

B—64 Kbps
H0—384 Kbps (= 6B)
H11—1.544 Mbps (= 23B + $1D_{64}$)—North America and Japan
H12—2.048 Mbps (= 30B + $1D_{64}$)—Europe

Control Data

D—Both 16 and 64 Kbps

Basic Service Options

$2B_{64} + D_{16}$ = 144 Kbps

Primary Service

$23B_{64} + D_{64}$ = 1.544 Mbps—North America and Japan
$30B_{64} + D_{64}$ = 2.048 Mbps—Europe

have not yet been identified, but applications that have been identified include:

Digital voice transmission

Local area networks (see Chapter 8 for additional information about this use of ISDNs)

Office automation (routing and access to documents)

Security via transmission of graphic images, such as signatures for check cashing verification or freeze-frame images to security guards

High-speed switched data lines

Video telephone service

Concurrent transfer of voice and data (for example, two users can be engaged in a telephone conversation while simultaneously transmitting data between their workstations)

Cellular Radio Telephone.   Cellular radio telephone provides mobile telephone connections. Often, the telephones are installed in vehicles, but that is not required. A mobile telephone can be carried by a pedestrian or cyclist. Currently cellular telephones are only available in major metropolitan areas because it is not economical to establish the facilities in areas of low population density. It is likely, however, that satellite transmission will be added to existing systems and thereby overcome this limitation.

Figure 3-31 shows a diagram of a cellular system. Transmission is via FM radio broadcast. Before cellular technology, signals for a major metropolitan area were broadcast from a central site like ordinary radio station signals. Because of the limited available channels (dictated by the assigned frequencies), only a limited number of calls could be in progress at one time. With cellular technology, the calling area is divided into cells, each of which is serviced by a transmitting station. The transmissions are low power and thus serve only that cell, allowing the same frequency to be used concurrently by nonadjacent cells. As a mobile user moves from one cell to another, the responsibility for transmission is passed from the cell being exited to the cell being entered. Since cellular telephone provides connection to line-based telephone networks, the full range of data transmission capabilities that exists for regular telephone service is available. For example, some cars are now equipped with facsimile machines for mobile fax transfers, and it is possible to connect portable computers in mobile stations to computer networks.

PBX and Centrex Services.   *PBX* is an abbreviation for *private branch exchange*. PBXs are discussed in more detail in Chapter 8 as a delivery mechanism for a local area network. *Centrex service* is essentially a PBX service provided by a common carrier. Instead of the switching equipment being located on the customer's premises, the common carrier provides the switching equipment on the common carrier's site. This allows several

Figure 3-31   A Cellular Radio Telephone System

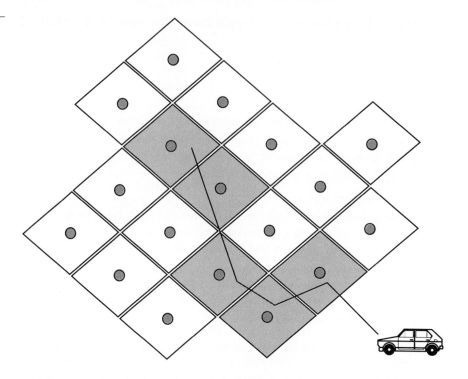

locations in a city to share the same switch and use the same calling prefix and allows extension dialing as though the telephones were located in one building and serviced by an onsite PBX. As with a PBX, Centrex service can be used to transmit data as well as voice.

Service Providers.   In the United States the following companies provide some or all of the above capabilities.

> AT&T
>
> MCI
>
> U.S. Sprint
>
> Western Union
>
> Allnet
>
> Contel/American
>
> CompuServe
>
> ITT
>
> IBM Information Services
>
> GTE
>
> Computer Sciences Corporation
>
> McDonnell Douglas
>
> Comsat

SUMMARY

There are three basic types of data flow: simplex, half duplex, and full duplex. Most business data communications systems use either full or half duplex. In half duplex mode, modem turnaround time may adversely affect terminal response time. Several different communications codes are used in data communications, the most common being ASCII and EBCDIC.

All media are subject to error. Detecting errors requires that redundant information be transmitted with the data. The three most common error detection schemes in data communications are vertical redundancy check (VRC), longitudinal redundancy check (LRC), and cyclic redundancy check (CRC). The most effective is CRC. In some protocols sequence checking is also used to improve the reliability of transmission.

Digital data transmission provides both higher transmission speeds and fewer errors. The common carriers are gradually making the conversion from analog transmission equipment to digital equipment. Digital transmission has led to new transmission capabilities, specifically the integration of different services over one medium. It is now common for both data and voice to be transmitted over the same circuits. One of the technologies rapidly being implemented to provide this capability is the integrated services digital network, or ISDN.

Interface standards exist regarding connections between data terminal equipment (DTE) and data communications equipment (DCE). There are both domestic and international standards regarding mechanical, functional, procedural, and electrical interfaces; unfortunately, these standards do not always agree.

Key Terms

ASCII
attenuation
Baudot
BCD
bit parallel transmission
bit serial transmission
block check character (BCC)
CCITT V.24, V.25, V.28, V.35, X.20, X.21, and X.24 standards
cellular radio telephone
Centrex
class 1 telephone center, or regional center
class 2 telephone center, or sectional center
class 3 telephone center, or primary center
class 4 telephone center, or toll center
class 5 telephone center, or end office
conditioning
crosstalk

cyclic redundancy check (CRC)
digital transmission
divestiture, AT&T
DS-1 signaling
DS-3 signaling
DS-4 signaling
EBCDIC
echo
echo suppressor
full duplex transmission
Gaussian noise
half duplex transmission
impulse noise
integrated services digital network (ISDN)
local access and transport area (LATA)
local (telephone) loop

longitudinal redundancy
   check (LRC)
modem turnaround time
parity check
phase jitter
point of presence (POP)
private branch exchange
   (PBX)
pulse code modulation
   (PCM)
regional Bell operating
   companies (RBOCs)
RS-232-C standard

RS-366 standard
RS-449 standard
SBT
simplex transmission
T-1 transmission
T-3 transmission
T-4 transmission
vertical redundancy check
   (VRC)
white noise
wide area telephone service
   (WATS)

Review Questions

1. Define:
   a. simplex transmission
   b. half duplex transmission
   c. full duplex transmission

2. What effect does modem turnaround time have on data transmission? Does it have a more significant effect on short messages or long messages? Why?

3. How is a reverse channel used?

4. What are the limitations of a 6-bit data code?

5. What are the limitations of an 8-bit data code?

6. Describe:
   a. white noise
   b. impulse noise
   c. echo
   d. attenuation

   Which of the four is most likely to cause an error in data transmission?

7. Describe four ways to *prevent* transmission errors.

8. Describe how parity checking works. If even parity is used, what will the parity bit be for the ASCII characters P, A, R, I, T, and Y?

9. Explain why CRC is a better error detection scheme than parity or longitudinal redundancy checks.

10. Explain how sequence checks can increase the integrity of data transmission.

11. What are the advantages of digital data transmission?

12. Explain how digital data transmission can obtain higher speeds than analog and at the same time have fewer errors.

13. Why are interface standards important?

14. What are ISDNs? Give two examples where ISDNs might be used for data transmission.

15. How does a cellular radio telephone system work?

Exercises

1. Label each of the following items as simplex, half duplex, or full duplex.
   a. commercial radio
   b. CB radio
   c. television
   d. smoke signals
   e. classroom discussion
   f. family arguments
   g. ocean tides
   h. shortwave radio communications

2. Calculate the line time and modem turnaround time required for the following transaction. Assume a modem turnaround time of 20 milliseconds, a line speed of 2400 bps, and 10 bits per character.
   a. Operator enters 10-character employee ID.
   b. System returns 500-character employee record.
   c. Operator changes zip code and retransmits only the 5-character zip code back to the system.
   d. System acknowledges receipt and positive action by sending operator 20-character message.

3. Identify instances other than those mentioned in the chapter in which a code with 256 different characters may be insufficient.

4. Obtain and examine the Japanese Industrial Standard (JIS) for data codes that contain a portion of the Kanji character set. What other characters are allowed? How many bits are required to support this standard? What, if any, special features are included?

5. Why is Morse code not a viable alternative for computers?

6. If the speed of transmission on a line is 7200 bps and that line is hit by lightning that causes an impulse distortion of 3.5 milliseconds, what is the maximum number of bits that could be in error?

7. Assuming the worst case in Exercise 6, what percentage of the errors incurred would be caught by VRC?

8. ISDN services are widely written about in data communications magazines and journals. Research the literature and describe four different applications that use this technology.

9. Interfaces are being defined for attaching microcomputers to ISDNs. Research the literature and find the cost and capabilities of one such interface.

10. Determine if cellular radio telephone service is available in your area. What are the distance limitations of the service? What is the cost?

References

Abrahams, John R. "Centrex Versus PBX: The Battle for Features and Functionality." *Telecommunications*, March 1989.

Bellamy, John. *Digital Telephony*. New York: Wiley, 1982.

Block, Ellen G. "ISDN: The Telcos are Ready, But Are the Users?" *Telecommunications*, May 1989.

Budwey, James N. "ISDN Progress in the USA." *Telecommunications*, March 1990.

Collie, Brian E., Larry S. Kayser, and Antony M. Rybczynski. "Looking at the ISDN Interfaces: Issues and Answers." *The Executive Guide to Data Communications*, Vol. 7. New York: McGraw-Hill.

Cypser, R. J. *Communications Architecture for Distributed Systems.* Reading, MA: Addison-Wesley, 1978.

Electronic Industries Association. *Interface between Data Terminal Equipment and Data Communications Equipment Employing Serial Binary Data Interchange.* RS-232-C Standards Document. Washington, DC: Electronics Industries Assoc., 1969, 1981.

Freeman, Roger L. *Telecommunications Transmission Handbook.* New York: Wiley, 1981.

Handel, Rainer. "Evolution of ISDN towards Broadband ISDN." *IEEE Network*, January 1989.

Harper, William L., and Robert C. Pollard. *Data Communications Desk Book: A Systems Analysis Approach.* Englewood Cliffs, NJ: Prentice-Hall, 1982.

Hertzoff, Ira S. "ISDN: A New Path to LAN Connection." *LAN Technology*, December 1989.

Jakubson, Joel E. "T3 Networks Require Strong, Flexible Management." *Networking Management*, February 1989.

Klinck, Courtney A. "Just When You Thought It Made Sense to Get Rid of Centrex..." *Data Communications*, March 1986.

Krechmer, Ken. "The Hidden Costs of ISDN." *Telecommunications*, October 1989.

Kuo, Franklin F. *Protocols and Techniques for Data Communications Networks.* Englewood Cliffs, NJ: Prentice-Hall, 1981.

Leddy, Donald, and Lori Rubin. "Here's How Pulse Code Modulation (PCM) Works in Converting Analog Voice Signals to Digital." *Communications News*, October 1986.

Leonard, D. J. "ISDN—The Next Decade." *Telecommunications*, August 1987.

Lubliner, Olivier. "ISDN Development in France." *Telecommunications*, July 1989.

Mantelman, Lee. "Tips from Europe's ISDN Pioneers." *Data Communications*, May 1989.

Mier, Edwin E. "Comparing the Long-Distance Carriers." *Data Communications*, August 1986.

————. "PBX Upgrades: Forget the Forklift." *Data Communications*, March 1990.

O'Brien, Brad. "ISDN: Users Think It's a Distant Prospect. Wrong." *Data Communications*, December 1985.

Pelton, Joseph N. "ISDN: Satellites Versus Cable." *Telecommunications*, June 1988.

Popko, John. "Assessing the ISDN Revolution: It's on Its Way and It Will Be Here Sooner Than You May Think." *Communications News*, October 1986.

Rosner, Roy D. "Can Packet Switching Survive ISDN and Fiber?" *Telecommunications*, April 1988.

Sazegari, Steven A. "Network Architects Plan Broadening of Future ISDN." *Data Communications*, July 1987.

Stallings, William. "CCITT Standards Foreshadow Broadband ISDN." *Telecommunications*, March 1990.

Underwood, Sarah. "ISDN on Trial." *Datamation*, February 1, 1987.

Valovic, Tom. "Will ISDN Replace LANs?" *Data Communications*, September 1987.

Weissberger, Alan J. "The Evolving Versions of ISDN's Terminal Adapter." *Data Communications*, March 1989.

_____. "Report Cards Out: Carriers Rated on Service, Quality." *Data Communications*, August 1987.

Terminal Equipment

Terminals
Terminal Capabilities
Terminal Attributes
Terminal Configuration
Case Study

INTRODUCTION

In the previous two chapters we discussed transmission media; the two methods used to represent data—analog and digital; how errors are introduced, detected, and corrected; various data codes; and one piece of hardware, the modem. In Chapters 4 and 5 we continue the discussion of the physical components of data communications systems, specifically, hardware, starting with the extremities of the system, the *terminal equipment.* The discussion then moves toward the primary processors of a system, *host computers,* examining along the way line-sharing devices that make the use of a medium more efficient, more cost effective, or both. One configuration of such equipment is illustrated in Figure 4-1. At the conclusion of this chapter, you should know about:

The difference between dumb, smart, and intelligent terminals

A variety of terminal attributes

What ergonomics means and the importance of ergonomically designed terminals

Ways in which two or more terminals can share the same communications line

Considerations for choosing the best terminal for a given task

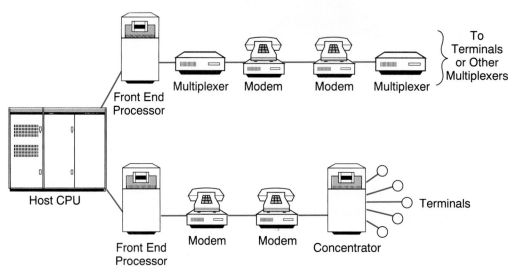

Figure 4-1   A Hardware Configuration

TERMINALS

Definition

What is a *terminal*? Here is the *Webster's New World Dictionary* definition:

> terminal (noun). 1. a terminating part; end; extremity; limit. 2. a connective device or point on an electric circuit or conductor. 3. either end of a transportation line.

Since this definition is too general for data communications, here is how terminal is defined for this book:

> terminal (noun). An input and/or output device that may be connected to a local or remote computer, called a *host computer*. The terminal is at certain times dependent on the host for either computation or data access or both.

The phrase "may be connected" allows for switched connections and devices that have some degree of processing power and are connected to a host on a periodic basis, such as a microcomputer. Even this definition is not quite as rigorous as is desirable, but further qualifications would make the definition unusable. In some environments, particularly distributed processing systems, data and/or processing functions are distributed among several host systems; to comply with this definition, each host would be classified as a terminal as well as a host. This text does not consider such systems to be within the main category of terminals.

Typical Uses of Terminals

A variety of terminal devices meet this book's definition, and they can be used in numerous ways.

Microcomputers.   A *microcomputer* can augment the host processing by doing a portion of the processing. Microcomputers are becoming an integral component of computer networks. In this capacity they are grouped together in a local area network or as terminal devices connected to a host computer or both. Some ways that microcomputers are being used in networks include:

1. Data stored on a host computer is transmitted to a microcomputer. The data is manipulated at the microcomputer with local database, spreadsheet, or word processing software. In some instances data is returned to the host for inclusion in the database or for additional processing.

2. Data is entered, edited, and stored at the microcomputer. When a batch of data is collected, it is submitted to the host for processing.

3. Applications on a microcomputer may be assisted by the greater capacity of a host computer. Thus, a scientific application may perform some data manipulation locally and pass data to a host for calculation and intensive processing.

4. A large project such as creating a technical manual can be divided among several microcomputer users. To complete the project, the separate manual sections are integrated into one document on a host system.

5. Microcomputers can function as standard terminals in many applications. In this role they emulate a specific brand of terminal. A software program and a hardware interface can effect the terminal emulation. A typical terminal emulation program allows one microcomputer to function as a variety of terminals in support of changing requirements.

6. Microcomputers operating on a local area network or directly connected to a host system can share hardware devices such as printers and disk drives. Sharing hardware peripherals helps reduce hardware costs and makes more effective use of existing equipment.

A microcomputer is shown in Figure 4-2, and Figure 4-3 lists several manufacturers of microcomputers. The price of microcomputers changes frequently as new products and processors are introduced. You can obtain current prices by consulting microcomputer-oriented magazines or weekly magazines like *Byte, PC Magazine, PC World, InfoWorld,* and *PC Week.* The use of microcomputers in networks is covered in more detail in Chapter 10.

Figure 4-2   A Micro-
computer

Figure 4-3
Microcomputer
Manufacturers

Acer America Corporation	Mitsubishi Electronics
Advanced Logic Research	NCR Corporation
Apple Computers	NEC
AST Research Inc.	Northgate Computer Systems
AT&T	Olivetti Corporation
Compaq Computer	Packard Bell
CompuAdd	Tandon
Dell Computer Corporation	Tandy Corporation
Epson Corporation	Toshiba
Gateway 2000	Wang Laboratories
Hewlett-Packard	Zenith Data Systems
IBM	Zeos International

Remote Job Entry Stations.   A terminal can be used to forward record images to a host system and possibly to receive updated reports back from the host. Historically, input from such terminals has been card images and the resulting output has been printed reports or punched cards. In some instances tape has also served as an input or output medium. This type of operation is sometimes referred to as *remote batch processing.*

Data Entry and Display.   A *video display unit* (*VDU*) or a hard-copy device such as a *teletypewriter* (*TTY*) can serve for data entry or data display

Figure 4-4   A VDU Terminal

Courtesy of TeleVideo Systems, Inc., Sunnyvale, CA.

or both. Such devices can carry on a dialogue with the host(s) and get data from and provide data to the business's applications. A VDU is also sometimes referred to as a *video display terminal* (*VDT*) or a *cathode ray tube* (*CRT*). A VDU terminal is shown in Figure 4-4.

Sensor Devices.   Sensor devices are used in laboratory, hospital, or data collection applications, frequently for input only. For example, many newer, large office buildings have a computer-controlled environmental monitoring system. Sensors located throughout the building alert the system to areas in which temperature is outside the comfort zone. The host responds by sending a message to an output-only terminal device that switches on either heating or cooling. When the temperature once again is within the comfort zone, the host sends a message to the thermal controller to discontinue its function. Sensor devices are also used in automobile testing to monitor engine performance and emissions, periodically transmitting data samples to a host for later analysis. In hospital and clinical laboratories, data collection devices and special terminals attached to host systems help in the classification and processing of clinical samples.

Display-Only Devices.   A display-only device frequently serves as a receiver of data. For example, the display monitors in stock market applications are display-only devices. Remote printers also fit in this class, although some also have the ability to transmit control information such as "out of paper" or "not ready to receive."

Point-of-Sale Terminals.   *Point-of-sale* (POS) terminals are used to help maintain inventory, record gross receipts, and—in some instances—participate in money transfers from a buyer's account to a merchant's account. The capabilities of POS terminals vary significantly. Many of these functions are described in the following example.

A customer brings several items to a checkout counter in a department store that uses POS terminals. An *optical character recognition* (OCR) reader attached to the terminal reads the sales tags for the item numbers (printed in a special OCR type font) and enters them into the system. Alternatives to OCR input include the *universal product code* (UPC) reader, which reads the bar codes on items, and manual entry by the store clerk. Once the product has been identified, the computer sends the items' current prices from the database to the terminal for totaling the sale, including tax, and for accumulating the terminal's daily sales. If the customer wishes to pay with a credit card or check, the terminal asks for a personal identification number (PIN) to authorize the sale. If a debit card is used, the funds are transferred from the customer's account to the store's account. At the completion of the transaction, the database inventory records are adjusted for the items sold.

Portable Terminal Devices.   One application for portable terminals or microcomputers is in direct sales. Some marketing agencies provide their sales force with portable terminals capable of storing information in memory. The salesperson records customer orders during the day and can use a telephone link to transmit the orders to the home office for processing. Figure 4-5 pictures a portable microcomputer.

Portable microcomputers like the one pictured in Figure 4-5 are increasingly being used by traveling businesspeople on airplanes and in hotel rooms for writing memos or letters, preparing budgets, generating graphics for presentations, and a myriad of other applications. Frequently data generated in this way is later transmitted to a host computer for dissemination, storage, or further processing.

Touch-Tone Telephones.   Touch-tone telephones can be used in bill paying, account inquiry or transfer applications, and student registration. Although not employed extensively because of their limited input and output capabilities, they work well for certain applications. Students at many colleges and universities use touch-tone telephones to register for courses, and some banks allow touch-tone telephones to be used for paying bills.

Automatic Teller Machines (ATMs).   Most banks now have networks of teller machines that enable the customer to handle simple banking transactions without the aid of a human teller and that also allow the customer to make withdrawals and deposits during nonbanking hours.

Credit Card Gas Pumps.   In California, Atlantic Richfield Co. and the Bank of America have joined forces so customers can use their ATM cards

Figure 4-5   A Portable Microcomputer

in microcomputer-controlled gasoline pumps. The customer enters the dollar amount of the sale, the pump dispenses that amount of gas, and the sales amount is transferred from the customer's account to that of Atlantic Richfield.

TERMINAL CAPABILITIES

Rather than discussing the wide variety of terminal types, we focus on terminal capabilities and go on to present a list of attributes to be considered in selecting the proper terminal for a given application. Terminals can be classified as dumb, smart, or intelligent, although the lines separating these classes are indistinct. Thus some overlap exists between smart and intelligent terminals; one type of terminal might be considered smart by one individual yet intelligent by another.

Dumb Terminal Capabilities

A *dumb terminal* does not participate. It passively serves for input and/or output and does no additional processing. Since dumb terminals usually have no memory to store entered data, each entered character must immediately be transmitted to the host, unsolicited, and the host must be always ready to accept data from the terminal. Of course, data entry errors are sent to the host, as well, so an additional load is placed on the communications medium. Transmission a character at a time, termed *asynchronous transmission,* is discussed in detail in Chapter 6. Because the dumb terminal rather than the host determines when data is transmitted, there is usually only one dumb terminal per line. Later in this chapter and in Chapter 5, you will learn how several dumb terminals can share a line.

Dumb Terminal Applications: An Example

Many dumb terminals are in use today, and they serve especially well in applications that are *conversational.* In fact, they are limited to conversational-type data entry, which is described in Chapter 1. The host prompts the terminal operator to enter the first field, and the operator responds with the data for the first field. Then the host edits the received data to determine if it conforms to predefined standards, such as all numeric, all alphabetic, or a mix of the two. The host also determines whether enough characters have been supplied, such as at least five digits for a zip code. The host checks that all required fields are present and that only acceptable values have been entered—for example, does the sex field contain only an F or an M? If the first field fails the data editing, the operator is asked to reenter the entire field; if the edit test is passed, the operator is prompted for the second data field. When the operator recognizes a keystroke error, the cursor must be backspaced the proper number of characters and all subsequent characters—not just the one in error—must be resubmitted. Every backspace is sent to the host, which adjusts the position for storing the next character received. This process continues until all necessary data fields have been entered.

There is a high degree of interaction between the dumb terminal and the host. With low-speed lines, operator efficiency may be impaired because of delays before each subsequent prompt signals that data entry can begin again. Consequently, data entry is somewhat slower than with smart or intelligent terminals. Should the operator realize that an input error has not been detected by the editing function, the operator must be able to request that the field be reentered, and this must be accommodated by the application, a more complex task than that required by more intelligent terminals.

Smart Terminal Capabilities

Memory, Addressing, and Host Control.   Unlike dumb terminals, *smart terminals* have a certain amount of memory, meaning they can receive, store, and display data and entry formats or screen templates from the host. Data entered by the operator can be saved in the terminal's memory until the entire record or some number of screens of data has been entered. The terminal can then transmit the entire data record in one or more blocks. This type of block transmission, called *synchronous transmission*, is covered in more detail in Chapter 6. *Block* (page) *mode* functions include the following.

Page mode editing: The cursor can be moved to any position in the displayed text to make corrections or alterations. Words and blocks of text can be moved around, and blocks of information, rather than just individual characters, can be received or transmitted.

Data entry: An input form or template is displayed on the terminal screen and the entire screen of data is entered before being transmitted to the host. The operator can move the cursor to any input field on the screen. The data transmitted may consist of multiple screens of data.

Windowing: The screen can be divided into multiple "windows," with each window portion of the screen representing a different object set. One window could represent the text being written, one could contain notes about the text, another could contain a graphic image of an item being described in the text, and a fourth could contain a menu of tasks or commands that are valid in the current window. Figure 4-6 shows a screen with windows.

Conversational mode can be used with smart terminals; thus, a smart terminal can handle applications designed for a dumb terminal, whereas the opposite is not necessarily true. Most smart terminals also are *addressable*, which means they can be given a name that both they and the host recognize. Thus, the host can transmit data addressed to that terminal, and the terminal will recognize that the data is intended for it and store

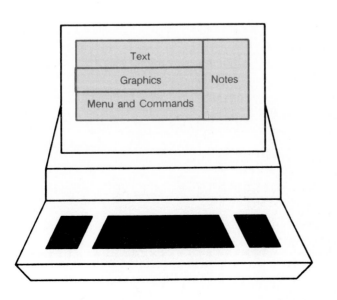

Figure 4-6 A
Terminal Screen
with Windows

the data in its memory. Smart terminals are subject to *host control*, meaning that the host can specify when the terminal is allowed to send or receive data; position the cursor on the display; designate that certain fields—such as an employee's salary—be protected from alteration; control the keyboard and disallow any data entry; specify the display attributes of fields such as blink and half intensity; and read from or write to selected portions of the display. Addressing, memory, and host control capabilities enable several terminals to share the same medium and thereby reduce transmission costs.

Auxiliary Data Entry Devices and Function Keys.   Some smart terminals support auxiliary data entry devices such as *light pens, mice,* and *touch-screens.* Many can have a printer attached, for printing a displayed page and for automatic logging of data received by the terminal. Many smart terminals have additional keys known as *function keys* or program attention keys, which transmit specific character sequences to the host. Function keys allow the operator to indicate to the application what function is to be performed on the data provided. Figures 4-7, 4-8, and 4-9 illustrate three data entry screen templates. The instructions at the bottom of the screen indicate actions that can be triggered by pressing the function keys F1, F2, and so on. The number of function keys per terminal varies from 4 to 32. Some special-purpose terminals have 50 keys or more.

Smart Terminal Applications: An Example

Since a smart terminal's memory can store multiple pages, the screen formats could be transferred into the terminal from the host. If the environment is host control, the host transmits an initial menu screen, as depicted

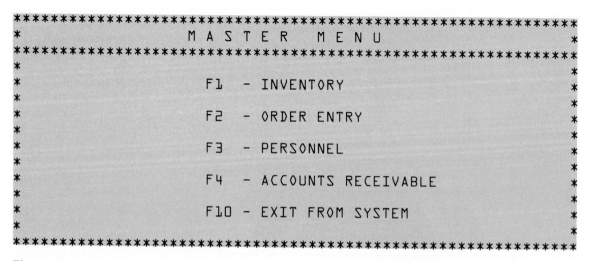

Figure 4-7   Master Menu Screen

```
************************************************************
*                C U S T O M E R   D A T A   S C R E E N            *
************************************************************
*                                                          *
*  DATE [            ]     PURCHASE ORDER NUMBER [          ]  *
*                                                          *
*  CUSTOMER NAME [                                      ]  *
*                                                          *
*  CUSTOMER NUMBER [                ]                      *
*                                                          *
*  ORDER PLACED BY [                                    ]  *
*                                                          *
*  CONTACT TELEPHONE [                    ]               *
*                                                          *
*  SHIP TO ADDRESS   [                                  ]  *
*                    [                                  ]  *
*                    [                                  ]  *
*                    [                                  ]  *
*  SHIP TO CONTACT NAME [                               ]  *
*                                                          *
*  SHIP TO TELEPHONE    [                               ]  *
*                                                          *
*  INVOICE ADDRESS   [                                  ]  *
*                    [                                  ]  *
*                    [                                  ]  *
*                    [                                  ]  *
*  INVOICE CONTACT NAME [                               ]  *
*                                                          *
*  INVOICE TELEPHONE    [                               ]  *
*                                                          *
*  SPECIAL SHIPPING INSTRUCTIONS                           *
*  [                                                    ]  *
*  [                                                    ]  *
*  [                                                    ]  *
*  [                                                    ]  *
*  [                                                    ]  *
*  [                                                    ]  *
*                                                          *
************************************************************
*  F1 - ENTER INFORMATION          F2 - GET CUSTOMER RECORD  *
*  F3 - CREATE NEW CUSTOMER RECORD F4 - DELETE CUSTOMER    *
*  F9 - DISPLAY HELP SCREEN        F10- EXIT TO MAIN MENU   *
************************************************************
```

Figure 4-8 Customer Data Entry Screen

```
************************************************************************
*          O R D E R    E N T R Y    L I N E    I T E M S           *
************************************************************************
*                                                                      *
*   DATE [            ]            CUSTOMER NUMBER [              ]     *
*                                                                      *
*                                                                      *
*     PART          QUANTITY        UNIT         DISCOUNT       TOTAL   *
*     NUMBER        ORDERED         PRICE        PERCENT        PRICE   *
*     ------        --------        -----        --------       -----   *
*   [         ]   [         ]   [          ]   [         ]   [         ] *
*   [         ]   [         ]   [          ]   [         ]   [         ] *
*   [         ]   [         ]   [          ]   [         ]   [         ] *
*   [         ]   [         ]   [          ]   [         ]   [         ] *
*   [         ]   [         ]   [          ]   [         ]   [         ] *
*   [         ]   [         ]   [          ]   [         ]   [         ] *
*   [         ]   [         ]   [          ]   [         ]   [         ] *
*   [         ]   [         ]   [          ]   [         ]   [         ] *
*   [         ]   [         ]   [          ]   [         ]   [         ] *
*   [         ]   [         ]   [          ]   [         ]   [         ] *
*   [         ]   [         ]   [          ]   [         ]   [         ] *
*   [         ]   [         ]   [          ]   [         ]   [         ] *
*   [         ]   [         ]   [          ]   [         ]   [         ] *
*   [         ]   [         ]   [          ]   [         ]   [         ] *
*   [         ]   [         ]   [          ]   [         ]   [         ] *
*   [         ]   [         ]   [          ]   [         ]   [         ] *
*   [         ]   [         ]   [          ]   [         ]   [         ] *
*   [         ]   [         ]   [          ]   [         ]   [         ] *
*                                                                      *
*   PAGE TOTAL   [             ]                [             ]         *
*                                                                      *
*   ORDER TOTAL  [             ]                [             ]         *
*                                                                      *
************************************************************************
*   F1 - ENTER INFORMATION          F2  - CLEAR SCREEN                 *
*                                                                      *
*   F9 - DISPLAY HELP SCREEN         F10 - RETURN TO FIRST PAGE        *
************************************************************************
```

Figure 4-9   Order Entry Line Items Screen

in Figure 4-7. The operator selects the order entry application by pressing the F2 function key. The host then transmits the first of the order entry screens, the customer data screen shown in Figure 4-8. The date is transmitted with the screen format by the host system. The operator enters customer number or customer name and presses the F2 function key, which instructs the host to read the data in the terminal's buffer. The host searches the database for particulars on that customer and displays the information. The operator then alters the information displayed if necessary and enters the information with the F1 key. The host reads and edits the data from the terminal. If edit errors are encountered, the host transmits an error message and identifies the erroneous field by changing the display attributes of that field, such as causing the field to blink or reversing the video ("highlighting" the field). The operator corrects the flagged data and retransmits either the entire screen or just the field that had to be changed. (The latter option is not supported by all smart terminals.) If the data is without detectable errors, the host transmits the next screen template, as shown in Figure 4-9.

On receiving the screen shown in Figure 4-9, the operator continues with data entry, entering the part number and the quantity ordered. On completion, the data is transmitted to the host for editing, for determining the unit prices and discount rate, and for calculating the line item, page, and order totals. The host sends the screen of calculations back to the operator so the operator can inform the customer of the total amount. If the terminal has an attached printer, the sales data can be printed for the office or the customer. The operator signals completion of the order by hitting the F10 key, which brings up the first data entry screen to start the cycle over.

Advantages of Smart Versus Dumb Terminals

The advantage of smart terminals over dumb terminals is a certain amount of independence between operator and host. Once a template is displayed, the operator is free to enter data at his or her own pace, unrestricted by the transmission speed of the line. Any errors made by the operator can be corrected without the host's involvement. The operator can move the cursor to any field in the record and can correct any data before transmission to the host. The host then controls the terminal and solicits inputs and outputs according to its priorities rather than being periodically interrupted by unsolicited inputs, as is the case with dumb terminals. The operator can use function keys to indicate which actions should be performed on the data entered, thus increasing operator efficiency.

Intelligent Terminals

An *intelligent terminal,* such as a microcomputer, has all or most of the capabilities of a smart terminal, but in addition it can participate in the data-processing requirements of the system. In some situations the intelligent terminal is completely independent of the host; however, to satisfy the definition of *terminal* given earlier, at some point the intelligent terminal must be connected to a host processor for processing or data access. It is also possible for an intelligent terminal to act as host for another terminal. An intelligent terminal is programmable.

Intelligent terminals generally have more memory than smart terminals, part of which is devoted to program code and program data storage. Some may also have secondary storage in the form of disk or tape. An attached printer is a common option. If there is no auxiliary storage, programs can be downloaded to the terminal from the host computer. *Downloading* is the act of transferring programs or data from a host to a terminal. *Uploading* happens when the terminal transfers files or programs to the host. Like smart terminals, intelligent terminals can be controlled from the host and can operate in both conversational and block modes. Processing functions available on intelligent terminals include storage and display of screen formats, data editing, data formatting, compression/decompression, and possibly some local database access and validation. In addition, intelligent terminals can allow local data entry if the communications link is disrupted.

Intelligent Terminal Applications: An Example

One example of an intelligent terminal is a microcomputer with disk drives and a printer. The disk contains the data entry screen templates, together with the data entry program for sequencing logic for the screens and data editing. The two major components of the order entry form are the customer portion and the product or order portion. Two or more screens of information are required to complete the order entry, as represented in Figures 4-8 and 4-9.

The data entry function of intelligent terminals is simplified. The same menu and entry screens as those for smart terminals can be used, although with an intelligent terminal the screen templates can be stored and displayed locally, thus reducing the amount of data transmitted over the communications link. The date of the order is supplied by the terminal from its date register. On entering either the customer name or customer number, the default customer information can be accessed and entered from a file on the local disk drive. The person taking the order can, of course, alter any default entries or bypass local access altogether. Hitting the F2 function key is a prompt to obtain local customer information. Other terminals might make the selection via transaction codes embedded in the data or by mouse, light pen, touchscreen, or similar data entry device.

On completing data entry for the first screen, the operator hits function key F1, causing the second screen of data to appear. The entered data is edited for consistency, and then the edited data is stored in a buffer in the terminal's memory. The operator enters the part numbers and quantities only. The unit price, customer discount, and total price are supplied from a local database; page and order totals are computed by the terminal. After editing the data and making the necessary calculations, the terminal performs *compression* on the data to be transmitted to the host. For example, repeating groups of characters such as blanks at the end of a name field are compressed into a repeat count and one-character sequence. This makes more effective use of the line. If the host uses a code different from that of the terminal—for example, an EBCDIC host and an ASCII terminal—the terminal also performs the code conversion.

The final step is to transmit the data to the host and await the reply. The data in this example will be transmitted in one or more blocks, depending on the length of the order. Any required blocking or deblocking of data is performed by the terminal. This example of the use of an intelligent terminal is referred to as *terminal emulation,* which means that the microcomputer appears to be a smart terminal. This application was chosen to compare and contrast the use of dumb, smart, and intelligent terminals. Of course, this is not the only way to use intelligent terminals.

Advantages of Intelligent Versus Smart Terminals

The advantages of the intelligent terminal over the smart terminal stem from the fact that control and processing are local. Customer information is maintained locally, where it is frequently used, and line time is not required for obtaining customer information, transmitting screen templates, or correcting edit errors.

TERMINAL ATTRIBUTES

Several terminal attributes are listed in Figure 4-10. These attributes are among the things to consider in selecting a terminal for a given application.

Output

The two different types of terminal output are hard copy and soft copy. *Hard-copy output* leaves a permanent record of the data sent to the terminals, whereas *soft copy display units* leave no record of the inputs or outputs. Hard copy uses some type of printed output, and soft copy format uses a display monitor such as a VDU or plasma display.

Cost	Synchronous	Auxiliary storage	EBCDIC
Conversational	Batch	Protected fields	Protocol support
Block mode	Point-to-point	Graphics	Attached devices
TTY-compatible	Multi-point	Formatting	Duplex
Dumb	Function keys	Character sets	Screen size
Smart	Editing	Keyboard	Character size
Intelligent	Cursor control	Blink	Modified data tags
Printer	Host control	Half intensity	CPU
Speed	Color	Reverse video	Interface
Asynchronous	Programmable	ASCII	Portability

Figure 4-10 Some Terminal Attributes

Hard Copy.   Being mechanical, hard-copy devices generally have a much slower output rate than CRT devices. In addition to the interactive class of terminals, hard-copy devices include output-only equipment such as printers and plotters. Having a hard copy of the dialogue between host and terminal is extremely important in certain situations and requires either a hard-copy terminal or a VDU with attached printer. Hard copy may be especially desirable for computer consoles where error and operator messages are displayed and for funds transfer applications where auditors require an audit trail of all transactions.

Soft Copy Display.   Soft copy display devices come in several variations, including VDU, plasma display units, and *light-emitting diode* (*LED*) display units. VDU technology is similar to television. A phosphor-coated screen is bombarded with directed electron beams that cause the phosphor to glow and thereby produce an image. Because the screen image fades without the electron beams, it is constantly refreshed by repeated electron beams. The rate varies with the phosphor coating, but 60 repeats per second is common. Slow refresh rates can result in flickering screens and washed-out images.

VDU technology is by far the most common in business data-processing systems. *Plasma terminals,* which are capable of higher resolution, are found primarily in graphics applications. The images in plasma terminals are created by arrays of neon lights that can be individually illuminated. The bulbs themselves are not separate lights but are integrated into a panel composed of several layers of glass, which provides a continuous image on the terminal screen. In LED display units, light-emitting diodes are used to form figure or character images much like a dot matrix printer forms images. In a variation of this technique, neon tubes or wires are used to form the character images. *Liquid crystal display* (*LCD*) panels similar to those found in digital watches and pocket video games are also used for terminals. LCD display units are found primarily in portable terminals.

Input

The most common input mechanism is the keyboard, in a variety of types. Other input devices include various types of readers—badge readers and OCR readers—and light pens, mice, trackballs, joysticks, touchscreens, sensors, voice recognition and generation equipment, and image processing devices such as digitizers that scan graphic images and create digital images of them.

Keyboards.   The standard keyboard has keys arranged like those of a typewriter. The keyboard can be augmented with additional keys such as function keys, numeric keypads, and control keys. Function keys indicate the functions to be performed on entered data or act as interrupt keys. When used to interrupt, striking a function key interrupts the process being run from the terminal and allows the operator to perform other functions such as stopping the process, starting a new process, or debugging the program. When a function key is struck, a character sequence associated with that key is transmitted to the host. Numeric keypads are convenient when much of the data to be entered is numeric. Control keys are used to transmit bit sequences that can be acted on by the program directly controlling the terminal, operating system, or application. Terminal control programs are discussed in Chapter 12.

Specialized keyboards also exist. In countries where the Kanji or Chinese character sets are used, the number of character symbols exceeds 30,000, though a 10,000-character subset is sufficient. Special expanded keyboards with multiple characters per key are used in these situations. Some keyboards are specially designed for certain applications, for example, specific medical laboratory applications, such as serology and urology, with the number of keys and the keyboard layout designed to enable the lab technician to characterize specimens with a minimum number of keystrokes. The urology keyboard might have several keys for describing specimen color, another group to describe clarity, and so on, with only one keystroke per attribute required.

Light Pens. *Light pens* are used to select from several options displayed on a VDU. The pen is essentially like a small, high-intensity flashlight. When the pen is aimed at a place on the VDU screen, the light image can be read and the coordinates of the point are determined. The data is translated into a selection displayed on the VDU screen. The process is similar to pointing to the object being selected.

Readers. *Reader devices* read images that have been encoded in various ways. One familiar reader device is the automatic teller machine (ATM), which reads a magnetic tape strip or holographic image to determine the identity of the user.

Touchscreens. *Touchscreens* vary in how they discern input. Some use a matrix of infrared light beams emanating from two sides, such as the top and the left side, with photosensors on the opposite sides of the screen. Touching the screen interrupts these beams, and the coordinates of the area touched are read. Another method uses a resistance technique wherein two conductive layers are separated by a small distance; the touching causes a connection between the two at the point of the touch. A third technique uses a conductive surface on the screen: When the screen's surface is touched, the electrical characteristics of the screen are disrupted, allowing the position of the touch to be discerned. Advantages of touchscreens include their ease of use, which makes them especially effective in applications for people unfamiliar with data processing. Many hotels have touchscreen information boards that allow patrons to inquire about news, events, and services.

Mice, Joysticks, and Trackballs.   The mouse, joystick, and trackball input devices have found application in both computerized games and business. They are used for cursor control and option selection. A user moves the cursor position on the screen by moving a *mouse*: Moving the mouse to the right causes the cursor to move to the right. A *trackball* is similar to a mouse except that the user rotates a ball mounted in a fixed holder: The cursor moves in the direction that the ball is rotated. A *joystick* also moves the cursor when the stick is moved in the desired direction. Most of these devices also contain additional input capabilities such as a button for selecting options. A mouse attached to a microcomputer is pictured in Figure 4-11.

Figure 4-11   A Mouse Attached to a Microcomputer

Courtesy of Logitech, Inc.

Graphics Imagers. *Graphics imaging equipment* scans images and translates those images into digital formats that can be stored and later modified or reproduced by a computer system. This technique, called *digitizing* or *image scanning,* can produce picture images as well as text images. One computerized business application of image scanning is facsimile acquisition, storage, transmission, and reproduction. This technique allows contracts bearing signatures and documents containing graphics images to be electronically acquired, stored, reproduced, and distributed to remote locations. This application of data communications and database technology is certain to expand.

Voice Synthesis and Recognition. *Voice synthesis* is an output technology, and *voice recognition,* an input technology. While more research is needed in this area its future looks promising; many applications are making use of what has already been developed. In one such application, telephone companies have implemented directory assistance in some areas with voice generation hardware and software. In shop floor applications, workers can enter voice commands, leaving their hands free to operate equipment. Voice store and forward systems allow users to enter data via a telephone, store a digitized image of the message, and later forward the message to a recipient. Currently, however, the technology and the costs prohibit voice as a cost effective input or output device for most business applications.

Cost

There is a dramatic range in the cost of terminals, from several hundred dollars for a dumb terminal to tens of thousands of dollars for special terminals such as RJE or very high resolution graphics terminals with imaging devices. Cost analysis is difficult, since cost factors like line utilization, operator acceptance, efficiency, and local processing ability are not always easy to quantify. In selecting a terminal for a given application, each of these factors must be considered in addition to the purchase and maintenance prices. Figure 4-12 represents a cross-section of terminal prices.

Speed

The speed at which a terminal accepts and transmits data is dependent on the terminal hardware, the type of line to which it is attached, and the

Terminal Type	Compatibility	Price Low	High	Typical
Dumb	TTY	$ 250	$ 1,500	$ 400–800
Smart	IBM 3270	1,500	8,000	1,500–4,000
Smart	TTY	250	5,000	500–1,500
Intelligent	IBM 3270	2,000	15,000	2,500–5,000
Intelligent	TTY	1,000	10,000	1,500–4,500

Figure 4-12 Representative Terminal Prices

types of modems used (if any). Any given terminal can receive and transmit information at a discrete set of rates. An unbuffered hard-copy terminal may have a maximum receive speed of 1200 bps because its print capacity is 120 characters per second. A CRT device, on the other hand, may be capable of receiving data at 19.2 Kbps or more. In addition to the maximum available speed, the intermediate speeds available should be considered. Some terminals have one or two speed settings, whereas others support several common speeds, such as 75, 300, 600, 1200, 2400, 4800, 9600, and 19,200 bps.

Maintenance and Support

Some computer manufacturers sell with their systems terminals that are manufactured by other companies. They usually also provide support for the terminals they sell. Many manufacturers also build terminals designed to complement their own computer systems. These terminals usually receive support consistent with the support for the rest of the system. An advantage of such vendor support is having only one organization to contact regardless of the problem. For instance, what appears to be a terminal problem actually may be an error in the software or hardware communicating with that terminal. Single-vendor support tends to eliminate the question of who is responsible for errors. In multiple-vendor installations, determining which vendor is responsible for a problem can become a difficult issue.

But single-vendor support has a disadvantage, for both terminals and computer equipment: Computer manufacturers sometimes charge more for their terminals than manufacturers who specialize in terminal equipment. For these specialty companies to survive they must offer better prices, equipment, or support than the computer supplier. Thus, you can frequently save considerably by getting terminals from an outside source, especially when many terminals are needed. However, when acquiring terminals from other than the computer vendor, be sure to have the terminal demonstrated *on your system*. Some terminals may not be supported by the vendor's software and hardware, and what appears to be an excellent purchase may turn into a colossal blunder. Furthermore, terminals advertised as being compatible with the computer vendor's terminals may have small areas of incompatibility that can adversely impact the application.

Memory

Not all terminals have memory available. Those that do may allow for different sizes of memory, some of which may not be available to a particular application. For instance, for intelligent terminals, a portion of the memory is needed to store programs run at the terminal. Therefore, a microcomputer with 640K bytes of memory may not have the entire memory space available for data. Typically, part of the space is for the operating system, the input/output routines that interface with the communications links and peripherals, and the application. If the application involves a spreadsheet, the program code would restrict the amount of data that can be stored in the terminal's memory.

Some smart terminals reserve a portion of available memory for the terminal's use. For example, suppose a terminal has enough memory to store the data for six screens of information and it also supports field attributes such as color, protection, and modified data tags. This terminal will allow only three pages of data to be stored, because the other three pages are used to store the field attributes. The terminal uses *modified data tags* to detect which fields on the screen have changed, which allows the terminal to transmit only those fields altered since the previous time the data was sent. To support these capabilities, a portion of memory is reserved to record the attributes of each character or field to be displayed.

Display Attributes

Hard-copy devices have very few display attributes to select, with the possible exception of colored pens for plotters, graphics, italics, underline, type fonts, or overprint. However, with video display units, many possibilities exist, including multiple colors, shading, and highlighting such as blinking fields. Also to be considered are screen size and character size, since the number of characters per line and the number of lines per screen can vary significantly.

Color Display. Color display units vary from two colors to 4096 colors or more. Common options are 4, 8, 16, 32, 64, or 256 different colors. Some also allow shading of colors or black-and-white. For example, if a display unit has 16 colors, the number of combinations of foreground or symbol colors and background colors is 16×15, or 240 different display capabilities. If each color has two intensities the number of combinations increases to 960, although some of these combinations may be rather difficult to read due to lack of contrast, such as white letters on a yellow background.

Monochrome Display. The users of monochrome displays—those that have only one foreground and one background color—also may have several options. *Half intensity* displays characters with half the intensity of full-intensity characters; the contrast between half intensity and the background is less than that of full intensity. In the screens shown in Figures 4-8 and 4-9 the prompts would probably be at half intensity and the data at full intensity so the operator's attention is drawn to the data entered, not to the prompts. *Reverse video* exchanges foreground and background colors: Instead of white characters on a black background, there are black characters on a white background. Half intensity can also be used in combination with reverse video to provide four different display modes. Reverse video is very effective in highlighting fields that are in error, error messages, and format headings. Another method for drawing attention to fields is to cause the field or a portion thereof to blink.

Ergonomics

Ergonomics is the study of how people physically adjust to their work environment. Currently, a very important consideration in terminal and microcomputer design and selection is the unit's human engineering. Several physical problems have been attributed to poor terminal design, including radiation side effects, headaches, eye strain, muscle and tendon problems, and arthritic conditions. Perhaps the major side effect of VDU terminals is their emission of radiation. In the 1960s parents were warned to keep children from sitting too close to color televisions due to low-level radiation emissions. Terminal and microcomputer monitors may also emit low-level radiation, but users cannot always distance themselves from the monitor. Some companies have noted a higher incidence of birth defects among women working at VDUs, and several lawsuits have been filed in this regard. According to U.S. law, radiation emitted from a terminal must be less than 0.0005 rems per hour at a distance of 2 inches from the screen. Reduction of radiation is usually achieved by filtering the radiation with a glass screen. In selecting monitors, one factor to consider is radiation emission.

Although there are a variety of ergonomic considerations for terminals and microcomputers besides radiation emissions, three other factors—monitor position, monitor display, and keyboard position—have significant impact on ease of use. The most common user complaints are head, neck, and eye strain. Head and neck strain can be caused because the user must adjust to the (relatively) fixed position of a monitor. An ergonomically designed monitor can be tilted and swiveled to a position that is comfortable for the user. Finger, hand, and wrist strains result from improper positioning of the keyboard. The keyboard should be detached from the monitor so the keyboard can be moved to a position comfortable for the user. Associated with positioning of monitors and keyboards is the furniture itself. Having a chair that can be raised and lowered and a keyboard platform that is movable helps the system be adjusted to the user. Again, the key is to have a unit capable of adjusting to a user rather than requiring a user to adjust to the equipment.

Eye strain can be caused by poorly formed characters, flickering screens, and poor foreground/background colors. A good monitor has crisp, well-formed characters and images. The contrast between foreground and background colors should be visually pleasing. Ergonomic studies have shown that green or amber foreground characters on a black background is easier on the eyes than other combinations, such as white letters on a black background. If you have a color microcomputer, you may wish to try different foreground and background color combinations to see this effect. Another factor affecting eye strain is screen flickering. CRT screen images are constantly refreshed by "repainting" the screen image. Low refresh rates cause screen images to fade before being refreshed, creating a flickering effect. Looking at flickering screens can cause headaches and eye strain.

Ideal Terminal Characteristics. The ideal display should be easy on the eyes, with a nonglare surface. Green phosphor or amber characters on a black background are preferred to white characters on a black background. The display should tilt and swivel for ease of reading. The keyboard should be detachable and should be at a convenient height. Keys should be sculpted and arranged for easy access. Display characters should be well formed and easy to read. The screen image should be refreshed at a sufficient rate to avoid flicker, and contrast should be adjustable to ease eye strain. The keyboard should emit a click to reinforce each keystroke, and the loudness of the click should be controllable, from inaudible to somewhat loud.

The ergonomics of terminals should not be taken lightly. Several lawsuits are currently in progress regarding excess emissions and debilitation of the fingers as a result of prolonged use of terminals. For international organizations, including ergonomic features is critical, since the laws in some countries require many of the features mentioned above. At least one corporation has found itself unable to use its terminals in some European countries because the terminals lack the required human engineering features.

Interface

How terminals interface with devices varies widely. In the United States, RS-232-C is currently the most common interface, with RS-449 gaining popularity. In many other countries, CCITT standards are used. Some terminals are attached to devices other than modems. For instance, most IBM 3270 terminals can be attached directly to a cluster controller rather than to a modem, in which case coaxial cable is used for the interface. Terminals on a local area network attach to the medium using a transceiver and controller. This interface is usually different from an RS-232-C or RS-449 connection. The type of interface depends on the terminal and the environment in which it is to be used. Terminals also have interfaces to other devices, such as light pens, printers, and other input or output systems. For printers, the two common interfaces are serial and parallel. These ports may also be used for attaching other types of equipment.

Protocol

Terminals communicate by a convention that transmits either a character at a time or a block at a time. These conventions, called *protocols,* are discussed in more detail in Chapter 6. Protocol support is a primary concern when purchasing a terminal. Many terminals communicate via only one of these conventions. Some terminals may have the option of being either asynchronous or synchronous. In addition to supporting a particular protocol, an asynchronous terminal usually is less expensive than a synchronous one.

Miscellaneous Attributes

There are many other terminal characteristics to be considered, including alternate character sets, addressability, codes, the central processing unit, and portability.

Alternate Character Sets.   Alternate character sets are available on some terminals. The alternate set may be a foreign language, a graphics character set, or both.

Addressability.   Some transmission techniques work on the principle that terminals have an address (see the section on polling later in this chapter). If this transmission technique is used, the terminal must be *addressable.* This characteristic is usually found in both smart and intelligent terminals.

Codes.   The code used by a terminal is important. Most terminals use either ASCII or EBCDIC data coding, but some 5-bit and 6-bit codes are still used. The terminal either must be compatible with the code used by the host or a code translation must be made. If implemented in host software, the translation can consume a significant portion of the processing power of the CPU.

Central Processing Unit (CPU).   Most smart terminals and all intelligent terminals have some type of microprocessor that controls the terminal functions. The type of CPU used can be important, particularly with intelligent devices. The terminal's processor is a significant factor in the speed with which instructions are executed and also with respect to expansion capabilities. Many of the newer intelligent terminals are based on a 16-bit or 32-bit CPU.

Portability.   At one time, terminal portability was confined mostly to dumb devices. Portable personal computers have made intelligent terminals portable as well. If the terminal operator may need to move from location to location, portability is beneficial. The traveling salesperson who enters orders on a portable computer during the day can quickly transmit those orders from a telephone to the data processing center at the end of each day.

TERMINAL CONFIGURATION

On any communications channel, there are two options for attaching terminals: point-to-point and multi-point.

Point-to-Point Connections

Point-to-point connections have one terminal at the end of a communications link from a host. There is little contention for the use of the channel in a point-to-point configuration, since only the host and the terminal are candidates for transmission. Point-to-point connections are very common in computer-to-computer communications, local connections, and remote connections with only one terminal. For communication among several terminals over a long distance, true point-to-point connections would be quite expensive, since each terminal would require a separate line with a pair of modems. Fortunately, there are hardware components (which we discuss later) that allow terminals to share a communications channel while logically operating in a point-to-point manner. The methodology for controlling which station is allowed to use the communications link is sometimes referred to as a *line discipline*. In a point-to-point configuration, data flow can be managed in several ways: contention, pure contention, and supervisor-secondary.

Contention.   One mechanism for managing data flow is known as *contention*. In the contention mode the host and the terminal contend for control of the medium. Each is considered to have an equal right to transmit to the other. To transmit, one station issues a bid for the channel, which means it asks the other party for control. If the other is ready to receive data, control is granted to the requestor. Upon completion of the transfer, control is relinquished and the link goes into an idle state, awaiting the next bid for control. A collision can occur when both stations simultaneously bid for the line. If this occurs, either one station is granted the request based on some predetermined priority scheme or each station waits awhile and then reattempts the bid. With the latter approach, the time-out intervals must not be the same, for having the same time-out intervals is likely to cause another collision.

Pure Contention.   A second method for point-to-point communication is also a contention method, but without line bids. This technique, known as *pure contention,* allows either of the two devices to transmit data whenever it is ready, the assumption being that the other station is ready to receive the data when it arrives. The sending station is made aware that the data was received correctly via a positive acknowledgment message from the recipient. Without a positive acknowledgment, and after a designated time-out interval, the sending station must assume the data was not received correctly and re-send it. Collisions can also occur with this technique. Pure contention is good in situations where modem turnaround times make line bids costly; dumb terminals often employ this method.

Supervisor-Secondary.   This form of control is more commonly used in the multi-point environment and is discussed in the following section.

Multi-Point Connections

In a *multi-point connection* multiple terminals share the same communications channel. The number of terminals allowed to share the medium is a function of channel capacity and the workload at the terminals themselves, and sometimes of other hardware employed. Chapter 2 discussed the calculations required to determine the optimum number of terminals on such a line: As the number of terminals on the line increases, the average time each terminal has access to the link decreases. A contention-type line discipline would work in a multi-point configuration. In fact, contention is a popular method in local area networks consisting of hundreds of stations. However, studies have shown that as the number of stations communicating in this manner increases, so does the number of collisions on the channel. When the number of collisions is high, the effective rate of data transfer declines because of the time required to resolve the collisions.

Polling.   The most common method of establishing line discipline in multipoint terminal networks is referred to as *poll/select,* or simply *polling.* In the polled configuration, one station is designated as the *supervisor* or *primary station.* This role is almost always assumed by the host computer, although other pieces of equipment such as controllers or concentrators may be used instead (see Chapter 5). There is only one primary station per multipoint link; all other stations are referred to as *secondary stations.* In the discussion that follows we assume that the host computer is the primary.

The primary station is in complete control of the link. Secondary stations may transmit data only when given permission by the primary station. This process of asking terminals whether they have data to transmit is referred to as polling. Each secondary station is given a unique address, and each terminal must be able to recognize its own address. Although there are several distinct methods of polling, essentially the process works as follows. The primary is provided a list of addresses for terminals on a particular link. Several multi-point lines may be controlled by one primary, although addresses on a given line are unique. The primary picks an address from the list and sends a poll message across the link using that address. The poll message is very short, consisting of the poll address and a string of characters that has been designated as a poll message. All secondary stations receive the poll message, but only the addressee responds. The poll message is an inquiry to the secondary station as to whether it has any data to transmit to the primary. If it has data to transmit, the secondary responds either with the data or with a positive acknowledgment and then the data. If the secondary station has no data to send, it responds with a negative acknowledgment. Upon receipt of either the data or the negative acknowledgment, the primary selects another station's polling address and repeats the process. For a terminal to operate in this manner it must have memory in which to buffer data until it is asked to transmit.

Selection.   When the primary has data to send to one or more secondary stations, it selects the station in much the same manner as that used for polling. Some terminals have two addresses, one for polling and one for selecting. In the *selection process*, the primary sends a selection message to the terminal. A selection message consists of the terminal's selection address and an inquiry to determine whether the terminal is ready to accept data. The terminal may respond positively or negatively. For instance, if the terminal's buffer is full, it cannot accept additional data and responds negatively. After a positive acknowledgment to the selection message, the primary transmits the data to the terminal. In some multi-point networks the primary can send a message to all stations simultaneously via a *broadcast address*, which is one address that all terminals recognize as theirs. Other addressing schemes allow terminals to be divided into broadcast groups by using a common prefix for their addresses.

A *fast select* is a variation of selection. With fast select, the data accompanies the select message. This is effective when the receiving stations are usually able to accept the data being transmitted. If a station is not ready to receive data, the message is lost and must be retransmitted. In this situation the primary could revert to the previously defined selection method for that terminal.

Types of Polling.   There are three basic types of polling: roll call, hub polling, and token passing. In *roll call polling* the primary obtains a list of addresses for terminals on the line and then proceeds sequentially down the list, polling each terminal in turn. If one or more stations on the link are of higher priority or are more likely to have data to send, their address could be included in the list multiple times so they can be polled more frequently. Roll call polling is illustrated in Figure 4-13.

Hub polling requires the terminals to become involved in the polling process. The primary sends a poll message to one station on the link. If that station has data to transmit, it does so. After transmitting its data or if it has no data to transmit, the secondary terminal passes the poll to an adjacent terminal. This process is repeated until all terminals have had the opportunity to transmit. The primary then starts the process again. Hub polling is more efficient than roll call polling because less of the line capacity is devoted to polling and acknowledgment messages. It also requires more intelligence at the terminal end, since the terminal must recognize the address of its neighbor and pass along the poll. Hub polling is illustrated in Figure 4-14. In the diagram, if T2 were not operational, T3 would pass the poll to T1.

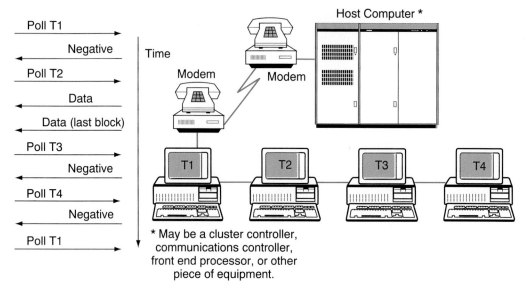

Poll T1

Negative   Time

Poll T2

Data

Data (last block)

Poll T3

Negative

Poll T4

Negative

Poll T1

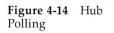

* May be a cluster controller,
communications controller,
front end processor, or other
piece of equipment.

Figure 4-13   Roll Call Polling

Figure 4-14   Hub
Polling

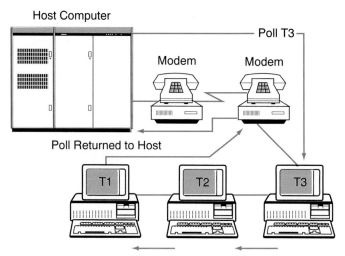

Device polling can be implemented in hardware or software. Software polling can have extensive overhead because it uses a significant number of CPU cycles and reduces the number of CPU cycles available for application processing. When software solutions are employed, the function is usually placed in a front end processor or communications controller to keep the main CPU from becoming bogged down with controlling lines. An additional overhead of polling is that a portion of the available line capacity is needed to exchange poll messages, which reduces the data-carrying capacity of the medium.

Token passing is more common in local area networks and multi-point configurations of intelligent terminals. This technique could be considered separate from polling, since there is no primary station and all stations have equal status. Token passing is similar in some respects to hub polling. A particular bit sequence is designated as the token. Whichever station has the token is the station allowed to transmit. The token is passed from station to station, together with the privilege of transmitting information. Since the token eventually arrives at each station, each receives the opportunity to send. Token passing is depicted in Figure 4-15.

Advantage of Multi-Point Connections.   The advantage of multi-point lines is economic. First, only one communications link is required for a host to communicate with several terminals; second, if modems are required on the link, fewer modems are necessary. In a true point-to-point link a pair of modems is often required for each terminal, one at the host end and one at the terminal end. For multi-point links, at most one modem per terminal and one at the host are required. In some instances a terminal cluster controller, discussed in Chapter 5, may be used at the terminal end, and if the terminals are sufficiently close to the controller, individual terminal modems are not necessary: Only a host and cluster controller modem are required. For example, if ten terminals are to be located remotely, ten point-to-point lines would require 20 modems. For a multi-point line, at most 11 modems would be required, and possibly two would be sufficient. Figure 4-16 presents several multi-point configurations, together with their required modems.

Disadvantages of Multi-Point Connections.   There are also disadvantages to the multi-point configuration. First, terminals used in this environment

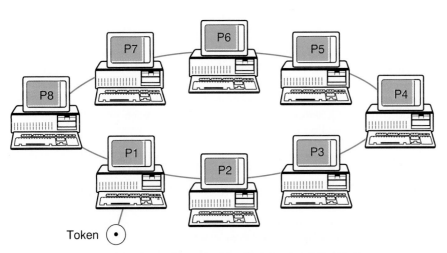

Token (•)

P1 has the token. P1 may transmit data to another station.
If P1 has no data to transmit, P1 passes the token to P2.

Figure 4-15   Token Passing

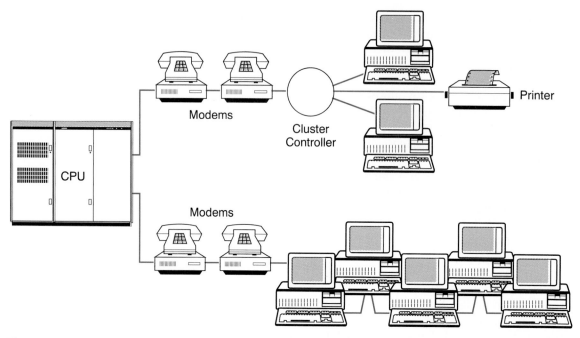

Figure 4-16   Multi-Point Configurations

must have some intelligence, making them more expensive than terminals in the point-to-point connection. This higher cost is usually negligible, however, when compared with the savings in medium and modems. Because the medium is shared among several terminals, a terminal may have to wait to transmit its information. If messages are short, the wait time should not be long; however, if messages are lengthy, such as when a microcomputer transfers a file, the other terminals may be required to wait an inordinate amount of time. Delays also have an impact on response times, and this delay should be factored into the response time calculations for a multi-point line. If half duplex lines with noncontinuous carrier are used for communication, the modem turnaround time can become significant. For roll call polling, two modem turnarounds are required for each poll message. As in the example in Chapter 3, where modem turnaround time was greater than the message time, such potential also exists in a half duplex polled environment.

Asynchronous Versus Synchronous Transmission

Polled terminals usually transmit information a block at a time rather than a character at a time; this is referred to as *synchronous transmission*. Although polled environments exist for transmission of one character at a time (referred to as *asynchronous* or *start-stop transmission*), the synchronous environment is more suitable because of its ability to transmit blocks of data. Terminals used in a multi-point configuration can also be used in a point-to-point configuration, providing configuraton flexibility while simplifying the portion of application design that deals with the terminal interface.

Microcomputers

Microcomputers are becoming an important force in data communications networks. Because of their intelligence they can be made to imitate any type of terminal, an important feature for protecting any investment in terminal equipment. With a microcomputer as a terminal, computer systems can be replaced by different models and the terminals will still be able to communicate with the new system. This compatibility is possible either because the new computer system supports the terminals or because the microcomputer has been reprogrammed to imitate a new type of terminal. Furthermore, the microcomputer is capable of performing several functions previously required of a host system or other piece of equipment, such as a front end processor (see Chapter 5). These functions include editing data, code translation, compression/decompression, and local processing such as totaling invoices and computing extended prices and discounts. For a microcomputer to be used as a terminal, it must be augmented by two items: a communications interface and software.

Communications Interfaces.   A *communications interface* is standard equipment in several systems; in other systems it must be added, usually as a printed circuit board occupying one of the microcomputer's expansion slots. Sometimes communications interfaces are added to printed circuit boards that provide other functions, such as additional memory. The communications interface enables the microcomputer to be attached to a communications line or modem and to physically receive and transmit data.

Software.   *Software* must provide the interface between the communications line and such microcomputer components as disk and memory. There are many pieces of software available for a variety of microcomputers, and they allow microcomputers to imitate a TTY device, an RJE device, or an IBM 3270-type terminal, as well as several terminals compatible with other computer models.

Other Selection Criteria.   Other factors that should be considered when selecting an intelligent terminal include the CPU, available software, auxiliary storage, and peripherals. Most early microcomputers used an 8-bit CPU; current systems use either a 16-bit or 32-bit CPU. The type of CPU influences the speed and capacity of the microcomputer. A 32-bit CPU typically allows the system to address more memory, provides faster access to memory, and executes instructions faster than an 8-bit CPU.

An extensive array of software is available for intelligent terminals, including database management, data communications, graphics, programming languages, spreadsheets, word processing, and a multitude of other applications. Use of these programs can increase the amount of processing done at the terminal and eliminate some of the need for accessing a host system. In selecting software, the interaction between the software and the host system should be considered. The amount of auxiliary storage—primarily disk and tape—the speed of these storage devices, and the peripherals available are important considerations, because these also affect the amount and type of work that can be accomplished at the terminal. For example, a disk's capacity partially determines the size and number of documents that can be stored at a word processing terminal: If the capacity is large, the terminal will have less need for the (usually) larger storage facilities of the host.

CASE STUDY

The Syncrasy Corporation is considering expanding operations into several major marketing areas. A preliminary analysis has been initiated to determine the costs of expansion; a portion of the analysis has already been completed. System design objectives and system goals have been formulated. A feasibility study is underway to determine if the design objectives can be met within the expense restrictions. One part of this study is to determine the number of terminals required in each location, which necessitates first estimating transaction time.

Transaction Time

The preliminary analysis has indicated that expansion needs will be met by a single host processor with multiple terminals at remote locations. For one location it has been determined that five types of transactions constitute the major transaction load. These transaction types are described in Figure 4-17.

Figure 4-17 Projected Transactions for Syncrasy Corporation

	Transaction Type				
	Order Entry	Credit Check	Customer Maintenance	Send Mail	Receive Mail
Think/wait time (secs)	10	5	120	60	180
No. of input characters	600	50	150	2000	50
No. of output characters	20	500	500	50	2000
Disk/CPU/ queuing time (secs)	1	0.5	0.5	1.5	1.5
Hourly peak	40	10	4	5	5

Think/Wait Time. *Think/wait time* for each transaction represents the amount of time the operator will wait or think before or during the entering of the transaction. The long think time for a customer maintenance transaction (120 seconds) reflects the time the operator is obtaining the information from the telephone. Other possible sources of think/wait time are drinking coffee or tea, reading documents, rearranging papers, and so on.

Data Entry (Input/Output) Time. The number of input characters represents the number of keystrokes the operator enters to complete a transaction. Depending on the type of data being entered, operators are capable of entering 5 characters per second or more. In the following analysis, a more conservative keystroke rate of 1.5 characters per second is assumed. Number of output characters is the number of characters received in response to the transaction. Both input and output create transaction time delay that is a function of transmission speed. Here, it is assumed that each character transmitted requires 10 bits.

Disk/CPU/Queuing Time. Disk/CPU/queuing time is the amount of time the transaction is held by the processor and the time spent waiting in queues at different places in the system. For this analysis the cumulative times for these activities have been given. In reality, some of these times are difficult to determine. *Disk access time* is important because each transaction type requires records to be read from or written into the database. For order entry transactions, the inventory levels of each ordered item are adjusted by reading and writing the inventory record for each item, which might require that one or more index tables be accessed and searched. Database access times depend on the type of disk drive used and the organization of the database. Usually, there are three major components of disk access time: *seek time, rotational delay* (latency), and *transfer time.* Some disks eliminate seek time by providing a read/write head for each track.

CPU time is the amount of time required for the CPU to execute the processing instructions, including those executed by the database management system, the operating system, the data communications software, and the application programs. It is a function of the speed of the processor and memory, as well as of the number and type of instructions to be executed, and it is small relative to disk access time and data transmission time. CPU time is difficult to estimate for a system that is being designed, and initial estimates could be off significantly. However, since most business transactions tend to be input/output (I/O) intensive, and since I/O time is usually much greater than CPU time, such deviations have little impact on the final calculations.

Queuing time is the amount of time the transaction must wait in queues for service. Like CPU time, this component is difficult to determine accurately; unlike CPU time, however, it can represent a significant portion of overall transaction time. A transaction can wait in queues in various places within a system—at the terminal waiting to be polled, at an application or data communications activity waiting to be processed, and at the disk drive awaiting the completion of other disk requests. Transaction queues can be compared to lines at a grocery store, where a customer might wait in one line for a parking space, another line for check approval, and a third line for checkout. In the store situation, wait time is a function of line length or customer arrival rate, mean service time for customers in line, number of servers available, and the service convention, such as first-in-first-out (FIFO) or last-in-first-out (LIFO). The same is true of computer systems. The specifics of how to calculate the disk, CPU, and queuing times are quite complex; a more detailed analysis can be found in Pritchard, 1976. These times have been provided without derivation for this exercise.

Number of Terminals

The amount of time required to completely process a single transaction is the total of operator think/wait time, data entry time, transmission time, and disk/CPU/queuing time. The minimum number of terminals required can be found by determining the total time required to process all transactions in a given period, such as 1 hour. Thus, if 1200 transactions per hour were to be processed, each requiring 30 seconds (0.5 minutes) to complete, the number of terminals required would be

$$\frac{1200 \text{ transactions}}{\text{hour}} \times \frac{0.5 \text{ terminal minutes}}{\text{transaction}} \times \frac{1 \text{ hour}}{60 \text{ minutes}} = \frac{600}{60}$$

$$= 10 \text{ terminals}$$

This is the minimum number of terminals required based on utilization.

For several reasons, a user might decide to install additional terminals. There may be more potential operators than there are required terminals, such as in an office in which every employee is given a terminal even though each employee uses it only part of the day. Or, to place ATMs more conveniently for customers, a bank might install more ATMs than actually required to meet transaction demand. Additional terminals might also be installed to accommodate expansion, to provide spares, and to provide a margin for calculation error.

It is assumed that all wait time components are included in the transaction times. If this were not the case, the calculated number of terminals would be less than the minimum number required. For instance, if only the transmission time on a line using polling were considered and not the average wait time for polling, the results would not reflect the total time of a given transaction because the calculation ignored wait time for access to the transmission medium. To determine the number of terminals required for Syncrasy Corporation, we calculate the transaction time for each type of transaction, multiply each transaction time by the number of transactions of that type per hour, and then total the results for each type of transaction. Shorter approaches could be taken, but they would be less instructive. Only the order entry transaction is computed in detail; the calculations for the remainder are left as an exercise.

Transaction time for the order entry transaction is given by

transaction time = think/wait time + data entry time

+ transmission time + disk/CPU/queuing time

To determine transmission time, a transmission speed must be selected; for this exercise a speed of 4800 bps is assumed. Order entry transaction time is

$$10 + \frac{600}{1.5} + \frac{(620)\,(10)}{4800} + 1 = 10 + 400 + 1.3 + 1 = 412.3 \text{ seconds}$$

The transaction times required for credit check, customer maintenance, sending electronic mail, and receiving electronic mail are, respectively, 39.9, 221.9, 1399.1, and 219.1 seconds. (Perform the necessary calculations yourself to test your understanding.) The total amount of time for all transactions in an hour is

$(412.3)\,(40) + (39.9)\,(10) + (221.9)\,(4) + (1399.1)\,(5) + (219.1)\,(5)$

$= 16{,}852 + 399 + 887.6 + 6995.5 + 1095.5$

$= 26{,}229.6 \text{ seconds}$

Thus, in one hour's time, 26,229.6 seconds of terminal, communications link, and CPU/disk/wait time will be required, and the number of terminals needed is

$$\frac{26{,}229.6}{3{,}600} = 7.29 \text{ terminals}$$

To provide for the total number of transactions from one location, eight terminals will be needed.

SUMMARY

There is a wide variety of terminals, terminal capabilities, and terminal prices. The industry has been moving toward terminals with more intelligence, which provide functions that are simple to use and may also reduce overall communications cost and host processor work. Microprocessors and intelligent terminals have begun to emerge as strong forces in the terminal marketplace. Their flexibility and local processing ability make them very effective in the modern communications network. Ergonomic features are important when selecting a terminal.

If several terminals are placed near each other in a remote location, it is impractical to have one line for each terminal, so the terminals must share one communications line. One way in which this is done is polling, which requires addressable terminals. In polling, a supervisor station asks each terminal in turn if it has data to send. A terminal that is polled returns either data or a negative acknowledgment that indicates it has no data to send. *Selection* is the name given to the procedure by which the supervisor sends data to a terminal.

Key Terms

addressable	multi-point connection
asynchronous transmission	optical character recognition (OCR)
block mode	poll/select
cathode ray tube (CRT)	point-to-point connection
compression/decompression	primary station
contention	remote batch processing
conversational mode	roll call polling
data editing	screen templates
data formatting	secondary station
downloading	smart terminal
dumb terminal	soft copy
hard copy	special-purpose terminals
host computer	synchronous transmission
hub polling	teletypewriter (TTY)
IBM 3270 terminal	terminal
intelligent terminal	token passing
joystick	trackball
line discipline	universal product code (UPC)
microcomputer	uploading
microprocessor	video display terminal (VDT)
modified data tags	video display unit (VDU)
mouse	windowing

Terminal Attributes

cost	function keys	reverse video
conversational	editing	ASCII
block (page) mode	cursor control	EBCDIC
TTY-compatible	host control	protocol support
dumb	color	attached devices
smart	programmable	duplex
intelligent	auxiliary storage	screen size
printer	protected fields	character size
speed	graphics	modified data tags
asynchronous	formatting	CPU
synchronous	character sets	interface
batch	keyboard	portability
point-to-point	blink	
multi-point	half intensity	

Review Questions

1. Describe each of the following uses of terminals:
   a. microcomputer workstations
   b. remote job entry
   c. data entry and display
   d. point-of-sale
   e. portable terminals or microcomputers
   f. touch-tone telephones

2. What are the characteristics of a dumb terminal?

3. What are the characteristics of a smart terminal?

4. What are the characteristics of an intelligent terminal?

5. Describe two terminal input devices.

6. Describe two terminal output devices.

7. Some applications have special terminal needs. Identify four such applications and the special keyboard options each needs.

8. Why is ergonomic design an important terminal selection criterion?

9. Describe the poll/select protocol.

10. What are the advantages of multi-point connections? What are the disadvantages?

11. Why are microcomputers a good replacement for terminals?

Exercises

1. Computer-aided design and computer-aided manufacture (CAD/CAM) use terminals in the design process. Graphics capability is essential to these applications. What other terminal attributes would be beneficial in such applications?

2. Some applications have unique needs. To meet these needs, special-purpose terminals are sometimes used. Research different applications and find three instances of custom-engineered terminals. What are the special properties of those terminals?

3. Besides the ergonomic requirements of terminals, what other environmental guidelines should be followed with respect to a terminal work environment? What lighting, noise level, and furniture should be available to protect the user? How frequently should breaks be taken?

4. Research the literature and find at least two cases in which employers are being sued as a result of terminal-related incidents.

5. Derive the transaction times for each of the transaction types described in the case study: credit check, customer maintenance, sending electronic mail, and receiving electronic mail.

6. A bank has decided to install ATMs in several locations. They have determined that the two major transactions at the ATMs will be withdrawals and requests for account balances. The characteristics for each transaction are

Figure 4-18 Projected ATM Transactions

| | Transaction Type | |
	Withdrawal	Account Balance
Think/wait time (secs)	15	15
No. of input characters	10	10
No. of output characters	100	100
Disk/CPU/queuing time (secs)	2	1
Hourly peak	1000	100

given in Figure 4-18. Determine the minimum number of ATMs required if the communications link speed is 2400 bps and assuming that each character transmitted requires 10 bits. Assume also that ATM users are able to enter 0.75 characters per second.

7. What are some reasons that a bank might install more ATMs than the minimum required?

References

Brear, Scott. "Assault on the 3270: Now There Are Choices." *Computerworld on Communications* 17 (September 28, 1983).

"*Computerworld* Buyer's Guide, Terminals and Peripherals." *Computerworld on Communications* 17 (October 5, 1983).

Foley, J. D., and A. Van Dam. *Fundamentals of Interactive Computer Graphics.* Reading, MA: Addison-Wesley, 1982.

IBM. *An Introduction to the IBM 3270 Information Display System.* Manual no. GA27-2739-7. IBM, September 1977.

Jones, James L. "A New Radiation Hazard." *Technological Review,* October 1983.

————. "Video Radiation: Fears Out of Focus." *Technological Review,* October 1983.

King, John. "Which Is the Fairest Terminal of All?" *Computerworld on Communications* 17 (May 18, 1983).

Martin, Lionel. "Ergonomics: A Growing Concern in CRT Design." *Mini-Micro Systems,* November 1980.

Miller, Frederick W. "CRT Terminals Get Smarter, Cheaper." *Infosystems,* September 1981.

————. "The World of CRT Terminals." *Infosystems,* June 1982.

————. "More Than Skin Deep." *Infosystems,* September 1982.

Morris, D. J. *Introduction to Communication Command and Control Systems.* Elmsford, NY: Pergamon Press, 1977.

Popper, Andrew. "No Truce Ahead in War over VDT Safety." *Business Week,* July 25, 1983.

Pritchard, J.A.T. *Quantitative Methods in On-Line Systems.* Rochelle Park, NJ: Hayden Book Co., 1976.

Puzman, Josef, and Radoslav Porizek. *Communication Control in Computer Networks.* New York: Wiley, 1980.

Raloff, J. "VDTs: User Stress and Eyestrain Largely Due to Job Design." *Science News,* July 16, 1983.

Tanenbaum, Andrew S. *Computer Networks.* Englewood Cliffs, NJ: Prentice-Hall, 1981.

Data Communications Hardware

Multiplexers
Concentrators
Front End Processors
Protocol Converters
Diagnostic and Miscellaneous Equipment
Summary of the Physical Layer
Case Study

INTRODUCTION

This chapter concludes the presentation of the physical layer of the OSI recommendation. We discuss the hardware components employed either directly or indirectly in data communications networks, continuing in the direction begun in Chapter 4—from the terminal equipment toward the host processors. The discussion of the various pieces of equipment that are configured in communications networks also presents the advantages and disadvantages of each. In addition, the chapter provides a brief overview of how some network problems are resolved. After this chapter you should know:

How multiplexers are used

How concentrators and front end processors work

The differences between concentrators and front end processors

The role of data communications controllers

How and why protocol converters are used

About data communications diagnostic equipment and how it is used

The roles of PBXs, facsimile, and LAN hardware in networks

167

In Chapter 4 you learned one way that terminals can share a communications line. There are several other ways for devices to share a communications line, one of the most common being multiplexing.

MULTIPLEXERS

In Chapter 4 you learned about polling and how it can be used to share a communications link. Polling requires the use of smart terminals because the terminals must be addressable and have memory. Another line-sharing technique, *multiplexing,* does not generally require the use of smart terminals. Multiplexing technology allows multiple signals to be transmitted over a single link. For many years, multiplexing has been used by telephone companies to combine multiple voice-grade circuits into a single high-speed circuit for long-distance communication. In data communications networks, multiplexers (*muxes*) allow several devices to share a common circuit.

How Multiplexers Function

Remote locations often have multiple devices that must communicate with a host. An obvious but expensive way to do this involves one line per device. Another alternative uses a single line and several smart devices that can be polled. Multiplexing provides yet another way for multiple devices to share a communications line. Figure 5-1 presents a general mux configuration. Several communication lines enter the mux from the host side. The mux combines the data from all incoming lines and transmits it via one line to a mux at the receiving end. This receiving mux separates the data and distributes it among the outgoing terminal lines. The number of lines going into the mux on the host side is the same as the number going out to terminals (or other muxes) on the remote side.

To the user, the multiplexer appears to function as though there were several physical lines as opposed to just one. The configuration of one high-speed link and a pair of multiplexers, however, costs less than that of several lower speed links with a pair of modems for each. Furthermore, applications written for a point-to-point terminal connection can be used without change. The multiplexer makes the line sharing transparent to the user. In essence, the application sees a point-to-point line.

Types of Multiplexers

A communications link is divided among several users in two basic ways. The first technique, known as *frequency division multiplexing,* separates the link by frequencies. The second technique, which has several variations, is known as *time division multiplexing;* it separates the link into time slots.

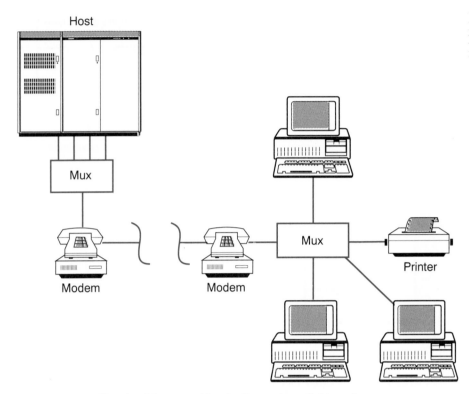

Figure 5-1 General
Multiplexer Configu-
ration

Host

Mux

Modem

Modem

Mux

Printer

Four host lines combined with one long distance line.
A modem is not required by all types of multiplexers.

Frequency Division Multiplexing (FDM).   In *FDM* the available bandwidth of the circuit is broken down into subchannels, each of which
has smaller bandwidths. Given a telephone circuit with a bandwidth of
3100 Hz, a frequency range of 300 to 3400 Hz, and a line-carrying capacity
of 1200 bps, suppose that instead of one terminal running at 1200 bps it
was desired to have three terminals, each at 300 bps. Although arithmetically it appears possible to have four 300-bps terminals on the line, this is
impossible because frequency separation of the subchannels must be maintained to avoid crosstalk. The recommended separation for a 300-bps circuit
is 480 Hz (Held, 1979). The subchannel separators are referred to as *guardbands*. This situation requires two guardbands of 480 Hz each. Each of the
three 300-bps subchannels therefore has a bandwidth of 713 Hz, derived as
follows: 3100 Hz (total bandwidth of circuit) − 960 Hz (two guardbands at
480 Hz each) = 2140 Hz/3 channels = 713 Hz per channel. Similarly, a
9600-bps channel can be divided into four 1200-bps channels. The higher
the speed of individual channels, the larger the guardbands must be. Figure 5-2 illustrates an FDM channel. An FDM configuration is given in
Figure 5-3. There is no need for modems in this configuration because the
FDM functions as a modem by accepting the signal from the data terminal
equipment (DTE) and transforming it into a signal within a given fre-

Figure 5-2 A Frequency Division Multiplexer Channel

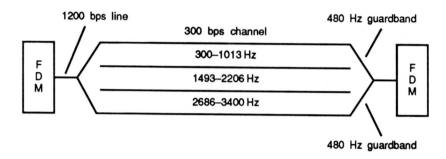

Figure 5-3 A Frequency Division Multiplexer Configuration

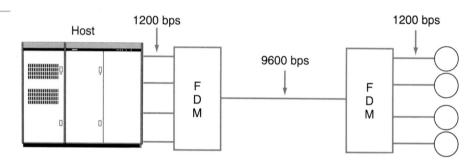

quency range. Thus, the modem is integrated into the FDM. Each line in FDM is mapped onto one of the subchannels. For example, the first line's signal is passed along the first subchannel, the second line's, along the second subchannel, and so on. If terminals on that line are not busy, that portion of the carrying capacity goes unused.

Time Division Multiplexing (TDM).   *Time division multiplexing (TDM)* is roughly equivalent to time-sharing systems. As with FDM, TDM has a group of lines entering the mux, one circuit shared by all, and the same number of lines leaving the mux at the other end. Instead of splitting the frequency, however, TDM shares time: Each line is given a time slot for transmitting, which is accomplished by interleaving either bits or characters. *Bit interleaving* is more common for synchronous (block at a time) transmissions and *character interleaving* is more common with asynchronous (character at a time) transmissions.

To understand how TDM operates, look at the four-port TDM in Figure 5-4. This mux combines signals from the four lines onto a single communications circuit. Data entering the TDM from the devices on the input line is placed in a buffer or register. With character interleaving, first a character from Line 1 is transmitted, then a character from Line 2, one from Line 3, one from Line 4, and back again to Line 1 to repeat the process. Bit interleaving works in the same manner except that a bit instead of a character is taken from each line in turn to form a transmission block. The mux at the other end breaks the data back out and places it on the appropriate line.

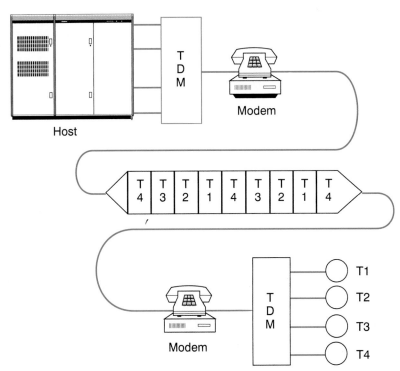

Figure 5-4 A Time Division Multiplexer

*A modem is not required for all TDMs; for example, an in-house digital TDM may not require modems.

As with FDM, each line gets a portion of the available transfer time. However, TDM requires no guardbands, so there is no loss of carrying capacity. Also as with FDM, lines are given a portion of the circuit's carrying capacity even though there is no data to be transmitted. Still, the improvement is significant: Instead of only three 300-bps sublines on a 1200-bps line, there can be four lines, each capable of 300-bps transmission. Likewise, a 9600-bps line can be multiplexed into eight 1200-bps lines or four 2400-bps lines, as illustrated in Figure 5-5.

Statistical Time Division Multiplexing (STDM). *Statistical time division multiplexing (STDM)* improves on the efficiency of TDM by transmitting data for only those lines with data to send, so idle lines take up none of the carrying capacity of the communications circuit. Figure 5-6 illustrates STDM. Because neither time slot nor frequency is allocated to a specific terminal, stat muxes must also transmit a terminal identification along with the data block. When all lines have data to transmit, an STDM looks just like a TDM; when only one line has data to send, the entire line capacity is devoted to that line.

Under good conditions, an STDM on a 9600-bps line can support five or six 2400-bps sublines, as illustrated in Figure 5-6, or three to four

Figure 5-5   Time Division Multiplexing

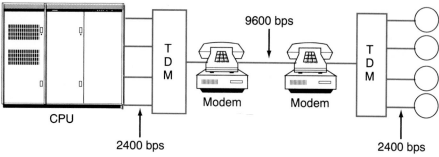

One 9600 bps line supporting four 2400 bps devices

Figure 5-6   Statistical Time Division Multiplexing

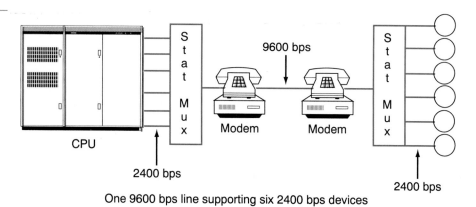

One 9600 bps line supporting six 2400 bps devices

4800-bps sublines. The reason for this apparent increase in carrying capacity stems from the probability that none of the incoming lines will be 100% busy. If each line is only 50% utilized, then four 4800-bps lines could be placed on one 9600-bps link. STDMs also have internal buffers for holding data from a line in case all lines try to transmit at once.

Newer stat muxes provide additional capabilities such as data compression, digital data support, line priorities, mixed-speed lines, integrated modems, network control ports for monitoring the multiplexed line, host port sharing where two or more lines at the terminal end are mapped onto one line at the host end, port switching wherein a terminal can be switched from one port to another, accumulation and reporting of performance statistics, automatic speed detection, memory expansion, and internal diagnostics. All of these features are not likely to be found in one mux. Different makes offer one or more of these capabilities as standard or optional functions. A few of these features can also be found in TDMs. Because of the higher performance of stat muxes, most of the development and enhancements in the last several years have been devoted to stat muxes.

Multiplexer Configurations

In addition to attaching terminals to muxes, other muxes can be added in *daisy chain* fashion, a configuration illustrated in Figure 5-7. Daisy chaining, also referred to as *cascading,* allows some circuits to be extended to another remote point, useful in a situation with two areas for data entry. With eight terminals in each area, a 16-port stat mux could provide linkage between the host and Area A, and eight lines from Area A could travel via an eight-port mux to Area B. The number of ports on a mux can vary, though commonly there are 4, 8, 16, 32, 48, or 64 ports. Multiplexer prices vary according to the number of ports and features provided. For a relatively plain four-port or eight-port stat mux, prices start at about $1000.

Inverse Multiplexer.   There is a less common type of mux known as an *inverse multiplexer*; its objective is to provide a high-speed data path between two devices, usually computers. An inverse mux accepts one line from a host and separates it into multiple lower speed communications circuits. The multiple low-speed circuits are recombined at the other end into a high-speed link, as illustrated in Figure 5-8. A 56-Kbps link from a computer to an inverse mux can be split into six 9600-bps lines and then back to a 56-Kbps line at the remote end. Telephone companies use this type of multiplexing to provide high-speed communications lines.

Multiport Modem.   A *multiport modem* is another multiplexing device. Essentially, it combines modem and TDM functions into one piece of equipment. Multiple terminal lines of varying transmission speeds enter

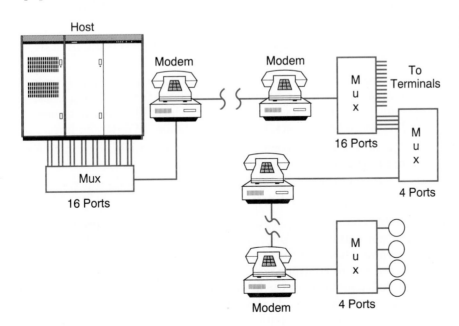

Figure 5-7 Cascading Multiplexers

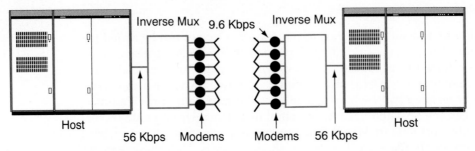

Figure 5-8   An Inverse Multiplexer

the multiport modem, and the modem multiplexes the data onto one line with a speed at least as fast as the aggregate data rate of all incoming terminal lines.

CONCENTRATORS

A *concentrator* is also a line-sharing device. Its primary function is the same as that of a mux: to allow multiple devices to share communications circuits. Because a concentrator is a computer, however, it can participate more actively than a mux in any application. In the early 1970s there was a marked distinction between a concentrator and a multiplexer. As multiplexers took on the additional functions just described, the difference between the two devices narrowed. Currently the principal differences between a mux and a concentrator are:

1. Concentrators are used one at a time; multiplexers are used in pairs.
2. A concentrator may have multiple incoming and outgoing lines, with a different number of incoming lines than outgoing lines; a multiplexer takes a certain number of incoming lines onto one line and converts back to the same number of outgoing lines.
3. A concentrator is a computer and may have auxiliary storage for use in support of an application.
4. A concentrator may perform some data-processing functions such as device polling and data validation.

One possible concentrator configuration is provided in Figure 5-9.

If the concentrator has disk drives attached, it can help the host(s) by storing terminal screen templates and sequencing their display; it can also enable terminals to continue some of their functions if the link between the host and the concentrator is malfunctioning. With disk storage, the concentrator can also provide store and forward functions, which means that if the communications paths become too busy, data can be stored on

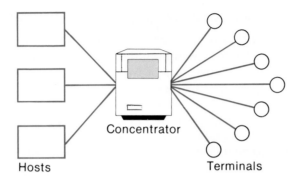

Figure 5-9 A
Concentrator
Configuration

Hosts

Concentrator

Terminals

the concentrator's disks for later transmission. Message logging functions are also made possible with auxiliary storage devices.

Concentrators can further aid an application by providing data editing, polling, error handling, code conversion, compression, and encryption. Concentrators can also switch messages between terminals and hosts. In a banking ATM environment where three regional processing centers are responsible for authorizing transactions, each city with multiple ATMs could use a concentrator to handle ATM traffic. The concentrator would have three lines, one each for the three hosts in the three regional processing centers. There would also be one line for each ATM or cluster of ATMs. Based on customer ATM card number, the concentrator would switch each transaction to the processing center closest to the customer's home branch.

FRONT END PROCESSORS (FEPs)

Front end processors (FEP) are employed at the host end of the communications circuit, much like a concentrator is used at the remote end. In many respects, front end processors and concentrators serve the same function. The FEP takes over much of the line management work from the host. An FEP configuration is shown in Figure 5-10. *Communications controller* and *message switch* are two other terms that refer to an FEP.

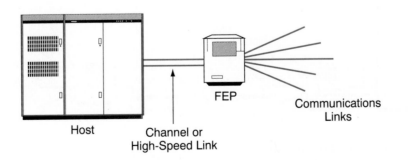

Figure 5-10 A
Front End Processor
Configuration

Host

Channel or
High-Speed Link

FEP

Communications
Links

Special-Purpose and General-Purpose FEPs

An FEP interface with a host system uses one or more high-speed links. The FEP is responsible for controlling the more numerous low-speed circuits. All functions of a concentrator can also be performed by an FEP, except, of course, concentrating message traffic for multiple remote terminals onto one communications line. FEPs may be either special-purpose or general-purpose. Special-purpose FEPs, such as the *IBM 3725* communications controller, Amdahl's 4705 communications processor, and Tandem Computers' 6100 communications processor, are designed specifically for data communications. Their operating system and software are totally communications-oriented. General-purpose FEPs, such as minicomputers by Digital Equipment Corporation, Data General, and Hewlett-Packard, represent the use of general-purpose computers primarily to perform data communications functions.

Communications Controllers

The IBM 37xx communications controllers or equivalents are used extensively in IBM installations for controlling communications lines. The 37xx family consists of the IBM 3725 and *3745* communications controllers (earlier models included the *3704* and *3705* controllers). The 3725 is the model used in this text to describe the functions of controllers. The 3725 can be used locally or remotely. In the remote configuration it actually functions as a concentrator. A local 3725 attaches to a channel on the host system; remote 3725s attach to a line from a local 3725. These configurations are depicted in Figure 5-11.

The IBM 3704 can control up to 32 half duplex lines; the IBM 3705 controls a maximum of 352 half duplex lines. Full duplex lines also can be attached, but this reduces the total number of available lines. One full duplex line is equivalent to two half duplex lines on the controller. Memory in the controller varies from 32K bytes to 1M bytes. Multiple hardware models are available, varying in memory, number of lines supported, and networking software available.

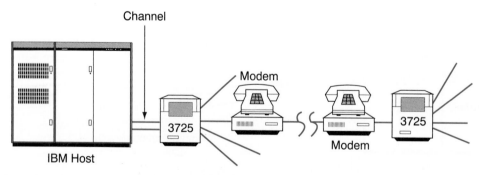

Figure 5-11   Local and Remote 3725 Configurations

Network Control Program (NCP). A *network control program* (NCP) is the controller's software. Several versions are available, each with its own capabilities. The most advanced NCP has *advanced communication function (ACF)*, which supports IBM's systems network architecture (SNA) (see Chapter 10). The NCP acts as interface between the host line-access methods and the lines to attached devices. An access method (see Chapter 12) provides input and output services as interface between an application and its associated devices. Access methods make it easier for application programmers to take advantage of the capabilities of different types of devices, which include polling, dialing, message buffering, code conversion, speed selection, error handling, and collection and reporting of statistics.

Message Switching Processors. A *message switching processor* functions to route messages to their proper destination, as described earlier in the banking application of concentrators. Message switching equipment can also serve as front end to one or more hosts in performing this function.

PROTOCOL CONVERTERS

To communicate with the many different types of data communications terminal devices requires conventions, or *protocols*. Protocols determine the sequences in which data exchanges may take place and the bit or character sequences required to provide device and line control (see Chapter 6). Not only are there many different devices, but there are many protocols as well. Each maker of terminals typically has its proprietary protocols, which means that a Unisys terminal probably will not be able to communicate with an IBM system as a 3270 terminal. IBM alone has over 25 different access methods. To bridge these differences, companies have developed *protocol converters*. A protocol converter is a special-purpose device that allows a terminal to look like a different type of terminal. A protocol converter also enables different computer systems to transmit to and receive from a given terminal model. Protocol conversion is accomplished by hardware, software, or both. This section considers only the hardware approach.

Functions of Protocol Converters

Protocol converters perform several functions, the primary one being to convert from one protocol to another. The significance of this function will become more apparent after you study the material on data link protocols in Chapter 6. Such a protocol change involves changing the characters that delimit the data, detecting errors, and providing control of the communications link; this may require reformatting the message data, changing a terminal's address to be compatible with the receiving device, segmenting a message into particular-size blocks or restoring such blocks to a complete message, translating one communications code (such as ASCII) into another (such as EBCDIC), or accommodating device characteristics.

A protocol converter is ordinarily treated as a "black box" on the communications line, or a piece of attached hardware that performs its function in a manner that is immaterial. Protocol conversion may be configured as illustrated in Figure 5-12. One purpose of protocol converters is to protect the user's investment in hardware. Suppose a user decides to change computer makes. The old processor from Company X may be kept or it may be exchanged for one from Company Y. If the user is fortunate, Company Y's processors will be able to interface directly with the Company X terminals. If Company Y has no support for the Company X terminals, there are three alternatives: sell the Company X terminals, probably at a great loss; write software that provides the capability; or attempt to find a protocol converter that can convert a Company Y protocol into that required by the Company X terminals.

Many different types of protocol converters are available. Some of the more common types are:

> Asynchronous to synchronous
>
> IBM 3270 to Unisys poll/select
>
> Unisys poll/select to asynchronous ASCII
>
> IBM 3270 to NCR poll/select
>
> IBM 3270 to IBM 2260 poll/select
>
> Teletypewriter (TTY) to IBM 3270
>
> IBM 2780/3780 to IBM 3270
>
> Asynchronous to IBM SDLC
>
> ASCII printers to IBM 3270
>
> IBM 3270 to IBM SDLC
>
> IBM 2780/3780 to IBM SDLC

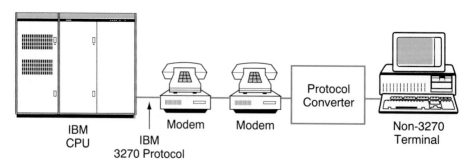

Figure 5-12   Protocol Conversion

PARS (airline reservations system protocol) to binary synchronous

Microcomputers to almost any of the above

An example of protocol converters connecting several different devices is depicted in Figure 5-13. Protocol converters also can accommodate differences in the keyboards of different terminals. Suppose that a simple TTY terminal without function keys needs to be used in an application that requires function keys. The protocol converter will take a combination of keystrokes and map them onto a particular function key, thus allowing a less expensive terminal to be used in an application that would require a more sophisticated terminal. Converters also exist that change from one code to another, for example, from ASCII to EBCDIC, and that change from one interface to another. An ICOT 352 asynchronous/ 3270 protocol converter is pictured in Figure 5-14.

DIAGNOSTIC AND MISCELLANEOUS EQUIPMENT

The hardware discussed thus far is involved in the transportation or receipt of data. Another set of hardware frequently is necessary to perform the following functions:

Provide security of transmission and facilities

Monitor the data

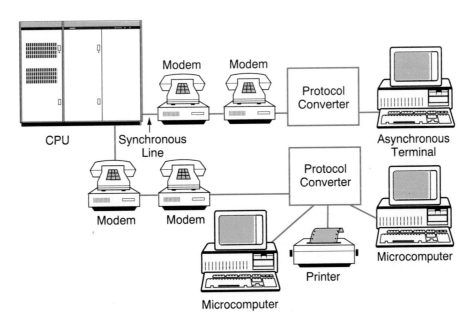

Figure 5-13   Protocol Converters Connecting Different Devices

Figure 5-14
An ICOT 352
Asynchronous/3270
Protocol Converter

Courtesy of ICOT Corporation

Control the sequences being transmitted

Provide connection for switched communications lines

Provide other functions necessary to control and manage the communications network

Some of these devices are described below.

Security

Security of data transmission and storage is becoming increasingly important. Several pieces of hardware are available to assist in the protection of data.

Call-Back Units.   One simple but effective device is a *call-back unit,* which participates in making switched connections. A person trying to access a system using a switched connection must identify himself or herself with an ID and a password. The opening connection is severed after the ID and password are entered, and the call-back unit looks in its tables for that user's number, calls the number, and the connection is made.

At least two problems exist with a call-back system. First, the host computer becomes responsible for the costs of the connection. Second, the call-back system prohibits portable terminal connections, such as that needed by a traveling salesperson with a portable terminal. However, some call-back units allow users with certain passwords to bypass the call-back. Call-back bypass can be allowed at all times for certain users or can be programmed to allow bypass only during specific hours. Of course, this feature has the disadvantage of lowering security.

Encryption Equipment. *Encryption equipment* allows transmitted data to be scrambled at the sending location and reconstructed at the receiving end. The U.S. National Bureau of Standards (NBS) has approved a standard called the *data encryption standard (DES)*, which uses a 64-bit pattern as the encryption key. The DES algorithm is available on a chip, and encryption boxes are commercially available. Figure 5-15 shows an encryption device installed on a communications link. Encryption is discussed in more detail in Chapter 13.

Line Monitors

The two types of line monitors are digital and analog. Analog monitors are used primarily by common carrier personnel to analyze their lines. Digital monitors are used by data-processing technicians to check for adherence to protocols. The following discussion refers to digital monitors.

Line monitors, also known as *protocol analyzers,* are used to diagnose problems on a communications link. Like all the equipment studied thus far, line monitors come in a wide variety of models and capabilities. Their basic function, however, is to attach to a communications circuit so the bit patterns being transmitted over the link can be displayed for analysis by a data communications expert who then determines what the problems are. Figure 5-16 shows a line monitor. Features commonly available on line monitors are:

Video display

Memory

Recording tape or disk

Programmability

Trap setting for selected bit patterns

Multiple protocol support

Variable character-length support

Multiple interfaces

Multiple speeds

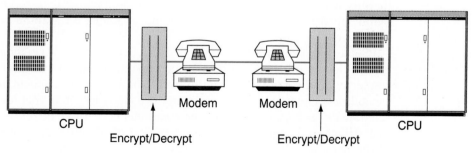

Figure 5-15   Data Encryption Box

Figure 5-16 A Digital Line Monitor

Courtesy of Atlantic Research Corporation

Function keys

Graphics display

Integrated breakout box

Importing/exporting data

If a corporation requires multiple line monitors to cover multiple locations, it is best to use models from one manufacturer. Each manufacturer usually has several models, with varying capabilities; this allows the user to buy the minimum required capability for a specific location. There are two reasons for using equipment from only one manufacturer. First, education of personnel is easier with only one manufacturer. Even though different models may be used, the operations typically are quite similar, especially for simple functions. Second, and more important, recordings made at one site may be shipped to another and analyzed, and since there is no industry standard recording mode, tape or disk recorded on Manufacturer A's machine probably is not readable on Manufacturer B's equipment.

Some microcomputers can be enhanced to provide line monitoring capabilities. A microcomputer may be enhanced with an adapter board, connector, and software that will provide network and protocol analyzer capabilities. The price for this capability is usually less than that for a dedicated analyzer because some of the components of an analyzer—monitor, disk drives, and cabinetry—are already part of the microcomputer. Some of the necessary hardware and software to equip a microcomputer with this ability is priced under $1500.

Protocol Simulators

Protocol simulators are used during development to debug systems. They can simulate a wide variety of terminals for testing of application-terminal interfaces. Simulators also can imitate the computer side of a protocol, which allows developers to test or evaluate terminals without computer software to drive the terminal. Simulators can be used to test software before terminals have been delivered or to test terminals in the absence of readily available new software.

Breakout Boxes

A *breakout box* is a passive multipurpose device that is patched into a circuit at an interface. Figure 5-17 shows a programmable breakout box. Once the breakout box is installed, it is possible to:

Monitor activity on the exchange circuits. Each exchange circuit has a light-emitting diode (LED) on the breakout box; if there is a signal on the circuit the LED lights up.

Exchange circuit leads. One of the causes of communication failure is crossed leads in the cable. A breakout box allows circuits to be changed without rebuilding of the connector on the cable.

Isolate a given circuit. If an interchange circuit is used by one device and not the other, that circuit can be isolated, which prevents the signal from being passed on to the device that does not accept that lead.

Measure voltage levels on an interchange circuit. This allows the user to detect if the voltages used to carry the signal are within acceptable tolerance limits.

Breakout boxes can be equipped with bit pattern generators and receivers, which allow for both transmitting and receiving a small number of selected bit patterns. This beneficial feature allows the individual doing the testing to determine what effect a known data pattern has on the circuit.

Auto-Call Units (ACU)

An *auto-call unit (ACU)* is used to place a telephone call automatically, without manual intervention. The ACU has the ability of opening the line (the equivalent of lifting the handset from its cradle), detecting the dial tone, dialing the number (through either pulse dialing or touch-tone dialing), detecting the ring indicator or busy signal, and detecting if the call is complete or incomplete. Incomplete calls can be the result of a busy signal, failure to answer, a busy circuit, a number out of order, or some other event. In the United States, ACUs originally could be sold only by the telephone companies. With the Carterphone decision, this policy changed. The ACU and auto-answer functions are now common in modem equipment. The

Figure 5-17 A Programmable Breakout Box

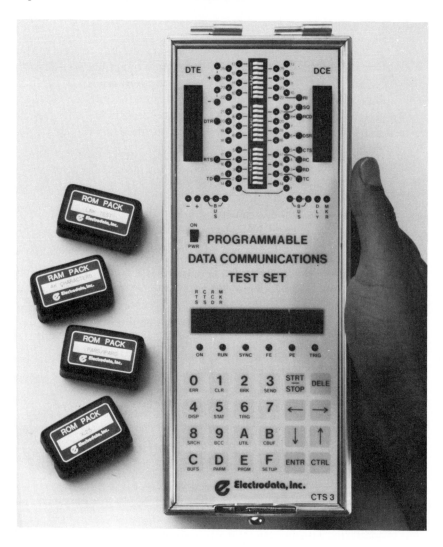

Courtesy of Electrodata, Inc.

interface to ACU equipment in the United States is via either the RS-232-C interface or the RS-366 interface. The latter specifically addresses the electrical and functional interface for automatic calling equipment.

Port Concentrator

Multiplexers allow multiple terminals to share one communications link. However, for each terminal attached to a multiplexer there must be one communicatons port at the host end to receive the signal, which is what makes the multiplexer appear to be a point-to-point connection for both terminal and host. All systems have an upper limit to the number of communication ports that may be configured, and, of course, there is a cost to providing ports. A *port concentrator* allows multiple input streams from a multiplexer to be passed to the host through a single communications port. This is beneficial not only in reducing the hardware cost of the host but also in allowing for expansion beyond the port limitations of a particular processor. Port concentration requires that a software module be available in the host to receive the multiple terminal messages and route them to the appropriate applications. The functions performed by this software are similar to what must be provided for a concentrator. A port concentrator is illustrated in Figure 5-18.

Port Selector or Data Switch

The function of a *port selector* is similar to that of a port concentrator: It helps determine which users are granted access in applications where the number of potential terminal users far exceeds the number of available lines, such as reservations systems and library systems. If a particular system allows a total of 1000 terminals—on either dedicated or switched links—to communicate with a host at one time and there are 8000 potential users, obviously not all of these users can have access to the system at once. A port selector helps to determine which users are granted access. For switched lines the port selector can act as a rotary, allowing users to dial one number and connecting the incoming calls to any available switched port. It can also enable switched users to connect to an unused

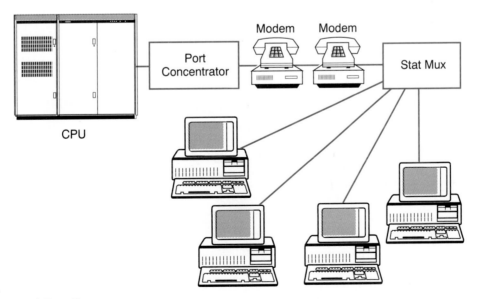

Figure 5-18   A Port Concentrator

dedicated port. Port selectors can also sometimes switch to ports on several hosts. Some port selectors give the user considerable control over how many ports will be used for switched calls, how many can be shared between dedicated and switched users, and how many can be routed to another host. Thus, the selectable ports and the class of users who may select them can be configured to meet specific needs. A schematic showing how a port selector is used is provided in Figure 5-19.

Cluster Controllers

A *cluster controller,* depicted in Figure 5-20, is designed to support several terminals. It manages the terminals, buffers data being transmitted to or from the terminals, performs error detection and correction, and polls. The controller may be attached to the host either locally or remotely. While every terminal attached to a cluster controller usually uses the same communications protocol, the devices themselves may differ. The remote cluster controller in Figure 5-20 has VDUs and a printer attached.

Figure 5-19   A Port Selector Schematic

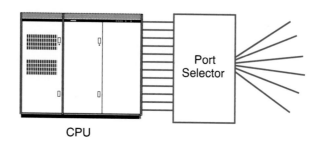

CPU

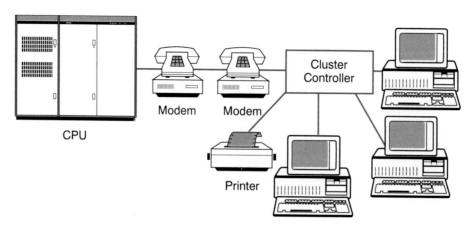

Figure 5-20   A Cluster Controller

Private Branch Exchanges (PBXs)

In the past, *private branch exchange (PBX)* telephone switches have been separate from data communications networks. More recently PBXs have been integrated into networks, primarily to provide local area networking capabilities. PBXs are discussed in more detail in the local area network section in Chapter 8.

X.3 PAD

In Chapter 1 the concept of a packet switching network (PDN) was introduced, and these will be discussed in more detail in Chapter 10. One requirement of these networks is the grouping of a specific number of characters, such as 128, into a transmission packet. Forming these packets is the responsibility of the sender, not the network (although some networks also provide this service). A CCITT standard, *X.3*, describes the function of *packet assembly/disassembly (PAD)*. Users wishing to use terminals that do not support PAD can purchase hardware that performs this function. One PAD device may provide support for several terminals. Figure 5-21 illustrates an X.3 PAD configuration.

Matrix Switches

Some installations have multiple host processors, and terminal users may attach to a specific host in a variety of ways. One way is through a *matrix switch,* such as that shown in Figure 5-22. The switch allows terminal connections to be switched among the available processors. This is effected

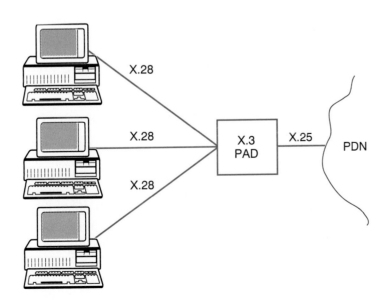

Figure 5-21   X.3 PAD Configuration

Figure 5-22   Matrix
Switch Hardware

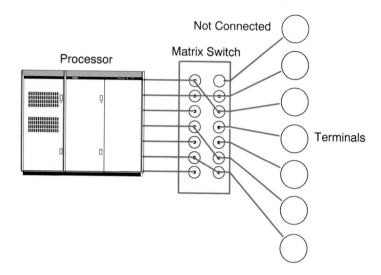

manually through a patch panel or automatically through program control. Matrix switches obviate the need to physically move communication
lines between terminals and processors. Functionally, these switches operate in the same manner as the early telephone PBX patch panels.

Three ways in which a matrix switch may be used include:

1. Users can be evenly distributed over several processors. If one
   processor in the system becomes saturated, some users can be
   quickly and efficiently transferred to another processor.

2. If a failure occurs in a line, the terminal(s) attached to that line
   are switched to a functional one.

3. More terminals can be distributed than direct physical line
   attachment would permit. For example, it may be necessary to
   have terminals in conference rooms, demonstration areas, and
   unoccupied offices where they are seldom used. For a system that
   supports 256 directly connected terminals, there may actually be
   275 installed terminals. Using a matrix switch, terminals in
   low-use areas can easily be connected or disconnected from the
   system as needed.

Facsimile

Facsimile (fax) transmitters/receivers are becoming standard office equipment. Early implementations consisted of one fax machine transmitting
images to another using telephone lines as a medium. Today, fax machines
are also attached as terminals to a processor, which is used to store and
forward fax images. In this capacity the processor is used as a repository
of fax images, which can be distributed to a variety of devices such as
other fax machines, terminals, and laser printers.

Local Area Network Hardware

File and Printer Servers.   On local area networks, it is common to share hardware components among users. This makes more effective use of devices such as printers and disks and reduces hardware costs. *File servers* allow data and disk drives to be shared among network users; *printer servers* accomplish the same function for printers. This capability is discussed in more detail in Chapter 9.

Database Servers.   One of the local area network technologies that was introduced in the late 1980s is the *SQL server*. *SQL* is a relational database language that allows users to create, access, update, and delete records in a database. The strengths of SQL are that it is nonprocedural and English-like. By *nonprocedural* we mean that the user enters a request without having to specify the way in which that request is to be carried out.

The SQL server provides greater efficiency for database access than does a file server. Consider the database request to find the average salary of all employees. With a file server, each database record is transferred to the user's workstation, where the total of the salaries and the number of employees is accumulated. After all employee records have been read the average is computed. In contrast, the same request directed to the SQL server results in only the final average being passed over the network. The SQL server performs all required disk accesses, computes the average, and sends only the result over the network. This is more efficient for two reasons. First, network traffic is significantly reduced because each employee record is not transmitted over the network. Second, the SQL server can be optimized for the work it accomplishes and thus can be more efficient than a workstation.

Terminal Servers.   One limitation on the number of terminals that can be connected to a computer is the number of I/O ports on the computer. With the advent of high-speed LANs, computer manufacturers now have another way to connect terminals to a computer that overcomes the port limitation on the host system. This capability, called a *terminal server*, is similar to a concentrator and is illustrated in Figure 5-23. Terminal servers provide from 8 to 64 terminal ports, allowing those terminals to share a single LAN port. Terminal servers can also save cabling costs, and some provide protocol conversion.

Network Interface Cards (NICs).   In a local area network, a workstation, node, or server must be connected to the network medium. When network nodes are large systems, a special adapter is required for the medium interface. The adapter is responsible for placing data onto the medium and for receiving messages. When the network node is a microcomputer, the interface is called a *network interface card* (*NIC*), which serves the same function as the adapter just described. NICs are discussed in more detail in Chapter 9.

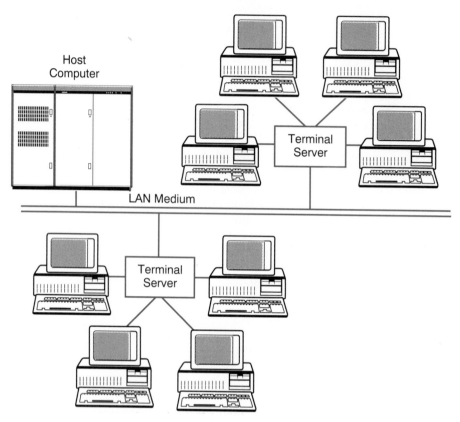

Figure 5-23   Terminal Server

Fax and Modem Pooling.   In local area networks, it is usually economical to share modems and facsimile machines. *Fax and modem pooling* operate in much the same manner as printer and file servers. Suppose four modems are attached to a LAN server. Modem pooling allows a user to attach to one of the available modems and establish a connection as though the modem were locally attached to his or her workstation.

SUMMARY OF THE PHYSICAL LAYER

This completes the survey of the physical layer of communications. What follows is a brief review of the different physical components and their advantages and disadvantages; the chapter concludes with a look at a case study in which these diverse elements are tied together.

There is a variety of transmission media from which to select. For local area communications the best alternatives are private wires, coaxial cable, fiber optics, infrared radio, and microwave radio. Long distances usually require that the medium be procured from a common carrier. The choices for long-distance routes include leased or switched wires, microwave, satellite, and packet distribution networks. The last option is discussed in Chapter 10. Wire connections obtained from a common carrier may include microwave, satellite, or fiber optics technology. A fiber optic link is treated as a wire because logically it is still a wire link and has the same transmission characteristics—speed and cost—as wire. The usual medium for long-distance transmission is a wire-like medium obtained from a common carrier. Microwave and satellite are usually selected when the volume of data to be transmitted per unit of time is large. Satellite has the added benefit of being able to reach many locations with a small cost for expansion. Propagation delay time, however, is a potential disadvantage of satellite transmission.

Other physical components also must be selected in addition to the transmission media. These include the host computers, terminals, and support equipment such as modems, multiplexers, concentrators, front end processors, security devices, and protocol converters. Speed, cost, functionality, and in some cases security are the determining forces in selecting these options.

When a connection is point-to-point, the configuration is straightforward. Required equipment includes a medium with enough speed to support the application, modems, and line drivers, where necessary. This type of configuration is typical in host-to-host communications, local terminal connections, and remote locations with only one terminal device.

Often a host must interface with multiple terminal devices; in this situation a greater number of alternatives exist. A wide variety of terminal equipment is available with each of the following options.

Multi-point (poll/select)

Multiple point-to-point links

Multiplexers

Concentrators

Concentrators with multiplexers

Front end processors

Front end processors with concentrators and/or multiplexers

Protocol converters

Dedicated links

Switched links

Packet switching networks

The number of potential combinations is enormous. In fact, configuring transmission links to multiple locations quickly becomes a matter of evaluating the many possible combinations. The difference between the low-cost link and the high-cost link can be significant. Fortunately, there are modeling systems that can sort through the possibilities and perform the time-consuming rate and distance calculations. These models may be either purchased or leased, and some are available on microcomputers. Anyone involved in planning an extensive system or planning multiple systems will surely find any investment in such a model beneficial, even if the model does no more than confirm initial speculations.

CASE STUDY

Seymour Opportunity, vice president of marketing for the Syncrasy Corporation, has convinced the other corporate executives that the future lies not only in mail-order operations but also in discount computer stores. Wanting to expand into several areas at once, Syncrasy is opening discount computer stores in Chicago, New York City, Atlanta, Houston, Los Angeles, San Francisco, and Kansas City. The home office and computer center are also being moved from Puma Flats to Kansas City. Penny Pincher, the comptroller, has exerted her influence by obtaining commitments that the cost of expansion will be held to a minimum.

The computer stores in Chicago, New York, and Los Angeles will have five terminals each; the other stores will have three each. Mail-order operations will continue, although on a diminished scale. The catalog stores in Kansas City, New York City, and Los Angeles will be located 15, 20, and 40 miles from the discount stores, respectively.

Computer Store Transaction Types

There will be two basic transactions at each computer store: (1) inventory and receipt transactions and (2) parts and customer inquiries.

Inventory and Receipts.   The first type of transaction deals with inventory control and receipts. Every time a sale is made, the part number, quantity sold, unit price, discount rate, and total amount of the sale are transmitted to the central computer. The line item for each part sold consists of 22 characters, and the total amount of the sale is a 10-character field. The usual response to the transaction is 10 characters. Orders that total more than $1000, however, are an exception. These exceptional transactions, which involve a credit check and which comprise an estimated 30% of all inventory transactions, have 10 additional characters in the response portion of the message. Average processing time for normal orders is 0.5 seconds; for orders over $1000 it is 0.8 seconds. There is an average of 6 items per order and an average of 20 orders per terminal per hour, with peaks of 40 orders per terminal per hour. Peak transaction periods are from noon to 1 P.M. and from 5 P.M. to 6 P.M. It is required that 95% of all transactions of this type have a response time of 3 seconds.

Parts and Customer Inquiries. The second type of store transaction is a parts or customer inquiry. Average input is 10 characters and average response is 500 characters. Average and peak rates for this transaction are both 10 per hour per terminal. A response time of 4 seconds is required. Processing time for these transactions is 1.5 seconds per order.

Catalog Store Activity

The third type of transaction will be in the catalog stores. Activity in the catalog store operations will decline as a result of having discount stores in the area. Catalog stores will have eight terminals each. The typical catalog store transaction has 500 characters of input data and a 100 character response. Each terminal averages 20 orders per hour, with a peak of 30 orders per hour. Five-second response time is required for these transactions. Processing time is 2.5 seconds per order.

Prices, Equipment, and Mileage

Only leased transmission lines from a common carrier are considered. Satellite transmission was considered by Syncrasy at the outset, but it was dismissed because of the relatively light amount of traffic from the stores and the effect of propagation delay on response times. The following rates are used in this case study (and in the exercises at the end of this chapter).

Modems. The cost of modems has declined in recent years so it is unlikely that modems will be leased. The following calculations are for monthly fees and hence modem costs are not included. Moreover, Syncrasy has opted to buy statistical multiplexers with integrated modems.

Interstate Communication Lines. The line can handle speeds up to 9600 bps. Line speed is governed by the modem.

First 100 miles	$2.52 per mile (including monthly fee)
Next 900 miles (101–1000)	$0.94 per mile
Each mile over 1000	$0.58 per mile

Local Communication Lines. The line can handle speeds up to 9600 bps. Line speed is governed by the modem.

Each mile $4.70

Statistical Multiplexer. Syncrasy chose stat muxes with additional memory and built-in modems. These muxes cost more than the entry-level price of $1000 quoted earlier in the chapter. The costs of the multiplexers Syncrasy has chosen are:

Number of Channels	Purchase Price	Monthly Lease Price
4	$1700	$150
8	2600	225
16	4300	358
32	6500	540

Concentrators. The price of concentrators can vary enormously. This case uses two configurations. The first configuration will handle up to 32 output lines, which could be point-to-point terminals, multi-point communication lines, or lines to another concentrator or multiplexer. It sells for $30,000, with a monthly lease price of $1500. The second configuration must be large enough for whatever is required. It sells for $40,000 and leases for $2000 per month. Each of these concentrators will be able to accommodate up to eight incoming lines from the host processor.

Front End Processors. The price of the FEP is the same as that for the more expensive concentrator, $40,000.

Terminals.

Dumb terminals sell for $500, with a monthly lease price of $50. (Syncrasy will not lease dumb terminals if they are used.)

Smart terminals sell for $1500, with a monthly lease price of $105.

Intelligent terminals sell for $2500, with a monthly lease price of $175.

Mileage. Airline miles are used for determining communication rates between cities. Figure 5-24 lists the mileage between cities.

Preliminary Considerations. A simple case study has been constructed, with few locations and a centrally located computer center. Even so, the

Figure 5-24   Mileage Chart

	Chicago	Houston	Kansas City	L.A.	N.Y.C.	S.F.
Atlanta	708	791	822	2191	854	2483
Chicago		1091	542	2048	809	2173
Houston			743	1555	1610	1911
Kansas City				1547	1233	1861
Los Angeles					2794	387
New York City						2930

variation between media costs of the best and worst cases alone can be significant. Because of the capabilities they provide, smart terminals have been selected. The line time delay for dumb terminals in conversational mode would be excessive, and the current transactions do not warrant the excessive expense for intelligent terminals.

Mileage Costs

In actual practice, several common carriers would be consulted and their bids solicited for the best configuration. If there were many more locations, one of the network modeling systems also would be utilized to analyze all possible routes and provide a listing of the best alternatives. Instead, this exercise uses the brute force method.

Long-Distance Line Costs.   Although it is unusual to do so, point-to-point costs are calculated first. This allows comparison of the best and worst case line costs. The cost of the Kansas City–Los Angeles link is computed in detail; mileage and line costs for the remaining cities are simply listed. Since mileage rates are different for miles 0–100, 101–1000, and over 1000, the 1547 miles between Kansas City and Los Angeles must be broken down into these increments, yielding 100 + 900 + 547 miles. The cost for the Kansas City–Los Angeles link, then, is:

$$(100 \times 2.52) + (900 \times .94) + (547 \times .58) = 252 + 846 + 317.26$$

$$= 1388.26$$

Monthly point-to-point link charges between the home city and all remote locations are:

Kansas City to:

Atlanta	$ 930.68
Chicago	667.48
Houston	856.42
Los Angeles	1415.26
New York City	1233.14
San Francisco	1597.38
Total	$6700.36

Minimum-Distance Configuration Costs.   To find the lowest rate based on a minimum-distance configuration, there are many combinations available. The easiest way is to start with the shortest link—Kansas City to Chicago—and work outward until all locations are accounted for. A simple program could also be written to evaluate all combinations and pick the

Figure 5-25   A Net-
work Configuration

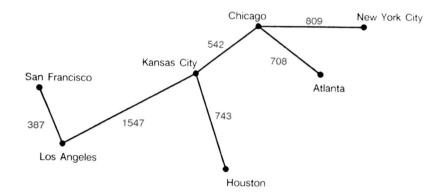

shortest route. A network configuration of the shortest routes is given in Figure 5-25. The costs of this network are:

From	To	Distance (miles)	Cost
Kansas City	Houston	743	$ 856.42
Kansas City	Chicago	542	667.48
Chicago	New York City	809	918.46
Chicago	Atlanta	708	823.52
Kansas City	Los Angeles	1547	1415.26
Los Angeles	San Francisco	387	521.78
Total			$5202.92

Local Line Costs. The costs of local links between the mail-order and discount stores in Kansas City, New York City, and Los Angeles must be calculated in addition to the costs of long-distance lines. These charges are easier to compute since there is a flat rate per mile. The costs are:

Location	Distance (miles)	Cost
Kansas City	15	$ 70.50
New York City	20	94.00
Los Angeles	40	188.00
Total		$352.50

The difference between the low-cost and high-cost configurations is $1497.44 per month ($6700.36 − $5202.92). However, this does not mean that the configuration is finalized. Yet to be determined is whether the capacity of the lines can support the application. For instance, the link from Kansas City to Chicago must be capable of supporting all message traffic from Chicago, New York City, and Atlanta. If one 9600-bps line is not capable of this, another alternative will be required, such as linking Houston and Atlanta.

Calculation of Line Utilization Costs

Five items must be considered in calculating the costs of line utilization: overhead, response time, aggregate data rate, line contention, and configuration. The first line speed calculation is for response time. Following that, the aggregate data rate for a given link is considered to make sure there is sufficient capacity to meet all terminals' demands. Contention issues are then addressed, followed by an analysis of configuration.

Overhead. Overhead includes costs for several components: control messages, polling, and terminal access. Overhead involves how efficiently the lines are utilized. As we discuss in the next chapter, some of the purposes of data link protocols are to delimit data, provide error detection and line control, and allow for addressing. Each of these functions requires that additional data be appended to the data message. In this case, control message overhead is approximated by using 10 bits per character rather than the actual 7 or 8 bits. While not entirely accurate, this measure is adequate, and it certainly simplifies calculation.

A second overhead factor is polling costs, if a multi-point configuration is used. Determining polling overhead involves figuring the amount of time a terminal must wait to be polled. This averages out to be:

wait time = polling interval × (number of terminals − 1)/2

On the average a terminal will wait for half of the *other* terminals. Sometimes a terminal will wait for all of the other terminals; at other times there will be no wait at all. Total wait time is the number of terminals that are waited for times the polling interval, or the amount of time required to send the poll message and wait for a reply. The amount of time required for a terminal to send data is not factored in because that is included in the contention calculations. Polling is ignored in this example.

The final component of overhead is the additional characters required for terminal access. Smart terminals using screen templates, protected fields, and video attributes require several characters to provide these capabilities. These include not only the characters needed for prompts but also the control characters that position the cursor, allow for video attributes and protected fields, and so on. The number of additional characters required to support these capabilities varies from terminal to terminal. Although these additional characters are ignored in this case, the number of characters required for terminal access can be significant. Polling wait time can also be significant, especially with many terminals and half duplex lines with slow modem turnaround times. These factors must not be ignored in real life.

Response Time: Inventory and Receipts. First, the inventory and receipts transaction is considered. The average number of line items per transaction is 6. Each line item consists of the part number, quantity, discount rate, and line item price, with a total of 22 characters per line item. For 6 line items, 6 × 22 = 132 characters are required, plus a 10-character total field, giving a total input record length of 142 characters. The response consists of 10 characters. The expected response time is 3 seconds. With 0.5 seconds required for processing, this leaves 2.5 seconds to transmit 152 characters, or 152/2.5 = 61 characters per second. At 10 bits per character for overhead of the data link protocol, a 610-bps line will be required. Thus, a 1200-bps line will be sufficient for this transaction's response time, hereafter referred to as transaction Type 1.

Transactions of this type that are over $1000 in total sales require the same response time but have an additional 10 characters in the response and an additional 0.3 seconds of processing time. The system must be able to transmit 162 characters in 2.2 seconds, which is 74 characters per second, or a 740-bps capacity. A 1200-bps line will also satisfy the response time for this transaction, hereafter called transaction Type 2.

Response Time: Parts and Customer Inquiries. The customer or inventory inquiry transaction requires 10 characters of input and generates a 500-character response, with 4-second response time and 1.5-second processing time needed. The line time allowed is 2.5 seconds. The system, then, must transmit 510 characters in 2.5 seconds, or 204 characters per second. This equates to 2040 bps, necessitating a 2400-bps line. This is hereafter referred to as transaction Type 3.

Response Time: Catalog Store Transactions. The catalog store transaction calculation was done in Chapter 2, where it was determined that 600 characters had to be transmitted in 2.5 seconds, for 240 characters per second or 2400 bps. This is hereafter called transaction Type 4. Overall, then, considering individual terminal response time only, a 2400-bps line will be adequate.

Aggregate Data Transmission Rate. In determining the aggregate data rate for Syncrasy's lines we can start with the line from Kansas City to Chicago, which must support five terminals in Chicago, eight catalog store terminals in New York City, five store terminals in New York City, and three store terminals in Atlanta. Computation of the aggregate data rate must also consider the peak transaction load. Figure 5-26 contains all of the pertinent information for this analysis.

In Figure 5-26, the Chicago Type 1 transactions have been separated from the East Coast Type 1 transactions. Since peak transaction rates occur during specific hours and the East Coast cities—New York City and Atlanta—are in a different time zone from Chicago, the worst condition of peak traffic on the East Coast has been assumed, for 40 transactions per hour; average load has been assumed for Chicago. Also, of the 40 transactions, 30% are of transaction Type 2. Thus, there are 28 Type 1 transac-

Transaction Type (Location)	Number of Transactions per Hour	Number of Characters per Transaction	Number of Terminals	Total Number of Characters per Hour	
1 (East Coast)	28	152	8	34,048	
1 (Chicago)	21	152	5	15,960	
2 (East Coast)	12	162	8	15,552	
2 (Chicago)	9	162	5	7,290	
3 (both)	10	510	13	66,330	
4 (mail order)	30	600	8	144,000	
			Total	283,150	

Figure 5-26 Transaction Analysis

tions and 12 Type 2 transactions per hour on the East Coast and 21 Type 1 transactions and 9 Type 2 transactions in Chicago. The total 283,150 characters transmitted per hour is the product of the number of terminals, the number of transactions per terminal, and the number of characters per transaction, as indicated in the last column of Figure 5-26.

An aggregate data rate of 283,150 characters per hour equates to approximately 78 characters per second, which is derived by dividing the number of characters per hour by 3600 seconds per hour. These calculations indicate that a 1200-bps line is sufficient to support the aggregate data rate. Thus far, response time is the dominant factor with respect to line speed.

Line Contention.   As discussed in Chapter 2, a 2400-bps line is adequate in a point-to-point environment, although not if two terminals attempt to start a transaction at the same time. If a random transaction arrival rate is assumed, the following formula (from queuing theory) may be used to determine the probability of several transactions arriving within the same interval.

$$P_k(T) = \frac{(LT)^k}{k!} \times e^{-LT} \quad \text{for } K = 0, 1, 2, 3, \ldots$$

where

$P_k(T)$ is the probability that k transactions will arrive in interval T

L is the average number of transactions per unit of time

T is the interval being considered

e is the natural base for logarithms

k is the number of arrivals

!   is the factorial function

In this transaction environment there is a total of 840 transactions per hour, which is derived by summing the products of the number of transactions per hour and the number of terminals performing that transaction rate, as shown in Figure 5-26. This results in an average of 0.23 transactions per second (840 divided by 3600). Thus, L in the formula is 0.23. Assuming an interval T of 5 seconds, which is the time for the longest transaction and which is actually more conservative than necessary, the probability of two transactions arriving within a given 5-second interval is:

$$P_2(5) = \frac{(0.23 \times 5)^2}{2!} \times e^{-(0.23 \times 5)}$$

$$= \frac{1.15^2}{2} \times e^{-1.15} = 0.21$$

The complete probability table is given in Figure 5-27, from which it can be determined that the probability of two or more transactions arriving in any 5-second interval is:

$$0.21 + 0.08 + 0.02 + 0.005 = 0.325$$

Thus, 33% of the time two or more transactions will be active in a 5-second time span. Doubling the line speed will allow two transactions within 5 seconds to meet the expected response time. The probability then becomes only 0.10, or 10%, that transactions will contend with each other (the probability that three or more transactions will arrive within 5 seconds). As stated above, a 5-second interval is actually quite conservative, since it is not entirely devoted to line time, the element of interest. During the 5-second interval, for a given transaction, the line will be idle approximately 50% of the time at a speed of 2400 bps. Increasing the line speed to 4800 bps should adequately eliminate slow response time due to contention.

Configuring the System: East Coast.   It would be most economical to use a short route-line configuration with cascading statistical multiplexers. If the configuration follows a path from Kansas City to Chicago, then from Chicago to New York City and Atlanta, and finally from New York City catalog store to New York City discount store, as shown in Figure 5-28, by the time the extremities have been reached, a stat mux is likely to have run out of capacity. Each time a line is dropped off, the speed generally steps down. In addition, cascading multiplexers down by five levels will likely result in performance problems. Another problem is the number of terminals in New York City that must be accounted for. Since smart terminals that require some degree of screen handling are being used, a concentrator in Chicago will provide a significant capability to the network, as follows:

Allows terminals to be polled from Chicago rather than Kansas City

Provides for later expansion

Figure 5-27   Transaction Arrival Probabilities

Number of Arrivals	Probability
2	0.21
3	0.08
4	0.02
5	0.005

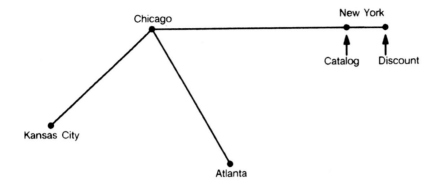

Figure 5-28 Syncrasy East Coast Network

Allows for more local terminal and error handling

Can provide some local support if the path to Kansas City is malfunctioning

Makes for a more workable configuration than extensive cascading of muxes

Can support higher speed circuits to the East Coast

Configuring the System: West Coast. A different configuration can be used for the West Coast link to Los Angeles and San Francisco: a direct link to Los Angeles and two separate drops—five terminals to the discount stores in Los Angeles and three to San Francisco. This contrasts with the link from Chicago to New York City, which involves 18 terminals. Cascading muxes are feasible for the West Coast. For the Houston link, a simple four-port statistical multiplexer on a 4800-bps line can be used. The final configuration is given in Figure 5-29.

Final Costs

The final monthly costs are summarized on the following pages, broken down into branches of the network.

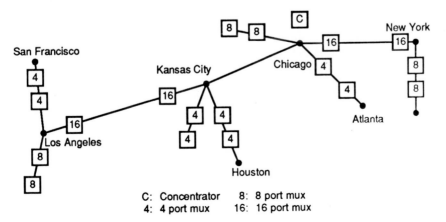

Figure 5-29 Syncrasy Configuration

Monthly Equipment Cost for the Kansas City, Chicago, New York City, and Atlanta Branches of the Network

Multiplexers

2	16-port muxes at $358 each	$ 716
4	8-port muxes at $225 each	900
2	4-port muxes at $150 each	300

Modems—purchased or integrated with muxes

Terminals

11 smart terminals at $105 each   1155
(Note: Two were available from the mail-order store.)

Concentrator

1 at $1500   1500

Subtotal $4571

Monthly Equipment Cost for the Kansas City to Kansas City Branch of the Network

Multiplexers

2	4-port muxes at $150 each	$ 300

Modems—purchased or integrated with muxes

Terminals

1 smart terminal at $105   105
(Note: Two terminals were available from the mail-order store.)

Subtotal $ 405

Monthly Equipment Cost for the Kansas City to Houston Branch of the Network

Multiplexers

2	4-port muxes at $150 each	$ 300

Terminals

3	smart terminals at $105 each	315

Subtotal $ 615

Monthly Equipment Cost for the Kansas City to Los Angeles to San Francisco Branches of the Network

Multiplexers

2	16-port muxes at $358 each	$ 716
2	8-port muxes at $225 each	450
2	4-port muxes at $150 each	300

Modems—purchased or integrated with muxes

Terminals

6	smart terminals at $105 each	630

(Note: Two were available from the mail-order store.)

Subtotal $2096

Total Monthly Costs for the Network

Total equipment	$ 7687
Total long-distance line costs	5203
Total local line costs	352
Total network costs	$13,242

Syncrasy will have to sell a lot of equipment to support this $13,242-per-month configuration. Another alternative exists, however: attaching to a packet distribution network (PDN). PDNs are discussed in Chapter 10. Because the amount of data being transmitted is relatively small and PDNs charge by the number of packets and not by connect time, the overall cost could be lower.

SUMMARY

Many alternatives are available when configuring a data communications system. The hardware components—multiplexers, concentrators, and front end processors—overlap in the functions they can provide. These components can reduce circuit costs significantly; they can also make more efficient use of the circuits and reduce some of the processing load of the hosts. Configuration modeling tools, which have been designed for telephone company or similar common carrier lines, are available to help system designers select the lowest cost or most efficient communications lines. A wide variety of protocol conversion equipment is available to enable different manufacturers' terminals to interface with host equipment. Such conversion equipment can protect a user's investment in terminals. Because errors can be encountered in connecting data terminal equipment to data communications networks, diagnostic tools are necessary. If properly used, these tools can reduce the time and effort in tracking down such problems.

Key Terms

auto-call unit (ACU)
bit interleaving
breakout box
byte interleaving
call-back unit
cascading
character interleaving
cluster controller
communications controller
concentrator
contention
daisy chain
data encryption standard (DES)

facsimile (fax)
file server
frequency division multiplexer (FDM)
front end processor (FEP)
guardbands
IBM 3704, 3705, 3725, 3745
inverse multiplexer
line monitor
matrix switch
multiplexer (mux)
multiport modem
network control program (NCP)

packet assembly/disassembly
  (PAD)
port concentrator
port selector
printer server
private branch exchange (PBX)

protocol converter
statistical time division multiplexer
  (STDM)
terminal server
time division multiplexer (TDM)
X.3 PAD

Review Questions

1. In general, how does a multiplexer work?
2. Describe frequency division multiplexing (FDM).
3. Describe time division multiplexing (TDM).
4. Describe statistical time division multiplexing (STDM).
5. Describe inverse multiplexing and give an example of its use.
6. How does a concentrator differ from a multiplexer? How are they similar?
7. Compare and contrast a front end processor and a concentrator.
8. What functions are performed by a protocol converter?
9. What advantages are afforded by protocol converters?
10. Who typically uses a digital line monitor and for what purpose?
11. What does an analog line monitor do?
12. What does a breakout box do?
13. Compare and contrast a port concentrator and a data switch.
14. What does a file server do?
15. Compare and contrast a file server and an SQL server.
16. What does a network interface card (NIC) do?

Exercises

1. Are there any situations in which an FDM is preferable to a stat mux? If so, what are they?
2. Give some examples in which multi-point configurations would be preferable to statistical multiplexing. Give an example where the opposite is true.
3. The costs of terminals and multiplexers are constantly changing. Research the literature and find current prices for these components. Are the prices more, less, or about the same as those given in the book?
4. Describe a situation in which a front end processor would be more desirable than a concentrator. Describe a situation in which a concentrator would be preferable to a front end processor.
5. What is the lowest cost communications configuration that will link each of the cities in the mileage chart below? Use the line costs presented in the case study.

	Cleveland	Houston	Las Vegas	Phoenix	Portland	San Diego	Washington, D.C.
Boston	657	1830	2752	2670	3144	2984	448
Cleveland		1306	2093	2032	2432	2385	360
Houston			1467	1164	2243	1490	1365
Las Vegas				285	996	336	2420
Phoenix					1268	353	2300
Portland						1086	2784
San Diego							2602

6. If Houston is the central location, what is the cost of a network connecting Houston to each of the cities in Exercise 5 via point-to-point links?

7. What line speed would be required to provide a 5-second response time for a transaction that transmits 600 characters of information and receives a response of 350 characters? Assume a processing time of 2 seconds and 10 bits per character.

References

Digital Equipment Corporation. *Introduction to Local Area Networks.* Bedford, MA: Digital Equipment Corporation, 1982.

Edwards, Morris. "Modem and Multiplexer Update: Compact and Cheaper." *Infosystems,* November 1981.

Forney, G. David, and Robert W. Stearns. "Statistical Multiplexing Improves Link Utilization." *Executive Guide to Data Communications,* 2nd ed. New York: McGraw-Hill, undated.

Guy, Kenneth R. "Stat Muxes Help Managers Reduce Data Comm Costs." *Government Computer News,* June 1983.

Harper, William L., and Robert C. Pollard. *Data Communications Desk Book: A Systems Analysis Approach.* Englewood Cliffs, NJ: Prentice-Hall, 1982.

Held, Gilbert. *Data Communication Components, Characteristics, Operation, Applications.* Rochelle Park, NJ: Hayden Book Co., 1979.

————. "Inverse Multiplexing with Multiport Modems." *Executive Guide to Data Communications,* 2nd ed. New York: McGraw-Hill, undated.

Kelley, Neil D. "Modems, Multiplexers and Concentrators: Diagnostics and Control Are Key." *Infosystems,* June 1980.

Miller, Frederick W. "Business Rides Networks on Mux/Modem Links." *Infosystems,* May 1982.

Riviere, Charles J., and Richard A. Cooper. "How Concentrators Can Be Message Switchers as Well." *Executive Guide to Data Communications,* 2nd ed. New York: McGraw-Hill, undated.

Sudan, Lee. "Mux Ado about Multiplexers." *Computerworld on Communications* 18 (May 2, 1984).

Vacca, John. "Front End Processors." *Computerworld on Communications* 18 (May 2, 1984).

DATA LINK

III

DATA LINK PROTOCOLS: THE DATA LINK LAYER

1. Data Link Protocols

Data Link Protocols

The Data Link Layer
Asynchronous Transmission
Synchronous Transmission
Character Synchronous Protocols
Byte Count Synchronous Protocols
Bit Synchronous Protocols
Carrier Sense Multiple Access with Collision Detection
(CSMA/CD) Protocol
Token Passing Protocols
Choosing a Data Link Protocol

INTRODUCTION

In this chapter we move to the data link layer in the OSI reference model and examine data link protocols. Asynchronous and synchronous transmission are emphasized. Topics covered in this chapter include:

Functions of the data link layer

Asynchronous transmission protocol

Byte synchronous transmission protocols

Bit synchronous transmission protocols

Token passing protocol

Contention bus protocol

At the conclusion of this chapter, you will be familiar with the functions of a data link protocol, the criteria used to evaluate the effectiveness of a data link protocol, and various types of data link protocols.

THE DATA LINK LAYER

You may recall from Chapter 1 that the functions of the data link layer are to establish and control the physical link between a computer and either a terminal or another computer. Suppose that a physical connection has been made between the two computing devices Device A and Device B. Before Device A can transmit data to Device B, Device A must gain control of the link. There are a variety of protocols for accomplishing this, and you will read about several of them in this chapter. Once a device has the right to transfer data (has control of the link), it must transmit the data in a way that is understandable to the receiving device. The receiving device must be able to tell where the data portion of the message begins and ends, and there ought to be a way to detect if errors have occurred during transmission. In this chapter, we examine the primary methods for effecting these objectives.

Objectives of Transmission Protocols

To move data from one point to another, sender and receiver must agree on a *transmission protocol* or *convention*. Protocols should have the following functions: delineation of data, error detection, contention control, transparency, addressing capability, permitting code independence, allowing multiple configurations, efficiency, and permitting system growth.

Delineation of Data.   Transmission of data includes not only message data but also control information and (almost always) error detection information. For receiving stations to discern which is which, the protocol must enable receivers to determine where the data portion of the message begins and ends, where the control portions of the message are and what they mean, and where the error control bits are. Several techniques are used to delineate data. A technique called framing *frames* the data with special begin-of-text and end-of-text characters. This technique is sometimes referred to as *enveloping*. Another technique, called *positional delineation*, relies on the message adhering to a fixed format. The beginning and end of the data are apparent from the relative *position* of fields on the message. The framing method of data delineation is illustrated in Figure 6-1(a).

Error Detection.   Data link protocols generate, append, and forward error detection codes. (Error detection algorithms are discussed in Chapter 3.) Protocols differ with respect to the specifics of their error detection algorithms and with respect to where in the message the error codes are placed. The error detection function is depicted in Figure 6-1(b).

Contention Control.   Data link protocols must establish the circumstances under which a station can transmit and receive data. If two or more sta-

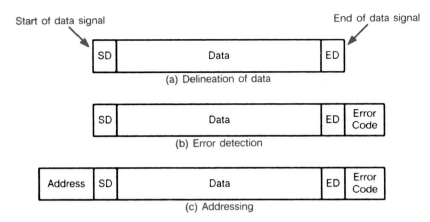

Figure 6-1 Some Data Link Functions

tions can transmit at once and thus possibly interfere with one another, the protocol must detect this situation and recover from it.

Transparency.   Transparency refers to the ability to transmit any bit pattern as data and have it accepted correctly. This may sound trivial, but it is not. For example, an EOT character may represent end-of-text and an STX character may represent the start-of-text, to delineate data. If special control characters are to be sent as data, the data link protocol must not interpret them as control characters. The transparency issue usually arises when data is transmitted between processors using a protocol designed for terminals or for displayable data. Interprocessor communications include transfer of binary files such as object code and data files containing binary number fields; transparency allows these binary fields, including characters ordinarily reserved for control purposes, to be accepted as data.

Addressing Capability.   For multiple stations to share a circuit, the data link protocol must enable a device address to be appended to the message. Each addressable device in turn must know where in the message the address appears—usually at or near the beginning. Addressing is shown in Figure 6-1(c).

Code Independence.   *Code independence* means the ability to successfully transmit data with any coding scheme, such as ASCII, EBCDIC, Baudot, or the like. Code independence enables two different devices—for instance, one that uses ASCII and one that uses EBCDIC—to share a line. As with addressing, code independence is not a strict data link requirement but is a desirable characteristic. Some of the protocols examined later in this chapter provide no code independence, although higher level data link protocols usually do.

Allow Multiple Configurations.   Multiple configuration capability enables the system designer to plan a network topology or layout that is

Figure 6-2 Multiple
Configurations

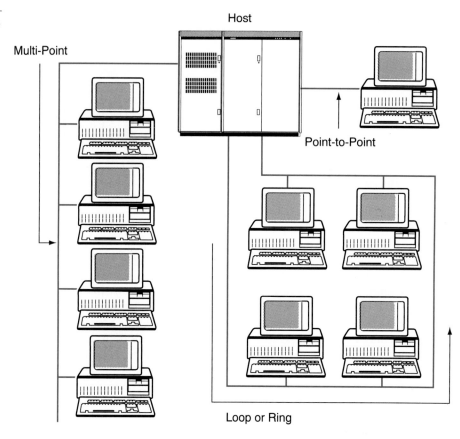

consistent with the application and that takes full advantage of the capabilities of the devices being used. In some protocols, only point-to-point or multi-point configurations are allowed. Alternatives such as *loop* or *hierarchical topologies* may also be supported, as can be seen from Figure 6-2.

Efficiency.   A protocol with very little overhead is desirable. Overhead refers to the number of additional characters or bits that must be appended to the message to meet the previously defined objectives. An efficient protocol allows more channel capacity to be devoted to carrying data.

Permit System Growth.   As new hardware components are designed and as features are added to old hardware, the data link protocol should be capable of supporting them. In addition, as the configuration itself expands with additional terminals or hosts, the protocol must not limit this growth. If the address field contains only eight bits of information, then growth would be limited to 256 distinct devices on that communications line.

ASYNCHRONOUS TRANSMISSION

Asynchronous (*async*) data link control is the oldest and one of the most common data link protocols. Like many of the techniques used in data communications, it is derived from the telegraph and telephone industries. *Asynchronous* is defined by *Webster's New World Dictionary* as "lack of synchronism; failure to occur at the same time." In asynchronous transmission, data are transmitted one character at a time, and sender and receiver are not synchronized with each other. The sender is thus able to transmit a character at any time. The receiver must be prepared to recognize that information is arriving, accept the data, possibly check for errors, and print, display, or store the data in memory. In addition, individual characters can be separated over different time intervals, meaning no synchronization exists between individual transmitted characters.

Most dumb terminals are async devices, and many smart and intelligent terminals can also communicate asynchronously. Many personal computers use async transmission to communicate with each other and with host systems. Async transmission is also referred to as a *start-stop protocol*. This term and the terms *mark*—which is the equivalent of a 1 bit— and *space*—which is equivalent to a 0 bit—are holdovers from telegraphy. Start-stop terminology derives from the fact that each character is framed by a start bit and a stop bit, as illustrated in Figure 6-3.

Compatibility of Sending and Receiving Stations

A communications link is either idling or transmitting data. In the idle state, an async line is held in the mark condition, which is continuous 1 bits. When establishing the communications link, the sending and receiving stations must agree on the number of bits per character. If parity is to be transmitted for error detection, both stations must agree on either even or odd parity and on whether the parity bit is to be checked. (The parity bit could be transmitted but not checked by the data link software or hardware.) Third, the stations must also agree on a transmission speed, because this determines the interval at which the line is sampled (see

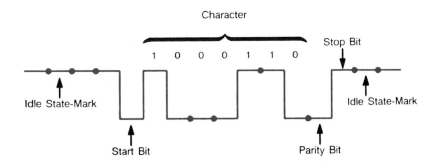

Figure 6-3
Asynchronous
Transmission of
the Character *F*

Appendix A). Finally, there must be agreement as to what will terminate the message. Usually, a message terminator is a defined set of characters called *interrupt characters*, a count of a specific number of characters, or a time-out interval. For the following discussion we assume that sending and receiving stations are the same with respect to the number of bits sent per character, parity, message termination, and maximum speed of the link (detected by the receiving modem). The line is in the idle state, meaning that a continuous stream of 1 bits is being transmitted. There are seven data bits and one parity bit, and odd parity will be checked.

Initial Transmission

A character's arrival is signaled by a start bit, which is a change in the state of the line from a mark to a space, or a 0 bit. Following the start bit are seven data bits, one parity bit, and a stop bit, which is a return to a 1 bit, or mark condition. If parity does not check or if the tenth bit is not a 1, it is assumed that an error has occurred. How checking for start, stop, data, and parity bits is physically accomplished is described in Appendix A. The ASCII representation for the character *F* is 1000110; the async representation for transmitting this character is given in Figure 6-3.

Transmission Termination

After transmitting a character, the line goes back to the idle state until the next start bit is encountered.

Interrupt Characters.   If *interrupt characters* are being used to end transmission, each character received must be examined to determine if it matches one of these characters. If it does, the message is considered complete and is delivered to the application for which it was intended. This is the usual way async communications are completed. On terminals, the character that is transmitted when the operator presses the Return key—usually a carriage return character— is frequently one of these termination characters. Other interrupt characters also can be specified.

Character Count.   *Character count termination* is used when the number of characters transmitted is large or when receiving data from a device that transmits continuously without sending termination characters. For example, some news wire services send large amounts of text for a story without including message termination characters. The receiving computer must be capable of accepting the entire story regardless of its length. Since the message is received by the computer into a buffer that may be smaller than the entire message, a character count termination allows the computer to save the data in blocks and avoid buffer overflow.

With character count termination, a read is posted on the communications line for a specific number of characters. When that number of characters has been received, the transmission is considered completed, and the data is delivered to the application. With this type of termination, it is the application's responsibility to make sense of the message, which includes determining the end of the transmission. With manned terminals, character count termination usually is used only for entering fixed-length data fields. Interactive questions with one-character answers often use this technique. Character count termination may be used with the other termination methods. With a continuous stream of data on the line as described above, another problem, buffer overflow, can occur.

Double Buffering.   *Buffer overflow,* or *overrun,* can arise when the data block being transmitted is larger than the receiving buffer area or when data from a subsequent block is received before the previous block's data has been emptied from the buffer. In such cases, there is no place to store the arriving characters, and they are lost. Frequently in such instances the data link protocol uses a technique known as *double buffering* to avoid losing characters.

Double buffering means there are two (or more) input buffers capable of receiving data. The buffers are alternated: When one buffer is filled, new incoming characters are stored in the alternate buffer. While an alternate buffer is being used, data in the full buffer can be passed to the application and that buffer made available for receiving new data. For example, double buffering might be used when transmitting data from a microcomputer's disk to the host. Such data may form a continuous character stream that can arrive at any time at nearly maximum data link speed and in variable-length blocks. With single buffering, the receiving computer may not be fast enough to empty its buffer and be ready to accept the next arriving characters.

Time-Out Interval.   Another termination mechanism is the *time-out interval.* This method is effective with a character count or when data is received from sensor-based or laboratory equipment. In the laboratory situation, a long interval between data arrival means the entire data stream has arrived or the equipment is out of order. In conjunction with character count, the time-out interval is beneficial when the size of a message can vary. Suppose that the termination character count is 100 and the message is 350 characters. If only character count termination is used, the first 300 characters would be received routinely in three data groups but the last 50 characters would be held in the buffer until it was filled, which would only occur when the next message is sent. A time-out termination prevents unnecessary delays in completing such a message. The time-out interval is not a good terminator for data being input by an operator, however: If the operator takes a break in the midst of input, a time-out interval would prematurely terminate the message.

Effectiveness of Asynchronous Transmission

The following rating of asynchronous transmission with respect to the data link objectives described earlier uses a three-level grading system— poor, adequate, and good. The data delineation and contention control objectives are not rated, since they are both essential functions; exactly how they are implemented, however, can influence the effectiveness rating.

Error Detection.   Recall from Chapter 3 that a common type of data transmission errors is an impulse error. Impulse errors can disrupt several bits. A parity check can detect only 50% of such errors (those in which an odd number of bits is affected). Therefore, parity checking alone is not an effective error detection scheme. In asynchronous transmission, it is also possible to append a longitudinal redundancy check (LRC) or cyclic redundancy check (CRC) block check character (BCC), but this is seldom done. The performance is poor.

Transparency.   The use of interrupt characters precludes transparency because the interrupt characters cannot be sent as data (unless special accommodation is made—see the discussion of binary synchronous transparency in Appendix B). Transparency can be achieved, however, with either character count termination or time-out termination. The performance is adequate, but use of transparency requires giving up part of the protocol: the ability to use interrupt characters. Transparency normally is not an issue in async transmission because transmission is either to or from display devices like terminals and printers. Most data transmitted to or from these devices is displayable characters that do not conflict with the interrupt characters.

Addressing.   Asynchronous transmission has no limitations with respect to addressing. The size of the address fields can be very large, allowing flexibility regarding station addressing. The performance is good.

Code Independence.   There is no code independence with asynchronous transmission. There must be agreement on the exact number of bits per character before communication. This limits the codes that can be used. If, for example, a seven-bit character size is used, an eight-bit code is precluded. Note that an eight-bit code could be divided and transmitted in two separate seven-bit entities, but this seldom is done. The performance is poor.

Configurations.   Often, asynchronous transmission configurations are either point-to-point or multi-point; however, no inherent restrictions in the protocol would inhibit the use of other configurations. A few local area network implementations use asynchronous protocols on ring and bus configurations. Performance is adequate.

Efficiency. In the earlier example, ten bits were transmitted for seven bits of data, making the overhead 30% for async transmission, which is high. In addition, transmission speed is limited. Performance is poor.

Growth. The ability to support growth is related to the functions described earlier—addressability, efficiency, transparency, support for multiple configurations, code independence, and so on. Asynchronous protocols are restricted with respect to several of these functions. Compared to newer data link protocols, the performance is poor.

Why Asynchronous Transmission Is So Popular

Despite the poor rating just given asynchronous transmission, it remains one of the most common data link protocols for several reasons. Async was the first protocol, and for several years it was the only way to transmit data. Consequently, many terminals and controller boards were designed for async operation. Thus, async technology is well developed, and a wide variety of hardware options is available at a relatively low price. Async also is very well suited to many types of applications. People performing data entry in a conversational mode or even in block mode operate at speeds compatible with async protocol. The primary penalty paid with async is its inefficient use of the circuit.

SYNCHRONOUS TRANSMISSION

Synchronous data link protocols can be divided into three groups: character oriented, byte count oriented, and bit oriented. The last is the newest technology and the basis for many data communications systems. With synchronous transmission, sender and receiver are synchronized with each other. Synchronous modems contain clocks that are set to the same time by a bit pattern transmitted at the beginning of a message. For long messages these *sync patterns* are periodically inserted within the text to ensure that the modem clocks remain synchronized. Synchronized clocks are one feature that separates asynchronous modems from synchronous ones; although there is a clocking function in async transmission, the clocks are not synchronized. The clocks on asynchronous modems are used to pace the bits onto the line on the sending side and to sample the line when awaiting data on the receiving side. Once data starts arriving, the sampling rate is adjusted to the pace of the arriving characters so the characters can be recognized (see Appendix A). Another difference between asynchronous and synchronous transmission is that instead of transmitting character by character, synchronous transmission involves sending a block of characters at a time. Block transmission means the sending and receiving modems must be in sync with each other; failure to remain synchronized results

Figure 6-4
Asynchronous vs.
Synchronous
Transmission

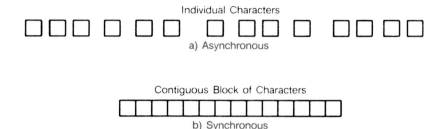

in lost data. Figure 6-4 graphically illustrates some of the differences between asynchronous and synchronous transmission; the differences are summarized in Figure 6-15, at the end of this section.

CHARACTER SYNCHRONOUS PROTOCOLS

Framing Versus Positional Protocols

Some synchronous protocols are positional, whereas others use a framing technique.

Framing Protocols.   These protocols use reserved characters or bit patterns to delineate data and control fields within the message. For a message that contains both a header and data fields, a *framing protocol* would use a special control character to indicate the start of the header, another control character to indicate the start of the data field, and a third control character to designate the end of the data field. This is illustrated in Figure 6-5. Other framed messages between the same sender and receiver could be in a completely different format. For example, the header field could be omitted.

Positional Protocols.   These protocols delineate fields by the use of fixed-length fields on the message (except perhaps on the data field); by indicating the size of the message with a character count embedded in the message; or both. A fixed-message format used in the Ethernet local area network is illustrated in Figure 6-17. All fields except the data field are a specific length and at a specific location within the message. The end of the message is indicated by dropping the carrier signal on the medium.

Figure 6-5 Framing for a Character Synchronous Message

Start of Header Character	Header	Start of Text Character	Message	End of Text Character

Neither framing characters nor character counts are used to define where address fields and data begin. The first 64 bits are always the preamble field; the next 48, the destination address; and so on. All messages in Ethernet adhere to this fixed format.

Byte count protocols delineate data by including the number of characters being transmitted within the message. If the number of characters being transmitted is placed in the first 16 bits of the message, a character count together with a fixed-format message enables the protocol to define the message components. The character count is used not only to identify the end of the message but also to allow the message to be decomposed into its constituent parts: address, data, block check character, and so on. Consider the message format in Figure 6-10. The first 16 bits contain the character count of the data portion. All messages will consist of the character count, the destination address, data, and a 16-bit cyclic redundancy check (CRC). Once the character count is known, the location of the CRC can be determined. The start of the message field is determined from the fixed format of the message.

Character synchronous protocols differ from byte count synchronous and bit synchronous protocols in that character synchronous message control is oriented toward specific transmission codes and specific characters within those codes. For example, in ASCII code (see Chapter 3), a specific character (STX) is used as a control character to indicate the start of text or message. Other types of data may be transmitted before the text, such as a message header. In bit-oriented protocols, specific characters have not been defined to perform these control functions.

Standards for Character Synchronous Protocols

There are both corporate and national standards that specify how character synchronous protocols are to be implemented. National standards include American National Standards Institute (ANSI) standards X3.1, X3.24, X3.28, and X3.36, all of which pertain to various aspects of character synchronous transmission. The IBM *binary synchronous communications (BSC or BISYNC) protocol* has become a de facto industry standard communications protocol that is supported by many manufacturers. Because it is so common, BISYNC is used as a model of character synchronous protocols in the following discussion. More details on binary synchronous transmission can be found in Appendix B.

Binary Synchronous Protocol: BISYNC

BISYNC was introduced by IBM in 1967 as the data link protocol for remote job entry, using the 2780 workstation. Since that time it has come to be used in many other applications and with many other devices. Only three data codes are supported by BISYNC: 6-bit transcode (SBT), ASCII, and EBCDIC. Technically, there is no reason that other codes could not be used. (SBT is an old code whose current use is minimal.) To synchronize sending and receiving modems, one or more synchronization characters are transmitted at the beginning of each transmission block. The receiving modem uses this bit pattern to establish timing and get in step with the sender. To maintain timing for long transmission blocks, additional sync characters are inserted at regular intervals. The number of sync characters required depends on the equipment being used, although two or three is the usual number. Figure 6-6 depicts a message with BISYNC control characters for *synchronization (SYN)*, the *start of text (STX)*, and the *end of text (ETX)*. BISYNC supports both point-to-point and multipoint configurations.

Point-to-Point Mode.   In the point-to-point mode, contention is used to determine which station is granted the right to transmit, which means both devices on the communications link are considered equal. To transmit a message, a station must gain control of the link, usually by issuing a bid for the line. If the other station is ready to receive messages, it grants control of the link to the requesting station. If both stations simultaneously issue a bid, some resolution mechanism is required. For example, each station could generate a random delay interval before retrying the bid, making it unlikely that both would issue another bid at exactly the same time. Another alternative is for both to agree ahead of time on which station has priority in case of simultaneous bidding. Short, one-character sequences are used to bid for the line. Point-to-point connections can be established via either switched lines or leased lines. Line bidding and data exchange sequences are illustrated in Figure 6-7.

Multi-Point Mode.   In the multi-point environment, one station is designated as supervisor and the others are tributary or secondary stations. The supervisor is aware of all stations on the line; secondary stations essentially see a point-to-point connection with the supervisor. The supervisor maintains absolute control over the link; secondary stations remain passive and monitor the link. Secondaries may transmit only when permitted

Figure 6-6 BISYNC
Control Characters

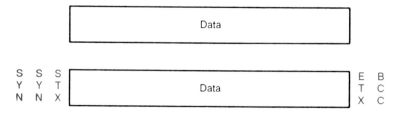

	SYN	Synchronization character
	STX	Start of text character
	ETX	End of text character
	BCC	Block check character—LRC or CRC

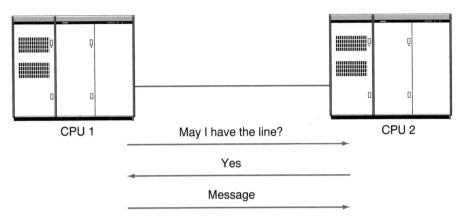

Figure 6-7 Line Bidding (Contention Mode)

to do so by the supervisor. Thus, all data transfers are initiated by the supervisor. Up to seven characters are allowed for addressing, providing for an extremely wide range of addresses (more than 100 billion different addresses are possible if only 40 different characters are used). All transfers of data are between the supervisor and the secondary stations. The protocol does not allow for direct transfer of data between secondary stations. Polling sequences are relatively short, usually consisting of the sync characters, the station address, and a one-character control sequence. Polling is illustrated in Figure 6-8.

Message Control. Each transmitted block can have an optional header field for message control that designates such things as routing information, priority, and message type (IBM, 1970). The beginning and end of text are identified by framing the data with control characters. For instance, an STX character signals that the data portion of the text is starting. One of several characters—such as ETX, ETB, or EOT—can be used to identify the end of a block of data, depending on whether an intermediate or final block is being transmitted. Lengthy messages ordinarily are broken into segments or blocks. The ETB control character designates the end of the transmission block; ETX signals the end of the text; and EOT means end of transmission. If a message were broken into four different transmission blocks, the first three blocks would terminate with the ETB control character and the last would terminate with the EOT character.

Transparency. Transparent transmission with BISYNC is rather cumbersome, involving the insertion of extra characters in the message. Appendix B includes a detailed discussion of the implementation. The original version of BISYNC was used for RJE. Because RJE was used to transmit card and printer images containing only displayable characters, transparent data transmission was unnecessary. Subsequent uses of BISYNC, however, such as file transfer between computers, created a need for transparent transmission. The implementation is workable but inelegant.

Figure 6-8 Polling
Example

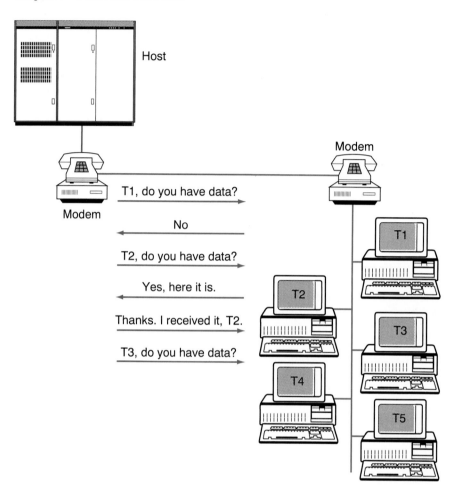

Error Control.   Error control is either CRC or LRC with VRC. CRC is used
with EBCDIC, with SBT, and with ASCII when ASCII is configured for
transparency. LRC and VRC are used with nontransparent ASCII.

BISYNC's Half Duplex Nature.   One limitation of BISYNC is that it is essentially a half duplex protocol, so each message transmitted must be
acknowledged by the receiver before the next message can be sent. This is
not a major concern for many applications, especially those involving terminal data entry, for which the amount of time required to acknowledge
is small compared with the speed of data submission. For host-to-host
communications, on the other hand, half duplex can be quite restrictive.
Consider a file transmitted between two processors: It would be efficient
for the sender to transmit several blocks before requiring an acknowledgment and for the acknowledgment to be transmitted in parallel with
the data, as would occur in full duplex mode. Unfortunately, the only

benefit to using BISYNC on a full duplex line is that it eliminates modem turnaround time.

The half duplex nature of the BISYNC protocol is also inefficient in conversational applications. A session to prompt a user for an employee's last name on a point-to-point connection would work as indicated in Figure 6-9. To overcome this problem, there is now a limited conversational mode that allows the receiver to acknowledge receipt of a message and send data at the same time. Another extension allows multiple blocks to be transmitted without individual acknowledgment, acknowledgment being made once for the entire group of blocks.

Effectiveness of the BISYNC Protocol

Error Detection. When CRC is used, BISYNC error detection is quite good. But CRC is not supported in every instance. The alternative of LRC and VRC is adequate. The performance is adequate to good.

Transparency. Transparency is possible but not cleanly implemented with BISYNC. Extra character insertion increases the overhead of the protocol. The performance is adequate.

Addressing. A wide range of BISYNC addresses is possible, from one to seven characters in length. The number of available addresses resulting from a seven-character address is large and provides considerable flexibility in address selection. The performance is good.

Code Independence. There is no code independence with BISYNC because only three codes—SBT, ASCII, and EBCDIC—are supported. It is not possible to use other codes nor to convert from one of the supported codes to another. The performance is poor.

Configurations. BISYNC configurations are essentially limited to multipoint and point-to-point modes on switched or leased lines. The performance is adequate.

Host		Terminal
May I have the line?	⟶	
	⟵	Yes.
Transmit: What is the Last Name?	⟶	
	⟵	I got your message
	⟵	May I have the line?
Yes.	⟶	
	⟵	Johnson
I got your message.	⟶	

Figure 6-9 Line Bidding and Conversational Exchange

Efficiency.   BISYNC is quite efficient with respect to the number of control characters required to transmit a message. If messages are very short, the amount of overhead is more significant than when messages are lengthy. This is because a fixed number of control characters must be transmitted regardless of the text length. Thus, when the text is short, the ratio of control characters to text characters is larger than when the text is long. Contrast this with the asynchronous case, where the number of control bits is directly proportional to the number of characters transmitted. The performance is good except in those applications where full duplex operations could be used or where the half duplex nature of the protocol impedes progress.

Growth.   BISYNC configurations are limited to multi-point and point-to-point configurations. This restricts the protocol's ability to support new configurations. Moreover, the lack of code independence might impede BISYNC's ability to accommodate emerging technologies. The performance is adequate.

BYTE COUNT SYNCHRONOUS PROTOCOLS

Byte count synchronous protocols are character oriented. The difference between them and BISYNC lies in how they signal the beginning and end of messages. They are called byte count protocols because the number of characters in the message is given in a required message header, as illustrated in Figure 6-10. The header is a fixed length, and the data field is variable length. One advantage of byte count protocols is that they are transparent. With the byte count provided, it is obvious where the message begins and ends: The header is a fixed length, such as x characters long. Therefore, the beginning of the data is x characters from the beginning of the message; the data spans the byte-count number of characters; and following that may be a block check character or CRC characters. Since there is no need to scan the input stream for termination characters, any bit pattern can be represented witin the data stream.

Message Sequence Numbers

Some implementations of byte count protocols also include *message sequence numbers*. Each transmitted message is given a number, in order,

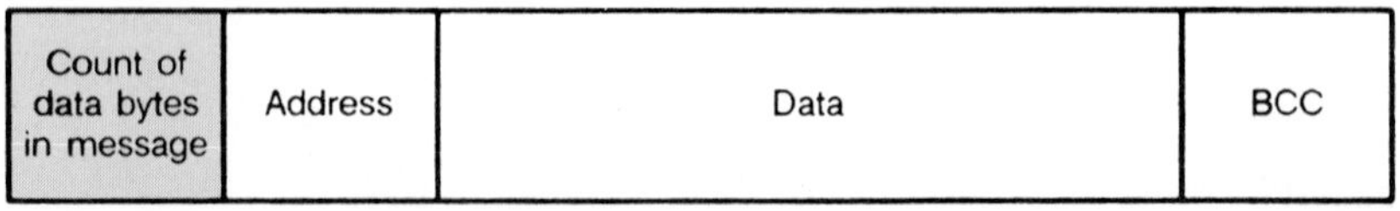

Figure 6-10 A Byte Count Message Format

Count of data bytes in message	Address	Data	BCC

thus allowing multiple messages to be transmitted without any acknowledgment. If three bits are used for sequencing messages, eight different sequence numbers—0 through 7—can be generated; when the count reaches 7, the next number assigned is 0. This allows up to eight messages to be transmitted before being acknowledged. The ability to send multiple messages without an acknowledgment can save a significant amount of time, especially on slower links or links with a high modem turnaround time.

Effectiveness of Byte Count Synchronous Protocols

The performance of byte count synchronous protocols is much the same as for BISYNC, the differences being in transparency and efficiency. Transparency is inherent in byte count protocols. In BISYNC, transparency is an option and induces additional overhead. Byte count protocols also have greater efficiency if message sequencing or true full duplex operations are allowed. An example of a byte count synchronous protocol is Digital Equipment Corporation's DDCMP protocol. Its message sequencing allows 256 message numbers.

BIT SYNCHRONOUS PROTOCOLS

The first *bit-oriented synchronous data link protocol* was introduced by IBM in 1972. It was appropriately named *synchronous data link control (SDLC)*. Since then, numerous other bit-oriented data link controls have surfaced. The major bit synchronous protocols are:

SDLC, synchronous data link control, from IBM.

BDLC, Burroughs data link control, from Burroughs Corporation.

UDLC, universal data link control, from Sperry Corporation.

CDCDLC, Control Data Corporation data link control, from Control Data Corporation.

ADCCP, advanced data communications control procedure, an ANSI standard data link protocol. (ADCCP is frequently pronounced "addcap.")

HDLC, high-level data link control, a standard of the International Standards Organization (ISO).

LAPB, link access procedure, balanced, designated as the data link protocol for the X.25 packet distribution networks. LAPB is an adaptation of HDLC.

All of these bit synchronous protocols operate similarly. Although there are both national and international standards, SDLC is used in the following discussion as the model for bit-oriented data link protocols because it is used in many IBM installations and thus represents most bit synchronous implementations. Many vendors also support SDLC to provide connection to IBM networks and devices. More detailed information regarding SDLC may be found in Appendix C.

Synchronous Data Link Control (SDLC)

SDLC operates in full duplex or half duplex mode on nonswitched lines in both point-to-point and multi-point configurations. In half duplex mode it also allows switched, point-to-point configurations. In addition, it is possible to configure stations in a loop, as depicted in Figure 6-11. Data is transmitted in one direction around the loop, as with hub polling. In all configurations, including point-to-point, one station is designated as the primary station and the others are secondary stations. The primary controls the link and determines which station is allowed to transmit.

The Frame.   The basic unit of transmission in SDLC is the *frame*; its general format is presented in Figure 6-12. The flag field is used to indicate the beginning and end of the frame. The bit pattern for the flag—01111110— is the only bit pattern in the protocol that is specifically reserved; all other bit patterns are acceptable. This is discussed further in the SDLC section on transparency. The second field within the frame—the address field—is eight bits. Thus, a maximum of 256 unique addresses is possible. Other data link protocols, such as ADCCP and HDLC, allow the address field to be expanded in multiples of eight bits, significantly increasing the number of addressable stations per link. The control field, also eight bits, identifies the frame type as either unnumbered, informational, or supervisory. Of

Figure 6-11   An SDLC Loop Configuration

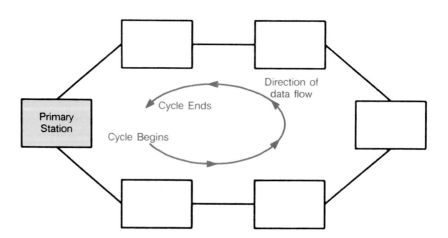

Figure 6-12   An SDLC Frame Format

8 bits	8 bits	8 bits	Variable	16 bits	8 bits
Flag 01111110	Address	Control	Data (Optional Octets)	Frame Check Sequence	Flag 01111110

these three types, only the first two are used to transmit data, with the primary data transport frame being the information frame.

The data field is optional. This field is always omitted for supervisory frames, is optional on unnumbered frames, and is usually present on information frames. The only restriction on the data field is that the number of bits must be a multiple of eight, each eight-bit group being called an *octet*. This restriction does not mean that an eight-bit code must be used; in fact, any code is acceptable. But if necessary, the data being transmitted must be padded with additional bits to maintain an integral number of octets (no partial octets). If the data being transmitted consists of five Baudot characters, for instance, at five bits each, only 25 bits would be required for the data and an additional seven bits would have to be appended to complete the last octet. Following the optional data field is a frame check sequence for error detection, which is 16 bits. The final field of the frame is the flag that signals the end of the message. The bit pattern for the ending flag is the same as that for the beginning flag; thus, the ending flag for one frame may serve as the beginning flag for the next.

SDLC is a positional protocol, which means each field except the data field has a specific length and location relative to adjacent fields. Thus, no special control characters (except for the flag characters) are used to delimit the data or headings in the message. For control frames, which are either unnumbered or supervisory, the control function is encoded in the control field. Unnumbered frames have five bits available to identify the control function, so 32 different function types are possible. The supervisory frame has only two bits available, and thus a maximum of four functions can be defined.

Number Sent (Ns) and Number Received (Nr) Subfields. For information frames, the control field contains two three-bit fields known as the *number sent (Ns)* and *number received (Nr) subfields*. The Ns and Nr counts are used to sequence messages. Three bits allow for eight numbers, 0 through 7. When transmitting an information frame the sender increments the Ns field value. The Ns or Nr number following 7 is 0; thus, the number sequence cycles through those eight values. The Nr field is used to acknowledge receipt of messages. Every time a message is received, the receiver increments the Nr count, which represents the number of the frame expected next. Thus, an Nr count of 5 means message number 5 should arrive next. The Ns and Nr counts are compared every time a frame is received to make sure that no messages have been lost. This scheme allows seven messages to be sent before an acknowledgment is required. Although the ability to receive up to seven frames without acknowledgment improves performance, it also places a burden on the sender, which must be ready to retransmit any unacknowledged frames. This requires that messages be saved in the sender's buffers until acknowledged, which can create problems for systems with small buffers or memory. Examples of how the Ns and Nr fields are used are found in Appendix C.

Figure 6-13   Control
Fields for Informa-
tion Frames

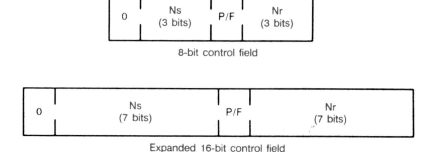

Both ADCCP and HDLC allow the control field to be expanded to provide for larger Ns and Nr counts, as illustrated in Figure 6-13. When expanded to 16 bits, the Ns and Nr fields can each be seven bits; this allows 128 sequence numbers, and up to 127 messages can be transmitted before being acknowledged. This arrangement is especially beneficial with satellite links, where, because of the propagation delay for response, a small number of unacknowledged frames could create undesirable delays. Recall from Chapter 2 that satellite signals incur a one-way propagation delay of approximately a quarter of a second. If 10,000 bit blocks are being transmitted on a 1 Mbps satellite link, then theoretically 25 blocks could be transmitted every quarter of a second. With three-bit Ns and Nr fields, only seven blocks could be sent before waiting for an acknowledgment. In this case, transmission time for 18 blocks would be lost, limiting the available capacity.

Transparency.   Transparency is implemented in SDLC by bit insertion, also known as *bit stuffing*. Since the beginning and ending flags use the only reserved bit sequence, their bit pattern—01111110—must never appear in the data portion of the record. This is accomplished by inserting a 0 bit after encountering five consecutive 1 bits in the data. After the control field, the receiver looks for two specific bit patterns: the ending flag and five consecutive 1 bits. If the ending flag is encountered the receiver knows that the preceding 16 bits are frame check characters and that all bits between the end of the control field and the start of the frame check are data. If, on the other hand, five consecutive 1 bits arrive followed by a 0 bit, the receiver also knows that the 0 bit has been inserted for transparency. The inserted 0 bit is then stripped out and the receiver continues evaluating the input stream. An example of transparency is illustrated in Figure 6-14.

Effectiveness of the SDLC Protocol

Error Detection.   SDLC uses CRC-16 to detect errors. Therefore, the performance is good.

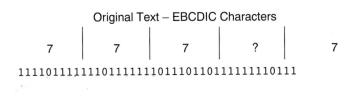

Figure 6-14   SDLC
Transparency

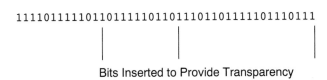

Bits Inserted to Provide Transparency

Transparency.   Transparency was designed into the SDLC protocol. The performance is good.

Addressing.   SDLC is limited in addressing capability because it can use only eight-bit addresses. The performance for SDLC is fair; protocols that allow the address field to be expanded provide good performance.

Code Independence.   All the bit synchronous protocols provide code independence. The only restriction—a minor one—is that the data field must be an integral number of octets. The performance is good.

Configurations.   Almost any combination of half duplex, full duplex, point-to-point, multi-point, dedicated, or switched links is supported in SDLC. In addition, loop configurations are allowed. The performance is good.

Efficiency.   Like BISYNC, SDLC has a fixed overhead. Each information frame has 48 bits appended for flags, control, addressing, and error detection. If the data to be sent consists of only a few bits, the amount of overhead is high. In the typical situation, the performance is good.

Growth.   Ability to accommodate growth and new developments was one of the original design objectives of SDLC. Thus far it has been flexible enough to satisfy all new developments. Despite being a relatively new protocol, it has gone through a period of significant expansion and new development in communications equipment and applications. The performance is good. A comparison of synchronous and asynchronous protocols is given in Figure 6-15.

Figure 6-15
Comparison of
Asynchronous and
Synchronous
Protocols

Asynchronous	Synchronous
Character-at-a-time transmission	Block transmission
Modems are not synchronized	Modems are synchronized
Error detection commonly is parity	Error detection commonly is CRC or parity plus LRC
Fixed overhead per character	Fixed overhead per block (may be less efficient for small messages but more efficient for large ones)
Less efficient use of communications link	More efficient use of communications link
Lower cost devices	Higher cost devices

CARRIER SENSE MULTIPLE ACCESS WITH COLLISION DETECTION (CSMA/CD) PROTOCOL

Carrier sense multiple access with collision detection (CSMA/CD) is used as the data link protocol in some local area networks (LANs), the best example being the Ethernet LAN designed by Xerox, Digital Equipment Corporation, and Intel. Where specifics are required in the discussion that follows, Ethernet serves as the example. CSMA/CD is a broadcast protocol. The typical CSMA/CD configuration consists of a length of cable with stations attached (a *bus* network), as illustrated in Figure 6-16. Each station attached to the LAN has a unique address. Messages are broadcast or sent across the medium, and all stations receive the message. Each recipient ex-

Figure 6-16   The
CSMA/CD Bus
Configuration

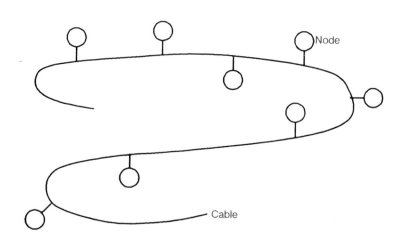

Node

Cable

amines the address field to determine if it is the addressee. Only the station(s) to whom the message is addressed act upon the message.

There is no supervisor station in Ethernet; all stations are equal. When a station has a message to send, it "senses" the carrier on the channel (CS, or carrier sense) to determine whether a message is being transmitted. If a message is in progress, the station waits until the circuit is clear. Any station detecting a clear channel is free to transmit (MA, or multiple access). If two or more stations attempt to transmit at the same time, the messages collide, since the medium only allows one message at a time, and the collision is detected (CD, or collision detection) by all monitoring stations. Any station detecting the collision reinforces it by also briefly broadcasting data, further jamming the circuit. After a collision, the stations responsible wait for a randomly selected time before attempting to transmit again, to decrease the probability that the same two stations will cause another collision.

CSMA/CD transmits messages in frames similar to those used by SDLC. The CSMA/CD frame consists of a 64-bit preamble, a 48-bit destination address, a 48-bit source address, a 16-bit field indicating the message type and how to interpret the data, a variable-length data field, and a 32-bit CRC field. The size of the data field ranges from 46 to 1500 octets. The CRC field is 32 bits rather than 16 as in HDLC and BISYNC, which improves error detection. The 64-bit preamble, which consists of alternating 1 and 0 bits (except the final two bits, which are both 1 bits), allows the receiver to become synchronized with the sender. The CSMA/CD frame format is given in Figure 6-17. Note that there is no end-of-block flag, as in SDLC; rather, the end of the frame is signaled by dropping the carrier signal.

Effectiveness of the CSMA/CD Protocol

Error Detection.   As implemented in Ethernet, a 32-bit CRC is used. This is an improvement over the error detection provided with 16-bit CRC. The performance is very good.

Transparency.   Transparency is inherent in the CSMA/CD protocol. The performance is good.

Addressing.   Ethernet address fields are 48 bits, which allows for an extensive address range. The performance is good.

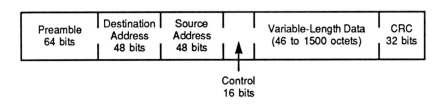

Figure 6-17 The CSMA/CD Message Format

Code Independence.   CSMA/CD's only restriction on code independence is that an integral number of octets must be transmitted. The performance is good.

Configurations.   Ethernet has basically one configuration, the bus. The access protocol is not limited to these configurations, however; star and other configurations can also be used. The performance is good.

Efficiency.   Efficiency of the CSMA/CD protocol is good when there are few collisions. As the number of collisions increases, efficiency decreases. The performance is adequate to good.

Growth.   Growth with the CSMA/CD protocol is inhibited by performance when large numbers of stations desire to transmit. The addressing scheme is not an inhibiting factor. The performance is adequate.

TOKEN PASSING PROTOCOLS

The *token passing protocol* is most frequently implemented in a ring architecture local area network, as depicted in Figure 6-18. Bus implementation is also possible. Data is passed around the ring from station to station in one direction only. Since all nodes on a token passing loop are considered equal, a mechanism is needed to determine which station has the right to transmit data. A predefined bit pattern called a *token* is used to accomplish this.

In Figure 6-19, Node B has possession of the token, which gives B the right to transmit data to another station on the ring. Maintaining possession of the token, Node B transmits its data to the next node on the ring, which examines the message's address to determine whether it is the recipient. If not, the node forwards the message to the next node. The node

Figure 6-18   Ring
Architecture LAN

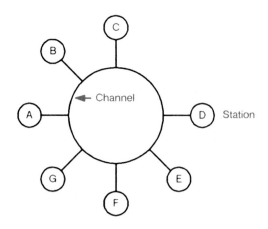

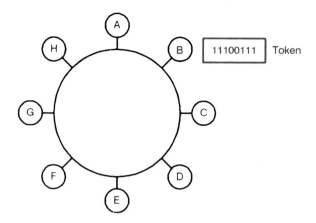

Figure 6-19
A Token
Passing Ring

11100111 | Token

that is the intended recipient of the data keeps the data and forwards an acknowledgment, which may be the message itself. On receiving the acknowledgment, Node B passes the token to Node C, giving C the right to transmit data. Of course, if Node C has no data to send, it immediately passes the token to its neighbor.

There are a number of variations of the token passing protocol. In some systems, a packet is sent around the ring. When the packet arrives at a node, the node removes the data addressed to it and appends its own messages to the others in the transmission block. Usually the block's maximum size is predefined, so a vacant spot must be obtained to transmit the message. Most ring networks are designed so a failed node will not disrupt the passing of data between the other nodes.

One advantage of a token passing ring is the predictability with which stations are granted the right to transmit data. For a given configuration the average wait time and transmit time can be determined and will not vary significantly. With the CSMA/CD protocol, in contrast, when the number of stations and messages increases, the wait time for use of the medium can be unpredictable. One of the criticisms of token passing is the potentially long delay time between transmissions from one station when the number of nodes is large, as it takes the token longer to reach a node wishing to transmit.

Effectiveness of the Token Passing Protocol

Error Detection. Error detection in token passing is determined by the specific implementation. When a CRC is used, the performance is good.

Transparency. The principal implementations of token rings—the IBM token ring, 802.4 token passing bus, and the IEEE 802.5 token passing ring standard—provide transparency. Performance is good. Note, however, that other token ring implementations are possible.

Addressing.   Addressing capability is implementation-dependent with the token passing protocol. The IEEE 802.4 and 802.5 standards allow for either 16-bit or 48-bit addresses. IBM's token ring uses 48-bit addresses. Performance is good.

Code Independence.   Token passing code independence depends on the implementation. The IEEE 802.4 and 802.5 standards and IBM's token ring implementation provide code independence. Performance is good.

Configurations.   The configuration of token passing is usually a ring or bus. Performance is fair.

Efficiency.   The efficiency of token passing is very predictable, given a specific number of stations. Performance is good.

Growth.   The growth of token passing protocols is inhibited by performance when many stations are configured: The more stations there are, the longer it takes for the token to reach a given node. Performance could degrade with many stations. Performance is adequate.

CHOOSING A DATA LINK PROTOCOL

Although several other data link protocols exist, those described in this chapter are the most common. The question is, which one is appropriate for which application? First, the network designer must choose a protocol supported by the hardware vendor. Most vendors support some version of asynchronous, character synchronous, and bit synchronous protocols. CSMA/CD and token passing are found primarily in local area networks. Second, the type of hardware used in an application partly dictates the data link protocol. Most terminals support one or possibly two protocols. The exception is intelligent terminals, which can support a wide variety of protocols. Third, the network support provided by the vendor affects the choice of data link protocol. Many newer network systems have been designed around a bit-oriented synchronous protocol; however, since not all users have compatible terminals, accommodations are frequently made to support other protocols, such as BISYNC. In practice, do not select a protocol and then gather the equipment to support it; rather, select a network design, a hardware vendor, and associated hardware, each of which dictates a particular protocol. Most current data link technology and development for wide area networks is based on bit-oriented synchronous protocols. There are several bit-oriented implementations and several standards exist. The industry trend is toward higher speed transmission and efficient use of the data link, which definitely favors synchronous transmission protocols.

SUMMARY

This chapter covered the OSI data link layer. The functions of a data link protocol were described and five protocols—asynchronous, character synchronous, bit synchronous, CSMA/CD, and token passing—were introduced. Additional details of asynchronous and both types of synchronous protocols can be found in Appendices A, B, and C. Asynchronous and synchronous protocols are used primarily for wide area networks, while CSMA/CD and token passing are used for local area networks. For wide area networks, bit synchronous protocols are preferable for most applications; however, asynchronous and character synchronous protocols are still widely used and have merits for some applications.

Key Terms

ADCCP ("addcap")
asynchronous
binary synchronous (BISYNC or BSC)
    protocol
bit synchronous protocol
byte count synchronous protocol
carrier sense multiple access with
    collision detection (CSMA/CD) protocol
character synchronous protocol
code independence
data link layer (OSI)
double buffering
enveloping
frame
framing protocol
high-level data link control (HDLC)
interrupt characters

link access procedure,
    balanced (LAPB)
local area network (LAN)
mark
message sequence numbers
number received (Nr)
    subfield
number sent (Ns) subfield
octet
positional protocol
space
start-stop protocol
synchronous
synchronous data link
    control (SDLC)
token passing
transparency

Review Questions

In answering some of the questions below, it may be helpful to refer to the material in Appendices A–C.

1. What are the functions of a data link protocol?
2. Explain why asynchronous protocols do not support code independence.
3. In asynchronous protocols, what function is provided by interrupt characters?
4. Why is double buffering necessary?
5. Explain the popularity of asynchronous protocols.
6. Distinguish between positional and framing synchronous protocols.
7. How does a byte count synchronous protocol work?

8. Name five implementations of bit-oriented synchronous data link controls. List those features indicated in the text that distinguish some of these from SDLC.

9. What is transparency? Why is it necessary?

10. What are the advantages and disadvantages of using BISYNC on a full duplex line?

11. How do asynchronous and synchronous protocols differ? In what respects are they the same? How do their modems differ?

12. What advantages does SDLC have over BISYNC?

13. Describe data link objectives in which CSMA/CD is inefficient.

14. In what respects does contention in BISYNC differ from that of CSMA/CD?

15. Explain how token passing protocols work.

Exercises

1. Make a chart that compares the overhead of asynchronous, BISYNC, and SDLC protocols. Make the chart for message sizes of 25, 50, 100, 500, and 1000 characters. The chart should look essentially as follows:

Number of Text Characters	Number of Bits Transferred		
	ASYNC	BISYNC	SDLC
25			
50			
100			
500			
1000			

In filling out the chart, assume a start, stop, and parity bit for async. For BISYNC, assume six control characters (SYN SYN STX ETX plus two for BCC). For BISYNC you should also include a point-to-point line bid (SYN SYN ENQ) and two acknowledgments (SYN SYN ACK0 and SYN SYN ACK1) of four characters each (ACK0 and ACK1 are two character sequences). One acknowledgment is for the line bid and one for the data. For SDLC, assume a frame overhead of 48 bits. Count the acknowledgment as 16 bits, since ordinarily several frames will be acknowledged at once. Which is the most efficient protocol and under what conditions? Assume seven-bit characters for each case.

2. Diagram a sequence of message exchanges between two stations using SDLC that shows the changing of the Ns and Nr subfields.

3. Is transparency a requirement of code independence? Justify your answer.

4. Can there be a start-stop flag in the address or control field of an SDLC message? If not, why not? If so, why does it not terminate the message?

5. Is there an analogy to CSMA/CD in other communications disciplines such as radio or television? If so, in what respects are they similar?

6. Examine the literature and describe what happens when the token is lost in a token passing protocol, such as when the node holding the token fails or is powered off.

7. Suppose you have a local area network consisting of 20 workstations with a low number of network messages. Which data link protocol would you choose for this situation? Why?

8. Suppose you have a local area network in which each node must have guaranteed equal access to the medium. Which data link protocol would you choose? Why?

References

Edwards, Jeri. *Network Protocols.* Cupertino, CA: Tandem Computers, Inc., September 1982.

Hewlett-Packard Corporation. *Guidebook to: Data Communications.* Santa Clara, CA: Hewlett-Packard Corp., 1977.

IBM. *General Information—Binary Synchronous Communications.* Manual no. GA27-3004-2. Research Triangle Park, NC: IBM, October 1970.

————. *IBM Synchronous Data Link Control General Information.* Manual no. GA27-3093-2. Research Triangle Park, NC: IBM, 1979.

Kuo, Franklin F. *Protocols and Techniques for Data Communications Networks.* Englewood Cliffs, NJ: Prentice-Hall, 1981.

McNamara, John E. *Technical Aspects of Data Communication.* Bedford, MA: Digital Press, 1977.

Sherman, Elton. "Implementing Distributed Networks with SDLC." *Digital Design,* March 1977.

Stallings, William. *Handbook of Computer-Communications Standards: Local Network Standards, Volume 2.* New York: Macmillan, 1987.

Tanenbaum, Andrew S. *Computer Networks.* Englewood Cliffs, NJ: Prentice-Hall, 1981.

————. "Network Protocols." *Association for Computing Machinery (ACM) Computing Surveys* 13 (December 1981).

SESSION

TRANSPORT

NETWORK

NETWORKS AND SYSTEMS SOFTWARE: THE NETWORK, TRANSPORT, AND SESSION LAYERS

Introduction to Networks

The Network Layer
The Transport Layer
Network Nomenclature
Network Topology
Message Routing

INTRODUCTION

In this chapter we move up another level in the OSI reference model to the network layer. Topics covered in this chapter include:

Functions of the network layer

Functions of the transport layer

Network terminology

Network configurations

Network routing

After this chapter, you will be familiar with computer networks and the terminology specific to them, computer network routing algorithms, and network configurations. Chapters 8, 9, 10, and 11 continue the discussion of networks. Chapters 8 and 9 cover local area networks, Chapter 10 presents wide area networks, and Chapter 11 presents considerations for network management.

THE NETWORK LAYER

The OSI *network layer* performs three major functions: routing, network control, and congestion control. Whereas the data link layer is concerned with moving data between two adjacent nodes, the network layer is concerned with end-to-end routing, or getting data from the originating node to its ultimate destination. In many networks, data may take a variety of paths from the originating node to the destination node. The network layer must be aware of alternative paths in the network and choose the best one. Which path is best depends on a variety of factors, some of which are congestion, number of intervening nodes, speed of links, and so on.

Network control involves sending node status information to other nodes and receiving status information from other nodes to determine the best routing for messages. Where priorities are associated with messages, it is the responsibility of the network layer to enforce the priority scheme. *Congestion control* means reducing transmission delays that might result from overuse of some circuits or because a particular node in the network is busy and unable to process messages in a timely fashion. The network layer should adapt to these transient conditions and attempt to route messages around such points of congestion. Not all systems can adapt to the changing characteristics of the communications links, however. In some instances — specifically, broadcast-type systems — very little can be done to overcome this problem.

THE TRANSPORT LAYER

The *transport layer* is involved in end-to-end transmission services and assists the session layer in establishing the connections for a session. The transport layer may accept messages of any length; however, the communications link may have limitations regarding message size. The transport layer must segment these large messages into smaller transmission blocks and establish sequence numbers for each. The transport layer is responsible for end-to-end sequence number control and error detection and recovery. For example, if a segment of a long message is lost, the transport layer effects recovery to ensure correct, complete message transfer.

Another service that may be provided by the transport layer is addressing. Each user of the system is identified by an address called a *transport service access point* (*TSAP*) to identify uniquely session entities. The transport layer is responsible for translating user identifiers into TSAPs. TSAPs of the source and destination session entity together with a checksum to detect errors are appended to the message received from the session layer. Before we get into the details of network routing and topologies, some new terminology needs to be introduced.

NETWORK NOMENCLATURE

Network and Node.   The term *network* as used in Chapters 7, 8, 9, 10, and 11 means a network of computer systems and their attached communications devices, such as terminals and multiplexers. Each computer system is called a network *node*. *Computer system* is the term used rather than *processor* or *computer* because of the existence of multiple processor systems. Thus, a node is one or more processors that collectively serve as a termination point for a communications link with another node.

Link, Path, and Circuit. In Chapter 6 you learned about the function of the data link layer: passing data and control information to the next node. This means sending data across a link to the next station—terminal, host, concentrator, or the like. There is a difference between a link and a path: A path represents end-to-end message routing, whereas a link connects one node to an adjacent node or one node to a terminal. In Figure 7-1, the rectangles represent host processors, the circles represent terminals, and the lines represent communications links. Figure 7-1 shows two paths available for communication between Node A and Node C (A $\rightarrow$ B, B $\rightarrow$ C and A $\rightarrow$ D, D $\rightarrow$ C), with two links on each path.

Session and User. *Session* refers to a communications dialogue between two users of a network. A *user* can be a terminal operator, an application, or any other originator of messages. In some systems, sessions are quite formal, with well-defined conventions for establishing, continuing, and terminating the dialogue.

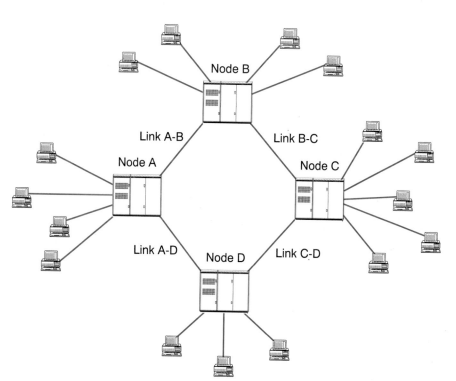

Figure 7-1 A Communications Network

Packet Switching, Packet Distribution Network (PDN), and Circuit Switching. *Packet switching* refers to the technology of transmitting a message in one or more fixed-length data packets. A packet switching network is also sometimes referred to as a *packet distribution network* (PDN), public data network (also PDN), an X.25 network (X.25 is a standard designation), or value-added network (VAN). Henceforth, the abbreviation PDN will be used. A PDN generally connects a user and the nearest node in the PDN. The PDN routes the data packets to their final destination by finding the best route for each packet (packet switching).

Store and Forward.   In a *store and forward* system, messages may be stored at nodes along the transmission path before these nodes deliver them to the next node. There are several reasons for using store and forward. First, there is the responsibility for being able to re-send the message. If Node A is transmitting a message to Node Z, the path between the two may pass through several intermediate nodes. To ensure delivery, either A must keep the message until it is delivered or an intermediate node that has received the message must assume this responsibility. In a store and forward system, a node that receives the message will write it to disk or store it in memory and then acknowledge to the sender that it has been received. This relieves the sender of accountability for the message. Store and forward is attractive for financial transactions as it provides a trace of the progress of the transaction.

Second, store and forward algorithms are used for time-staged delivery systems. These systems allow users not only to send messages but also to specify a required delivery time. There are several benefits of such systems. For corporations with offices in several time zones, mail messages can be given a delivery time. If the delivery time is not immediate, the system can process the message during a period of low activity. For example, suppose that a mail message is posted at 2 P.M. for delivery to a time zone that is four hours later, where it is 6 P.M. If the delivery time is set as 9 A.M. the next day, the message can be stored locally and sent at midnight when both the sending and receiving systems are less busy. Time-staged delivery of large files can also allow their transmission to be paced over time, making the communications links more available for other transmissions. Third, store and forward systems may be used when no path to the destination is available. If a link fails during the process of sending the message and the message cannot be delivered, the node at the point of failure can store the message. When the link is restored, the message is forwarded to the next node in the path. This practice relieves the message originator from the responsibility of saving the message until it reaches its destination. Finally, store and forward techniques can be used in systems where messages have different priorities. Low priority messages may be stored for later delivery to give higher priority messages better access to a link during periods of congestion.

Local Area Network (LAN) and Wide Area Network (WAN). The two broad categories of networks are *local area networks* (*LAN*) and *wide area networks* (*WAN*). A LAN is almost always privately controlled with respect to both data terminal equipment (processors, terminals, and so on) and data communications equipment (media, repeaters, and so on). A LAN serves a limited geographical area, typically within one building or building complex. The maximum allowable distance between nodes varies with the system, but it is generally a few miles. A WAN, on the other hand, usually consists of data terminal equipment owned or controlled by the user, together with data communications equipment provided by a common carrier. In a few instances WANs have been implemented as totally private networks. A LAN is depicted in Figure 7-2, and a WAN, in Figure 7-3.

Network Architecture and Topology. The general configurations used to describe networks are sometimes referred to as *network architecture* or *network topology*.

NETWORK TOPOLOGY

Network topologies come in several varieties, defined by how the nodes are connected: star, hierarchical, interconnected, ring, bus, or combinations of these.

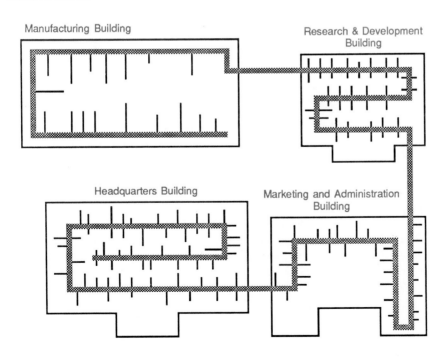

Figure 7-2 A Local Area Network Connecting Devices in a Building Complex

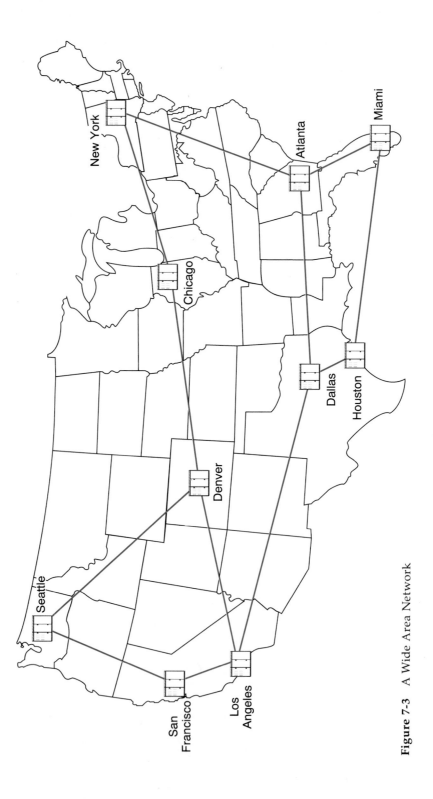

Figure 7-3 A Wide Area Network

Star Network

A *star,* or centralized, *network* is illustrated in Figure 7-4. In a star network, one node serves as a message switch, accepting a message from the originating node and forwarding it to the destination node. A star configuration has several advantages. First, it makes for a short path between any two nodes with a maximum of two links, or hops, to traverse. And if the message is to go from the central node to a peripheral node, or vice versa, only one hop is required. Thus, the time needed for a message to get from source to destination can be quite short. On the other hand, having the central node involved in the transmission of every message can lead to congestion at the central site, with consequent message delays, and such congestion is exacerbated when the central node is functioning for more than just message switching. If, as is frequently the case, the central node is also the central processing system, higher priority processing requirements could make the processor temporarily unable to attend to communications functions, a problem that is more likely to occur in a uniprocessor system than in a multiple processor system.

A star configuration also provides the user with a high degree of network control. Since the central node is in direct contact with every other node and all messages flow through it, a centralized location exists for message logging, gathering of network statistics, and error diagnostics and

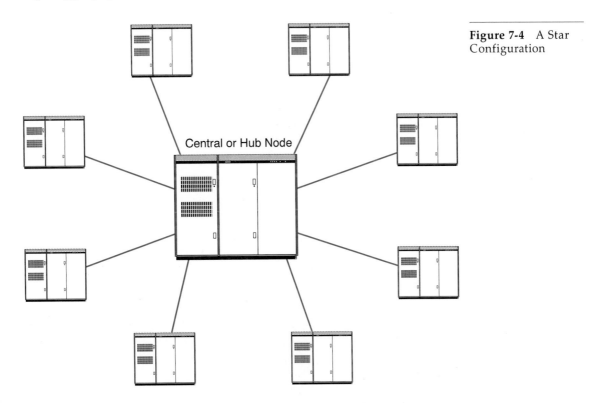

Central or Hub Node

Figure 7-4 A Star Configuration

recovery. In some situations, however, this centralized control and dependence on a centralized system are considered a disadvantage rather than an advantage. In a corporate network, having a centralized system may be consistent with a centralized management control philosophy. Close control of all other data-processing centers by a main data-processing center may be consistent with corporate management objectives. However, in a network of peer organizations, having one organization act as a point of centralized control may be undesirable. Consider a network of major universities. It may be difficult to reach agreement as to which university will serve as the centralized controller. Even after the decision is made, dependence on one data center for communications services may be undesirable for the other nodes.

Expanding a star network is easy, for only the new node and the central node need be involved. All that is required is to obtain the communications link, connect the two, and update the network tables in the other nodes. Some instances also require that a new system generation be performed for the other nodes. If adding a new node exceeds the limits of memory allocated to the network routing tables, a new system generation is usually required. For relatively dynamic networks it is common to allocate space for potential nodes to reduce the number of system generations that must be performed.

Star systems have a relatively low reliability. The loss of the central node is equivalent to loss of the network. Failure of a peripheral node has little impact on the network as a whole, as only messages bound for that node are undeliverable. The best candidate for central node is a fault-tolerant system that is almost immune to failure.

Star systems have an additional disadvantage in a long-distance network: possibly higher circuit costs. This is exemplified in the case study in Chapter 5, in which the point-to-point configuration has a monthly circuit cost almost $1500 higher than that of the shortest path configuration. This is particularly true when the centralized node is not geographically in the center of the network.

Hierarchical Network

Hierarchical topology, shown in Figure 7-5, is also referred to as a tree structure. There is one root node (Node A). Directly connected to Node A are several nodes at the second level. Each of these can have several cascaded nodes attached. This type of network closely resembles corporate organization charts, and corporate computer centers are one instance in which this topology can be found. With the corporate computer center as root node, division systems are attached directly to the root, regional systems to divisional systems, districts to regions, and so on. Corporate reports from a lower level are easily consolidated at the next higher level, and the network generally mirrors the information flow pattern in the corporation. Thus, information flowing from a district in one division to

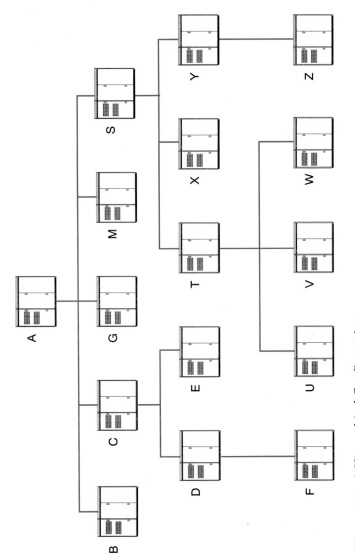

Figure 7-5 A Hierarchical Configuration

a district in a different division would need to go through the root or corporate node. As with a star system, this allows for a great deal of network control.

Media costs for the hierarchical system are likely to be less than for star topology, assuming that the lower level nodes are in closer proximity to the next higher level than they are to the root. It is possible, of course, to devise configurations in which media costs are higher than for a centralized system. The number of hops for a hierarchical system can be quite large. If Node F in Figure 7-5 needed to send a message to Node Z, the message would have to pass through five intermediate nodes (F $\longrightarrow$ D $\longrightarrow$ C $\longrightarrow$ A $\longrightarrow$ S $\longrightarrow$ Y $\longrightarrow$ Z). In the hierarchical topology, the number of instances of this type of data transfer is presumably small compared to the number of messages that remain within one branch of the tree.

Expansion and reconfiguration of a hierarchical network can pose problems. In the configuration of Figure 7-5, to split Node C into Nodes C and K, with D and F under C and E under K, would require more work than in the star configuration. Node K would have to be linked to Node A, and Node E would have to be unlinked from C and relinked to K. Although this may not sound difficult, it costs time and money to change circuits from one location to another, especially with circuits provided by a common carrier. As with most configuration changes, network routing tables must be updated, and a system or network regeneration may be needed. Failure of the root node in a hierarchical configuration is less costly than in a star configuration, but it does present a serious problem of reliability. In fact, the failure of any node other than those at the extremities will make it impossible to reach that node or any of its subordinate nodes. Congestion at the root and higher level nodes is also a potential problem.

Interconnected (Plex) Network

Two forms of *interconnected* (*plex*) architecture are portrayed in Figure 7-6. In the fully interconnected network, Figure 7-6(a), every node is connected to every other node with which it must communicate. In the past, fully interconnected topology was required because the available network software was not sophisticated enough to perform the routing and forwarding functions. The more typical topology does not require all nodes to be connected. Message traffic patterns are used to determine where links should be installed. As might be expected, the cost of the links in a fully interconnected network is high. The number of links required for a fully interconnected network of n nodes is $n(n - 1)/2$. The performance of an interconnected system is generally good, since direct links can be established between nodes with high amounts of data to exchange. Costs can also be controlled because interconnected topology is capable of the shortest or least expensive configuration. In fact, any of the other topology types can be mimicked by an interconnected topology, although routing and control mechanisms probably would be different.

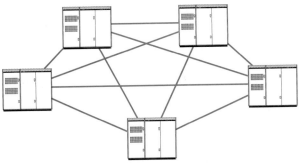

Figure 7-6
Interconnected
Configurations

(a) Fully Interconnected Network

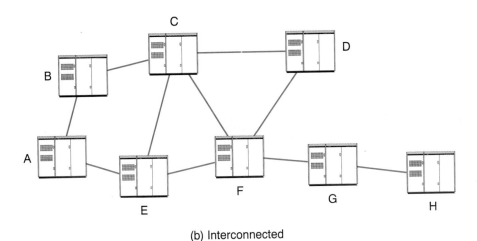

(b) Interconnected

The expandability of interconnected configurations depends upon the type of network and how the new node is to be connected. In the fully interconnected network, expansion is costly and time-consuming because a link must be established to every node with which the new node must communicate. In networks that do not require full interconnection, insertion of a new node can be simple. For example, adding Node H in Figure 7-6(b) would be very simple, requiring only adding a link from Node G to the new Node H. Adding a node such as Node C in Figure 7-6(b) would be more involved and costly, however. The impact of node failure depends on the specific configuration. In some instances, alternate paths around a failed node are available, such as Node C in Figure 7-6(b). The loss of Node F, however, would isolate Nodes G and H. Since all nodes in interconnected topology are equal, control is distributed rather than centralized.

Ring Network

A *ring* architecture is depicted in Figure 7-7. In a typical ring configuration, data flows in one direction. In some implementations, the use of two

Figure 7-7 A Ring
Configuration

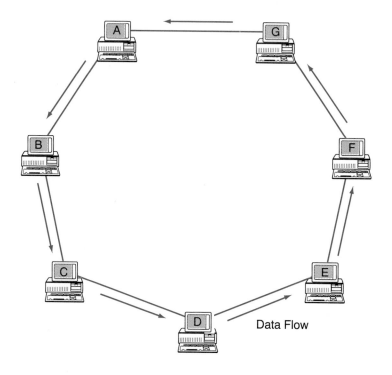

Figure 7-7 A Ring
Configuration

Data Flow

channels allows data to flow in both directions. The usual ring implementation uses token passing to determine which station is allowed to transmit information. One node might be designated as the primary station and the others as secondary stations, as required in the SDLC ring configuration. This implementation is generally referred to as a loop rather than a ring. However, all nodes are typically at the same level of priority, and consequently there is less control than in the star and hierarchical topologies. This can be advantageous or disadvantageous, depending on the user's perspective. With central control all enhancements and monitoring are done centrally. On the other hand, if the nodes are autonomous entities, each node is allowed to make any local changes that do not affect the network.

The number of hops a message must take is a function of the number of nodes in the network, or n. On the average, a message must pass through $n/2$ links. When token passing is used, it serves as a flow control mechanism, and congestion is not as apparent as with star, hierarchical, or interconnected architectures. Reliability of the ring is high, assuming that messages are routed to the next node when one node fails, meaning the ring remains unbroken, which is the usual case. Thus, when a node fails, only that node is lost, and all other nodes can communicate as usual. Expandability is easily achieved with ring architecture. Only the two adjacent nodes are physically affected; only one link must be abandoned and two new ones added. Ring architecture usually costs less than the star or hierarchical network. The links are usually chosen to minimize media costs.

Bus Network

A *bus architecture* is like a ring in which the ends are not connected. A bus, shown in Figure 7-8, is defined as a conductive medium to which multiple devices (in this case, nodes) can be connected. Bus topology and ring topologies are common in local area networks. In the usual implementation, all nodes on the bus are equal, so control is distributed. Either token passing or CSMA/CD access can be used. The most common bus implementation currently is CSMA/CD.

When token passing is used on a bus, a logical ring is established through station addressing. Consider the nodes on the token passing bus illustrated in Figure 7-9. Each station has an address, and the transmit token is passed from one station to another in address order. Suppose that each station passes the token to the station with the next lower address and that the station with the lowest address then passes the token to the station with the highest address. The logical ring thus formed is depicted by the dashed line in Figure 7-9. Each station must know its address and the addresses of both its successor and predecessor stations. Of course, it is necessary to insert and remove stations from the ring. For example, a workstation may be powered off and need to be removed or a new one brought online. A station is dropped whenever its address is skipped when passing the token. This will occur if a station fails to accept the token from its predecessor. New stations are inserted via a special control frame. Periodically, stations will issue this special solicit successor message. This message contains the sending station's address and the address of the next station. A node with an address between these two addresses will respond to this message and insert itself into the network. This is illustrated in Figure 7-10.

Reliability on bus networks is good, unless the bus itself fails. The loss of one node has no effect on any of the other nodes. Cost comparisons with other topologies do not make much sense, since bus architecture is limited to a LAN. Expandability is excellent with a bus architecture. All

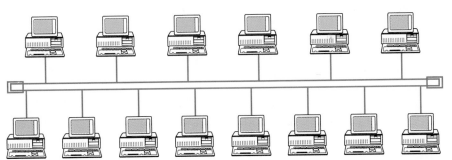

Figure 7-8 A Bus Configuration

Figure 7-9   Token
Passing Bus

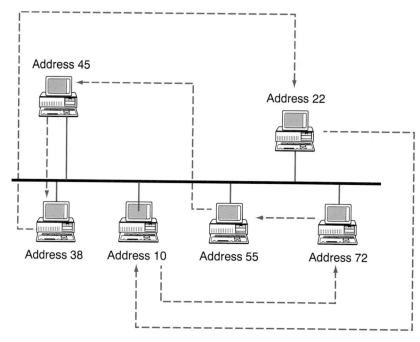

Address 45

Address 22

Address 38   Address 10   Address 55   Address 72

- - - - - ▶   Path of Passing the Token - Based on Descending Station Address

Figure 7-10   Inserting a New Station in
a Token Passing Bus

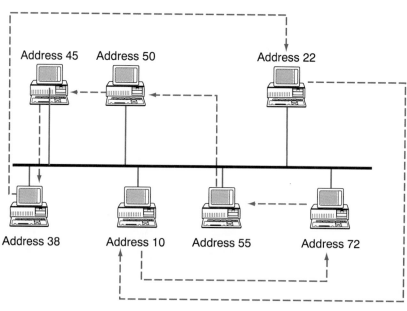

Address 45   Address 50   Address 22

Address 38   Address 10   Address 55   Address 72

- - - - - ▶   Path of Passing the Token - Based on Descending Station Address

that is required to add a new node is to tap into the medium. The ability to add new nodes is one of the strengths of bus architecture.

Another LAN topology that can be derived from bus interconnections is illustrated in Figure 7-11. The different branches, or *spurs*, might represent cables on different floors in a building or in different buildings. These individual buses are connected to a common bus. If the distances involved are great, repeaters must be used to enhance the signals.

Combination Networks

Combinations of the above topologies are sometimes integrated into one network. One such combination is a backbone network—for instance, a ring—with spurs attached. The backbone nodes can be dedicated to message transfer and data communications while the other nodes are used for both data processing and data communications. In widely distributed systems with many nodes, this helps reduce the number of hops, the length of the links, and congestion problems. If the backbone is implemented as a ring or with multiple paths available, reliability is also high.

Summary of Network Topologies

Figure 7-12 summarizes the different types of topology with respect to cost, control, number of hops (speed), reliability, and expandability.

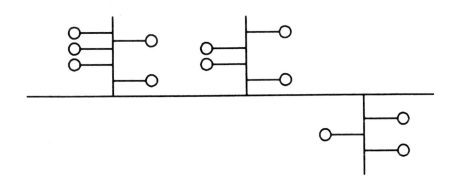

Figure 7-11 A Bus Configuration with Spurs

ology Type	Cost	Control	Number of Hops	Reliability	Expandability
	Can be high	Very Good	Maximum of two	Poor	Good
rarchical	Can be high	Good	Can be many	Fair	Fair to good
rconnected					
ull	Highest	Distributed	One only	Good	Very poor
ther	Can be lowest	Distributed	Can be many	Good	Good
g	Good	Distributed	Can be many	Good	Good
	Good	Distributed	N/A	Good	Good

Figure 7-12 Network Topology Characteristics

MESSAGE ROUTING

Routing, one of the functions of the network layer, is achievable through several algorithms used to direct messages from the point of origination to final destination. Determination of message routing can be either centralized or distributed. Routing itself can be either static, adaptive, or broadcast and is governed by a network routing table resident at each node. The network routing table is a matrix of other nodes together with the link or path to that node. Thus, if a message destined for Node X arrives at Node K, the network routing table is consulted for the next node on the path from K to X. Network routing tables can also contain more information than just the next link, such as congestion statistics. The following discussion does not cover all varieties of routing techniques. For more detail, refer to Tanenbaum, 1981, and Kuo, 1981.

Centralized Routing Determination: The Network Routing Manager

In centralized determination of routing tables, one node is designated as the network routing manager to whom all nodes periodically forward such status information as queue lengths on outgoing and incoming lines and the number of messages processed within the most recent interval. The routing manager thereby is provided with an overview of network functioning, where bottlenecks are occurring, and where facilities are underutilized. The routing manager periodically recalculates the optimal paths between nodes and constructs and distributes new routing tables to all nodes. The disadvantages of this form of network routing are manifold. That the routing manager can receive many messages from the other nodes increases the probability of congestion, a problem that can be exacerbated if the routing manager is itself a node used to accept and forward messages. And networks are sometimes subject to transient conditions such as when the internode transfer of a file saturates a link for a short period of time. By the time this information is relayed to the routing manager and a new routing is calculated, the activity may have already ceased, making the newly calculated paths less than optimal. Also, some nodes will receive the newly calculated routing tables before others, leading to inconsistencies in how messages are to be routed. For example, suppose that under the old routing mechanism the route was A ⟶ B ⟶ D ⟶ X, whereas the new path is A ⟶ C ⟶ D ⟶ X, as indicated in Figure 7-13. Also, the new path from Node B to Node X is B ⟶ A ⟶ C ⟶ D ⟶ X. If Node B receives its new routing chart while Node A is still using the old chart, then for a message destined from A to X, A will route it to B and B will route it back to A, continuing until A receives the new routing table. In addition, transmission of the routing tables themselves may bias the statistics being gathered to compute the next routing algorithm.

An additional problem with centralized route calculations is the amount of processing power needed—a considerable amount of CPU time could be

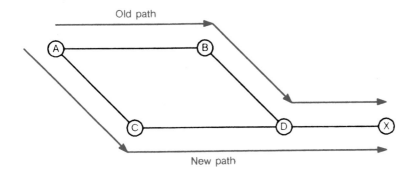

Figure 7-13 A Network Configuration

consumed. Reliability of the routing manager is also an important factor. If this node fails, either the routing remains unchanged until the system is recovered or an alternate routing manager must be selected. The best situation is to have alternate routing managers available in case the primary routing node fails. This is implemented most easily by having the routing manager send the alternates "I'm alive" messages at predefined intervals; if the backup manager fails to receive this message within the prescribed interval, it assumes the manager has failed and takes over, its first responsibility being to broadcast the fact that network status messages should now be routed to it.

Distributed Routing Determination

Distributed routing determination relies on each node to calculate its own best routing table, which requires each node to periodically transmit its status to its neighbors. As this information ripples through the network, each node updates its tables accordingly. This technique avoids the potential bottleneck at a centralized route manager, although the time required for changes to flow through all the nodes may be quite long.

Static Routing

The purest form of *static routing* involves always using one particular path between two nodes; if a link in that path is down, communication between those nodes is impossible. Fully interconnected networks sometimes used to utilize this approach. The only path between any two nodes was the link between them. If that link was down, the available network software was incapable of using any of the potentially alternate paths. Fortunately, that type of system has largely disappeared. In general, static routing now refers to the situation in which a selected path is used until some drastic condition makes that path unavailable; then an alternate path is selected and used, until the route is switched manually, a failure occurs on the alternate path, or the original path is restored.

When multiple paths exist, some implementations weight each path according to perceived utilization, which is referred to as *weighted routing*.

Figure 7-14
Weighted Routing

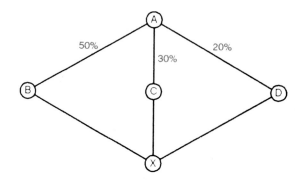

The path is then randomly selected from the weighted alternatives. Figure 7-14 shows three paths from Node A to Node X, via Nodes B, C, and D. Suppose the network designers had determined that the path through Node B would be best 50% of the time, the path through Node C would be best 30% of the time, and the path through Node D would be best 20% of the time. When a message is to be sent from Node A to Node X, a random number between 0 and 1 is generated: If the random number is 0.50 or less, the path through Node B is traversed; if the random number is greater than 0.50 and less than or equal to 0.80, the path through Node C is selected; otherwise, the path through Node D is selected. The path may alternate, but each path is used with the same frequency as in the routing tables. This type of routing can only be changed by altering the route weighting in the routing tables.

Adaptive Routing

Adaptive routing is occasionally referred to as dynamic routing. (Although in some instances a distinction is made between these two terms, this text makes no such distinction.) Adaptive routing attempts to select the best current route for the message or session. The best route may be determined by several different parameters, such as link congestion, link speed, and so on. Link congestion occurs when message traffic on a link is heavy, similar to freeway congestion during rush hours.

Quickest Link.   The simplest adaptive routing algorithm is to have a node pass along the message as quickly as possible, with the only restriction being not to pass it back to the sending node. Thus, the receiving node looks at all potential outbound links, selects the one with the least amount of activity, and sends the message out on that line. There is no attempt to determine if that path will bring the message closer to its destination. This type of algorithm is not very efficient and causes messages to be shuffled to more nodes than necessary, thereby adding to network congestion. The message could conceivably be shifted around the network for hours before arriving at its destination.

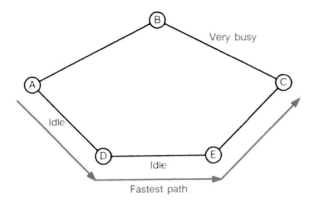

Figure 7-15 Routing
Based on Congestion

Best Route. The more intelligent adaptive routing techniques attempt to select the best route, as determined by one or more of the following parameters: the number of required hops, the speed of the links, the type of link, and congestion. Routing of this type requires current information on the status of the network. If a node is added to the network or if one is taken off the network, that information must be relayed to the nodes doing route calculation. Knowing the speed of the links as well as the number of hops is important. Traversing two links at 4800 bps is more costly than traversing one link at 2400 bps. The line time for both will be the same, but some time is lost in receiving and forwarding the message. Avoiding congested areas will prevent messages from being stuck on inbound and outbound queues. In the configuration of Figure 7-15, if Node A is transmitting a file to Node C, the route from Node A to Node C through B is the shortest but probably not the quickest at that time. The route through Nodes E and D would be more efficient, since the link from B to C is congested.

Broadcast Routing

A third type of routing is *broadcast routing*, exemplified by the CSMA/CD type of link protocol discussed in Chapter 6. Routing is quite easy, the message is broadcast to all stations, and only the station to whom the message is addressed accepts it. Token passing, also described in Chapter 6, is most commonly used in ring architectures: The data flow, in one direction only, is passed from node to node along the medium until the destination is encountered, at which point the receiving node removes the message. Alternatively the message is passed back to the originator as an acknowledgment, and the originator then removes the message and passes the token to its neighbor. The network layer of the OSI recommendation has little function in broadcast routing and token passing networks.

SUMMARY

The general overview of networks started by defining some terms common to all networks. Networks can be configured in a variety of ways. These configurations are called network topologies. The most common topologies are the star, hierarchy, interconnected or plex, ring, and bus. These topologies were compared relative to cost, control, number of hops, reliability, and expandability. The network layer is responsible for message routing, and there are a variety of methods for accomplishing this. Routing can be determined by a centralized routing manager, or this function can be distributed among all or several nodes. Common routing algorithms include static, weighted, quickest link, best route, and broadcast.

Key Terms

adaptive routing
broadcast routing
bus network
centralized routing
circuit
hierarchical network
interconnected network
link
local area network (LAN)
network
network architecture
network layer (OSI)
network routing manager
node

packet distribution network (PDN)
packet switching
path
plex
quickest link routing
ring network
session
star network
static routing
store and forward
topology
user
weighted routing
wide area network (WAN)

Review Questions

1. Distinguish between a link and a path.
2. Describe the functions provided by a store and forward system.
3. Compare wide area networks (WANs) and local area networks (LANs).
4. Which network topology provides the greatest amount of control? Which provides the lowest link costs? Which will have the highest link costs?
5. What are the advantages and disadvantages of centralized routing calculations?
6. What are the advantages and disadvantages of local route determination?
7. Distinguish between static and adaptive routing.
8. What are the advantages and disadvantages of the quickest link routing algorithm?
9. What are the problems inherent in the quickest link routing method?
10. Describe the weighted routing algorithm.

Exercises

1. List two network configurations for which calculation of routes is not required. Why is it unnecessary to determine a message route in each of these configurations?

2. In the chapter it was stated that the line time to traverse two 4800-bps links is equivalent to that for one 2400-bps link. Perform the calculations to verify this.

3. Suppose you need a wide area network and want a topology that provides a low cost with good reliability and expandability. You also need good response times, which implies a limited number of hops. Which topology would you choose? Why?

4. Investigate three network implementations and answer the following questions.
   a. What topology does each use?
   b. What type of routing does each use?
   c. Are alternate paths available? If so, under what conditions are they used?

References

Hewlett-Packard Corporation. *Guidebook to: Data Communications.* Santa Clara, CA: Hewlett-Packard Corp., 1977.

Institute of Electrical and Electronic Engineers (IEEE). *Computer Networks: A Tutorial.* Document no. EH0162-8. Geneva, Switzerland: IEEE Computer Society, 1980.

Kuo, Franklin F. *Protocols and Techniques for Data Communications Networks.* Englewood Cliffs, NJ: Prentice-Hall, 1981.

McNamara, John E. *Technical Aspects of Data Communication.* Bedford, MA: Digital Press, 1977.

Tanenbaum, Andrew S. *Computer Networks.* Englewood Cliffs, NJ: Prentice-Hall, 1981.

Tropper, Carl. *Local Computer Network Technologies.* New York: Academic Press, 1981.

Wen-Ning and Israel Gitman. "Routing Strategies in Computer Networks." *Computer* 17, June 1984.

Introduction to Local Area Networks

LAN Definition

The Rationale behind LANs

LAN Applications

LAN Components

LAN Software

LAN Standards

The Private Branch Exchange (PBX)

LAN Implementations

INTRODUCTION

One of the biggest growth segments of the communications industry during the 1980s was local area network (LAN) technology. The LAN boom has resulted from lower hardware costs, availability of network and application software, and the integration of microcomputers into the workplace. This is not to say that all LANs use microcomputers as workstations. LANs were in operation before microcomputers became commonplace, and high-speed LANs are used to connect large computing systems.

In this chapter we first define a LAN and review applications that lend themselves to this type of network. Next, you learn about the hardware and software components of LANs and variations in LAN technology. Finally, overviews of several prominent or unique LAN implementations are presented. In Chapter 9, you learn about microcomputer LANs and criteria for their selection. After this chapter, you should have a knowledge of common uses of a LAN, LAN terminology, and the basics of LAN implementations.

LAN DEFINITION

Local area networks are high-speed networks confined to a limited geographical area. High speeds over limited distance make LANs very suitable for joining computers in a building or building complex. Typically, LAN speeds are 1 Mbps or faster. In the laboratory, speeds of 2 billion (G) bps have been attained. The distance spanned depends on the specific implementation. Usually workstations are not dispersed over a distance of more than a few miles; a few LAN implementations support distances of 100 miles or more. For example, the fiber distributed data interface (FDDI) LAN can span up to 200 kilometers (about 124 miles). The LAN itself consists of communications software, a communications medium, nodes, connectors that attach the nodes to the medium, and network software. The two varieties of network software are the system software that provides networking services and application software for solving user problems. These components are discussed below. First, let us examine why LANs came into being and how LANs are used.

THE RATIONALE BEHIND LANS

Originally most LANs were implemented for two reasons—data transfer and resource sharing. Consider the following scenarios.

Large Data Transfers

In a large data-processing installation with a variety of processors, moving data from one system to another once was accomplished by tape or low-speed communications links (less than 100 Kbps). If a file is to be moved from System A to System B, one approach is to write the file to a tape on System A, move the tape to System B, and load the data from the tape to System B's disk. This approach provides high data transfer rates but has two disadvantages. First, manual intervention is required to effect data transfers. Operators are required to mount and dismount tapes. Not only does this tend to slow down the transfer but also it often means that the transfer must be scheduled, reducing the potential for as-needed transfers. Second, incompatibilities between tape formats on different systems must be accommodated when tapes are used as a transfer medium.

A second approach used to transfer data between systems is a standard communications link using protocols such as RJE and BISYNC. This technique requires that both systems support the same protocol. Moreover, these communications links are often limited to speeds under 100 Kbps. Large file transfers at this speed are very time-consuming. If we consider the standard speed of 56 Kbps in transferring one million records of 100 bytes each, the transfer would require

$$\frac{(1{,}000{,}000 \text{ records}) (100 \text{ bytes per record}) (8 \text{ bits per byte})}{56{,}000 \text{ bits per second}}$$

$$= 14{,}286 \text{ seconds} = 238 \text{ minutes} = 3.97 \text{ hours}$$

For the above figures we assume that the line is operating at 100% capacity and there is no protocol overhead, both ridiculous assumptions. The actual transfer time would likely be more than 6 hours.

A LAN implementation can provide the best attributes of each of the above solutions: high speed coupled with an operator-free implementation. LANs used for high-volume transfers between large systems operate at speeds of 10–100 Mbps, or roughly 200–2,000 times faster than the link described above. A caveat is required at this point: Although the medium can transmit data at a rate of 100 Mbps, actual transfer between two systems is often considerably slower. Still, the transfers are both time efficient and can be initiated under program or terminal control without operator intervention.

Resource Sharing

Resource sharing is best exemplified by microcomputer LANs. By today's standards, original microcomputer hardware was primitive and, in most cases, expensive. The first systems had no hard disks at all, and when hard disks were introduced, they had small capacities (10MB or less) and were expensive (about $900). Printers were also quite expensive, particularly those capable of providing letter-quality output at high speeds. For organizations that purchased several microcomputers, equipping each with hard disks and printers was an expensive proposition. A printer dedicated to one microcomputer frequently was not used full time. Moreover, a user typically would not be able to use completely either the space or the access capacity of a hard disk drive (remember that applications at that time took relatively little disk space).

Suppose that during the early days of microcomputers, you were a manager of an organization with a need for several workstations. You would want to find a way to minimize the costs of the hardware and software and at the same time have the necessary hardware and software available for each user. Hardware and software sharing is one way to reach this goal. Printer sharing can be effected using switches, but the workstations and printer thus shared needed to be located near each other, within 50 feet. However, switches solve only half the problem: They cannot provide disk sharing. Fortunately, LAN technology had already been developed for larger systems. It was simply necessary to port that technology down to microcomputer systems.

Early microcomputer LAN systems were primarily oriented toward printer and disk sharing—*printer* and *disk server* technology. You should already be familiar with the concept of printer sharing. Disk sharing means that several users can access the same disk drive, but not in the same way we share disks today. Recall that early microcomputer software was single-user oriented. Neither programs nor data could be effectively accessed by two users at the same time. Disk sharing on early LAN systems partitioned the hard disk and provided a private area for each user. Each application a user needed was placed in the user's private area. Thus, if five users needed to use a word processing program, a copy of that program existed in each of five user partitions. Naturally, the organization needed to purchase five copies of the software to honor the software company's license agreements. Being able to share software and hardware provided a cost effective way to improve individual productivity. Disk sharing quickly evolved to file sharing and the introduction of *file servers*. With file sharing, two or more users can share a single file. This was made possible through both application and operating system improvements. For LAN use, applications needed to be rewritten to allow several concurrent users. This sounds easier than it actually is. For example, some application programs create temporary work files for a user. In going from single-user to multi-user capabilities, the application must be able to distinguish one user from another and to create individual work files for each.

In the operating system, improvements had to be made to prevent contention problems. Suppose that you and your work partner both decide to edit a paper that you are jointly writing. If you retrieve the document and make changes concurrently with your partner, what do you think will happen? Probably the last person to save the file will erase the changes made by the other person. This contention problem is illustrated in Figure 8-1. For many years, solutions to such contention problems have been used in minicomputer and mainframe computer systems. LAN file server operating systems also need to provide these safeguards. In some cases, applications designed to work in a stand-alone manner can operate on a LAN in a shared environment without modification. However, such software typically does not allow a profile to be set for each user. A *user profile* allows each user to tailor the application to his or her needs, such as hardware attributes and default parameters.

File sharing was an improvement over disk sharing but still had a disadvantage for database usage. Suppose that a personnel manager needs to find the average salary of all employees. From her workstation, she can start a database application and use it to access the personnel file stored on a file server. To complete this request, all employee records are transferred to her workstation, the salaries are totaled and averaged, and the manager obtains the final result. For a large company, transferring each employee record to a workstation can place a significant load on the network. A better solution is to send the request to a server, have the server do all the accesses and calculations, and send only the necessary results

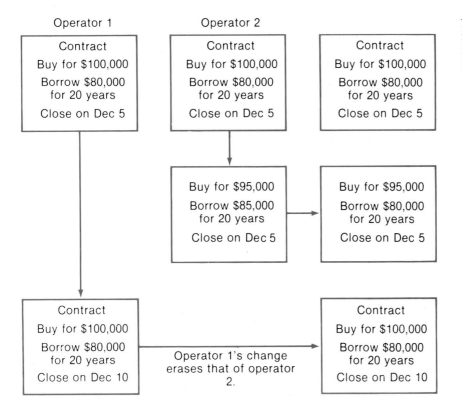

Operator 1   Operator 2

Contract
Buy for $100,000
Borrow $80,000
for 20 years
Close on Dec 5

Contract
Buy for $100,000
Borrow $80,000
for 20 years
Close on Dec 5

Contract
Buy for $100,000
Borrow $80,000
for 20 years
Close on Dec 5

Buy for $95,000
Borrow $85,000
for 20 years
Close on Dec 5

Buy for $95,000
Borrow $80,000
for 20 years
Close on Dec 5

Contract
Buy for $100,000
Borrow $80,000
for 20 years
Close on Dec 10

Operator 1's change
erases that of operator
2.

Contract
Buy for $100,000
Borrow $80,000
for 20 years
Close on Dec 10

Figure 8-1 Word Processing Operators Interfering with Each Other

back to the requester—in this case, one number. This is the service provided by a *database server*, more commonly referred to as an *SQL server* (*SQL* is an abbreviation for structured query language, a standard database access language).

Today LANs are used to share more than printers, disks, and data. Other things shared on a LAN are facsimile (fax) machines, modems, and terminals. You might have observed that sharing resources is not completely simple. One of the objectives of LAN implementations, however, is to hide the complexity of sharing. Often this is referred to as *user transparency* or *seamless interfacing*. For users, transparent access means that using network facilities should be no more difficult than using the same facilities via a different interface. Again, using a microcomputer workstation as an example, a LAN user should not be expected to learn several complicated procedures to accomplish a simple task. If a user needs to access an application stored on a file server, invoking that application from the server should be accomplished with relatively the same ease as invoking it from a local hard disk.

Another transparency issue when using shared resources arises from contention. This problem can be avoided by placing controls on records, files, or documents. The usual control is a lock that disallows concurrent access or concurrent update. Lock controls can create deadlock, however,

		Application A	Application B

Figure 8-2 Dead-
lock Situation

		Application A	Application B
T		Read Record 1 with Lock	
			Read Record 2 with Lock
I			Request Record 1
		Request Record 2	
M			Wait
		Wait	
E			

as when User A reads and locks Record 1 and User B reads and locks Record 2. If A then tries to read Record 2 while B tries to access Record 1, a deadlock occurs. Without arbitration, A and B might both wait forever, since A cannot proceed while needing a resource controlled by B and B cannot proceed while needing a resource controlled by A. This deadlock condition is illustrated in Figure 8-2. If deadlock occurs and is not resolved by the LAN software, a user will likely think the workstation is hung and will reboot it. This can cause operator frustration and the loss of work.

Groupware, a New Motivation for Using LANs

As microcomputer and LAN technology evolved, the ability to share has been greatly enhanced. Sharing of applications and data is common, and most software today can operate in a multiple-user environment. These advances have expanded the potential of LANs from individual productivity applications to work group productivity. Work group productivity tools, collectively referred to as *groupware*, allow a group of users to communicate and coordinate activities. The 1980s was the decade in which microcomputers were used to increase personal productivity, and the 1990s is the decade in which they will be used to increase work group productivity. Work group productivity tools include:

Electronic mail. *Electronic mail,* often referred to as E-mail, allows users to communicate with each other electronically. E-mail allows messages to be delivered to all recipients' mail addresses almost instantaneously.

Electronic appointment calendars. *Electronic appointment calendars* are stored on the network. One user can consult other users' appointment calendars to find a time at which each user is available for a meeting. The electronic calendar system can then schedule the meeting for each participant.

Electronic filing cabinets. E-mail and other machine-readable documents can be stored in disk folders that are equivalent to file folders in conventional filing cabinets. Messages and documents in the folder can later be retrieved, modified, or deleted. Most filing systems maintain an index of the folders and their contents.

File exchange utilities. *File exchange utilities* allow files to be easily copied from one network node to another.

Project management. *Project management systems* give managers a tool that assists in planning projects and allocating resources.

Decision support software. *Decision support software* assists individuals and groups in the decision-making process and helps them set objectives. Group decision support software is also used in brain-storming exercises.

Thus, the motivation for using microcomputer LANs has evolved from that of simple hardware resource sharing to data and application sharing to idea sharing and personnel coordination. While LANs are still used to share hardware, software, and data, the biggest benefit of LANs may lie in groupware applications.

LAN APPLICATIONS

There are many LAN applications. Some of the more common include office automation, factory automation, computer-aided design (CAD), computer-aided manufacturing (CAM), and computer-aided instruction (CAI). Some of the functions performed in these application areas are described below.

Office Automation

Over time, a few technologies have significantly affected office procedures. Among these are telephones, calculators, copy machines, and computers. Two of the most recent influences are microcomputers and LANs. Microcomputers have provided office workers with some autonomy regarding their processing needs. The vast array of microcomputer software with user-friendly interfaces has given end users significant local processing capability. This ability, coupled with shared access to centralized databases and documentation, has added a new dimension to data access and manipulation. Together with electronic mail and document exchange systems, these capabilities have significantly changed the way many offices conduct business.

Some LAN activities an office worker can perform include:

1. Distributing memos to a list of recipients using the electronic mail system.
2. Scheduling a meeting by accessing electronic appointment calendars for the participants. The scheduler software chooses a time at which all participants are available. The calendars of the

attendees can be accessed over the network, a common convenient time determined, and appointments made in affected calendars without contacting each participant personally.

3. Running an application that is stored on a file server's disk. The speed at which the application is transferred to the workstation is relatively equal to that of executing the software from a locally attached disk drive.

4. Accessing an expensive, shared plotter or color printer to output a graph.

5. Accessing a document for editing and returning the changes to a central repository, the shared disk drive.

6. Extracting data from a centralized database and manipulating it locally with spreadsheet, database management system, word processor, or other software.

7. Composing a portion of a document and submitting it to a centralized system for integration with work accomplished elsewhere.

8. Inputting transactions for processing on another node in the network.

9. Transmitting data from the LAN through a gateway to other corporate users on a wide area network (WAN) or another LAN.

10. Accessing public or quasi-public networks such as CompuServe, Prodigy, or Bitnet. These networks and similar ones provide a wide range of services including electronic mail, information databases, and services such as banking, stock trading, and catalog shopping.

CAD/CAM

In addition to the office automation functions above, LANs can serve as the communications medium for *CAD/CAM applications*. In a CAD/CAM application a user can check out a drawing and continue work on it, compose a new drawing, and exchange information with other users of the system. The draftsperson can access a designer's notes, change or create a drawing from those notes, and print the drawing on a shared device such as a plotter. Engineering drawings are usually represented by very large data files; LAN transmission speeds are essential to effectively transfer these drawings from one node to another. CAD is used extensively by automobile, aerospace, computer, and engineering corporations. With a CAD system, an engineer can go directly from drawings to constructing a model of the system to sending the plans to manufacturing in a seamless operation. By *seamless*, we mean that the flow of work and control is highly integrated and the system user is not aware of the interfaces in going from one operation such as engineering drawing to another such as model construction.

CAM systems control assembly line operations, robots, manufacturing processes, and machinery. The objective of CAM systems is to make the manufacturing process more efficient through automation. In the aerospace industry computer control of machinery effects precision fabrication of parts. Computer-controlled robots are used to weld bodies on automobile assembly lines. As in CAD applications, transmission speed is critical in many CAM applications because events must be triggered at precisely the right time.

Computer-Aided Instruction

Educational institutions have found that LANs can facilitate the education process. Most of the education capabilities of stand-alone microcomputer systems are also available on LANs. These capabilities include computer-based instruction and testing. In educational institutions the LAN may be used for many reasons—device sharing, access to application software, and electronic mail. Other potential uses include assignment, collection, and return of exercises. An English professor could assign a term paper, require that it be "typed" on a word processor, have the papers submitted electronically, grade the papers, insert grading comments, print a copy for archival purposes, and return the graded papers to the students. Clubs and committees can use the LAN to post information for other students on electronic bulletin boards. *Electronic bulletin boards* are the computer equivalent of the physical bulletin board. Users of the LAN typically access the electronic bulletin board through a switched telephone connection. Once attached, the user can "post" notices on the board, such as ask how to interface a specific device to a microcomputer. Alternatively, a user could post answers to existing questions or make software or hardware available. In general, the electronic bulletin is a clearing house for public (group) dialogue and equipment exchange.

LAN Characteristics

The applications described above have several things in common:

1. Communication between a variety of devices in a limited geographical area
2. Utilization of several different applications
3. High-speed data transfer
4. High reliability
5. Device and data sharing
6. Transparent interface to shared resources
7. Adaptability to meet changing hardware and software requirements
8. Potential access to other networks such as a wide area network, a PDN, or another LAN

9. Potential access to a multi-user host system like a minicomputer or a mainframe

10. Security from interference from other users, either accidental or intentional

11. Ease of management

12. Private ownership

This, then, is the basis for a local area network: multiple devices of different types and capabilities providing transparent access to diverse applications in a limited geographical area, all requiring reliability and rapid response for common services needed by the devices. The network must be manageable, be able to accommodate changing requirements and devices, and be able to interface to other communication networks. Most important, the LAN must contribute to the solution of business problems. Let us now look at the components that are integrated to form a LAN.

LAN COMPONENTS

A LAN is a combination of hardware and software working together to allow communications between network nodes. The basic hardware and software components are listed in Figure 8-3. Some of the components may not be required in a specific LAN implementation and other components may be required only under certain circumstances. An explanation of the components and where they are used follows.

Network Interface Card and Transceivers

A physical connection must exist between the medium and the node's I/O bus. This connection consists of a *bus interface unit* (*BIU*), which connects to the computer's I/O bus, and a *communications interface unit* (*CIU*), which connects to the medium. The BIU and CIU can be combined on one logic board, the *network interface card* (*NIC*), or can be on separate boards. The BIU and CIU are illustrated in Figure 8-4. The functions of the connection are to: (1) monitor the medium, (2) serve as a buffer between the medium and the node's memory, (3) give a unique address to each node, (4) recognize data on the medium addressed to that node, and (5) place data on the medium on behalf of the node.

The NIC contains logic for implementing the *media access control* (*MAC*) protocol (see Chapter 6) and the physical layer requirements of the medium. This means the NIC will be specifically oriented to Ethernet, token ring, ARCnet, or another MAC protocol and will have connectors suited to the specific medium used. A *transceiver* is responsible for physically placing data onto the medium and taking data off the medium. *Transceiver* is a shortened expression for transmitter/receiver. The NIC and the

Figure 8-3 LAN
Components

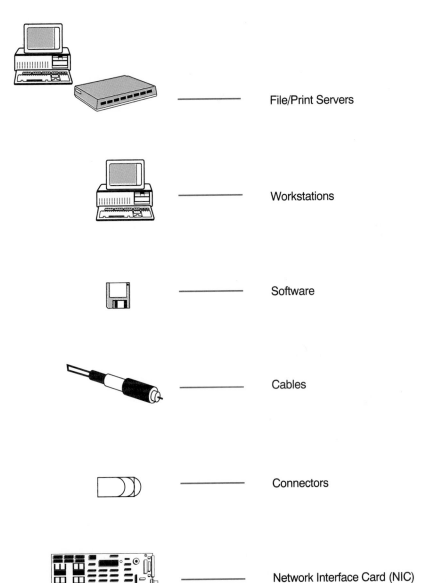

File/Print Servers

Workstations

Software

Cables

Connectors

Network Interface Card (NIC)

transceiver are often packaged on the same printed circuit board; however, in a few implementations, the transceiver is separate from the NIC.

Connectors, Terminators, and Repeaters

The NIC must be connected to the medium. A variety of *connectors* are used. Often the type of connector is determined by the medium. For example, BNC connectors are frequently used for coaxial cables. A variety of BNC (Bayonet-Neill-Corcelman) connectors are illustrated in Figure 8-5(a).

Figure 8-4 Bus/
Communications
Interface Units
and Transceiver

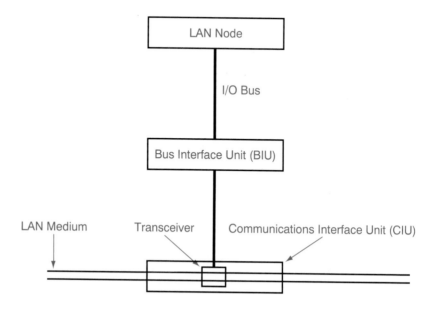

For twisted wire pairs, an RJ-11 or RJ-45 telephone jack connector is commonly used. These connectors are illustrated in Figure 8-5(b). *Terminators*
are required in some LANs. On bus networks, terminators are usually required at the ends of the bus to eliminate signal loss and echo. They are
also sometimes required on unused wiring hub ports to prevent signal
loss. The use of a terminator is illustrated in Figure 8-5(c). *Repeaters* provide signal amplification for LANs that span long distances. For example,
one LAN standard states that the longest single medium segment is
500 meters. A cable span of 1000 meters can be accomplished by using a repeater. In the middle of the 1000-meter span, a repeater is inserted to provide signal regeneration, as illustrated in Figure 8-6.

Medium, Wiring Hubs, and MAUs

Unlike WANs, where a variety of media may be used in a single network,
LANs usually consist of only one type of medium. The most commonly
used media are coaxial cable, twisted wire pairs, and fiber optics. Most
early LANs used coaxial cable; however, starting in the late 1980s, coaxial
cable has lost market share to twisted wire pairs and fiber optics. This loss
of market share is attributable to the higher speeds available on twisted
wire pairs and to the maturation of fiber optic technology. Twisted wire
pairs support speeds up to 20 Mbps and fiber optic cable is increasingly
being used for the higher speed LANs. A few LANs use wireless media,
usually either infrared light or radio-frequency broadcast.

   Wiring hubs are used to interconnect workstations as illustrated in
Figure 8-7(a) or to provide cable junctions in a wiring closet as illustrated
in Figure 8-7(b). Hubs are not required in all networks. Hubs can be active

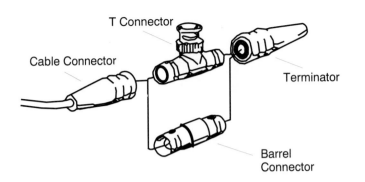

Figure 8-5(a) Cable Connectors and Terminator

T Connector

Cable Connector

Terminator

Barrel Connector

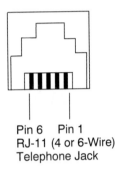

Pin 6 Pin 1
RJ-11 (4 or 6-Wire)
Telephone Jack

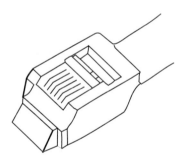

Figure 8-5(b) Telephone Cable Connectors

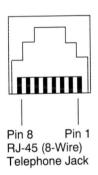

Pin 8 Pin 1
RJ-45 (8-Wire)
Telephone Jack

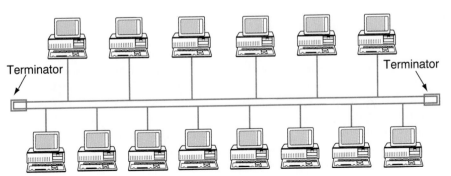

Terminator

Terminator

Figure 8-5(c) Use of a Terminator

Figure 8-6 Network
Extension with a
Repeater

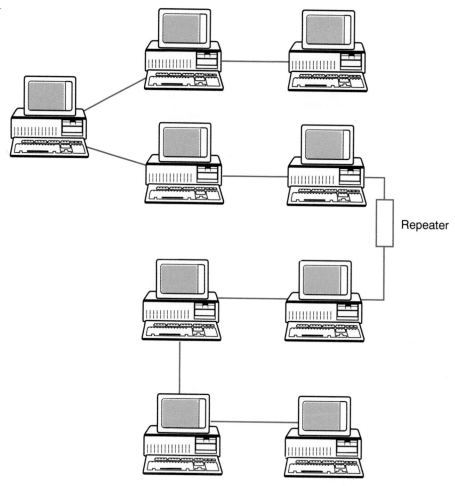

Repeater

or passive. *Active hubs* provide signal regeneration and *passive hubs* simply
provide workstation connection. *Multi-station access units* (*MAUs*) serve
the same purpose as wiring hubs and are used in token ring networks for
station interconnection. A MAU is illustrated in Figure 8-8.

Servers and Workstations

LAN nodes cover a broad spectrum. At one end of the spectrum are
relatively low-cost devices such as microcomputer workstations. Other
types of nodes include minicomputers, CAD workstations, disk drives,
tape drives, large-scale computing systems, laboratory equipment, and
manufacturing equipment. Examples of laboratory equipment include
apparatus for monitoring the environment, analyzing clinical specimens,
and monitoring engine emissions. Manufacturing equipment includes
robots and numerical control machinery. Small LANs may consist of fewer

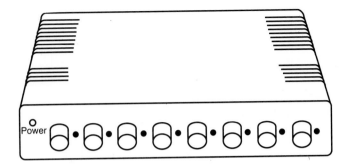

Figure 8-7(a)
Wiring Hub

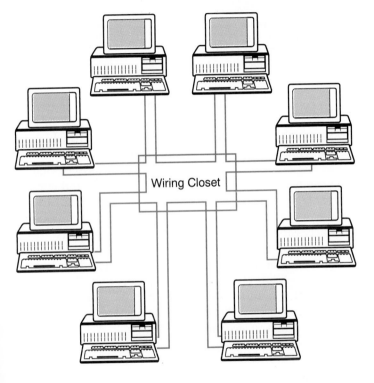

Figure 8-7(b)
Wiring Closet

than ten microcomputers connected primarily to share disks and printers. At the other end of the spectrum are LANs of large computing systems manufactured by corporations like Cray, IBM, Unisys, DEC, Tandem, and Control Data.

Large microcomputer LANs usually have one or more server nodes; small microcomputer LANs may have none or may have a node that operates as both a workstation and a server. Networks without servers are called *peer-to-peer networks*. In peer-to-peer LANs each workstation can provide server functions. Interestingly, peer-to-peer LANs are often used when connecting large systems; thus, they are found on both ends of the size scale. The advantage of peer-to-peer networks is that you do not have

Figure 8-8 Multi-Station Access Unit (MAU)

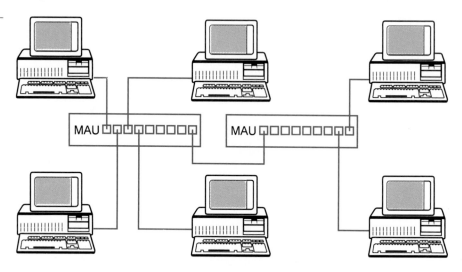

to change your computer configurations. In a server-oriented LAN, shared resources like printers and disks must be attached to the servers. In a peer-to-peer LAN, printers and files can remain on the computer to which they were originally assigned. Those resources can then be shared without reconfiguration. On the other hand, keeping track of resources that can be on any node on the network presents a few management and control problems. A disadvantage of peer-to-peer LANs is security. Since the disks on each node are accessible from other nodes, all files on each node may thus be network accessible. Typically, peer-to-peer LAN software does not provide security to protect confidential files and directories. In most microcomputer LANs, one or more computers are designated as servers. The server(s) almost always has more processing power and disk storage than workstations. In a LAN with IBM PC, XT, and AT workstations the server may be based on an 80386 or 80486 processor, a Motorola 68000-family processor, or might be a large system like a DEC VAX. A wide variety of options is available for server nodes.

LAN SOFTWARE

It takes more than hardware to make a network function successfully—the software is equally important. Generally speaking it is the software that provides the shared access to devices, effects file transfers, and forms the logical connections between users. A discussion of LAN software becomes somewhat difficult if one considers the wide variation in LAN implementations. Some are low-speed microcomputer-oriented nets accommodating only a few workstations and intended primarily for hardware sharing. Some are microcomputer oriented, but on a much larger scale, accommodating hundreds of users sharing not only hardware but also files and software. Some are oriented toward interfacing to other equipment and networks. Still others are oriented to high-speed data transfers. Rather than attempting to address such diverse applications, we make some general software observations and discuss several key software products.

File Server Software

The primary function of a server is to provide a service to network users. The two most common types are file servers and print servers. Each has unique requirements. *File servers* allow users to share one or more disk drives. To effectively provide disk sharing, the file server must perform the following functions.

Concurrent Access Controls. Many microcomputer-oriented software systems were designed for single users on a stand-alone system. When software and files are placed on a server multiple users may be able to access them concurrently. This poses a problem with some software for several reasons. Some systems create temporary files using specific naming conventions. If this occurs, a second user of that software may conflict with the first user because of file name conflicts. Many software systems can be somewhat customized for a particular user. Accommodating multiple user profiles is a desirable capability for network software, but it may not be found in single-user-oriented systems. Moreover, when sharing data or text files, server software must prevent the contention problems described earlier.

Single-user software can sometimes be used effectively when installed on a file server. A software package that is used by several users but is used by only one user at a time may be installed on the file server. To avoid the problems inherent in multiple users attempting to use such software concurrently, controls are placed over the software. For example, there may be a user-count watchdog program that controls access to the software. When a user accesses the software, the watchdog program makes note that the application is being used. If another user attempts access while the software is in use, that user receives a file busy or locked message. Other controls that might be used are record or file locks.

License Agreements. Most purchased software has license agreements. *License agreements* specify the way in which the software may be used and typically stipulate how many users can concurrently use the software. It is important that LAN users understand and adhere to the provisions of a software license; to do otherwise is illegal and might subject the company to a lawsuit. License agreements differ substantially from one software vendor to another. Some stipulate that the software can be installed on one and only one workstation. Others stipulate that the software can be installed on several workstations but cannot be used concurrently by two or more users. Still other license agreements (typically those for LAN software) allow a specific number of concurrent users, while others allow unlimited concurrent usage (an unlimited site license). Understanding software vendors' licensing agreements is not only important from the legal aspect but also has financial impact. If a particular vendor's license agreement allows for ten concurrent users and a corporation needs to have 105 workstations concurrently using that software, then 11 such software modules must be purchased.

Access Optimization. If the file server's primary responsibility is to provide access to files and software, the file system ought to be optimized to meet user requests in a timely manner. For example, Novell, Inc., a leader in microcomputer LAN technology, has written an operating system specifically for server file optimization. Features incorporated in this system include fault tolerance, file recovery, disk caching, and multiple disk channels. Fault tolerance is usually attained by adding backup components to the system. With a fault-tolerant system, one component of the system such as a disk drive can fail and the system continues to operate at full capacity. *File recovery* means that data can be recovered subsequent to a problem causing data loss, such as accidentally erasing a file or a disk failure. *Disk caching* is a technique whereby main memory is used to store frequently used disk data. Caching provides rapid access to that data because no physical disk access is needed. Multiple disk channels can be used to spread disk accesses over several paths and thus increase the disk access capacity. Basically, the server's operating system is designed to make user access to data faster.

Reliability. If the file server is the repository of data necessary for users to perform their work, the server must be reliable. Failure of a server node can make the network inoperable and cause a loss of productivity. Several LAN vendors have integrated fault tolerance into their systems. An alternate approach to fault tolerance is to have multiple file servers. Then, if one server fails, another is available to continue processing. Multiple fault-tolerant file servers provide even better reliability.

Transparent Access. LAN users often are not computer experts. For them to make effective use of server capabilities, access to the server's files should be no more difficult than local access. Simple interfaces and help functions make using a system more effective. One of the functions that the LAN software needs to accomplish is making the interface to the LAN transparent to the users, also known as a seamless interface. The LAN software, running in both server and workstation nodes, allows the workstation user to access server resources as though those resources were locally attached and dedicated to that workstation. It is impossible, however, to completely separate a workstation user from the shared nature of a network. Print jobs may take longer to print because multiple users are sharing one printer, database records may not be immediately available because another user is updating them, applications may not be available because the number of users has reached the license agreement maximum, and response time may increase because of peaks in system use. Other than consequences of sharing resources like those just mentioned, the network user should not need to work differently because he or she is on a network.

Network transparency is not always completely provided. For example, on one network, a word processing user must operate differently when printing a document. In a stand-alone mode, the user can simply select the print option and return to document edit mode. On the network in question, after selecting the print option, the user must select a network printing option and then exit from the word processing program to have the print job queued for printing. On the same system, Pascal programs cannot write directly to the printer; instead, the programs write to a disk file that is subsequently printed using a network print utility. These are two examples of network interfaces that are not transparent.

Interfaces.   Often one LAN must *interface* to another network or to a variety of terminals, workstations, and processors. A file server may be called upon to provide these connections. This means that a variety of software interfaces may need to exist, for example, to an X.25 network, a WAN, or a large host computer.

File Transfer.   One of the basic LAN software functions is the ability to transfer data from one node to another, and all LANs have software to effect this. Another frequent requirement is the ability to transfer data from the LAN to a device not directly connected to the LAN. This could be a node on another network or a stand-alone host computer. File transfer software must exist in at least two places, the sending node and the receiving node. If there are intermediate nodes, file transfer functions must exist there as well.

Node-to-Node Communication.   Both servers and workstations must have LAN software to communicate. Workstations must have software to identify and accept network requests and pass those requests down to the data link control layer. On the receiving end, network software accepts data from the data link control layer and passes it to the application layer. Thus, the LAN software essentially performs presentation and session layer services for the network.

On the server side, the same type of software is required. However, server software tends to be more complex than workstation software. Workstations typically must deal with one request at a time; servers can receive multiple service requests at one time. To handle multiple requests efficiently, the server must be able to perform multi-tasking or multi-processing. This means that the server should not be single-threaded. A single-threaded server accepts a request, processes it until completion, accepts the next request, processes it to completion, accepts the next request, and so on. This service mechanism causes some workstations to wait a considerable time for requests to be acted on. Multi-tasking or multi-processing allows the server to work on multiple requests at the same time. For example, while waiting for a disk read to complete for one request, the server can be transmitting data for another request.

Network Management.   Once installed, a network must be managed. Management functions include adding and deleting users, setting security, establishing user profiles, detecting and correcting faults, and so on. Network management software and hardware diagnostic tools can greatly simplify the management tasks. Network management is discussed in more detail in Chapter 11.

Security.   *Security* is intended to allow users access to those resources necessary for performing their job functions while restricting them from access privileges that do not fall under their job scope. In stand-alone systems, security is not so great an issue. However, when data is shared among multiple users, often there is a need to control how that data is used. For a given individual file, some users may not even find out that it exists; some can read it; others can write to it; and a few can possibly erase it. If it is an executable file, users may be allowed to execute it but are forbidden to copy it. If licensing restrictions exist for the object program, the system may be required to limit the number of concurrent users of the program. Security details are discussed in Chapter 13.

Application Program Interface (API).   A convention must be used to pass requests and data from an application to the network. *Application program interface (API)* is a term that refers to such a convention. There is a wide variety of APIs available. As a result, you will find that applications that run on one LAN might not run on another because the interface conventions differ. Examples of APIs are IBM's NetBIOS, named pipes, and Novell's Internetwork Packet Exchange/Sequenced Packet Exchange (IPX/SPX). An application interfaces with an API through procedure calls or by generating an interrupt. Regardless of the method, the objective is for the application to signal that it needs a network service. The service may be to read or write a record or to send output to a printer. The API accepts the application's request and acts on it on behalf of the application.

Printer Server

One of the LAN resources commonly shared is a printer. Because only one job can be printing at a time and because multiple users may simultaneously request the use of the same printer, a mechanism is needed to allow orderly printer sharing. One such device is a software system called a *spooler* (*spool* is an acronym for simultaneous peripheral operation online). A spooler is an interface between users needing print service and printers.

The spooler manages print jobs by placing them in a print queue for printing, establishes print job priorities, prints jobs from the queues on the proper available printer(s), and provides for print job management. Print job management includes items like:

Collection of printed output

Direction of print jobs to the correct printer(s)

Management of print job statuses, such as hold after printing; number of copies to be printed; priority queuing of jobs to be printed; printing of selected portions of documents, such as a specific page or pages; and print job origination

Other management functions, such as providing a user interface, manual deletion of print jobs, changing print job priorities, adding/deleting printers, sensing printer status, starting/stopping printers or taking on/off line, printing statistical reports, adding/deleting locations, associating locations with printers, printing banner or trailer pages to separate print jobs, and starting/stopping the spool process itself

After reading the list of print management tasks above, you might correctly draw the conclusion that shared printer management is not necessarily a simple task. Any resource sharing requires management and control, and print management is often one of the most challenging to manage because of the relatively low speed of printers, occasional high demand for their use, conflicts regarding the paper stock used, and the likelihood of printer faults due to out-of-paper or similar conditions. Moreover, users often like to have nearly immediate access to their printed output. Some of the challenges faced by LAN administrators regarding print management are capacity planning, printer distribution, job queuing, forms management, and printer maintenance.

Print Capacity Planning.   There are several aspects to print capacity planning. First, print jobs are routed to a file on disk. Sufficient space must be allocated to hold these jobs. Insufficient space allocation may result in jobs being lost or the inability to initiate or complete print functions. Therefore, the LAN administrator must ensure that sufficient job storage space is available and monitor the storage area to ensure that space is not becoming limited. This is particularly the case when users can cause their printed output to be held on disk indefinitely, such as with spooler systems allowing print jobs to be held for printing at a later time. Poor management can result in these jobs consuming a significant portion of the available space and creating out-of-space conditions. Of equal importance is the management of large print jobs. Suppose that one user is printing a 200-page document. Such large documents can result in considerable delays for other users. The LAN manager may wish to avoid such delays by having printers designated as "large-job" printers and "small-job" printers.

Lengthy or time-consuming jobs such as printing of graphic images are routed to the large-job printer, where longer waits are anticipated. Other jobs are routed to the short-job printers.

Printer Distribution.   As mentioned earlier, transparency is one objective of network management and network systems. Easy access to printed jobs is one facet of transparency. If a user's printed output is not located near his or her workstation, the effectiveness of the network is diminished. Thus, printers need to be strategically placed to provide easy access to users. Moreover, there is typically a variety of printing devices available— laser printers, plotters, color printers, and so on. Printer distribution must consider not only having a printer conveniently available to users but also having the *right* printer available.

Job Queuing.   With a variety of available printers and a variety of job types—long jobs, short jobs, graphic jobs, and so on—it is important that jobs be routed to the correct printing device(s). Users at each workstation may, for example, route their output to the same local printer, say LPT1 in a DOS environment. However, these jobs designated for printing on the same local port will likely need to be printed on a variety of network printers. Establishing the proper mapping of local printer ports to local or network printers is essential in promoting user productivity. Also, as previously stated, it may be necessary to queue long jobs to certain printers to avoid printer congestion.

Forms Management.   Printer output needs vary. Some users require plain paper, others may require corporate letterhead paper, and still others may require special forms such as envelopes, checks, or invoices. Not only that, but one user may require one set of forms for one print job and a different set of forms for another. As a result, conflicts can occur. Checks may end up being printed on corporate letterhead paper and invoices, on envelopes. The LAN administrator and the spooler must make provisions for these needs. One technique is to specify a forms option for a printer loaded with special forms. Only jobs specifying that form option will be allowed to print on that printer.

Printer Maintenance.   Printers are usually the most unreliable part of a network. They run out of paper or toner, paper jams occur, and users accidentally leave them offline and thus unable to accept additional print jobs. The spooler software ought to have warning messages that alert LAN administrators to printers that are unable to accept jobs. Upon being advised of printer errors, someone must be responsible for correcting them. It is commonplace for users to clear faults such as out-of-paper, paper jams, or offline conditions. Other problems may require action by LAN administrators or technicians.

LAN Topologies and Protocols

In Chapters 6 and 7 the basic network protocols and topologies were introduced. Three of these topologies—bus, ring, and star—and two media access protocols—CSMA/CD and token passing—are used extensively in LAN implementations. The topics of topologies and protocols as they apply to LANs are reviewed in this section.

Bus with CSMA/CD. To date most of the LAN implementations have used a bus configuration with CSMA/CD as the access protocol (Cashin, 1987). This is not necessarily because this combination is superior to other implementations but because much of the early research and development, such as Ethernet, used this technology.

Token Ring. A token passing ring is probably the second most common LAN implementation. This architecture has been selected by IBM.

Token Bus. Instead of using CSMA/CD on a bus architecture, some implementers have chosen to implement token passing as the media access protocol on a bus configuration.

Star. The third major topology is the star. Several access protocols are used in this configuration, including contention, token passing, polling/selecting, and CSMA/CD.

Baseband Versus Broadband Revisited

An additional configuration option, baseband or broadband transmission, must be considered when implementing a LAN. This topic was introduced in Chapter 2 and is covered in somewhat greater detail here. The discussion of transmission media in Chapter 2 briefly covers the differences between baseband and broadband transmission for coaxial cable. In fact, baseband and broadband transmissions are not limited to coaxial cable; both can also be implemented via twisted wire pairs or fiber optics, or any other medium. In practice, such transmission on twisted wire pairs makes little sense because the bandwidth is too small. The following discussion assumes coaxial cable as the medium, since that is the one commonly used. With small alterations, the discussion could also apply to fiber optic cable.

In baseband transmission, the entire bandwidth of the medium is used to carry data, which is represented as voltage fluctuations. In baseband, only one signal is transmitted on the medium. In broadband transmission, a frequency division multiplexing technique allows multiple, both high-speed and low-speed, channels on one cable and also permits use of the cable for other purposes such as voice and video. A discussion of one potential use of a broadband system follows.

Coaxial cable has a bandwidth of approximately 400 megahertz (MHz), which can be divided into several channels, each of which will support

Figure 8-9 Suggested Broadband Frequency Allocation

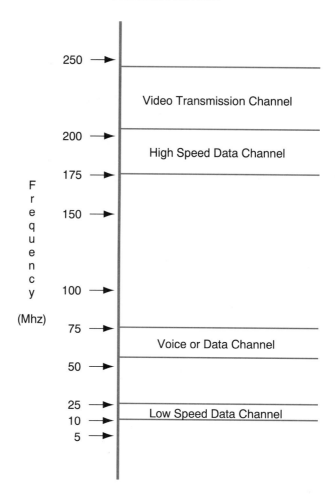

Figure 8-9 Suggested Broadband Frequency Allocation

a particular function. For instance, the total bandwidth can be separated into a voice channel, a video channel, a high-speed data channel, a low-speed data channel, and switched channels. Harris et al. (1983) suggest the following channel allocations, which are illustrated in Figure 8-9. One band can span the frequency range of 10 to 25 MHz, to be used for low-speed data transmission. A band that spans the range from 55 to 75 MHz can be used for switched voice or data transmissions. Another band, from 175 to 210 MHz, can be dedicated exclusively to high-speed data exchanges. A fourth band, from 210 to 240 MHz, can be assigned for video transmission.

A 10-Mbps channel using CSMA/CD access can be implemented on the high-speed data band, yielding a band equivalent to that of the baseband Ethernet system. The low-speed data band can be separated into several 56-Kbps circuits as well as lower speed 9600-bps circuits. Because video requires a channel capacity of approximately 6 MHz, five video channels could be allocated on the video band. The interface with the broadband system is via modems specifically designed for that purpose or similar devices. On the low-speed channels, almost any type of terminal can be attached. The high-speed channel can be used to attach devices capable of transmitting at higher speeds, such as workstations and processors.

From the above description, broadband transmission may seem the obvious way to go. It provides flexibility as well as a channel that is equivalent to many of the baseband systems. However, there are some disadvantages to broadband. A broadband system is inherently more complex than a baseband system, for the channels must be carefully designed and allocated among users. A baseband system does not need the same amount of planning and design. A broadband system is more expensive to implement, on the order of $100 to $200 more per station (Greaney, 1989). Baseband is more suitable for the extremely high transmission rates sometimes required for communication between large-scale processors or many lower speed devices. Current implementations on coaxial cable operate at up to 100 Mbps, and fiber optic systems have been planned with data rates of over 2 Gbps.

Broadband networks may increase in popularity as the cost for these systems decreases. Another use for broadband technology is as a backbone network medium connecting multiple LANs. Broadband technology is well suited for this use because of the high data rates it can sustain and because broadband LANs can span longer distances than most wire-based baseband technologies. For example, a single Ethernet LAN with repeaters is limited to 2,500 meters. A broadband backbone can span distances up to 20,000 meters (the IEEE 802.3 10Broad36 specification provides for maximum network distances of 3,600 meters). An example of a broadband backbone used to interconnect stand-alone workstations and baseband LANs is shown in Figure 8-10.

For a LAN user interested only in the transfer of data, a baseband system is the easiest to implement. With careful prior planning, it could be implemented initially and later converted to a broadband system if necessary. This would, of course, necessitate buying additional equipment. Future uses of LANs will probably require the flexibility and diversity provided by a broadband system, which allows almost any device to interface with the system, with both high-speed and low-speed interfaces available. More important, broadband also easily accommodates voice and video.

LAN STANDARDS

You have probably already sensed that there are a wide variety of LAN implementations and ways to install them. In the early days of LAN technology, 1979, there were 44 identified LAN implementations that could be grouped into seven different categories (Myers, 1982). Since then more

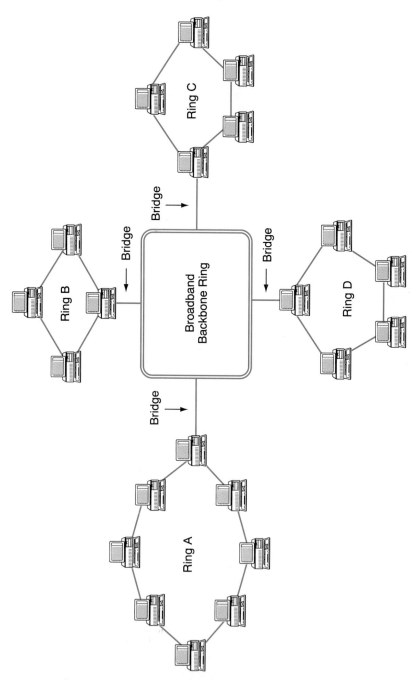

Figure 8-10 Broad- band Backbone Network Connecting Local Area Networks

288

have been added. The communications industry quickly realized that standards were necessary not only to define LANs to meet specific application needs but also to bring control to a burgeoning technology and provide for open architectures. In an *open architecture* the interface specifications are published. Open architectures allow multiple manufacturers to design and market network components. In contrast, a *closed architecture* is proprietary to one or a few companies. Thus, only those companies can build network components. One of the principal organizations to address the problem of multiple architectures and to establish an open architecture is the Institute of Electrical and Electronics Engineers (IEEE).

IEEE LAN Standards

The IEEE recognized that different applications can call for different LAN architectures. For example, the needs of process control differ somewhat from those of office automation. A guaranteed response time is relatively unimportant in the automated office, but in process control a guaranteed response time may be critical. The manufacture of silicon chips, for instance, is a combination of time-sensitive photographic, chemical, doping, and heat processes. If a LAN is used in the process control cycle, it is essential that a node controlling a time-sensitive operation have a guaranteed access window into the network. As described in Chapter 6, such guarantees are impossible to make in the CSMA/CD access protocol, whereas response times are quite predictable with token passing protocols. The IEEE formed a standards project designated Project 802 to address the various needs of different LAN applications. The 802 project is composed of several subcommittees with specific areas of responsibility. These subcommittees are described below.

IEEE Project 802 Recommendations

The IEEE recommendations cover four areas: (1) topology, speed, and data link protocol; (2) transmission medium; (3) addressing; and (4) voice and video transmission. We provide a brief overview of each.

Topology, Speed, and Data Link Protocol.   Rather than proposing a standard representing a single approach, the committee decided to propose a standard representing two topologies—ring and bus—and three data link protocols—carrier sense with multiple access and collision detection (CSMA/CD) for bus topology and token passing for either ring or bus topologies. In 1987 the IEEE recommended inclusion of a star topology as well. LAN designers and implementers are thus free, within standard guidelines, to adopt a strategy that meets the requirements of their particular application. IEEE standards also include minimum requirements for speed, number of accessible devices, and distances. Some of these restrictions eliminate several LAN alternatives, such as PBXs, where the minimum speed characteristics cannot currently be met.

Transmission Medium. The standards subcommittees are primarily considering three media: coaxial cable, twisted wire pairs, and fiber optics. The committee recommended twisted pairs and coaxial cable—both baseband and broadband—in the first completed standards. Fiber optic cable will also be incorporated. Microwave, radio broadcast, and infrared transmission have been recognized as possible alternatives but have not yet been included in the standards.

Addressing. The committee proposed various addressing alternatives. On one hand, users of larger networks are interested in inter-network connections involving addresses that are internationally unique. On the other hand, some users desire local access only and are concerned about the extra address space required for international addressing. A compromise proposal allows both alternatives. The scheme for local access uses a 16-bit address, and the internationally unique address uses 48 bits.

Voice and Video Transmission. Video has not been specifically addressed by the IEEE standards. Integration of voice and data is being considered for the 802.9 standard.

IEEE Project 802 Subcommittees

By mid-1984, the institute had adopted two standards: IEEE 802.3, which describes a CSMA/CD bus architecture, and IEEE 802.4, which describes a token passing bus configuration. Since that time, additional standards have developed. The IEEE 802 subcommittees that are formulating standards and their objectives are described below.

802.1—High-Level Interface. The high-level interface subcommittee is addressing matters relating to network architecture, network management, and network interconnection, and all other issues related to the higher OSI layers.

802.2—Logical Link Control. IEEE has divided the data link layer into two sublayers: *logical link control* (*LLC*) and *media access control* (*MAC*). The MAC sublayer implements protocols such as token passing or CSMA/CD. Figure 8-11 illustrates the relationship between the LLC and the MAC sublayers. The objective of the LLC is to provide a consistent, transparent interface to the MAC layer, so that the network layers above the data link layer are able to function correctly regardless of the MAC protocol.

802.3—CSMA/CD. This standard covers a variety of CSMA/CD architectures that are generally based on Ethernet. Several alternatives are available under this standard. Some of these are:

1Base5	1 Mbps baseband medium with a maximum segment length of 500 meters. The segment length is the length

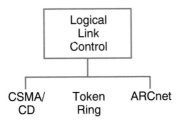

Logical Link Control
Media Access Control, e.g., Token Ring

Figure 8-11 OSI Data Link Control Layer

of cable that can be used without repeaters to amplify the signal. This standard encompasses implementations commonly known as *Starlan*.

10Base5   10 Mbps baseband medium with a maximum segment length of 500 meters.

10Base2   10 Mbps baseband medium with a maximum segment length of 200 meters. The cable used in this implementation is commonly called Thinnet or Cheapernet.

10BaseT   10 Mbps baseband medium with twisted wire pairs as the medium.

10Broad36   10 Mbps broadband medium with a 3600-meter segment length.

You may infer from this nomenclature that, in general, the initial number represents the speed of the medium in millions of bits per second; the "base" or "broad" designator represents baseband or broadband, respectively; and, with one exception, the last number represents the segment length of the medium in hundreds of meters.

802.4—Token Bus. This subcommittee sets standards for token bus networks. The standard describes how the network is initialized, how new stations can insert themselves into the set of nodes receiving the token, how to recover if the token is lost, and how node priority can be established. The standard also describes the format of the message frames.

802.5—Token Ring. This subcommittee sets standards for token ring networks. The standard describes essentially the same functions as those described by the token bus network.

802.6—Metropolitan Area Networks (MANs). This subcommittee sets standards for networks that can cover a wide area and operate at high speed. Distances of up to 200 miles and speeds on the order of 100 Mbps are being considered for metropolitan area networks. A metropolitan area network could transmit voice and video in addition to data.

802.7—Broadband Technical Advisory Group. This group's purpose is to provide guidance and technical expertise to other groups that are establishing broadband LAN standards, such as the 802.3 subcommittee for 10Broad36.

802.8—Fiber Optic Technical Advisory Group. This group's purpose is to provide guidance and technical expertise to other groups that are establishing standards for LANs using fiber optic cable.

802.9—Integrated Data and Voice Networks. This committee sets standards for networks that carry both voice and data. Specifically, it is setting standards for interfaces to the Integrated Services Digital Networks (ISDNs).

IEEE and the OSI Reference Model

One of the first actions of IEEE was to endorse the International Standards Organization's OSI reference model. Because the top three layers are application-oriented and the next two are interface layers between application and transmission functions, only the bottom two layers, divided into three separate layers as illustrated in Figure 8-12, were chosen for the LAN standard. The lowest layer encompasses the physical medium, either twisted wire pairs, coaxial cable, or fiber optics. The second layer designates the physical attachment to the medium and includes the techniques for encoding data onto the medium and decoding data from the medium. The third layer, the data link layer, includes the LLC and MAC protocols.

The ANSI Fiber Distributed Data Interface (FDDI) Standard

Two major uses have been suggested for high-speed LANs. The obvious one is the high-speed exchange of data among computers located within a large urban area. Frequently, companies have several offices distributed throughout a large metropolitan area, and a MAN will allow computers in these locations to exchange large amounts of data almost instantly. The second purpose is as a backbone network to interconnect distributed LANs. This is illustrated in Figure 8-13.

A high-speed LAN standard was also addressed by the American National Standards Institute (ANSI). ANSI has established a standard, the Fiber Distributed Data Interface (FDDI), for a high-speed LAN using fiber optic cable. The FDDI is similar to the metropolitan area network (MAN)

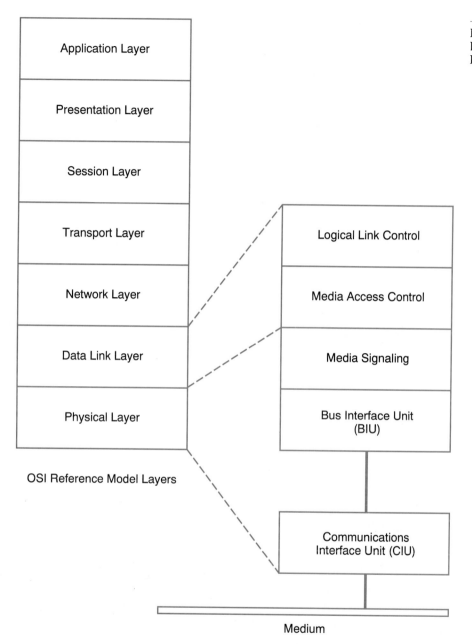

Figure 8-12 Two Bottom Layers of IEEE Standard

LAN being proposed by the IEEE. ANSI completed its specification before IEEE, and, as a result, the impetus for the IEEE effort has waned.

The FDDI specifications call for a token ring LAN operating at a speed of 100 Mbps over distances up to 200 kilometers. As the name implies, the medium is fiber optic cable. The maximum cable segment allowed without repeaters is 2 kilometers. The 200 kilometer distance can be attained by

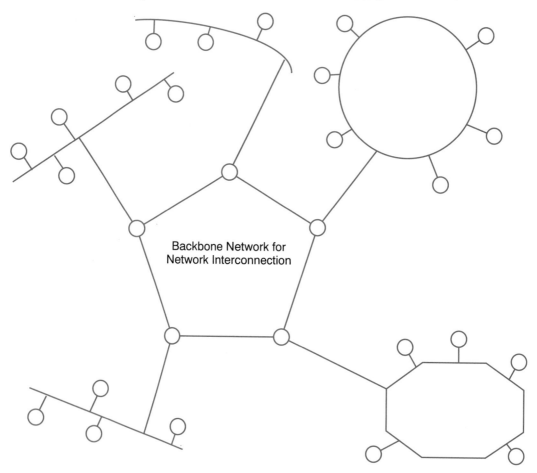

Backbone Network for
Network Interconnection

Figure 8-13   A Backbone Network

connecting 100 such segments. Up to 1000 nodes can be connected to the ring. With a LAN spanning this distance, it is not realistic to have only one message on the ring at one time. Multiple messages may be circulating at a given time. The protocol for doing this is as follows: Only one token circulates around the line. When a station receives the token, such as Node A in Figure 8-14(a), it removes the token from the ring and transmits its message. At the end of its message, A appends the token as illustrated in Figure 8-14(b). The next node, Node B, sees the token and can piggy-back a message onto the existing message. Node B then appends the token onto the message as illustrated in Figure 8-14(c). A's message continues to circulate around the ring until it gets to the recipient, Node X. X returns the message to A as an acknowledgment, and A removes its message from the ring as illustrated in Figure 8-14(d). The specification also allows a node to transmit multiple messages in succession. A transmit time limit is established during which a node is allowed to send multiple messages while it holds the token.

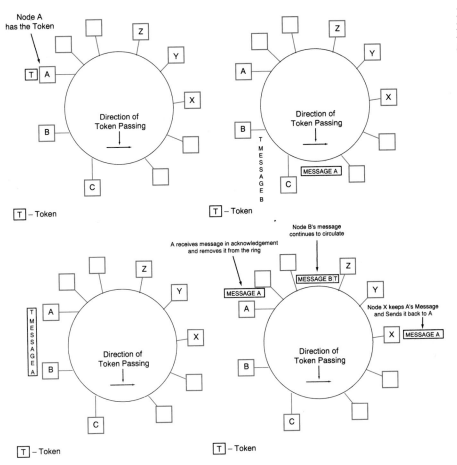

Figure 8-14
Message Passing in
an FDDI LAN

Two addressing modes are allowed in an FDDI network. One mode uses a 15-bit address and the other uses a 46-bit address. The standard does not, however, stipulate the exact format of addresses. The FDDI LAN can be used as a backbone network to connect multiple LANs, as a high-speed LAN connecting large computing systems, and as a high-speed document delivery system for office automation and graphics applications.

THE PRIVATE BRANCH EXCHANGE

In the discussion of broadband technology above, it was mentioned that one of the broadband channels can be used to carry voice signals. The *private branch exchange (PBX)* is another way that voice can be accommodated on a LAN. PBXs have changed dramatically in the last two decades. This section highlights the potential of PBX as a medium provider and data switch for LAN systems.

PBX History

The PBX system has been a standard fixture in business offices for many years. As the number of people occupying offices grew, so did the required number of telephone installations. This increased demand eventually became a drain on the telephone companies' ability to supply individual telephone lines. PBX equipment was meant to alleviate this problem. In essence, with a PBX, a business becomes a private telephone branch switching office.

One of the basic assumptions of telephony is that telephone calls are relatively infrequent and of short duration. Telephone switching systems therefore have been set up with capacities of approximately 10%–20%. Thus, no more than 20% of the subscribers in a given exchange can place a call at a given time (McNamara, 1977). The same assumption was brought to PBX installations, excluding intra-office connections. Thus, for a business with approximately 50 telephones, sufficient line capacity would be installed for only approximately 5–10 outside calls (Digital Equipment Corp., 1982). Add to this the intracompany calls made within the same business location via a PBX (which does not utilize outside-line capacity) and the total number of connections possible is greater than 20%.

Until 1967, the only vendors of PBX systems were the telephone companies. With the Carterphone decision (see Chapter 1), the market opened up for other vendors to design and sell PBX equipment. This spurred developments such as electronic switching, computer-based PBX systems, and finally digital PBX systems. All of these technologies were developing concurrently with LAN technology.

PBX Implementation

Suppose that you are the head of a business in an established office building. Your office has a PBX system. You have recently noticed that your current LAN, sneaker-net, is occupying a good deal of personnel time. Sneaker-net is the network whereby users exchange files by walking between workstations to obtain what they need. To eliminate the time wasted in personal data delivery, you decide to install a LAN system. Having done your homework, you realize that some software will need to be purchased, perhaps some special hardware for servers, connectors, and a medium. The major issue among these requirements is how to wire the building for a LAN. One solution to this problem, the PBX system, is already in place.

PBX systems typically use shielded or (more commonly) unshielded twisted wire pairs as the medium. This same medium can also be used to convey data and serve as the medium for a LAN. The problems faced in accomplishing this are ensuring that (1) both voice data can be transmitted on the same medium, (2) data transfer rates are sufficient to meet response and throughput requirements, and (3) the existing telephone service will not be impaired. For some PBX users, these problems can be successfully resolved.

The first concern is the ability to use the same medium for both voice and data transmission. This problem has been resolved using both analog and digital PBX systems. The new wave in PBX systems is digital PBX, sometimes referred to as a *digital branch exchange* (*DBX*). This system uses digital transmission not only for data, but also for voice. Digital telephone sets, some integrated into terminals and workstations, transmit digital rather than analog signals. The more common analog telephone sets can also be used when accompanied by an analog-to-digital conversion board, a device called a *codec* (short for coder-decoder). Digital PBX systems eliminate the need for modems for local access. However, access to remote locations through analog telephone transmission still requires modems. For example, a workstation may need to connect to a bulletin board system that uses an analog telephone connection. Interfacing the data network with the outside telephone network may require changing digital signals to analog for transmission along telephone companies' wires. This, too, is likely to change in the future as telephone companies gradually convert to digital networks.

The second concern is transmission speed. For earlier PBX systems the maximum data transmission rates supported by a PBX-based LAN were approximately 56 Kbps for synchronous transmission and 19.2 Kbps for asynchronous. Using LAN access protocols, the speeds have increased to between 1 and 10 Mbps on unshielded twisted wire pairs. This speed rivals that of the higher speed, general-purpose LAN networks. Although most PBXs cannot support such high speeds, the potential is there.

The third and last concern is being able to maintain telephone availability and quality with a shared medium. The integration of voice and data on the PBX network has altered its characteristic usage. Previously, PBXs served exclusively for relatively infrequent calls of short duration. With the integration of data onto the network, it is not uncommon to have workstations connected for the entire day, with nearly continuous data exchange. This has dictated changes in the operations of the PBX system. To provide enough circuits for both periodic voice transmissions and continuous data transmissions, a PBX uses proprietary protocols or time division multiplexing. In the time division multiplexing approach, each connected device is given a time slot on the medium. This prevents one station from transmitting a large amount of data and monopolizing the medium and makes the system appear to be 100% available to all user categories. PBX technology should definitely be considered as a LAN delivery and control mechanism.

The Potential of ISDN

Recall from Chapter 3 that ISDN is an integrated services digital network provided by telephone companies. In essence, ISDN provides the same services as PBX systems do. Therefore, one possible use of ISDN is as the medium and message routing for a LAN. Workstations in an office complex can attach to the ISDN and allow the ISDN facilities to take care of routing

Figure 8-15 An
ISDN-Based LAN

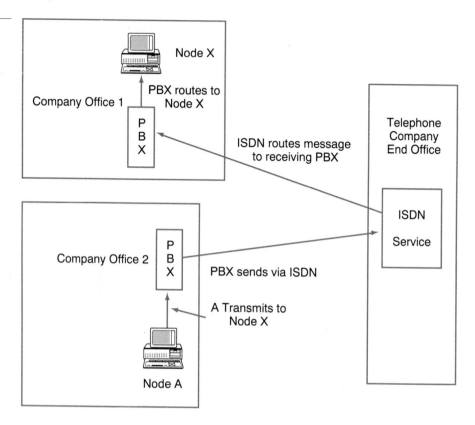

messages from one node to another. Thus, ISDN can do for LANs what
X.25 providers have done for WANs—provide the medium and data switching. A graphic illustrating an ISDN-based LAN is shown in Figure 8-15.

There is also a negative side to using ISDN for a LAN. One of the
characteristics of LANs is private ownership and control. Using ISDN requires that a company give up a portion of this control. With local ownership and control, a company owns the medium and the hardware. Using
ISDN, a portion of the network is owned and controlled by the telephone
company. Data, therefore, is transmitted offsite to the telephone company's end office and then back to the corporate premises. Thus, a portion
of the network is outside the control of the company. Disruption of services
at the end office or the wires between the end office and the company will
disrupt network availability. Depending on the company's philosophy,
this can be an advantage or a disadvantage. Although ISDN promises a
variety of speeds, including some that rival today's office LAN implementations, it remains to be seen how well ISDN-based LANs will perform.
Moreover, the higher speed ISDN lines will come at a higher cost, and
these costs will be recurring. Perhaps ISDN's best LAN use will be as a
gateway to connect two widely separated LANs.

LAN IMPLEMENTATIONS

Having introduced the basic concepts of LANs, let us now look at several specific implementations. The implementations presented in this chapter were chosen for three reasons: (1) they are historical, (2) they are general in nature, meaning that they apply to microcomputer networks as well as large system LANs, or (3) they are implementations commonly used only to connect large computing systems. In the next chapter, you learn more about microcomputer LAN implementations.

The AlohaNet

The prototype of CSMA/CD LANs is the *AlohaNet*, developed by the University of Hawaii (UH) and placed in operation in 1971. UH had a unique problem to resolve in establishing a data communications network in the islands—how to link the main computer center in Honolulu with outlying campus and research facilities, some of them in areas where telephone service was poor. The distances involved and the ocean made it impractical to establish private communication lines. Satellite communications might have been a good solution, except that satellite technology was still in its infancy. The solution adopted by UH was ultra-high-frequency radio broadcast utilizing two broadcast frequencies, one emanating from the Honolulu computer center to all outlying stations and one from outlying stations to the central station. Outlying stations were not allowed to transmit directly to one another. The transmission rate was 9600 bps.

Stations on the inbound channel operated in contention mode for the right to broadcast, much like the CSMA/CD broadcast protocol described in Chapter 6. Outbound message traffic was not subject to contention, since only the central station was allowed to broadcast on that channel. All remote stations monitored the central station's frequency and accepted those messages addressed to them. This is illustrated in Figure 8-16. System performance was good when the number of stations was small. As more stations were brought online, however, contention on the inbound channel increased, as did the number of collisions. Modifications have since been made that reduce the number of collisions and also increase performance. One of these improvements is the slotted Aloha protocol. A modification of the original protocol, called the *slotted Aloha protocol*, was introduced to correct the contention problem. The slotted protocol is similar to time division multiplexing or statistical time division multiplexing (see Chapter 5). In the slotted Aloha protocol, transmit time is essentially broken into intervals of a length required to transmit the maximum-size block or packet. Variations of the slotted technique exist, but the general idea is that one station may not occupy successive transmission slots, thus helping to avoid contention. Suppose that two stations each have a long message to send and each message requires multiple transmission packets. Using nonslotted CSMA/CD, Station A transmits its first packet, waits

Figure 8-16
The AlohaNet

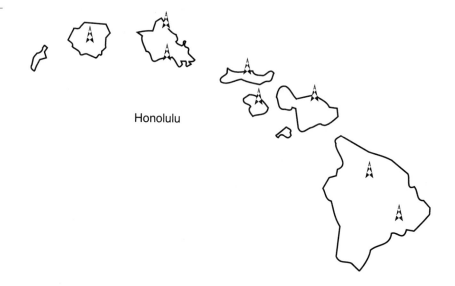

Honolulu

for the medium to clear, and then attempts to transmit Packet 2. Station B, also waiting for a quiescent channel, transmits at the same time as Station A; a collision occurs and both stations back off for a random interval. In the slotted protocol, on the other hand, Station A would not have the option of transmitting in two successive slots. The slotted Aloha protocol is illustrated in Figure 8-17. The slotted protocol, or variations thereof, is used in some LAN configurations.

Ethernet

Ethernet has probably been the most publicized and utilized LAN implementation, in part because it was one of the earliest implementations. Loosely based on the AlohaNet, Ethernet was originally proposed in 1972 by Xerox Corporation, which was later joined by Digital Equipment Corporation and Intel Corporation to implement and standardize a LAN. Ethernet specifications preceded the IEEE standards efforts. The 802.3 standard was considerably influenced by Ethernet; consequently, Ethernet is very similar to that standard. What follow are the most current guidelines for Ethernet implementation.

In formulating the specifications for Ethernet, the designers focused on 11 requirements of a LAN: high data transmission rates, distance, ability to support several hundred devices, simplicity, low error rates and good error detection, efficient use of shared resources, stability under high load, fair access to the medium, ease of installation, ease of reconfiguration, and low cost (Shoch and Hupp, 1980). The resulting specifications are described below.

Transmission Rates and Distance.   Ethernet uses coaxial cable with baseband transmission at 10 Mbps and a maximum allowable distance of

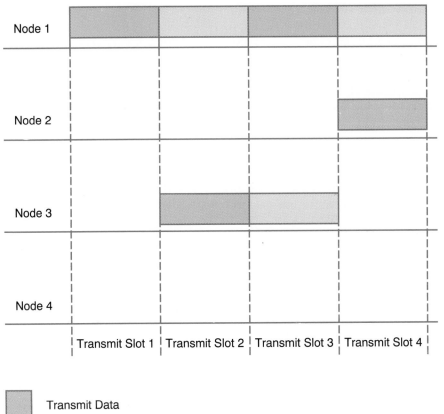

Figure 8-17 Slotted Aloha Protocol

Transmit Data

Cannot Transmit Data

2.5 kilometers (1.55 miles). The distance restriction relates to the length of the cable and not the distance between stations. The 2.5-kilometer distance is sufficient for most applications. For greater distances, two or more interconnected LANs can be used.

Ease of Installation and Reconfiguration and Error Characteristics. Because coaxial cable is the medium, adding and removing stations without disrupting the network is relatively easy. The technology for tapping into the network, developed by community antenna TV (CATV), allows stations to be added while the network is live. Thus, it is easy to configure and reconfigure the network. As mentioned in Chapter 2, coaxial cable provides very low error rates, which, coupled with 32-bit CRC, provides excellent error characteristics for the net.

Number of Supportable Devices and Medium Accessibility. The specifications state that a maximum of 1024 devices may be attached to the network, although the range of allowable addresses is much larger—a 48-bit address field yields over 281 trillion unique addresses. This address size was chosen not to support so many devices but to allow for unique international addressing or network interconnections. A very large office complex where it is likely that more than 1024 devices will be required can get around the limitation by interconnecting two or more Ethernets. There is also a tradeoff regarding the number of supported devices and ability to access the net: As the number of stations increases, so does the probability of contention for the medium. A limit of 1024 stations is realistic.

Performance under Heavy Load and Efficiency.   The ability to configure 1024 devices on the network does not necessarily mean that all the devices will be supported satisfactorily. One of the potential problems of the CSMA/CD protocol is poor performance under heavy load; however, prototype office networks with over 200 stations have not proven much of a stress to the Ethernet system.

Installation and Data Packets.   Stations are attached to the network via a transceiver and an NIC that performs the CSMA/CD and packet assembly/ disassembly functions, buffers messages, and recognizes the station address. Data is transmitted on the Ethernet in packets, with a minimum data field width of 46 characters (octets) and a maximum of 1500 characters. The minimum allows the network's most distant station to detect a message before transmission ends; without this delay, some stations would have difficulty knowing whether a collision had occurred. Likewise, each station waits a propagation delay interval after sensing the end of a message to ensure that the message has cleared the channel. Both the sender's address and the receiver's address are transmitted. The frame check sequence is a 32-bit CRC. A 16-bit data field designates the message type. The general format of a data packet is given in Figure 8-18.

Cost.   The current costs to interface to an Ethernet LAN vary with the type of device. Representative costs in 1990 were approximately $300 for a personal computer interface (logic board and software). Connecting a minicomputer or mainframe system to a LAN is more expensive. A controller board and software prices for these systems start near $1000, and, usually, the bigger the computer, the bigger the cost.

Ethernet does not solve all users' problems. Some deficiencies of CSMA/CD have already been mentioned. Certain other attributes also are not provided by Ethernet: The broadcast technology prohibits full duplex

64-bit Synchronization Pattern	48-bit Destination Address	48-bit Source Address	16-bit Field Type	Data 46–1500 Octets	32-bit CRC

Figure 8-18   An Ethernet Packet Format

operations. This limits interstation message exchange. In addition, no provisions have been made for priority of stations or messages, which would be advantageous for applications that need guaranteed rapid access to the medium such as process control applications. However, the ability to assign priorities to stations has been part of other implementations similar to Ethernet. Of course, priority schemes run counter to the design objective of fair access to the medium.

MAP and TOP

Two LAN standards and implementation efforts have grown out of specific application requirements. The General Motors Corporation has spearheaded specifications for a *manufacturing automation protocol* (*MAP*) while the Boeing Corporation has led an effort to establish a standard for a *technical and office protocol* (*TOP*). These two distinct efforts are oriented toward different application areas; however, the two are closely related—so much so, in fact, that there is a MAP/TOP Users Group.

MAP is implemented using the IEEE 802.4 broadband token bus standard. However, the significance of this LAN is not in its low-level protocols but in its ability to interface with a wide variety of equipment and in its application layer. MAP is designed specifically to support manufacturing applications with interfaces to robots, numerical controlled machines, and similar manufacturing components. It has been adopted by companies in addition to General Motors.

TOP has not received the same degree of acceptance as MAP. TOP is based on the IEEE 802.3 CSMA/CD bus architecture. In April 1987, it was expanded to include interfaces to token ring and token bus protocols as well as to X.25 networks. Like MAP, TOP's appeal is in its interface capabilities and the application layer. It is intended to support the multitude of functions required by office automation, including document transfer and ability to accommodate multiple document formats and graphics.

Attached Resource Computer Network (ARCnet)

Datapoint's *attached resource computer network* (*ARCnet*), one of the early commercial offerings, has gone through several generations since its introduction. ARCnet is a token passing bus-and-star architecture that originally used baseband coaxial cable as the medium. Current implementations also use twisted wire pairs and fiber optic cable. As implemented by Datapoint, network nodes are either for database processing or for application processing. Though each node can have its own disk, a database node is meant to serve as a central repository of data to be shared by the application nodes, making it a database server. The maximum distance spanned by ARCnet is 4 miles. ARCnet has also been adopted for microcomputer LANs and has enjoyed widespread use. Details on this use of ARCnet can be found in the next chapter.

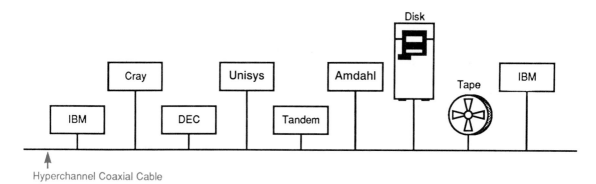

Figure 8-19   A Representative Hyperchannel Configuration

High-Speed LANs

Ethernet and similar LANs are well suited to office automation and process control environments, where the messages to be exchanged generally
are small and users do not require extremely high speed transmission.
This is in contrast with (1) a LAN consisting of only large computing systems, in which the LAN could be used to transfer large files, provide database service to multiple hosts, and provide high-volume printing and tape
archiving or (2) a LAN used as a backbone network to interconnect several LANs in a metropolitan area. To be successful in these industry segments, the LAN must be capable of operating at very high speeds.

The most widely used high-speed LAN for connecting large computer
systems is Network Systems Corporation's Hyperchannel (HC). A representative Hyperchannel configuration is given in Figure 8-19. The HC uses
a bus architecture on a baseband coaxial cable with a CSMA/CD bus access
protocol at a transmission speed of 50 Mbps. Distances up to 3000 feet have
been attained with high-quality coaxial cable (Thornton and Christiansen,
1983). Each node in the Hyperchannel can be connected to up to four cables.
The additional cables provide backup and increase the aggregate data
transmission rate to 200 Mbps. They also reduce the probability of collisions on the medium: If many collisions are detected and only one cable is
used, then the CSMA/CD access protocol is augmented with a priority
scheme. This reduces contention and enables higher priority messages to
be transmitted first.

HC interfaces to many different CPUs have been implemented, including systems from Control Data Corporation, IBM, Cray, Unisys, Digital
Equipment Corporation, and Tandem. It is also possible to attach HC to
controllers for IBM-compatible tape and disk drives, common memory,
and high-speed data communications channels, such as AT&T's T1,T2, and
T3 services and satellite. The ability to attach to tape, disk, and memory

allows these units to function as servers for the rest of the system. Thus, any CPU can have access to a common database; use the tape drives for archiving, logging, or data access; and share common memory. Access to these facilities also can reduce data redundancy and minimize the amount of independent storage units connected to each CPU.

SUMMARY

There are many different LAN implementations and several basic LAN topologies; popular configurations include bus, ring, and star. The common network protocols are CSMA/CD and token passing. There are also great variations in LAN speeds and standards. LAN speeds range from 1 Mbps to over 1 Gbps. Common data rates for office-type LANs with microcomputer nodes range from 1 Mbps to 20 Mbps. Higher speed LANs typically are used as an interface for mainframe and minicomputer systems or to provide a backbone network to interconnect subnets.

The media most often used to implement LANs are twisted wire pairs, coaxial cable, and fiber optics. Other media, such as infrared and radio wave, have limited usage. The medium may be dedicated to LAN transmission or may be shared. For example, if the medium is the telephone network wires, LAN data shares the medium with voice communications. This usage is characteristic of PBX, ISDN, or broadband LANs. In broadband systems, the medium may carry LAN data, video, and voice signals as well as other data communications signals. A LAN implementation exists for most application requirements. Some companies have installed several different LANs, each chosen to meet specific application needs.

Key Terms

AlohaNet
ANSI standard for fiber optic
   interface (FDDI)
application program interface (API)
attached resource computer
   network (ARCnet)
baseband
broadband
bulletin board system (BBS)
bus
carrier sense with multiple access
   and collision detection (CSMA/CD)
computer-aided design (CAD)
computer-aided manufacturing
   (CAM)

connector
contention, data or file
database server
digital branch exchange (DBX)
disk server
download
Ethernet
fiber distributed data
   interface (FDDI)
file server
groupware
Hyperchannel (HC)
IEEE 802.1
IEEE 802.2
IEEE 802.3

IEEE 802.4
IEEE 802.5
IEEE 802.6
IEEE 802.7
IEEE 802.8
IEEE 802.9
integrated services digital
   network (ISDN)
local area network (LAN)
manufacturing automation
   protocol (MAP)
multi-processing
multi-station access unit (MAU)
multi-tasking
NetBIOS
network interface card (NIC)
open architecture

printer server
private branch exchange (PBX)
repeater
ring network
server
single-threaded
slotted Aloha protocol
software license
spooler
SQL server
technical and office protocol
   (TOP)
terminator
token passing
transceiver
upload
wiring hub

Review Questions

1. What were the motivating factors for the development of LANs?

2. What are the distinguishing features of a LAN?

3. Describe three LAN applications.

4. Describe four LAN hardware components.

5. Describe three LAN software functions.

6. What features of a PBX make it unsuitable for a local area network? What features make it attractive?

7. Compare and contrast Ethernet and the Hyperchannel.

8. Is a broadband LAN superior to a baseband LAN? Justify your answer.

9. Why are there multiple LAN standards?

10. Compare and contrast the MAP and TOP LANs.

11. List two advantages of each of the following IEEE standards:
    a. 802.3
    b. 802.4
    c. 802.5

12. Distinguish between an open and a closed network architecture. Give a LAN example of each.

13. Describe how ISDN can be used to implement a LAN.

14. Describe two uses for a high-speed metropolitan area network like the fiber distributed data interface (FDDI).

15. What does a spooler do and why is a spooler important for efficient LAN operation?

Exercises

1. Investigate the licensing agreements of five leading vendors of microcomputer software. How are they the same? How do they differ?

2. Is having multiple LAN standards beneficial? Justify your answer.

3. Choose a specific LAN installation. Describe the hardware, software, and vendor details. Cover such items as maintenance policies, support fees, cost of adding a station, number of stations that can be supported by the system, system management procedures and costs, and the type of work accomplished by workstations.

4. Do you believe MAP and TOP are necessary? Defend your answer.

5. Find two examples of PBX LAN implementations. What are the characteristics of each? How do they differ from an IEEE 802.3 or token ring LAN?

6. On a token ring, what happens if the token is lost? For example, suppose the station owning the token fails before passing the token along.

References

Allinger, Doug. "A Look at Low-End LANs." *LAN Technology*, December 1989.

Bracker, William E., Benn R. Konsynski III, and Timothy W. Smith. "Metropolitan Area Networking: Past, Present, and Future." *Data Communications*, January 1987.

Brodsky, Ira. "Tapping Into ISDN." *Data Communications*, April 1990.

Burr, William E. "An Overview of the Proposed American National Standard for Local Distributed Data Interfaces." *Communications of the ACM* 26, August 1983.

Campbell, Greg. "10Base-T: Strategies for Implementation." *LAN Technology*, July 1990.

Campbell, Greg. "10Base-T: The UTP Standard Arrives." *LAN Technology*, June 1990.

Carlo, Jim, and John Hughes. "Token Ring Compatibility: It's Time to Plug and Play." *Data Communications*, November 21, 1989.

Cashin, Jerry. "Local Area Networks Play the '20% Game'." *Software News* 7, April 1987.

Cashin, Jerry. "LAN Markets Mandate Multiuser Standards." *Software News* 6, November 1986.

Cooper, Stephen. "ANSI Network Holds Promise for Fiber's Future." *Data Communications*, December 1986.

Digital Equipment Corporation. *Introduction to Local Area Networks*. Bedford, MA: Digital Equipment Corporation, 1982.

Dixon, Roy C. "Synchronous Data Multiplexing Technique Ensures Minimum Delays." *Data Communications*, February 1986.

"Ethernet Performance of Remote DECwindows Applications." *Digital Technical Journal*, Summer 1990.

Frank, Howard. "Broadband Versus Baseband Local Area Networks." *Telecommunications*, March 1983.

Franta, William R., and John R. Heath. "Hyperchannel Local Network Interconnection through Satellite Links." *Computer* 17, May 1984.

Greaney, Joseph E. "Linking LANs with Broadband." *LAN Technology*, November 1989.

Greenfield, David. "Multivendor Token Ring Networks Come of Age." *Data Communications*, November 21, 1989.

Greenfield, David. "Super Servers Energize Networks." *Data Communications*, March 1990.

Gregory, Peter. "A Topology of Local Area Networks." *Data Communications*, August 1986.

Harris, Fred H., Frederick L. Sweeney, Jr., and Robert H. Vonderohe. "New Niches for Switches." *Datamation* 29, March 1983.

Haugdahl, J. Scott, and Carl R. Manson. "FDDI: The Next-Generation LAN." *LAN Technology*, October 1989.

Hertzoff, Ira S. "ISDN: A New Path to LAN Connections." *LAN Technology*, December 1989.

Hinden, Eric M. "IBM Serves Up a Gold-Plated LAN Strategy." *Data Communications*, October 1989.

Hirsh, Don. "Terminal Servers: Here to Stay." *Data Communications*, April 1990.

Keiffer, Tom, Leslie Richey, and Tim Christian. "Charting Network Topologies." *LAN Technology*, March 1989.

Liu, Ming T., Wael Hilal, and Bernard H. Groomes. "Performance Evaluation of Channel Access Protocols for Local Computer Networks." *Proceedings of the COMPCON Fall 82 Conference*, 1982.

McCool, John F. "The Emerging FDDI Standard." *Telecommunications*, May 1987.

McHale, John. "Building LANs with Twisted-Pair Cabling." *LAN Technology*, March 1989.

McNamara, John E. *Technical Aspects of Data Communications*. Bedford, MA: Digital Equipment Corporation, 1977.

McQuillan, John M. "Broadband Networks: The End of Distance?" *Data Communications*, June 1990.

Metcalfe, Robert M., and David R. Boggs. "Ethernet: Distributed Packet Switching for Local Computer Networks." *Communications of the ACM* 19, July 1976.

Mier, Edwin E. "Appraising PBXs with an Eye toward ISDN." *Data Communications*, May 1990.

Myers, Ware. "Toward a Local Network Standard." *IEEE Micro*, August 1982.

Puttre, Michael. "Wireless Networks Connect at the End of the Line." *MIS Week*, June 25, 1990.

Rauch-Hindin, Wendy. "Revamped MAP and TOP Mean Business." *Mini-Micro Systems*, November 1986.

Ross, Floyd, E. "Rings are 'Round for Good." *IEEE Network* 1, January 1987.

Saal, Harry. "LAN Downtime: Clear and Present Danger." *Data Communications*, March 21, 1990.

Sarto, Dan, and Greg Campbell. "An Inside Look at Premises Wiring." *LAN Technology*, February 1990.

Shoch, John F., and Jon A. Hupp. "Performance of an Ethernet Local Network—a Preliminary Report." *Digest of Papers—COMPCON Spring 80*. Los Alamitos, CA: IEEE Computer Society, 1980.

Shoch, John F., Yogen K. Dalal, David D. Redell, and Ronald C. Crane. "Evolution of the Ethernet Local Computer Network." *Computer* 15, August 1982.

Stallings, William. *Handbook of Computer-Communications Standards, Volume 2*. New York: Macmillan Publishing Company, 1987.

Strole, Norman C. "The IBM Token Ring Network—A Functional Overview." *IEEE Network* 1, January 1987.

Swastek, Mary Rose, and David J. Vereeke. "Migrating to FDDI on Your Next Big LAN Installation." *Data Communications*, June 21, 1989.

Thornton, James E., and Gary S. Christiansen. "Hyperchannel Network Links." *Computer* 16, September 1983.

Thurber, Kenneth J. "Getting a Handle on FDDI." *Data Communications*, June 21, 1989.

Microcomputer LANs

INTRODUCTION

Although originally designed to connect minicomputers, mainframes, and supercomputers, most LANs being installed today are used to link microcomputers. In many of these LANs, larger systems are also available, either through direct connection as a LAN node, through a micro-to-mainframe link, or through a network-to-network connection. In this chapter, you learn about the selection, implementation, and use of microcomputer-oriented LANs and alternatives to microcomputer LANs. You also learn ways in which microcomputer LANs can be connected to larger computer systems and to other networks, both local and wide area.

LAN ALTERNATIVES

In the preceding chapter you learned some of the reasons for establishing a LAN, the principal ones being resource sharing and communicating. Suppose that two or more users need computational power and that these users can have their computing needs satisfied by microcomputer applications. Would you immediately begin looking for a LAN solution, as many companies have done? Before deciding on a LAN solution, a good analyst examines all alternatives. In this section you learn about the major alternatives, specifically:

Large, centralized computer systems

Service bureaus

Multi-user microcomputer systems

Sub-LANs

Zero-slot LANs

Large, Central Computer Systems

For years, the traditional approach to computing was to have a central host computer as shown in Figure 9-1, and large, central computers are still the mainstay of many data-processing operations. They are the primary means for processing large volumes of data, producing big reports, supporting special-purpose hardware devices like check reader/sorters, and so on. For example, it is unlikely that a large bank would be able to process its daily closing work with a microcomputer or a network of microcomputers; however, most companies augment their processing capabilities with microcomputers for personal productivity applications.

Each computer, regardless of size, has a maximum number of users it can realistically support. The large computer alternative is, in general, capable of supporting many users. Large computers are very expandable, although such expandability sometimes must be gained by upgrading to a larger model computer. The primary disadvantage of a large, centralized computer is cost, both initial and recurring. The initial cost varies according to both the size of the system and the vendor. Initial hardware and software costs in the hundreds of thousands or even millions of dollars are not uncommon. Moreover, large systems often must be housed in an expensive computer room that is air-conditioned and has special power outlets, a raised floor, and a custom fire suppressant system. The recurring costs are hardware and software maintenance, floor space, and salaries for the staff required to run and program the system. Another disadvantage of large computers is their inability to support microcomputer applications. With today's systems, the interface between microcomputers and host systems is not highly developed. Frequently, multiple steps must be taken to extract data from a host, format the data properly for microcomputer use, download the data to the micro, and import the data into the micro application. The same problems exist when uploading data to the host. Considerable development effort is being devoted to this problem, and you can expect this disadvantage to become less serious.

Service Bureaus

Another alternative that a potential LAN user might consider is contracting with a computer *service bureau*. Basically, this alternative provides the

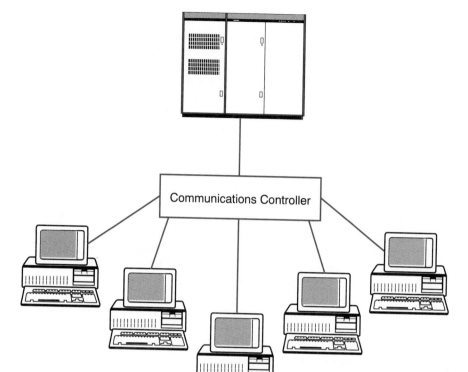

Figure 9-1 Central Host Computer

Communications Controller

same computing and connectivity capabilities as the large, central host alternative but without the high initial costs. The subscriber pays for the amount of computing resources—disk storage, processing time, and printed output—actually used. In addition, subscribers pay for custom software modifications and possibly pay a monthly subscription fee. This pricing structure is similar to that offered by the telephone systems, with a monthly connection charge regardless of usage and a second charge based on the amount of use. If usage is high, costs can be significant.

With the service bureau approach, personnel and system management costs are low. These costs are borne by the service bureau and are usually bundled into the overall charges. The exception occurs when custom software must be created. Service bureau software design and implementation rates can be substantial; therefore, if extensive application customization is required, these costs can be significant. The number of users is large and expandability is good. Again, as the number of concurrent users increases, so does the cost.

The disadvantage of this solution is that it does not provide all of a LAN's capabilities. For instance, loading application software can pose a problem because of the slow speed of the communication links. With a 9600-bps communications link, a 300,000-byte program will take over

5 minutes to download. This assumes 100% line utilization, an unrealistic assumption. Thus, the link is most useful only for exchanging small amounts of data. Application program files need to either reside locally on each microcomputer or be programs that run on the host. For example, the subscriber's database can be maintained entirely on the host using the host's database management system. The database then can be accessed via host resident programs.

Multi-User Microcomputer Systems

Several years ago, a *multi-user computer system* required a large computer. However, today's microcomputers are as powerful as some low-end mainframes and minicomputers. Thus, a high-end microcomputer equipped with the right operating system can provide multi-user capabilities for a small number of users. As microcomputer technology expands, the number of users that can be supported will grow. This solution can provide complete compatibility with microcomputer software at a cost lower than that of most LANs.

The key to a multi-user system is the operating system. The hardware can be an off-the-shelf microcomputer as long as it has sufficient memory, disk space, and speed to support multiple users. However, the operating system must be able to support multiple concurrent users, display devices, and peripherals—features not available in common microcomputer operating systems like MS-DOS and OS/2. Several multi-user operating systems are available today, and more are likely to be added. In addition to the operating system, a multi-user system needs a printed circuit board that provides the interface to user terminals or microcomputers. A diagram of such a configuration is shown in Figure 9-2.

A variation of the multi-user microcomputer system is to cluster microcomputers. With *clustered microcomputers*, each user's terminal is attached to a microprocessor board housed in the host computer. The terminal functions as the monitor for the microprocessor to which it is connected. This is illustrated in Figure 9-3. Each user has a microprocessor and a copy of DOS. The host's peripherals—disk drives and printers—are shared by all users. As with the multi-user microcomputer configuration, the host computer itself must use a customized operating system to service the various users.

Clustered microcomputers are most commonly found in systems in which users must access microcomputer software from a remote location, such as their residence or a hotel room. This configuration overcomes the problem of downloading software remotely; for example, downloading a 300,000-byte program over a 2400-bit per second (bps) dial-in communications link will take about 20 minutes. Clustered microcomputers are also used in LANs to provide remote access. The disadvantage of such systems is that they are not as expandable as microcomputer LANs. The number of workstations supported by such systems is 12 or fewer. However, as the

Figure 9-2 A
Multi-User System

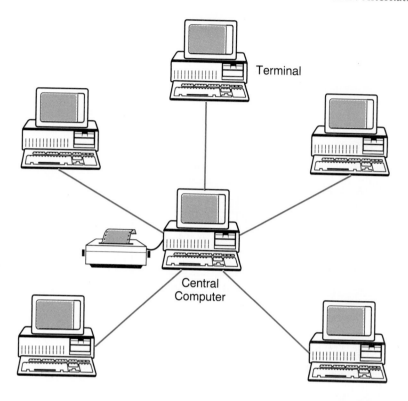

Terminal

Central
Computer

capabilities of microcomputer hardware and multi-user operating system
software expand, you can expect an expansion in the number of concurrent users. Another disadvantage is the limited ability to interface to other
computer networks.

Sub-Local Area Networks

Sub-LANs provide a subset of LAN capabilities, primarily peripheral
sharing and file transfer. They differ from a LAN in two ways: (1) a sub-
LAN's data transfer rates and costs are lower than those of a LAN and
(2) file transfer capabilities are typically less transparent than on a LAN.
On most sub-LANs, if a user needs to transfer a file to another workstation, the sender must first call the person operating the receiving workstation to establish manually the setting for data transfer. Sub-LANs are
implemented with *data switches*. Data switches provide connection between microcomputers in much the same way a telephone company provides connections between callers. A switch configuration is shown in
Figure 9-4. If Device A needs to connect with Device B, the switch establishes the connection as illustrated in Figure 9-5. Many data switches are
designed specifically for sharing peripheral devices like printers and plotters and use manual switching. This means that a user must turn a switch
selector knob on the switch box to make the proper connection. Some of

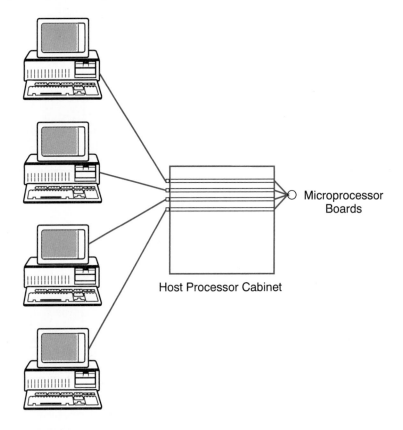

the more advanced switches allow switching via keyboard commands and
support file transfers and modem pooling. With keyboard command
switching, a user can enter the address of a desired device. If the device is
not already in use, the connection is made; otherwise, the user must wait
until the device is available. The connection remains active until one of
the two stations requests a disconnect; alternatively, a disconnect may
occur after a specified time of inactivity. Keyboard command switching
does not solve the file transfer problem described above: Operators at the
sending and receiving computers still must coordinate file transfer by
starting the file transfer software at each end of the connection.

Sub-LANs are relatively inexpensive. A serial or parallel interface is
used between the microcomputers and the switch. Since serial and parallel
ports are either standard or low-cost options, the cost for the microcomputer components is limited to those ports and a cable. A switch that can
support eight devices together with the essential operating software can
be purchased for less than $2500. Thus, the cost per connection will be
about $325.

The disadvantages of a data switch are the low speed of the communications link; lack of user transparency, expandability, and ability to interface to other networks; and contention. The line speeds supported are

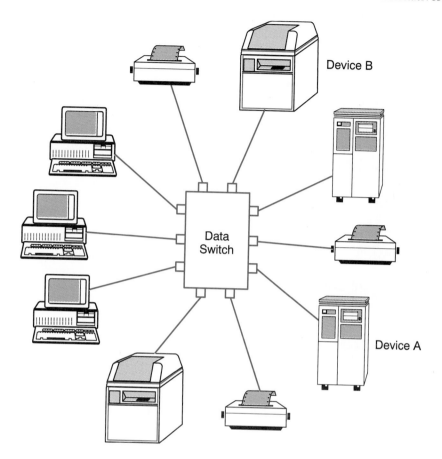

Figure 9-4   A
Sub-LAN
Configuration

typically 19.2 Kbps or lower. This speed is adequate for small file transfers and individual database records but not for large data transfers such as downloading program files, large documents, or large portions of a database. The ability to connect to other networks is generally poor. Although one of the switch ports might be connected to a terminal port on a large system, making the connection is not simple. The number of such connection ports is also limited.

Contention can also occur when using a data switch. If two users want to connect to a device such as a printer, only one of the connections can be made. The first request received is granted, and the second user must wait until the first connection is severed. Some data switches have on-board random access memory (RAM) to alleviate this contention problem. If multiple outputs for the same printer are received, one can be held in the switch's RAM until the device becomes available. Thus, in the above situation, both users would perceive that their connection request was honored. Data switches are an effective, low-cost way to share peripherals and accomplish infrequent transfers of small files. They are not well suited

Figure 9-5 Data
Switch Connection
in a Sub-LAN
Configuration

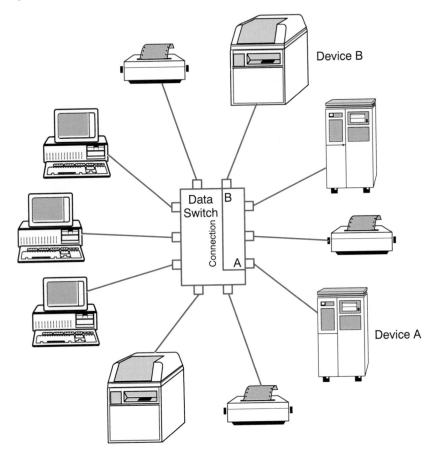

for downloading software programs or large data files or for frequent file exchanges.

Low-Cost LAN Alternatives

Just as there is a broad range of microcomputer workstations capable of meeting a variety of user needs, there is a broad range of microcomputer connection technologies collectively referred to as LANs. One of the major variants among these technologies is transmission speed, with speeds ranging from a low of 9600 bps to over 2 billion (G) bps. In this text, the major emphasis is on technologies supporting speeds of 1 Mbps or greater. In this section, you learn about several low-speed LAN alternatives. The advantage of these alternatives is low cost. The disadvantages are low transmission speeds and, in general, the inability to add many workstations. Low-speed LANs function well for small file transfers, database record access, and printer output; they perform poorly in an environment with many users or where large files and programs are downloaded.

The least expensive LAN alternatives use existing microcomputer hardware for connection. High-speed LANs use a network interface card (NIC) as the interface between the communications medium and the workstation. Low-speed LANs use "standard" microcomputer components such as a serial or a parallel port. These LAN implementations are sometimes referred to as *zero-slot LANs* because they do not require an additional slot on the motherboard for an NIC. When an NIC is used, each station is assigned a unique address, which is set on the NIC through *dual inline package (DIP)* switch settings. Sometimes two serial or parallel ports are required by zero-slot LANs, as illustrated in Figure 9-6. Thus, the costs of implementing this type of LAN are cables, LAN software, and perhaps server hardware.

Low-cost alternatives other than zero-slot LANs exist. These systems use NICs that run at speeds of 1 Mbps or lower and that cost less than the higher speed NICs. Usually, the number of supported workstations is fewer than that supported on more expensive LANs, and the network software is not as developed as that used with most of the higher speed LANs. The software limitations are in support for file sharing, microcomputer applications, security, and network management. With zero-slot LANs based on the DOS operating system, the ability to perform multi-tasking operations is limited, resulting in less responsiveness to concurrent users. In the area of security, some low-cost LANs do not support user passwords; of those that do, some provide only limited file protection schemes, such as the ability to provide certain file attributes—read, write, create, erase, and execute—to users and user groups.

Comparison of Alternatives

Figure 9-7 compares the LAN alternatives just discussed. Conventional LANs, the topic of the remainder of this chapter, are also rated in Figure 9-7. The evaluation rates several criteria on a scale of 1 to 5, with 1 being best.

MICROCOMPUTER LAN SELECTION CRITERIA

Once an organization has evaluated its application needs and has decided that for its purposes a LAN is superior to the LAN alternatives, it needs to

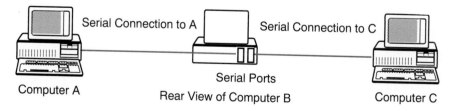

Serial Connection to A   Serial Connection to C

Computer A

Serial Ports

Rear View of Computer B

Computer C

Figure 9-6 LAN Connection Using Two Serial Ports

Figure 9-7 Rating
of LAN Alternatives
and a "Conven-
tional" LAN

	A	B	C	D	E	F
Number of workstations	1	2	3	3	3	1
Initial cost	5	4	2	1	1	3
Personnel costs	5	1	1	1	1	2
Operations/maintenance costs	5	4	1	1	3	3
Expandability	1	2	3	3	3	1
Microcomputer workstation support	4	3	2	2	1	1
User transparency	3	3	2	4	1	1
Accommodation for multiple users	1	1	4	4	3	2
Ease of use	3	4	2	4	2	1
Ease of management	5	1	2	2	4	3
Interface to other networks	1	5	5	5	4	1

A = large, centralized computer systems
B = service bureau
C = multi-user microcomputer systems*
D = sub-LANs
E = zero-slot and low-cost LANs
F = conventional LAN such as Ethernet or token

set about selecting the type of LAN that best meets its needs. The LAN
selection process can be difficult because a host of selection criteria and
different types of LANs and LAN vendors must be evaluated. The first and
most important aspect of LAN selection is to understand fully current
and projected application needs. Then you must enter an investigation and
analysis process to select the LAN that best meets those needs. A formal
process for doing this is described in Chapter 14. Factors influencing LAN
selection are given in Figure 9-8. A brief explanation of each is provided
below. How these factors influence the selection process will vary from
one organization to another, as each factor may carry different weight in
different organizations and possibly even between different departments
within the same company.

Applications

The purpose for having computing resources is to solve business problems; therefore, the LAN you select must be capable of supporting both
current and projected applications. Microcomputer software that runs correctly on a stand-alone micro or on some LAN implementations may not

Applications	Number of workstations	Type of workstations
Number of users	Type of usage	Number of printers
Medium and distance spanned	Speed	Cost
Expandability	Device connectivity	Interconnectivity with other networks
LAN software and hardware	Adherence to established standards	Support
Vendor	Manageability	Security

Figure 9-8 LAN Selection Criteria

run correctly on all LAN implementations. Application software communicates with the network via an application program interface (API), and a variety of such interfaces exist. The way these interfaces are invoked by an application differs from one API to the next; a spreadsheet package that runs correctly on Network A may not work on Network B because of API differences.

An application also may be deficient in its ability to service multiple concurrent users. Even if an application runs correctly on a network when only one user uses it at a time, problems may arise when two users attempt to run the application at the same time. For instance, the application may create temporary files during execution; if only one set of these work files is allowed, two users will conflict with each other as they attempt to use the software. Another aspect to consider is the ability of the application to support multiple workstation configurations, such as color and mono-chrome monitors; hard and floppy disks; CGA, EGA, and VGA graphics; and so on. CGA, EGA, and VGA are common graphic interfaces for IBM and IBM-compatible microcomputers. A well-designed network application will support individual workstation and user profiles to tailor the application to each user's environment. A less well designed network application will provide the same usage profile to all users, which limits the effectiveness of the application. When implementing a LAN, the safest procedure is to have prospective network vendors demonstrate multiple users sharing required software packages. Problems likely to be encountered are: (1) lack of network licensing provisions from the software vendor, (2) failure to support concurrent users, and (3) inability to run on a particular LAN software/hardware configuration. Each of the above should be thoroughly investigated before the final network decision is made.

Number and Type of Workstation

The number of workstations in the network is an important consideration. All LANs have a maximum number of workstations that can be connected, but this number differs. Novell, the leader in microcomputer LAN installations, provides several LAN alternatives. *Novell's Entry Level System (ELS)* versions I and II support a maximum of four and eight concurrent users, respectively, although more stations can be connected to the network than four or eight. Novell's largest network implementation, *NetWare 386*, supports up to 250 concurrent users, and more users can be accommodated by linking two separate networks together. Note that the number of workstations that can be connected is not the true measure of LAN capacity. The LAN must be able to provide good service to all concurrent users as well.

The type of workstations connected to a LAN is equally important. Some LANs support IBM or IBM-compatible workstations only, others support only Apple computers, and some LANs can support most types of workstations. Some LANs also can support larger systems like a DEC VAX. An organization that needs to connect a variety of workstations must ensure that the mixture they anticipate using is supported. There is more to workstation support than just type. In LANs, much of the focus is placed on servers and the media access strategy used. Somewhat lost in this are the workstation requirements. Each workstation must also have LAN hardware and software. The hardware is the NIC or other type of physical connection; the software is responsible for intercepting certain application requests, such as reading a record, and determining if the request is to be satisfied locally or remotely. If the request is remote, the workstation LAN software must connect to the server, send the data over the network, and receive the reply. Furthermore, this software must remain resident in the memory of the workstation and be able to operate with the application and resident operating system. One factor to consider with workstation LAN software is how it interfaces to the application, the APIs supported, and how much workstation memory it requires. LAN software that requires a large amount of memory may leave insufficient memory for application software.

Number of Users and Type of Use

The number of workstations is a measure of LAN connectivity. The number of concurrent users may be fewer than this number: A company may need to have a workstation on each employee's desk, but not all employees will use the network at the same time. The number of concurrent users together with user profiles has a big impact on the selection process. For example, in an office where the primary application is word processing, the major LAN activities will be downloading the application software (perhaps only once per user), document printing, and occasionally downloading or uploading documents. An office that extensively uses a database will have a different usage profile. This type of application may require many small data transfers as records are moved from the file or database server to workstations and back again. A college using the LAN for educational purposes may need to download application software to a large number of workstations at the same time at the beginning of a microcomputer application class. Usage has a big influence on the LAN speed and number of servers.

Number of Printers, Medium, and Distance Spanned

Like workstations, there is a limit to the number of printers that can be supported. Some LANs support a maximum of five printers per server. In this instance, one server may be adequate to support the number of concurrent users, but if eight printers are needed, an additional server is required just to provide printing capability. Other networks provide a variety of ways in which printers can be deployed. Some network operating systems allow sharing of printers attached to workstations, while other systems allow printers to be attached to terminal or printer servers. In the latter case, the number of printers supported can be much more than five per file server.

The type of medium used will affect speed, distance, cost, and ease of expansion. In Chapter 2 we discussed the relative advantages of various media. The most commonly used media for microcomputer LANs are twisted wire pairs, fiber optic cable, and coaxial cable. Coaxial cable was originally the most popular medium, but recently twisted wire pairs and fiber optic cables have gained market share. Another medium option is the existing telephone wiring with either the PBX system or possibly a common carrier's ISDN services. Moreover, wireless LANs that use infrared light, microwave, or radio frequency transmission are becoming more common.

Every LAN is designed to operate in a limited geographical area but the limits vary from one LAN to another. The FDDI LAN described in the preceding chapter is designed to span 200 kilometers; the ARCnet system can span approximately 6.2 kilometers; the Ethernet specifications provide for distances up to 2.5 kilometers; and AppleTalk can support a cable length of only 0.3 kilometers. Therefore, if the distance between nodes on the network is 5 kilometers, you might choose ARCnet or bridge two Ethernet networks together. Network interconnection can be used to solve distance restrictions as well as to increase the number of connected workstations.

Speed, Cost, and Expandability

LAN speeds tend to be deceptive. Each LAN implementation has a rated speed. For microcomputer LANs the speeds range from 1 Mbps to 20 Mbps. This speed is the rate at which data moves over the medium. Because it is impossible to always use the entire capacity of the medium, the actual number of bits transferred per unit of time will be considerably lower than the rated speed. Despite this, the faster the rated speed, the better the performance. Speed and cost are closely related factors. As the LAN speed increases, so does the cost. The cost for a 10 Mbps Ethernet NIC is approximately $250, while a 2.5 Mbps ARCnet card can be obtained for approximately $80. The cost of NICs also varies according to microcomputer architecture. NICs for industry standard architecture (ISA) buses are less expensive than those for microchannel architecture (MCA) and extended industry standard architecture (EISA) systems. Moreover, as the sophistication of the network software increases, so does the cost of that software.

A LAN configuration often is dynamic. Existing nodes may receive hardware and software upgrades, new workstations may be added, printers or servers may be added, and new functions such as a facsimile server or database server may be included. It is important that the LAN be able to accommodate these changes without incurring a large additional cost. If the initial LAN configuration calls for eight workstations, purchasing a LAN system with an eight-station maximum may be cheaper initially but more costly in the long term. Adding a new station to this LAN will require upgrading and will cause the network to be unavailable while upgrading and testing are done. Therefore, when evaluating LAN costs, you need to look at the future costs as well as the immediate costs. Another cost to be concerned about is recurring costs: the costs for maintenance, support, spare equipment, LAN management, and training that continue through the life of the LAN. There can be a wide variation in these costs. Installing the LAN medium is often a major expense. Adding extra wiring for expansion during the initial cable installation is almost always a good investment. Planning is important when wiring for expansion because distances between future workstations and wiring must be considered. For example, in Ethernet, the maximum length of the cable connecting the workstation to the Ethernet medium is 165 feet; the distance between an ARCnet passive hub and a workstation is 100 feet; and the distance between an eight-unit multi-station access unit (MAU) and a workstation in a token ring network is 330 feet.

Device and Network Connectivity

Associated with expandability are the abilities to add new devices to the network and to attach to another LAN or to a WAN. It is important to choose a LAN that offers these capabilities. A LAN with a real or widely adopted de facto standard is more likely to provide connectivity than a nonstandard LAN or one that has a small user base.

Adherence to Standards

Choosing a LAN that conforms to well-established standards or that has a large user base supported by a well-established company (or companies) protects a company from obsolescence. Real or de facto standards create a competitive situation in which several vendors can build LAN software and hardware. The LAN user is the beneficiary of this competition.

Vendor and Support

One of the most important things to remember when selecting a LAN is that you are also selecting a LAN vendor. A variety of vendors can pro-

vide you with the same type of LAN. Selecting the vendor that will provide the lowest cost is not always the most cost effective alternative.
Critical to the success of the LAN, particularly during the installation,
training, and early operations, is a vendor that can provide not only equipment but also training and support. During the selection process, it is im-
perative that you evaluate the vendor as closely as you do the technology.
Interview current (and past) clients of prospective vendors, evaluate support and maintenance policies, and choose the vendor that has the personnel and financial backing to support you in the long term.

Also realize that you will have a variety of vendors involved: the one
providing you with the hardware and software and the ones that manufacture the medium, hardware, and software. Building a LAN can be
compared to building a house. You can have a prime contractor who is responsible for the complete project or you can be the prime contractor and
select all the subcontractors and coordinate their activities. You may elect
to have one company assemble the entire LAN for you, or you may assume
the role of integrator. In the first instance, you will probably have one vendor that will be responsible for any problem that arises. In the second
instance, you must assume the responsibility of determining which of several vendors are responsible for a problem and resolve differences among
your subcontractors.

LAN Software and Hardware

Obviously, the hardware and software are major evaluation criteria. In
the preceding sections you have already learned about hardware and software, and more coverage is provided in following sections. Having multiple sources of LAN software (electronic mail, utilities, LAN management
tools, and so on), LAN hardware (NICs, servers, disk drives, and so on),
and application software is to an organization's advantage. Moreover, interoperability of these components is important, because you may wish to
have different versions of operating systems in workstations and different
types of operating systems running in the servers. Some LANs are more
adept at accommodating these variations than others.

Manageability and Security

Although LANs solve many application needs, they also present organizations with a new set of problems: LAN management and security. With
stand-alone systems, each user manages and operates a microcomputer
and is responsible for safeguarding the data stored on that system. With
LANs, some central management and security provisions are required.
Moreover, by nature, a LAN system is more sophisticated than a stand-
alone micro and requires a higher level of expertise to operate and manage it. For example, the LAN manager must add users, establish their
access privileges, install new software, diagnose and repair problems, and

so on. LAN management is discussed in more detail in Chapter 11, and security is addressed in Chapter 13. One way in which a measure of control can be exercised is a diskless workstation.

Diskless Workstations

With the widespread use of microcomputer LANs, a new model workstation has been introduced, the *diskless microcomputer*. As the name implies, these workstations have no local disk drives. For booting, diskless workstations contain a read-only memory (ROM) chip that contains the logic to boot the system from a file server's disk. All files used by the workstation are located on the LAN's file servers. These workstations provide companies with several advantages, three of which are lower cost, greater security, and more control.

Cost.   The cost savings for a diskless workstation are realized in three areas: initial system cost, supplies, and maintenance. Since the system does not have a local disk drive, the initial system cost is less. A diskless system does not need disk controllers, cables, or the disk drive itself. Eliminating a single floppy disk drive from a workstation configuration can result in savings of $150 or more; greater savings are realized if a company can avoid configuring workstations with hard disk drives. Savings on supplies result because diskettes, diskette holders, backup capabilities such as local tape drives, and storage facilities are not required for diskless systems. Finally, maintenance costs for diskless systems ought to be less than for systems with disk drives. Typically, mechanical devices like disk drives and printers are more susceptible to failures than electronic components are. Because of this, mechanical devices are significant components of maintenance costs.

Security.   A serious concern facing the computer industry today is security. LAN workstations pose three security problems over those found in terminal-oriented networks. First, microcomputers provide an easy way for users outside a company to access the company's computer network. Second, workstations with local disk drives provide employees a convenient way to establish local databases. This can be useful in many applications. On the negative side, however, it also provides a means for copying sensitive corporate data and removing it from corporate premises. Studies indicate that employees are responsible for most corporate security violations; disk-based workstations make it easier for employees to engage in such activities. Finally, software piracy is a major concern to companies and software vendors alike. A company that does not take proper measures to prevent employees from illegally copying software might be sued by the software vendor. Diskless systems are an excellent way to prevent software piracy.

Control. Workstations have added new dimensions to the workplace. They have brought processing and data manipulation directly to the end user. These capabilities also are subject to employee abuse. For example, workers may use their workstation for personal projects during work hours, or they may play computer games rather than doing their work. These problems do exist with terminal-based systems; however, in a terminal-based system the personal applications and game programs must reside on a host processor, which can be easily monitored. Diskless systems provide the best of both worlds—central control of the available software combined with local processing and data manipulation. Because a diskless workstation does not allow workers to copy files onto a separate disk, it reduces the potential of employees working on private projects.

MAKING THE SELECTION

In selecting a LAN, consider your needs regarding each of the above criteria (as well as others you may devise), establish a weighting for each, and determine which implementation best satisfies your particular needs. Bringing everything down to basics, you essentially have three things to choose—architecture, LAN software, and vendor(s). Vendor considerations were briefly discussed in the preceding section. Now we look at the other two basic options, architecture and LAN software.

Before getting into more LAN specifics, let us first discuss what we mean when we talk about a LAN. If you talk to two different people in the same company and ask them to describe the same LAN you might get two different answers. One respondent may say they have a Novell LAN or an IBM LAN. Another may say they have an Ethernet or token ring LAN. Both would be right. The first respondent chose to characterize the LAN according to the vendor that supplies the LAN software, Novell or IBM. The second chose to describe the LAN in terms of architecture—the topology and media access control. To be more definitive, one should describe both the LAN software and the architecture used. For example, Novell's software supports the three most common architectures, Ethernet, token ring, and ARCnet.

LAN ARCHITECTURES

A variety of architectures is available, but three predominate—IEEE 802.3, or Ethernet; IEEE 802.4, or token bus; and IEEE 802.5, or token ring. Descriptions of each implementation follow.

Ethernet, or IEEE 802.3

Ethernet is the oldest of three architectures. The preceding chapter discussed the objectives of Ethernet. It has been used as the architecture for large system LANs as well as microcomputer LANs. You may wish to review the material on Ethernet in Chapter 8 and the CSMA/CD media access protocol in Chapter 6; both are descriptive of Ethernet.

The medium used for Ethernet LANs was originally coaxial cable. Today, two cable types are commonly used: standard Ethernet shielded cable, which supports distances of up to 500 meters without repeaters, and Thinnet or Cheapernet coaxial cable, for distances up to 185 meters. The Thinnet cable conductor gets its name from the fact that it is 0.25 inches in diameter as opposed to the 0.4-inch diameter conductor of the standard Ethernet cable. Often, the standard cable is used for the backbone of the network, and the Thinnet cable, for spurs off the backbone or for networks spanning only a short distance, such as an office. Figure 9-9 illustrates a common configuration employing both thin and thick cables. Instead of coaxial cable, many Ethernet LANs use twisted wire pairs or fiber optic cables. Twisted wire pairs are covered by the IEEE 802.3 10BaseT standard; fiber optic cables have yet to be standardized.

Figure 9-9 Thin and Thick Cable IEEE 802.3 LAN

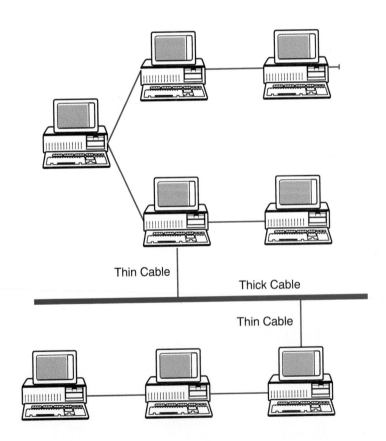

IBM's Token Ring

IBM supports two LAN systems, *PC Network* for small configurations and a token ring for large ones. PC Network conforms to the IEEE 802.3 standard, and there is both a baseband and a broadband implementation. However, IBM's major LAN product is the token ring. IBM's implementation generally conforms to the IEEE 802.5 standard, but there are several inconsistencies because IBM chose to implement a superset of the IEEE 802.5 standard. One of the enhancements over the standard requirements is an extension of the number of available message formats. This means that a message format generated by an IEEE 802.5 standard network would be correctly accepted by an IBM ring, but the opposite is not necessarily true. A representation of an implementation of IBM's token ring network is given in Figure 9-10.

The token ring LAN uses baseband transmission on shielded or unshielded twisted wire pairs. Wires are connected to the token ring NIC in the workstation at one end and to a multi-station access unit (MAU) at the other end. The MAU provides interconnection among the workstations as illustrated in Figure 9-11. MAUs are available in 4-, 8-, and 16-port configurations. IBM's initial implementation had a transmission rate of 4 Mbps; subsequently, the speed was increased to 16 Mbps on shielded twisted wire pairs, and some implementations now support the higher speed on unshielded twisted wire pairs. Both speeds are currently supported. On unshielded twisted wire pairs, the type typically used for telephone transmission, 72 workstations can be attached. With shielded twisted pairs, 260 nodes per ring are possible. If additional nodes are required, multiple rings can be connected via bridges, as illustrated in Figure 9-12.

ARCnet

As mentioned in the previous chapter, ARCnet was developed by Datapoint to connect minicomputers. This architecture was readily adopted for

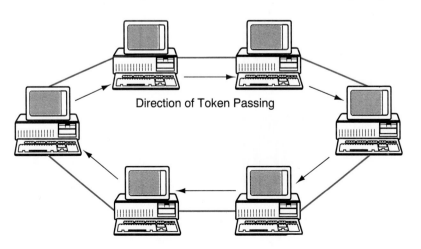

Figure 9-10 Token Passing Ring

Direction of Token Passing

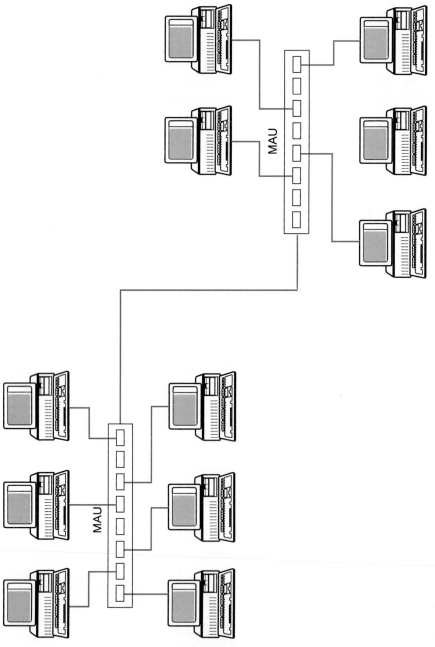

Figure 9-11 A Token Ring Using a Multi-Station Access Unit (MAU)

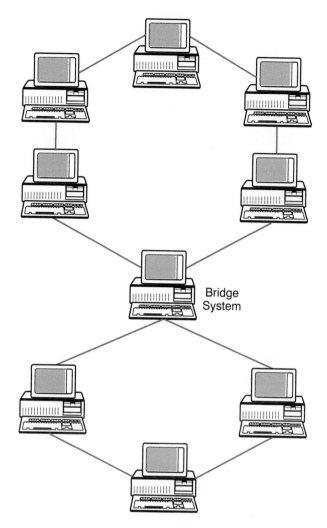

Figure 9-12 Two
Token Rings
Connected by a
Bridge

Bridge
System

microcomputer LANs. ARCnet uses a token passing bus or star architecture but does not conform to the IEEE 802.4 token passing bus standard. Despite its lack of adherence to an established standard, ARCnet is one of the more popular architectures, and it has been submitted to the American National Standards Institute (ANSI) for approval. Reasons for its popularity include early availability in the race for microcomputer LAN implementations, relatively low cost, flexibility of configuration, and a well-established de facto standard.

Original microcomputer ARCnet implementations operated at speeds of 2.5 Mbps over coaxial cable; current implementations allow that speed on twisted wire pairs or fiber optic cable as well. Furthermore, ARCnet has been enhanced to allow 20-Mbps implementations using coaxial cable; the enhanced, high-speed version of ARCnet is called ARCnetplus. As

Figure 9-13(a)
ARCnet Bus
Configuration

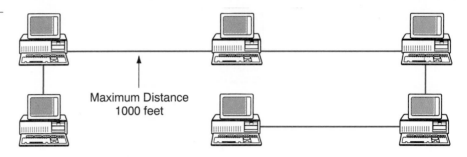

Maximum Distance
1000 feet

Figure 9-13(b)
ARCnet with Active
and Passive Hubs

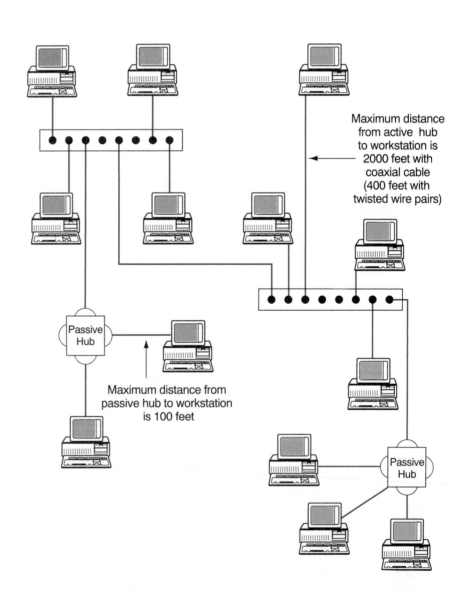

Maximum distance
from active hub
to workstation is
2000 feet with
coaxial cable
(400 feet with
twisted wire pairs)

Passive
Hub

Maximum distance from
passive hub to workstation
is 100 feet

Passive
Hub

mentioned earlier, one of the advantages of ARCnet is configuration flexibility. Figure 9-13 illustrates a variety of possible network layouts. In Figure 9-13(a), workstations are connected to a bus, providing a true token passing bus architecture. Figure 9-13(b) shows a more typical ARCnet implementation where stations are interconnected through active and passive hubs.

Active hubs can have a varying number of stations, with 4-, 8-, 16-, and 20-port hubs common. An active hub not only serves as the interconnection among workstations, it also provides signal amplification, allowing workstations to be up to 2000 feet from an active hub. A *passive hub* typically has 4 ports and does not provide signal regeneration. Workstations connected to a passive hub have a maximum cable distance of 100 feet from the hub. Active hubs can be daisy chained as illustrated in Figure 9-13(b), but passive hubs can only be connected to workstations or an active hub, not to another passive hub. Through daisy chaining, the maximum cable distance supported by ARCnet can be extended to 20,000 feet. An ARCnet LAN can have 255 stations connected to it, but the low-speed version has trouble supporting this many active users. For LANs needing more than 255 workstations, individual ARCnet LANs can be bridged together.

Starlan

AT&T entered the LAN market with an architecture known as *Starlan*. Starlan, which has also been adopted by other companies such as Hewlett-Packard and Western Digital Corporation, uses unshielded twisted wire pairs to provide a transmission speed of 1 Mbps. Starlan has been standardized by the IEEE 802.3 subcommittee under the 1Base5 standard. A CSMA/CD access protocol is used to support an unspecified number of nodes on a cable 500 meters long (original Starlan specifications cited a maximum of 50 nodes). With a wiring hub, a star configuration can also be used. The star configuration is illustrated in Figure 9-14.

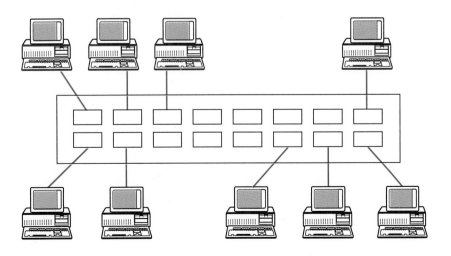

Figure 9-14 Starlan Configuration

AppleTalk

With the increasing popularity of Macintosh microcomputers in the business environment, it is natural to want to connect them to a LAN. Several approaches have been taken in doing this. Interfaces exist that allow Macintoshes to connect to LANs having IBM or IBM-compatible workstations. Thus, it is possible to have a mixture of IBM (compatibles) and Macintoshes on the same LAN. For Macintosh-only LANs, Apple Computers provides the AppleTalk LAN.

Many of the AppleTalk networking capabilities are built into a standard Macintosh, making the creation of an AppleTalk network relatively simple. Moreover, other manufacturers have engineered AppleTalk interfaces to allow non-Apple devices like IBM microcomputers to participate in an AppleTalk network. Compared to the LANs described earlier in this section, however, AppleTalk is relatively limited. The maximum number of stations that can be supported without bridging is 32, the maximum cable length is 300 meters, and the transmission speed is a relatively slow 230 Kbps. Thus, an AppleTalk network would be satisfactory for a rather small LAN but not for a large, active one. AppleTalk uses a CSMA/CD medium access protocol and the workstations can be arranged in a bus or star configuration much like the Starlan configurations illustrated above. The medium can be coaxial cable, twisted wire pairs, or fiber optic cables but twisted wire pairs are most commonly used.

Architecture Comparison

A comparison of the architectures just described is given in Figure 9-15. Additional LAN options are available, particularly for low-cost LANs. Some of these implementations use one of the four architectures shown in Figure 9-15, while others use proprietary media access control protocols. For networks having few workstations and simple resource sharing requirements these implementations warrant consideration. A list of a few of these implementations and their vendors is given in Figure 9-16.

LAN OPERATING SYSTEMS AND SERVER SOFTWARE

The preceding section looked at LAN architectures. Just as important as the architecture is the software that drives the network. A fast transmission speed can be rendered inconsequential by an operating system and server that take extensive time to access required data. Since operating systems (OSs) are tightly coupled with LAN-specific software, both are discussed in this section. Recall that each workstation must also have LAN software, which runs on top of the workstation's OS, such as DOS. While the workstation's software is important, the major LAN differences

	IEEE 802.3, or Ethernet	IBM's Token Ring	ARCnet	Starlan	AppleTalk
Speed	10 Mbps	4 or 16 Mbps	2.5 or 20 Mbps	1 Mbps	235 Kbps
Medium	Twisted wire pairs, coaxial cable, or fiber optic cable	Twisted wire pairs	Twisted wire pairs or coaxial cable	Twisted wire pairs	Twisted wire pairs or coaxial cable
Distance	500 meters for thick cable, 200 meters for Thinnet cable	1,200 feet for the main ring. Can be extended to 750 meters with repeaters and to 4000 meters with fiber optic cable	20,000 ft. Maximum distance between active hub is 200 ft. and between passive hub, 100 ft.	500 meters	300 meters
Number of Stations	802.3—100 per thick cable segment, 30 per Thinnet segment. Ethernet— 1024	255	255	Not stated by 1Base5 standard (early Starlans set limit at 50)	32
Standards	IEEE 802.3	Based on IEEE 802.5 but does not adhere strictly to that standard	De facto	IEEE 802.3 1Base5	De facto
Cost for NIC and Connectors Only	High (approx. $250 per station)	High (approx. $600 per station)	Medium (approx. $150 per station)	High (approx. $400 per station)	Low (approx. $80 per station)

Figure 9-15 LAN Architecture Comparison

**Figure
9-16** Additional
LAN Systems

LAN Name	Vendor Name	Topology	Protocol
LANtastic	Artisoft, Inc.	Bus	CSMA/CD
TOPS	Sun Microsystems, Inc.	Bus, star	CSMA/CD
ViaNet	Western Digital Corporation	Bus, star	CSMA/CD
PC/NOS	Corvus Systems, Inc.	Bus. The PC/NOS OS also will support Ethernet, IBM token ring, and ARCnet.	CSMA/CD
Vines	Banyan Systems, Inc.	LAN OS supporting Ethernet, IBM token ring, and ARCnet	CSMA/CD Token passing

are found in the server software. In some LAN implementations, the LAN software runs on top of a general purpose OS such as OS/2 or Unix. Other implementations have been designed explicitly for LAN operations, such as Novell's NetWare 386. Thus, when we speak of LAN server software, we sometimes refer to the OS and LAN software as one software package.

Selecting the LAN software and hardware is as important as selecting the architecture. Some LAN operating systems, such as Novell's NetWare, can support all of the architectures described above. Others, such as IBM's OS/2 LAN Server, support only one—in this case, the IBM token ring. Therefore, sometimes your choice of LAN software will determine your architecture; in other instances, you must choose both. Currently, the leader in installed base for microcomputer LANs is the Novell Corporation so our discussion of LAN software starts with Novell's products.

Novell LANs and Operating Systems

Novell offers seven network OSs as well as custom server hardware on which those operating systems run. The custom server hardware is not essential, as the operating systems can run on standard platforms. Of the seven operating systems (OSs) currently offered by Novell, five run on IBM or IBM-compatible systems, one on Apple Macintosh systems, and one on DEC VAX systems. Of the five IBM-compatible OSs, two are Entry Level Systems (ELSs), version I and version II, which support a maximum of four and eight concurrent users, respectively. For higher end networks, Novell offers Advanced NetWare, SFT NetWare, and NetWare 386. NetWare 386 is designed to run on hardware based on the 80386 and 80486 processors only. Other versions will run on those platforms as well as on 80286-based systems.

One significant feature available from Novell is *system fault tolerance* (*SFT*). SFT provides an environment in which certain hardware failures will not cause network failures. For example, SFT provides mirrored disk drives. Thus, if one of the mirrored disk drives fails, the other is available to provide continuous service. Mirrored disk drives also provide for redundant data storage, further enhancing the reliability of the system. In all OS versions, Novell has designed the OS to optimize LAN performance. An efficient file server must be able to quickly retrieve data from its disks. Novell provides optimized disk directory support and disk caching to maximize performance. With disk caching, data is held in memory buffers after being read from the disk. Thus, if the data is needed by two users or needs to be re-used by one user, physical disk accesses can be eliminated. For example, if two LAN users start a word processing program at nearly the same instant, rather than the program file being read from disk for each user, it is read only once, improving the response time to the requests. The Novell operating system supports all four of the architectures previously described.

Other Novell Products

In addition to LAN operating systems, Novell provides LAN-oriented hardware and network interface software.

Novell Hardware. Novell provides both standard and custom LAN hardware. The standard hardware includes products like NICs for Ethernet and adapters to interface to synchronous communications lines and X.25 networks. The custom hardware, such as disk coprocessor boards to optimize disk access, is designed to provide higher performance than that typically found in standard microcomputers.

Novell Software. Novell provides a variety of network interface products and utilities. Among these are:

LAN to SNA gateway

LAN to IBM minicomputers such as System 38 systems

X.25 gateway

LAN-to-LAN interconnection products using X.25 or T1 lines

Structured query language (SQL) server

Btrieve, a file management system

The breadth of interface products makes it clear that Novell does not view its LAN systems as isolated islands of computing. Instead, Novell is active in building bridges and gateways to other networks and systems.

Network Training and Support. In addition to its hardware and software products, Novell has a comprehensive education and support organization. Its education classes start with introductory courses on LANs and data communications and proceed through detailed network installation, trouble-shooting, and management courses. In support it offers telephone assistance, remote diagnostics services, and onsite consulting.

IBM's LAN Server and OS/2 Operating System

The second generation of operating systems for IBM and IBM-compatible microcomputers, *OS/2*, incorporates several data communications capabilities. These capabilities include both LAN interfaces and terminal emulation features. Although this chapter is oriented to LANs, both the LAN and data communications facilities are presented in this section. The two versions of OS/2 are standard and extended. The standard OS/2 version provides multi-tasking, presentation services, and data communications capabilities similar to those of the original IBM PC operating system, DOS. The extended OS/2 version contains enhanced data communications capabilities—the LAN Server and a communications manager—and a database manager. Capabilities of the LAN Server and the data communications manager are given below. In addition to the two basic versions of OS/2, several vendors are providing different extended versions of OS/2. Each provides different combinations of the LAN and communications manager capabilities. For instance, IBM's LAN Server supports only IBM token ring LANs. Microsoft's version supports both token rings and IEEE 802.3 LANs. Additional vendors that have announced extended OS/2 communications alternatives include AST Research, Inc., Rapid Software, and Digital Communications Associates, Inc. It is likely that other companies also will release extended version communications products either to compete with existing products or to augment existing capabilities. The following discussion does not distinguish among vendor offerings; instead, an overview of the major capabilities is given.

Communications Manager Capabilities.   The communications manager's function is to provide terminal and gateway support. Most vendors provide a variety of asynchronous terminal emulation, IBM 3270 terminal emulation, X.25 services, and a program-to-program gateway to an IBM host system. Other capabilities include a variety of interfaces to IBM's Systems Network Architecture (SNA) (see Chapter 10). Some of these communications manager functions also exist under DOS; however, OS/2 provides these functions in one comprehensive package rather than as a variety of individual packages provided by various vendors. Moreover, OS/2's multi-tasking capabilities allow more terminal sessions to be active than in the DOS environment. Connections to multiple hosts as well as to a LAN can be supported concurrently.

LAN Server.   IBM's *LAN Server* supports IBM's token ring LAN only. Other vendors also support IEEE 802.3 networks. Some LAN managers provide components that allow a microcomputer to function as a server or as a workstation. A variety of LAN hardware components from multiple vendors can also be accommodated by some vendor offerings.

Banyan Vines

Banyan Vines is recognized for its support for large networks and network interconnections. Banyan Vines runs on Unix-based servers. Being Unix-based gives Banyan a distinct advantage because many WANs contain nodes running the Unix operating system. This makes it easier for Vines systems to connect to those nodes. Moreover, a server based on Unix can be used effectively as an application system in addition to providing LAN services. OS/2 operating systems allow multi-tasking but not multi-user capabilities and thus cannot match Unix-based machines in allowing several users to run applications.

One major strength of Vines is a global naming strategy called *StreetTalk*. StreetTalk is a database that identifies network resources—users, files, hardware, and so on. This database is replicated on each server in the network, thus providing a measure of fault tolerance as well as making resource lookup more efficient. Applications use StreetTalk to locate needed resources; for example, a mail application can use it to find the location of mail recipients. LAN managers use StreetTalk to assist in controlling the network and network users; for example, the access rights of each user can be placed in the StreetTalk database. A unique feature of StreetTalk, particularly for international networks, is the ability to store certain information like status and error messages in several languages, such as German, French, and English. Although several other LAN vendors have announced or released such a product, none yet has matched StreetTalk's capabilities.

3COM 3+Open and Microsoft's LAN Manager

3Com, founded by the inventor of Ethernet, Bob Metcalfe, has been a leader in LAN technology from the beginning. 3Com's current contribution to LAN operating systems, *LAN Manager,* runs under Microsoft's OS/2 operating system. Microsoft and 3Com in a cooperative effort created the counterpart to IBM's OS/2 token ring LAN manager. *3Com 3+Open* is the OS/2–LAN Manager product sold directly by 3Com; Microsoft also provides its own version of LAN Manager. These products are distinct but have the same roots and many of the same capabilities. Although the products may diverge over time, they are discussed collectively here. 3+Open goes beyond IBM's implementation by supporting Ethernet as well as token ring architectures.

Like Novell's NetWare with SFT, LAN Manager provides fault tolerance via mirrored disk drives. In addition, there are provisions to have designated files replicated across several servers. This provides a degree of data reliability in addition to the potential of providing better response for accesses to such files. The security and management capabilities of LAN Manager rival that of its competitive products. 3Com also has announced a name directory service similar to that of Banyan Vines.

Other LAN Operating Systems

There are more LAN operating system options than the four described above. The ones listed in Figure 9-17 are competitive with those just described.

Interoperability of Server Software

If you have a large LAN you may need more than one file server. (The point at which a second server becomes necessary varies according to number of active, concurrent users and usage profiles.) If two or more servers are required, you must ensure that they will operate correctly. Usually, if all servers are using the same hardware and software platforms, they will operate correctly in concert. It is not always true, however, that two different server software packages will interoperate correctly. As an example, there has been a reasonable amount of press coverage regarding the compatibility of IBM's LAN Server with Microsoft's LAN Manager system. Note that both are based on the OS/2 operating system and have common roots.

Figure 9-17   Other Operating Systems for Large-Scale LANs

Company	LAN Name	Base OS	Comments
AT&T	StarGROUP	Unix	Ported from Microsoft's LAN Manager
DSC Communications Corporation	Nexos	Proprietary	Supports all major MAC protocols
Performance Technology	POWERserve	Proprietary	Good connectivity to other LANs
Digital Equipment Corporation	VMS Services for PCs	DEC VMS	Can run on DEC VAX computers

INTERFACES TO OTHER NETWORKS AND COMPUTERS

We often find that LANs do not exist in isolation. Many need to communicate with other networks with large computers. The general characteristics of a LAN are given above, but it is also worth noting how a LAN differs from other types of networks, specifically PDNs and wide area networks. The following differences exist.

1. A LAN is restricted in geographical area. Other networks may span long distances.

2. LAN speeds are usually much greater than the transmission speeds in other networks.

3. LANs are almost completely owned by the organization that uses them. Other networks, particularly long-distance ones, often use the transmission facilities of a common carrier. The latter networks consist of components owned by the using organization and other components leased from a network facilities provider.

4. Many LANs have an open architecture, which means the details of attaching to the LAN are made public and a variety of equipment manufacturers can attach their products to the network. This is true of many but not all LANs. Long-distance networks tend to be more closed. Computer manufacturers are the main sources of long-distance networks, and the networks are designed to support that company's equipment. Again, this does not mean that only Vendor A's equipment can be to be attached to Vendor B's network. The difference here is mainly in approach: Many LANs encourage attachment of differing equipment; many long-distance networks tolerate it, but do not encourage it. The vendors would naturally prefer to sell their own equipment for attachment to their network.

5. In most LANs the nodes have equal stature, which means no single node has a higher media access priority than other nodes. In many long-distance networks there is a distinction among nodes. For example, in IBM's SNA networks, some nodes have a systems services control point (SSCP), which is a focal point for many network functions (see Chapter 10).

6. Several national and international standards exist for LAN implementations. Except for PDNs, most long-distance networks conform only to corporate standards.

In some companies, the LAN represents the company's complete computing resources. In others, it is simply one facet of the computing capabilities. When other computing facilities exist, it frequently becomes necessary to connect them with the LAN. These connections can be LAN-to-LAN, LAN-to-WAN, or LAN-to-host computer. The type of connection plays a large part in determining how the connection can be made. First, let us look at network-to-network connections and then, LAN-to-host connections.

Network-to-Network Connections

The most common inter-network connections are repeaters, bridges, routers, brouters, and gateways. As illustrated in Figure 9-18, each of these operates at different layers within the OSI reference model; however, all provide the same general functions, allowing nodes on one network to communicate with nodes on another network. Network differences dictate that different interconnection methods be used; connecting two Ethernet LANs in the same building is a much simpler task than connecting them over distance or connecting with an IBM SNA network.

Figure 9-18   Network Interconnection and the OSI Model

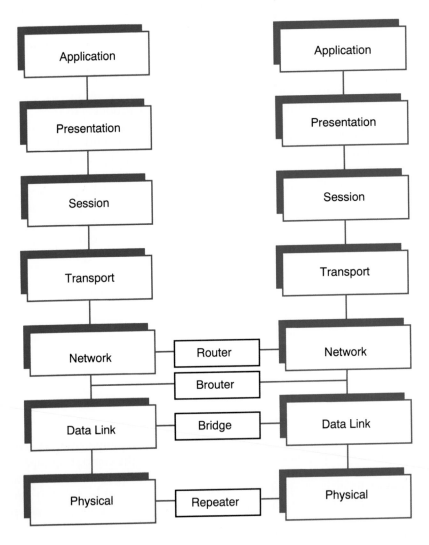

Repeaters. You have already learned a little about *repeaters* in the previous chapter. You may also recall from Chapter 3 that signals lose their strength through attenuation. At some point along the medium, the signal weakens to such a degree that it cannot be recognized by a receiver. To prevent this, the signal must be regenerated, and a repeater is one device that does this. Repeaters operate at the OSI physical layer to join segments of the same type of network. A repeater does not recognize messages, only signals. It faithfully regenerates and retransmits any signals it receives. Figure 9-19 illustrates the use of repeaters on an 802.3 10Base5 network. The objective of the repeaters in this instance is to allow a longer length of cable.

Bridges. *Bridges* are used to link networks of the same type. Bridges operate at the media access control (MAC) level of the OSI data link layer and recognize data packets. Usually, a bridge is used to connect the same type of network, such as Ethernet to Ethernet or token ring to token ring. The typical bridge implementation is to have one node, the bridge node, connected to two different networks, as illustrated in Figure 9-20. Some bridges are dumb and pass all messages they receive on to both networks.

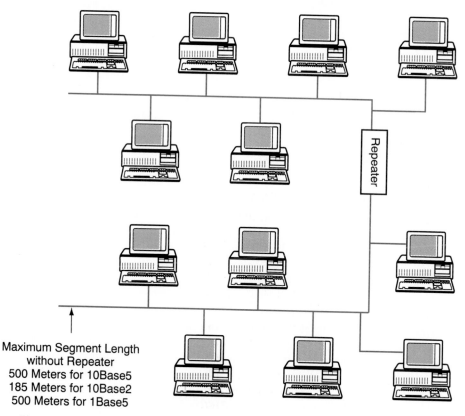

Maximum Segment Length
without Repeater
500 Meters for 10Base5
185 Meters for 10Base2
500 Meters for 1Base5

Figure 9-19 Repeater on an IEEE 802.3 LAN

Figure 9-20 Bridge Connecting Two LANs

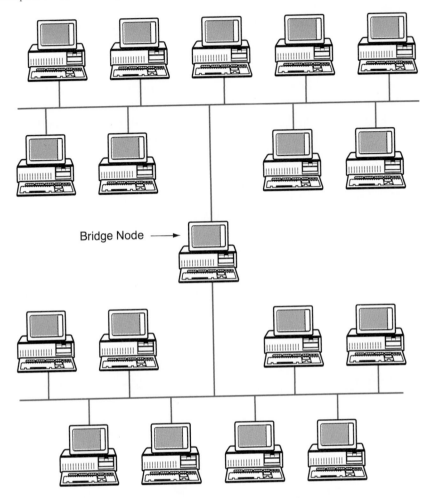

Bridge Node →

More intelligent bridges examine each message and, using a routing table, determine to which network the message is addressed. If the message is local, the bridge node simply passes it along on the same network. If the message is an inter-network message, the bridge node generates the proper address for the receiving network's node and transmits the message onto the other network.

Routers. Above bridges in the inter-network connection hierarchy are *routers.* Routers operate at the OSI network and transport layers. Applications address data packets to a router module. The router examines the address of the packet and either forwards it to a router node on another network or passes it on for delivery on the local network. Suppose that two networks support a message interchange protocol like Transmission Control Protocol/Internet Protocol (TCP/IP). The procedure followed by the TCP/IP protocol is as follows.

1. The TCP receives data from the application through the presentation layer services. It attaches a header to this data and passes the message down to the IP. The message header contains the destination address and error detection fields such as a cyclic redundancy check (CRC) and message sequence number.

2. The IP determines if the destination is an inter-network address. If the address is on the local network, the IP passes the message to the local network routing facility, which transports the message to the proper node.

3. If the destination is on another network, the IP finds the best path to the destination and forwards the message to the next IP node along that path. Thus, an IP node in one network communicates with an IP node in another network.

4. When the message is received at the next node, it is passed to that node's IP. If the destination is local to that IP's network, the IP delivers it to the local network routing facility as in step 2; otherwise, the IP follows step 3. Ultimately the message arrives at the proper network node.

5. When the message arrives at the final destination node (through the services of the IP and local network routing facilities) it is passed up to the TCP. The TCP decodes the header and checks for errors, such as message sequence errors. If no errors are detected, the TCP determines the destination program and sends the message to it.

TCP/IP's role as just described is as a router or file transfer facility. TCP/IP is more than just a file transfer program. It is a collection of protocols oriented toward communication between network users. The users communicating might be people at a terminal or workstation or the users could be application programs. The users might be on different nodes in the same network, on nodes in two directly connected networks (two LANs connected via a bridge), or on nodes in two networks that are interconnected by intermediate networks. TCP/IP is primarily noted for its ability to transfer files or messages between users; however, its scope is broader than that and currently is increasing. Thus, TCP/IP is best described as a collection of protocols capable of carrying out several tasks. Some of the current tasks are:

File transfer

Electronic mail

Logging in to remote nodes

TCP/IP networks also typically provide user services such as remote printing, sharing files over a network (as opposed to file transfer), allowing a user to start programs on remote nodes, and providing a name service that allows users to find network resources (for instance, providing the address of a particular node or user in a participating network). The details of these services are too extensive to cover here.

Brouter.   A *brouter* has characteristics of both bridges and routers. Brouters operate at the data link layer while also performing some degree of protocol conversion. For two LANs separated by a long distance and connected via a T-1 telecommunications link, a brouter can be used to establish the connection and convert from the LAN protocol to the T-1 protocol and then back to the LAN protocol.

Gateways.   The interface between two different networks is called a *gateway*. A gateway functions to reconcile the differences between the two networks. The functional components of the gateway are the network interfaces and the translator process that forms the heart of the gateway. For example, suppose that two LANs are able to interface to an X.25 network. The X.25 network can then serve as an intermediary and allow the stations on the two LANs to communicate; in this case, there are two gateways, one from a LAN to the X.25 network and one from the X.25 network to the other LAN. This is illustrated in Figure 9-21.

Example of a Network Gateway Interconnection.   A corporation with the same type of local area networks in its Milwaukee and St. Louis offices desires to connect the two LANs so electronic mail, document images, and

Figure 9-21   X.25 as a Gateway Connecting a LAN and a WAN

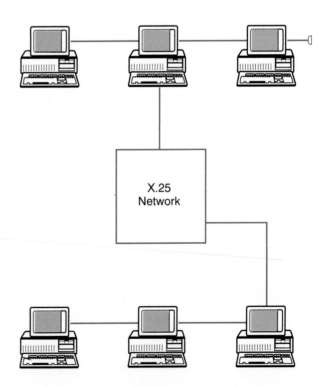

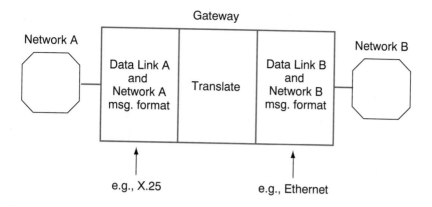

Figure 9-22
Gateway Functions

data can be exchanged, as shown in Figure 9-22. There are two gateway nodes, one in Milwaukee and the other in St. Louis. To further simplify matters, the connection between the two is a single communications link with a speed of 9600 bps using an HDLC data link protocol. To transmit a 10,000-character document image from Milwaukee to St. Louis, the LAN formats the message as though the recipient were local. This requires that both the sending and receiving addresses be present and uses a 32-bit CRC for error detection, a data field of 1500 characters, and a transmission speed of 10 Mbps. (This is essentially a description of an Ethernet LAN.)

The gateway machine that is monitoring all messages in the Milwaukee LAN detects the message with a St. Louis address, accepts it, and translates it into HDLC format. (The sending station's address is probably included at the beginning of the data.) The message can be broken into smaller blocks and transmitted to the St. Louis gateway machine, where the opposite procedure is performed to make the message acceptable to the St. Louis LAN. Meanwhile, back in Milwaukee, the additional message frames are arriving at a pace greater than the long-distance channel can accommodate, which means the gateway in Milwaukee must either buffer these messages or hold the sender off until the first frame is completely transmitted. A combination of both procedures could also be used, whereby the gateway could accept data until the buffer was full and then hold off further frames. Alternatively, the gateway could operate in a store and forward manner.

Network Directory Services. When we discussed the capabilities of Banyan Vines, it was noted that one of the strengths of this LAN was the naming directory, StreetTalk. The value of such a facility has not been lost on the standard-making groups. The CCITT has developed a standard, X.500, to provide a global directory service. When implemented, it will allow one network, regardless of type, to find users and resources on any other network defined in the directory. It will serve much like an international telephone directory, only the contents will be the names and addresses of users and the locations of network resources and data.

Figure 9-23
LAN-to-Host
Connection

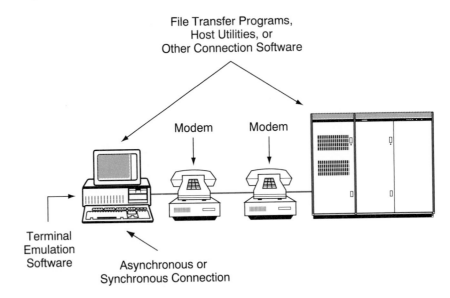

File Transfer Programs,
Host Utilities, or
Other Connection Software

Modem　　　Modem

Terminal
Emulation
Software

Asynchronous or
Synchronous Connection

LAN-to-Host Connections

Suppose that a company has a large computer (a host) and several micro-computers connected via a LAN, as illustrated in Figure 9-23. LAN users may on occasion need to access data stored on the host or may need to use a host application not available on the LAN. A connection between the LAN and host is needed to fulfill this requirement. One method of con-nection is to have the host become a LAN node; however, for reasons of hardware interface, security, or company policy, this alternative may not be possible. In such instances, another interface, a host gateway, must be devised. If the host is an IBM computer or supports IBM protocols, a vari-ety of LAN-to-host connections may be available. One or more nodes on the LAN can serve as a host gateway machine; thus, LAN workstations will communicate with the host via a host gateway server. Common inter-faces of this type include IBM 3270 terminal emulation, SNA logical unit (LU) 6.2 interface, or IBM 5251 interface for connection to IBM minicom-puters (for example, System 38 or AS400).

More generic gateways also exist. Workstations can attach to the host using terminal emulation, for example, as an asynchronous or synchro-nous terminal. On the LAN side, a terminal emulation program is re-quired, and there must be a connection between the LAN and the host. A user could logon to a gateway server, invoke the terminal emulation soft-ware, and use the gateway connection to login to the host. Alternatively, a dial-up connection can be established. A workstation, either through a lo-cally attached modem or a modem server, can use a terminal emulation program to dial an access port on the host and establish a session. When operating in these modes, the communications path between the work-station and the host is usually equivalent to terminal communication speeds—19.2 Kbps or lower. Therefore, these links are not well suited for high-volume data transfers.

Once connected to a host, the workstation user can run host applications like standard terminal users. Many times, however, the objective is to download or upload data, which requires a file transfer utility. A variety of such utilities is available. One of the most popular is called Kermit. Kermit provides an RS-232-C transfer capability between a wide variety of microcomputers, minicomputers, and mainframe systems.

CASE STUDY

LAN Requirements

Syncrasy has decided to connect all the home office microcomputers using a LAN. They soon found that choosing a microcomputer LAN is no easy task. There are four primary architectures—CSMA/CD bus, Starlan, token bus, and token ring. Each of these has several variations, which may include speed and baseband or broadband as well as hardware and software. It became apparent to Syncrasy that the most important aspect of choosing a LAN implementation was to understand and define the problem they were attempting to solve. The following points were formulated as their LAN requirements.

Data Sharing. Data maintained on the host system must be available to be used on microcomputer workstations. This data includes data in the database, text files, and graphics images.

Software Downloading. Most of the software that is to be run on the micros must reside on one or more file servers. A user needing access to a particular program will run it from one of the file servers. The requirement is subject to software licensing agreements.

Printers. Approximately 20 printers will be distributed throughout the work areas. These will consist of laser printers, high-speed dot matrix printers, and plotters, and they must be accessible to all users, which means they must be attached to printer servers.

User Access. Users must be able to easily access the resources of both file and printer servers.

Remote Access. Remote access to the network must be available. Users on the wide area network already installed must be able to attach to the LAN and utilize its resources.

Attachment to Computing Resources.   LAN users must have access to all computing resources of the corporation. Thus, they must be able to attach to all computing systems as terminal users.

Switched Connection.   A user must be able to access the LAN via switched connection, either directly or through the central computer.

Productivity Functions.   In addition to application software, the LAN must support office productivity functions such as electronic mail and electronic calendars.

Compatibility.   The LAN should support all the IBM-compatible microcomputers currently owned by Syncrasy. New workstation technology should also be able to attach to the LAN and coexist with the existing technology.

Other Hardware.   Other hardware should be able to be attached to the LAN as well, such as minicomputers and mainframe systems.

Tools.   LAN management tools must be available. This includes the ability to define, change, or delete users; file security; operating statistics; diagnostics; and so on.

Fault Tolerance.   Some level of fault tolerance is required either through hardware and software features or through multiple components such as file and print servers.

Support of User Base.   The LAN must have the ability to support the current user base of 150 workstations.

Expansion.   The LAN must have the ability to expand in a modular fashion. Support of up to 250 workstations within two years is considered essential.

Vendor Requirements.   Vendors are requested to provide system configuration and costs for hardware, software, cabling, education, manuals, maintenance, and installation for the system capable of supporting 150 workstations. Moreover, they are required to explain how the system could be expanded to accommodate 250 workstations and to estimate the cost required to effect this expansion.

   To obtain the best information on obtaining and implementing a LAN, Syncrasy launched a three-pronged effort. A request for information (RFI) was drafted asking LAN vendors to indicate how their systems would meet the above requirements. Application software vendors were contacted to determine whether their software was LAN compatible, which LAN implementations were certified, and their licensing agreements. Finally, the selection committee made arrangements to visit a variety of comparable LAN implementations.

Hardware Evaluations

When the LAN vendors returned their responses, Syncrasy was amazed at the variations in suggested approaches. Twenty responses were received. LAN speeds of 1, 2, 4, 10, 16, and 20 Mbps were proposed. Implementations included token rings, token buses, CSMA/CD buses, and Starlans. The number of file servers recommended to provide service for 150 workstations varied from one to six. Moreover, for the configuration proposing one file server, the apparent processing capacity of the file server was equivalent to that of one of the file servers in the configuration proposing six servers! The supporting operating systems included MS-DOS, OS/2, Unix, and custom server-oriented ones. Equating capabilities among the alternatives was not an easy task. After reviewing all responses, Syncrasy decided to attempt to reduce the systems being considered to a more manageable size of five. The company established a set of criteria to provide a fair elimination process. A summary of the process used to do this follows.

Resolve Areas of Uncertainty.   Some RFI responses were not clear on certain points. These vendors were contacted for clarification.

Cost.   At the outset Syncrasy had anticipated the cost for workstation LAN controllers, cabling, servers, server software, installation, education, and manuals at $252,000. This estimate did not include the costs of workstations or application software. This cost was based on the following rough calculations:

LAN network interface cards—150 at $500 each	$75,000
(included workstation software)	
Cable—2000 feet at $2 per foot	4,000
Cable installation	10,000
Education	20,000
Servers	100,000
Manuals	10,000
First-year maintenance	15,000
Miscellaneous—network management and so on	18,000

The only figure in the entire original estimate in which there was a high degree of confidence was the LAN controller cards. Syncrasy knew how many they needed and documentation was available indicating that the per-unit cost was a reasonable approximation. The other figures were mostly speculation.

The variation between vendor responses was considerable. Some vendors did not propose a configuration or price. The lowest cost was approximately $100,000, and the highest, over $500,000! Because there were

several attractive proposals under $300,000, it was decided to table all pro-
posals over that figure.

Speed.   Syncrasy wanted to run file server software at close to floppy
disk speed. Some of the literature they had read indicated that they would
be fortunate to realize 50% of the rated LAN speed. In fact, some literature indicates that only 20% effective use may be attained (Cashin, 1987).
Floppy disks have a transfer rate of about 250 Kbps. Factoring in seek and
latency time, Syncrasy estimated an effective transfer rate of 100 Kbps for
a program located on adjacent tracks. Running a 100-Kbyte program would
thus require transferring 1 million bits. This would take 10 seconds on a
floppy disk drive using the 100 Kbytes per second speed. Empirical tim-
ings on some software packages indicated that this figure was reasonable.
     Using the 50% LAN utilization factor (which some thought optimis-
tic), a 1-Mbps LAN would be required for a 2-second download time for a
100-Kbyte program. Because there were to be 150 users on the LAN, multiple requests for downloading could be received simultaneously—
particularly at common start times such as the first thing in the morning
and after lunch. The selection committee decided that the minimum speed
for their network should be 4 Mbps. Had there been fewer users, lower
speeds would have been sufficient.
     The speed decision eliminated several proposals, specifically Starlans
operating at 1 Mbps and implementations based on their PBX system.
Again, these implementations were ideal for many applications. With the
number of users on their system, however, Syncrasy decided that higher
speeds were necessary to provide everyone with reasonable access times.
The speed decision also resulted in a higher price for the network.

Manageability.   There is a cost of managing the network. Network management consists of establishing user IDs, setting security on files, taking
backups, managing disk usage, monitoring performance, tuning, and so
on. Without working with a system it is difficult to determine the management involvement. Syncrasy believed, however, that the greater the number of components involved, the more difficult the management tasks.
Several viable solutions that used three or fewer file servers were proposed. Therefore, Syncrasy decided that all solutions calling for more than
three file servers would be tabled. It also turned out that some of the solutions that had the most file servers also were among the most costly.

Connectivity.   One of the requirements Syncrasy had placed on the system was to be able to connect existing computers to the LAN. While they
did not have plans for this at the outset, it was an option they wanted to
hold open for the future. Some of the LANs proposed were limited in this
capability. Interfaces must exist on two sides to make connections, the
LAN side and the equipment side. While almost everyone supported connections such as asynchronous interfaces, Syncrasy desired a direct LAN

attachment that could operate at LAN speeds. Connectivity also pertains to the number of workstations that can be added, the configuration for workstations, and how many printer servers can be supported. All LANs have limits; however, these limits are encountered in different areas. Some examples of limitations include a maximum of five shared printers and a maximum of 64 workstations per file server.

Adherence to Established Standards. Syncrasy decided to implement a LAN for which a standard existed. This meant adherence to one of the IEEE 802 standards, MAP, TOP, and so on. It was Syncrasy's belief that a standardized implementation would protect them from future isolation regarding attaching equipment to the LAN and the ability to take advantage of new technology.

Vendor Reliability. One or two vendors were rejected because Syncrasy was skeptical of their reliability, ability to support the product, and/or the reliability of the manufacturer of the equipment they proposed.

Viability of Proposal. As mentioned above, there was a considerable difference in the proposed solutions. A small number of proposals were rejected because they did not seem plausible.

Syncrasy drew two key conclusions from this research: First, do not assume anything, and second, ask questions even if they seem obvious. We do not divulge Syncrasy's final selection; it is left as a reader exercise. There is another reason for not indicating the final selection. There are many LAN alternatives and all fulfill certain user needs. Picking one over another here could be erroneously construed as an endorsement of that technology. There are many good solutions to a given LAN problem, and different constraints and emphases will lead to different implementations.

Software Evaluations

Just as there were considerable differences in the hardware proposals, Syncrasy found considerable differences regarding how application software vendors approached site licensing. For an organization to use software, it must comply with the software vendor's licensing agreements. Most software for microcomputers is licensed to operate on one system only, or at least on only one system at a time. Networks have added a new dimension to software use. The software resides on a file server and is available for any LAN user to access. For leading software packages, Syncrasy encountered all the following variations.

1. There was no such thing as a site license.
2. Running the software on the LAN was a violation of the licensing agreement, even if the site purchased one package for each potential user.

3. The site license required that an individual package be purchased for every workstation.

4. The site license required that an individual package be purchased for each simultaneous user. A counter was used to control simultaneous access to the program.

5. The site license was a one-time fee for the software, which allowed as many multiple users as the site needed.

6. The site license was based on a per-server charge. There were no restrictions regarding concurrent use.

7. There was a license fee for each server and for each workstation that would have access to the software.

There was also the situation where leading software packages would not run on a LAN because of copy protection or because they were not capable of supporting multiple users. Some software would work on one LAN implementation and not another. Syncrasy decided to adopt a standardized set of software for common functions such as word processing, database management, graphics, spreadsheets, desktop publishing, and statistics. Before Syncrasy made the final selection, the vendor was required to demonstrate each of these programs running on the proposed network in a multi-user environment.

SUMMARY

Microcomputer LANs are increasing in number. You can expect to encounter them or a LAN alternative whenever two or more microcomputers are located near each other. There are a variety of LAN alternatives. The alternatives include large mainframe systems and service bureaus on the high end and multi-user microcomputers, sub-LANs, and zero-slot LANs on the low end. These alternatives ought to be considered before implementing a LAN. Once the decision has been made to install a LAN, a host of selection criteria must be evaluated. Among these are the applications, the number and type of workstations, number of users and how they will use the LAN, number of printers, medium, distance, speed, initial and recurring costs, expandability, connectivity of devices and other networks or computers, hardware, software, adherence to standards, support, vendor, manageability, and security. The most common LAN architectures used for microcomputers are IEEE 802.3 compliant systems (including Starlan), token ring, and token bus. A variety of implementations exist under each architecture.

One of the important considerations in LAN selection is the LAN software. There are many options from which to choose. They vary in the number of users that can be realistically supported, the hardware they run on, and the base operating system. Some network software runs under an existing operating system like Unix or OS/2, while others are integrated into a custom operating system designed for LAN server systems. Some networks are server based, some are peer-to-peer, and some allow nodes identified as servers to also function as workstations. The multitude of options and vendor claims makes LAN selection a difficult process.

LANs often need to be connected to other LANs, to a WAN, or to a host computer. A variety of connection options is available. Among these are repeaters, bridges, routers, brouters, and gateways. Connection to host systems can be via asynchronous, synchronous, or HDLC communications lines. The ability to interface to a variety of networks and computers is important and ought to be considered when acquiring a LAN.

Key Terms

active hub (ARCnet)	Novell Entry Level System (ELS)
AppleTalk	Novell LAN
Banyan Vines	OS/2
bridge	passive hub (ARCnet)
brouter	repeater
clustered microcomputers	router
data switch	service bureau
diskless workstation	Starlan
gateway	StreetTalk
host computer	sub-LAN
LAN Manager	system fault tolerance (SFT)
LAN Server	3COM 3+Open
multi-user computer	zero-slot LAN
NetWare	

Review Questions

1. Describe how a data switch works. What are its weaknesses as a LAN alternative?

2. What is a zero-slot LAN? What are the advantages and disadvantages of zero-slot LANs?

3. How does the type of usage affect LAN selection?

4. Is the number of workstations and number of users of a LAN the same? Why or why not?

5. Why is security a critical issue on LANs when it is not such a critical issue with stand-alone microcomputers?

6. Why is the vendor an important LAN selection criterion?

7. Describe three differences between IBM token ring LANs and an IEEE 802.3 LAN.

8. What operating systems are commonly used in LAN servers?

9. Compare Starlan and ARCnet.

10. What is a repeater? How are they used?

11. Compare routers and bridges.

12. How does a gateway differ from a router?

13. Identify three functions that a bridge between a 1-Mbps CSMA/CD Starlan and a 16-Mbps token ring must perform.

14. What are the advantages of diskless workstations?

Exercises

1. Suppose you have decided that a LAN alternative is the correct solution for your application. You want to connect five microcomputers in one 20 × 30-foot room of your office complex. You want to share printers extensively and do a limited amount of file sharing. Cost is a critical consideration in your implementation. What LAN alternative should you use? Explain why you reached your decision.

2. If in Exercise 1 user transparency were a critical issue, which LAN alternative would be best? Which alternative would likely be unsuitable? Explain your decisions.

3. Research the literature and find three ways in which IBM or IBM-compatible workstations can coexist on a LAN with Apple Macintosh workstations.

4. Consider the case study at the end of the chapter. What LAN presented in the chapter will best fit Syncrasy's needs? What factors influenced your selection?

5. Select several leading microcomputer software applications and determine:
   a. their ability to run on a LAN
   b. the LAN licensing agreement
   c. the cost of licensing
   d. any LANs with which they are incompatible

6. You need to connect your LAN to an IBM SNA network. Find and describe three ways this can be done. What software and hardware are needed for each solution?

7. Research the literature and find the characteristics and cost of a bridge to connect:
   a. two IEEE 802.3 LANs
   b. two IBM token ring LANs
   c. an IEEE 802.3 LAN with an IBM token ring LAN

8. Suppose that you want an IEEE 802.3 LAN based on the 10Base5 standard and that the cable distance for your LAN is 2200 meters. How many repeaters will you need to do this? What is the cost of a repeater? Draw a diagram of your network showing the segment lengths and location of each repeater.

References

Allinger, Doug. "A Look at Low-End LANs." *LAN Technology,* December 1989.

Bates, Richard J.S., Lee C. Haas, Robert D. Love, and Franc E. Noel. "Transmission—The IBM Token Ring Will Handle up to 72 Stations at the Full 4-Mbit/s Data Rate." *Data Communications,* March 1986.

Bederman, Sy. "Source Routing Controlling Message Routing Is Key to Interconnection." *Data Communications,* February 1986.

Cashin, Jerry. "Choosing a LAN OS: Proceed with Caution." *Software Magazine,* March 1990.

Cashin, Jerry. "Local Area Networks Play the 20% Game." *Software News,* April 1987.

Catchings, Bill, and Mark L. Van Name. "Growing Pains." *Byte,* June 1990.

_____. "Electronic Peripheral Sharers Counter 'LAN Overkill'." *PC Week,* November 28, 1988.

Cavanagh, James P., Robler L. Guaraldi, Kathleen McKinney, and Mary Anne Cleary. "Anatomy of a Network OS Selection." *LAN Technology,* June 1990.

Cavanagh, James P., Tyrone Pike, Charles Tartaro, and Roosevelt Giles. "Anatomy of a Network OS Selection." *LAN Technology,* July 1990.

Coffee, Peter. "Software Tools Support Decision Making." *PC Week,* June 25, 1990.

Corrigan, Patrick H., and Guy Aisling. *Building Local Area Networks with Novell's NetWare.* Redwood City, CA: M&T Publishing, Inc., 1989.

Derfler, Frank J., Jr. "Building Workgroup Solutions—Low-Cost LANs." *PC Magazine,* March 28, 1989.

_____. "Building Workgroup Solutions—The X.25 Alternative." *PC Magazine,* May 15, 1990.

_____. "Building Network Solutions: Is ISDN Tomorrow's Interoffice Network?" *PC Magazine,* February 13, 1990.

_____. "The LAN Survival Guide." *PC Magazine,* May 29, 1990.

_____. "The Next Wave: LANs without Wires." *PC Magazine,* May 29, 1990.

_____. "Building Network Solutions: Is ISDN Tomorrow's Interoffice Network?" *PC Magazine,* February 13, 1990.

Derfler, Frank J., Jr., and Keith M. Thompson. "Lan Operating Systems: The Power behind the Server." *PC Magazine,* May 29, 1990.

Dern, Daniel P. "Groupware Can Leverage the Most from Your LAN." *MIS Week,* June 25, 1990.

Fisher, Sharon. "Getting Away from Cables." *Infoworld,* April 30, 1990.

Greenfield, David. "Super Servers Energize Networks." *Data Communications,* March 1990.

Hertzoff, Ira S. "ISDN: A New Path to LAN Connections." *LAN Technology,* December 1989.

Kelly, Paul. "Connecting LANs with Bridges." *Telecommunications,* June 1990.

Klein, Mike, and Mary Petrosky. "ARCnetPlus: New Life for an Old Standby?" *LAN Technology,* June 1990.

Martin, James, and Kathleen K. Chapman. *Local Area Networks, Architectures and Implementations.* Englewood Cliffs, NJ: Prentice-Hall, 1989.

Maxwell, Kimberly, and Patricia A. McGovern. "Building Workgroup Solutions: Zero-Slot LANs." *PC Magazine,* April 24, 1990.

O'Dell, Peter. *The Computer Networking Book.* Chapel Hill, NC: Ventana Press, Inc., 1989.

Sanz, Steve. "AppleTalk Grows Up." *LAN Technology,* April 1990.

Stallings, William. *Handbook of Computer-Communications Standards, Volume 2.* New York: Macmillan Publishing Company, 1987.

_____. "What You Need to Know about Bridge Routing." *LAN Technology,* March 1990.

Wilkinson, Stephanie. "As LAN Operating Systems Get Better, Choices Get Tougher." *MIS Week,* June 25, 1990.

Packet Distribution Networks and Wide Area Networks

Packet Distribution Networks
Wide Area Networks
IBM's Systems Network Architecture
International Networks
Microcomputers in Networks
Case Study

INTRODUCTION

In Chapter 7 you were introduced to the concepts of networks, and you learned about local area networks (LANs) in Chapters 8 and 9. In this chapter you learn about wide area networks (WANs). Specific topics covered in this chapter include:

Packet distribution networks (PDNs)

An overview of major PDN implementations

Advantages and disadvantages of PDNs

Distinguishing characteristics of LANs, PDNs, and WANs

IBM's WAN, systems network architecture (SNA)

International networks

Microcomputer connections to WANs

The chapter concludes with a case study that illustrates some considerations for implementing a WAN.

PACKET DISTRIBUTION NETWORKS

The concept of a *packet distribution network* (*PDN*) was first introduced in 1964 by Paul Baran of the Rand Corporation. Baran defined a process of segmenting a message into specific-size packets, routing the packets to their destination, and reassembling them to re-create the message. In 1966, Donald Davies of the National Physics Laboratory in Great Britain published details of a store and forward packet switching network. In 1967, plans were formulated for what is believed to be the first packet switching network, ARPANET, which became operational in 1969, with four nodes. The ARPANET has since expanded to more than 125 nodes and was renamed to NSFNET.

Packet switching networks specify several different packet sizes, with sizes of 128, 256, 512, and 1024 bytes being common. All packets transmitted will conform to one of the available packet lengths. Individual users subscribe to a service providing one of the available packet sizes. Eliminating a large number of variations in packet size makes management of message buffers easier and evens out message traffic patterns.

Terminology

A packet distribution network (PDN) is a special kind of a WAN and is variously referred to as an X.25 network, a packet switching network, a *value-added network* (*VAN*), or a public data network. *Packet distribution* and *packet switching* both refer to how data is transmitted—as one or more packets with a fixed length. The X.25 designation stems from CCITT's recommendation X.25, which defines the "interface between data terminal equipment (DTE) and data circuit-terminating equipment (DCE) for terminals operating in the packet mode on public data networks" (Tanenbaum, 1981). The term *public data network,* which derives from the X.25 recommendation, is somewhat of a misnomer, since packet switching networks have also been implemented in the private sector. When the network is public, users subscribe to the network services much like they subscribe to telephone services. The term *value-added network* is used because the network proprietor adds not only a communications link but also message routing, packet control, store and forward capability, network management, compatibility between devices, and error recovery.

PDNs and the OSI Layers

Only three OSI layers—physical, data link, and network—have been described for PDNs, because a PDN is only responsible for message delivery. Although all seven OSI layers exist for the user, the application, presentation, session, and transport layer functions are the responsibility of the user portion of the network.

Current PDN Implementations

The use of PDNs has increased significantly since the first one was established, and most computerized countries currently have access to at least one. In addition to the privately implemented NSFNET, in the United States there are public networks offered by AT&T, Computer Sciences Corporation, McDonnell Douglas, ITT, MCI, Motorola, RCA, and Western Union, to name a few. Implementations outside of the United States include Datapac in Canada, Transpac in France, EuroNet in Europe (essentially an extension of Transpac), Britain's Packet Switching Service (PSS), West Germany's DATEX-P, and Japan's Nippon Telephone and Telegraph (NTT) DDX-2 system. Interconnections exist between these networks, providing international networking capabilities at a reasonable cost. The general configuration of a PDN is given in Figure 10-1. Several CCITT recommendations, covering different aspects of PDN access and use, are listed in the figure at the points where they apply; this section acquaints you with the basic workings of packet switching networks.

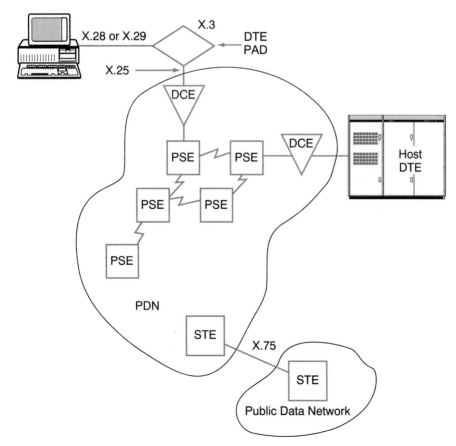

Figure 10-1
A PDN General
Configuration

Connection Options

A PDN provides up to three types of connection options: switched virtual circuit, permanent virtual circuit, and datagram service. A virtual circuit is a communications path that is established between the sending and receiving nodes.

Switched Virtual Circuit.   A *switched virtual circuit* (SVC) is similar to a switched communications link. When a session is established between two users, an end-to-end circuit is determined and allocated for the duration of the session. This is accomplished via a call-setup request that is initiated by the user. On receiving a call-setup request, the X.25 network establishes a transmission link for the session. At the end of the session, the switched virtual circuit is dissolved. Breaking the switched virtual circuit is referred to as *call clearing.*

Permanent Virtual Circuit.   A *permanent virtual circuit* (PVC) is usually selected when two nodes require almost continuous connection. A PVC is similar to a leased communications link, as described in Chapter 2. With a PVC, no call-setup is required. The circuit is permanently established between the communicating nodes.

Datagram Service.   The third type of connection option is a *datagram,* which is a message that fits completely into the data field of one packet. Since a temporary path is established for each datagram, two datagrams from the same source can have two different circuits established. Datagram service, which avoids the overhead of establishing a virtual circuit, has the potential of fast service for short, unrelated messages. Certain features of datagrams make them undesirable for many applications. First, the arrival order of datagrams is not guaranteed, since each datagram sent by a particular node may take a different route. Second, and more important, arrival itself is not guaranteed, since the PDN establishes datagram arrival queue depths, and a datagram is discarded if the queue is full when the datagram arrives. This problem is compounded by the fact that recovery of lost datagrams is the responsibility of the user, not the PDN, making datagrams best suited to messages of relatively low importance and messages where speed is more critical than the possibility of loss (such as in process control environments and certain military situations). Datagram service, though included in the X.25 standard, seldom has been implemented in existing systems.

Example of a Packet Distribution Network

To see how a PDN functions, let us follow a message as it proceeds from the starting terminal to its destination address, using a switched virtual circuit connection.

Establishing the Virtual Circuit.   The user connects to the PDN by dialing the nearest PDN access port (a local telephone call in most large cities). After a log-in procedure, the address of the other node is supplied. The PDN then goes through the process of establishing the virtual circuit. The call establishment sequence is as follows:

1. A call request packet is sent from the sending node to the receiver. The call request is delivered to the receiver as an incoming call packet. The receiver may accept or reject the call.

2. If the receiver wishes to accept the connection, it transmits a call accepted packet that is presented to the sender as a call connected message. This establishes the connection, and data exchange may begin.

3. To terminate the connection, either node can transmit a clear request to the other. The recipient of the clear request acknowledges the disconnect with a clear confirmation control packet.

Data Exchange.   Once the virtual circuit has been established, data exchange can begin. The recommended data link protocol is link access procedure, balanced (LAPB), an HDLC-type protocol (see Chapter 6). Other data link protocols also have been specified for use on an interim basis, since there are so many pieces of data terminal equipment that do not support LAPB. The data portion of the frame is restricted to a specific maximum length, recommended at 128 octets, with 16, 32, 64, 256, 512, and 1024 specified as options. The Ns and Nr subfields (see Chapter 6) are defaulted to 3 bits each, as in SDLC, but they may optionally be expanded to 7 bits. In the defaulted situation, up to seven frames can go unacknowledged, although the X.25 specification recommends that no more than three be sent before acknowledgment. This acknowledgment limit can be altered at the discretion of the implementer and would almost always be increased when the Ns and Nr subfields are expanded to 7 bits. The PDN uses a portion of the data field for control information—circuit addressing, packet sequence numbers, and packet confirmation. Three or four octets are used in information packets for this purpose, four when the sequence numbers are 7-bit entities. Figure 10-2 illustrates the format of a PDN packet.

Packet Assembly/Disassembly (PAD).   The first step in sending the data is to assemble the packets, a function performed by a *packet assembly/ disassembly (PAD)* module. The PAD function is not considered a part of the PDN; rather, it is the responsibility of the data terminal equipment. However, since many of the terminals used in PDNs lack the intelligence to perform this function, most PDNs still provide this capability. PAD functions are specified in the CCITT X.3 standard. The PAD acts on one end to transform a message into one or more packets of the required length and then reassembles the message at the other end. The PAD is also

Figure 10-2
Call Request and
Incoming Call
Packet Format

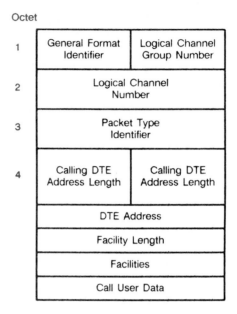

responsible for generating and monitoring control signals such as call setup and clearing.

Once the message has been transformed into packets, the packets are passed to the PDN in accordance with the X.25 interface. The PDN then moves the data through the network for delivery to the destination. The standards do not discuss the internal workings within the PDN, such as routing and congestion control. The receiving PAD takes the information from the data portion of the packet and reassembles the message.

PDN Equipment

Two types of machines have been defined for use within a PDN: *packet switching equipment* (*PSE*), which accepts and forwards messages, and *signaling terminal equipment* (*STE*), which is used to interface two different PDNs according to CCITT standard X.75. The standards for a packet switching network specify interfaces and functions of the PSEs and STEs but not the nature of the equipment itself. Figure 10-3 illustrates the connections between users' equipment and a PSE, connections between PSEs, and STE connections.

Advantages and Disadvantages of the PDN

PDNs have several advantages. For one, the user is charged for the amount of data transmitted rather than for connect time. Applications that send low volumes of data over a relatively long period will find the charges for

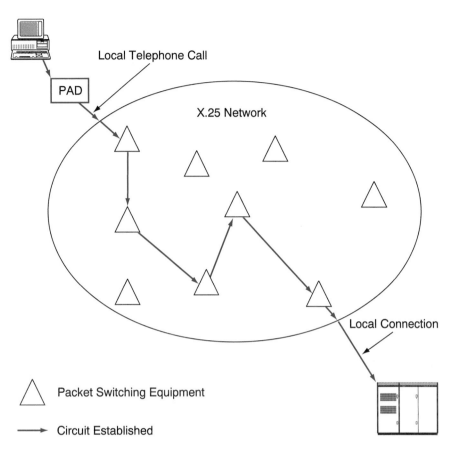

Figure 10-3
Connections in
an X.25 Network

a PDN lower than those for either leased lines or switched lines. The PDN also gives access to many different locations without the cost of switched connections, which usually involve a charge for the initial connection plus a per-minute use fee. Access to the PDN is usually via a local telephone call, which also reduces costs (unless telephone companies begin using measured billing). Maintenance of the network and error recovery are the responsibilities of the PDN.

There are also disadvantages to using a PDN. Because the PDN is usually shared, users must compete with each other for circuits. Thus, it is possible for message traffic from other users to impede the delivery of a message. In the extreme case, a virtual circuit to the intended destination may even be unobtainable. This is also true for a switched connection from a common carrier. If the number of data packets to be transferred is great, the cost of using a PDN can exceed that of leased facilities. Because the PDN is controlled by its proprietor, the individual user is unable to make changes that might benefit an individual application, such as longer messages or larger packets, longer message acknowledgment intervals, and higher transmission speeds, all of which are set by the PDN administrators.

WIDE AREA NETWORKS

Vendor offerings play a major role in network implementation and configuration, and almost every major computer vendor offers a networking capability. Vendor networks compete with each other, with packet switching or X.25 networks, and with common carrier networks. In Chapters 8 and 9 you learned about LANs. A WAN can be distinguished from a LAN in several ways. The primary difference between a WAN and a LAN is distance. A LAN serves a limited geographical area. A WAN may cover a large geographical area or can be limited to a small one. In the latter case it would be distinguished from a conventional LAN based upon the speed of the links, the media used, and the architecture. Figure 10-4(a) illustrates a local area network, and Figure 10-4(b), a wide area network serving the same geographical area. In Figure 10-4(a) the nodes are connected via a high-speed communications path (1 Mbps or higher) and use either a CSMA/CD or token passing access protocol. In Figure 10-4(b) the speed of the links is 56 Kbps using a data link protocol such as HDLC. There

Figure 10-4   Local Area Network and Wide Area Network in a Limited Geographic Area

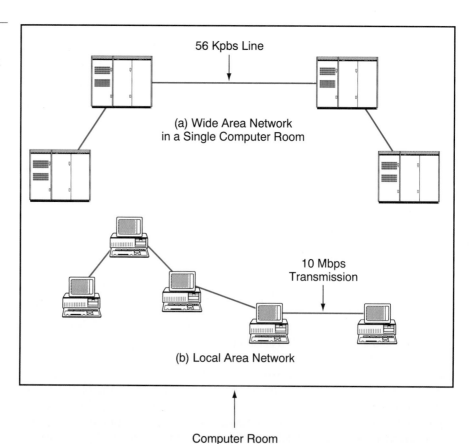

56 Kpbs Line

(a) Wide Area Network in a Single Computer Room

10 Mbps Transmission

(b) Local Area Network

Computer Room

is a host processor, which is responsible for controlling access to the communications link.

Admittedly, the distinction between the two networks may seem artificial, as it is primarily based upon transmission speed and media access method. Even though both networks serve the same geographical area, their basic architectures differ. There are also more subtle differences in these networks with respect to other network functions such as routing, store and forward capability, and expansion. The key is that a WAN can easily be expanded to cover long distances using the same technology, while the LAN cannot.

In general, a WAN can be characterized as a private network serving either a wide area or local area (or both). The network uses lower speed links (generally under 100 Kbps) or special high-speed services such as T1. While some of the transmission facilities may be obtained from a common carrier, all network routing, error detection and recovery, and network management functions are the responsibility of the network owner. Even if the nodes connected serve a limited geographical area, the network can be expanded to a wider area using the same software and hardware technologies.

The following section is devoted to one particular network that has become a de facto industry standard: IBM's *systems network architecture* (*SNA*). Currently, most networks being designed on IBM mainframe systems use SNA. Other vendors' equipment interfacing with an IBM network is likely to do so via an SNA interface. Many computer manufacturers have implemented or are implementing the ability to attach to an SNA network as some type of SNA node.

IBM'S SYSTEMS NETWORK ARCHITECTURE

SNA, announced by IBM in 1974, provides the framework for implementing data communications networks using IBM or IBM-compatible equipment. It is not a product per se; rather, it is a blueprint for how hardware, software, and users interact in exchanging data on IBM systems. A network based on SNA consists of a variety of hardware and software components in a well-defined configuration.

Why SNA?

For years, IBM has been the leader in computer sales and installations. The move to SNA was prompted not so much by competition from the outside but by competition from within IBM itself. Before 1974, the implementation of communications systems had been somewhat random: If a new terminal was developed, a new or modified access method and data link protocol were likely to accompany it. By 1974 IBM was offering more than 200 different models of communications hardware, 35 different device access methods, and over a dozen data link protocols. Continuing this product proliferation would have given IBM an enormous burden for support and maintenance. SNA was the result of the corporate objective of integrating all these functions into one cohesive network architecture.

The objective of any network is to enable users to communicate with one another. Users in SNA are either people working at a terminal or operator's console or they are applications that provide services for other programs or terminal users. A user is thus an entity with some degree of intelligence. A terminal is not a user, though the terms *terminal operator* and *terminal* are frequently used synonymously. SNA has been developed to provide communications paths and dialogue rules between users. This is accomplished via a layered network architecture similar to the OSI reference model.

SNA Layers

The early releases of SNA referenced either six or four functional layers. The discrepancy between a six-layer and four-layer definition is explained by the fact that layers three through five are sometimes referred to as a single layer known as the *half-session layer*. The lowest OSI reference model layer, the physical layer, is not usually specified in SNA, nor is the application layer included. However, both of these layers obviously must exist. The four-layer definition is given in Figure 10-5. The six layers are identified in parentheses, where applicable. In the current version of SNA, the layering has been somewhat redefined. The presentation service layer is omitted from the earlier definition and the services manager is now referred to as the function management layer. Even though the layering carries different names, the functions each performs are similar to those for the OSI reference model.

SNA also defines four distinct hardware groupings called *physical units* (*PU*). The four physical units are numbered 1, 2, 4, and 5, with no PU currently assigned to number 3. These device types are listed in Figure 10-6. The hardware configuration, then, consists of IBM or IBM-compatible CPUs, communications controllers, terminal cluster controllers, and terminals, printers, or workstations, all connected by any of the media discussed in Chapter 2. Other vendors' equipment may also be included in the network if it conforms to the SNA protocols. The preferred data link protocol

---

Figure 10-5
SNA Layers

Layer 1	Data link control
Layer 2	Path control
Layer 3	Half-session layer, consisting of:
	Transmission control (Layer 3)
	Flow control (Layer 4)
	Presentation service (Layer 5)
Layer 4	Services manager (Layer 6)

Physical Unit	Hardware Component
Type 1	A terminal device, e.g., 3278
Type 2	A cluster controller, e.g., 3274
Type 4	A communications controller, e.g., 3725
Type 5	A host processor, e.g., 4381 or 3094

Figure 10-6
SNA Physical Units

is SDLC, but accommodations have been made for other protocols such as BSC and asynchronous.

Logical Units and Sessions

Users of SNA are represented in the system by entities known as *logical units (LU)*. An LU is usually implemented as a software function in a device with some intelligence, such as a CPU or controller. The dialogue between two system users is known as a *session*. Since a logical unit is the agent of a user, when one user wants to establish a session with another user, the LUs are involved in establishing the communications path between the two. Since a session involves two different LUs, the activities and resources used by one LU in a session are called a *half-session*. In the SNA layering above, the half-session layers represent the functions that would be performed by an LU for its user.

Session Types. Many different types of sessions can be requested, such as program to terminal, program to program, or terminal to terminal. Each of these categories can be further stratified as to terminal type (interactive, batch, or printer) and application type (batch, interactive, word processing, or the like). To further complicate matters, one logical unit can represent several different users, and a user can have multiple sessions in progress concurrently. For example, suppose a terminal (operator) desires to retrieve a record from a database. The terminal will need to use the services of an application program to obtain the record. Each user—the terminal and the database application—is represented by a logical unit. The terminal LU issues a request to enter into a session with the database application LU. The application LU can either accept or reject the session request. Rejection is typically for security reasons, because the requesting LU lacks authority to establish a session with the application LU, or because of congestion, meaning the application LU has already entered into the maximum number of sessions it can support. If the session request is granted, a communications path is established between the terminal and the application. The two users continue to communicate until one of them terminates the session. Figure 10-7 shows several sessions between users communicating through their respective logical units.

LU Types. Seven LU types have thus far been defined within SNA. These are numbered from 0 to 7, with the definition for LU Type 5 omitted. It is

Figure 10-7 Several
SNA Sessions

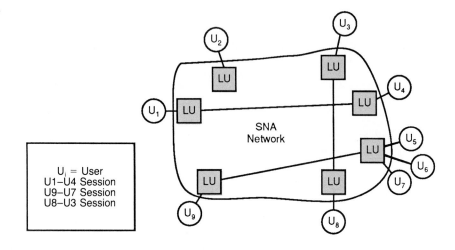

U_i = User
U1–U4 Session
U9–U7 Session
U8–U3 Session

important to note that the LU types refer to session types and not to a specific LU. Thus, one specific LU can participate in a Type 1 LU session with one LU and a Type 4 LU session with another. For two LUs to communicate they must both support and use the same LU session type. Of the seven LU types all but Types 0 and 6 address sessions with hardware devices such as printers and terminals. LU Type 6 is defined for program-to-program communication. It has evolved through two definitions, LU 6.0 and LU 6.1, to its current definition, LU 6.2. LU 6.2 has recently been given considerable attention as a key SNA capability. There are several significant aspects of LU 6.2.

First, LU 6.2 defines a protocol for program-to-program communication. Most of the other LU types are somewhat hardware oriented, involving sessions between 3270 devices, printers, and so on. A program-to-program communications interface is more general and can have wider uses than hardware-oriented ones. Second, program-to-program sessions provide a communications path for applications distributed over multiple nodes. Two applications communicating with each other are not required to be in the same node. This capability supports transaction processing systems with multiple processing nodes. For example, an inventory inquiry can start on a network node in a sales office and communicate with a warehouse node application to determine if stock exists to cover a pending order. Finally, and perhaps most significantly, a program-to-program interface is more generic than a session type involving specific hardware devices. This means that other vendors' equipment can enter into SNA sessions with an application process running in an IBM processor so long as the communicating program in the vendor's processor adheres to the session rules. An application on Vendor A's hardware could enter into a transaction with a database application running on an IBM node.

Many vendors have implemented an LU 6.2 capability for their SNA interface because such an interface can be made device-independent.

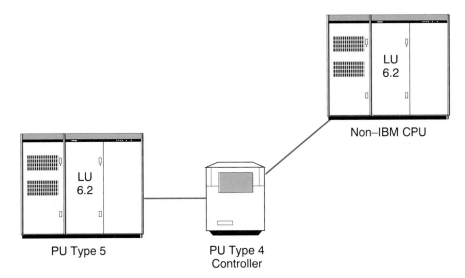

Figure 10-8
Non-IBM Vendor in
an LU 6.2 Session

Given a configuration as illustrated in Figure 10-8, a program in Vendor X's system can interface to its terminal device on one side and to an IBM application on the other. This logically provides the ability for a non-IBM terminal to interface to an IBM application system. Without LU 6.2, Vendor X would need to appear to the IBM application as one of the supported hardware types, such as a 3270 terminal or cluster controller. Moreover, the International Standards Organization (ISO) has agreed on a transaction interface that is compatible with IBM's LU 6.2 session. Some of the computer manufacturers that have committed to an LU 6.2 interface include Tandem Computers, Inc., Hewlett-Packard Co., Apollo Computer Corp., Prime Computers, Sun Microsystems, Inc., Banyan Systems, Inc., Cincom Systems, Inc., and AT&T.

Systems Services Control Point (SSCP)

As mentioned above, a dialogue between two users within the SNA environment is called a session. A supervisor or intermediary is involved in establishing a session. In SNA this extremely important entity is known as the *systems services control point (SSCP)*; it resides in a host processor, which is a physical unit Type 5. Not all PU Type 5 devices house an SSCP. The SSCP is the software controlling its host's portion of the network. The devices controlled by the host and its SSCP represent a *domain.*

Networks implemented under early versions of SNA had only one SSCP and thus only one host computer. Therefore, all of the network was controlled by this one host. In 1979 SNA was enhanced to allow multiple host systems, and hence multiple domains. This became necessary because large SNA networks were being implemented. Multiple SSCPs were better able to manage many devices and sessions. A two-domain SNA configuration is shown in Figure 10-9.

Figure 10-9   The
IBM SNA Network

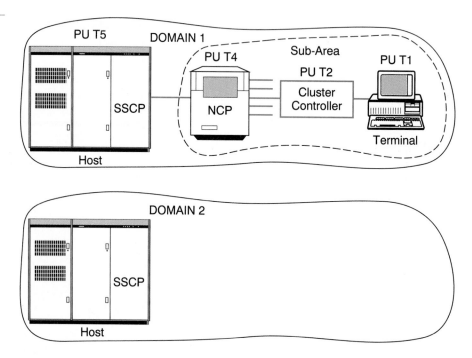

Within a given domain the SSCP is the controlling entity. It is responsible for the physical and logical units within its domain. In fulfilling this
obligation, it manages its units, including unit initialization, maintaining
the status of individual units, taking units on- and offline as necessary,
and serving as mediator in the establishment of sessions. Physical units
subordinate to an SSCP must be able to carry on a dialogue with the SSCP.
To accomplish this, a subset of the SSCP functionality, called a *physical unit
control point (PUCP)*, resides in SNA nodes that do not contain an SSCP. A
PUCP is responsible for connecting and disconnecting the node from the
SNA network.

Addressing

For one user to communicate with another, an address is required because
messages are sent to a specific unit by using its address. Addressable components in SNA are called *network addressable units (NAUs)*. An NAU can be
an SSCP, an LU, or a PU. Network addresses are hierarchical in nature. You
have already learned that an SNA network consists of domains. Domains
consist of sub-areas. A *sub-area* consists of a communications controller (for
example, a 3725) and all its NAUs or of a host/SSCP together with all of the
locally attached NAUs. Figure 10-10 shows two sub-areas. Each sub-area
has an address different from all other sub-areas. NAUs within one sub-
area are known by a local address. An example is a 3278 terminal attached
to a cluster controller. An SNA address consists of two parts, a sub-area

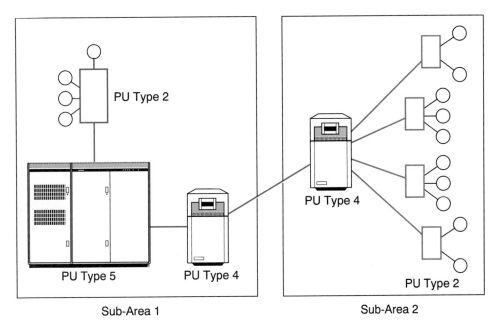

Figure 10-10 SNA Network with Two Sub-areas

address and a unit address. The unit address uniquely identifies an NAU in the sub-area. The combination of sub-area address and unit address uniquely identifies an NAU in the network. In SNA, addresses may be either 16 or 23 bits. The longer address is known as *extended addressing.* The extended address allows for a larger number of NAUs in the network.

In the extended addressing mode the first 8 bits represent the sub-area, and the last 15 bits, the device within the sub-area. The 16-bit address can be decomposed into a sub-area and device address on a network-by-network basis, which allows two networks to decompose the address in different manners. One could have an 8-bit address for both sub-areas and devices, while another could adopt a split of 7 bits for sub-area and 9 bits for devices.

Communication Between Users

If Users A and B are in the same domain, communication between them is established as follows. The logical unit representing User A sends a message to the SSCP requesting a session with User B. On behalf of User A, the SSCP contacts the User B LU to request a session and also to provide information about User A, including User A's access profile and type. User B either accepts or rejects the session request. If the session is rejected, User A is so notified. If User B accepts the invitation to enter into a session with A, a communications path must be established. Communication between users in different domains is established in a way similar to that for a single domain, except that the SSCPs in both domains are involved: The request goes from an LU to its SSCP to the SSCP in the other domain and then to its LU.

Path establishment was easy in early SNA implementations because there was only one path between LUs. Presently, two routing methods are supported: end-to-end routing and virtual routing. In *end-to-end routing*, for which at least one of the nodes must be a Type 5 physical unit or terminal, the path is determined and maintained through the entire session (unless the path is broken). In *virtual routing*, there is no permanently established path; instead, each node consults its routing table to determine to which node the message should be forwarded. The path control half-session layer is responsible for path allocation. Each available path is given a weighting that assists in route determination. A route might be selected based on best use according to such factors as security, speed, and propagation delay (as for satellite links). Up to five different paths between any two LUs can be described.

Additional SNA Elements

Network Control Program (NCP). The *network control program* (*NCP*), which resides in a communication controller such as the 3725, controls communications lines and the devices attached to them. It works with the *virtual terminal access method* (*VTAM*) that resides in the host. VTAM serves as the interface between application programs and the network.

Advanced Communications Facility (ACF). The *advanced communications facility* (*ACF*) was introduced in 1979. It provides such features as interdomain communication, improved error and testing capabilities, and dynamic device configuration.

Network Performance Analyzer (NPA). The *network performance analyzer* (*NPA*) provides performance information for the system, including information on lines, buffers, errors, queue lengths, and data transmission rates.

Network Problem Determination Aid (NPDA). The *network problem determination aid* (*NPDA*) collects, maintains, and reports information on error conditions within the network. It also allows for testing of the system concurrent with production operations.

Netview and Netview/PC. In 1986 IBM announced two network management packages for use in SNA systems. *Netview* runs on IBM hosts, and *Netview/PC,* on microcomputers. With Netview IBM has consolidated several previous network management facilities (including NPDA) and enhanced them to provide more comprehensive management capabilities. The functions found in Netview are covered in Chapter 11, which addresses network management.

SNA Distribution Services (SNADS). *SNADS* allows users to exchange documents using the SNA network. Document interchange differs from the typical SNA session. In a typical SNA session the sender and receiver are synchronized regarding information exchange. By *synchronized* we mean that the users communicate (through their LUs) and agree to carry on a conversation. In contrast, with document exchanges the users may not be synchronized. A sender may dispatch a document without first coordinating the transmission with the recipient. The recipient can then request access to the document as its convenience. SNADS provides the ability to distribute documents in such a manner. This is particularly helpful for office automation applications such as network mail and document distribution.

INTERNATIONAL NETWORKS

Data communications networks are not confined to national boundaries. Today many companies are international in scope. International computer networks help many of these companies manage their data and provide communication among employees. International networks are used by banks for money transfer and financial planning applications. With international networks, manufacturing companies can schedule production of parts in multiple locations for assembly at a central location. All international companies can use international networks and electronic mail for immediate, timely communications; moreover, electronic mail helps eliminate the problems of time zone differences. For example, there may not be an overlap of working hours between offices in England and Australia. Electronic mail allows quick communication during an employee's normal working hours. Designing and implementing international networks is more difficult than building one that is national in scope. The problems we encounter are ones of politics, regulations, hardware, and language.

Politics

On occasion the problems to be resolved with international networks are political rather than technical. For example, one company reported that it was given permission to install a microwave link in a particular country. That country's government, however, suggested that the company double the capacity of the network. Upon completion, the microwave system was nationalized by the government, and the company that built it was "given" half of the carrying capacity of the network (Jenkins, 1987).

Regulations

Networks require communication links. In many countries the communications networks are controlled by an agency we shall call the postal, telephone, and telegraph (PTT) authority. Often the PTT is a government agency or government-regulated agency with exclusive rights to provide communication facilities. The regulations under which the PTTs operate generally were designed for their original mission of postal, telephone, and telegraph communications. These regulations sometimes impede the establishment of international data communications.

For example, sometimes regulations are established to protect or subsidize certain interests. In some countries restrictions exist regarding which equipment can be connected to a network. A few countries require that hardware used in a network be manufactured in whole or in part within the country. Pricing regulations in some countries are structured so data communications services help subsidize individual telephone services. Frequently regulations prohibit competition in providing communication facilities. Thus, it is often difficult to set up a network using services provided by a single communications carrier. Many PTTs recognize that regulations need to be changed to meet the needs of international networks; therefore, some countries have begun to deregulate their communications industry. Deregulation typically means opening competition regarding equipment that can be attached to the network and the cost and provision of communications facilities.

International networks sometimes also conflict with other national interests. Some countries impose an import duty on software. Sometimes the duty is on the value of the carrying medium, such as a magnetic tape; other countries tax the value of the imported software. International networks provide the ability to import software over the network, making the collection of tariffs more difficult. Some countries view international networks as potential threats to national security. Data regarding national resources, the economy, and people can be more easily collected and transmitted to another country through international networks. Several nations are attempting to legislate solutions to these concerns.

Hardware

When discussing regulations we mentioned that in some countries restrictions exist regarding the source or type of equipment that can be attached to the communications facilities of a PTT. Several countries require that all or part of the equipment used within the country be locally manufactured. Some do not require the equipment to be manufactured in-country but still restrict the equipment that can be used to that manufactured by a select group of companies. Most countries require that equipment attached to communications networks meet minimum technical specifications. Moreover, the specifications differ among countries. A communications controller that is certified for operation in the United States may not meet the tighter specifications for grounding that exist in Australia.

Another technical difference that must be accommodated is variations in power supplies among countries. When ordering equipment for a specific node, we must be sure that the equipment's power supply needs are consistent with the power available in that location. Many times new hardware also must be certified by a host country before it can be attached to the communications network. For example, a company that introduces a facsimile controller that connects to the common carrier's network must first undergo testing and evaluation by the host country. It is not unusual for certification to take several months and require that equipment and circuit schematics be provided for the evaluation process. Thus, introduction of new equipment into a network can incur substantial delays.

Language

Another problem needing resolution in international networks is language related. Network managers at different locations must be able to communicate to resolve differences. On occasion, several different countries and hence several different languages may be involved in solving one problem. It is thus necessary to have not only technical expertise but also linguistic expertise in the network management organization. Furthermore, data generated in one location in the in-country language may need to be translated when used in another country. Such translation may be manual or through language translation programs. Accompanying the need to translate from one language to another is the need to have hardware and software capable of displaying local character sets, such as Kanji in China and Japan, Hongul in Korea, and Farsi in Arab countries. Accommodations also must be made when the number of characters in a national character set exceeds the capacity of a particular code. For example, 7-bit ASCII codes can accommodate 128 distinct characters, but the number of Kanji characters exceeds 30,000.

Other Issues

Typically, an international network involves the coordination of several communications providers. One of the easier methods of creating an international network is to use the services of existing X.25 networks. The ease derives from the fact that most public X.25 network providers have established interconnections and the network implementer need not be concerned about PTT interfaces. If a company decides to procure exclusive links such as leased lines, creating the network may be more difficult. Determining the correct interfaces and problem resolution must be assumed by the company. Problem resolution can be somewhat difficult in an international network. Consider a link from Australia to France. The end-to-end connection may use links from Australia to the United States, to England, and then to France. Thus, four PTTs, several protocols, a variety of vendor equipment, and several time zones may be involved. If a problem arises in transmitting data between the French and Australian nodes, the multiplicity of involved vendors can cause delays in resolution. On more than one occasion a problem has been allowed to continue while two PTTs debated which was responsible for the problem.

Costing an international network can present several difficulties. First, collecting tariff information can be time-consuming. When multiple nodes exist within a country, we typically must deal with local tariffs and international tariffs. In some cases, there may be multiple circuit providers, a variety of available rates, and variations between local and long-distance rates. In addition to tariffs for the use of lines, in some countries we must also determine the costs of taxes applied to the movement of data over a country's borders and taxes on imported software.

The International Telecommunications Union (ITU), the Consultative Committee on International Telegraph and Telephony (CCITT), and other international communications organizations realize the existing limitations and problems in implementing international connections and are addressing the issues. Standards like OSI, X.25, and X.400 electronic mail interface ease the burden of establishing international networks. Deregulation of the communications industries in some countries has allowed the introduction of new equipment and competition among providers of communications links. Issues such as the rights of communication facilities provided from a foreign country, such as a Canadian PTT operating circuits in the United States, are being discussed. All these efforts should make establishing international networks easier; however, the problems inherent in international networks will always be greater than those for domestic networks. Another international body, the General Agreement on Trade and Tariffs (GATT), an organization of 97 nations, has proposed a treaty that will ease the problems of international networks. Among the treaty provisions are stipulations regarding the use and cost of private lines.

MICROCOMPUTERS IN NETWORKS

When we use the terms *microcomputers* and *networks* together, usually the image that comes to mind is that of a LAN with microcomputer workstations. Microcomputers are becoming increasingly important elements of WANs as well. In this section we discuss how microcomputers are used in a WAN.

Advantages of Microcomputers

The trend of using micros in networks that began in the early 1980s is continuing because of their advantages, which include:

Relatively low cost

Ability to emulate a variety of terminals

Compact size

Ability to operate in office environments

Relatively wide-ranging processing capabilities

Large base of applications software

Large base of network-related software

Ease of adaptation: adding software or a printed circuit card allows the microcomputer to accommodate changing conditions

Low Cost.   The cost of microcomputers has steadily declined since their introduction. Currently they are price competitive with many smart terminals that have fewer processing capabilities. Furthermore, because microcomputers can emulate a wide variety of terminals, they are a sound investment: If the user changes hardware vendors or data communications products, the micro probably will be able to function in the new environment. For a micro to emulate a terminal, a synchronous or asynchronous logic board and certain software are required. With these components, a micro can function as either an asynchronous or synchronous terminal, and within each of these data link protocols it can represent a variety of terminal types, such as IBM 3270, IBM 2780, and DEC VT100.

Fewer Special Requirements.   Because most microcomputers are designed to operate in an office environment, they have none of the special requirements for air-conditioning or power that typify many larger systems. Their compact size means they fit in about the same desk space as a conventional terminal or typewriter. These attributes also help keep their overall cost down, as both office space and air-conditioning can be expensive.

Ease of Use and Versatility.   Next to cost, perhaps the most significant reason that micros have become important components of data communications networks is their ease of use and wide-ranging processing capabilities. The ability to function as multiple terminal types, cited above, and the applications and network software available, in addition to an increase in processing power and storage capacity, have expanded the range of possible applications. Programs once available only on mainframe systems are now available on micros, including presentation services, CAD, scientific and statistical packages, simulation models, database management systems, and others. Moreover, microcomputer application software is typically easier to use than mainframe software. The former is usually designed for nontechnical users while the latter often assumes that the user has well-developed computer skills.

With large-capacity disk drives and memory, together with increased processing power, significant amounts of data can be stored or downloaded from a host system for processing. This information then can be printed locally and distributed to other systems within the network. This not only provides more local control of such functions but also can reduce the workload of the host system. The combination of powerful hardware and software has led to an environment where data is distributed over multiple processing nodes at both host systems and workstations. Workstation users now satisfy many of their data processing requirements locally without assistance from the computer center.

Microcomputer-Host Connections. As the power of workstations increases, we will likely see a change in how they attach to the host. In the future it is likely that microcomputers will function more like network nodes rather than as terminal devices. In this type of connection the software residing in the workstation will need to be more sophisticated than that required for terminal emulation. The operating system will need to provide multi-programming capabilities, and the communications software will need to perform host-type functions. This type of connection is important but is not our concern in this section. The reason for this is that this role of microcomputers is not very common and it is essentially a node-to-node connection equivalent to connecting two mainframes together in a network.

When a micro is attached to a WAN as a terminal device, several components are required in making the connection. From the perspective of the host computer, the micro appears as a particular terminal type with which it can communicate. It may appear as a synchronous or asynchronous device using a specific protocol such as an IBM 3270 or DEC VT220. The host communication software usually does not make any accommodations for the fact that the device with which it is communicating is a microcomputer. Thus, almost all the connection accommodation is done at the micro end. The major exception to this is with respect to file transfers between the two.

The first communication component that must be included in the micro configuration is a communications controller. This is usually an asynchronous or synchronous board that fits in one of the micro's expansion slots, providing a port to which the communication line can be connected. Between the communications card connector and the host processor, the connection looks just like that for any terminal, such as a modem cable, modem, circuit to the host, host modem, and connection to a port on the host's communications controller. Like all terminals, under certain circumstances the workstation also may be connected directly to the host without a modem.

At the micro end of the communications link, software that interfaces to the communications port is required. This software performs two basic functions. On the communications side it must provide the low-level support to interface to the line. This is the line driver function that handles line interrupts and performs error detection and recovery, modem interface, and data link protocol functions. The second function of the micro software is the terminal emulation logic and the micro interface function. Many communications packages are available that allow a micro to communicate with another micro or a host system. Some of the features found in these packages are described below.

Terminal Emulation. A wide variety of terminals may be emulated through micro software. These range from primitive capabilities such as TTY devices to fairly sophisticated capabilities such as an SNA 3270 terminal. Virtually all the major terminal types have micro emulators, including terminals from IBM, Digital Equipment Corporation, Unisys, Hewlett-Packard, and Tandem.

File Transfer.   One of the key functions when using a micro as a terminal and workstation is the ability to transfer data between the host and the micro. Data resident on the host can be transmitted to a workstation, where it can be manipulated and from which reports can be generated. In some applications the manipulated data is returned to the host for further processing or to make it available to other users. This capability on the surface seems simple; in actuality, it poses several complexities.

If the data to be transferred to the micro is stored in a database on the host system, several steps may be required before the micro's software can use the data. The data may exist in more than one database file, and each file may contain many records—more than can be stored locally at the workstation. If this is the case, the required records need to be extracted from the database. As an example, the data of interest may be all orders that are still open, together with the order line items. There may be one million order records in the database but only 1000 that meet the processing requirements. The line items for these orders may be stored in a separate file. The first step in the transfer process would be to extract the required data to a file on the host.

Once the data has been extracted from the database, it may need to be placed into a format compatible with the workstation software. This could be accomplished on the host or at the micro. Because the host probably has a higher processing speed and supports the data formats of the extracted data, formatting often is more efficiently done on the host. In some cases the data extraction program may even accomplish it. After extraction and formatting, the data is ready for transfer to the micro. A sending program on the host side must communicate with a receiving program on the micro to accomplish transfer. There are numerous file transfer software capabilities. Some have a component that runs on both ends of the connection, while others use standard host utilities and a micro file transfer utility.

An example of the first case is a file transfer utility called *Kermit*. Kermit allows files in ASCII format to be transferred over an asynchronous communications link using a half duplex protocol. Data being transmitted is packetized, and Kermit provides CRC error detection for these packets. On the micro side of the communications link, Kermit stores the data on the disk. Other general-purpose file transfer utilities include XMODEM and YMODEM. Some vendors offer proprietary software packages to accomplish this.

In the second case data can be transferred between a host and a workstation using standard utilities on the host processor. For example, to transfer data from the host to a workstation, a text editor or file transfer program can be used on the host side to output to the terminal. From the perspective of the host software, it is simply listing the data on a terminal.

At the workstation end, the terminal emulation program receives the data and writes it to the workstation's disk. The same utilities could be used when transferring from the workstation to the host. In this case the file transfer program or text editor would act as though it were receiving data entered from the terminal's keyboard; in fact, the terminal emulation program would be reading the disk file and writing the data to the host. The disadvantage of this type of transfer is that the data may have additional control characters embedded in the text. These would be placed there by the host software that transferred the data. For instance, a carriage return and line feed character would likely appear at the end of each line transferred, since the host software would be formatting the data for terminal display.

Modem Support.   Most terminal emulation packages provide some level of modem support. Modem capabilities include keyboard dialing, storage of commonly used telephone numbers, and automatic redialing. These functions obviously apply to switched connections. Most emulators also support direct connection and interface conventions such as XON/XOFF for pacing control.

Miscellaneous Features.   The major features of a terminal emulation package are given above. Many provide additional user convenience features such as:

> Scripts that provide automatic logon
>
> Online help
>
> Integrated text editors
>
> Background operation for file transfer and print spooling
>
> Clock and session timer

These are convenience features. Manufacturers of these packages periodically add such features to maintain their market share and remain competitive. Terminal emulators vary in price. A relatively full-featured package may be obtained for under $100.

Microcomputer Applications

Having made the connection between a host computer and the microcomputer, the terminal operator can access information on the host. While it is possible to interact with the host only as a terminal (that is, the host-workstation interaction is exactly the same as what could be done on the terminal being emulated), the real power of this type of connection is using the processing capabilities of the workstation to augment host processing. Database access and file transfers have been covered above. Other uses are identified below.

Participating in Host Application.   A PC can be an active participant in an application system running on the host. When data has been entered on the PC, a local process edits the data to ensure that it meets editing characteristics. The data is then compressed (to minimize utilization of the communications link), encrypted for security, and transmitted to the host. The PC can also be responsible for the display and sequencing of screen templates, which not only eliminates that portion of the data being transmitted over the communications link but also assumes some of the processing load usually required of the host node.

Efficient Use of Terminal Operators.   Another advantage of microcomputers as opposed to smart or dumb terminals is the ability to keep an operator productive even when the host is unavailable. For an operator using a less intelligent terminal in an application where the data is ordinarily entered directly into a database residing on the host, a failure of either the host or the communications link would result in the operator's being unable to continue with data entry. With a microcomputer, however, it is possible for the operator to have the data stored locally and to continue with data entry. When communications to the host computer are reestablished, the transactions already entered can be forwarded to the host. If the microcomputer's operating system supports multi-tasking, the stored transactions can be forwarded while the operator enters additional transactions. With the use of switched connections, this mode of operation can be very cost effective. Data is transmitted at line speeds rather than operator input speeds, which reduces the connect time.

Home Computers.   Network applications involving personal computers in the home have started to emerge. Home banking is implemented in some areas, enabling customers to transfer money between accounts and to pay bills. Videotex applications enable consumers to shop at home and to obtain information from a variety of sources, such as news wires, stock exchanges, and travel agencies. When the home computer becomes as common a household appliance as the telephone, its use in computer networks is likely to expand even further.

Microcomputers and Host Processing

Whether the use of microcomputers in communications networks will bring about a significant savings in host processing remains to be seen. In one installation the amount of host CPU savings was slight—approximately 5% (Campbell, 1984). On the other hand, microcomputers might actually increase the load on host processors, since they will open up new kinds of applications. The ease of access to host data, coupled with local processing and output, is likely to aid the development of previously impractical applications. These new applications will surely increase demand for host computer services.

CASE STUDY

The Syncrasy Corporation, once again expanding, intends to open retail outlets in several additional cities. A tentative list of these new cities is given in Figure 10-11.

Network Requirements

Each city on the network will have at least one processor, and the existing network, discussed in Chapter 5, might be abandoned if a better configuration exists.

Reliability.   The requirements of the new network include high reliability among the major centers in New York, Chicago, Kansas City, and Los Angeles and among the European cities. For the Pacific area, however, it has been decided that distance and the related communications costs prohibit the redundant links required for reliability. Reliability for Syncrasy means that all nodes can continue to communicate should a link fail and that all remaining nodes can still communicate should a node fail.

Low Cost.   The second design criterion is cost. Syncrasy wants the lowest cost network that can provide the necessary functions.

U.S. Network Configuration

The long-distance network in the United States must, of course, interface with the local area network, designed in Chapter 9, with the gateway function being performed by a processor attached to both networks.

Backbone Network.   The need for reliability in the four major U.S. cities demands a loop configuration, as depicted in Figure 10-12. As a minimum, the network routing algorithm must be able to alter paths if a node or link fails. This type of configuration is sometimes called a *backbone network*, and the nodes are referred to as *backbone nodes*. From the mileage chart given in Figure 5-24, it can be determined that the backbone network in Figure 10-12 is the minimum-distance configuration.

One possible U.S. configuration is depicted in Figure 10-13. The backbone network serves as the delivery system for many of the nodes, such as

---

Figure 10-11
Expansion Cities

Seattle	Detroit	Rome
Phoenix	Denver	Oslo
Boston	Montreal	Hong Kong
Miami	Toronto	Sydney
Dallas	London	Tokyo
Washington, D.C.	Paris	Mexico City
Philadelphia	Frankfurt	

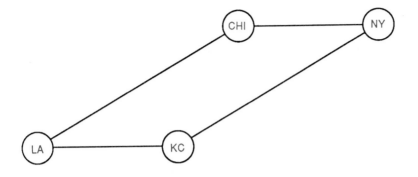

Figure 10-12
A Backbone Network

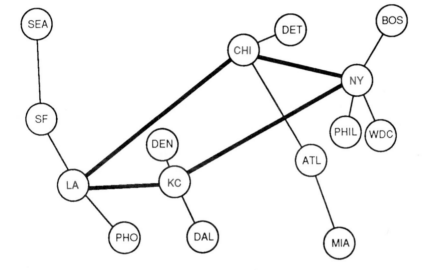

Figure 10-13
A Possible United
States Network

from Seattle to Boston. However, a message sent from Seattle to San Francisco will not make use of the backbone system. Syncrasy has decided that the backbone nodes should be dedicated to the network task, so they will not be used for application processing. This decision was made because the amount of anticipated message traffic is high enough to allow dedicated backbone nodes. To increase the reliability of the backbone network, fault-tolerant computers were chosen.

Remaining U.S. Network. Three primary options were considered in configuring the remainder of the network: leased media, switched media, and public data network (PDN). Which of these is most cost effective is a function of distance and message traffic. Distance becomes a factor when determining the rates charged for leased and switched connections; it usually is not a factor with respect to PDN rates. Message traffic affects the connect time for switched connections and the packet charges for a PDN. For all U.S. nodes not in the backbone network, an analysis was performed to determine which of the three options would be most cost effective. The analysis for the Seattle node follows.

Figure 10-14
Leased Line
Rates, Seattle to
San Francisco

First 100 miles	$2.52 per mile (includes monthly service charge fee)
Next 900 miles (101–1000)	$0.94 per mile
Each mile over 1000	$0.58 per mile

Figure 10-15
Switched Line
Rates, Seattle to
San Francisco

First minute of connect time	$0.60
Each additional minute	$0.40

Figure 10-16   PDN
Charges, Seattle to
San Francisco

Connection charge per node	$400 per month
Packet charge	$1.50 per 1000 packets
Packet size	128 characters

Seattle–San Francisco Line Costs.   The following rate information on the three options for connecting the Seattle node to the San Francisco node (the closest) are approximate and are intended for use only in this case study. Actual rates may vary. Leased line rates are given in Figure 10-14; switched telephone rates, in Figure 10-15; and PDN rates, in Figure 10-16. Additional comparison information must be derived. To evaluate the switched connections, the number of connections per day and the total amount of connect time must be approximated. Seattle, being a relatively low volume node at a network extremity, will not be involved in store and forward operations. In contrast, the San Francisco node will originate and receive its own messages and will forward messages to and from Seattle and other nodes. It is estimated there will be three connections per day, requiring 250 minutes total connect time. A message traffic of 30,000 characters per day also is anticipated. A 23-day work month is assumed. The total distance between Seattle and San Francisco is 810 miles. Leased line charges are:

(first 100 miles @ $2.52 per mile) + (710 miles @ $0.94 per mile)

$$= 252 + 667.40 = \$919.40$$

Daily switched line costs are:

(3 connections @ $0.60 per first minute) + (247 remaining minutes

@ $0.40 per minute) = 1.80 + 98.80 = $100.60

Monthly switched line costs are therefore:

23 days @ $100.60 per day = $2313.80

No additional telephone service charges are included in the analysis because telephones are already installed on the premises. If one or more telephones were dedicated to data communications, then their cost would have to be included.

PDN charges are derived as follows: Two stations must be connected at a fee of $400 each. There are 30,000 characters transmitted per day, which, at 128 characters per packet, is 235 packets. This assumes that all packets are full, which will not be the case. A message of 140 characters requires two packets to be sent. The 30,000 characters transmitted per day was approximated to include this variance. There is a charge of $1.50 per 1000 packets, and there are 23 workdays per month. Thus, the monthly PDN charges are:

$$(2 \times 400) + (30,000/128 \times 1.50/1000 \times 23)$$
$$= 800 + (235 \times 0.0015 \times 23) = 800 + 8.11 = \$808.11$$

This analysis shows that PDN will be the most economical link between Seattle and San Francisco. This configuration has the added benefit of allowing the Seattle node to transmit directly to any node with a PDN port, meaning that such messages would not always need to be routed through San Francisco.

Break-Even Point. One more computation will complete the analysis of the link between Seattle and San Francisco. A break-even figure will show the amount of message traffic necessary to make the cost of a leased link the same as that for a PDN. (From the above analysis, it seems unlikely that a switched connection will ever be practical.) The break-even number of characters per day, x, is given by:

$$(2 \times 400) + (x/128 \times 0.0015 \times 23) = \$919.40$$

$$x = 442,991 \text{ characters per day}$$

This is not a significant amount of message traffic; a 120-page typed document, at 80 characters per line and 55 lines per page, with no compression, exceeds this amount.

The above calculations assumed that neither node had a PDN port and that there was one connection charge per node. However, if one of the nodes already had a PDN connection, then the cost for that port either should not be included or should be distributed throughout the network. Thus, if San Francisco already had been configured with a PDN port, the PDN cost would decrease by $400, or the cost of that port should be apportioned among the nodes that must be connected to San Francisco.

San Francisco–Los Angeles Line. A similar analysis was performed for the San Francisco–Los Angeles connection. A switched line was not considered in this instance; a leased line was the most economical. The leased line rates between San Francisco and Los Angeles are different from those given in Figure 10-14 because the link is intrastate. A leased line is available for $425. Since approximately 200,000 characters per day are transferred between the two cities, PDN charges are:

$$400 + (200,000/128 \times 0.0015 \times 23) = 400 + 53.90 = \$453.90$$

International Lines. All the European cities will be connected by a backbone network. The connections between Europe, the United States, Canada,

Mexico, Japan, Australia, and Hong Kong will be made via X.25 networks. The amount of message traffic between these entities does not warrant the use of leased facilities. Configuring the other parts of the network is left as an exercise.

SUMMARY

Packet distribution networks have evolved into an efficient, effective networking alternative to private networks. PDNs offer circuit acquisition, message routing, error detection and correction, and maintenance. Interconnection of PDNs provides users with an instant international network. The cost of a PDN is reasonable so long as the number of data packets being transferred is low. However, this advantge comes at the price of contending with other users for the facility and a lack of control over network operations. The success of packet switching networks has made them a potential standard for future network implementations as well as for gateways between different network systems.

Wide area networks are usually built around a particular vendor's network software. Although most major computer vendors offer network capabilities, the leader in proprietary network software is IBM's SNA. SNA provides an architecture for building networks, and many vendors support some type of connection to SNA networks. One of the ways that vendors can communicate with an SNA network is via the LU 6.2 protocol. Microcomputers are increasingly found as wide area network components. Their versatility makes them a cost-effective network tool.

SNA continues to evolve and mature as a network product. Internally, new network functions such as those provided by LU 6.2 and SNADS are being included in the architecture. Gateways to other networking products continue to be implemented, together with SNA interfaces between IBM SNA components and other manufacturers' equipment. Some vendors have gone so far as to implement PU Type 4 and PU Type 5 capabilities within their systems. SNA may be the most significant influence in WAN implementations today.

Key Terms

advanced communications facility
  (ACF)
backbone network
data link control (SNA layer)
datagram
domain
end-to-end routing
flow control (SNA layer)

function management (SNA layer)
half-session
half-session (SNA layer)
logical unit (LU)
LU 6.2
Netview
Netview/PC
network addressable unit (NAU)

network control program (NCP)

network performance analyzer (NPA)

network problem determination aid (NPDA)

path control (SNA layer)

permanent virtual circuit (PVC)

physical unit (PU)

physical unit control point (PUCP)

presentation service (SNA layer)

PU Type 1

PU Type 2

PU Type 4

PU Type 5

server

services manager (SNA layer)

session

sub-area

switched virtual circuit (SVC)

systems network architecture (SNA)

systems network architecture distribution services (SNADS)

systems services control point (SSCP)

transmission control (SNA layer)

user

virtual routing

Review Questions

1. Why are only three layers defined for PDNs? Do the other OSI layers exist? Explain.

2. Why is datagram service generally unsuited to business applications?

3. Are there any business applications for which datagram service is useful? If so, list them.

4. What are the four types of physical units in SNA? What is the role of each in the network?

5. What is a half-session layer in SNA? What is its purpose?

6. Explain how a session is established in SNA.

7. Describe what a gateway between SNA and Ethernet must accomplish.

8. Compare and contrast a LAN and a WAN.

9. Compare and contrast a WAN and a PDN.

10. Discuss the influence of SNA on other computer vendors.

11. How does SNA relate to the OSI reference model?

Exercises

1. Suppose that the message traffic between New York City and Boston is 600,000 characters per day. If the cost of a leased line is $650 per month, which will be more economical, a leased line or a PDN? Assume that New York City already has a PDN port. How many characters must be exchanged for a leased line to cost the same as a PDN? Use the costs included in the case study in your analysis.

2. Would a PDN be a suitable network for the Syncrasy Corporation's network of catalog and discount stores (see Chapter 5)? What would be the advantages and disadvantages of using a PDN for that application?

3. Obtain the costs for subscribing to a PDN. What are the monthly charges and what are the packet charges?

References

Baer, David M., and Jim Sturch. "An SNA Primer for Programmers, Part 1." *Computerworld on Communications* 17, November 14, 1983.

————. "An SNA Primer for Programmers, Part 2." *Computerworld on Communications* 17, November 21, 1983.

Bellamy, John. *Digital Telephony.* New York: Wiley, 1982.

Benhamou, Eric, and Judy Estrin. "Multilevel Internetworking Gateways: Architecture and Application." *Computer* 16, September 1983.

Campbell, B.W. "The Planning Side of Success with Micros." *Data Communications* 13, October 1984.

Cypser, R. J. *Communications Architecture for Distributed Systems.* Reading, MA: Addison-Wesley, 1978.

Herman, James G. "How to Expand and Modernize a Global Network." *Data Communications* 14, December 1985.

IBM. *Systems Network Architecture, Concepts and Products.* Manual no. GC30-3072-1. Research Triangle Park, NC: IBM, 1981.

————. *Systems Network Architecture—Sessions between Logical Units.* Manual no. GC20-1868-2. Research Triangle Park, NC: IBM, 1981.

Jenkins, Avery. "Networks in a Strange Land." *Computerworld Focus—Critical Connections* 21, September 9, 1987.

Kuo, Franklin F. *Protocols and Techniques for Data Communications Networks.* Englewood Cliffs, NJ: Prentice-Hall, 1981.

Martin, James, and Kathleen Kavanagh Chapman. *SNA: IBM's Networking Solution.* Englewood Cliffs, NJ: Prentice-Hall, 1987.

O'Connor, Walter F. "Information—The Next Trade Problem?" *Data Communications* 15, March, 1986.

Tanenbaum, Andrew S. *Computer Networks.* Englewood Cliffs, NJ: Prentice-Hall, 1981.

Tropper, Carl. *Local Computer Network Technologies.* New York: Academic Press, 1981.

Network Management

Brief History of Network Management
Network Management Objectives
Meeting the Objectives
Network Management Organization
Network Management Systems
Managing a Local Area Network
Network Management Tools
Network Management Protocols

INTRODUCTION

This chapter begins with a discussion of the objectives and functions of network management and how those objectives can be met. You then learn about both generic and specific network management systems and some of the issues surrounding managing a local area network (LAN). Specific topics you learn about in this chapter include:

Network management history

Objectives of network management

Meeting the objectives of network management

Network management organization

Functions performed by a network management system

IBM's Netview and Netview/PC network management systems

LAN management

Network management tools

Network management protocols

391

BRIEF HISTORY OF NETWORK MANAGEMENT

The network management team historically has been responsible for the selection, implementation, testing, expansion, operation, and maintenance of the data communications portion of the data-processing environment. With the introduction of computerized branch exchanges, digital branch exchanges, and the associated integration of voice, data, and video transmissions on a common medium, this role is expanding to include management of the entire telecommunications needs of an organization. In the past, voice, video, and data communications were usually separate and were managed by different groups. In today's communications environment, sharing media and hardware components and integrating these functions can produce significant savings for a company.

The role of network manager, like that of database administrator, is a relatively new position within the data-processing industry. Both positions were created by the technological expansion of the 1970s and the recognition of the increasing importance of these technologies to the storage, retrieval, and maintenance of business data. These positions are similar in several respects. Both have high visibility among system users. The database administrator is called when the required data is unavailable. If terminals do not work or response time is unsatisfactory, the network manager is notified. Both roles are responsible for configurations, planning, tuning, and establishing standards and procedures in their respective areas. Both positions require personnel with a strong technical background, good leadership qualities, and an ability to work well with people with wide ranges of technical expertise. In the remainder of this chapter, the term *network manager* refers to the function of network management and therefore to a team of people, rather than to a single individual.

NETWORK MANAGEMENT OBJECTIVES

The two primary objectives of network management are to satisfy system users and to provide cost-effective solutions to an organization's telecommunications requirements. If these two objectives are met, the network management team will be successful.

User Satisfaction

User satisfaction implies a host of requirements, the three most obvious of which are performance, availability, and reliability. User satisfaction can also be enhanced by keeping users informed of system changes and through formal and informal training.

Good Performance. Good performance means a predictable transaction response time. Response time depends on the nature of the transaction.

Transactions differ in the amount of work to be accomplished and the number of characters to be transmitted. For every transaction in the system, a realistic response time objective should be established. Predictable response times require that most transactions be completed within a small range around the established response time goal. For example, for an expected transaction response time of 10 seconds, it is realistic to expect 95% of all transactions of that type to be completed within 9–11 seconds and 100% of such transactions to be completed within 20 seconds. Erratic response times are generally perceived by users to be worse than slow but predictable responses. Of the two response time components—processing time and communications time—the network manager ordinarily has little or no control over the application processing and database access components, but does have control over configuration and line speed. The configuration aspects include the number of terminals on a given line, hardware employed (such as multiplexers, front end processors, and concentrators), types of terminals used, number of intermediate nodes through which the message must travel (hops), networking software, and error characteristics. Each of these affects the performance of the system.

Availability. Availability means that all necessary components are operable when a user requires them; for a terminal operator, these include the terminal, cables, connectors, modems, medium or media, controllers, processors, and software. Three factors influence availability: operational considerations, mean time between failures (MTBF), and mean time to repair (MTTR).

Operational considerations may require that portions of the system be taken out of service. Some portions of the online system may be available only during standard working hours. Thus, the payroll system may be unavailable at night, when payroll transactions are not anticipated. In some installations the online system is given in priority during the day, whereas batch operations have priority on night shifts, when all or portions of the online system may be stopped. Other operational requirements such as preventive maintenance and installation of new hardware or software can remove all or parts of the system from use. Generally, operational considerations can be planned so online users are able to work around them.

Mean time between failures (MTBF) is the average period that a component will operate before failing. For example, a CRT terminal with MTBF of 2000 hours that operates an average of 8 hours a day, 23 days a month, would be expected to fail once every $2000/(8 \times 23) = 10.86$ months. *Mean time to repair (MTTR)* is the average amount of time required to place a failed component back into service. For certain components, repair time is relatively constant, such as replacing a failed modem with a spare (unless travel time is required). For a CPU, however, there may be considerable variations in repair time. Often CPU repairs require the repair person to travel to the site and run a varying number of diagnostic routines and testing procedures.

Availability can be defined by the following probability function (Nickel, 1978):

$$A(t) = \frac{a}{a + b} + \frac{b}{a + b} e^{-(a+b)t}$$

where $a = 1/\mathrm{MTTR}$, $b = 1/\mathrm{MTBF}$, e is the natural logarithm, and t is a time interval. The equation gives the probability that a component will be available when required by a user. For a terminal with an MTBF of 2000 hours and an MTTR of 0.5 hours (typical of replacement with an onsite spare),

$$a = 1/0.5 = 2, b = 1/2000 = 0.0005$$

Availability for an 8-hour period, then, is

$$A(8) = \frac{2}{2 + 0.0005} + \frac{0.0005 e^{-(2+0.0005)8}}{2 + 0.0005}$$

$$= \frac{2}{2.0005} + \frac{(0.0005)(0.0000001121)}{2.0005}$$

$$= 0.99975 + 2.8 \times 10^{-11}$$

$$= 0.9997$$

On the average, an operator can expect the terminal to be unavailable three times in every 10,000 tries. And since the exponential term approaches zero and becomes insignificant as the time interval increases, availability in such cases becomes

$$A = \frac{MTBF}{MTBF + MTTR}$$

For the terminal with an availability of 0.9997, if the operator used it 20 times an hour, it would take 500 hours for the terminal to be used 10,000 times. At 8 hours a day that equates to 62.5 days. Thus, three failures can be expected every 10,000 uses, which means that, on the average, the terminal will be unavailable once every 20.8 days. Superficially this may seem to be too frequent for a terminal that fails only once every 10.86 months (assuming use is based on 8-hour days). With the use pattern described, the operator will be denied approximately 10 access attempts to the system (since access is attempted every 3 minutes on the average and MTTR is 30 minutes); thus, being unavailable once every 20.8 days equates to 10 times every 208 days, or 9.04 months. A different use pattern would give a different availability profile. For instance, if used 10 times an hour, the terminal will be unavailable an average of once every 41.6 days.

Availability with Multiple Components.   If several components must be linked together to make the system available to the user—for instance, terminal, modem, medium, and CPU—then system availability is given by the product of the availabilities of the component parts (Nickel, 1978):

$$A_s = A_t \times A_m \times A_l \times A_m \times A_c$$

where A represents availability and the subscripts s, t, m, l, m, and c represent the system, terminal, modem, link, modem, and CPU, respectively. If each component has an availability of 0.999, the user will see a system availability of

$$A_s = 0.999^5 = 0.995$$

In this situation, statistically the user would find the system unavailable five times every 1000 attempts, or once every 200 attempts. The availability factor is important in determining how many spare components to stock and how much productive time might be lost when the system is unavailable. System availability as a function of MTBF and MTTR is illustrated in Figure 11-1.

Reliability. Reliability is the probability that the system will continue to function over a given operating period. For example, if a transaction requires 3 seconds for a response to be received, then the reliability of the system is the probability that the system will not fail during that 3 seconds. Reliability of the network involves error characteristics of the medium and stability of the hardware and software components. More specifically, network reliability is a function of the MTBF. In some cases the user will see circuit errors in the form of slow response times. Data received in error will cause retransmissions, slower response times, and congestion of the medium. If the errors are persistent, the retry threshold for the link might be exceeded and the link consequently removed from service. For some modems, a large number of errors will cause the modem to change to a

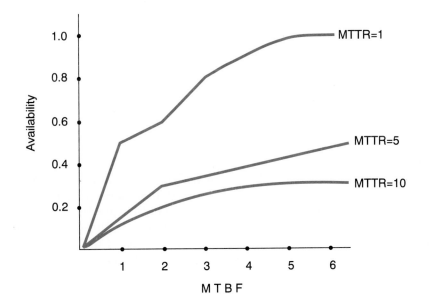

Figure 11-1 Availability, MTBF, and MTTR

lower speed to minimize the impact of the errors. Failure of hardware and software components is usually seen by the user as a down system. With fault-tolerant systems the effect is either negligible or somewhat slower response times, depending on the system load. Even though the processor and all components of the system except one are functioning properly, the user, who is unable to continue working because of that one failed component, views the system as being down.

The reliability function, which is the probability that the system will not fail during a given period, is given by (Nickel, 1978):

$$R(t) = e^{-bt}$$

where b is the inverse of the MTBF, as described above. If the MTBF for a terminal is 2000 hours and a transaction requires 1 minute to complete, then the reliability is

$$R\left(\frac{1}{60}\right) = e^{-(1/2000)\,(1/60)}$$

$$= e^{-(1/120,000)}$$

$$= 0.999992$$

All times are expressed in hours. Thus, if the terminal is available at the beginning of the transaction, the probability is high that it will remain available throughout a 1-minute transaction.

Reliability with Multiple Components.   Like availability, system reliability is the product of the reliability of its components. Thus, if a system consists of a terminal, a medium, two modems, and a CPU, the reliability of the system from the user's perspective is

$$R_s = R_t \times R_m \times R_l \times R_m \times R_c$$

where s, t, m, l, m, and c represent the reliability of the system, terminal, modem, medium link, modem, and CPU, respectively. Reliability as a function of the MTBF is graphed in Figure 11-2.

Overall Effectiveness.   The overall effectiveness of a system is a measure of how well it serves users' needs. Mathematically it is given by the following formula (Nickel, 1978):

$$E = A \times R$$

where E is the effectiveness, A is the availability, and R is the reliability of the system. From the formula it can be seen that, for a given system effectiveness, when R is greater than A the amount of time available for repairing a fault increases, whereas if A is greater than R the repair time is reduced (Nickel, 1978). Since R is entirely a function of the MTBF, an increase in R means that more time can be devoted to repairing the system to attain the same overall effectiveness. This is illustrated in Figure 11-3.

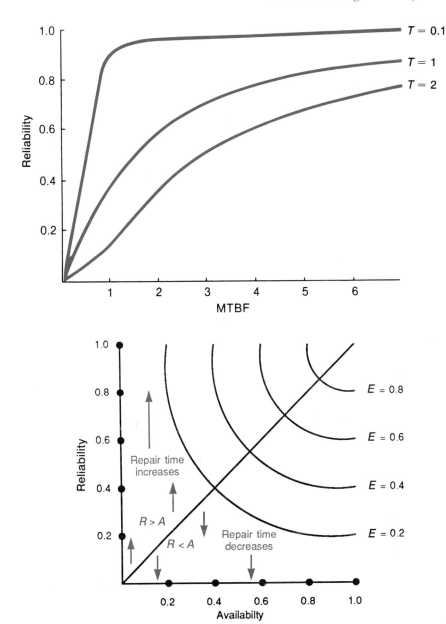

Figure 11-2 Reliability and MTBF

Figure 11-3 Reliability, Availability, and Effectiveness

Reliability of Backup Components. In many networks, alternate components are available should one component fail. Communication paths frequently have alternate links available, and fault-tolerant systems have available a backup CPU, disk drive, or other components. These backup components decrease the MTBF of the system. A decrease in the MTBF increases reliability, availability, and effectiveness. With backup components available, the reliability of the components operating in parallel is given by (Nickel, 1978):

$$R_p = 1 - (1 - R_s)^2$$

where R represents reliability, p represents the components operating in parallel, and s represents a single component. If the reliability of a communications link is 0.995, the reliability of the link with a backup is

$$R = 1 - (1 - 0.995)^2 = 0.999975$$

Clearly, backup components significantly increase the reliability and effectiveness of a system.

Selecting a hardware or software system involves selecting more than just a system; a vendor is also being selected. The vendor's ability to maintain, enhance, and expand the components may well determine the selection's overall success. Therefore, both the components and the vendor must be evaluated with equal care. In addition to performance, availability, and reliability, there are several less obvious factors that affect user satisfaction. Keeping the user community informed is one of the easiest and most overlooked of these. Users should be informed of scheduled down time, imminent down time, periods when other processing requirements are likely to adversely affect response times, certain changes in hardware or software, and changes in personnel with whom users will be interfacing. This information can be disseminated in several ways, the most direct being to reserve a portion of the terminal output area for system or network news bulletins. Users ordinarily understand the inconveniences when down time is unanticipated and no prior warning is possible. On the other hand, it can be difficult for users to remain civil when they arrive at 4 A.M. to catch up on some work and find the system down for a scheduled but unannounced reason. Many systems can send notices to users when they logon to the system and can send notice of system status for short-term, emergency network interruptions.

Another useful communication medium is newsletters, which can alert users to down times scheduled for preventive maintenance and reconfigurations, announce new capabilities, serve as a training aid, answer frequently asked questions, solicit comments and suggestions, and generally help people feel they are an integral part of the network team. Newsletters have the advantage of being able to reach all users of a system. Meetings between users and the network management team should be held at least quarterly. Mature systems not undergoing change require meetings less frequently than those that are new, changing, or experiencing problems. Such forums can serve to air grievances, disseminate information, propose new ideas, educate both users and network managers, resolve problems, plan for future changes, and establish new goals. Again, one important side effect is to get groups communicating with one another and to help users feel they are an important part of the network.

Another form of user communication is formal and informal training. Some companies find informal seminars at lunchtime or after hours a very effective way to exchange information. Formal training classes serve not only to educate users but also to establish contacts within the organization. New users especially usually develop an association with training instructors, giving them an expert to call on should a problem arise.

Cost Effectiveness

The second objective of network management is to provide cost-effective solutions to the telecommunications needs of an organization. As shown in previous chapters, there are many solutions to communications problems. Network management is charged with selecting those that are feasible and cost efficient. If the network is unable to contribute positively to the financial position of a company, it probably should not be implemented.

Prior Planning.   Proper prior planning is one way to save money. In configuring a network two basic alternatives exist: installing equipment to meet immediate needs and paying the price of upgrading when the time comes—which sometimes leads to lower immediate costs but a higher cost of expansion—or immediately buying equipment in anticipation of future needs—which creates higher immediate costs, with relatively low cost, easy expansion. Buying immediately for future needs is sometimes risky because of the rapid rate at which technology changes. Usually the best alternative is to purchase modular equipment, which can be upgraded in small increments so over-purchasing is seldom necessary and expansion is relatively easy. A variation of this approach is the planned movement of equipment, whereby lower capacity equipment is gradually pushed outward and absorbed elsewhere in the network as newer, higher capacity equipment is acquired.

Modular Expansion.   Modular growth is available for several network components, the most fundamental being the processor. Many computer vendors offer a broad line of systems that allow growth within the product line. Most vendors have several different models spanning the distance between small systems and very large systems, and within one model there is also a certain amount of growth potential. The transition from one model to another is not always easy, often requiring a recompilation of programs, as a minimum, and too frequently causing significant rewrites. When an organization has finally reached the top of one model line and is ready to move up to the next model, even through the same vendor, the processors, operating systems, and network software too frequently are not the same as those in current use, so a conversion is required. At such a time the vendor typically is very positive regarding the ease of conversion to their new model, because the user is probably examining other vendors' alternatives, which may be no more complex than conversion to the incumbent's next model.

This approach can be contrasted with those vendors' systems that allow modular expansion from a relatively small system to an extremely powerful one by adding more of the same type of processor. There is no need to remove, sell, or return the existing equipment; it is simply augmented to provide the additional processing power. Several computer vendors offer this capability; some of them, such as Tandem Computers, Inc., and Stratus Computers, Inc., also have systems designed for the transaction processing market, where expansion is very common. Modular expansion is also possible with front end processors (FEPs) and multiplexers. Some vendors offer muxes that can be expanded from 4 to 32 or more lines, in increments of 4, 8, or 16 lines, so the user pays for the cost of expansion only when necessary. Sometimes making this upgrade is effected simply by inserting a printed circuit board. Many FEPs can have increases in memory capacity and number of lines controlled; some allow users to add processors as well.

Planned Equipment Moves.   Planned migration of equipment is useful when modular expansion is not possible. For example, the central site could begin with a 4-port multiplexer, with remote sites also having 4-port muxes. As the number of applications in a remote site grows, the central-site 4-port mux could be moved there, a new 8-port mux added to the central site, and the old 4-port mux used in a new location or cascaded off the 8-port mux. This is illustrated in Figure 11-4. Similarly, low-speed modems

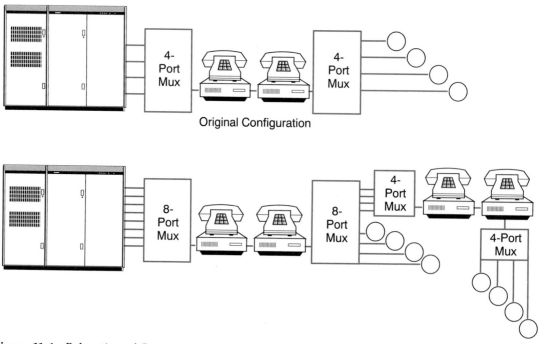

Figure 11-4   Relocation of Components

can be moved to lower traffic locations as they are replaced by high-speed modems. If there is no need for the older equipment, it could be kept in inventory to be used as replacements for failed equipment. This type of activity requires longer range planning than the other options; however, the financial rewards may make it preferable to the disposal of old equipment— possibly at a significant loss—every time a new piece is acquired.

MEETING THE OBJECTIVES

The objectives of network management are met by a combination of competent staff, hard work, careful planning, good documentation, implementing standards and procedures, communicating with users, and being able to work with other people to resolve problems. Although every one of these elements may not be present in a successful network, the probability of success is directly proportional to how well they are realized.

Competent Staff

The most important element is creating a competent staff, which can even overcome deficiencies in other areas. While specific staff qualifications depend on the hardware and software employed, some generalizations can be made. The functions of network management can be grouped into the areas of design and configuration, testing, diagnosis, documentation, repair, and, on rare occasions, coding. The team must have detailed knowledge of both hardware and software; ideally, every person would know both areas. The staff should be versatile and creative in resolving problems, because many solutions are ad hoc, temporary ones that require ingenuity.

Design and Configuration

The staff should be skilled in use of the diagnostic and planning tools described later in this chapter. In design and configuration, they should be knowledgeable of configuration alternatives and their strengths and weaknesses. They must be willing and able to learn to keep up with changes in hardware and software of the existing system as well as capabilities continually offered by other vendors, including a multitude of different tariff structures from a growing number of common carriers. Finally, and perhaps most important, staff should be able to work well with both technical and nontechnical personnel. Being able to describe the technology to those not "in the know" and to elicit the necessary technical information from nontechnical users is critical to the success of system design.

Diagnosis

Skill in diagnosing the cause of problems is essential, and being able to do so under considerable pressure is very valuable. Whenever a problem in a production system is encountered that disables all or a portion of an online application, immediate resolution is desirable. A failed system usually means financial loss: Personnel being unable to perform certain of their job functions leads to a loss in productivity. In some situations, direct revenue is also lost, such as in an airline reservation system.

Planning

Planning is another key to success. Because of the dynamic nature of networks, constant planning and replanning is necessary to ensure that objectives are met. Too often, network managers are so caught up in day-to-day activities they ignore longer range planning. This type of behavior is both common and self-perpetuating. Without good planning, problems occur more frequently and require a greater amount of time to be solved. There is often truth to the adage, "If you fail to plan, you plan to fail." Corporate goals are set by upper-level management. Planning that defines the actions essential to accomplishing these goals should include short-term and long-term objectives. Short-term planning includes scheduling of personnel, hiring, training, budgeting, and network maintenance and enhancement activities. Long-term planning involves predicting and resolving expansion issues, integrating new technologies, and budgeting.

Documentation, Standards, and Procedures

Documentation, standards, and procedures are an outgrowth of good planning. Good documentation increases the productivity of the staff. It includes listings of the software, logic diagrams, internal and external specifications for the system, wiring and connection diagrams, hardware specifications, and users' manuals. These tools are used in all phases of the management of the network. Standards and procedures together provide consistency in system management. Standards set minimal acceptable levels of performance and implementation. Procedural guidelines aid in operating and maintaining the system and are especially necessary in resolving problem situations.

In summary, meeting network management objectives requires a group of talented individuals who have the right tools in place, have a well-defined but flexible direction for the short term and the long term, are willing to work unusual hours in sometimes difficult or stressful environments, and can work effectively with people at all levels of capability. The growth in network management has prevented the supply of competent people from meeting the demand; as a result, network management personnel are currently among the hardest to find and highest paid in the computer industry.

NETWORK MANAGEMENT ORGANIZATION

Once a system has been successfully installed, tested, and brought into operation, the day-to-day management of the network begins. Operations deals with monitoring, control, diagnostics, and repair. As application developers design a system to solve business problems, network managers should design a system—part manual, part automated—that solves the problems of operations. The manual portion of the system is necessary for restoring a down system, a task that cannot be accomplished with software when the hardware is not running.

Control

Control functions to be performed include putting failed lines or terminals back in operation, adding new lines or terminals, and taking failed components out of the system. Control of a geographically separated, multiple computer network is somewhat more difficult, since parts of the control function must also be distributed. The distributed case is discussed here, since a subset of it applies to single-node or colocated-node networks.

Control Center.   The control center is responsible for monitoring the network and taking corrective action where necessary. In a distributed network, it is not uncommon to have more than one control center. In a network of cooperating, independent users—for example, a network of universities—each node can participate in the management and control functions, with each installation being responsible for control of its part of the network. Usually, however, there is a control point—the central control site—that has the ability to resolve any problem.

In very large networks, a processor may be dedicated to the control function. Several companies provide computers and software designed specifically for network control. Typically a network control system consists of special microprocessor-based modems that collect network statistics that are periodically transmitted to the network monitor node for storage and analysis. The monitoring systems gather information such as error rates, data rates, and the number of retransmission attempts resulting from errors. Trend analysis of this data can help determine gradual degradation so faults are immediately reported and corrective measures taken.

Network Monitors.   The control facility must have a minimum of one or more hardware/software monitors so the management team can probe every node for problems and gather network parameters and statistics. The monitors also enable managers to make any necessary changes to the system, such as bring lines and terminals into and out of service; bring network applications to an orderly halt and start network applications; alter network parameters, such as the process controlling a terminal;

check for line errors and implement corrections; initiate and evaluate line traces; run diagnostic routines; add and delete users from the system; control passwords for local and remote nodes; and maintain the control center database. A network database contains data about the network configuration, the release level of all software and hardware components, the names of contact individuals at remote sites, histories of problems and solutions, outside contact points for vendors, and documentation.

Problem-Reporting System.   Ideally an online problem-reporting system should also be available for retrieving trouble reports via keywords. This capability is especially helpful in managing a distributed network. In a distributed network, problems can be encountered and resolved in multiple locations and one problem can be worked on simultaneously in multiple locations. An online problem reporting system can help avoid having to repeatedly solve the same problem.

Problem-Reporting Procedure

Another important function of a control center is the acceptance and resolution of problems. In some instances, a solution may lie outside the control center itself; however, the center should remain active as an intermediary in resolving the problem. This section describes a prototype control center's operation with respect to problem reporting and resolution. Although a computerized problem-reporting system is assumed, a manual system with the same functionality could exist.

Network managers should publish a problem-reporting procedure that describes the information that users must gather to report a problem and to whom the report should be made. It is assumed that users have been directed to contact their control center about network problems by telephone rather than by any automated problem-reporting system. An end user such as a terminal operator ordinarily should not be expected to interface with an automated problem-reporting system. When the problem report call is received, the network manager obtains all relevant information, including date and time of the call; date and time the problem was first observed; name of the caller and how the caller might be reached; names and contact information for any other personnel involved in the problem; and a brief but detailed description of the problem—its severity as well as consequences expected before a solution is available, whether the problem is reproducible or intermittent, and possible contributing external influences such as installation of a new software release, reconfiguration, power glitches, or the equipment being used.

A problem report containing the relevant information is generated and a copy returned to the reporting person. As soon as the problem is resolved, the solution is noted in the trouble report, a final copy is sent to the reporting installation, and the trouble report is marked closed. If the solution is not immediately known, the control center begins its evaluation, first searching the problem database to determine whether such a problem was ever resolved before. If not, then problem investigation begins. The first objective of such an investigation is to isolate the problem and pinpoint the source of the difficulty, which can involve looking at statistics and system console or log messages, initiating line traces, using line monitors, taking program dumps or traces, debugging, or running hardware diagnostics. If the problem is isolated to an area of vendor responsibility, such as network control programs, the vendor is contacted and the supporting documentation is passed to them for analysis. The degree of vendor involvement varies among vendors, and even within one vendor company, the support level can vary among individual customers, depending on the expertise available. Some users provide a vendor with a complete analysis and suggested solution, whereas others simply report the existence of a problem and leave the diagnostics to the vendor.

Additional Control Center Responsibilities

The additional responsibilities of the control center are creating and maintaining documentation, security, establishing procedures, release control, and training of personnel. Documentation, which should be kept current, includes operations manuals, procedures for emergency and routine activities, notification lists, contingency plans, inventory, program listings, statistics, and manuals. Security measures include creating and assigning passwords, setting user access levels, monitoring and reacting to unsuccessful logon attempts, ensuring that passwords are changed periodically, and checking physical security where applicable. Procedures should cover normal operating guidelines as well as those for handling abnormal situations such as network failures. Escalation policies that bring problems to the attention of higher management levels if the problem persists and contact names and numbers are also included. Release control involves the installation, testing, and implementation of new versions of hardware and software, to ensure compatibility of new features with existing software and hardware and to uncover any new problems (frequently introduced with new releases). Training involves all levels of personnel that use or maintain the network.

NETWORK MANAGEMENT SYSTEMS

A network should be under continuous scrutiny to ensure that the objectives of customer satisfaction and cost effectiveness are met. Too often, network problems are found through user complaints. This is usually not the way a network manager wants to learn about problems. A far better way is to have potential problems detected and reported by a network management system, so that problems can possibly be corrected before users become aware of them.

A network management system is a combination of hardware and software used by network supervisors to monitor and administer the network. The network management system must be able to determine the status of network components such as modems, lines, terminals, multiplexers, and so on. If a device's status indicates that malfunctions are occurring, the network management system will either take automatic corrective action or alert a network supervisor of the condition. The network supervisor may then use network control functions of the network management system to take corrective action. A network management system also gathers network statistics, such as line utilization information, together with capabilities for evaluating those statistics. The information produced assists network supervisors in capacity planning.

Most network software vendors originally neglected the area of network management. With few exceptions, the network software and hardware were built and installed with little support for managing it. With small networks, management is not difficult. However, as more businesses have made the move to online systems, the compositions of networks have changed. Two of these changes have had a significant impact on the ability to manage networks. First, the number and complexity of network nodes have increased. Early networks may have consisted of one central processor with communications controllers and terminal devices. The host assumed a supervisory role and provided a centralized point of control and management. Often the communications links were point-to-point leased or switched lines. In contrast, many of today's networks have multiple processing nodes and hundreds or thousands of connected devices. The network may consist of local area networks, X.25 networks, leased lines, satellite and microwave links, switched lines, and PBX systems. Numerous interfaces between different types of equipment and networks are relatively commonplace.

Second, many of today's networks are a mixture of vendor equipment. It is common to find processors, terminals, controllers, modems, and other components from different vendors. Just managing a homogeneous network where all the components are provided by one vendor is difficult; in the past, effectively managing a large network with components from multiple vendors has approached the impossible. Fortunately, this problem is being recognized by network users and vendors alike, and *network management systems* (NMSs) are being sold from both sectors. Let us first look at the requirements of a generic network management system and then discuss the capabilities provided by IBM's Netview and Netview/PC. These products were picked for two reasons: their applicability to a large body of users and functionality. The reader should be aware that other products exist, some of which provide more comprehensive management features.

A Generic Network Management System

To understand a network management system, consider a hypothetical network of a large, international manufacturing firm. This company has pro-

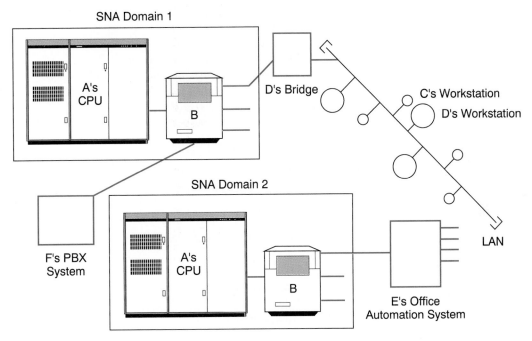

SNA Domain 1

A's
CPU

B

D's Bridge

C's Workstation

D's Workstation

LAN

SNA Domain 2

F's PBX
System

A's
CPU

B

E's Office
Automation System

Figure 11-5   Integrated Network

cessing nodes in many locations throughout the world. A small portion of
this network from one manufacturing location is depicted in Figure 11-5.
The backbone network is an SNA network, and there are two domains. The
major components of the system come from seven different vendors. The
host processors in both domains are from Company A. The communications controllers were purchased from Company B but run IBM NCP
(Network Control Program) software. The engineering and development
department has a local area network of systems to support its design efforts. The LAN is an IEEE 802.3-compatible system. The workstations are
special purpose and were provided by two companies, C and D. A bridge
to the SNA network is provided using Company D's equipment. The interface to the SNA network is via LU 6.2. The office automation system uses
equipment from Vendor E and interfaces to the SNA system in the same
way as the engineering bridge. The PBX system obtained from Vendor F is
also tied into the network. Modems and multiplexers all were obtained
from Vendor G. What will the network management team need to know to
keep this network running efficiently? A summary listing of this appears
in Figure 11-6.

  In a large network, if all of the data being gathered is sent to the network managers, both the network and the network managers would have
a difficult time keeping up with it. Simply receiving the data is not
enough; it must be received in a usable format. The network management
system is responsible for ensuring that the correct data is received and that

Figure 11-6
Network Management Information

A. Host processors
  1. Status
  2. CPU busy rates
  3. Internal queues, for example, on TCP
  4. Transaction turnaround time in the CPU
  5. Buffer utilization
  6. Peak activity times
  7. Performance during peak activity
B. Communications controllers
  1. Status
  2. Processor busy rates
  3. Buffer utilization
  4. Queues
  5. Peak activity time
  6. Performance during peak activity
C. Lines
  1. Status
  2. Number of failures
  3. Number of retries
  4. Aggregate data rate
  5. Peak activity time
  6. Performance during peak activity
  7. Active devices on the line
  8. Line quality
  9. Changes in line quality
D. Modems
  1. Status
  2. Errors
E. Terminals
  1. Status
  2. Number of failures
  3. Failure types
  4. Number of transactions
  5. Type of transactions
  6. Transaction response time
F. Processing nodes
  1. Status
  2. Number of transactions
  3. Response time
  4. Type of transactions

it is in a usable format. The network segment illustrated in Figure 11-7 shows a network component, a portion of the NMS, and the connection to the control center. The NMS will continually obtain status and operational data from the component(s) it is monitoring. Ordinarily the data will be

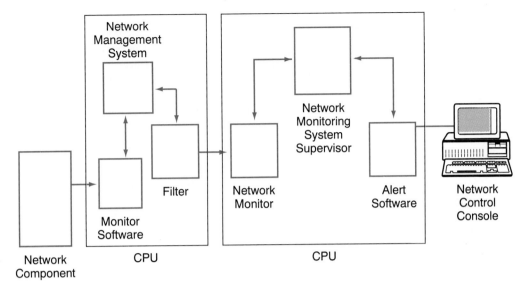

Figure 11-7 Network Management System

routine and either ignored or logged for later evaluation. Specifically, if the component being monitored is a communications line, some of the information the NMS will receive could be the number of errors encountered since the last status report, status (up or down), line quality, number of retries on the line, and number of characters transmitted or received. When some statistic changes, it must be brought to the attention of the network managers. If a problem has occurred, the NMS should also assist the managers in solving the problem by indicating the potential causes and perhaps even solutions. Bringing a problem to the attention of network managers is called an *alert*.

If the values received are within tolerance and if data collection is enabled, the data will be logged. Later it may be evaluated for trend analysis and capacity planning. If the data is not within accepted tolerance levels, this must be brought to the attention of the network managers. For a data communications line, an alert is necessary if the line is down, the error rates have exceeded some threshold, the number of retries is excessive, or the line is congested. For a component that is being closely monitored, a change in service level may also be cause for an alert. For example, if the line has been operating between 20% and 25% capacity and suddenly is experiencing 50% load capacity, the change might be cause for an alert. Frequently network managers are interested not only in malfunctions but also in changes in normal status.

When an alert condition has been detected, it must be forwarded to the network management center. Steps that may be taken in this process include:

1. Identification of probable causes of the alert condition.

2. Formatting the message for the NMS presentation services. Component addresses, status, and probable causes must be identified. In Figure 11-7 this function is performed by the software component identified as a filter, which is used to screen and format data sent to the management center. A filter can perform many functions, one of which is to control the flow of data to the center. Flow control avoids flooding the control center with repetitious status messages.

3. Transmission of the data to the control center for display.

4. At the control center, passing the message through a formatter, which determines where and how the message is to be displayed. Many NMS presentation services utilize color monitors to present the data. Warnings may be displayed in yellow, outages in red, and major catastrophes in blinking red with an audio signal. The message will also usually be logged to an alert history file.

5. The network management team acting on the alert as necessary and documenting the event and its solution.

As mentioned above, obtaining the proper information to manage a network is difficult enough in a homogeneous network environment. In a mixed-vendor configuration, additional complexities must be resolved. In Figure 11-7 the network management control center is attached to one of the host processors and uses software provided by that vendor, Vendor A. Vendor A's network management tools are designed to monitor only its equipment and to present messages in a specific format. In the configuration shown, terminals attached to Vendor E's processors may be involved in a session with a host logical unit. Moreover, this terminal may be of a type unsupported by the host system.

The problems that must be resolved in such an environment are: obtaining status information from each vendor's equipment, formatting the alerts in a manner consistent with the host's requirements, and routing alerts and their associated data to the host node for display. Once the alert has been raised, the system managers must react to it. For example, if a device is malfunctioning and disrupting the network, it needs to be deactivated until the problem is fixed. The network management system will provide an interface that allows the network managers to deactivate the device and later bring it back online. In our example, several vendors are represented; each vendor is likely to have different peripheral control utilities and different command languages for them. For example, in Vendor A's environment the command to bring a failed terminal, such as the terminal known to the system as TERMINAL-X, back online may be RESTORE TERMINAL-X, while in Vendor E's system the same command may be DEVICE TERMINAL-X UP. The important point is that once the alert has been received correction in a mixed vendor network may not be simple. One cannot expect network managers to know the command languages required to remedy faults on a variety of vendor systems. Even on one system there may be several interfaces for fault correction. One interface may be used for physical devices and another for logical devices and connections. For example, if a terminal has failed and needs to be restored, it may be necessary to activate the terminal on the line via a peripheral utility program and, using a different utility, notify application programs that the terminal is again available.

To reduce the complexities of dealing with multiple vendor equipment and sometimes even a variety of interfaces from one vendor, the NMS may provide a command mapping function. This allows the network managers to work with one command language with a consistent interface. The command mapping function will select the proper interface program(s) to receive the message and translate the command into a format acceptable to these programs. With this general overview of network management we now look at a specific implementation of an NMS system, IBM's Netview and Netview/PC products.

IBM's Network Management System

Netview and *Netview/PC* were introduced by IBM in 1986. Netview consolidated and extended several network management packages that had been used to monitor and control SNA networks. Netview is thus oriented to managing the host SNA environment. Netview/PC is a new element within IBM's network management offerings. It contains logic for monitoring IBM's token ring network, PBX systems from Rolm, and other vendors' equipment.

Netview. Netview runs on an IBM host system. It provides diagnostic and control capabilities for an SNA network. The functions it provides include hardware monitoring, session monitoring, status monitoring, and control services. Hardware monitoring collects status information from physical devices, and session monitoring provides information on SNA sessions. Status monitoring provides display information regarding system components and assists in restarting system elements following a failure. The control function provides the ability to activate and deactivate devices. In addition to the management and control functions, Netview provides two other basic facilities: help and a user interface. The help function provides users with online assistance in using Netview; an operator tutorial is also supplied. The user interface allows scripts called *Clists* to be prepared by users to monitor devices and/or to automate startup and shutdown sequences.

Netview/PC. Netview/PC, as the name indicates, runs on a microcomputer. Netview/PC is an important component in IBM's *open communications architecture (OCA)*. IBM recognizes that networks are apt to contain a mixture of vendor equipment. OCA opens an IBM network from a management perspective by providing other vendors with interface specifications.

Through these, other vendors can have their equipment integrated more completely into the network. Within Netview/PC this is effected through an application program interface (API).

API allows users to write applications to interface to non-IBM devices. These applications can use device-specific interfaces on one side and interface with Netview on the other, which allows them to make the management connection between the device and IBM's network management tools. Within Netview/PC, IBM provides this interface to its token ring LAN and to Rolm computerized PBX systems. Status information collected by the microcomputer running Netview/PC may be stored on the microcomputer's local disk and/or forwarded to Netview, which runs on the host system. If alerts are received, they may either be handled at the microcomputer or be forwarded to the host for operator intervention and resolution. The interface between the host and the microcomputer is either via an SNA 3270 terminal or as an LU 6.2 session type.

Netview Architecture. The Netview architecture identifies three types of control points—focal points, entry points, and service points. *Focal points* provide host-oriented functions. A focal point is a central point for network management and monitoring functions. It also provides functions related to network billing, line optimization, and performance analysis. *Entry points* relate to IBM or IBM-compatible network elements. Functions contained at entry points include remote management and control modules, which allow the element to be controlled remotely from the control center and to communicate with Netview. *Service points* are gateways into the Netview system from non-SNA devices. Service points are characterized by Netview/PC and the devices it monitors and controls.

To summarize Netview and Netview/PC, IBM has created a system that allows centralized control of a distributed system that consists of IBM, IBM-compatible, and non-IBM equipment alike. Netview provides the ability to monitor and control the SNA network, and Netview/PC has the ability to provide the same function for other network components.

MANAGING A LOCAL AREA NETWORK

Suppose that you are a member of a six-person office in which each person has a microcomputer workstation. How do you imagine the management and operations of the workstations are conducted? In most such offices:

Each person is responsible for backing up his or her data (if it is done at all).

Each person is responsible for operating a micro.

There is no office data-processing manager (although there may be a local "expert" upon whom others rely for help).

There are no provisions for security.

If resource sharing exists, it is done via diskette exchange or printer switches.

If someone makes a mistake or if one system fails, it has little impact on the others.

There is a certain amount of "trading" of software because the office does not have one copy for each user.

Everyone wants the best printer attached to their computer.

Now, suppose that the office manager informs everyone that a LAN is about to be installed and that, after the dust settles, a more effective computing system will be available. The manager is correct with respect to using and sharing the available resources—hardware, programs, and data. However, let us look at another implication of a LAN: LAN management.

In switching from a stand-alone microcomputer environment to a LAN, it is essential to have two or more people designated as LAN managers. If the LAN is large, several people may be actively involved as LAN managers; if the LAN is small, one person may be the principal manager and the second the alternate. (What constitutes a small, medium, or large LAN is difficult to define. For our purposes, small LANs are those with fewer than 50 workstations and only one server; a medium-size LAN will have from 50 to 150 nodes and three or fewer servers. Large LANs will be all other LANs. Be aware that some small LANs can be as complex to manage as a large one.) The alternate LAN manager assists the primary manager as necessary and fills in when the primary is absent. It is important to have a backup manager available if the primary manager cannot fulfill his or her duties.

During installation, LAN management is a full-time job. After the LAN is in operation, management tasks are less time-consuming. For a small LAN, management tasks may take less than one hour a day; for a large LAN, management may be a full-time position and may even require more than one full-time person. It is easy for a business to overlook the costs of LAN management.

LAN Management Tasks

Before the LAN is installed, LAN managers should be hired or existing personnel trained. The amount of training varies according to the complexity of the system. As a minimum, managers should know the fundamentals of data communications and how to:

Connect and disconnect workstations

Diagnose and correct medium problems

Add and delete users

Implement security

Create, modify, and manage the printing environment

Install and modify applications

Take system backups

Recover from system failures

Monitor and evaluate performance

Add new resources, such as a new server

Maintain LAN documentation and procedures

Connect and Disconnect Workstations.   Often, a LAN is not static. New workstations need to be added and existing ones moved or removed, particularly during LAN installation and the initial stages of operation. The procedures for installing a new workstation vary from one implementation to another, but usually the following steps are required:

1. Determine a unique address for the new workstation.
2. Install the network interface card (NIC) in the workstation and set the workstation address (usually on the NIC).
3. Establish a connection on the medium for the new workstation. This may require a new port on a MAU or wiring hub, a new BNC connection on a coaxial cable, or simply a tap into a cable.
4. Connect the workstation to the medium by establishing a connection between the NIC and the medium.
5. Install network software in the workstation.
6. Boot the new workstation and test its ability to communicate over the network.
7. Add new user identifiers and security as necessary.

Once the new workstation is working, the network documentation ought to be updated to reflect the new address and wiring circumstances.

Diagnose and Correct Problems.   In some LANs, the most common problems are medium faults—wiring breaks, loose connectors, and unterminated cables. Being able to locate and correct these faults is critical to the success of the LAN. A host of other problems can occur as well. Some of these include:

Two workstations with the same network address

Improperly installed network software

Improperly installed application software

User errors

Broken equipment

Improper security settings

Network has not been started correctly or other operational errors

Add and Delete Users.   Each LAN user must identify himself or herself when logging onto the LAN. Moreover, each user is authorized to run certain applications and perform a set of actions on selected files. These privileges are described in the following section on security. The network manager must assign user IDs to individuals and delete or modify user IDs when a user leaves or changes job functions. Furthermore, users are usually associated with a group: There may be a group of LAN managers, one for personnel administration, one for payroll administration, and so on. Like users, groups have assigned privileges on the LAN. Again, it is the responsibility of the LAN manager to define the required groups and to assign individuals to one or more groups. Sometimes, the LAN manager will pass user and group administration functions to unit managers.

For each new user, the LAN administrator typically will create or assist in creating the user's environment. Some of the tasks that might be completed are:

Create a home directory for the user

Add the user to the network mail system

Create a user login script—a set of actions to be taken when the user logs in, such as setting search paths, initial menus, and so on

Set default security parameters

Set limits on resource utilization, such as the maximum amount of server disk that the user can consume

Set printer mappings

Implement Security.   In making the transition from a stand-alone to a LAN environment, resources that once were private may become shared. A file that resided on a stand-alone system may be placed on a file server; a program that existed on one or two microcomputers may be placed on a file server; or a printer available to only one micro might be attached to a printer server. Being placed in a shared circumstance does not mean, however, that any user ought to be able to read or modify the file, run the application, or use the printer. Instead, the LAN manager must create an access profile for each user, group, file, application, and hardware device. Some of the attributes thus defined may include:

File capabilities

    Ability to examine a directory listing

    Ability to read or write a file

    Ability to delete, rename, or create a file

    Ability to execute an application

    Ability for several users to simultaneously use a file

    Ability to restrict a file to one user at a time

    Ability to define file ownership

    Ability to pass privileges on to another user

User and group capabilities

> Allow file access according to the capabilities just described by user and group
>
> Require a password
>
> Require passwords to have a minimum number of characters
>
> Require passwords to be changed at certain intervals
>
> Allow logins only during specified times
>
> Allow a user to login only from selected workstations
>
> Inclusion of users in a group
>
> Specify account expiration date
>
> Restrict amount of disk space used
>
> Detect multiple login attempts and deactivate workstation or account

Monitoring capabilities

> Identify users logged on to system
>
> View information about users
>
> View information about jobs
>
> View a user's activity on servers
>
> View what is displayed on a workstation
>
> Take control of a workstation's keyboard

There may be more or fewer capabilities depending on the particular implementation. Frequently, additional utilities can be purchased to enhance the capabilities provided with the LAN software. For example, most LANs do not provide the ability to view what is displayed on a workstation's monitor or to take control of the keyboard. Several utilities exist that do this.

Create, Modify, and Manage the Printing Environment.   There may be two types of printers on a LAN: dedicated and shared. *Dedicated printers* are attached to workstations and can be used only by a person at that workstation. *Shared printers* are those controlled by a server and available to designated users. It is the latter type of printer that is considered in this section.

The general layout for a LAN printing system, a *spooler*, is illustrated in Figure 11-8. The steps an application might go through to print a document on a shared printer are as follows:

1. The application opens a printer port, such as LPT1 in a DOS system, and begins writing to that device.

2. The LAN printer software intercepts the print stream and routes it over the network to the server.

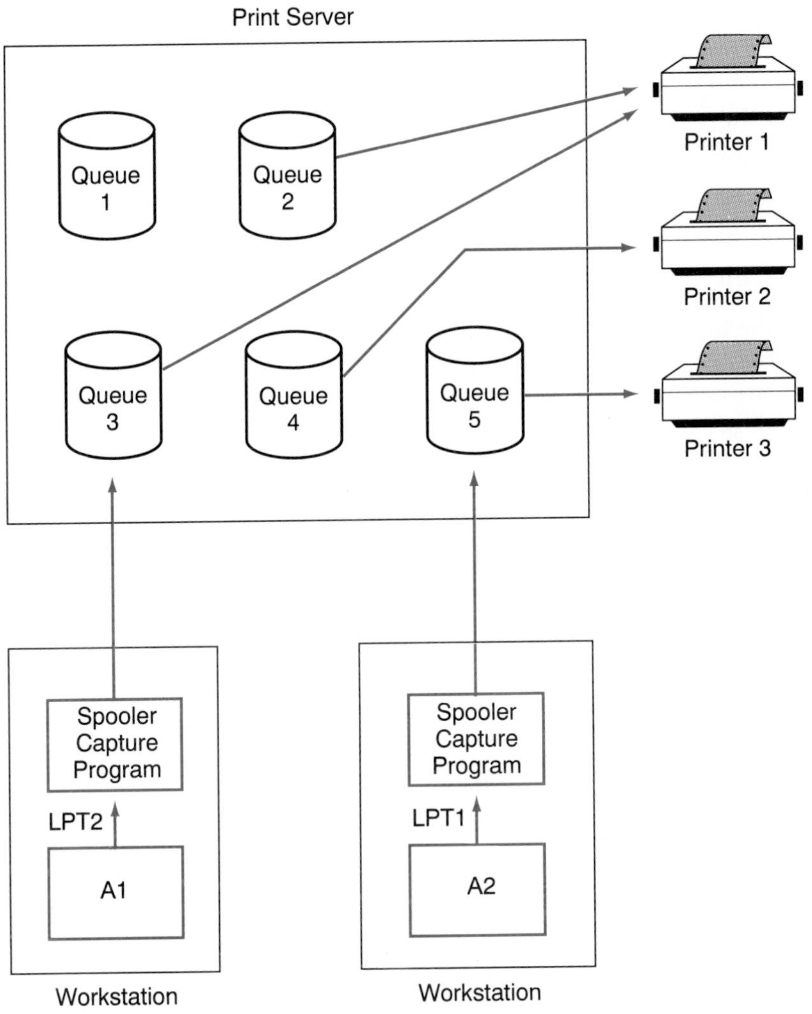

Figure 11-8 Spooler Configuration

3. The server print collector accepts the print stream and stores it in a file.
4. Steps 2–3 continue until the application closes the connection to the printer port or until a time-out limit of no print output is reached. In either case, the workstation software sends an end-of-job designator to the server.
5. The server closes that print job and schedules the job to be printed.
6. The printer driver looks at the scheduled jobs, selects the one with the highest priority, and prints it on the printer.
7. On completion of printing a job, the printer driver selects the next available job and prints it, and so on.

From each user's perspective, the needed printer is always available and dedicated to that user. It is the spooler that provides this virtual printer capability. The spooler can also provide other functions such as:

Printing multiple copies

Printing a document on several printers

Holding a document on disk after printing or instead of printing

Printing selected portions of a document

Printing banners before each print job

At the more detailed level, there are many factors to consider and parameters to set when installing and controlling a printing subsystem. The factors are too many to cover in detail here, and the ways in which they are established vary from one LAN to another. In essence, the LAN administrator carries out the following tasks:

Mapping printer ports on workstations to a print queue

Mapping print queues to one or more printers

Associating a printer with one or more print queues

Changing the configuration described in the three preceding steps

Assigning a printer priority scheme, for example, small jobs print before large jobs

Monitoring the print jobs on disk

Removing print jobs from disk

Starting or stopping print jobs or printers

Adding or deleting printers

Being able to obtain printed output is one of the basic needs of a LAN system. With all the configuration options typically available, the LAN administrator can provide an environment that meets or exceeds the needs of the LAN users; on the other hand, a poorly designed configuration can hinder printing effectiveness.

Install and Modify Applications.   When installing a new application, the LAN manager must plan how the application will be used, which users will need it, and on which server(s) the application will reside. Applications not designed for shared use must be installed in a way that prohibits concurrent usage. Applications that can be used concurrently need to be installed in a manner that maximizes their capabilities for each user. Most important, the LAN administrator must understand and comply with the application vendor's license agreements. License agreements vary considerably. Some software programs are licensed for only one workstation; some are licensed for a specific number of concurrent users, such as four concurrent users; some are licensed to allow access for all users on a specific server; and some are licensed to allow access for all users on all servers. Obviously, understanding the license agreements is important both for application selection and installation.

Ideally, each application user will be able to match his or her hardware with the application's features. Thus, a user with a color monitor ought to be able to tailor the application and have it display that user's preferred foreground and background colors. A user with a monochrome monitor will have a different user profile that runs correctly on his or her workstation. Other features that might be accounted for include the type of graphics adapter, display size, amount of memory available, and so on. Once the application is operational, the LAN administrator is responsible for installing application upgrades. Sometimes, a major application release will provide significant changes in how the system works and the user interface to the system. The LAN manager must plan for the transition from the old system to the new one. In such cases, it is usually prudent to have both application versions available. This makes the transition to the new application easier.

Take System Backups.   Recall that in the stand-alone microcomputer environment, each user is responsible for backing up his or her data files. On a LAN, this responsibility is assumed by the LAN administrator. The administrator must design a backup policy that will allow data files and programs to be recovered. A variety of backup devices is available. The main options are given in Figure 11-9. Associated with the backup devices is backup software. Most LAN systems provide this software. Some installations choose to purchase separate backup software that provides a more robust set of capabilities than the LAN version. Some of the common backup capabilities are given in Figure 11-10.

Recover from System Failures.   The main purpose of taking backups is to recover from failures. The LAN administrator must prepare procedures that will be implemented if the LAN fails. Because some failures do not affect files, the recovery procedures must encompass more than file recovery. For example, a workstation may fail in the middle of an application. The LAN administrator ought to have a procedure for recovering the application and lost work.

Monitor and Evaluate Performance.   LAN usage will likely change over time. New users might be added, some workstations deleted, and applications added or deleted. The LAN administrator must monitor the LAN usage and plan necessary changes. If usage increases, a new server may

Diskette	Hard Disk	Magnetic Tape (several different technologies)
Optical Drive	Digital Audio Tape	Digital Video Cassette

Figure 11-9 Backup Device Alternatives

Figure 11-10
Common Backup
Options

Timed backups where the backup is scheduled to start at a specific time	Only backup files that have been modified since the last backup	Ability to specify a list of files or directories to backup
Ability to specify a list of files to exclude from the backup	Ability to backup files for a specific user	Ability to backup hidden and system files
Ability to change the directories of the files being backed up	Ability to preserve or change file ownership and attributes during backup and restore	Data compression to reduce the number of bits stored on the backup medium
Allow wildcard naming conventions	Ability to backup open files	Ability to backup local drives on a workstation
Data verification during backup	Ability to resume backup after interruption	Ability to create and review backup audit and error logs

be needed or, if multiple servers exist, the usage may need to be better balanced among them. Some of the things the LAN administrator may monitor include:

Printing environment

Disk usage

Number of active users

Application usage

Transmission faults

Server busy statistics

Based on the performance statistics, the LAN administrator will plan corrective action as necessary.

Add New Resources. If new LAN resources are necessary, the LAN administrator must plan their acquisition and integration into the system. Suppose that a new file server is added. The LAN administration must decide which files are to be placed on the new server and which users it will primarily serve. After integrating the new server, the administrator will monitor the LAN activities to ensure that service is satisfactory and that all components are effectively used.

Maintain LAN Documentation and Procedures. Much of the success of data-processing administration stems from having good, current documentation and procedures. The LAN administrator is responsible for creating and updating this documentation.

LAN Management Tools

One of the tasks carried out by the LAN administrator is diagnosing and correcting system faults. To properly perform all aspects of this, the administrator needs the proper tools. Some of the functions LAN analysis tools can perform are given in Figure 11-11. A cross-section of software and hardware tools exist that perform one or more of these functions. A representative list of these tools and the functions they perform is given in Figure 11-12. The tools listed in Figure 11-12 may not work on all LANs; some are designed for Ethernet LANs, some for ARCnet, and others for token rings.

NETWORK MANAGEMENT TOOLS

To carry out its various duties, the network management team frequently employs a variety of tools. In addition to the tools just described for managing a LAN, a variety of other tools exist. These can be divided according to their function—diagnostic tools, monitoring tools, and management tools. These tools differ from the LAN tools just discussed because they can be used for both LANs and WANs.

Monitor network traffic and performance	Set triggers and traps to detect transmission errors	View what is displayed on a workstation's monitor
Take control of a workstation's keyboard	Raise an alert when a problem is detected	Detect faulty NICs
Detect incorrectly installed workstations, such as duplicate addresses	Identify bottlenecks	View and analyze data packets
Detect cable problems, such as loose connectors and cable breaks	Print a map of the network nodes	Monitor stations for activity and/or faults

Figure 11-11 Functions of LAN Management Tools

Figure 11-12 Representative Network Management Tools and Their Functions

	A	B	C	D	E	F	G	H
Monitor network traffic	x		x			x		x
Set traps	x							
View workstation monitor		x			x			
Control workstation keyboard		x			x			
Raise alerts			x					
Detect faulty NICs				x				
Detect improperly installed workstations								
Identify bottlenecks			x	x	x	x	x	
View data packets	x		x	x	x	x		
Detect cable problems	x		x	x	x	x		
Print network map							x	x
Station monitoring	x		x				x	x

A = LANalyzer by Excelan
B = Close-up/LAN by Norton-Lambert Corporation
C = Watchdog by Network General Corporation
D = Emonitor and ARC Monitor by Brightwork Development, Inc.
E = HP 4972A and LAN Probe by Hewlett Packard
F = Sniffer by Network General Corporation
G = NetWare Care by Novell
H = NWRanger by Sarbec

Diagnostic Tools

Digital Line Monitors and Breakout Boxes.   Two diagnostic tools are discussed elsewhere in the book (Chapter 5), *digital line monitors* and the *breakout boxes* with or without bit-sequence generation.

Analog Line Monitors.   Another type of line monitor is also available — the *analog line monitor*. Where the digital line monitor looks at digital signals on the data terminal side of the modem, and so has the same view of the data as the data terminal equipment, an analog line monitor measures and displays the analog signals on the communications circuit or on the data communications side of the modem, enabling the user to check for noise and proper modulation. Analog line monitors are seldom employed in a user's environment; more often they are used by a common carrier to evaluate their circuits.

Emulators.   An *emulator* is a diagnostic tool that enables the user to check for adherence to a specific protocol. For example, a vendor must have its X.25 software certified by a packet distribution network before being allowed to connect to the system, to avoid disrupting other system users, and one way the software can be tested is with an emulator. The emulator acts like an X.25 node, generating both correct and incorrect messages to ensure that the system reacts according to the X.25 specifications. Usually, emulators of this type allow the user to specify the types of messages to be transmitted. A scenario or script can be defined on which the emulator acts. Emulators can also be used during the development process to ensure that the interfaces between software levels are correct.

Current Documentation.   One of the best diagnostic tools is current documentation, including software listings that reflect the correct release and patch levels, logic diagrams, internal documentation, maintenance manuals, and any other supporting documents. Although documentation may seem obvious as a diagnostic tool, its importance cannot be overstated.

Whereas diagnostic tools help locate problems in the network, monitoring and management tools are used to avoid problems in the network, including areas such as capacity planning, general project management, performance, and configuration. Several of these tools have been developed for microcomputers and are affordable for many users. Capacity planning is an extremely important function of network managers, who must recognize when resources are approaching full utilization and plan for expansion or reconfiguration to avoid saturation and potentially degraded service. Three tools are very effective in this area: performance monitors, simulation models, and workload generators.

Monitoring Tools

Performance Monitors.   *Performance monitors* provide snapshots of how a system is actually functioning, typically capturing such information as number of transactions, type of transaction, transaction response times, transaction processing times, queue depths, number of characters per request/response, buffer utilization, number of I/Os, and processing time by process or process subprogram. When collected over time, information of this nature enables the management team to spot trends in the use or misuse of the network—for instance, whether the number of a specific type of transaction is steadily increasing and whether the capacity for handling that transaction type is being reached, or whether an increasing number of users is playing Star Trek or Adventure during lunch, which period may also coincide with the day's peak processing load.

Simulation Models.   *Simulation models* allow the user to describe network and system activities and receive an analysis of how the system can be expected to perform under the described conditions, which is useful during the development stage to predict response times, processor utilization, and potential bottlenecks. During operational situations, simulation models help determine what size of transaction load will reach or exceed full capacity and the effect of adding new transactions, applications, and terminals to the existing system. A good simulation model in the development stage can avert performance issues during the design stage. Simulation models vary significantly with respect to the amount of information provided and the manner in which the user defines the workload. A simple model for line utilization and polling overhead might interactively prompt the user for the speed of the line, data link protocol, number of polling characters, modem turnaround time, and number of stations on the line, resulting in a report indicating the processing and line overheads of the polling and the maximum and average wait times a device might expect between polls. A comprehensive model, on the other hand, uses a network configuration file and a transaction file as input (both user-supplied). The configuration file will contain the complete hardware configuration, including disk drives, disk drive performance characteristics, line types, data link protocols, terminal types, database files and their locations, and access methods. The transaction file will contain a list of transaction types and the activities each transaction type performs, such as number of inputs/outputs to which disk using what type of access method, number of instructions executed, and number of characters input from and output to a terminal.

In addition to the two user-supplied files, the simulation model is driven by software performance characteristics, such as polling overhead, instruction execution times, and disk access times. Such a model outputs information similar to that provided by a performance monitor: expected response times, line utilization, processor utilization, disk utilization, and so forth. In essence, the model enables the user to see, without ever writing it, how an application will run. For example, if the model predicts that a particular communications line will have 300% utilization and a response time of 10 minutes, either a faster circuit or more circuits will be needed to support the workload.

The time required to set up a simulation run varies with the amount of detail needed. The comprehensive model just described requires a considerable amount of information regarding the application. Usually it is unnecessary to have the correct initial configuration, as the model will indicate areas of over- and under-utilization. If the processor is 150% busy, either a larger or an additional processor is needed. The benefit that can be realized from a simulation model is considerable.

Workload Generators.   Another helpful tool, a *workload generator*, is similar to the simulation model. But where the simulation model predicts system utilization and can be run on a system much smaller than that required for the actual application, a workload generator actually generates the transaction loads and pseudo-application processes for execution on the proposed configuration. If the model and the workload generator were perfect, the results would be identical; in actual practice, however, some variation between the two is likely. A workload generator together with a performance monitor can illustrate how the system will actually function in the proposed configuration. It also can be used for stress testing. As with any model, the above models are only as good as the inputs, the people who use and interpret them, and the closeness of the models to real life. Their value decreases with the amount of time required to utilize them and increases with their ability to portray an application accurately. This means that they should be used carefully and the results interpreted sensibly.

Log Files. *Log files* are another tool valuable in monitoring a system. Certain logs—such as logs of system messages (system log) or network messages—should be maintained continually, whereas others can be used only when necessary—for example, a line trace, which is a log of the activity on a particular line that is normally used only when a problem has been detected. Some software has been designed to log its activities on demand; the network manager would enable or disable the logging, depending on what information is required. Log files are used both for diagnostic functions and predictive or management functions.

Network Configuration Tools. *Network configuration tools* are used to plan the optimum network configuration with respect to sources and types of circuits. In the past these have been relatively expensive to purchase or use, and some were limited to one common carrier's facilities or geographical locations. These systems are now available on microcomputers and at more affordable prices.

Management Tools

Project Planning Tools. *Project planning tools* are beneficial in the administration of the network, and they can help in planning the activities of the team members, the installation of new equipment and software, and numerous other management activities. Many of these tools are now available on microcomputers, bringing them to more users at a relatively low cost.

Database Management Systems and Report Generators. Database management systems and report generators are also useful management tools. The database can be used to store statistical and operational information; a good query/report writer can select, synthesize, and summarize this data. These systems can schedule members of the network management team, store and retrieve error and trouble report information, and produce reports on modeling, among a multitude of other uses. Database management systems are available on most systems today and can be very useful in storing, modifying, and retrieving data about the network management function. State-of-the-art systems enable users to define a database; enter, modify, and delete information; and generate reports without writing any or much code. Many of the microcomputer-relational model database systems provide all these features and are oriented toward users with little expertise in programming or systems.

NETWORK MANAGEMENT PROTOCOLS

Network interconnection raises an additional network management problem. The problem is how to monitor nodes on one subnetwork from a node on a different subnetwork, for example, monitoring a node on a token ring from a network management console attached to an IBM SNA network. To facilitate the exchange of management data among network nodes, a network management standard or protocol is essential. If such standards exist, network designers can build their networks with the ability to exchange management and control data. Two such standards have evolved: the *Simple Network Management Protocol (SNMP)* and the *Common Management Information Protocol (CMIP)*.

Simple Network Management Protocol (SNMP)

Since the first SNMP products appeared in 1988, they have rapidly gained in acceptance and popularity. The protocol is endorsed by companies like IBM, Hewlett-Packard, and Sun Microsystems. SNMP has four key components: the SNMP protocol, the structure of management information (SMI), the management information base (MIB), and the network management system (NMS). The SNMP protocol is an application layer protocol that outlines the formal structure for communication among network devices. The SMI details how every piece of information regarding managed devices is represented in the MIB. The MIB is a database that defines the hardware and software elements to be monitored. The NMS is the control console to which network monitoring and management information is reported.

SNMP allows network managers to get the status of devices and set or initialize devices. If problems occur, an event mechanism generates a message that is displayed on the network monitoring console. Being a simple protocol, SNMP has a few shortcomings. Its command set is limited, there are limited provisions for security, and, lacking a strict standard, there is some inconsistency among different vendors' implementations.

Common Management Information Protocol (CMIP)

In competition with SNMP is the International Standards Organization's (ISO) CMIP. CMIP has a more complex protocol for exchanging messages among network components and has the potential for better control and the ability to overcome the limitations of SNMP. Unfortunately, there currently are no provisions for interoperability of SNMP and CMIP. Because CMIP was developed later than SNMP, operational systems are just beginning to emerge. It will take some time for it to overcome the impetus of SNMP. CMIP has been endorsed by the Digital Equipment Corporation, and its capabilities are being implemented in DECnet Phase V.

SUMMARY

As the use of data communications expands, so will the role and importance of network management. The keys to effective network management are personnel who are competent and knowledgeable and who can work well with a broad spectrum of users; planning; and the effective use of network management tools. Network management is involved in the design, testing, and operations of a system. In some installations a certain amount of implementation or development is also required.

Network management is both a function and an application. The application portion should be designed and implemented like any other business application. The primary functions for computerized implementation are problem-reporting systems, tools, network management software that reacts automatically to problems in the network, and diagnostic systems. With careful management, the network can be a valuable asset to a company; with poor or no management, even the best designed application system can fail. If the network is incorrectly designed, is not modified to meet changing demands, or is frequently inoperable and if problems are not readily resolved, users will lose confidence in the system, and the network's effectiveness will be diminished.

Key Terms

alert
analog line monitor
breakout box
Common Management
  Information Protocol (CMIP)
digital line monitor
emulator
entry point
filter
focal point
log file
login script
Netview
Netview/PC

network management protocols
network management system
network statistics
performance monitor
problem-reporting systems
service point
Simple Network Management Protocol
  (SNMP)
simulation model
software license
spooler
system log
trouble reports

Review Questions

1. What are the two main objectives of network management?
2. Why is user satisfaction an important network management objective?
3. Describe the functions performed by the network management team.
4. How do problems get reported and resolved? What documents are generated as a result of the problem-reporting system? Who receives copies of these documents?
5. How are statistics used in network management?
6. Describe the documentation created and maintained by the network management team.
7. What functions are performed by network management systems?
8. Describe how IBM's Netview and Netview/PC interact with each other.
9. List ten LAN management tasks.
10. What must a LAN manager do when installing a new workstation?
11. How is LAN security implemented?
12. Explain how a spooler works.
13. Explain five functions you might find in a file backup system.
14. Why is file backup important?
15. Describe the function and use of four LAN management tools.
16. Describe the function and use of:
    a. analog line monitor
    b. emulator
    c. simulation model
    d. log files
17. How are project management tools used in network management?
18. Compare the Simple Network Management Protocol (SNMP) and the Communications Management Information Protocol (CMIP).
19. Why are SNMP and CMIP necessary?

Exercises

1. Identify and describe five sub-objectives of network management. To which of the two main objectives would each of your five pertain?
2. Investigate a network management system other than IBM's Netview. How does it compare to the features provided by Netview?
3. Explain how five of the statistics listed in Figure 11-6 might be used in managing the network.
4. Design a problem-report form. What are the essential elements of a problem-reporting form?

5. Suppose you were assigned to recruit a LAN manager. What experiences would you require of qualified candidates? What salary can a LAN manager expect?

6. A personnel file contains data regarding an employee's name, address, date of birth, date of hire, performance rating, and salary. You have been assigned the task of setting security for this file for all employees and employees in the personnel and payroll departments. Suppose that you can set security attributes on each data item. What attributes would you assign to:
   a. all employees?
   b. employees in the personnel department?
   c. employees in the payroll department?

   Explain your decisions.

7. How are backup files used in recovering from a disk head crash that destroys both the disk and the data stored thereon?

8. Describe two situations in which it would be beneficial to have a LAN utility that allows the network manager to view what is displayed on a workstation's monitor.

9. Describe a situation in which it would be beneficial for a network manager to take control of a workstation's keyboard.

10. Find two software applications that perform the functions described in Exercises 8 and 9. What features do these applications provide? What do they cost?

11. A company has decided to install a local area network and has collected data from two vendors regarding their equipment reliability. The figures they obtained are as follows:

Device	Vendor A		Vendor B	
	MTBF	MTTR	MTBF	MTTR
Workstation	4000	2.5	3500	1.5
Network interface card	8000	1.0	8500	1.0
File server	3500	4.5	3500	4.0

Which vendor has the best availability? Which vendor has the best reliability? Which vendor has the best effectiveness?

References

Armstrong, Thomas R. "An Automated Network Management System." *Mini-Micro Systems* 12, March 1979.

_____. "Managing the Communications Menagerie." *Computerworld on Communications* 17, September 26, 1983.

Bailey, Robert B., and Jack Drescher. "Game Plan." *Data Communications*, March 1987.

Brown, Jacqueline, Shelley Dews, Denise Kanyuh, Gretchen Moore, Lynn Percival, and Jeff Weiner. "Usability." *Data Communications*, April 1987.

Capps, Jim, and Ron Martin. "Partners." *Data Communications*, March 1987.

Chessman, Ed, and Arvind Shah. "The Service Point." *Data Communications*, April 1987.

Chu, Van. "Monitoring Network Performance." *Computerworld on Communications* 17, May 18, 1983.

Deal, Richard L., and P. C. Wood. "Data Communications: Putting It All Together." *Datamation* 18, December 1972.

Derfler, Frank J., Jr. "LAN Analyzers." *PC Magazine* 9, June 26, 1990.

Doll, Dixon R. "Strategic Planning." *Computerworld Office Automation* 18, April 11, 1984.

Evans, Bill, and Arvind Shah. "Voice." *Data Communications*, April 1987.

Fitzgerald, Jerry. *Business Data Communications, Basic Concepts, Security, and Design.* New York: Wiley, 1984.

Gafka, Gerry, and Ron Martin. "API." *Data Communications*, March 1987.

Harper, William L., and Robert C. Pollard. *Data Communications Desk Book: A Systems Analysis Approach.* Englewood Cliffs, NJ: Prentice-Hall, 1982.

Hurwicz, Michael. "Network Management Tools." *Computerworld.* May 1, 1989.

IEEE Computer Society. *Computer Networks: A Tutorial.* Catalog no. 297, Document EH0162-8. Long Beach, CA: IEEE Computer Society, 1980.

Kanupke, William C. "Network Management." *Computerworld on Communications* 17, May 18, 1983.

Kaufman, Bob. "Cost-Effective Telecommunications Management." *Computerworld on Communications* 17, May 18, 1983.

Levin, David P. "Needs Assessment in Data Communications Networking." *Journal of Information Systems Management* 1, Summer 1984.

McCann, John T., Adam T. Ruef, and Steven L. Guengerich. *NetWare Supervisor's Guide.* Redwood City, CA: M&T Books, 1989.

McCormick, J. H. "Controlling the Data Exchange." *Infosystems* 30, March 1983.

McDonald, Thomas W. "Controls for Wider Reach." Spotlight no. 2. *Computerworld Spotlight*, February 2, 1987.

Mandell, Steven L. *Computers, Data Processing and the Law—Text and Cases.* St. Paul, MN: West Publishing Co., 1984.

Miehe, William H. "Remote Diagnostics." *Mini-Micro Systems* 10, October 1977.

Nickel, Wallace E. "Determining Network Effectiveness." *Mini-Micro Systems* 11, November 1978.

Painter, Melinda R. "Structure." *Data Communications*, March 1987.

Ryan, Jerry. "Considering Network Management Software." *Computerworld on Communications* 17, May 18, 1983.

Soudant, Robert. "Managing the Remote Computing Function." *Data Management* 12, April 1974.

Stephenson, Peter. "Network Monitoring: Don't Launch a LAN Without It." *MIS Week*, June 4, 1990.

Stiefel, Malcolm L. "Network Diagnostic Tools." *Mini-Micro Systems* 12, March 1979.

Network System Software

The OSI Session Layer
Software Overview
Access Methods
Transaction Control Process

INTRODUCTION

In this chapter we discuss some of the major software components of a data communications network. In the OSI reference model, software exists at every layer from the data link level up. Thus, this chapter covers functions of the six highest levels of the reference model. Consistent with prior approaches, the discussion moves from the level closest to the terminals and proceeds toward the host processor. In this chapter you learn about systems level software functions. By *systems level software,* we mean the software that is typically provided by a hardware or software vendor and that supports the applications in accomplishing its tasks. Specific topics you learn about include:

The OSI session layer

The operating system

Device drivers

Database and data communications access methods

Database management systems

Teleprocessing monitors

How each of the preceding subsystems interfaces with application level software

How transactions flow through an online system

Chapter 13 addresses other software topics such as security, editing, formatting, and message routing. The emphasis in this chapter is on how

431

these components can be integrated into a comprehensive applications support system.

THE OSI SESSION LAYER

Whenever two entities in a network need to communicate, a session is established between them. The session may be established formally as in IBM's systems network architecture (SNA) or informally as in Tandem's Expand network. Regardless of the way in which it is established, several things are accomplished in setting up a session. In this section, you learn about the functions of the OSI session layer.

The major objectives of the session layer are to establish the dialogue rules between two entities, manage the exchange of data between the entities, and dissolve the session. The dialogue rules include the method of flow control, which can be either full duplex or half duplex. Simplex transmission is not supported in the OSI reference model. Another aspect of the dialogue rules is establishing synchronization points. If a session is interrupted for any reason, the synchronization points help reestablish and recover the session. Other parameters that the session layer might stipulate for a session are message lengths and quality of service. Quality of service parameters include the ability to set priorities, security, and speed and quality of the communications link. When the entities involved in a session need to terminate the dialogue, the session must be dissolved. Dissolution may occur at the request of either session member. Prior to a session being dissolved, all data in transit must first be received and acknowledged. In summary, the function of the session layer is to establish a connection between two entities, regulate the flow of data between them, and dissolve the session when all data transfer has been completed.

SOFTWARE OVERVIEW

Applications Software

A generic software configuration is depicted in Figure 12-1. At the heart of the system is the applications software. The goal of applications software is to solve a business or scientific problem, not to solve computer system problems. An example of a system problem is the details of how to display data on a terminal. In the early days of computer programming, an applications program needed to contain logic for communicating with specific hardware devices. If a new terminal was introduced into the system, application programs had to be changed to support the differences between the new terminal and terminals the program already supported. Thus, if all currently supported terminals have monochrome screens and

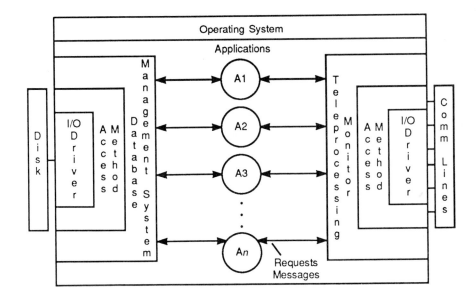

Figure 12-1
An Applications
Environment

the new terminal has a color screen, the application program must be modified to be able to display colors. When application software is responsible for device handling, the application programs take longer to create, test, and modify. Moreover, the application programmer must be knowledgeable of device interface skills as well as application design skills.

Most current systems provide systems level software to remove programming for device dependencies from applications software. This allows programmers to focus their attention on business problems. To support this objective, software such as database management systems, teleprocessing monitors, and file and data communications access methods were developed. These provide functions common to most application programs and insulate the applications from the details of file and device access. This follows a trend of systems level software: making the system easier to program and use. Programmers interface to devices via well-defined user interfaces. As the adjacent levels of the OSI reference model have interfaces that allow data to flow between layers, messages and data flowing between application programs and the database or data communications system pass through interfaces to reach their destination. Perhaps the most important piece of software in effecting this is the operating system.

Operating System

The *operating system* (*OS*) helps applications by performing the functions listed in Figure 12-2. It performs all of these functions in a manner largely transparent to the applications program and programmer. The OS performs many functions for an executing program, but these functions are carried out without the programmer explicitly requesting them. The OS is

Figure 12-2
Operating System
Functions

Interface functions—provide interface to:
    Users
    I/O system
    File system

Process functions
    Schedule processes for execution
    Start/stop processes
    Establish process environment
    Enforce process priorities
    Prevent processes from interfering with each other
    Allow multiprocessing/multitasking

Management functions
    Manage memory
    Manage I/O system and devices
    Manage access to CPU
    Manage user access through security provisions

File management functions
    Allocate disk space
    Maintain disk directories
    Manage file attributes—owner, date and time updated, and
    so on
    Provide file security

the overall manager of the computing system. It is loaded when the system is started and portions of it remain memory resident so it is always available to provide its management and interface functions. One of the functions provided by the OS is managing the input/output (I/O) subsystem. The parts of the operating system that perform this task are called I/O drivers.

I/O Drivers.   The *I/O drivers* in Figure 12-1 provide the low-level access to devices. On the database side the devices are tapes and disks, and on the data communications side they are communications lines. In data communications, low-level access involves implementing the data link protocol, such as asynchronous or HDLC, error detection, buffer management, and so on. For disk drives the I/O driver issues seek, read, and write commands. The specifics of I/O drivers are system- and device-dependent.

Access Methods.   *Access methods* exist for both database and data communications systems. Generally, access methods separate the application from physical characteristics of the data or devices it is accessing. An access method essentially functions as a black box to translate user read and write requests into lower level requests tailored to the file or device being accessed. Database access methods allow users to retrieve data. Often an application must provide a variety of methods for data retrieval. With personnel files, for instance, an employee record might need to be accessed via the employee's name, employee number, and Social Security number. Moreover, sometimes we must retrieve records in order on each of these fields, such as accessing records in employee name order to produce a corporate telephone directory. Database records can be physically ordered in only one way. For example, personnel records may be physically stored in order by employee number or in the chronological order in which records are inserted. Access methods provide the ability to select a specific record from the database with a small number of disk accesses regardless of the physical ordering. Some access methods also allow records to be retrieved in order on a key, which provides a logical ordering to the records. Thus, one access method might be used to retrieve personnel records in employee name order and another access method might be used to retrieve personnel records in department order.

The mechanisms used to effect this type of access are beyond the scope of this text; however, a real-world analogy may assist in illustrating this concept. Suppose our database is a library and the books are the records. We can find books based on title, subject, and author, or we can retrieve them in author name order, subject order, or title order. Physically the books are not maintained in any of those orders. Two things make a library system work: Each book has an address or location, and a set of indices has been built to point us to the addresses. In addition, the index has several levels: a gross level that consists of the catalog, a finer level consisting of individual trays of index cards, and individual pointers from the index cards to books on the shelf.

The access method that is similar to the library card catalog is called *index sequential* and is illustrated in Figure 12-3. To find the record of employee Adams, for instance, would mean looking first in the root index (the card catalog) to find the next-level index table (the specific tray) where Adams's name would reside. (Note that in the library the book for which you are looking may not exist, and the same is true in finding an employee's name. However, you do not know this until the search is done.) The index table is searched, and if the search is successful there will be a pointer to where the record is located. By following the entries in the index one after another, records can be retrieved in employee name order. The ordering is preserved in the index tables just as book ordering is established by the library card catalog. Index-sequential access methods are but one of several access methods used in databases. Some provide faster access but do not provide ordering on the data item. Data fields on the records that are used for retrieval in this manner are called access keys or simply keys.

Data communications access methods allow users to display data on a terminal and to retrieve data that has been entered on the terminal. How data is displayed on terminals may vary from one terminal to another. In Chapter 4 several terminal attributes were presented, including color, reverse video, protected fields, and so on. Data communications access

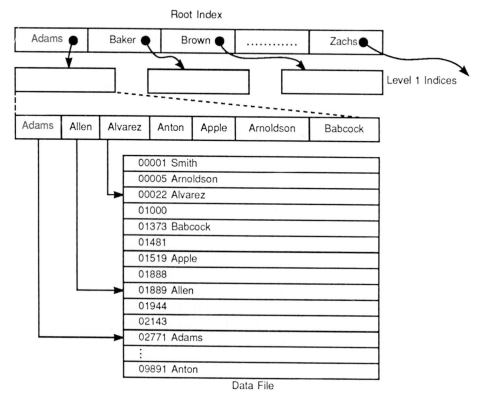

Figure 12-3   An Index-Sequential Access Method

methods allow the user to utilize these attributes. Access methods are covered in more detail later in this chapter.

Database and File Management Systems

A *database management system* (*DBMS*) organizes data into records, organizes records into files, and provides access to the data based on one or more access keys. A DBMS also provides a mechanism for relating one file to another. For example, in a university database, records are maintained on students, classes, and teachers. File relationships allow users to answer questions such as "What students are enrolled in Section 4 of tapeworm taxonomy?" and "List the advisors for all students majoring in mathematics." Both of the above requests require that data be extracted from at least two files via relationships (for example, a teacher advises a student) that exist between the files. A *file management system* (*FMS*) provides a subset of the capabilities found in a DBMS. An FMS is basically oriented toward one file and hence does not provide file relationships. Database and file management systems provide data services to application processes. Applications issue database requests to store, modify, retrieve, or delete data, and the database management system carries out these requests.

Transaction Control Process

Whereas the database management system provides an application with access to data, application access to terminals or other nodes is provided by a *transaction control process (TCP)*, also referred to as a *teleprocessing monitor* or *message control system (MCS)*. Without a TCP, a data communications access method can partially fulfill this function. Just the DBMS allows applications to share data, insulates the applications from the physical details of data storage, and provides data independence, the TCP enables different terminals to interface with multiple applications and insulates an application from the physical differences between terminals and between network nodes. Whereas the DBMS uses different data access methods to provide multiple paths to data, the TCP uses different terminal access methods to give access to different terminal types. A more detailed description of the transaction control process and its associated access methods is found later in this chapter.

Example of Transaction Flow

With this brief overview of the applications software environment, let us now see how the software components cooperate in processing a transaction. It is assumed that our system is configured to allow recovery from most system failures. Our transaction will be entered by a user at a terminal.

Preparation for a transaction begins before the user enters the information. Let us assume that the system has just been powered up. The first thing that happens during a system startup is loading the operating system. Following that, the mainline software such as DBMS, TCP, spooler, and electronic mail systems are started. At this stage all components in Figure 12-1 are available for use.

The application programs in Figure 12-1 receive their inputs from the TCP. Once the applications start, they must establish a session with the TCP. In some systems, such as IBM's *customer information control system (CICS)*, applications run under the control of the TCP. In other systems, applications are relatively independent of the TCP. In the first case the applications are tightly coupled to a single TCP. In the second case applications can receive messages from one or more TCPs as well as from other sources.

Regardless of the implementation, a data path always exists or can be established between applications and a TCP. Once this path exists, the application issues a read request on its message file or otherwise indicates its readiness to accept a message for processing. A TCP typically controls several terminals. The TCP displays an opening screen on each terminal under its control and then initiates a read for each terminal. Typical opening displays are a menu of available transactions or a user login screen.

There may be multiple TCPs in operation concurrently, each of which will exclusively control several terminals. Terminals may be moved from one TCP to another, but at any one time will be attached to only one.

Moreover, not all terminals in the system need to connect to a TCP. Some terminals may be used outside the TCP for applications such as program development. Terminals also may alternate between use for transaction processing under TCP control and for other applications outside of TCP control.

At this point in the transaction environment, each application is awaiting a transaction from the TCP, and the TCPs are awaiting data from their terminals. We shall assume that a user has successfully logged on to the system, a menu of transactions the user can perform has been displayed on the user's terminal by the TCP, and the user is ready to enter a transaction. When a terminal transmits a transaction (such as admitting a patient to a hospital), the following actions are taken:

1. The user selects the admit patient transaction from the menu. This selection is transmitted to the TCP.

2. The TCP responds to the user's selection by displaying a patient identification form on the terminal and issues a read request for that terminal. The user fills in the form and transmits it to the TCP.

3. The TCP receives the transaction from the terminal, which completes the read that has been posted on that device. The TCP usually handles several terminals. For each of the other terminals, the TCP also has an outstanding read. Thus, at any time, a terminal operator may complete a task and transmit data to the TCP. The TCP must be able to accept these messages when they arrive.

4. The TCP sends the patient's ID to an application with a request to find a patient record with that ID. The objective is to determine whether this patient already has a hospital record.

5. The application issues a database read request to obtain a patient record with the ID sent to it by the TCP. If the record exists, it is returned to the application; otherwise, the application receives a message from the DBMS stating that the record does not exist.

6. The application returns the result to the TCP. In this case we shall assume that the patient does not have a record on file.

7. The TCP displays a patient registration form and posts a read on the terminal. The user enters data into the form and sends it back to the TCP. At this point the TCP has all the data necessary for admitting the patient.

8. Data edits are performed on all fields for which they have been specified. For example, the TCP determines whether the patient's name has been entered, whether the data entered for the patient's gender is either M or F, whether the birth date entered is a valid date, and so on. If fields are found to be in error, the TCP displays an error message on the terminal and highlights

the field to be corrected. The operator then corrects the mistake and the TCP rereads the data (ideally, just the corrected field).

9. When all data edits have been successfully completed, the TCP writes the data received to a *transaction log*. The transaction log is used for recovering from failures and sometimes for system auditing.

10. Since this transaction will modify the database, the TCP starts a transaction for recovery purposes. A transaction that changes data in the database must leave the database in a consistent state, which means the transaction must be completed in its entirety or leave the database as it was before the transaction started. Thus, a transaction is a unit of work as well as a unit of database recovery. Starting a transaction is typically not necessary for read-only transactions because read-only transactions do not change the database and do not need to be recovered. For example, the admissions clerk may check the database to see if the patient already has a record on file. This activity does not require that a transaction be started.

11. The TCP examines the transaction and determines which application(s) should process it. Some transactions require the services of more than one application process. In this example, one application will create a patient record, another will locate a room and calculate room charges, and still another will generate a standard patient supplies issue and build supply charge records. The TCP may send each participating application its work at the same time; alternatively, the TCP may wait until one application finishes before sending the second application its portion of the work.

12. An application receives its portion of the transaction and begins processing. We shall consider only the activity performed by the application that creates the patient record. The application uses the data received from the TCP to create a database record for the patient. The application sends the record to the database management system with a request to insert the new record.

13. The DBMS receives the request from the application and acts on it. Each time a record is updated or a new record inserted, images of the records being changed are inserted into the DBMS recovery log. Images of the record before and after the changes are written to the log. This allows the transaction to be reversed if it cannot be completed and allows it to be re-created at a later time if necessary.

14. After logging the before- and after-images, the DBMS inserts the patient record and returns a successful result status to the application.

15. After the application has performed all of its work, including the database requests, it formats a reply message and returns it to the TCP. In this case, the reply is a status code indicating the success of the transaction. If the database operation is unsuccessful, the response code will be an unsuccessful result code and a message or data to be returned to the terminal. For example, the insert might have failed because the patient file was full.

16. The TCP determines whether another application process must become involved in the transaction. The other applications are given their work to accomplish, and they respond to the TCP with the result. When all applications have successfully completed their work, the TCP posts a transaction completion message on the transaction log, formats a response, and sends it back to the terminal.

17. The application process(es), having finished the transaction, posts another read request on the message file, which indicates its ability to accept another transaction (another transaction may already be queued on the application's input file). The TCP posts another read on the terminal, thus enabling additional transaction input.

While all of this activity is being accomplished for this transaction, other transactions may also be in various states of completion. Examples of other transactions that may be in progress include:

Another admission clerk may be admitting a different patient.

A nurse may be reading a patient's record to find the patient's work telephone number.

An accounting clerk may be consolidating the fees for a patient being dismissed.

A clerk in the radiation laboratory may be entering a charge for a patient who has just been X-rayed.

Let us now look in more detail at the data communications software components, beginning with the access methods.

ACCESS METHODS

Data communications access methods give system users easier access to terminal devices. They relieve users from the device-specific attributes of terminals and provide connection, disconnection, and data transfer services to the applications. As with TCPs, the scope of access methods differs with the vendor and even within different access methods from one vendor. A generic description is provided below, with a specific implementation included in Appendix E.

Application-Terminal Connection

Several approaches have been used to provide access methods, but we shall discuss only the most practical implementation. One of the functions of an access method is to provide terminal-application connections. This is accomplished by having a pool of applications and a pool of terminals available, as illustrated in Figure 12-4. The access method serves as a switch to connect terminal requests with the proper application(s).

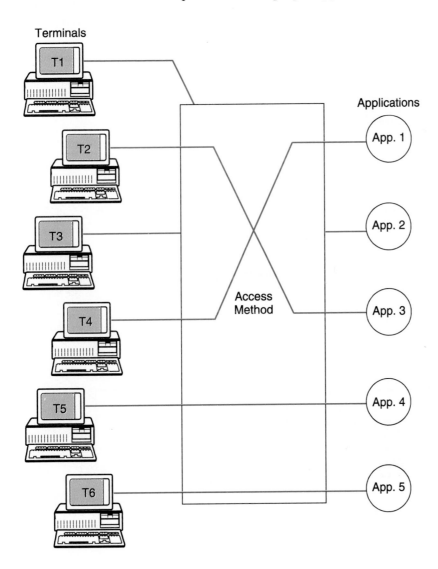

Figure 12-4 Access Method and Pooled Application-Terminal Connections

Accessing a Terminal

Because an access method separates the application program from the terminal access logic, access methods can be used with or without a TCP, depending on the environment. Figure 12-5 illustrates two situations: TCP present and TCP absent. The access method performs fewer functions when the TCP is present because some functions, such as message routing and data editing, are performed by the TCP.

The first requirement of accessing a terminal from a program is to connect the two. The access method serves as an intermediary in this case. Either the application initiates a connection by issuing an open or connect request to the access method or the terminal initiates the action by issuing an application logon request through the access method. Once the connection has been honored, a communication path exists, and the terminal and

Figure 12-5 An Access Method with and without a TCP

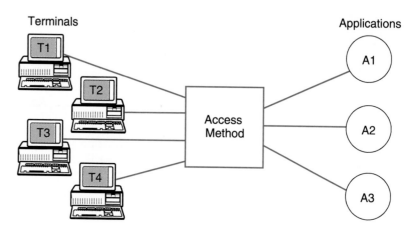

(a) Access Method without a TCP

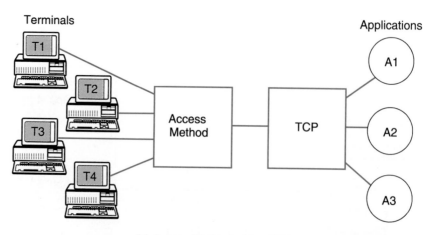

(b) Access Method with a TCP

application can exchange data. Connection requests can be denied for security reasons or because the application or device is already occupied.

Without a TCP, the access method makes the connection between an application program and a terminal. In some implementations the connection is static: The application and terminal are attached to each other and the terminal can run only those transactions provided by that particular application. For the terminal user to access another application process, the terminal must first be disconnected from its current access application and then reconnected to the new one. Other systems provide more flexibility in making the connection between a terminal and an application. IBM's *virtual telecommunications access method* (*VTAM*), described in Appendix E, provides several methods for terminal-application connections.

TRANSACTION CONTROL PROCESS

This section covers the general functions of the TCP. Appendix F presents a specific implementation.

TCP Configuration

The configuration of the transaction control process is depicted in Figure 12-6. Since the TCP serves as a switch between applications and terminals, it must be aware of the terminals attached to it, the transactions that can be submitted, and the applications responsible for processing those transactions. In this environment, any terminal can access any application known to the TCP. Implementation can be as a monolithic process, as in Figure 12-7(a), or as multiple processes, as in Figure 12-7(b).

Single Threading Versus Multi-Threading

The efficiency of the application environment is a function of how quickly transactions can be processed. If multiple transactions can arrive at once, good performance requires that parallelism in transaction processing be provided. From the TCP's perspective, this means that it may need to be involved in processing several transactions concurrently, a concept known as *multi-threading*. With *single threading*, a process accepts an input, processes the input to completion, produces an output, and then is ready to accept another input for processing. If a TCP were to operate in this manner it would accept an input from one terminal, send the transaction to an application process, wait for the response, and send the result back to the terminal. Then, the TCP would accept another transaction and process it. Meanwhile, other terminals may be waiting to be serviced. This processing method will result in long delays for terminals with queued requests.

The difference between single threading and multi-threading can be likened to what happens in a grocery store when people queue up at the

Figure 12-6
A Generic TCP
Configuration

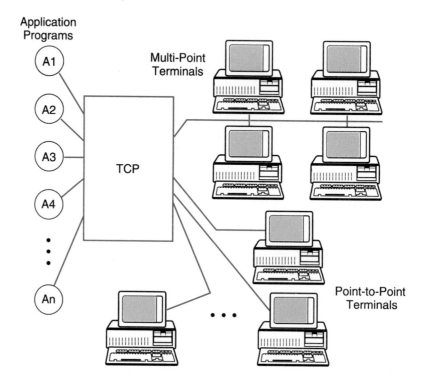

checkout counter. The checkout clerk represents the TCP process, and the customers represent the terminals. The clerk ordinarily operates in a single-threaded manner, processing one customer and one customer only until the total order has been tabulated and the money collected before turning to the next customer. If an object is unpriced, everyone waits while an assistant locates the price. Looking up the price is analogous to accessing a disk, with the assistant as the DBMS. Everyone waits while the price is being determined, the check written and verified, and comments about the weather exchanged. To improve efficiency, the clerks could be multi-threaded: Everyone in the queue would get attention as time allows. The clerks would maintain separate totals for each customer. While a missing price was being located, the clerk could move on to the next customer and process that customer's order. While the checks were being written, another customer could be served. The multi-threaded clerk must, of course, be much more flexible than the single-threaded clerk. Multiple totals are accumulated, items are taken from the correct basket and placed in the proper sack, and the bill is delivered to and collected from the proper customer. Multiple application theads, then, are active within a multi-threaded process at the same time. A comparison of single-threaded and multi-threaded processes is presented in Figure 12-8.

Figure 12-7   TCPs

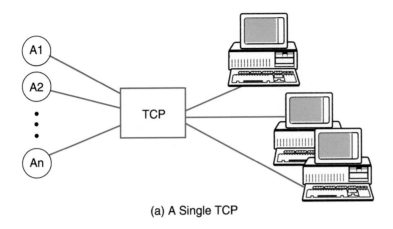

(a) A Single TCP

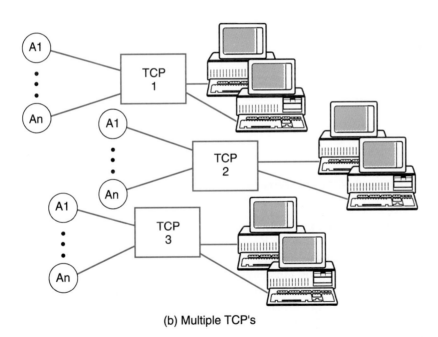

(b) Multiple TCP's

Maintaining Context

An additional requirement of multi-threaded processes is maintaining context. Whereas each single-threaded transaction is completely self-contained, in a multi-threaded process, a transaction might be separated into several parts, and somewhere, some process must keep track of the parts that are completed and those yet to be performed and continue the

Figure 12-8 Single Threading vs. Multi-Threading

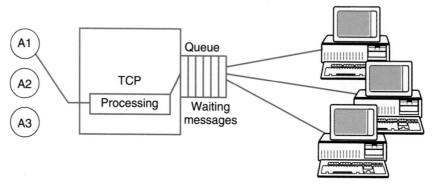

(a) Single Thread: Only One Transaction Active

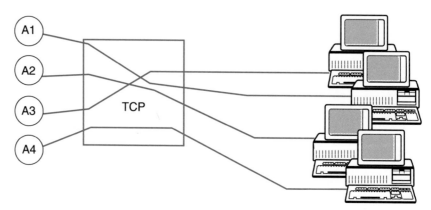

(b) Multi-Threading: Multiple Transactions in Progress

transaction from the point at which it was discontinued. In some instances the action to be performed is contingent on a previous activity. For instance, in searching a database for an employee named Smith, an application might select and display the first ten Smiths plus additional identifying information; if none of the ten names is correct, the next ten are displayed, and so on until the proper Smith is found. The search for the next ten names is contingent on where the previous search stopped.

Like the multi-threaded grocery clerk, the TCP must handle multiple customers at once. For example, suppose the TCP controls four terminals— T1, T2, T3, and T4—and three applications—A1, A2, and A3. At the start of the system, all three applications request to open, or connect to the TCP. The TCP records this information and issues a command to open, display the first screen, and post a read on each of the four terminals. At this point, the TCP is awaiting input from the terminals or a process. A chronological record of its activities is outlined in Figure 12-9. This type of interleaved processing continues throughout the workday.

For the activities in Figure 12-9, context was maintained in the TCP. It could also have been maintained within the application or the terminal. The TCP is the most logical place for maintaining context. The application is not as logical a place because multiple copies of one application may be used to increase efficiency, in which case the TCP would have to send the second part of a transaction to the same process that worked on the first part. Furthermore, saving context in applications programs makes them more complex. Some designers prefer to remove this type of complexity from the application. Since many TCP processes are supplied by software houses or computer vendors rather than being written by the end user, it benefits the user to have the multi-user complexity in the TCPs and not in the applications.

Memory Management

To manage context information and accept data from both terminals and applications, the TCP must provide *memory management* functions. At any time it can receive a message from either terminals or applications; multiple messages may be queued up at one time. The way in which TCPs manage memory varies. Essentially, they must have sufficient memory available to provide storage for terminal and application messages as well

Accept update transaction from terminal T2

Write T2's transaction on audit log

Accept inquiry transaction from T4

Route T4's request to application A1

Receive *write complete* on T2's audit log write

Begin transaction for T2

Route T2's transaction to A2

Receive inquiry transaction from T3

Route T3's transaction to A1

Receive A1's return message for T4

Write response to terminal T4

Receive A2's return message for T2

End T2's transaction

Receive inquiry transaction from T1

Receive request for next ten records from T4

Send T1's request to A3

Receive notice that T2's transaction has ended

Send response to T2

Send T4's request together with stored context to A1

Figure 12-9
Multiple TCP
Transaction Threads

as for context data. Sometimes this requires virtual memory algorithms similar to those employed by some operating systems: The disk is treated as an extension of memory and data is swapped back and forth between real memory and disk.

Transaction Routing

The TCP also must provide *transaction routing,* which means routing the transaction received from a terminal to one or more application programs. Several techniques are used to determine how to route a transaction. One method uses a transaction code embedded within the data message itself. For example, the terminal operator enters the transaction code in the text of the message, as illustrated in Figure 12-10. The TCP must recognize this code and route the transaction accordingly. Another method is based on context and a signal from the terminal. The signal is usually either a transaction code or the operator pressing a certain function key. Other signals may be indicated by using a light pen, mouse, or touchscreen.

Transaction routing requires that the TCP know which application handles a given transaction and the path or connection that leads to that application. Transaction routing could be table driven, in which case the TCP would look up the transaction ID in a table that provides directions

Figure 12-10
Transaction
Routing in a TCP

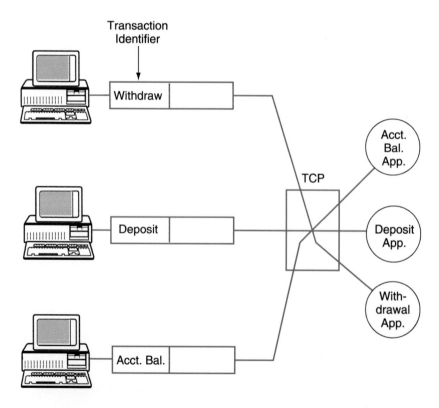

to the proper application process. Alternatively, a procedural interface with a case statement or similar construct would result in a program call or a message being sent to that process.

Transaction Log

The TCP is a logical place to implement transaction logging. A *transaction log* captures the transaction inputs, usually on tape or disk. Once inputs are captured, the system can assure the user that the transaction will be processed. This does not mean that the transaction will be successfully completed (errors could prevent that); it does mean that the transaction will not be lost by the system should a system failure occur. In addition to its use in recovery, transaction logging is sometimes required by auditors, especially in financial transactions. Electronic data processing (EDP) auditors will periodically check transaction sources and trace them through the system to determine if they were correctly processed. If transaction logging is implemented, as soon as a transaction is received by the TCP, it is written on the log file. Usually the TCP appends additional information to the message, such as a date-time stamp, transaction ID, or similar identifying information. Sometimes the completion of a transaction is also logged. In recovery situations this prevents a transaction being processed twice.

In some systems the transaction log is synchronized with the database logging function to ensure that a message received by the system will be processed and that no duplicate transactions will be processed if a failure occurs. One system even guarantees that transactions that must be reprocessed in the event of a failure will be processed in the original processing order. This last is an important feature in banking applications, such as when an account with a $100 balance first has a $500 check deposited and then a $200 check cashed. In the time-compressed recovery situation, the transaction could possibly be processed in reverse order, meaning the check-cashing transaction would be rejected for insufficient funds, leaving the account in an inconsistent state.

Security and Statistics

Since a TCP can be a focal point for online transactions entering the system, it is a logical place to collect statistics and provide for security. Several statistics that are necessary to effectively manage a network system can be collected in the TCP, including the number of transactions, types of transactions, number of characters transmitted to and from a terminal, application processing time per transaction, and number of transactions per terminal. Security at the terminal and transaction level could be enforced at the TCP. Since all online transactions for terminals managed by a TCP must be routed through it, the TCP is a logical place to implement security, possibly through security application processes.

Message Priorities

If message priorities are desired within the online system, the TCP is in an ideal position to assist with implementing them. Every message received could be examined for priority, or priorities could be assigned by the TCP. Priorities could be established according to the source and type of message. Priority messages could then be given service first and routed to special server applications to expedite message processing.

Application Development

It is necessary to establish test environments consisting of terminals, access methods, TCPs, applications, and a database when designing an online system. This environment is also used after a system has been placed in operation to develop and test enhancements and problem fixes. The TCP can provide features to make testing and debugging easier, including the ability to trace or examine transactions received by the TCP, the ability to store transactions in a transaction file and pass them through the TCP as though they were entered at a terminal, and the ability to vary the rate of transaction submission. The TCP should also allow concurrent running of production applications and test applications.

Operations Interface

An *operations interface* must be provided for control of the TCP environment. This may be accomplished through an operations interface program, illustrated in Figure 12-11. The operations interface provides some or all of the following capabilities:

TCP startup

TCP shutdown

Figure 12-11   TCP-
Operations Interface

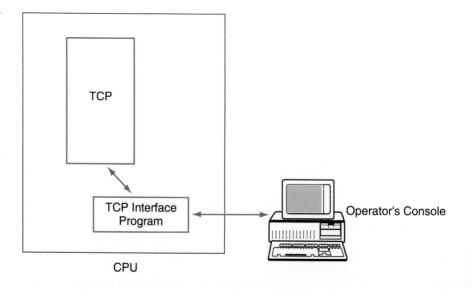

CPU

Defining lines, terminals, applications
Starting lines, terminals, applications
Stopping lines, terminals, applications
Adding lines, terminals, applications
Deleting lines, terminals, applications
Displaying statistics
Enabling/disabling statistics gathering
Moving lines, terminals, applications from one TCP to another

Other TCP Functions

Additional functions that a TCP might carry out include:

If an application fails, the TCP should be able automatically to restart it.

If a transaction arrives for a process that is not currently running, the TCP should be able to activate the process.

If one application receives so many requests that response times become degraded, the TCP should be able to initiate additional copies of that process to enhance performance.

If a process has been inactive for a long time, the TCP can optionally delete that process to free the resources it is holding.

Figure 12-12 summarizes the activities of a TCP.

Provides a user interface with the TCP subsystem
Manages memory
Provides an interface between applications and terminals
Manages applications
Logs messages
Participates in recovery
Provides transaction definition
Edits data fields
Formats data for terminals and applications
Routes messages to server processes
Gathers statistics
Provides testing and debugging facilities
Assists in providing security
Assists in implementing a priority system

Figure 12-12 TCP Activities

SUMMARY

Data communications software works closely with the applications, database, and operating system software to provide the functions required of today's systems. Two major components of networking software are access methods and transaction control processes. In some cases, access method software provides the linkage between application programs and terminal devices. In all cases, access methods provide an interface with different terminal devices, providing terminal and application independence. Transaction control processes also provide a link between applications software and terminal equipment. A TCP will also use the access method software to interface with terminal devices. The functions provided by TCPs in interfacing applications and devices go beyond those provided by the typical access method. These added capabilities include data edits, message switching, data formatting, and transaction definition and recovery.

Key Terms

access methods

context data

customer information control
    system (CICS)

data communications access
    method

data independence

database management system
    (DBMS)

I/O driver

memory management

message control system (MCS)

multi-threading

operating system (OS)

recovery

single threading

teleprocessing monitor

transaction control process (TCP)

transaction log

virtual telecommunications access
    method (VTAM)

Review Questions

1. What functions are performed by the operating system? Explain how two of these functions support applications.

2. Describe how a database access method is used to access a record.

3. Describe the functions of a data communications access method.

4. Describe how a transaction flows through an online system.

5. Describe the functions of a TCP.

6. Compare and contrast the functions of a TCP and a data communications access method.

7. Compare and contrast the operations of a TCP and an operating system.

8. Why are audit (log) trails important?

9. Why is multi-threading of a TCP an attractive feature?

Exercises

1. Other than the banking example given in the chapter, describe two transactions that could create inconsistencies in a database if not recovered in the same order in which they were originally processed.

2. Is the saving of context necessary for multi-threading? Why or why not?

3. Is it necessary for all user transactions to be recoverable units? If so, why? If not, give an example of a transaction that would not have to be recovered if the system failed.

4. Some data-processing professionals claim that a TCP uses a considerable amount of system resources and thus has a high overhead. This statement has some validity. How would you respond to such a statement in supporting the use of a TCP?

5. Research the literature to find an example of a TCP other than IBM's CICS. What features does it provide?

6. Do TCPs (or TCP-like functions) exist on microcomputer systems? Explain your answer.

7. Compare and contrast the functions of a local area network file server and a TCP.

References

IBM. *Introduction to VTAM Logic.* Manual no. SY27-7256-3. Kingston, N.Y. IBM, 1976a.

_____. *OS/VS TCAM Concepts and Applications.* Research Triangle Park, NC. Manual no. GC30-2049-1. IBM, November 1983b.

_____. *Customer Information Control System/Virtual Storage (CICS/VS) System Programmer's Reference Manual.* Manual no. SC33-0069-4. IBM, 1981.

_____. *Advanced Communications Function for VTAM General Information: Concepts.* Manual no. GC27-0463-3. Kingston, N.Y. IBM, 1982a.

_____. *Customer Information Control System/Virtual Storage (CICS/VS) General Information.* Manual no. GC33-0155-1. Kingston, N.Y. IBM, 1982b.

_____. *Customer Information Control System/Operating System/Virtual Storage (CICS/OS/VS) Installation and Operations Guide.* Manual no. SC33-071-3. IBM, 1982c.

Lim, Pacifico Amarga. *CICS/VS Command Level with ANS COBOL Examples.* New York: Van Nostrand Reinhold, 1982.

Tanenbaum, Andrew S. *Computer Networks.* Englewood Cliffs, NJ: Prentice-Hall, 1981.

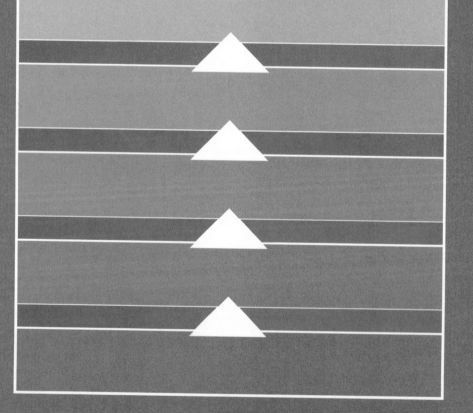

ANALYSIS AND MANAGEMENT: PRESENTATION AND APPLICATION LAYERS

Application and Presentation Layer Software

The Presentation Layer
The Application Layer
Security
Data Editing
Formatting
Error Detection and Recovery
Other Software Functions

INTRODUCTION

In this chapter we continue the discussion of software begun in the preceding chapter. At the chapter's conclusion, you should be familiar with some of the more common data communications software functions. Specifically, you learn about:

Security

Encryption

Data editing

Message and screen formatting

Data compression

Error detection and recovery

Electronic mail

Time-staged delivery systems

THE PRESENTATION LAYER

The presentation layer accepts the data from the application layer and provides generalized formatting of the data. Thus, if there are data preparation functions common to a number of applications, rather than embedding them in each application, they can be resolved by the presentation services. The types of functions that can be performed at this level are encryption, compression, terminal screen formatting, and conversion from one transmission code to another (such as EBCDIC to ASCII).

THE APPLICATION LAYER

The application layer is functionally defined by the user. Sometimes, application programs must communicate with each other. The content and format of the data being exchanged are dictated by the needs of the organization. The application determines which data is to be transmitted, the message or record format for the data, and the transaction codes that identify the data to the receiver. For example, an order entry transaction started on a sales node may need to pass product shipping information to a warehouse node. In this application, the message will contain the ship-to address, part identifiers, quantities to be shipped, and a message code indicating the action to be taken by the receiving application.

SECURITY

Security is a delaying tactic. It does not prevent unauthorized access to a system but simply makes it more difficult. Such delay should be long enough either to make unauthorized access too costly or to give time to detect and apprehend the perpetrator, or both. In the first case, the rewards of unauthorized access would be less than the cost of breaking into the system. In the second, the attempted penetration would be detected and further attempts squelched. From the system owner's perspective, the cost of security should be no more than the potential loss from system penetration.

Note also that levels of security may exist. No security means that any user can do anything on the system. For example, a user could give himself or herself a raise or a good performance rating. On the other hand, total security means that no one can do anything. Obviously, selecting the proper security level for each user is important. Security ought to protect data from intentional or accidental loss or disclosure without adversely affecting employees' ability to perform their jobs.

Vendor-Provided Security

Security needs are as various as the number of users. Each organization has its own security objectives. It is therefore difficult to provide one security system that meets everyone's needs; the security features provided by the vendors of hardware or systems software systems tend to be oriented toward meeting basic security needs. This security is generally found only in vendor-provided user interfaces such as command interpreters and operator- or programmer-level interfaces. When provided, such facilities generally are limited to user identification and authentication. Usually, there is also additional protection at the data level. These protections include the following:

Layered security for access to files

Operating systems safeguards such as prohibiting one process from interfering with the data of another process and viewing the data of an active or recently terminated process

This section does not concern operating system security; instead, it addresses security concerns that more directly affect the data communications network.

Physical Security

A good place to start establishing a secure system is with *physical security*. Since physical security is independent of hardware or software, it can be planned long before the installation of a network and hardware. By preventing access to physical components of the system such as terminals, communications circuits, processors, and modems, the likelihood of unauthorized access is significantly decreased. It will not prevent an authorized user from accidentally or intentionally misusing the system. This is significant because studies have shown that the biggest security risk companies face is the accidental or intentional destruction or misuse of data by their employees (Tucker, 1987).

Security has always been a requirement for some applications. In the past, however, enforcement of security was much easier than it is in most of today's systems. Consider the security implications of a batch system. All the computerized data can be contained within the computer room. Paperwork used for generating batch inputs and printed outputs are the only data that need to leave the computer facility. These inputs and outputs can be controlled through corporate policies for dissemination and protection of paperwork.

Security of batch systems can be established through physical measures. Physical security means using techniques such as door locks, safes, and security guards to deny physical access to areas containing sensitive information. Because gaining access to computerized data in a pure batch facility requires gaining access to the computer room, security locks on computer room doors and proper staff training regarding computer room access provide a security level adequate for many installations. While the computer staff is on duty, they control computer facility access. Without 24-hour staffing of the computer room, however, a company must consider physical access controls during off-shift times, such as security guards.

A common physical security measure is a surveillance system. Security personnel can use it to screen entry to the premises. The premises may be the property on which the facility is located, individual buildings, rooms within a building, or combinations of these. Additional security can be provided for sensitive areas with closed circuit television monitors, motion sensors, alarms, and other such intrusion-detection devices. Many installations can justify features such as closed-circuit television and motion sensors because they provide for equipment protection as well as data protection. Use of these devices may result in reduced insurance rates and partially offset their cost.

Other physical security measures that may be used include:

For sensitive applications, all equipment should be located in secure areas with controlled personnel access.

Nonsecure transmission media such as broadcast radio should be avoided where possible because such transmissions are easier to intercept. Use a conducted medium rather than a radiated one for such transmissions.

If broadcast radio must be used, all transmitted data should be encrypted (encrypting only sensitive data identifies it as such to a potential penetrator and makes his or her work easier).

Switched lines should be avoided, if possible. Recall that switched lines are those that can be accessed through the telephone company's switching equipment. If you have a switched line, any person with a computer and a modem has the ability to access your system. When required, switched lines should be physically disconnected during the hours they are not required, thus limiting the potential for unauthorized use and other protective devices like a call-back unit should be used.

Computers being used for highly sensitive applications should be disconnected from networks whenever possible placing an additional barrier to access from other network nodes. For example, some of the United States military computers are connected to a national network; however, those that are used for highly classified data are not connected to the network.

In most of today's processing environments, protecting computer rooms from physical access is not sufficient to protect data. Access to data is available via terminals distributed throughout the organization. Many online systems also have the ability to access the system remotely via switched circuits. Because physical security is not enough, other security levels, encryption and access security, must be added.

Encryption

Encryption should be used with all media carrying sensitive data. The particular encryption algorithm chosen should be capable of deterring unwarranted use by making the cost or time to decipher the message too great.

Data Encryption Standard (DES).   One of the most common yet controversial encryption algorithms is the *data encryption standard* (*DES*) adopted by the National Bureau of Standards. The controversy surrounds the effectiveness of the standard. In 1976 it was estimated that it would take an average of 91–2000 years to break the DES code (Diffie, 1978; Kinnucan, 1978; Meyer and Tuchman, 1978; Solomon, 1978). Opponents of the algorithm countered that the code could be broken in 6 minutes to 12 hours at a cost of $20–$5000 (Solomon, 1978). The primary criticism of the DES is that only 56 bits are used for the encryption key, a size critics believe allows for too few different possible data permutations because systematic attempts to decrypt the message would allow message decryption within a reasonable time. With the increasing speed and lower cost of computer hardware, most critics and proponents agreed that the algorithm had an effective life of approximately 10 years, meaning it should now be nearing the end of its effectiveness.

Most DES algorithms make use of integrated circuits designed for that purpose. The chips may be integrated onto processor or controller boards or used in stand-alone external boxes. The encryption devices can be placed between individual nodes or at the origin and destination of the message. Figure 13-1 illustrates several configuration options. If the encryption devices are placed at each node, some degree of security is lost, since the message must be decrypted at each intermediate node. This increases the likelihood of interception. In end-to-end encryption, only the text body can be encrypted, and end-to-end addressing must remain clear so intermediate nodes can perform the routing correctly.

How the DES Algorithm Works.   The DES algorithm uses a 56-bit encryption key (plus 8 bits for parity) to encrypt and decrypt the data. Known only to the sender and receiver, the encryption key locks and unlocks the meaning of the message. In general, unencrypted data (called *plain text*) is translated into encrypted data (known as *cipher text*) by rearrangement of the order of the bits, substitution of one bit or character for another, or a combination of the two techniques. There must exist a deterministic algorithm that takes the plain text to its equivalent cipher text so the same data used with the same key always yields the same cipher text. The process must also be reversible so the data can be reclaimed. The DES

Figure 13-1   Encryption Configurations

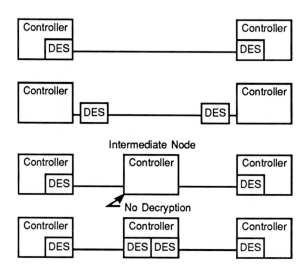

algorithm uses 16 iterations of a combination of rearrangement and substitution. Each of the 16 iterations is essentially the same and involves the following actions:

1. A 64-bit data entity is broken into two 32-bit pieces.

2. One piece is rearranged and augmented, yielding a 48-bit group.

3. The 56-bit encryption key is manipulated to produce a 48-bit entity.

4. The 48-bit key and the bits in the data string are combined and a 32-bit string is extracted. The two bit strings are combined using a technique called an exclusive OR (XOR). An exclusive OR is a logical operation that returns a 1 if the bits are different and a 0 if the two bits are the same. For example, 1 XOR 0 is 1 and 1 XOR 1 is 0.

5. The 32 bits are again rearranged.

6. This 32-bit string and the untouched 32-bit data half are exclusively ORed, forming a new 32-bit entity.

7. The resulting 32-bit string is then used as input to Step 2.

With 16 such iterations, a 56-bit key yields over 70 quadrillion possible outputs. Lengthening the key to 128 bits or more would, of course, further extend the number of possible encrypted strings and increase the average expected decryption time. The lack of a longer key string is cited as one of the current weaknesses of the DES.

Example of Encryption

The complexity of the DES algorithm provides its usefulness but makes the working through of an example quite tedious. However, the basic mechanics can be illustrated with the less complex algorithm outlined in Figure 13-2. The second step in the figure is a rearrangement step; the third through sixth steps form the substitution phase. The algorithm of Figure 13-2 can be illustrated by applying it to the plain text string, DATA COMMUNICATIONS, using the key PROTOCOL. The first eight characters are encrypted in Figure 13-3; the remainder is left as an exercise.

Unlike anagrams, which simply substitute one letter for another, encrypting a letter in the plain text can produce different letters in the cipher text. Thus, the clear text letter A is encrypted as both the letter Q and the letter P in our example. The algorithm of Figure 13-2 will work only for text containing letters. The more general case could use ASCII or EBCDIC decimal equivalents and a divisor of 128 or 256. *Decrypting* the data, or changing it from cipher text back to plain text, is a reversal of the encryption process. The procedure for doing this is given in Figure 13-4. The decryption of the encryption example given in Figure 13-3 is illustrated in Figure 13-5. Decrypting the remainder of the message is left as a reader exercise.

1. Divide the plain text into groups of eight characters. Pad with blanks at the end as necessary.

2. Select an 8-character key.

3. Rearrange the plain text characters by interchanging adjacent characters—that is, making the first character the second and the second the first, and so on.

4. Translate each alphabetic character into an ordinal number—that is, A becomes 1, B becomes 2, and so on, with a blank being a zero.

5. Add the ordinal number of the key to the results of step 3.

6. Divide the total by 27 and retain the remainder (which will be between 0 and 26).

7. Translate the remainder back into a character to yield the cipher text.

Figure 13-2
Example Encryption Steps

1.	DATA COM								Separate into groups of eight.
2.	ADATC MO								Rearrange the characters.
3.	01	04	01	20	03	00	13	15	Translate characters to decimal.
4.	01	04	01	20	03	00	13	15	Add key values.
	_16_	_18_	_15_	_20_	_15_	_03_	_15_	_12_	
	17	22	16	40	18	03	28	27	
5.	17	22	16	13	18	03	01	00	Remainder after division by 27
6.	Q	V	P	M	R	C	A	space	

Figure 13-3
Example of Encryption

Figure 13-4
Example Decryption
Steps

1. Divide the cipher text into groups of eight characters. Pad with blanks at the end as necessary.

2. Translate each cipher text alphabetic character and the encryption key into an ordinal number: A becomes 1, B becomes 2, and so on, with a blank being a zero.

3. For each eight-character grouping, subtract the ordinal number of the key value from the ordinal number of the cipher text. Subtract the ordinal number of the first character of the key from the ordinal value of the first character of the eight-character group, and so on.

4. Some numbers obtained in Step 3 may be negative. These values must be "normalized" by adding 27. Recall that in Step 6 of the encryption algorithm, numbers larger than 26 ended up being changed to a value between 0 and 26 through the division and remaindering process.

5. All numeric values will now be between 0 and 26. Translate these numbers back to their alphabetic equivalents: 0 is a blank, 1 is an A, 2 is a B, and so on.

6. Rearrange the text resulting from Step 5 by interchanging adjacent characters: Make the first character the second and the second the first; the third character the fourth and the fourth the third; and so on.

Figure 13-5
Example of
Decryption

	Q	V	P	M	R	C	A	space
1.	Q	V	P	M	R	C	A	space
2.	17	22	16	13	18	03	01	00
3.	17	22	16	13	18	03	01	00
minus	16	18	15	20	15	03	15	12
	01	04	01	−7	03	00	−14	−12
4.	01	04	01	−7	03	00	−14	−12
plus				27			27	27
	01	04	01	20	03	00	13	15
5.	A	D	A	T	C	space	M	O
6.	D	A	T	A	space	C	O	M

For encryption to be useful, the key must be derived as randomly as possible and changed frequently, and the key value should be carefully safeguarded. Additional iterations with a different key will also impede unwarranted decryption. Thus, in Step 6 of Figure 13-3, the cipher text QVPMRCA could be used as plain text and another algorithm with a different key applied, which is analogous to the iteration process in the DES algorithm.

Key administration is an important function in an effective encryption program. Administration includes:

Key creation

Key distribution

Key storage/safeguarding/restoration

Setting standards for frequency of changing keys

Standards organizations have recognized the critical nature of key management and have adopted several standards to guide key administrators. Among these are ANSI X9.17, which addresses key management for financial institutions, and U.S. Federal Standard 1027, for security requirements of equipment using the DES standard. An organization that is serious about security and encryption should have one or more persons designated as security administrators whose function is to implement procedures to effect security measures and detect attempts to breach security. Some of the measures that might be implemented are given in Figure 13-6.

Other encryption algorithms have been proposed, although none has gained the acceptance of the DES. One of the more promising, referred to as the *trapdoor* or *public key* method, utilizes large prime numbers and two keys, one key made public and the other kept secret by the message recipi-

All users must have a password.

Passwords must be at least 6 characters long.

Passwords must be changed at least monthly.

Passwords will be changed immediately if there is suspicion that the password has been compromised.

Passwords will not contain users' initials, month abbreviations, or other obvious character strings.

Passwords must not be written down.

Passwords must be created randomly so they do not contain sequence numbers or other instances of succession.

Unsuccessful attempts to logon to the system will be recorded. Data recorded will include the time, terminal from which the attempt is made, and the user ID for which the login is attempted.

All unsuccessful login attempts will be investigated.

All sensitive data will be encrypted.

Encryption keys will be changed regularly.

Two people will be responsible for encryption key administration.

No single individual can change the encryption key.

Switched (dial-up) lines will be disconnected when not in use.

Manual answer and user verification must be used for all switched connections or call-back units will be used.

Figure 13-6 Sample Security Measures

ent. The public key encrypts the data; the private key decrypts the cipher text. For further information regarding this method, consult Solomon, 1978.

User Identification and Authentication

Encryption is only one aspect of security. In most systems the first level of security is user identification and authentication. *User identification* runs the gamut from simply providing a user name to more exotic biological measures like retina scans, voice prints, palm prints, or fingerprint identification. Biological security measures are usually employed only in high-security systems like those of the intelligence and military communities. In business applications, identification is generally via user name, or by badge, in which case the system must be equipped with a badge reader. After identification comes *authentication*, which requires the user to provide additional information ostensibly known only to that particular user—something the person knows (like a password) or has (like an ID card) or something unique about him or her (such as a fingerprint or voice print).

Passwords. *Passwords* are the most common form of authentication. They are maintained in a file of information about system users, typically including user ID, password, defaulted security attributes for any files created, and possibly an access profile. Because this file contains the information needed to access any portion of the system, it should be carefully secured and encrypted. Passwords should be changed frequently, either centrally by the network administrators or in a decentralized manner by the users. Centrally changed passwords are assured of being changed regularly and assigned on a random basis. The major flaw of this approach is in the timing of their distribution to users: Dissemination of new passwords must be timely and well coordinated. The logistics in a large, distributed network are considerable. Furthermore, the distribution process is likely to be the weakest element in the security system: Since passwords are usually distributed in written form via mail or courier, there is ample opportunity for unauthorized users to obtain them.

Decentralized password changes rely on users to change their passwords regularly, either by themselves or through their managers. Individual users can change their passwords without leaving any written record of the password, and they can make changes as often as they like. The password file periodically can be centrally examined, and if users have not changed their password within a specified time, they can be so notified or their access privileges can be revoked. Some systems contain provisions for password aging. For example, the security administrator can specify that users must change passwords at least monthly. Users who have not changed their passwords in the allotted time are warned during their login. The security administrator may allow the user several such "grace" logins. If the user still fails to make a password change under the rules, his or her account is deactivated. The user will then need to see the security administrator to have the account reactivated. The biggest problem with user-assigned passwords is that they are typically nonrandom, since users like to select a password that is easy to remember, like their initials, birth date, or names of loved ones. Unfortunately, this type of password is also more easily guessed by a potential intruder. Some dos and don'ts regarding password selection are given in Figure 13-6.

Ultra-Sensitive Applications.   Identification and authentication are usually insufficient for sensitive applications, since we must also identify what functions a given user may or may not perform. The two most common ways of controlling user access are by adding layers of identification and authentication or by employing user or application profiles.

Layered IDs.   Layers of identification and authentication help to screen access to sensitive transactions. Once users have been logged on to the system via the initial identification procedures, they can be asked to provide additional identification and authentication information every time they attempt to access a new application or a sensitive transaction within an application. Thus, in a banking application, an operator might be required to provide another password or authorization code to transfer funds from one account to another. The operator will use one user ID and password to gain access to the system. This level of access will allow the operator to check account balances and make changes to data other than account balances. If the operator needs to run a transaction that will change an account balance, he or she must first provide another password. If the transaction exceeds a certain limit, an additional password may be required. The advantage of layered IDs is that each application or transaction can have its own level of security, so applications that are not sensitive can be made available to everyone, and those that are very sensitive can be protected with one or more levels of security. The disadvantage of layered IDs is that the user must remember several different authentication codes, thus increasing the probability of their being written and made accessible to others.

User Profiles.   A *user profile* contains all the information needed to define the applications and transactions a user is authorized to execute, such as when a user in a personnel application is authorized to add new employees, delete employee records, and modify all employee data fields except salary. The profiles maintained in a user file can be very detailed, covering each application or transaction, or relatively simple, with only a brief profile. With a brief profile, for example, a user might be assigned an access level to the system for each of four functions: read, write, execute, and purge. Specifically, suppose a user has been given Level 8 read access, Level 6 write access, Level 8 execute access, and Level 2 purge access. Each file and transaction is also given an access profile. A user is granted access to the file or transaction only if his access number is equal to or greater than that of the file or transaction. Thus, if the payroll file has access attributes of 8, 8, 10, and 10 for read, write, execute, and purge, respectively, the user just described will only be able to read the information in the file. This is because the read-access meets or exceeds the file's security profile. A write-access of 6 is insufficient to allow the user to write to the file.

The advantage of the brief profile is its simplicity. Its disadvantage is the difficulty in stratifying all users across all applications and files in this manner. Of course, such a profile could be provided for all files or applications, which then becomes a complex profile that is difficult to maintain and administer. Another effective aspect of user profiles is the restriction of logins to specific days and times. In some systems, the security administrator can define a calendar specifying when a given user is allowed to be logged in. Thus, most workers can be given a profile restricting their access to the system to normal working days and hours. Attempts to login during times outside this profile will be unsuccessful.

Menu Selection and User Profiles.   User profiles can be very effective when used in combination with a menu selection system that displays user options on the terminal so the user can select the transactions or applications to perform. If a user profile is available, the menu can be tailored to the individual user, and the only transactions the user will see are those to which the user has access. Thus, in the example above, the user who could only read the payroll file would see only that option displayed on the menu, whereas the payroll manager would likely have all options displayed. The security of the system is enhanced by denying users visibility to transactions and files to which they have no access.

Time and Location Restrictions

Time and location with identification and authentication can play an important part in bolstering security. Intervals can be established during which a transaction is legal or during which a user can be logged in. In a stock trading application, for instance, buying and selling stock on the exchange is limited to a specific period, so any attempt to trade stock outside of that period will be rejected. In a personnel application, it would be prudent to restrict to normal working hours those transactions that affect employee salary or status. This kind of security can be further enhanced by making sensitive portions of the application system unavailable during nonworking hours.

Transactions also can be restricted by location. For instance, a money transfer transaction would be disallowed from a bank teller terminal if such transactions had to be initiated by a bank officer. Also, money transfer transactions will always be disallowed if the terminal is attached to a switched (dial-up) communication line. In a manufacturing plant, a shop floor terminal would be unable to start an accounts receivable or payable transaction, such transactions being limited to a set of terminals in a given location. This can be implemented either by attaching applications to specific terminals or by terminal identification coupled with its location and a transaction profile. A terminal profile could list the location of the terminal and the transactions valid from that terminal. Time and location restrictions with user controls provide a hierarchy of security precautions.

Switched Ports with Dial-In Access

Perhaps the most vulnerable security point of any system is a switched port that allows dial-in access. The dangers of this should be evident: It enables any person with a telephone and a terminal to access the system. For that reason, extra security precautions should be taken. The switched line should be operational only during the periods when transactions are allowed. In a university environment, for instance, this might be 24 hours a day. In an order entry application, this would likely be between 8 A.M. and 8 P.M. During the period when transactions are disallowed, the line should be disabled. A call-back unit as described in Chapter 5 can be used to ensure that only calls from authorized locations are received.

User identification and authentication procedures and the restriction of allowed transactions become of greater concern when switched lines are used. The telephone numbers of the switched lines should be safeguarded as carefully as possible. In high-security installations a manual answer arrangement should be used, thus allowing person-to-person authentication as well as the usual application-based authorization. Another method used to stall unauthorized users of switched lines is to hide the carrier tone until an authentication procedure has been provided, a solution that is most practical when telephones are manually answered. This method is meant to foil hackers who try to gain access to systems by randomly dialing business telephone numbers until a computer installation is reached.

Recognizing Unauthorized Access Attempts

As we said at the outset of the discussion of security, all the techniques discussed are simply delaying tactics; their implementation alone may not provide adequate security. A tight security system should recognize possible unauthorized access attempts and provide some type of corrective assistance. In the movie *Wargames*, a computer was used to generate passwords until a correct one was found. Even relatively unsecure systems would discourage this type of activity. A very simple way to counter such attempts is to mark the terminal down altogether, or to temporarily retire the terminal, meaning that the system would not accept input from that terminal for a specified period. Such an algorithm might work as follows: After three unsuccessful access attempts, no input from that terminal would be accepted for 5 minutes. Assuming a six-character password of only letters and numbers, which gives over 2 billion possible passwords, if a billion of these were tried, with a 5-minute delay between each try, over 9500 years would be needed to gain access.

There is a second algorithm employed in some systems that acts to simulate a successful logon. After a certain number of unsuccessful logon attempts, the user receives a successful logon message. Rather than actually being granted access to the system, the user is provided with a fake session. While this session is being conducted, security personnel can determine the terminal from which access is being made and the types of transactions the user is attempting to run. This type of simulated session can also help keep the penetrator busy while security personnel are dispatched to the location for investigation. Again, switched connections make such an activity more difficult, especially with respect to apprehension. You may wish to read Stoll, 1989, to gain some insight regarding an actual case of security violations and detection.

Automatic Logoff

People are often the weakest link in security. All too frequently, operators write their passwords on or near the workstation or they leave the area with their workstation still logged on, allowing anyone to perform transactions on their behalf. This not only jeopardizes the security of the system but can also place the employee's job in jeopardy. The system can assist operators by logging off any user who has not entered a transaction within a certain amount of time, such as 2 minutes. Then, operators who leave their terminals for more than 2 minutes will have to go through the identification and authentication procedures on returning. Alternatively, the user can be required to go through an authentication procedure for every transaction. Unfortunately, this adversely affects operator performance. The first alternative is relatively simple to implement on most systems, and if the logoff interval is chosen well, operator efficiency will be unimpeded.

Transaction Logs

Transaction logs are an important adjunct to security. Every logon attempt should be logged, including date and time, user identification, unsuccessful authentication attempts (with passwords used), terminal identification and location, and all transactions initiated from that terminal by that user. If several unsuccessful logon attempts are made, the information could also be written on the console of the operator or security personnel so other actions—such as investigation—can be initiated. Transaction logs are also of benefit to electronic data processing (EDP) auditors and diagnostic personnel.

Computer Viruses

The need for a new type of security surfaced in the latter part of the 1980s. Most security countermeasures until that time were oriented toward individuals actively attempting to breach security for personal gain, revenge, or gratification. During this type of security violation, the perpetrator of the breach or the perpetrator's system was actively connected to the network. In contrast, computer viruses operate independently of the person who implanted them. A virus infection can be implanted intentionally or accidentally.

A variety of viruses have been discovered. Although their implementation differs, there is usually a common objective—to break a system or disrupt users. A virus typically is a section of code that is attached to a legitimate program or file. The virus has the ability to duplicate itself to other programs and files. Once attached, the virus may attack a variety of resources. Some have destroyed or altered disk files, some simply display annoying messages, and others have caused system failures. A widely publicized situation of the last type, the Internet Worm (Spafford, 1989, and Rochlis and Eichin, 1989) was not technically characterized as a virus but had much the same effect: It caused the failure of network nodes connected to the Internet network.

Detection and correction of viruses or viral equivalents can be time-consuming and expensive. They disrupt proper system operation and often require both time and investment in detection and eradication. Often, special anti-viral software is purchased to eliminate and detect viruses. Viruses can be introduced intentionally or accidentally and new viruses are continually appearing. An unintentional infection might occur, for example, when an employee uses an infected diskette, unaware that the disk carries a virus. Within a short time, the entire network might be infected. Moreover, detection may be made more difficult because some viruses remain dormant for a period, propagating themselves before becoming active.

For most known viruses, antidote programs exist. Using these anti-viral programs can help keep a system healthy. Additional measures should also be taken to prevent infections. Procedures to prevent employees from using personal diskettes in workstations, checking new software in an antiseptic environment before installing it for general use, and closely monitoring the source of all new files are effective countermeasures. Using diskless workstations is another excellent way to limit exposure.

DATA EDITING

Data editing has been a part of data processing almost since its inception.

Batch Verification and Editing

In the batch environment the data was collected in source form and then entered into machine-readable form, such as punched card, paper tape, magnetic tape, or disk. The next operation was likely to be a verification process. With punched cards this meant passing the cards through a verifier. Essentially, another operator would reenter the data so the verifier could compare the second input with the original; if there was a difference, a notch would be cut in the card to notify the keypunch operator that a correction was necessary. This means that the transfer from source document to machine-readable form was performed twice. Once in machine-readable form, the data would be checked by an editing program to ensure that it conformed to predefined constraints. Records that did not pass the edit checks were rejected and printed on an exception list for immediate correction, or they were removed for later correction and placed in later batch runs. The records that initially passed the edit checks were input to batch programs that processed the data.

Several problems are inherent in such a system. They can be illustrated with a personnel transaction—hiring a new employee. New employees must fill out several forms with such information as name, address, telephone number, Social Security number, and dependents. The forms are checked by a personnel administrator to ensure they are complete, placed in a collection basket, and forwarded to the data-processing department, where they are distributed to data entry personnel for translation into machine-readable form—punched cards, for this example. After being punched, the cards are verified and input to the edit program. A card that fails the edit test is reunited with its source document to determine whether the data is punched incorrectly. If not, the source documents are sent back to the point of origination for correction, and the process begins again.

Compared to an online system, the problems with such a system are excess handling, increased potential for document loss, separation of data capture from data entry and verification, and slow reaction of the system to data entry or edit errors. Because the data is captured in one location and processed in another, it must be packaged and transmitted. Each handling or move increases the probability of loss. The personnel ultimately responsible for entering the data into the system are less able to catch errors than the personnel involved in the original capture of the data. Finally, if errors in the data are encountered, it may take several hours or days for the corrections to be made. An online system avoids these problems because the personnel who capture the data are also usually the ones who enter the data into the system. Errors in input are immediately flagged and corrected at the source. In addition, the resulting database is more current and accurate.

Edit Test Types

Numerous types of edit tests are employed in online systems and batch editing systems. The most common are described below.

Existence.   A field can be designated as optional or mandatory. Mandatory fields must be provided. The edit check for a mandatory field simply checks that some entry has been made in that field, it does not assure that the data is correct.

Class Tests.   A *class test* checks a data field for class or type, most commonly numeric and alphabetic. The first name of an employee would be checked to ensure that it contained only letters, and a Social Security number field would be checked to ensure that it contained only numbers. More sophisticated systems contain additional classes of data, such as dates and currency types.

Size Tests.   A *size test* can ensure that a minimum and possibly maximum number of characters have been entered. A size test might require a U.S. postal zip code to have either five or nine digits and a state abbreviation to have exactly two characters. It is seldom necessary to specify a maximum data size in an edit check since the amount of space allocated on the input record or the database record will establish the maximum length. However, in some instances field lengths defined on records are sometimes made larger than the size required for current usage. This allows for ease of future expansion. For example, the field for a U.S. postal zip code could have been sized at ten digits during the era of five-digit zip codes. In this situation a user could accidentally enter a code greater than five digits, and thus a maximum size edit would be prudent.

Range Tests.   *Range tests* ensure that data falls into prescribed ranges. An employee's salary may be checked to ensure that it is within salary guidelines or a numeric field representing a student's grade point average can be checked to ensure that it is between 0.0 and 4.0, inclusive. Range checks can also be used to flag unusual data entries and mark them for special attention, such as in the following example of a city tax assessment system. When the tax base was computed, a key-punch error gave a 10-year-old automobile an assessed valuation of $7 million rather than $700. This incorrect figure was used in calculating the amount of property tax each resident would have to pay so the city could meet its budget. The owner of the car refused to pay a tax in excess of $200,000 and the city had to borrow money. A range check in the edit program could alert tax assessors to such inconsistencies or draw attention to excessively high property valuations.

Value Tests.   *Value tests* are similar in some respects to range tests. Where a range test checks the limits of a field's value (such as, is the field greater than zero and less than 100?), a value test checks for discrete values, such a M or F for sex or O, A, B, or AB for blood type.

Hash Totals.   In data entry and other applications where groups of numbers are entered, a hand-computed total may also be included as input. When the data is edited, the total is recomputed and compared with the input total. If the two agree, it is assumed that the data was input correctly; otherwise, the batch is rejected and checked for errors. A related technique is the *checksum*, a number computed from the input data by the sending system and transmitted to the receiver so that when the edit tests are performed, the checksum can be computed again and checked.

Data Consistency versus Data Accuracy

The more that is known about a set of data, the more accurate the edit checks can be. However, edit checks do not ensure the accuracy of the data, only its consistency. Thus, when a blood of type O is mistakenly entered as type A, the value is consistent with acceptable values, even though the data is in error.

When to Perform Edit Tests

Data editing can be employed at any point in an online system, preferably as close to the terminal as possible. For an intelligent terminal that would be at the terminal itself. When intelligent terminals are not being used, the edit tests could be performed at the TCP or in the application program, with the TCP being the better of the two. Performing the edit tests as close to user input as possible decreases the amount of processing required for records that do not pass the tests.

FORMATTING

Formatting of application messages is a function of the OSI presentation layer. When working in page mode, formatting also includes screen formatting, which is generally done by the access method or the TCP. Data or message formatting can include encryption, as discussed earlier. One type of formatting, compression, can be used to make more efficient use of the communications link. The objective of compression is to reduce the number of characters that need to be transmitted.

Data Compression

A message can be compressed by several techniques, all of which attempt to reduce the size of the message and thus allow more efficient use of the communication links.

Repeating Character Compression.   Perhaps the most common compression technique is *repeating character compression*. This algorithm replaces repeating characters with one character plus a character count. For instance, with a 40-character address field, an address consisting of only

123 Main Street

Uncompressed

Figure 13-7 Data
Compression

```
000000000011111111112222222222233333333334
12345678901234567890123456789001234567890
```

2

123 Main Street5

Compressed

15 characters would contain 25 blanks, which by repeating character compression would be replaced with a byte-count field and a character field, as illustrated in Figure 13-7.

In the compressed message in Figure 13-7 the "25" represents a binary encoded byte. Thus, up to 255 bytes can be represented. It is also necessary to be able to distinguish a byte count field from an actual data field, which can be done by setting the high-order bit in the field to on (and thus limiting the repeat count to 127 characters). Alternatively, it can be done by using two bytes for the repeat count, the first byte being a reserved flag byte to indicate that compression is being used and the second representing the actual character count. The important aspect of compression is that the system be able to distinguish repeat counts from actual data.

Common Word Compression. *Common word compression* is a technique whereby commonly used words can be represented by one or two bytes. In a hospital application, common words like *patient, insurance, bill, x-ray, doctor,* and *nurse* can each be represented by one character. Again, the encoding or compression scheme must include a flag of some sort to distinguish compressed data from uncompressed data. For example, the word *insurance* can be represented by the two-character sequence ESC I.

Front End Compression. *Front end compression* is a technique whereby records with like beginnings are compressed. This algorithm is similar to that of repeating character compression, except the repetition is of the first characters in a record. It is used more frequently in database management systems for index compression than in data communications applications. Figure 13-8 gives an example of front end compression performed on a subset of a personnel file that is arranged by employee last name.

Uncompressed	Compressed
LAMB, CAROLYN	LAMB, CAROLYN
LAMB, MARY	6MARY
LAMB, RICHARD	6RICHARD
LAMBDEN, RON	4DEN, RON
LAMBDIN, PEGGY	5IN, PEGGY
LAMBERT, DONNA	4ERT, DONNA
LAMBIRD, GEORGE	4IRD, GEORGE

Figure 13-8 Front
End Compression

Other Types of Formatting

Other types of formatting may also be required. At each of the OSI levels above the physical level, headers and control characters can be added to a message. Header information would include transaction identification, originating terminal, time stamp, transaction type, destination information, routing information, sequence numbers, and so on. Examples of the type of formatting that could be done at each of the OSI levels follows.

Application Layer Formatting.   The basic concern at the application level is to provide the data that will be sent to the application layer on the receiving side. Formatting by the application layer is meant to organize the data into fields and to order the fields into records. Some systems, such as the U.S. bankwire system, use variable-length fields, with separators as field delimiters. Most business systems use fixed-length fields organized into records of variable or fixed length, like those in a COBOL program. The only requirement is that the sending and receiving applications agree on the message format. The application can also attach a descriptive header to the message, possibly containing a transaction identification, date and time stamp, originating terminal or application, and an identifier telling the receiving application what to do with the message—for instance, add to database, modify a database record, or database inquiry. One possible message built by the application level is given in Figure 13-9.

Presentation Layer Formatting.   The application layer passes the message to the presentation layer. In the example of Figure 13-10, the only change made by the presentation layer is compression.

Session Layer Formatting.   The next layer is the session layer, responsible for establishing the connection, recovery should the session be disrupted, flow control, and dialogue rules. For the message in Figure 13-11, the ses-

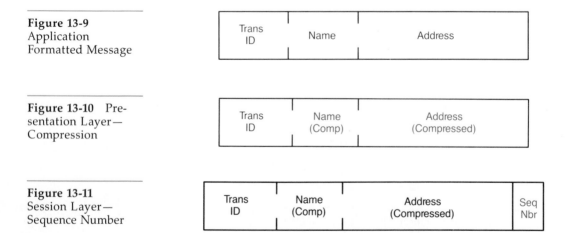

Figure 13-9
Application
Formatted Message

Figure 13-10   Presentation Layer—
Compression

Figure 13-11
Session Layer—
Sequence Number

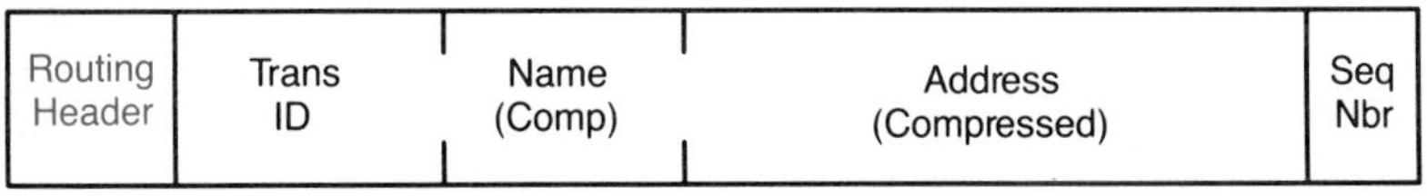

Routing Header	Trans ID	Name (Comp)	Address (Compressed)	Seq Nbr

Figure 13-12
Network Layer—
Destination Header

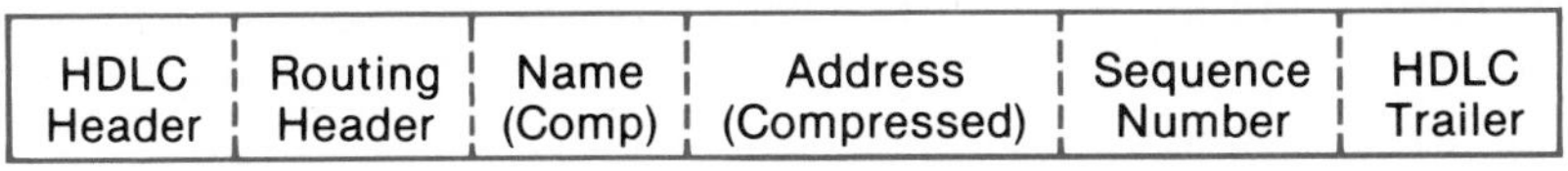

HDLC Header	Routing Header	Name (Comp)	Address (Compressed)	Sequence Number	HDLC Trailer

Figure 13-13 Final Message Format with HDLC Protocol

sion layer has appended only a message sequence number, which can be used for recovery and possibly flow control. This is not the same sequence number as the data link control sequencing for HDLC.

Transport Layer Formatting. The transport layer in this example assists in making the connection between the session layers at each node; however, this activity does not affect the message. The transport layer also breaks a long message into smaller transmission blocks if necessary and enables its peer on the receiving side to reconstruct the message. Since the message is relatively short, the transport layer adds nothing to the message in this example.

Network Layer Formatting. One function of the network layer is routing. In performing this function it can append the routing information to the message, as illustrated in Figure 13-12.

Data Link Layer Formatting. At the data link layer, the control information is included in the message. This includes the headers, block check characters, and transparency control characters if needed. The changes that would be made to the messages at this level are described in Chapter 6.

Device Formatting. The formatting of messages is only one part of the formatting that must be done. The other factor in data communications is *device formatting*, which means preparing the message for display on a specific type of terminal, printer, log file, or similar output device. For page mode terminals, the message and data fields within the message must be defined by control or escape sequences. The formatting capabilities are described in Chapter 4. For printed output, field alignment, page numbering, titles, subtitles, column headings, and carriage control must be inserted. For log files, record blocking and message formatting must be accomplished. The message in its final transmission format is shown in Figure 13-13.

ERROR DETECTION AND RECOVERY

Certain aspects of error detection and recovery have already been discussed in previous chapters, specifically with regard to the various redundancy checks and the send and receive counts in HDLC. These checks provide detection of lost or garbled messages, and the recovery technique is usually to retransmit the message or messages that are in error. Another level of recovery in data communications systems is the recovery of the system once a message has arrived and before it is processed and its response returned to the user. In the ideal situation this type of recovery is coordinated with database recovery. Although individual implementations may differ somewhat in their approach, the basic elements of such a recovery system are outlined in this section.

When a message arrives at a node, a certain amount of processing must be accomplished to satisfy the message requirements, such as forward the message immediately to the next node, store the message and forward it as time allows, or process the message and return the results to a terminal or other output device. During this processing cycle the application(s) processing the message, or the system itself, may fail. This section discusses how recovery might be effected. Not all systems adopt the approach discussed here; of those that do, some have yet to implement all the features in the following discussion.

When a node receives a message and acknowledges receipt to the sender, responsibility for the message is transferred from the sender to the receiver. This means the receiving node must be able to re-create the message and ensure its correct processing in the event of almost any possible failure. Designers of simple terminal systems sometimes take the view that it is the responsibility of the terminal operator to resubmit any possibly lost messages in the event of a failure. This approach can be justified only on the grounds that it is easier than implementing more sophisticated software that would resolve most of the problems automatically. Although such recovery systems slow the system and increase processor utilization, these resources still usually cost less than does relying on an operator to recover transactions, usually without sufficient knowledge of what occurred.

Message Logging (Safe Storing)

To be sure that a message can be re-created, it should be logged to a file before being acknowledged. The object of the recovery process is to close all windows of vulnerability and create a system in which no messages are lost and all are processed exactly once. If message receipt is acknowledged and then the message is logged to an audit file, there is still a small window of time—perhaps 50 milliseconds—during which a system failure could prevent the message from being re-created. For example, the failure might occur after acknowledgment has been returned but before the write to the log file has been completed. In this case the message will have been lost. Furthermore, it is insufficient to initiate the write to the log file and acknowledge the message before the log write is successfully completed. In this case queues on the log device might delay the write, or a file error could occur that prevents the write from being completed. Thus, the acknowledgment will have already been sent and a failure could again cause the message to be lost. Since it is typically the responsibility of the receiver to be able to re-create the message once it has been acknowledged, it is important to design the system so that reception acknowledgment is sent only after the message is logged.

Database-System Consistency

In addition to the message being logged, a transaction must be started for update transactions. A transaction is a logical collection of processing activities that either will be completely accomplished or will leave that database in the same state as before the transaction started. This complicated-sounding idea is actually uncomplicated and can be shown by a simple example. Consider a banking application in which a customer wants to transfer money from her checking account to her savings account. We will designate the checking account record by the letter C and the savings account record by the letter S. At the beginning of this transaction, Record C has a balance of $1000 and Record S has a balance of $3000.

A transaction will be started indicating that $500 is to be deducted from the checking account (Record C) and deposited into the savings account (Record S). After attempting to process the transaction, the database can be in only two possible states: Records C and S contain either $500 and $3500 or $1000 and $3000. The combination of $500 and $3000 and the combination of $1000 and $3500 are inconsistent states. If a failure should occur when Record C has attained the value $500 and Record S still has the value $3000, recovery must be invoked. The recovery process must either roll the value of Record C back to $1000 or roll the value of Record S forward to $3500. This transaction is used in the following discussion. Figure 13-14 illustrates the various states of the database for the transaction.

Message Processing

Once the message has been written to the log file (also referred to as *safe storing* the record), the acknowledgment returned to the sender, the data edited, and a transaction started, the message can be processed. The transaction is forwarded to an application process. The unique transaction ID created when the transaction began is passed along with the message.

Database Update.   The application accesses the two records to be updated in the database and issues a database write request for both records. Before the updates are posted to the database, the database management system writes the before- and after-images to an audit file. The *before-images* are balances of $1000 and $3000 for Records C and S, respectively. The *after-images* for those records are $500 and $3500. After the audit writes have been completed, the writes to the database can be initiated. Just as it was

Figure 13-14 Database States during Transaction

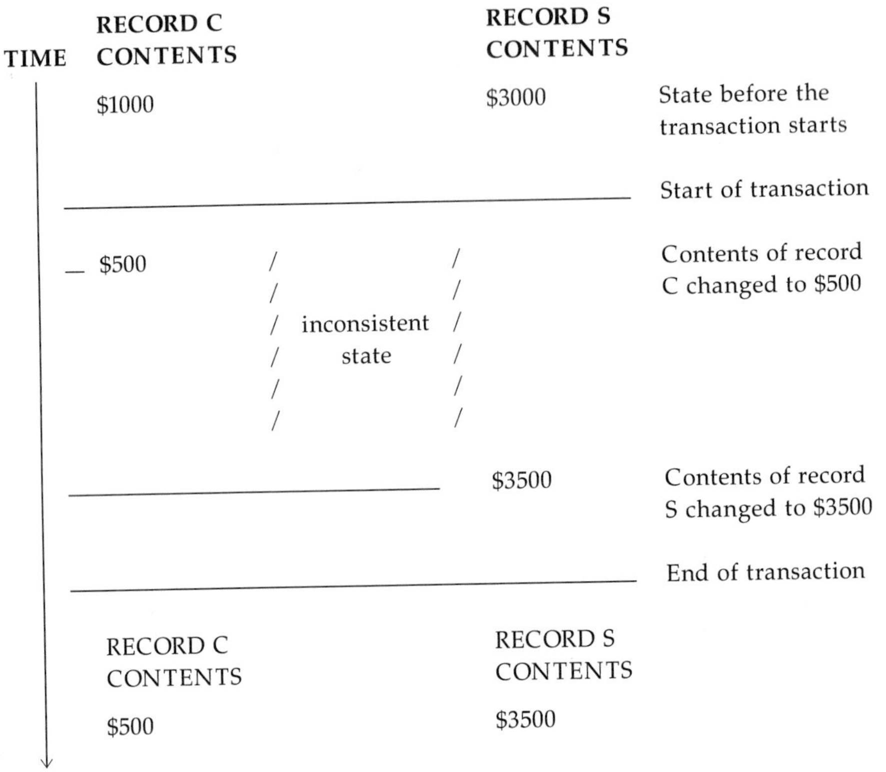

TIME	RECORD C CONTENTS	RECORD S CONTENTS	
	$1000	$3000	State before the transaction starts
			Start of transaction
	— $500		Contents of record C changed to $500
	/ / / inconsistent / / state / / / / /		
		$3500	Contents of record S changed to $3500
			End of transaction

RECORD C CONTENTS	RECORD S CONTENTS
$500	$3500

*The data base must be left in a consistent state—either the state at the beginning of the transaction or the state at the end of the transaction

incorrect to acknowledge the message before completing the write to the log file, it is incorrect to write to the database before the before- and after-image writes are completed, for to do so would create a small time window that would make recovery impossible: The database could be updated before the audit writes are made. If a failure occurs before capturing the audit images on disk or tape, the transaction might be unrecoverable. In some systems both the database and audit writes may be deferred until a later time, with the records held in memory for some time to expedite processing. Deferring the writes does not alter the fact that writes to the audit trail must be completed before the writes to the database.

Response Message.　Having completed the database updates, the application prepares a response and returns it to the TCP. The TCP then ends the transaction by writing an end transaction record to the transaction log and ensuring that all audit buffers have been written to the audit file. After both of these events have occurred, the transaction is completed and the response message can be sent back to the originating terminal.

Recovery Is Possible after Safe Storing

Recovery following failure is a joint effort between database and data communications systems. At any point after the safe storing of the original message, recovery to a consistent state is possible. Suppose that a failure occurs after the application has received the message and modified the first but not the second database record. The database system begins the recovery process first. When the system is restored to operational status, the transaction will be observed to be incomplete. The database management recovery system will use the before-images it captured to restore the database to its state before the beginning of the transaction. The before-image of the updated record is written back to the database, thus erasing the update. Next, the database recovery process sends a message to the TCP advising that the transaction was unsuccessful and the before-images have been posted. The TCP retrieves the message associated with that transaction, starts a new transaction, and forwards the message to the application.

Retry Limit. The same transaction could fail again, always possible because of problems with database files being full, access method tables being full, or unusual data conditions, such as division by zero. To protect against an infinite recovery loop, the recovery system should have a retry limit that prevents a transaction from being restarted indefinitely. If the retry limit is exceeded, the failed transaction must be dealt with. One outcome is to display an appropriate error message on the computer operator's console and to notify the initiator of the transaction that it cannot be completed. The computer operator must then follow the necessary procedures to have the problem corrected. When the cause of the failure has been removed, the transaction can be resubmitted. The transaction can be restarted from the transaction log or from the user. In some cases it is not appropriate to restart from the transaction log. For example, the transaction may have been to book a traveler on a flight. If the system were unable to process the transaction, the traveler may have booked the flight with another carrier. Thus, the exact recovery procedures that are followed are application-dependent.

Audit Trails. Like security systems, recovery systems are not completely reliable. If system failure includes failure of the device (tape or disk) containing the transaction and database audit logs, automatic recovery becomes impossible. In such instances a database backup version is reloaded and as many after-images as possible are reposted to the database to bring it forward in time. Those images on the medium that failed are not available, of course, so some processing is lost. To limit the exposure due to failure of the audit media, many systems allow the user to have multiple copies of the audit trails. If both a tape drive and a disk drive are available, then although for most recovery processes the disk drive would be used because of the random access capability it provides, the tape could be used when the disk is inaccessible. The next chapter contains further discussion regarding transaction design in an online system.

OTHER SOFTWARE FUNCTIONS

Some of the capabilities discussed in previous chapters can also be implemented in software. These functions include the gathering of statistical information, polling, speed conversion, queue handling, flow control, network control, buffering, blocking and deblocking, dialing and answering a telephone line, performance monitoring, and the person-machine interface. These functions are found in many data communications systems as adjuncts to applications. They make the applications more secure, reliable, or efficient. Two applications, electronic mail and time-staged delivery systems, are frequently found in data communications systems, and information regarding these applications is often found in the literature on data communications systems. Therefore, we provide a brief description of each.

Electronic Mail

Electronic mail, also referred to as *E-mail*, is the ability to transfer messages electronically. A data communications system serves as the delivery medium, with E-mail software providing the network mail delivery function. Corporations using electronic mail may use a private system, a public system, or a combination of both. A private mail system is one under the complete control of a corporation. Naturally, electronic messages may flow over circuits not controlled by the corporation, such as leased lines or X.25 networks. However, a private mail network is used only by the members of the corporation or their designated agents. A public mail system is similar in some respects to an X.25 network. Corporations subscribe to the mail service from an electronic mail provider. The provider is responsible for managing a delivery network, administration of the network and mail software, and providing ancillary mail services such as hard-copy backup. U.S. providers of public network mail systems include General Telephone and Electronics (GTE), Western Union, Tymshare, and MCI.

Some corporations use both a private and public electronic mail system. The private mail system is used exclusively for intracompany communication. Reasons for using a public system include access to personnel at locations that do not have direct access to the private system and communication between corporations. For example, a service organization could use a public mail system to communicate with its customers and a private mail system to correspond with its employees.

Perhaps the most significant advantage of an electronic mail system is ease of use. A message may be sent from one user to another without having the message typed, placed in a mailing envelope, routed through a public or private mail delivery system, and delivered to a specific location. By contrast, in many systems, an electronic mail user may access electronic mail from any location having a terminal. Thus, a manager who is traveling from one office to another can access mail regardless of her location.

For corporations with correspondents spread over multiple time zones, an electronic mail system can augment the telephone system and assist in eliminating the problems of communications across time zones. Consider a company with offices in London, England, and Sydney, Australia. Because of time differences, there may be no overlap in the normal working hours. Electronic mail messages can be used to provide much of the necessary communication. When personal communication is required, the mail system can be used to make an appointment for a telephone conversation.

Distribution of mail electronically is rapid; messages usually are available to recipients almost instantly. If a message is distributed to several people, all will have access to the message at nearly the same time. By contrast, conventional mail systems may allow a local user to receive the mail almost at once while a remote recipient may not receive it for several days. For corporations with a network already in place, an electronic mail system can be quite cost effective. It can eliminate or reduce telephone and conventional mail costs while providing a fast, convenient form of communication. In contrast to telephone systems, an electronic mail system allows users to peruse and respond to messages at their convenience.

Mail System Features

A wide variety of features is provided by mail systems. Some of the common ones are given below.

Create and Edit.   All systems provide the ability to compose and change messages. Some provide a text editor for this purpose. Others not only provide a text editor but also allow a variety of word processing systems to be used for message composition.

Send and Receive.   Another essential feature is the ability to send and receive messages. There are a variety of ways in which recipients can be designated; most are based on individual names, such as SMITH, JOHN, or user groups, such as ACCOUNTING.MANAGER. Some systems allow a variety of schemes for identifying recipients. Mail users are also associated with a mail address to which messages are sent, such as a network node.

Broadcast and Distribution Lists.   Messages may be broadcast to mail users in a variety of ways. Some systems provide a true broadcast capability to all users; for instance, announcement of corporate stock prices could be distributed to *.*. This designation places the message in all users' mailboxes. Using the same user identification scheme, a narrower broadcast to all members of the accounting work group could be designated with an address of ACCOUNTING.*.

A third dissemination mechanism for reaching a group of users is the distribution list. Users are often able to create a list of recipients. A list of all members of the corporate ski team, for example, could be placed in a list called SKIERS. A message could then be sent to SKIERS and the mail system would extract the names from the list and send the message to each person or group on the list. Some systems allow distribution lists to be embedded in other distribution lists. The list SKIERS could be composed of distribution lists for EUROPEAN-SKIERS, US-SKIERS, and ASIAN-SKIERS. Furthermore, US-SKIERS could be composed of distribution lists for WEST-COAST-SKIERS, ROCKY-MTN-SKIERS, and EAST-COAST-SKIERS. Distribution lists may be private and thus restricted to use by the originator, or they may be public and available for use by all mail users.

Classes of Mail.   Some systems allow multiple mail classes, such as "first," "second," and "third" class. First-class could be used for business correspondence between individuals and groups, second-class for corporate broadcast information such as stock quotes and product announcements, and third-class for junk mail such as that regarding garage sales. Within first-class mail it is often possible to have "registered" or "certified" messages. These two categories provide the sender with notification of message arrival at the destination or notification that individual recipients have examined the mail message. Thus, a mail message announcing an important meeting can be distributed as certified mail, and the sender would receive a certification for each person receiving the message. Included within mail classes may be a priority scheme, in which priority mail may be given higher consideration by the delivery algorithm. Urgent mail messages may be flagged as such and listed in a special area of the recipients' mailbox so they can receive special attention.

Message Forwarding and Routing.   In most mail systems the recipient of a mail message can forward it to other mail users. In addition to passing the letter along, the forwarder may also be able to edit the letter before redirecting it. A variation of this that is sometimes supported is memo routing. A message may be sent to a distribution list in a way similar to a paper memo with an attached circulation list. The first person on the list gets the message, examines it, possibly adds comments, and then releases it. Upon release, the memo is then automatically routed to the next person on the distribution list, and so on. This feature allows automatic circulation of a letter down a management chain of command, enabling each level of managers to include their comments within the communique.

Electronic Filing and Printing.   All mail systems provide a mechanism for printing mail messages. Most also allow messages to be filed on a storage medium, usually a disk drive. Often a system comes with a named set of folders, such as "in-basket," "out-basket," and "waste-basket," where letters may be placed. In many mail systems, the user can also define electronic folders into which messages may be placed. Folders logically provide the same capability as folders in filing cabinets. For example, a user can create electronic message folders for budget, personnel, meeting notes, and so on.

Mail Agents.   Some systems allow users to create programmatic mail agents. These would allow capabilities such as:

1. Deleting all third-class mail
2. Notifying all senders of a mail forwarding address
3. Automatically forwarding mail to another user (for example, a user who is traveling or on vacation specifying another recipient for his messages during his absence)
4. Automatically filing messages in a folder

Some systems provide default agents such as the vacation agent function described in Point 3.

Security and Expiration.   Most systems provide security mechanisms for electronic mail; ordinarily this is an identification and authentication scheme. A smaller number of systems provide an ability to encrypt messages. To reduce storage requirements, mail messages may be accompanied with an expiration date. Thus, third-class mail can be automatically removed from all system nodes if not read within a given period. All messages may be given a default expiration date; moreover, expiration dates can typically be assigned for individual messages.

Security of electronic mail messages raises several concerns. Laws that cover tampering with post office mail do not usually apply to electronic mail messages. As noted above, password security cannot guarantee that the confidentiality of mail messages is protected. Moreover, system managers may have the ability to examine mail messages and mail messages will also be backed up to tapes during an installation's standard backup procedure. In one instance of a public subscription electronic mail system, users have complained that the mail administrators examined personal mail messages. Companies having or using electronic mail systems need to have a policy regarding the type of data that should not be entered into an electronic mail system and the safeguarding of the backups of electronic mail messages.

Help and Interactive Messages.   Some mail systems support an interactive mail capability wherein users can essentially carry on an electronic mail conversation. With this feature messages are immediately displayed on the work station of the recipient. Most systems also provide online help capability, and some have levels of help. With different help levels new users can get detailed instructions on the use of commands, while more experienced users receive condensed help messages.

Mail Administration

Administering a mail system can be a time-consuming responsibility. User lists and distribution lists must be established and maintained. Periodically old mail messages may need to be manually removed from the system. There is also the potential for mail to be misused, which may include sending a high volume of broadcast junk mail, hate/love letters, and advertisements for personal gain. One responsibility of mail administration is to set corporate policy for acceptable and unacceptable use of the mail system.

Electronic mail is becoming a significant communication tool for many companies. For some corporations, it has become the fundamental means of communication. In a private mail system where the communications network already exists, an electronic mail system can help reduce telephone and postage charges. It allows messages to be quickly composed and delivered. Recipients can review their mail at their convenience, eliminating some of the interruptions of telephone communications.

Electronic Mail Interchange Standard—X.400

One of the first standards for the application layer of the OSI model pertains to the interface of electronic mail systems. The *X.400 standard*, developed by the Consultative Committee on International Telegraph and Telephony (CCITT), provides a platform for the implementation of a worldwide electronic message-handling service. A variety of electronic mail systems is in use today. Connecting these systems to provide message exchange between heterogeneous mail systems is the focus of the X.400 standard. X.400 is to mail systems as the OSI reference model is to the interconnection of different networks.

The implementation of X.400 is based on a hierarchy of entities. The hierarchy is used for implementation of worldwide message distribution and for addressing. At the top of the hierarchy is a country, followed by a public administration agency or private regulated operating agency, a company, and a user. Addresses for the senders and recipients of a mail message are generated from this hierarchy. An address is a country name plus a public utility name plus a company name plus a user name.

An X.400 system allows users to exchange electronic messages. The users can be in the same or different companies, can be using the same or different mail systems, and can be in the same or different countries. Mail transfer is accomplished via mail agent processes. Each user has a mail agent called a *user agent* (*UA*). A user agent allows a user to compose a message, provides recipient addresses, and receives messages. The inter-

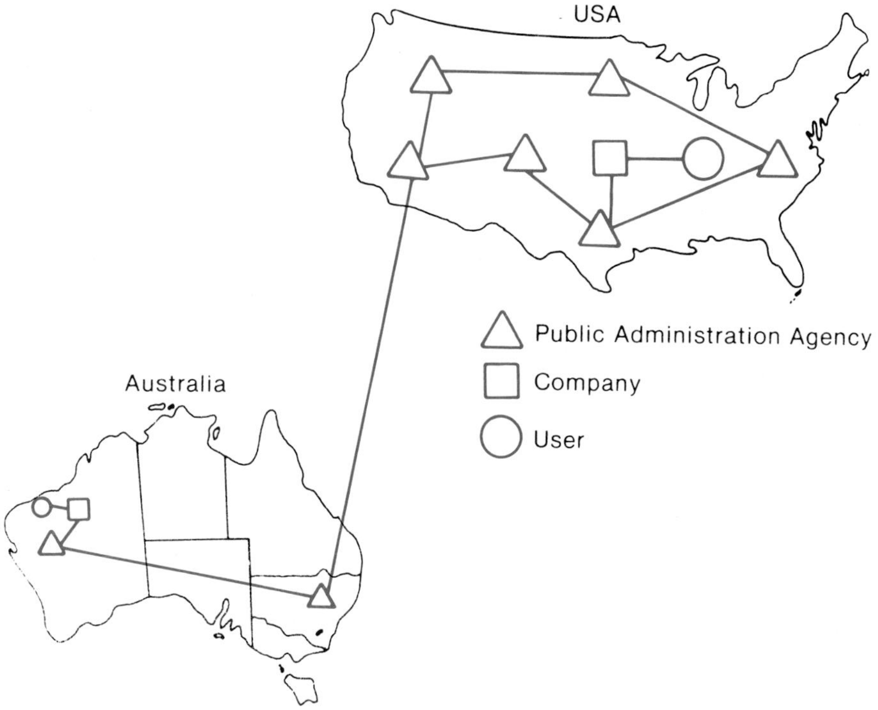

Figure 13-15 X.400 Connection

△ Public Administration Agency

□ Company

○ User

face between UAs is accomplished by *message transfer agents* (*MTAs*). An MTA can service none, one, or several UAs. The network of MTAs is responsible for taking a message from a sender's UA and delivering it to the recipient's UA. This is depicted in Figure 13-15. In the figure a U.S. user is communicating with an Australian user.

The X.400 standard describes two different domains, a *private domain*, which represents a private electronic mail system represented by a company in the above hierarchy, and a *public domain*, which represents a delivery and interconnection network corresponding to the public administration agency in the hierarchy. In some ways the public domain provides a function similar to that provided by an X.25 network—the ability to provide connections and message routing among systems. The public domain is called an *administrative management domain* (*ADMD*) and the private domain is called a *private management domain* (*PRMD*). An interdomain interface is defined to establish protocols for passing messages among different domains. Protocols are defined for communicating between ADMDs, between PRMDs and ADMDs, and for the contents of the message itself. X.400 is significant because it establishes a standard for user communication. It has been implemented in several systems. If universally followed, computer users anywhere will be able to communicate with each other electronically.

The CCITT X.500 Standard

Imagine the complexities of managing a worldwide X.400 electronic mail system. Currently, there are over 2.4 million users of public electronic mail and 12.8 million users in private companies. By 1993, these numbers are expected to rise to 6 million and 48 million respectively (Whitten, 1989). Keeping track of all these users and their mail addresses is a complex task that is addressed by the *X.500 standard*. The X.500 standard specifies how to create a directory system to maintain electronic mail user names and their network addresses. Thus, if a user needs to send a mail message to another user but does not know that user's mail address, a search of the X.500 directory will provide the necessary information. The directory will contain the addresses of mail users worldwide.

Time-Staged Delivery Systems

Time-staged delivery systems have some characteristics of a mail system. Time-staged delivery software allows users to identify a transmission package, designate one or more recipients of the package, initiate the delivery of the package, and specify a delivery priority. If we relate time-staged delivery and electronic mail to regular mail service, electronic mail is like express mail service while time-staged delivery is like parcel post or surface mail. Electronic mail is usually oriented toward short messages of several pages or less. Time-staged delivery systems may be used for short messages, for transaction routing, or to transmit entire files.

With time-staged delivery, the user specifies a required delivery time. The system then schedules the message transmission to meet the requested goal. Suppose that a user needs to send a lengthy report from New York to each of five manufacturing plants and that the message must be available at each plant by 9 A.M. local time. The report to London needs to arrive several hours before the one destined for California, so it will have a higher priority in transmission than the California-bound package. The delivery system can use the delivery time to defer transmission until a more convenient time. Rather than sending data in real time when the system may be quite busy, it can delay transmission until a less busy time, such as early morning hours. In distributed processing environments, the ability to designate transmission packages and delivery times can be an important capability. An example of a time-staged delivery system is IBM's SNA delivery system (SNADS).

SUMMARY

Security is a delaying factor used to deter unauthorized personnel from gaining access to a system and to provide time to catch those who try.

Security of systems and networks is of growing concern to system implementers. Security can be implemented at multiple levels within a system. There is an overhead to implementing security precautions, and the cost of the security system should not exceed the potential loss from unauthorized use of the system. Reliability and presentation of data are very important to the success of any system. Many software functions in a data communications network handle these requirements. Data is encrypted to prevent unauthorized disclosure, compressed to economize on line time and disk storage, edited to eliminate as many errors as possible, and formatted to make it understandable and presentable. Data is formatted for output as well as for exchange between processes and media.

The error detection and recovery discussed in this chapter are different from the error checks made by VRC, LRC, and CRC discussed earlier. This chapter discussed error detection and recovery in connection with system and application recovery. The data communications and database systems should work together to provide a comprehensive recovery that leaves the system in a consistent state, with no transactions lost or processed more than once. The recovery system should also recover the users of the system and establish or help establish their restart points. Two network applications that are becoming commonplace in networks are electronic mail and time-staged message delivery systems. These provide communication among network users and move data from one node to another in an orderly, timely manner.

Key Terms

after-image	physical security
audit trail	plain text
authentication	public key encryption
before-image	range test
cipher text	rearrangement
class test	recovery
common word compression	repeating character compression
compression	safe store
data editing	security
data encryption standard (DES)	size test
electronic mail	substitution
encryption	time-staged delivery
existence test	trapdoor encryption method
front end compression	user profile
hash totals	value test
identification	verification
message logging	virus
National Bureau of Standards (NBS)	X.400
password	X.500

Review Questions

1. What is the greatest security risk a company faces? Why is this so?
2. How has data communications complicated the ability to provide security of data?
3. Describe a number of physical security features and how they protect unauthorized access.
4. What is data encryption? What benefits does it provide?
5. What are the basic operations used to encrypt data? What happens if the encryption key(s) is lost?
6. What is user identification and authentication? Describe three methods for accomplishing identification and authentication.
7. How can you recognize and overcome unauthorized access attempts?
8. What is a computer virus? How can you protect against computer viruses?
9. Why are data edits necessary? Can they ensure the accuracy of data? Explain your answer.
10. Describe:
    a. range test
    b. existence test
    c. size test
    d. class test
11. Why is data compression helpful in a communications network?
12. Why is error detection and recovery important?
13. Describe the steps a system might take to provide a good recovery environment.
14. Describe eight features that might be found in an electronic mail system.
15. Describe the motivation behind the X.400 and X.500 standards.
16. What are the benefits or uses of a time-staged message delivery system?

Exercises

1. Complete the encryption example for the message DATA COMMUNICATIONS started in Figure 13-3.
2. If you did Exercise 1, decrypt the message using the algorithm given in Figure 13-4 and the example of Figure 13-5.
3. Investigate the security features of a system to which you have access. Describe the strong and weak points of the security provided.
4. Research the security capabilities of Novell Corporation's Netware version 2.15 or later. Describe how users and groups are managed. What file security attributes are there? What provisions exist for password administration (requiring users to change passwords, time and location restrictions, and so on)?

5. Research the literature and find three incidents of virus or viral-like infections. What problems were caused and how were the problems corrected? Were the perpetrators apprehended? If so, what happened to them?

6. Computer crime can result from a lack of security. Find three instances of crimes (including intentional destruction of data) and describe the nature of each. What security measures could have prevented these crimes?

7. Using the recovery mechanism described in this chapter, discuss how recovery would be implemented if a failure occurred (a) after safe storing the message and before sending it to the application and (b) after all the database writes have been completed (assume two writes) but before the end of the transaction.

8. What will happen in an online system if a data edit check fails?

9. Investigate an application to which you have access and describe the data edit checks it uses. If you do not have access to an application, pick one, describe two data records used in the application and the edit checks you would use for those fields.

10. Design an input record for registering a student in a class. Describe the edit checks that could be used to verify each field.

11. Investigate an electronic mail system and determine which of the features described earlier in the chapter it provides. Does it provide any capabilities not listed in the chapter? If so, what are they?

12. Research the literature and find three applications that use a time-staged message delivery system.

References

Ball, Michael. "To Catch a Thief: Lessons in Systems Security." *Computerworld*, December 14, 1987.

Berg, John L. "Security Report." *Infosystems* 22, July 1975.

Bryce, Heather. "The NBS Data Encryption Standard: Products and Principles." *Mini-Micro Systems* 14, March 1981.

Bush, John. "Vendors Want Electronic-Mail Blueprint. Will X.400 Be It?" *Data Communications*, Vol. 15, No. 1, January 1986.

Cook, Stephanie. "U.K., West Germany to Connect via First European X.400 Link." *Data Communications*, Vol. 16, No. 3, March 1987.

"Cryptography and Data Communications." *Infosystems* 22, July 1975.

Diffie, Whitfield. "The Outlook for Computer Security." *Mini-Micro Systems* 2, October 1978.

Edwards, John. "X.400 Protocol Will Benefit Users, E-mail Firms." *PC Week* 3, October 14, 1986.

"Electronic Mail: User Boom." *Data Communications*, Vol. 15, No. 4, April 1986.

"Encryption Algorithm: Key Size Is the Thing." *Datamation* 22, March 1976.

Fiderio, Janet. "Voice, Finger, and Retina Scans: Can Biometrics Secure Your Shop?" *Computerworld*, February 15, 1988.

Fischer, Kristian, and Wilhelm F. Racke. "Integrating X.400 Message Handling into the IBM VM/SP Environment." *Sigcomm '87 Workshop Proceedings— Frontiers in Computer Communications Technology*, Vol. 17, No. 5. Stowe, Vermont, August 11–13, 1987. Menlo Park, CA: ACM Press, 1988. Special Issue.

Hellman, Martin E. "Commercial Encryption." *IEEE Network*, Vol. 1, No. 2, April 1987.

Hurst, Rebecca. "Don't Get Locked into Too Much Security." *Computerworld Focus: Corporate Assets in Peril*, Vol. 21, No. 22A, June 3, 1987.

Kinnucan, Paul. "Data Encryption Gurus: Tuchman and Meyer." *Mini-Micro Systems* 2, October 1978.

Meyer, Carl H., and Walter Tuchman. "Putting Data Encryption to Work." *Mini-Micro Systems* 2, October 1978.

Nabut, Martin. "Insider Crimes Threaten." *Computerworld Focus: Corporate Assets in Peril*, Vol. 21, No. 22A, June 3, 1987.

Naecker, Philip A. "Security: Security Checklist." *DEC Professional*, Vol. 8, No. 4, April 1989.

Newman, David B., Jr., Jim K. Omura, and Raymond L. Pickholtz. "Public Key Management for Network Security." *IEEE Network*, Vol. 1, No. 2, April 1987.

Rochlis, Jon A., and Mark W. Eichin. "With Microscope and Tweezers: The Worm from MIT's Perspective." *Communications of the ACM*, Vol. 32, No. 6, June 1989.

Seeley, Donn. "Password Cracking: A Game of Wits." *Communications of the ACM*, Vol. 32, No. 6, June 1989.

Solomon, Richard J. "The Encryption Controversy." *Mini-Micro Systems* 11, February 1978.

Spafford, Eugene H. "Crisis and Aftermath." *Communications of the ACM*, Vol. 32, No. 6, June 1989.

Stoll, Clifford. *The Cuckoo's Egg: Inside the World of Computer Espionage*. New York: Doubleday, 1989.

Tanenbaum, Andrew S. *Computer Networks*. Englewood Cliffs, NJ: Prentice-Hall, 1981.

Tucker, Michael. "Security in the First Degree." *Computerworld Focus: Corporate Assets in Peril*, Vol. 21, No. 22A, June 3, 1987.

Valentine, Ian R. "Why X.400?" *Telecommunications*, Vol. 21, No. 10, October 1987.

Whitten, David. "X.400: Breaking Vendor Boundaries for Enterprise-Wide E-Mail." *Telecommunications*, Vol. 23, No. 7, July 1989.

Systems Analysis

The Design Process
The Product Life Cycle
Transaction Design
Selecting Hardware and Software
Case Study
Additional Evaluation Considerations
System Configuration
Case Study Revisited

INTRODUCTION

In this chapter we discuss aspects of data communications analysis and design that have not been covered in previous chapters. This chapter includes:

An overview of the analysis and design process
The product life cycle
How to design efficient transactions
A method for selecting hardware and software
How to evaluate system availability and reliability
What should be included in a request for proposal
Considerations for configuring a system

At the conclusion of this chapter the Syncrasy case study shows how the chapter material can be applied.

THE DESIGN PROCESS

All design processes are oriented toward one goal: producing a product. In building a product designers need a plan that takes them from the point of conceptualization through implementation. The plan must have a progression of steps for defining the problem, proposing and evaluating solutions, selecting an approach, identifying constraints, designing the solution, and then implementing the solution. Some of the typical constraints that must be satisfied are cost effectiveness, good performance, ease of maintenance, ease of use, and so on.

THE PRODUCT LIFE CYCLE

The product life cycle recognizes that a product goes through several well-defined stages during its life. Designers identify four to six major product life cycle phases. Five phases are listed in Figure 14-1, and the characteristics of each are defined below. Other design approaches may use different descriptions for the phases or a different number of phases. Even though approaches may differ, the objectives and items produced remain generally the same. Throughout all phases of the design, there are feedback loops to previous steps. The design phases and feedback loops are illustrated in Figure 14-2. The significance of the feedback loops is twofold.

First, they recognize that designers must sometimes make design changes. For instance, designers may find in the design phase that one of the product requirements cannot be met within established cost constraints. In this event, there are four alternatives: (1) the cost constraints in the product requirements can be relaxed; (2) the product requirements can be relaxed to meet the cost constraints; (3) the problem definition can be changed to eliminate the need for the particular product requirement; or (4) the entire project can be canceled because none of the above is practical, meaning the problem cannot be satisfactorily solved within the established parameters and there is no viable alternative set of parameters. Feedback loops are used when evaluating and making these changes. Second, at the completion of each phase, a review is conducted to ensure that the results are consistent with the outputs of previous phases. Management approval is usually necessary before proceeding to the next phase. Feedback loops provide a self-checking mechanism to ensure that the project is staying on track.

Figure 14-1 Product Life Cycle Phases

1. Investigation
2. Analysis
3. Design
4. Implementation
5. Operation and Maintenance

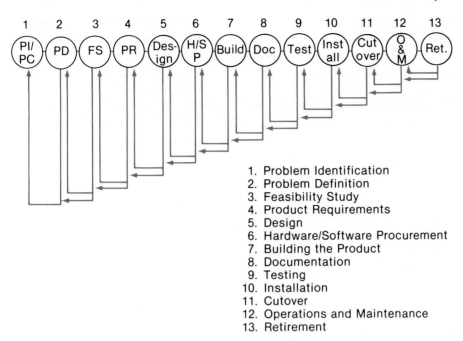

Figure 14-2 Product Life Cycle Feedback Loops

1. Problem Identification
2. Problem Definition
3. Feasibility Study
4. Product Requirements
5. Design
6. Hardware/Software Procurement
7. Building the Product
8. Documentation
9. Testing
10. Installation
11. Cutover
12. Operations and Maintenance
13. Retirement

Life Cycle Phases—Investigation

The first phase of the product life cycle is oriented toward identifying and defining the problem the product will solve. It consists of three subphases: problem identification/product conceptualization, problem definition, and the feasibility study. In our discussion we use a two-tiered numbering system in defining the phases. The first number represents one of the five major phases given in Figure 14-1, while the second number represents a subphase.

Phase 1.1—Problem Identification/Product Conceptualization. Products start from a need or problem, which can be real or anticipated. Once a problem has been identified, it must receive management attention. Management then allocates resources to investigate the problem. This phase is the only one of the 13 life cycle phases that may not have formal output. If there is a product, it is a problem statement.

Phase 1.2—Problem Definition. The first formal step in the design process is to define fully the problem being solved. It is very important at this point to distinguish between a problem to be resolved and solutions to the problem. If solutions work their way into the problem statement, the ability to examine all potential solutions is limited. The product of this phase is a document that fully identifies all facets of the problem.

Phase 1.3—Feasibility Study.   When the problem being solved is understood and defined, a feasibility study begins. A feasibility study is the first step in solving the problem. The objective of the feasibility study is to examine all possible solutions, identify the best ones, and determine if they are realistic. The product of this phase is a document detailing all solutions considered, their strengths and weaknesses, and why they were rejected or accepted. At the conclusion of this phase, the best solutions are examined in considerable detail before starting the process of developing or acquiring the solution. The best solutions are those that solve the problem in a cost-effective manner. In addition to documenting the alternatives considered and which will be the best approach, the feasibility study contains a recommendation for proceeding to the next phase, for abandoning the project because no realistic solutions can be found, or for revising the problem definition to permit a feasible solution (a feedback loop).

Life Cycle Phases—Analysis

The product investigation stage provides an organization with a basic understanding of the problem being solved. The analysis phase has one subphase, the purpose of which is to identify the requirements of the product.

Phase 2.1—Product Requirements.   This phase is sometimes referred to as preliminary design or the design objectives phase. The outcome of this step is a statement of both the design objectives and design constraints. Essentially this document is a contract between management and the designers as to what is to be produced and at what time and cost. This document is sometimes called a *functional specification* because it specifies the functions that must be included in the product.

Life Cycle Phases—Design

The design phase is sometimes divided into two subphases, preliminary or systems-level design and detailed design. For large projects a two-tiered approach is usually preferred. For smaller designs a one-level approach is often suitable. Only one subphase is described below.

Phase 3.1—Design.   This is one of the longest phases in the life cycle. There are many outcomes from this phase, and depending upon the specific design approach, the outcomes may vary. As a minimum, the outcomes will include an internal specification, an external specification, and a database design. Other deliverables typically include prototypes, product models, and logic and data flow diagrams. For a software system, the *internal specification* details how the developers view the system. It describes the modules and algorithms for building the system. You can think of the internal specification as the product's blueprints. The *external specification* details end-user interfaces to the system and the information users can get from the system. For example, one item in an external specification may be a terminal screen layout and the functions it provides. The external specification is somewhat similar to a user's manual.

Life Cycle Phases—Implementation

The implementation phase consists of six subphases, some of which may not be required. During the implementation phase the product and its supporting components are built and installed.

Phase 4.1—Hardware/Software Procurement. If all of the equipment needed to solve the problem is already available, this phase will not exist. If additional hardware or software is necessary to implement the design, it must be selected, ordered, and installed. This may require a detailed investigation of vendor capabilities and a formal bidding process. One of the tools used in the formal bidding process is a request for proposal (RFP). The RFP is discussed in a later section. Following vendor selection, site inspections and preparations may be necessary. The equipment required should be completely installed and operable by the beginning of the final testing phase.

Phase 4.2—Building the Product. Once the design specifications have been completed, the system can be created. The products of this step are a variety of documents, prototypes, functional test results, and the (almost) completed product. We define *functional testing* as the testing of individual modules to ensure that they produce the correct results. It is different from integrated and stress testing, which come later.

Phase 4.3—Documentation. Documentation is an integral part of each phase. It is also identified as a separate phase to emphasize its importance and to identify some of the documents that need to be produced. The products of this phase are the formal documents that must accompany the product. Some of these are reference manuals, maintenance manuals, users' manuals, and operators' manuals.

Phase 4.4—Testing. Functional testing is completed during the building phase. The formal testing phase is for integration and stress testing. The products of this phase are a test plan, a test bank, test reports, and eventually the formal acceptance of the product by the operations group. *Integrated testing* ensures that all parts of the system function well together. For instance, if the outputs of one program are the inputs to another, integration testing determines if the interface between the two works correctly. Likewise, if two processes exchange messages in processing a transaction, integrated testing checks the compatibility of their message formats. *Stress testing* ensures that the system can sustain the designated workload. This may include the ability to process a specific number of transactions per unit of time, provide a stated response time to a set of transactions, or complete a given set of work, such as a batch job, within a specified amount of time.

Phase 4.5—Installation.   Upon successful completion of the testing phase, the system is ready to be installed. The results of this phase are an installation plan and an operational system.

Phase 4.6—Cutover.   The cutover phase consists of phasing out the old system and making the new one fully operational. The eventual result of this phase is an active working system. Preliminary outputs are a plan for how cutover will be accomplished and contingency plans if the new system does not meet expectations.

Life Cycle Phases—Operations and Maintenance

The last phase in the life cycle of a product is the operations and maintenance phase. It consists of two subphases: (1) operations and maintenance and (2) retirement.

Phase 5.1—Operations and Maintenance.   During this phase the product is enhanced to provide new capabilities, the system is monitored and tuned to maintain adequate performance levels, and system bugs are fixed. The products are change requests, updates to the existing documentation to reflect changes, and a myriad of statistics and reports necessary for the monitoring and control functions.

Phase 5.2—Retirement.   At some time the product will be replaced. The results of this phase are utilities to assist in transforming to the replacement system and archiving the retired one.

TRANSACTION DESIGN

A *transaction* is defined as a user-specified group of processing activities that are either completed or, if not completed, that leave the database and processing system in the same state as before the transaction started. Thus, a transaction always leaves the database and the system in a consistent state. A transaction is also a unit of recovery, an entity that the recovery system manages. Recovery and contention have a great influence on transaction design. From the perspective of an application, it makes little difference as to how or when the transaction begins, ends, or is recovered. From a systems design and system recovery perspective, good transaction design is very important.

Review of Transaction Activities

Before discussing transaction design, it is useful to discuss the activities needed to start, end, and process a transaction. As in Chapter 12, a generic recovery system is assumed; details vary with implementations. Beginning and ending a transaction require a certain amount of work, and additional work is required when processing a transaction. Starting a transaction demands that a unique transaction identifier be generated. A beginning transaction record is then written to the transaction log. Each record updated by the transaction must be locked to avoid concurrent update problems. Some records that are read but not updated may also have to be locked. All updates must be posted to the before- and after-image audit trail before being written to the database. At the end of the transaction all audit buffers must be flushed to disk and end-of-transaction markers written to the audit trail.

A simple transaction that updates one record may therefore result in five writes—the begin-transaction record, the end-transaction record, the before-image, the after-image, and the record itself, as illustrated in Figure 14-3. This may appear to be a rather high overhead, but it is not. The cost of inconsistent data can be much greater, and many systems use techniques to optimize the capturing of audit images. Audit images are like insurance policies—they cost a small amount over time but pay large dividends when needed.

Grouping Activities in a Single Transaction

Transaction design covers two areas: the grouping of activities into one transaction and how that transaction is implemented within the system. In many cases, the need for a transaction to leave the system in a consistent state dictates the transaction's composition. In other cases the composition is not quite so obvious. In transferring funds from one bank account to another, for instance, it is clear that the deposit and withdrawal must be

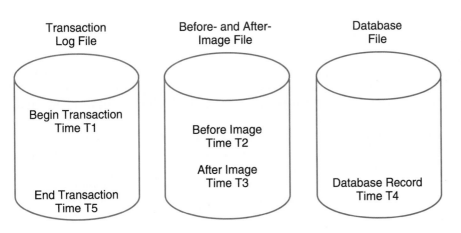

Transaction Log File — Begin Transaction Time T1 — End Transaction Time T5

Before- and After-Image File — Before Image Time T2 — After Image Time T3

Database File — Database Record Time T4

Figure 14-3 Records Written for a Simple Transaction

placed together in one transaction, for to do otherwise would make the database inconsistent. A trial balance would not balance if funds are taken from one place but not deposited in another.

An example of a transaction with less obvious boundaries is adding a new employee to a company database. This statement assumes that the transaction activities required are selection and assignment of an employee number, addition of an employee record, and addition of zero to several associated records—employee history, payroll, dependents, and benefits. The employee number is selected so that employee numbers form an increasing numeric sequence with no gaps. This requires reading a control record that contains the next number in the sequence, incrementing the sequence number on the control record, and rewriting the control record.

Although the employee will not be fully entered into the system until all these activities have been completed, it may be unnecessary to group all activities in a single transaction. The selection and assignment of an employee number and the creation of an employee record are tightly coupled events. Thus, if an employee number has been removed from the control sequence, there should be an employee record with that number, which number should be available for reuse if adding the new employee to the file fails. However, adding a dependent record, which requires only that an employee record exist, is not so tightly linked with the process of creating the employee record. Indeed, dependent records are frequently added long after an employee has been hired. The same can be said for payroll records, benefits, and work history. In this example, there might be one or several transactions.

Advantages and Disadvantages of Single Versus Multiple Transactions

What would be the advantages and disadvantages of making the employee transaction a single or multiple transaction?

Brief Versus Long Transactions.   A single transaction requires only one begin-and-end transaction activity. Although not an overriding consideration, there is an overhead to starting and ending a transaction that a careful designer will attempt to minimize. On the other hand, a long transaction has a greater risk—albeit very slight—of a failure that would involve a recovery. Long transactions also require that records be locked for a longer period, which both increases the likelihood of deadlock and increases the time the records are unavailable. When record locking is used to resolve the multiple update problems of contention (which arise when two or more users attempt to access the same records), deadlock can occur. As discussed earlier, deadlock results when two different users (in this case, transactions) have controls over records and attempt to access records the other has already locked, as illustrated in Figure 14-4.

	Transaction 1	Transaction 2
T	Read and lock Record A.	
		Read and lock Record B.
I	Attempt to read Record B.	
		Attempt to read Record A.
M		
	Wait.	Wait.
E		

Figure 14-4
Deadlock Situation

Multiple Sessions with One Operator. The major consideration in whether to group multiple updates into one transaction is none of the above, however. Because the weakest link in a transaction is perhaps the operator, good transaction design avoids multiple sessions with the terminal operator whenever possible. If it is decided when adding a new employee to treat all activities as one transaction, complications could arise, as follows: The terminal operator begins the transaction by entering the employee data, triggering updates to the employee number assignment file, the employee file, and perhaps a number of access method files, all accomplished by one interaction with the terminal. Having been updated, the employee number assignment record and the new employee record are locked. The operator next enters job history information. If the operator takes a lunch break at this point, putting the transaction on hold with its records locked, then, because the employee number assignment record must be used every time a new employee is added, no new employees can be added during this interval.

The problem with having a transaction span sessions with one operator is not just the operator's potential absence; it is also the amount of time that a transaction must be held in limbo while the operator enters more information. Compared to the milliseconds required to update databases and process transactions, the minutes required to enter the data are rather long. This situation is further complicated when records are locked across sessions with the operator. Fortunately, techniques exist for avoiding such delays.

How to Avoid Multiple Sessions. If system design requires all the activities described for adding a new employee to be a single transaction, the transaction should be planned to avoid multiple sessions with the operator once the transaction begins. Essentially the solution is to gather all necessary information before beginning the transaction. One way that this could be accomplished is described here. The operator enters the information for the new employee. The data is edited, and if there are no inconsistencies the record is safe stored. The operator is then prompted for job history data. Again, edit checks are performed and the record is safe stored. The same is done for dependent, payroll, and benefits data. If a failure occurs during this process, the data already input will be available, so the operator will not need to enter it again. Once all of the data has been entered, the transaction is initiated. The database locks are kept for the minimum required time, since no additional sessions with the operator are required. Upon completion, the result is returned to the operator. Should the operator leave the terminal in the midst of the transaction, no records are left locked during the period.

To summarize, transactions should be designed to be as brief as possible and to avoid multiple interactions with an operator. The overriding consideration is to design transactions so the database is always left in a consistent state and so recovery can be assured. The participation of a terminal operator in the recovery process should be kept to a minimum. Operators should be notified of the last activity completed on their behalf so they can continue from the correct place.

SELECTING HARDWARE AND SOFTWARE

When implementing a new online application, it is sometimes necessary to acquire additional hardware and software to support the application, especially if the online application is the first break from the more traditional batch operating environment. In addition to the hardware and software, new services such as communications media, support personnel, and education may be needed. If the new application fits the existing equipment as is or with minor enhancements, selection of hardware and software is a relatively simple task. In those situations where major acquisitions are necessary, the prudent systems group should evaluate the offerings of several vendors. In the remainder of this section we assume that support of the new application requires a major upgrade of hardware and software. Selecting a hardware or software system involves selecting more than just a system: A vendor is also being selected. The vendor's ability to maintain, enhance, and expand the components may well determine the selection's overall success. Therefore, the components and the vendor must be evaluated with equal care.

Request for Information

Sometimes a company may want to simply investigate hardware and software solutions to a problem. One way to do this is a *request for information (RFI)*. An RFI consists of a brief statement of a problem to be solved and a list of questions regarding solutions to the problem. Vendors are asked to respond to the RFI and propose solutions. For example, a company intending to install a local area network might release an RFI asking vendors to describe the type of network they would propose to support 150 workstations. Some of the questions that might be included in the RFI are:

What media access control is recommended?

How many file servers are necessary?

What type of hardware is used for file servers?

How many printers can be supported in the recommended configuration?

What type of wiring is required?

What is the cost of the configured equipment?

What are the names of three references with comparable systems?

The RFI may be a preliminary step for the more formal equipment procurement process discussed below, or it may form the basis for the selection itself. The advantages of an RFI are the ease of creation and response. In general, it is not as detailed as the request for proposal discussed in the next section, and it does not usually entail benchmark tests or other time-consuming analyses like detailed system sizing and transaction analysis.

Request for Proposal

Most smaller companies and private companies can use the rather informal approach of the RFI or alternate methods to system selection. In larger corporations and most government implementations, equipment selection involving a large cash outlay must be based on a competitive bid process and fair appraisal. This is accomplished when the user creates and issues a *request for proposal* (RFP), sometimes referred to as a *request for quotation* (RFQ). In some countries this is called a request for a tender offering. Regardless of the name, the process yields a document describing the problem to be resolved and requesting qualified vendors to submit plans and costs for solving the problem. Henceforth, the term *RFP* refers to the document describing the problem to be solved. An RFP, which has no well-defined format, is used to procure a broad range of equipment from low-cost items such as terminals and multiplexers to large-scale processing systems and software. The RFP for the first category of equipment might consist of fewer than 20 pages, whereas the latter might require several hundred pages of description. It is up to the user to determine what is pertinent to the proposal.

Format and Content of the RFP

The arrangement of the following topics in an RFP is not set, except that within a document the ordering should be logical (for example, descriptions of how responses are to be delivered should not be placed between descriptions of the hardware and software components).

Table of Contents.   A table of contents should be included for any lengthy RFP document and for some shorter ones. Because the RFP is usually aimed at a team of specialists from several disciplines, a table of contents gives the responders a quick reference to specific topics.

Introduction.   The first section of the RFP should be a brief introduction. It can include overviews of the company, the problem to be solved, and the anticipated schedule for completion of the proposal, evaluation, selection, installation, and live operation.

Response Ground Rules.   The ground rules for responding to a proposal are ordinarily placed at the beginning or end of the RFP. This establishes the schedule for the selection process, how responders interact with the user during the process, the format for a proposal, the manner in which proposals are evaluated, and how multiple vendor responses are to be treated. The schedule should include:

The date proposals are to be submitted

The place, date, and time for submission of all proposals

The dates during which vendor presentations can be made

The date the winning proposal will be selected

The anticipated delivery dates of the equipment being procured

The anticipated date the system will be operational

The time and place of proposal submission are quite important. Most RFPs specify a specific date and time after which proposals will no longer be accepted. RFP responders often are allowed to make a presentation to the selection committee. The presentation enables the vendor to provide additional technical information and to answer any questions the selection committee may have. Since such presentations tend to be time-consuming, it is usually a good practice to narrow the field of candidates to a small number of final presenters, perhaps five.

The date of selection tells vendors when they will be notified of success or failure. All responders to the RFP should receive a minimum of two notifications, the first an acknowledgment of proposal receipt and the second a notification of proposal acceptance or rejection. Although the equipment delivery date applies only to the winning proposals, it is important to all responders, because companies frequently need considerable lead time to manufacture or obtain equipment. If the specified delivery date is too soon for a particular vendor, the vendor can suggest a more realistic date in the proposal. The anticipated date to commence operations is important in helping the vendor to determine the number of employees needed for development and installation and to evaluate the costs and risks involved. Some vendors may have the needed equipment in stock, whereas others might require a significant development investment. As with delivery date, responders might wish to propose their own operational date.

Fair Appraisal. If the appraisal process is to be conducted fairly, all responders should be treated equally. This can be difficult if one of the responders is the incumbent vendor and because personal associations frequently exist between vendor personnel and the selection committee. Furthermore, vendors' sales representatives like to use the selection period to practice their salesmanship—with lunches, dinners, entertainment, and an increased presence. One common practice during submission and evaluation is to require all communications between a vendor and the selection committee to be made through a small group of user personnel, thus providing each vendor with consistent intermediaries and response. While evaluating the RFP, vendors frequently need to ask questions of the user. The user can distribute to all vendors a list of relevant questions and answers, which is especially helpful to clarify points in the RFP. However, distribution of questions that disclose information regarding a particular vendor's solution should be avoided.

Response Format. The format of the response is a user option. It is customary to have the response submitted in two volumes, one consisting of technical responses and the other for the financial and contractual response. Each of these sections might be evaluated by a different group, thereby preventing the technical evaluation from being biased by price. In the final analysis a combination of the two reports determines the winner. Providing an outline for responders to follow in their proposals makes for consistency in content and format that decreases the work of evaluation. Question sheets and checklists also provide a quick means of obtaining information.

Evaluation Criteria. The RFP should contain information regarding how the proposal is to be evaluated. Otherwise it is like giving an examination without saying how it will be graded or giving the relative point values for each question. A complete description is usually impossible, but, as a minimum, features should be defined as "mandatory," "highly desirable," or "optional but influential." The more influential features should be pointed out so the responder can more completely describe these critical aspects of the system. This also assists the vendors to determine whether their solution is viable and describes the key points to make in the response. In the final analysis, a grading of key requirements plus a weighting applied to each requirement usually makes the overall evaluation easier. For example, 5 points could be assigned for meeting a requirement completely, 3 for meeting it partially, and zero for deficiencies. Weights that reflect relative importance can then be assigned to each requirement. For a communications system, being able to interface with IBM's SNA network might carry a weight of 10, and an interactive screen design feature might carry a weight of 2, which implies that an SNA interface is 5 times as important as interactive screen design aids. A portion of a sample evaluation sheet is illustrated in Figure 14-5. The technical winner would

Figure 14-5 Sample
RFP Evaluation
Sheet

Item	Weight	Vendor 1		Vendor 2		Vendor 3	
		Score	*Tot.*	*Score*	*Tot.*	*Score*	*Tot.*
Cost	10	5	50	7	70	6.3	63
Documentation	6	3	18	9	54	6	36
Support	5	2	10	8	40	7	35
Education	5	4	20	8	40	5	25
Page Total			98		204		159

be the responder with the highest number of points. If a point value is
given to the pricing as well, the technical and financial evaluations can be
combined to make the overall best response even more obvious.

Multiple Vendor Bids. Several vendors can cooperate in proposing a
solution for very large projects, one vendor providing the hardware and
system-level software while another contracts for custom application software. In other instances, one vendor might supply the processors, another
the terminal subsystems, and a third the software. Users should specify
any special rules regarding multiple vendor bids. As a minimum, users
generally prefer to have one vendor as prime contractor with overall responsibility for the entire proposal. Of course, as long as the implementation goes smoothly, multiple independent vendors pose no problems. But
when delays occur, it is much easier for the user to contact one responsible
vendor for resolution. Having one vendor as the primary contractor simplifies problem resolution for the user and eliminates finger pointing
between vendors.

User Characteristics. It often helps a vendor to be provided with a description of the user's company, personnel, and current processing environment. This perspective enables the responder to address the proposal
more appropriately. For instance, since there are a multitude of payroll
and accounts receivables applications, a section describing the user's company would give insight into how the company works and how the payroll
or accounts receivable applications differ from those of other companies.

Problem Description. The major portion of the RFP is devoted to a description of the problem to be solved. This should not include any perceived solutions because such solutions are usually biased by a particular
hardware and software environment. For instance, an RFP that states that a
processor is "capable of executing 2 million instructions per second (MIPS)

and supports line speeds in excess of 56 Kbps" is presenting the vendor with a perceived solution to the problem. What is preferable is a problem described in sufficient detail to allow responders to configure a system based on their own hardware and software capabilities. In actuality, many RFPs are released with the anticipation of only one or a few viable contenders. In some instances the RFP is written in such a way that only one or two vendors even stand a chance of successfully competing. In these cases it is up to the vendors to determine their chances of success and weigh the risk of losing their investment in preparing a response.

CASE STUDY

Consider again the Syncrasy Corporation. They continue to be successful and are again expanding. The company has decided to become a developer of software and an original equipment manufacturer for minicomputer systems as well as personal computers. Their target market is office automation systems. The software development department is to be located in Austin, Texas, and sales offices with computer equipment will be located in 13 large cities throughout the United States and international offices in Montreal, Toronto, London, Paris, Rome, Frankfurt, Oslo, Tokyo, Hong Kong, Sydney, and Mexico City. The objective is to network all of these systems to allow software to be quickly distributed to all sales sites, provide problem communication on a timely basis, manage corporate inventory and accounting, and provide interoffice communication of letters and graphics. To obtain the network equipment an RFP will be prepared. A proposal committee consisting of data-processing personnel and several key users of the system has been formed. A synopsis of the first draft of the RFP as submitted to Link Editor, the vice president for data processing, follows.

Syncrasy Corporation's Draft 1 RFP

Each of the 13 domestic offices must have processors capable of executing the same object modules. The speed of the processors will vary between 1 million instructions per second (MIPS) and 5 MIPS. The processors must be capable of communicating with each other using HDLC protocol as well as an interface to X.25 networks and IBM 3270 or compatible terminals must be supported.

This first draft was rejected because it contained too many solutions and not enough problem definition. The object code compatibility is only one solution to the problem of developing software at one location for execution at another; cross compilers might also work. A better problem definition would state that it must be possible for system and application software to be generated at one node and transported to another node for execution. Within a particular vendor's product line, then, the solution might differ from object code compatibility.

ADDITIONAL EVALUATION CONSIDERATIONS

MIPS Rates

The quoted MIPS rates represent the perceived processing power, most likely based on the amount of work accomplished by one or several processors with which the committee has experience. MIPS rates are a measure of instructions executed per unit of time, but not necessarily of throughput. Operating systems, database systems, and data communications systems all consume processing resources while providing varying levels of function. A system that provides complete recovery of database and data communications networks can be expected to execute more instructions than one without those capabilities. Furthermore, the application software can vary significantly in the number of instructions required, depending on the efficiency of the written code as well as the efficiency of the code generated by the compilers. Higher level languages such as database query languages and interpreters also can consume more machine cycles.

More on Problem Description

The statement of the problem should be a description of the applications to be run, together with the type of transactions expected to be executed. For instance, a transaction might be described as being local to one node or requiring communication between nodes and might also define the number of input and output characters, transaction frequency, peak transaction rate, and work performed by the transaction. This type of definition is covered in more detail in the section on system configuration. The amount of work necessary to provide such information appears to be more than that required in the rejected solution stated above. However, it is impossible to derive the solution without doing the same analysis internally. There are benefits to be derived from this type of problem statement as well: The vendor's response might come up with a novel and economical solution, or it might provide some preliminary design solutions. Regardless, the vendor is allowed to configure the system in a manner fitting their hardware and software rather than some preconceived solution.

Subrequirements

If the system to be procured is large, the requirements can be broken into subsections dealing with data communications, terminals, hardware, and software. Sufficient transaction and batch processing detail should be provided to enable the vendor to size and price the system.

Benchmarks

A benchmark test is one or more programs that are run on a proposed hardware configuration to verify the ability of the hardware to meet the application requirements. The benchmark programs usually simulate the activity required by the proposed application. Thus, benchmark testing is useful in assuring that the proposed configuration will actually solve the problems. However, care must be taken when using a benchmark. Benchmarks are also a measure of how well a group of experts can run benchmark programs. A far better measure of performance is the analysis of an already operational system that supports a processing load similar to that of the anticipated system. If benchmark programs are necessary, they should not be required of all responders. Instead, the field of candidates should be narrowed to a small number, such as five, and these finalists should run the tests. This does not preclude other responders from eventually running the benchmark as well. For instance, the five finalists might fail to perform the benchmark as expected on the proposed configuration, thereby elevating the responses of other vendors. The rationale behind having only a selected group run the benchmark test is that such tests are expensive for both vendor and user. Equipment must be allocated and configured, tests written, system tuned to maximum performance, results evaluated, and reports written. The user should be involved in the testing as a monitor at least and ideally as a participant. A great deal of information can be gained by such participation.

Other Points in the RFP

Other factors that should be addressed in the RFP include education offered, including cost and location; maintenance costs and hours; extended maintenance coverage; software license; microcode; maintenance and user fees for the software; location of maintenance offices; escalation procedures for maintenance; locations of spare parts and the time required for delivery; number, location, and type of available support personnel; national and international support policies where applicable; and the availability of backup systems in the event of a prolonged failure for whatever reason.

References

Every vendor should be asked to submit at least three reference accounts for contact; those unable to supply three good reference accounts should be scrutinized very carefully. The requester should also attempt to contact three additional accounts not listed as references; this can prove very informative. Sometimes the references themselves can provide names of other accounts. If the vendor's customer base is large, references in a similar business or within a similar transaction load as that of the user should be contacted.

Final Selection Considerations

Once the responses to the RFP have been evaluated, the field should be narrowed to three to five finalists. These are the vendors who can be expected to run a benchmark. These vendors' references should be contacted at this time, and contract negotiations should begin. The vendor's standard contract should be reviewed by the user's attorneys. If nonstandard components are to be used, the user should attempt to make contractual agreements about when the components are to be delivered, what constitutes acceptance of the components, and what penalties, if any, will apply for nonconformance. Support and maintenance issues should be resolved. The user should know from which office their support is coming, what the expected response time will be, what charges are involved, what the escalation procedures are, and whether the vendor is willing to provide backup systems should the purchased system malfunction for any significant length of time. The user should ascertain how frequently new releases are made and what the policy is for fixing bugs of various levels of severity, distributing the solutions, and what this service costs. The user should determine if enhancements to the product are planned, how frequently they will be made, and the costs involved in receiving them.

Unfortunately, the history of user-vendor relationships is full of well-intentioned but unfulfilled promises of things to be delivered and services to be provided. There is also a history of hidden costs and of support problems. For a sizable purchase, the purchaser should make every attempt to protect the investment. Standard contracts provided by a vendor are designed to protect the vendor. In many instances this does not adequately protect the purchaser. For any significant purchase, attorneys representing the purchaser should review and modify the standard vendor contracts. A thorough analysis of a number of vendor's solutions to a processing problem provides a user with a higher probability of success in selecting the equipment best suited to an application. The time invested in this activity is frequently regained several times over in project implementation.

SYSTEM CONFIGURATION

Sizing and configuring a system is an ongoing activity. Over time, the manner in which an online system is used tends to vary. New transactions may be introduced and existing ones changed or discontinued, or the frequency with which they are invoked might change. In addition to changes in online activity, changes in batch processing requirements and hardware can alter the response characteristics of a system. For example, in a virtual memory system, memory pages are swapped to disk. So long as sufficient real memory is available, paging does not seriously affect response times. As more applications are added to the system, the paging rate increases and performance decreases. Eventually a point will be reached where the system spends more time satisfying memory management requests than it does processing data. This is just one of a number of potential system bottlenecks. Sizing and configuring a network requires a comprehensive knowledge of the application, system, and performance objectives. In this section the focus is on the information that must be collected to make an educated estimate of the resources required to meet the response time requirements of the online system. Batch processing and the transfer of large amounts of data are not considered.

Response Time

Good response times are important to the success of an online system. During the design process, response times are set for each transaction, the response times for critical transactions are included in the RFP, and response times are measured during benchmark tests. Response time consists of two components: data communications and processing. The data communications component is the time required to transmit a message from source to destination and receive any necessary response. The processing component consists of the activity required by one or more processors in satisfying the request, including field editing, message routing, message formatting, data manipulation and calculation, recovery overhead, and database access. All of these factors must be known to properly size and configure a system. One can start to analyze response time either at the processing or data communications component. It is usually easier to begin with the processing component and then determine the required line speeds needed to meet the data communications component.

Processing Time Requirements.   Processing time requirements start with a detailed definition of the transaction. Because input-output access time is almost always the most time-consuming factor in the processing component of a transaction, the number and type of accesses must be determined. For example, a banking transaction in which the account record must be retrieved using the customer's name may have a higher overhead than the same transaction using the account number. This would occur if the account number were the primary key of retrieval and the customer name were a secondary key. Furthermore, account numbers are unique, whereas the name may not be. Thus, the transaction using customer name requires the retrieval and search of an index and multiple accesses to the account file if duplicate names exist. The transaction using account number may require only one access to the account file.

Disk Access Time.   For each transaction the number of database or file accesses must be counted, including in the count auxiliary accesses for indices. If optimization features such as cache memory (which reduces disk accesses) or storage of indices on the same cylinder as related data are available, they should be considered in determining the required access times. Being able to complete this step requires a knowledge of the database design, the manner in which records are accessed, and how the transaction requests records from the database management system.

CPU Time.   Another component of transaction processing is the amount of CPU time required. This is difficult to approximate unless the transaction has been measured by a performance monitor. In most cases a very rough estimate based on the number of instructions executed or just the processing time itself is sufficient. For the majority of transactions the amount of time spent executing instructions is minor compared to the amount of time waiting for I/O completions. CPU time becomes a concern only when transactions are CPU-intensive or when CPU time is in short supply. Thus, CPU times become a critical element in a statistical transaction where the solution requires iterative techniques and little or no I/O. In the banking situation mentioned above, CPU time is negligible when compared to the I/O time.

Data Communications Time Requirements.   A transaction's I/O time and processing time make up the processing component of response time. The data communications component consists of line time plus time to handle the message at any intermediate nodes. Line time is a function of the type of line used, the transmission speed of the line, and the total number of characters transmitted.

The preceding considerations will result in the minimum expected response time. A number of other factors—all dealing with contention for system resources—will potentially add to the minimum response time. If the communications links are shared by a number of devices through multi-drop, multiplexing, or similar techniques, the links may not be immediately available or the terminal's apparent line speed may be less than that of the link. In such cases the average time spent waiting in the transmit queue must be included in the total response time. In most instances it is also beneficial to determine the worst case response time as well. Queuing at the TCP, the application, and the disk are other places where delays can occur. The TCP ordinarily handles multiple terminals, but only one terminal receives the attention of a TCP at a given time. The same is true of the application and disk processes. The service times for these potential delays are derived by calculating the expected transaction arrival rates and mean service times.

Example Computation of Transaction Response Time

This example assumes that disk access time has three components—seek time, latency, and transfer time. *Seek time* is the time it takes to move the read/write heads to the proper cylinder. A seek time of 20 milliseconds (ms), which is typical of a number of disk drives, is used in this example. *Latency* is the average time required for the data to be read to revolve under the read/write heads. After the seek, the data may have just passed under the heads, thus requiring a full revolution of the disk, or it could be just arriving at the heads, thus requiring no latency. Some disks revolve at 3600 rpm, resulting in a full latency of 16.6 ms and an average latency of 8.3 ms. *Transfer time*, usually negligible compared to the other two components, is the amount of time required for the data to be sent over the channel to the CPU's memory. If the channel speed is 5 million characters per second and the block size being transferred is 500 characters, then the transfer time is approximately 0.1 ms (approximately because a small amount of processing time is also required). These figures represent the amount of time required for random access to the disk.

Consider a library transaction. A patron wants to renew two books but does not have a library card available. The transaction requires the following processing:

1. Read the patron record using the name as a key. This requires an index record. On the average three names will qualify. These three records, with address and library card number, are displayed on the operator's terminal. This requires reading one index record and three data records.

2. Select the proper patron and retrieve the books checked out records, one for each book borrowed. In this instance two records are retrieved using the library card number and requiring an index record search of one index record and two data records.

3. Update both book records to reflect the new due date. This requires two writes to the book file and no updates to the index file.

Processing Time.   Total disk activity for this transaction involves seven reads and two writes. Furthermore, the system uses transaction auditing, which requires writes to the before- and after-image audit files and two writes to the audit trail for the beginning and ending of the transaction. An efficient audit system is assumed, so the two before-images and two after-images are written with one disk write each. Thus, there is a total of 13 disk accesses, nine for the transaction and four for the audits. Disk time is therefore

13 seeks @ 20 ms each	260.0 ms
13 latencies @ 8.3 ms each	107.9
Total disk time	367.9 ms

There is approximately 20 ms of processing or CPU time and approximately 100 ms of queuing time within the system (waiting for disk and application). Total processing time, then, is

Disk access time	367.9 ms
Processing time	20.0
Queue wait time	100.0
Total processing time	487.9 ms

Data Communications Time. The number of characters transmitted to the terminal is

Input last name	10
Output three records	150
Input selected record	10
Output two records	100
Input updated data	100
Output completion status	10
Protocol, formatting	190
Total no. of transmitted characters	570

If the expected response time is 2 seconds, then (without considering the overhead of the data link protocol) approximately 4560 bits must be transferred in 1.512 seconds, requiring a transmission speed of at least 3015 bps. This equates to a standard speed of 4800 bps and represents the minimum line speed. A higher speed link may be needed. For example, if asynchronous transmission is used, 10 bits per character will be required and the minimum line speed will be 3770 bits per second. With a multi-point line, polling overhead and possible modem turnaround times must be factored in. This example, however, assumes a point-to-point line.

Sizing exercises almost always make numerous assumptions. For instance, the previous example assumed an average number of disk accesses and average queue times and processing time. With a multi-point line, assumptions would have to be made regarding the number and size of messages transmitted before a particular terminal's poll was received. Prediction of performance becomes easier once the system has been installed and is operational, when variables such as queue time can be more readily determined. Sizing in the case of an already operational system helps determine the impact of changing the transaction load, adding new transactions, or changing the batch component of the processing load. Even though sizing analysis is partly an imprecise estimate, it is still valuable in predicting initial system sizing and components, as well as in anticipating the growth of an established system.

Network Modeling. The larger the network, the more difficult it is to conduct sizing and performance estimates. The use of formal modeling tools in these instances is often required. Modeling tools run the gamut from simple spreadsheet templates to formal simulation and modeling systems, which allow components to be described and connected, different forms of arrival rates to be generated, transactions to be described, and critical system factors calculated. These factors will include items such as:

Response times
   Best
   Average

Percentile, for example, 95% will be under 3 seconds

Disk accesses

Disk access times

Number of characters transmitted

Line times

Line speeds

Processing time

Peak performance characteristics

Some modeling systems, in addition to producing the performance fig-ures, also generate software to measure the results on a live system. Trans-action scripts are prepared and run on the proposed hardware to find the actual performance information. Live terminals can also be used to input transactions and give prospective users a feel for system performance.

Network Configuration Tools. Design aids also exist to help configure the optimal network links. These tools allow users to indicate the nodes that must be connected and the expected traffic between nodes. Using this information and existing tariff data, the configurator will recommend the lowest cost network connections to connect all of the nodes. Again, if the system being designed is complex, this type of design aid can help econo-mize on the recurring communication costs of network links.

CASE STUDY REVISITED

Having installed their network, the Syncrasy Corporation has begun de-velopment of a distributed order-processing system. A number of transac-tions have been identified for the system, one of the most complex of which is the order entry transaction. The analysis that went into the de-sign of this transaction follows.

Order Entry Design Requirements

The order entry transaction is to serve the customers in North America. Orders will be filled from the closest warehouses in New York, Chicago, Kansas City, or Los Angeles. Each warehouse location maintains its own computer system and inventory. The network configuration is depicted in Figure 14-6. Placing an order involves the following activities.

Customer Identification. The operator enters the customer's name. If the name is already in the database, order entry commences; if the name is not on file, a customer entry screen is presented and the required information, such as billing and shipping address, is entered. A credit limit is estab-

Figure 14-6 The
Syncrasy Order
Entry Network

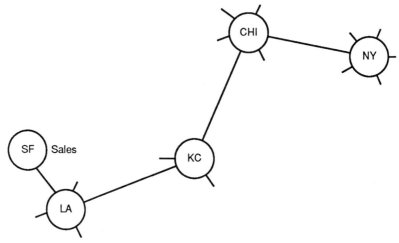

San Francisco searches Los Angeles, then Kansas City, then Chicago, then New York City.

lished for the customer. When the customer records have been set up, the order can be entered.

Order Entry.   Order line items are entered, consisting of part numbers together with the quantity for each part. Any number of line items can make up an order. It has been determined that the average Syncrasy order has eight line items, 10% of all orders have more than 20 line items, and 2% have more than 30 line items.

Total Order Value/Credit Limit Check.   The total value of the order is computed by summing the products of line item price and quantity. This value is then compared with the customer credit limit; if the limit is exceeded, the customer is advised and credit can be extended by manual authorization procedures if necessary.

Inventory Check.   Inventory is checked to determine which ordered parts are in stock, with the closest warehouse checked first. If the entire order cannot be filled from the nearest warehouse, the others are checked. The operator is notified of any line items unavailable from inventory. The customer then has the options of canceling all or part of the order or entering the entire order and back-ordering the out-of-stock items. It has been determined that 5% of all transactions encounter the out-of-stock condition and that in only 10% of these situations (0.5% of all situations) are ordered items canceled as a result of insufficient stock.

Inventory/Credit Update.   If an order is placed, the inventory in each shipping warehouse is updated, and if it is not a cash transaction, the customer's credit limit is adjusted.

Receipt and Order Confirmation.   A receipt and order confirmation are printed at the order entry location.

Packing Lists/Shipping Labels.   Packing lists and shipping labels are printed at each of the affected warehouses.

Billing.   Billing information is generated and accounts receivable files are updated. If the customer pays cash, no invoice is generated, but the general ledger files are updated.

Transaction Design Selected

Syncrasy wants the transaction designed so records can be locked for update as briefly as possible and remain unlocked while awaiting operator inputs. If the entire logical transaction is to be decomposed into multiple database transactions, the subtransactions must be individual elements; for recovery to be consistent, it would be improper to debit the accounting files without a corresponding credit entry. However, the primary design consideration is to provide the best possible response for the customer, meaning that customer identification and order verification must be performed in the minimum possible time. Page mode terminals were selected for this application. They have no local processing capabilities. A number of transaction designs can meet the above criteria. The design selected by the Syncrasy analysts and the rationale behind their decisions are described below.

Customer ID/Credit Check.   The operator first enters the customer identification, either customer number or name. This information is transmitted to the local host and the database is searched to determine whether the customer has already been defined. If the customer is on file, the customer's billing and shipping address are displayed on the operator's terminal. If the customer is not on file, a customer definition form is displayed on the operator's terminal. When the customer data has been entered, it is edited for consistency; if the edit checks are successful, a credit check is performed. If the credit check is positive, the transaction to add a new customer record is started, the customer data is added to the database, the transaction is completed, and the information is displayed on the operator's terminal together with the order entry line item screen. The new customer who fails to pass the credit check is asked to pay cash or is referred to the credit department for approval.

Customer Order.   Once the customer has been properly identified, the operator enters order line items. This part of order entry can be quite complex, since orders can be open-ended. A virtually unlimited number of line items is allowed and the customer can cancel any or all of the order on an out-of-stock condition or insufficient credit condition. Ten line items can be entered on the first screen; subsequent screens allow 20 line items. Since orders are open-ended, a design decision must be made regarding long orders. The first design alternative basically consists of limiting the number of items per order, and the second allows any number of items and makes a special case of extremely long orders. The problem with long orders is essentially that the transaction control process (TCP) buffers line items as they are received; however, a maximum buffer size is set for storing them. If more line items are ordered than can fit in the buffer, either a buffer overflow algorithm must be employed or the transaction must be limited to a specific number of line items.

In Syncrasy's case, optimization is meant to favor the customer, not the programmer. Because a customer may decide to cancel all or part of an order if a line item is unavailable, dividing a logical transaction into two or more separate recovery transactions was considered impractical. Thus, if an order for 40 items was divided into two transactions of 20 items each, the customer could find a line item unavailable in the second transaction and cancel the entire order. This presents a number of problems for the system. Once the first transaction was completed, picking and packing lists were printed at warehouse locations. These actions need to be reversed. Moreover, a completed transaction would need to be backed out, requiring an interface with the audit logs or necessitating that the application keep track of all line items. The first case is usually too difficult in vendor-supplied recovery systems, which are designed to back out a particular uncompleted transaction or to roll all or a group of transactions forward. Very seldom is the recovery system able to back out one particular transaction that has already been completed.

Backing Out a Transaction.   Indeed, backing out one completed transaction could affect other already completed transactions. If, for example, a part were ordered in both transactions A and B, with B starting after A, then to back out A, it would be insufficient to replace A's before-images in the file because that would erase B's update. All transactions completing after A would have to be examined to determine if they affected A's records, or A's order quantity would have to be added back into the inventory. Even this could create problems if automatic reordering is used. B's transaction could have precipitated a reorder, and adding A's quantity back in could place the quantity back over the reorder point. Subsequent orders could again trigger a reorder. In either case, if the item is expensive, then an overstock condition could be reached, which might adversely affect profits. Syncrasy has decided that for transactions in excess of 30 line items (the first two screens), those items over 30 will be written to an overflow disk file. Experience has indicated that only 2% of all transactions fall into this category. Thus, the operator enters line items until all have been completed. All line items are held in the TCP, with some records possibly in the overflow disk file. The number of line items is maintained in the data entry record, so it is known whether overflow has been used.

Inventory Check. The next stage of the transaction is to determine if there is sufficient inventory to fill the order. Since there are four warehouse locations in North America from which the goods can be shipped, the application uses a search priority, with the first search being at the closest warehouse. Two alternatives were considered in doing the database searches. The first involves locking records as the search progresses and the second involves scanning all items without locking them and then rereading the records for update. In the first case, when out-of-stock conditions are encountered, locks must either be released or held across the operator sessions. In the second case, extra reads are required, and the record could be changed by other transactions in the interval between the initial read and the subsequent update read, which could create an out-of-stock condition that was not identified in the initial read.

Inventory Check/Update Alternatives. Analysis of orders indicates that in only 5% of the transactions is there insufficient stock in all warehouse locations and that in only 10% of those situations are one or more line items canceled as a result. The first of these numbers is the more significant, for in 5% of all transactions the operator must be prompted to determine whether any line items should be canceled. This portion of the overall transaction presented the most significant dilemma for the analysts. The five basic approaches considered follow. In each of them, the customer record is read and locked unless it is a cash transaction, thus prohibiting the same customer from placing orders concurrently and exceeding the credit limit.

1. Read records without locking them. If all stock levels could be met then the records would have to be reread, locked, and updated. In 5% of the cases, the operator would be consulted before proceeding. In 95% of the circumstances the records would be read twice and updated once. In rare situations, the stock levels could be decreased by other transactions. In this situation, an insufficient stock level would be recognized, thus defeating the intent of deferring the updates.

2. Lock records as they are read and defer updates until the entire order can be completed. If an item is out of stock, the records can be unlocked and the operator informed of the out-of-stock items and the transaction started again if the order is placed.

3. Same as Transaction 2, except do not unlock the records during the operator session. This ensures that other transactions will not decrease stock levels already checked.

4. Read the records with lock, update them as read, and back out all updated records when an insufficient stock level is encountered. The database management system being used can support this situation. A transaction can be started and if an insufficient stock level is encountered, the transaction can be aborted, which automatically reverses all updates.

5. Lock records and update them as read. If an out-of-stock condition is encountered, all locks can be maintained across the session with the operator. This option has the problem of potentially locking a large number of records and keeping them locked over a session with the operator. It is possible that the customer will take a long time to decide about canceling line items.

The design team considered Options 2 and 4 as the best approaches. Option 4 was selected because the number of exceptions is low and because transaction backout creates less overhead than locking and releasing locks, rereading records, or spanning sessions with an operator. Option 4 optimizes the transaction for the typical situation; the atypical situation results in more overhead. (If the number of exceptions increases, however, then one of the other approaches might be preferable.) As an integral part of the transaction, an order record is written to a log file. This record is important with respect to completing the rest of the transaction. Rather than having the customer wait while picking list algorithms are processed, packing lists written, shipping labels created, accounting records updated, and so on, the order confirmation is returned to the order location as promptly as possible. The log entry is used to activate the rest of the transaction after customer notification. In all of the above scenarios, the transaction would be defined for the updating of the inventory records and the entering of the log file record.

Customer Order Confirmation.   Once the inventory has been updated, the order is confirmed with the customer. The order, together with shipping information, is printed at the order point. A background process used to complete the order reads the transaction log record and produces the packing lists, shipping labels, and accounting entries. While this background activity is occurring, other order entry transactions can be started. Since this design separates the noncustomer portions of order processing from those directly affecting customer wait time, the customer is delayed for the minimum amount of time and the order is divided into recoverable, indivisible components: customer identification, order entry and verification, and background processing.

SUMMARY

The acquisition of hardware, software, and services is a time-consuming process. For potential vendors to adequately size and price a system, a significant amount of information must be collected, organized, and presented to them. The information should be in the form of a statement of a problem to be solved rather than a response to a solution. This request for proposal (RFP) allows the vendors to configure their systems in the way in which they work best. The evaluation of responses is also time-consuming. Careful preparation of the RFP can simplify the evaluation process. The field of viable vendors should be narrowed down to a small number who can best solve the problem. This select group can then be evaluated in depth and can be required to make presentations and run benchmarks. System configuration and sizing is an ongoing process. It also requires a good knowledge of the equipment and application involved. By modeling a developing system or monitoring an existing system, performance problems can be anticipated and avoided.

Key Terms

availability	request for proposal (RFP)
benchmark	request for quotation (RFQ)
effectiveness	seek time
latency	sizing
reliability	transaction
request for information (RFI)	

Review Questions

1. Suppose that you eliminated the feasibility study phase in the product life cycle and proceeded directly into designing a solution. What problems might result from this?

2. What are the implications of having transactions involve multiple sessions with a terminal operator? Are there any benefits to having multiple sessions with an operator?

3. What impact will long transactions have on a system?

4. Why is transfer time considered insignificant in sizing a system?

5. When a request for proposal (RFP) is released to vendors, why should a single contact point for questions be established?

6. Why should an RFP focus on problem definition rather than problem solutions?

7. Compare and contrast an RFI and an RFP. Give an example where an RFP will likely be required.

Exercises

1. Are there any applications where long transactions are necessary? If so, what are some examples?

2. Write a request for information to solicit information about statistical time division multiplexers.

3. A banking application is defined below. Calculate the response time for each transaction.

Banking Application Parameters

A banking application is designed to provide ATM and teller services. During the peak application period, 20 ATM transactions and 10 teller transactions must be processed per second. These 30 transactions are of three types: cash withdrawal, account balance inquiry, and account transfer. Cash withdrawals account for 15 of the transactions, 10 are account balance inquiries, and 5 are account transfers. A description of each transaction is given in Figure 14-7.

Figure 14-7
Transaction Activity

Cash Withdrawal Transaction

Data communications input: 50 characters
Disk accesses: 10
Data communications output: 100 characters
Line speed: 4800 bits per second

Account Balance Inquiry Transaction

Data communications input: 20 characters
Disk accesses: 4
Data communications output: 50 characters
Line speed: 4800 bits per second

Account Transfer Transaction

Data communications input: 50 characters
Disk accesses: 12
Data communications output: 50 characters
Line speed: 4800 bits per second

4. A hospital patient admission transaction generates a large number of database updates. Some of the files updated include:
   a. patient file
   b. room file
   c. several records in an inventory file for patient supplies
   d. insurance coverage file
   e. multiple records in the patient fee file for room costs, supplies, and so on

   How would you define the transaction for these activities: Would you define one transaction or multiple short transactions? Justify your decision.

References

Bronner, L. "Overview of the Capacity Planning Process for Production Data Processing." *IBM Systems Journal*, Vol. 19, No. 1, 1980.

Cooper, J. C. "A Capacity Planning Methodology." *IBM Systems Journal*, Vol. 19, No. 1, 1980.

Guerrieri, John A., Jr. "How to Develop Effective RFPs." *Journal of Information Systems Management*, Vol. 1, No. 4, Fall 1984.

Martin, James. *Systems Analysis for Data Transmission*. Englewood Cliffs, NJ: Prentice-Hall, 1972.

Nguyen, H. C., et al. "The Role of Detailed Simulation in Capacity Planning." *IBM Systems Journal*, Vol. 19, No. 1, 1980

Schiller, D. C. "System Capacity and Performance Evaluation." *IBM Systems Journal*, Vol. 19, No. 1, 1980.

Seaman, P. H. "Modeling Considerations for Predicting Performance of CICS/VS Systems." *IBM Systems Journal*, Vol. 19, No. 1, 1980.

Yuvall, A. "System Contention Analysis—An Alternate Approach of System Tuning." *IBM Systems Journal*, Vol. 19, No. 2, 1980.

Distributed Systems

Distributed Systems Definitions
Evolution of Distributed Systems
Remote File Systems
Distributed System Examples
Advantages and Disadvantages of Distributed Systems
Database Management in Distributed Systems

INTRODUCTION

Thus far, we have looked at networked systems primarily from the perspective of using them for their communications capabilities. However, there is another application of networking: distributing and sharing resources. One of the directions of network technology has been creating the ability to effectively distribute processing resources such as hardware, software, and data as well as their management and control. In this chapter you learn about this technology and its advantages and disadvantages. Specific topics you will read about include:

Distributed systems terminology
The evolution of distributed systems
The requirements of distributed systems and distributed databases
Advantages and disadvantages of distributed systems
Distributed database considerations

DISTRIBUTED SYSTEMS DEFINITIONS

There are a variety of ways in which systems can be distributed. In Chapters 8 and 9 you read about local area networks (LANs), and although it was not explicitly stated, a LAN's resources are distributed. A LAN's processing load is split among servers and workstations, both acting in concert to help knowledge workers attain their objectives. In this use of the system, processing is distributed. In other instances data is distributed over two or more nodes, such as on file servers, SQL servers, and workstations. However, usually in LANs, although data is distributed, there is no distributed data management. Instead, the distributed data is treated as "islands of data" without the benefit of the comprehensive, coordinated management of a distributed database management system. Let us more precisely define the various aspects of distributed systems.

First, there is a distinction between distributed processing and distributed databases. From the preceding paragraph, you may have an intuitive idea about these distinctions. *Distributed processing* refers to the geographic distribution of hardware, software, processing, data, and control. The data communications system is the glue that holds the distributed system together and makes it workable. Geographic distribution does not mean great distances. As stated earlier, a LAN is a distributed processing system and, by definition, serves a limited area. Moreover, a company can have a distributed system contained in a single computer room. The key factor in having a distributed processing system is networking two or more independent computing systems where there is an interdependence among the nodes thus connected. The dependence can be for processing power, data, application software, or use of peripherals.

Often distributed systems also are characterized by distribution of control. Thus, if the nodes are placed in different locations, there is local responsibility for each node. For example, a manufacturing organization may have processing nodes in the headquarters offices, regional offices, and warehouses. In each of these locations, there will be an operations staff responsible for running the systems. There may also be a local support and development organization responsible for developing, installing, and maintaining applications and databases.

Data is often one of the objects distributed in a network. Frequently people refer to data distribution as a distributed database. Simple data distribution, however, is not sufficient for having a distributed database. To have a true distributed database, there must be a comprehensive, coordinated system that manages the data. Later in this chapter, you learn about the requirements of a distributed database management system and how it differs from distributed file systems. Because distributed data and databases are an important aspect of distributed system, a large portion of this chapter addresses the issues surrounding this topic.

One objective of distributed processing is to move data and processing functions closer to the users who need those services and thereby to improve the system's responsiveness and reliability. A second objective is to make remote access transparent to the system user, so the user has little or nothing special to do when accessing the other nodes of the system. How these objectives are met is explained below. First, however, let us review how distributed systems evolved.

EVOLUTION OF DISTRIBUTED SYSTEMS

At the dawn of the computer age, computers were big and expensive, and operating systems were either nonexistent or incapable of supporting multiple job streams. As a result, for the organizations that could afford it, computer systems were acquired for every department needing computational power. Thus, in a manufacturing organization, one computer would be dedicated to inventory, one to accounting, one to manufacturing control, and so on. These were *decentralized processing systems,* but they were considerably different from the current concept of distributed systems in one important respect, the sharing of resources.

Duplicated Databases and Inconsistent Data

Processors in those early systems usually were not connected via communications links. As a result each maintained its own database, often with duplicated data. Thus, both the warehouse database and the accounting department database contained the same customer information, the former for shipping and the latter for invoicing. When a customer moved, the address change was not likely to be reflected in both databases at once, and in some instances not before a considerable amount of time had elapsed. Thus, redundant storage of data, with the attendant update problems, created data inconsistencies. Data inconsistencies often are manifested by conflicts in reports. Managers are generally intolerant of such conflicting reports. Perhaps more importantly in the example just given, shipments or invoices could be sent to the incorrect address and perhaps be lost. Because each department was essentially the proprietor of its own system, there was little sharing of computer resources. Thus, one system might be completely inundated with work while another is relatively idle. One possible early decentralized processing system is depicted in Figure 15-1.

Centralization

The early decentralized systems were far from ideal. In addition to data inconsistencies, there were extra costs for hardware, operations, maintenance, and programming. Therefore, as systems grew larger and operating systems more comprehensive, there was a movement to large, centralized systems, as illustrated in Figure 15-2. Large, centralized systems had the benefits of a single operations center, control, and—according to some—economies of scale, since a single, large system was likely to cost less than several smaller decentralized systems. In many organizations having centralized systems, a single programming department was established for all application development and maintenance. To reduce data redundancy and promote data sharing among users, centralized databases were also established.

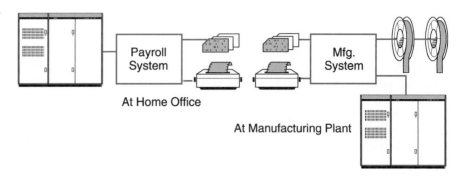

Figure 15-1 Early Distributed Processing System

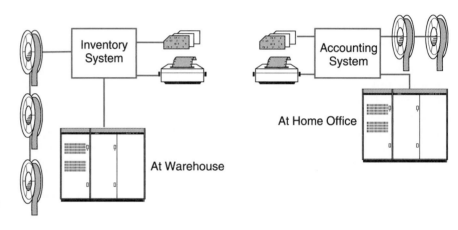

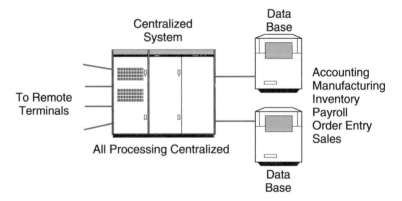

Figure 15-2 A Centralized System

Disadvantages of Centralization

It was later found that large, centralized systems also have inherent problems. First, if the large, central system fails, the entire system fails and if a component fails, all or part of the application system may also be unavailable. In the decentralized approach, failure of one node results in part of the overall system being lost, but many processing functions can be continued. In this respect, decentralized systems are more reliable than the single, centralized system.

Many end users of centralized systems—the accounting department, warehouse, and so forth—found their needs inadequately met by a centralized system. Because the system was shared, users often found it unresponsive, particularly regarding when jobs would be run and getting resources for new development. With a departmental system in a distributed or decentralized environment, a user contends only with other users in the department, so it was relatively easy to establish priorities. Setting inter-department priorities, however, sometimes was not easy. The same held true for programming: In the centralized environment, a programming team may have been assigned to develop an application or a new report for a department. Because developers were not under the direct control of the department, it was sometimes difficult for the department to change priorities and directions.

Expansion and growth of the large, centralized system posed another problem for some companies, that of controlling system growth. Too often growth was not in small, manageable increments but in giant steps, such as conversion to a larger processor with a different operating system. This conversion meant down time while the new system was being installed. Sometimes programs had to be revised and new program bugs were encountered. The change was usually disruptive to all users. In contrast, when upgrading a distributed system growth was generally in smaller, more manageable increments. Moreover, if a new processor became necessary, only those using that node were affected, not the entire user community.

Networked Systems

Networking provides some of the benefits of both centralized and distributed environments—more localized processing and control with shared data, processing power, and equipment. Let us again use a LAN as an example; the same comments generally apply to wide area networks as well. In a LAN end users have a workstation capable of performing a variety of application functions such as word processing, working with spreadsheets, and so on. Each workstation is also able to call on the processing power and database capabilities of a larger system—a server or host processor—to accomplish more complex and time-consuming processing tasks. Some of the data required frequently by a user at a workstation may be resident on the workstation's local disk drives. This may include documents in process and budget data for spreadsheets. Data that either is infrequently used or is too big for the workstation's local disks can be maintained at a larger host. Despite its being maintained by another node, the workstation can access that data as though it was stored locally. Workstations are also able to share other network resources such as printers and magnetic tape drives. The key to distributing systems is making resource distribution transparent to the users of the system. When the resources being distributed are data, sophisticated network software is necessary. The software responsible for doing this is called a *distributed file system.*

DISTRIBUTED FILE SYSTEMS

In distributed systems, users must have the ability to locate and use remote files as though they were locally resident. Software systems that provide this service are called *distributed file systems* (*DFS*). The objectives of a DFS are given in Figure 15-3 and are described below. Again, do not confuse a DFS with a distributed database management system. While there are similarities between the two, distributed database systems significantly extend the capabilities of a DFS.

Transparent Access.   *Transparent access* means that a user at one node must be able to access distributed files as though they were located on the user's local node. This means that a user should be able to use the file system commands of the local system to access remote files—even if the remote file is located on a node with a different operating and file system.

Operating System Independence.   In building a distributed system, a user should be able to configure heterogeneous systems. This may mean that different operating systems and file systems are involved. Not only should designers be able to build a system composed of different hardware and software but they must also make these differences transparent to users.

File System Independence.   With *file system independence,* different file systems, such as DOS, UNIX, and VMS, may be used in one network. Just as important, the differences between the file systems should be transparent to users. For example, the local file system commands should be functional when accessing a file on a remote node having a different file system.

Figure 15-3
Distributed File
System Objectives

Provide transparent access to distributed files
Provide operating system independence
Provide file system independence
Provide architecture independence
Provide contention resolution
Provide security
Provide file directory information
Provide location independence

Architecture Independence.   The DFS should allow any network configuration—star, bus, ring, interconnected, and so on. Neither the architecture nor the network software should limit the ability to distribute files.

Contention Resolution.   The DFS ought to provide a mechanism that prevents data corruption due to contention. This can result when two or more users try to access and update the same file or record.

Security.   A DFS must provide the requisite level of security. Files should be able to be secured for local access only or for remote access. When remote access to a file is allowed, the DFS must be able to grant or deny requests based upon the requester's ID. Inherent in this requirement is the ability to (1) provide user identities for users on a node that does not support user IDs, such as a single-user microcomputer, and (2) reconcile network differences among user IDs.

File Directory Information.   The DFS is responsible for transparently satisfying user requests. This means that it must maintain a directory of remote files and their locations. When a user requests access to a file, the directory is consulted to find the node(s) that house the file.

Location Independence.   *Location independence* means that a file can be located at any node in the network. Moreover, a file must be able to be moved from one node to another without disrupting applications or end-user access to that file.

Several DFS implementations exist. The one most often used for networks with equipment from a variety of vendors is the *network file system* (*NFS*), developed by Sun Microsystems. It is implemented not only on Sun systems but also on a variety of Unix-, VMS-, and DOS-based systems. Sun Microsystems has placed the NFS protocol specifications in the public domain to allow other vendors to implement it. The objective of publishing the protocol was to spread its use and establish NFS as a standard.

A Unix operating system DFS, *remote file sharing* (*RFS*), currently runs only on Unix-based systems. This protocol is supported by the American Telephone and Telegraph Company (AT&T), the originator of the Unix operating system. One of the current limitations of RFS is its restriction to Unix-based systems. With RFS, files that physically exist on one node can appear as though they are resident on other nodes. Thus, a user can access the remote file as though it were a local file.

DISTRIBUTED SYSTEM EXAMPLES

Let us now look at several examples of distributed processing and subsequently describe the extended requirements for distributed databases. A large national bank has decided to regionalize its bank card authorization system. The area served by the bank has been divided into five regions, each with a data center for authorizing credit card purchases. Each region contains files for the customers it serves. Merchants within a region call a toll-free number to get authorization for purchases. The toll-free number connects them with a computer that services the region in which the merchant is located. A graphic of the network is given in Figure 15-4.

In the usual situation, customers make charges within their own region. For a smaller percentage of transactions, credit card customers make charges in a region outside their home region. In these cases, the transaction being authorized in a center other than the one called by the merchant must be transparent to both the merchant and the customer. The merchant still telephones the local region for authorization; the credit card number is identified as being that of another region and the authorization system sends a message to the remote node for authorization. Suppose that a customer from Region 3 in Figure 15-4 makes a charge in Region 1. The merchant's interface to the authorization system automatically telephones the authorization center in Region 1. The card number is read from the magnetic strip on the card by a card reader and transmitted together with the charge amount totaled in the cash register. The software in Region 1 recognizes that the card number is from Region 3 and sends a message to that processing center. The application software in Region 3 authorizes the charge and updates the customer's record. The authorization message is then routed back to Region 1's node, from which an authorization code is displayed on the merchant's terminal to complete the transaction.

Figure 15-4   A Distributed Bank Card Authorization Network

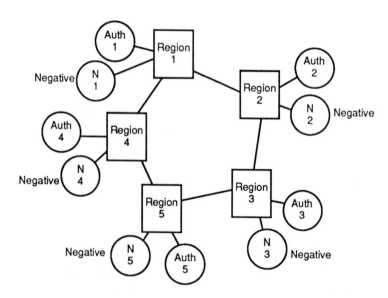

Negative File

If a communications failure occurs, it may be impossible to reach a remote node for authorization. In such instances a *negative file* is used for authorization. The negative file, replicated at each node, contains a list of all bad credit risks from all regions. The negative file is maintained centrally and updated periodically.

Local Node Failure

If a local node fails, authorizations can still be made. Suppose, for instance, that the northwest region's system is unavailable. Authorizations initiated at other nodes for Region 4 are made using the negative files at those nodes. Calls to Region 4's authorization center can still be processed. In these cases, calls are automatically switched to another region's system. Authorizations for Region 4's customers are made using the negative files. Foreign authorizations are made in the usual manner by routing them to the proper regional node.

Distributed Data

In the bank card authorization system, the credit card being from another region is transparent to both the merchant and the customer. Neither had to do anything different to authorize the sale. With distributed files, the data was distributed to be located where used most often. On occasion it was necessary for one node to access and update the data at another node. One file, the negative file, was replicated on all nodes, since each node would have occasion to use it. These negative files were kept up-to-date from a centralized location.

Distributed Processing

In the credit card authorization system it was primarily the data that was distributed, and one center used very few processing resources of another. In other distributed systems the opposite is true. In some university networks, for instance, it is primarily the processing that is distributed. A few universities have supercomputers suitable for processor-bound tasks such as nuclear, seismic, or atmospheric research. Jobs that are compute intensive are routed to such processors. Moreover, if one academic network node becomes saturated with student programs, some programs might be routed to another, less congested node for processing. In this academic situation it is not the data that is shared among the different nodes as much as it is the processing power.

Combination Distributed Data and Distributed Processing

Between these two situations is a continuum of sharing of data and processing. Consider a computer manufacturer with manufacturing and marketing facilities in several locations. Each manufacturing location maintains its own inventory database, each warehouse has its inventory maintained locally, and marketing offices have local databases describing their customers, prospects, and installed systems. The home office contains information on personnel, accounts receivable and payable, and so on. The distributed software makes the distributed data accessible to all authorized users. Some of the distributed uses of the system follow.

1. If inventory shortages occur in one manufacturing area, the other manufacturing plants' databases are checked to determine if the parts are available. A shipping clerk must access each remote file individually to make these checks.

2. Marketing offices can check the inventory at any warehouse to determine if a piece of equipment is available for shipment to a customer. Salespeople ordinarily have equipment shipped from the nearest warehouse. They have the added flexibility of being able to determine the stock levels at any warehouse and have one composite order shipped from several locations. The application system provides this capability automatically; however, within the application, each inventory file is treated as an individual file, which means each file must be opened separately and manipulated separately.

3. Home office managers can initiate reports at remote nodes for forecasting and planning. Suppose the vice president of manufacturing is interested in a summary report on the inventories at all the plants. She can start a process at each of the manufacturing nodes to access and summarize the information there and transmit these separate summaries to the corporate node, where they would be consolidated and printed. In this instance, it is less time-consuming to access the large volume of data at multiple local nodes, summarize it, and transmit the results. Both remote data and processing facilities are used.

4. Because of time zone differences, one area of the country can use the processors in another area when they might otherwise be idle. For instance, if the system in a West Coast office is busy at 4 P.M., a user could start a job at an East Coast node, which at 7 P.M. Eastern time would be relatively uncongested.

5. The network provides instant access to documents and personnel files within the corporation. Documents and graphic images can be made immediately available to those who need them regardless of which node they are attached to.

ADVANTAGES AND DISADVANTAGES OF DISTRIBUTED SYSTEMS

Advantages

Each of the distributed systems just described has numerous advantages. For one, storing data close to the location that uses it most in a network situation minimizes the amount of data that must be transmitted between nodes and provides better response times. Since maintenance of the data is a local responsibility, there is more of a vested interest in keeping the data current. Third, nonlocal transactions are still possible, as are transactions that must span several nodes, the only penalty being slower response times due to slow transmission speeds on the communications links. Distributed systems also give local users more control over their data-processing system. This provides them with the flexibility to tailor changes to their own particular needs without disrupting other network nodes. In addition, reliability is higher than with a centralized system, for the failure of one node does not mean the entire system is down. Each node has most of the data it needs to continue local processing so applications can continue with only a slight degradation in service.

Disadvantages

There are also disadvantages to the distributed approach.

Multiple-Node Transactions Are Slower. Whenever a transaction must span more than one node, response time is longer than if the transaction ran on one node only. Suppose that a salesperson for a computer vendor enters an order for a new system consisting of processors, disks, and terminals. The response time for placing the order will be faster if all the equipment is available in the local warehouse than if each component must come from a different location. In the latter case, a message would have to be sent to the other warehouses in sequence until the order was filled.

Maintaining Transaction Integrity. You have already read in Chapter 14 that a transaction is an atomic piece of work. In a centralized database, this atomic property is guaranteed by the database management system's recovery system. However, when a transaction updates files on several nodes, several independent database management systems are involved. Each may be capable of guaranteeing the integrity of the *portion* of the transaction processed on its system but there is no coordination among the various database management systems. In fact, it may be difficult to even establish a consistent, unique transaction identifier for node-spanning transactions.

Contention and Deadlock. Update transactions on multiple nodes increase the risk of *contention* and *deadlock*. As discussed in previous chapters, a record being updated is locked until the end of the transaction, to avoid the problems of concurrent updates. Since a transaction that spans several nodes is slower than one on a single node (because of data communications transmission time), the records locked by the transaction remain locked longer. Thus, the probability increases that the records will be needed by another transaction, and hence the amount of contention and the potential for deadlock increase.

Potential for Failure.   The longer response time for transactions that span multiple nodes also increases the probability of a failure that will produce an unsuccessful transaction.

Determining Participating Nodes

Most database management systems available today were not designed for distributing data over several nodes. With a transaction that accesses and updates records on multiple nodes, the system must determine which other nodes must be involved. It is unthinkable to require the user to do this, because one of the objectives is to make the distributed nature of the system transparent to the user. Also, it is desirable to reserve the ability to redistribute data and processes without disrupting users.

One approach to identifying the location of resources is to programmatically define the nodes that are to participate by coding the locations into the programs. This requires that the programming staff know the location of data their programs are using. As additional nodes are added or data are relocated, it is likely that program changes also will be required. This approach is preferable to relying on the user to decide the location of files, but presents considerable problems with respect to maintaining the system, extending the system, and redistributing its resources.

Network Dictionary of Locations.   A better way to identify resource locations is to have a network dictionary that describes the locations of all distributed data and processing entities referenced in the system. The application or transaction control process can access the dictionary to learn where the required resources are located. Redistribution of files requires a simple update to the dictionary and programs are unaffected by such changes.

Central Versus Distributed Dictionary.   The dictionary can be either centrally located and maintained or replicated at all nodes, like the negative file in the bank authorization example above. The centralized approach, with several weaknesses, is the less desirable of the two. First, when the central node becomes unavailable, the distributed system is inoperable. Local operations could continue, but finding remote resources would be impossible. The centralized dictionary approach could be augmented by establishing one or more alternate nodes with backup dictionary capability. The backup nodes are used if the primary fails.

A second problem with a centralized dictionary is that additional access time is required to obtain the information and the possibility of the central node becoming a performance bottleneck. In a local area network with high-speed links communication time might not be significant. Accessing data via a slow communications link with several hops through intermediate nodes can significantly slow the application response time, especially if the dictionary must be consulted several times for each transaction.

A distributed dictionary resides on all nodes or strategically located nodes. This provides faster access to the dictionary than in the centralized approach. The disadvantage of distributed dictionaries is keeping all dictionaries properly updated, particularly if the contents change frequently. Despite this shortcoming, a distributed dictionary usually gives better performance than a centralized one.

Routing, Transmission, and Processing

Once the locations of the distributed resources have been determined, a strategy must be developed for accessing and processing the data. Designers of distributed systems have several options in determining how the remote processing and accesses will be handled. In general, which strategy is selected depends on the type of transaction.

Remote Access and Local Processing. One method for processing with distributed data is remote access and local processing. This type of transaction is used effectively when most of the data being accessed is needed at the local node. Consider a system for a state's highway patrol force. Suppose that a state trooper stops a car and inquires regarding the driver's record. The application on a local node will issue a read request for the driver's files on a remote node. The set of records for the driver is transmitted to the local node and from there to the display device in the trooper's car. In this case, there was a local request for remote access, and all data satisfying that request was sent to the local node for processing. It is possible that the driver is cited for a violation as a consequence of the trooper's work. In this case, the driver's record might be modified locally and then a local request for updating the record in the remote file will be made. The revised record will be transmitted over the network and the database updated as a consequence of the remote update request. The characteristics of the police transaction are that every record accessed was transmitted over the network to the local node, all processing was done locally, and all updates were brought about via local requests. This is similar to the way in which a LAN file server operates.

Partial Remote Processing.   A second method for handling distributed processing requires that the remote node perform some amount of application processing. Consider a transaction to list all employees having more than 10 years of service and a salary less than $20,000: For a company with 100,000 employees, all 100,000 records will need to be accessed to satisfy the query. To pass each of the 100,000 records to the requesting node for selection would place a large load on the communications subsystem and take considerable extra time. A much better alternative is to have a server process on each remote node access the records, perform the selection, and then transmit only the results to the requesting node where the list will be consolidated.

Total Remote Processing.   Consider a transaction that updates records at a remote node. When the record is required locally, the remote record is transmitted to the local node, an update is made, and the record is sent back to the remote node for updating in the database. In some instances the entire update can be performed remotely, as in giving an across-the-board pay raise to employees.

Suppose that a company has decided to distribute the personnel and payroll applications and maintains that data in each of five regional processing centers. A manager in the corporate headquarters may have the responsibility for administering a 6% pay raise for all 100,000 employees. If the first strategy is used, each of the 100,000 records must be read remotely, transmitted over the network, updated, sent back over the network, and updated in the database. For this transaction, however, there is no need to transmit any data to the local node. A better alternative is to send the request to a server process on the remote node and have all the work done there. You should recognize this type of processing as being equivalent to the capabilities of the local area network's SQL server described in Chapter 9.

Many other examples of the division of activity between nodes could be cited. In essence, there are only the three basic methods just discussed: (1) access remote records, pass them to the local node, process the records locally, and then return them to the remote node(s) for updating as necessary; (2) send messages to remote application servers that accept and process data and then return only the required information to the requesting nodes; and (3) a combination of the two approaches is sometimes the best alternative. The design objective is always to make the transaction as efficient as possible, which means minimizing the transmission of many records between nodes.

DATABASE MANAGEMENT IN DISTRIBUTED SYSTEMS

Having discussed how data can be manipulated with remote file systems, let us now look at the more complex problem of distributed databases.

Most current database management systems were designed to operate on only one node. Thus, there was no need to keep track of files or databases on another node or to manage transactions that span multiple nodes. In some instances the problem of distributed transactions is compounded by having two different database systems involved. One example is when one node uses one vendor's hardware and software and another node uses a different vendor's hardware and database management system. In such cases, it is not likely that the database management systems will cooperate with each other except through user-written programs or routines.

It is significant to note that distributed file systems provide a mechanism for remote file access and manipulation but they do not provide for distributed data management. For example, in the manufacturing company, each inventory file had to be treated as a separate entity even though in contents and structure the inventory file on one node was identical to the inventory files on the other nodes. Moreover, in the distributed file example, there was no transaction integrity for node-spanning transactions. These are but two of the problems inherent in distributed file systems that a distributed database management system overcomes. Thus, a distributed database management system goes beyond the capabilities provided by distributed file systems.

Rules for a Distributed Database

You have already read about the objectives of distributed file systems. A similar set of objectives or rules has been established for distributed databases (Date, 1987). These rules, given in Figure 15-5, are explained below. Note that in some instances the rules are comparable to those for distributed file systems and that the rules extend the capabilities of remote file systems

1. Local autonomy.
2. No reliance on a central site.
3. Continuous operation.
4. Location independence.
5. Fragmentation independence.
6. Replication independence.
7. Distributed query processing.
8. Distributed transaction management.
9. Hardware independence.
10. Operating system independence.
11. Network independence.
12. DBMS independence.

Figure 15-5 Date's Twelve Rules for a Distributed Database

Rule 1. *Local autonomy* means that users at a given node are responsible for data management and system operation at that node. A local node has a certain amount of independence regarding these local operations. This independence is not unrestrained, however. As with individuals in a free society who have individual independence, the independence extends only where it does not adversely affect another member of the society. Thus, a local node does not typically have the independence to arbitrarily remove their node from the network if that action is detrimental to operating the distributed system. Another implication of local autonomy is that users at a node accessing only data local to that node should neither experience performance degradations nor need to interact with the system differently as a result of being part of a distributed system.

Rule 2. No reliance on a central site means that all nodes in the distributed system shall be considered as peer nodes with no node identified as a supervisor. Furthermore, there shall not be one node upon which other nodes must rely, such as a single node that contains a centralized data dictionary or directory.

Rule 3. *Continuous operation* means that adding new nodes to the network, removing network nodes, or having one node fail will not discontinue availability of other nodes. Naturally, a single node failure will likely disrupt access for the users local to that node; however, users at other nodes can continue to use the distributed database, and their disruption will be limited to an inability to access data stored only at the failed node.

Rule 4. *Location independence* means that data can be placed anywhere in the network and that its location is transparent to those needing access to it. Data can be moved from one node to another, and users or programs needing access to that data will not be disrupted.

Rule 5. In the personnel and payroll example cited earlier in this chapter, each regional node had personnel and payroll files for the employees in that region. Physically, these were separate files, but logically their combination formed the *corporate* personnel file and payroll file. *Fragmentation independence* means that data that appears to users as one logical file can be transparently partitioned over multiple nodes. Thus, the personnel file is fragmented over several regional nodes. The corporate personnel director must be able to make inquiries regarding all employees, such as finding the average salary of all employees, and receive the answer consolidated from all fragments. Moreover, the manager must be able to initiate the query in the same way he or she would have if the table had not been fragmented. The distributed database management system is responsible for making the various fragments appear as a single file.

Rule 6. In the banking example cited earlier, one file, the negative file, needed to be resident at each node. Storing the same file in multiple locations is called replication. *Replication independence* means that any file can be replicated on two or more nodes and that such replication is transparent to both users and applications. Replication is desirable for files that need to be accessed by several nodes, such as a network directory. Replication can enhance performance and availability. The distributed database management system is responsible for managing updates to replicated data and keeping the replicated data consistent.

Rule 7. When we discussed access strategies for distributed files, three alternatives were given—remote access and local processing, partial remote processing, and total remote processing. Which was used depended on the application program's logic. *Distributed query processing* means that a user at one node can start a query involving data on other nodes. Access and processing strategies like those discussed earlier must be supported. The location of the data must be transparent to the user and the application. Moreover, the query must be completed in an optimum way. This might mean that database servers on several nodes cooperatively work on a portion of the query. In this way, the minimum amount of data will be transmitted over the network to the requesting node. The database management system is responsible for determining the access strategy and carrying it out.

Rule 8. *Distributed transaction management* means that node-spanning transactions must be allowed. Moreover, transactions that update data on several nodes must be recoverable. This requires that a transaction started on one node can update records on other nodes and that the database management systems on those other nodes coordinate their activities regarding locking records and effecting transaction backout and recovery.

Rule 9. *Hardware independence* means that the distributed network can consist of hardware from a variety of vendors. Thus, nodes in the distributed system can come from a variety of vendors, such as IBM, DEC, and Tandem.

Rule 10. When different hardware vendors supply network nodes, it is likely that different operating systems will be used. This capability is known as *operating system independence.*

Rule 11. Another consequence of Rule 9, hardware independence, might be that different network architectures, software, and protocols be used. If the vendors designed their network systems according to the OSI reference model and related standards, such interconnection will be easier. *Network independence* means that multiple kinds of network software may be used in connecting the nodes together. For example, some network nodes may be part of an SNA network, others may be members of a DECNET network, and still others may be nodes on an Ethernet local area network.

Using disparate network systems must not adversely affect distributed database capabilities.

Rule 12. *Database management system independence* means that a variety of database management systems may be used in the distributed database. For example, one node might use an IMS database, another might use DB2, a third might use ENCOMPASS, and still another might use Oracle. Each of these database management systems has a different data access and manipulation language, has different recovery mechanisms, and stores data in different formats. The distributed database management system must make these differences transparent to both users and applications. Moreover, a user shall be able to access data managed by such a variety of database management systems without learning a variety of data access languages. Specifically, the user should be able to access distributed data using the same interface he or she uses to access data stored locally. This rule implies that database recovery systems be coordinated and database language differences accommodated. Implementation of this rule is very complex.

Currently, there is no system that adheres to all of these rules. Creating a distributed environment that encompasses all twelve rules will require a considerable investment. Until then, those who want to implement distributed databases will need to settle for less than the capabilities implied by these rules. The best way to implement distributed databases today is to use hardware and software from one vendor only and to choose a vendor having a database system that supports distributed capabilities. Key to a distributed database system is the underlying model on which the database management system is based. Most databases in use today are based on one of two models: the relational model or the older network model.

Relational Model and Network Model

Distributed database technology continues to be a development project for developers of database management systems. In a few implementations, many of the required features described above are available; however, some complex problems must still be resolved. One of the fundamental capabilities of a database management system is its ability to establish associations between records in one file and records in another (or even the same) file. For instance, student records can be associated with class records and teacher records, and an employee record can be associated with another employee record, such as the record of the employee's manager. These associations allow system users to answer questions like "What is a student's schedule?" and "Who is an employee's manager?"

In the *network model*, an association is frequently created by storing the disk address of one record on the related record as illustrated in Figure 15-6. The figure shows a relationship between an employee record and several employee dependent records. Moving a record being pointed at

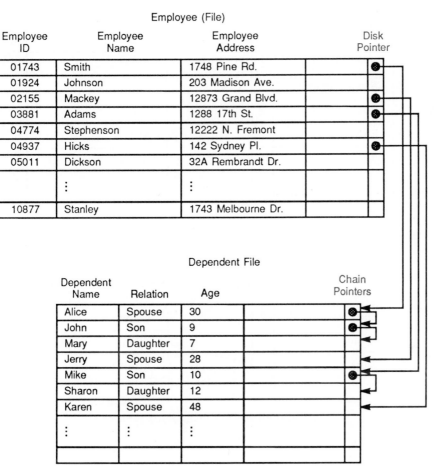

Figure 15-6
Network Model

either requires that the pointer be updated or renders the pointer invalid. For example, in Figure 15-7(a) the pointer on Record 2 in File A points to Location 5 in File B. Suppose that Record 5 in File B is moved to Location 6 to allow a new record to be inserted. This results in File B's organization as shown in Figure 15-7(b). Since the pointer on Record 2 in File A has not been changed, it is now pointing at an incorrect record.

In the network model, a list of pointers or a chain of records implements relationships among records. In the list approach shown in Figure 15-8, a list of pointers maintained on the employee record or an associated record contains the disk addresses of the related dependent records. The chain approach is illustrated in Figure 15-9. The employee record contains a disk pointer to the first and possibly the last dependent record. Each dependent record in turn contains a pointer to the next and possibly the prior related record. In some implementations the dependent record also may have a pointer back to the employee record. With the network approach, moving

Figure 15-7 Invalid Pointer Resulting from Record Movement

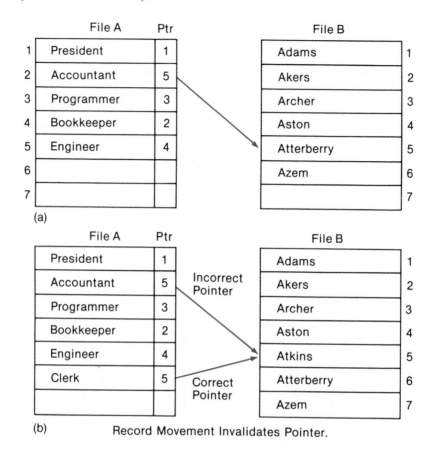

(a)

(b)   Record Movement Invalidates Pointer.

Figure 15-8
A Relationship Using a List of Pointers

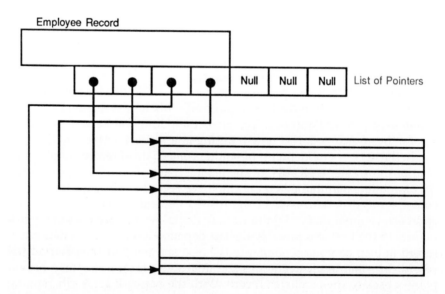

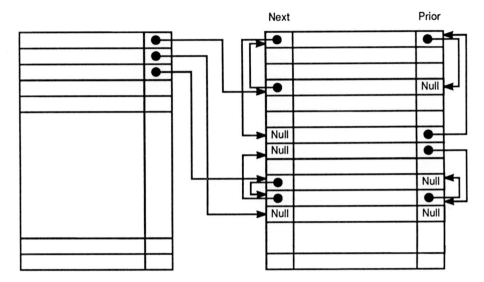

Figure 15-9 A Relationship Using Chain Pointers

a dependent file from one location to another will possibly invalidate all record pointers, making it necessary that the records be reloaded and the relationships reestablished, a time-consuming process. As a result, the network model has limited location independence. Implementation of distributed databases using network model systems is not impossible; it is just more difficult than with use of the relational model.

In contrast, the *relational model* is location independent. The relational model database system uses the content of data records or relations to form associations between files. This model allows data to be distributed and relocated without altering record pointers. Figure 15-10 illustrates the relational approach to relating employees and dependents compared to the network approach shown in Figure 15-6. Note that in the relational system the employee identification number is on each record in the dependent file as well as on the employee record. To find all dependents of a particular employee, the employee ID column of the dependent file is searched for the matching ID. Ordinarily, it is not necessary to examine every record to satisfy the search. Indices or other search strategies make the search very efficient.

File Distribution

A second obstacle that distributed database management systems must overcome is how files are distributed. In the personnel application mentioned above, it should be transparent to the manager administering the salary increase that the records are actually stored in multiple locations. Most current systems require that data in multiple locations be in separate

Figure 15-10
Relational Model

Employee Relation (File)

Employee ID	Employee Name	Employee Address	
01743	Smith	1748 Pine Rd.	
01924	Johnson	203 Madison Ave.	
02155	Mackey	12873 Grand Blvd.	
03881	Adams	1288 17th St.	
04774	Stephenson	12222 N. Fremont	
04937	Hicks	142 Sydney Pl.	
05011	Dickson	32A Rembrandt Dr.	
⋮	⋮	⋮	
10877	Stanley	1743 Melbourne Dr.	

Dependent Relation

Employee ID	Dependent Name	Relation	Age	
01743	Alice	Spouse	30	
01743	John	Son	9	
01743	Mary	Daughter	7	
02155	Jerry	Spouse	28	
03881	Mike	Son	10	
03881	Sharon	Daughter	12	
04937	Karen	Spouse	48	
⋮	⋮	⋮	⋮	

Association
made via
this field

files and run under separate database managers. Thus, for the five portions of the personnel files, the application software must open five database files and access each separately. Rather than having a view of one logically consolidated file, the application must access and merge records from each of the individual files. It becomes the user's responsibility to make the five separate files look like one logical file.

An ideal solution to the five personnel files is to have the database management system present them to the application as one file with partitions or subdivisions in five separate locations, which provides fragmentation independence. The application would then have only one file to open and one access path to the entire set of data, thus shifting responsibility for creating one logical file from files in five separate locations from the user or application to the database management system where it belongs.

This type of file partitioning would enable the user to specify rules regarding the node on which a record would be stored and would allow restriction of access to the local node or to all nodes. It would also require that the loss of one node not prohibit any other node from accessing the other available file fragments. The techniques for realizing this type of distributed file exist, but the capability has yet to be implemented. Expansion of distributed systems will make this a requirement of future database management systems.

Transaction and Database Recovery

Very few database management systems permit transactions to span nodes or allow transactions and database recovery between two or more nodes. However, the number of systems providing this ability is rapidly growing. It is important for a database management system operating in a distributed environment to maintain the integrity and consistency of the database by providing node-spanning transactions and transaction recovery. Without this ability, transactions such as a transfer from an account on one node to an account on a different node would be treated as two separate transactions, allowing one but not the other to complete successfully and leaving the database in an inconsistent state. For those systems that do handle such transfers between accounts as separate transactions, it is up to the application to recognize the failure of any transaction and to effect recovery. Again this capability should be provided by the database management system. An abbreviated explanation of how this is accomplished follows.

Example.   A transaction is started on Node C to transfer funds from Account X on Node A to Account Y on Node B. A network-wide unique transaction ID is created, its uniqueness guaranteed by appending a node identification number to a date-time stamp. Every application that works on the transaction receives this unique transaction ID and performs work for that transaction. Account Record X is retrieved on Node A and the transfer amount is subtracted from the balance. Before- and after-image records are written for recovery purposes. In updating the record to reflect the new balance, the record is locked and will remain locked until the end of the transaction, thus preventing any other transaction from interfering with the balance until the transfer is completed. A message is sent to Node B requesting that the transfer amount be added to the Account Y record, which is retrieved, locked, and updated. A message is returned to the application at Node C indicating that the update was successfully completed.

With the updates successfully completed, the transaction can end successfully. The database management system at the initiating node sends a message to all participating nodes that the transaction is ready to end. After each node has ensured that its audit buffers are flushed to the audit medium and that the transaction's integrity at that node can be assured, it sends a completion message to the originating node. When all involved nodes have successfully responded, the transaction is completed by writing the end-of-transaction record to the log. This two-phase commit procedure guarantees that the transaction is fully recoverable. The database management system does all of this through the database and recovery managers. The application is responsible only for identifying the records to be updated. If for any reason a part of the transaction cannot be completed, a transaction abort message requesting that the transaction be backed out is transmitted to all participating nodes.

Deadlock. When updates involve several nodes, records are locked for longer time due to the relatively low speed of the communications medium. Furthermore, since the lock management systems at the various nodes are almost always independent, they are unaware of locks on remote nodes, thus increasing the probability of deadlock. This situation is further complicated by the fact that the deadlock could result from locks on more than one node. A deadlock condition is illustrated in Figure 14-4. These conditions lead to a deadlock for the two transactions, but recognition of this fact is made difficult because two nodes are involved and the lock management systems are unaware of each other's activities. Deadlock detection algorithms to resolve this problem have been proposed, but as yet, few, if any, have been implemented commercially.

Archiving. *Archiving* of database files, also known as backup and restore, also presents unique problems in the distributed environment. Archiving means to keep a historical copy of a database as it existed at a specific point in time. Such copies can be used to recover the database if a catastrophic failure occurs such as fire, program logic errors, or head crashes on a disk. The recovery procedure requires the historical copies to be restored to disk and the after-images from the audit trails to be posted to the database to bring it forward to a consistent point in time.

Synchronizing Files. Files in a distributed database must be kept in synchronization to ensure consistency. In the account transfer example, it would be unsatisfactory to have yesterday's files reloaded onto Node B and today's files loaded onto Node A. If this occurred, Node A's files would then reflect the transfer that had just occurred, whereas Node B's files would reflect the previous day's balance. Keeping the files synchronized following a major failure is an operations problem, one made more difficult when the archival copies have been created at different times on different nodes. The recovery system will reestablish the database on individual nodes, but there is currently little or no help from the database management system software to ensure that files on different nodes are at the same level of update.

Data Placement

A critical factor affecting performance in the distributed system is placement of the data. In most online applications, accessing data is the most time-consuming function, and is even more so when accessing data from a node through several intervening nodes.

Centralized Database. The simplest approach for the database management system is to centralize the data. All or most of the database is made resident on one or several nodes, a situation that eliminates many of the database problems described earlier, since a transaction spanning several nodes is quite rare. The disadvantage of such an implementation is that most accesses must span a data communications link and will thus be somewhat slower. With a star network, having the central node as the database node provides reasonable performance. In an interconnected configuration with many nodes, a centralized database approach may be impractical. This is illustrated in Figure 15-11. This approach is viable for a LAN but usually not for a long-distance network. In Figure 15-11 Node K's request must pass through three intermediate nodes, resulting in increased response time and network congestion.

Replicated Files. Files common to applications on several nodes can be *replicated* to reduce or eliminate accessing those records across the network. In the bank card authorization application discussed earlier, a negative file was replicated at each node. This type of file is ideal for replicated files. The negative file was potentially required by every node, its use was required whenever the communications link to another node was severed,

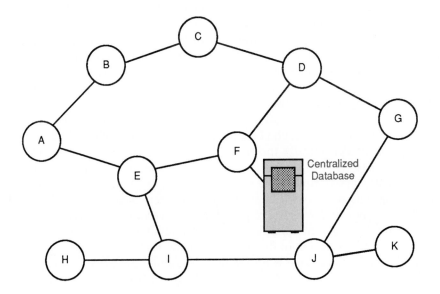

Figure 15-11 A Centralized Database

and the file was not volatile, which means it was not updated frequently. The last consideration is a very significant factor.

To illustrate the significance of volatility and file replication, consider again the credit card authorization system. An alternative to the negative file is to replicate the customer file on all nodes. Thus, each node in each of the five regional authorization centers would contain the entire customer database, meaning that all authorizations would be run very efficiently because the needed data would always be available locally. The bank's risk of loss from improper authorizations would decrease somewhat because a negative file would no longer be necessary. (The only purpose of the negative file was to allow an authorization when the path between the authorizing node and the customer's home node was unavailable.) These are the advantages of full replication. Unlike the negative file, however, the customer file is very volatile. Every time an authorization is made, the customer credit limit must be adjusted. For an authorization in the fully replicated configuration, then, a message must be sent to every other node to update its copy of the customer record. Instead of only a small percentage of the transactions requiring network transmission, every transaction would result in four update messages being transmitted, an unsatisfactory solution for many applications.

Updating replicated files in real time is further complicated by disruption of network communications. In the above example, if the link between two nodes is severed, there are three alternatives: disallow further transactions until the link is repai ed, batch the updates for the unavailable nodes and send them along when the link is restored, or continue processing and restore consistency in a batch-type operation as soon as possible. Disallowing transactions until the link is repaired is rarely viable. Saving the transactions until the link is reinstated is the best alternative in most cases because the replicated files are inconsistent for the shortest time. When the link is restored this solution creates a high level of network traffic and impedes the speed of the current transactions. Even if the batch transactions are paced to the remote nodes, the additional traffic and workload will affect system performance. Restoring file consistency in batch mode is satisfactory for certain types of files, such as the negative file. For customer files, however, the risk of inconsistent data would be too great.

Variations of the alternatives just described can be effective for certain types of data files. One such variation is to update the replicated file in one location only. Periodically the entire file or changed portions thereof are distributed to the rest of the nodes. This restoration would normally be effected at off-peak times. The types of files that generally qualify for this type of update are those that are frequently referenced and for which absolute currency of data is not required. In an inventory application, a parts description file might qualify for such treatment. If the part number changes or a description of the part changes, a day's delay in changing the description at every node is not likely to present a problem. The negative file update in the banking application might also qualify for such treatment.

SUMMARY

Distributed systems are becoming viable processing systems. They are currently at the frontier of database management systems and data communications systems. Many of the problems that impede their widespread use are in the area of database technology rather than data communications. Distributed data and distributed transactions may have a significant impact on the utilization of network resources. Specifically, data transfers, message transfers, and recovery messages can cause increased media traffic. Development in the problem areas should be spurred by potential advantages of distributing data to where it is most often used, by sharing of processing and data resources, and by providing more control to end users.

Key Terms

architecture independence
centralized system
database management
  system independence
deadlock
distributed database
distributed file
  system (DFS)
distributed processing
file directory
file system independence
fragmentation independence
hardware independence

local autonomy
location independence
negative file
network file system (NFS)
network independence
network model
operating system independence
relational model
replicated files
replication independence
synchronization of files
transparent access

Review Questions

1. What are the disadvantages of replicating data on multiple nodes?
2. What types of files are candidates for replication?
3. Describe three methods for keeping replicated files current.
4. What benefits do relational model database management systems provide in distributed database applications?
5. List four current problems in distributed processing.
6. List four applications that are good candidates for distributed processing.
7. Distinguish between distributed processing and distributed databases.
8. Describe the objectives of a distributed file system.
9. What are the advantages and disadvantages of distributed systems?
10. List and describe the 12 rules for distributed databases.

Exercises

1. Research the literature for database management systems that are or claim to be distributed. Determine how they resolve the problems cited above.

2. Suppose you were asked to design the placement of files for a personnel database. Your company has four regions, each of which has a personnel office, and there is a personnel office in a separate world headquarters complex. The files in the system are: employee, benefits, job history, payroll, department, skills, insurance, and insurance claims. Devise a plan for placing each of these files assuming each location has computer facilities. Would you recommend a distributed database solution? If so: Would you replicate any files? Would you partition any files? Document your decisions.

3. Research Digital Equipment Corporation's implementation of the remote file system. Describe how files are distributed and how users are able to access them.

References

Bernstein, Philip A., James B. Rothnie, and David W. Shipman. *Tutorial: Distributed Data Base Management.* IEEE Catalog no. EHO 141-2. New York: IEEE Computer Society, 1978.

Borsook, Paulina. "New Pains, New Gains: Distributed Database Solutions Are on Their Way." *Data Communications,* Vol. 17, No. 3, March 1988.

Champine, G. A. "Six Approaches to Distributed Data Bases." *Datamation,* May 1977.

Date, C. J. *An Introduction to Database Systems,* Vol. 2. Reading, MA: Addison-Wesley, 1983

————. "Twelve Rules for a Distributed Database." *Computerworld,* June 8, 1987.

Kallis, Stephen A., Jr. "Networks and Distributed Processing." *Mini-Micro Systems,* March 1977.

Moore, William G., Jr. "Going Distributed." *Mini-Micro Systems,* March 1977.

Q. E. D. Information Sciences. *Distributed Processing: Current Practice and Future Developments,* Vols. 1 and 2. Wellesley, MA: Q.E.D. Information Sciences and Online Expertise Limited, 1978.

Appendix A
Asynchronous Transmission

This appendix supplements the discussion of asynchronous transmission protocols in Chapter 6. You may wish to refer to that material before continuing. Asynchronous transmission occurs one character at a time. Sending and receiving stations are not synchronized with each other, which means that a sending station can send a character at any time, with no prescribed interval to the next character. Of course, the receiving station must also be ready to accept a character at any time. In the discussion that follows, an asynchronous point-to-point line with a transmission speed of 1200 bps is assumed.

The UART

At the heart of asynchronous transmission is a processing chip called the *universal asynchronous receiver/transmitter* (*UART*). The UART accepts characters via parallel transmission from the terminal or host and places them on the circuit serially. It also accepts bit serial transmissions from the communications line and passes the characters to the data terminal equipment in bit parallel fashion.

Detecting Incoming Characters

To detect an incoming character, the UART samples the state of the communications circuit at a rate 16 times the expected bit rate. On a 1200-bps line, one bit passes every $1/1200 = 0.000833 = 0.833$ milliseconds, so a sampling of the line is taken every 52 microseconds. Figure A-1 illustrates this situation. The line is sampled so frequently to identify immediately when the state of the line has changed from the mark condition to the space condition. When a line transition is detected, the sampling interval is changed to ensure that the line is always being sampled in the middle of a bit interval. This is far safer than attempting to interrogate the line at the beginning or ending of a bit, when a slight timing error could cause the bit

553

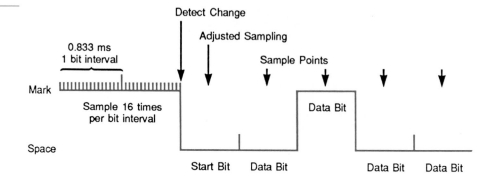

to be missed. Thus, when it appears that a start bit has arrived, there is a delay of 7/16th of a bit interval (0.364 milliseconds in the current example) before the line is sampled again, so that the sample is taken approximately in the middle of the bit interval. If the line is in the space condition, it is assumed this represents a start bit. Line sampling timing is adjusted to sample the line during every bit interval (every 0.83 milliseconds), and the line is sampled once for each bit and nearly in the center of the bit interval. As discussed in Chapter 6, four items must be agreed on by sender and receiver before asynchronous communications can begin—line speed, number of bits per character, presence of a parity bit, and message termination characters. Line sampling makes use of the agreed-on line speed.

Receiving Incoming Characters and Parity Check

Knowledge of the number of bits expected per character is used to receive the bits making up each character. This discussion assumes seven bits per character plus one parity bit. Having detected the start bit, the UART then assembles the next seven bits that should make up the character. The ninth bit, the parity bit, follows the start bit and the seven data bits. The parity bit is received and checked against the seven data bits already received. If parity does not check, then a parity error message is sent to the transmitter so the character can be retransmitted. If parity checks, the next bit is examined to see if it is a stop bit or a mark condition. If a stop bit or mark condition is not detected, a transmission error is assumed to have occurred. If everything is correct, the UART returns to sampling the line. It is necessary to know how many bits compose a character, as well as whether parity is being transmitted and checked, to know when to expect the stop bit.

Message Termination

If termination characters have been specified, the communications process driving the line must examine the character to determine if it matches any of the defined termination characters. If there is no match, the character is placed in memory awaiting the rest of the message. If an interrupt character is detected, appropriate action is taken, depending upon the interrupt character.

Suppose two interrupt characters have been designated, a backspace and a carriage return. The backspace is used to cancel a character just received, and a carriage return, to signal the end of the message. If a backspace character is received, it causes the end-of-buffer pointer to be decreased by one, meaning it essentially erases the previously received character. The next character transmitted (if not another backspace) is placed in the buffer over the previously received character. Since every keystroke in asynchronous transmission is transmitted immediately to the host (with dumb terminals, anyway), hitting an incorrect character followed by backspace transmits two characters to the host: the incorrect character and the backspace character. On the other hand, if the carriage return character is received, the end of the message has been indicated. On receiving this interrupt character, the system makes the data available to the application program.

Data Overruns

A UART usually has two registers available for receiving data from the line and two for receiving data from the data terminal equipment (DTE). This allows a received character to be checked for parity and placed into memory while another character is being received. Even so, *data overruns* are still possible, especially when an intelligent or smart terminal is transmitting data from its buffer. At such a time the data may be transmitted at intervals much faster than operator typing speeds. Even when the line speed is not exceeded, the receiving hardware or software may be incapable of receiving a continuous stream of characters at that speed. One solution to this problem is to increase the interval between transmitting characters.

Appendix B
BISYNC Transmission

Binary Synchronous Transmission

Binary synchronous (BISYNC) protocols transmit data a block at a time. This requires that the sender and receiver be in sync with each other. To achieve this timing, synchronous modems contain clocks synchronized with each other during transmission. This timing can be compared to joggers and their watches: The jogging watch can be set to a pace related to the length of the runner's stride and the distance to be run. The watch determines the necessary number of strides per minute and emits a beep every time the jogger's foot strikes the ground. There must be synchronization between the watch's beeping tone and the runner's feet. Likewise, the clocks in the synchronous modems must be in time with each other so the receiving modem will look for an arriving character at the correct time.

Establishing Synchronization

To establish this timing ordinarily requires two or more synchronization (SYN) characters. The sending station prefixes all transmissions with a number of SYN characters. If the modems are not in sync when the first SYN character arrives, the entire character will not be received correctly, although the receiving modem will be aware that a character stream is arriving. The second SYN character assures synchronization. Additional SYN characters are transmitted with equipment that requires more than two characters for synchronization. SYN characters are hexadecimal 32 in EBCDIC, hexadecimal 16 in ASCII, and hexadecimal 3A in SBT; these are the three codes supported by BISYNC.

In BISYNC transmission, the line is continuously monitored, awaiting the SYN character that signals the beginning of a message. A copy of the SYN character is maintained in a register and compared with the data received. When the first SYN character has arrived, the next character is checked to determine whether it is also a SYN character. The first SYN character sets bit synchronization; the second sets character synchronization. Once synchronization is established, individual characters can be received and processed.

Transmission Control Characters

BISYNC uses a number of special transmission control characters to indicate the beginning of the data or header information, the end of the data or transmission block, the end of transmission, acknowledgments of data received, and so on. A listing of these follows.

SYN.   The SYN character establishes synchronization. It precedes all message blocks and may be inserted in long messages to maintain synchronization.

STX.   STX indicates start-of-text; what follows it is data.

SOH.   SOH means start-of-header. The optional header field follows. Headers may contain application-dependent data such as transaction codes and terminal ID.

ETX.   ETX indicates end-of-text. It tells when a complete text message has been received. If lengthy text is broken into blocks for transmission, only the final block will contain the ETX character.

ETB.   ETB signals the end of the transmission block and requires an acknowledgment. See ETX, above.

ITB.   ITB marks the end of an intermediate transmission block. In some cases a number of blocks may be transmitted without being acknowledged. An ITB character is used to signal the end of these blocks. The actual character used to represent the ITB is IUS in EBCDIC and US (unit separator) in ASCII and SBT.

EOT.   EOT means end-of-transmission and is used to terminate a transmission. It differs from ETX in that ETX signals the end of a logical message. Multiple messages may comprise one transmission; EOT signals this condition. Following the transmission of EOT, the transmitting station relinquishes control of the link. All stations are reset following EOT. EOT can also be used as a response to a poll and to signal an error condition that precludes message completion.

ACK0.   Positive acknowledgment is signaled by ACK0, which is actually a two-character sequence consisting of a DLE character (see below) plus a character that is code-dependent. In ASCII, 0 is the second character. BISYNC uses ACK0 and ACK1 in an alternating acknowledgment scheme.

ACK1.   Positive acknowledgment. See ACK0 above. ACK1 is a two-character sequence consisting of DLE (see below) and a second code-dependent character, a 1 in ASCII.

NAK.   NAK, meaning *negative acknowledgment*, is used to indicate that the previous block was received in error and should be retransmitted. It is also used as a negative response to a poll message.

ENQ.   ENQ, meaning *inquiry*, is used to bid for the line in contention mode, to initiate a poll or select message, or to ask that a response to a previous transmission be resent.

DLE.   DLE—data link escape—is used to implement transparency. It is also used to form other control characters such as ACK0.

WACK, TTD, RVI.   These are used for special control situations, defined later. Each represents a special kind of positive acknowledgment.

Control for Long Messages.   Messages, particularly long ones, can be broken into blocks for transmission to minimize the amount of data that might have to be retransmitted in case of errors and to accommodate buffer sizes in the receiving equipment. In the case when all intermediate blocks can be transmitted before acknowledgment is required, the ITB control character is used to terminate the block. If ETB is used instead, each block must be acknowledged. Alternating acknowledgments—ACK0 and ACK1—are used to provide a small amount of error control. ACK0 is always a positive response to a line bid or to selection.

Transmission Sequences

In the examples that follow, the character sequences should be read from left to right, with the first character transmitted appearing on the left. BCC represents the block check character, either LRC or CRC.

Point-to-Point Contention Mode.   In point-to-point contention, a station must first bid for and be granted access to the line. This sequence is given in Figure B-1. At this point the line is available for either station to issue a bid. A negative response to the line bid would be NAK. If a station were unable to receive data for some reason, it would NAK the line bid.

Multi-Point Mode.   A polling sequence with positive and negative responses is shown in Figure B-2. A selection sequence is portrayed in Figure B-3. In the selection sequence in Figure B-3, the station being selected at first gave a negative acknowledgment to the selection, or a NAK. A printer would respond in this manner if its buffer was not empty and it

Figure B-1 A
BISYNC Contention
Mode Line Bid

Line Bidder		Responder	Comment
SYN SYN ENQ	⟶		Line bid
	⟵	SYN SYN ACK0	Positive response
SYN SYN STX text ETB BCC	⟶		Message block 1
	⟵	SYN SYN ACK1	Positive response
SYN SYN STX text EOT BCC	⟶		Last block
	⟵	SYN SYN ACK0	Positive response

Figure B-2 BISYNC
Polling

Supervisor		Secondary	Comment
SYN SYN address1 ENQ	⟶		Poll to station 1
	⟵	SYN SYN EOT	No data to send
SYN SYN address 2 ENQ	⟶		Poll to station 2
	⟵	SYN SYN STX data EOT BCC	Data sent
SYN SYN ACK0	⟶		Positive response
SYN SYN address3 ENQ	⟶		Poll to station 3

Figure B-3 A
BISYNC Selection

Supervisor		Secondary	Comment
SYN SYN EOT SYN SYN address ENQ	⟶		Selection
	⟵	SYN SYN NAK	Negative response; unable to receive
SYN SYN EOT SYN SYN address ENQ	⟶		Retry
	⟵	SYN SYN ACK0	Positive response
SYN SYN STX text ETX BCC	⟶		Data sent
	⟵	SYN SYN ACK1	Positive reponse
SYN SYN EOT	⟶		End of data

was unable to accept more data. A positive acknowledgment was given to the subsequent selection, and the data was transmitted. EOT in the selection stream ensures the status of the link.

WACK. On occasion a station may wish to positively acknowledge receipt of a block and also advise the sender that it is not ready to receive the next block, such as when a printer with limited buffer size is out of paper or otherwise unable to empty its buffer. The WACK character is used both to positively acknowledge receipt of a block and also to tell the sending station to wait before transmitting further. WACK is a two-character sequence—DLE followed by a code-dependent character (a semicolon in ASCII and a comma in EBCDIC). The message sequence for WACK is presented in Figure B-4. The WACK response in Figure B-4 delays the sender from transmitting the remainder of the text block. The sender would continue prompting the station with ENQs until the receiver is able to receive. A positive response to ENQ will allow the sender to continue with the message.

TTD. Sometimes a sending station becomes temporarily busy and so is unable to continue sending its message. If the sender wants to maintain

Sender		Receiver	Comment	
SYN SYN ENQ	$\longrightarrow$		Line bid	**Figure B-4** BISYNC WACK
	$\longleftarrow$	SYN SYN ACK0	Positive response	
SYN SYN STX text ETB BCC	$\longrightarrow$		Data	
	$\longleftarrow$	SYN SYN WACK	WACK	
SYN SYN ENQ	$\longrightarrow$		Line bid	
	$\longleftarrow$	SYN SYN ACK0	Positive response	
SYN SYN STX text EOT BCC	$\longrightarrow$		Data	
	$\longleftarrow$	SYN SYN ACK0	Positive response	

control of the communications circuit during such an interval, it can do so with the temporary text delay (TTD) control sequence. TTD consists of STX followed by ENQ. The transmitting sequence for this is given in Figure B-5. The TTD sequence must be repeated within 2 seconds to avoid time-out. The usual time-out value of 3 seconds avoids a long wait for a station that is not online.

RVI. When a receiving station has a high-priority message to transmit to a sending station, the receiver can indicate this by acknowledging a message with a reverse interrupt (RVI) character sequence. RVI is a two-character sequence—DLE plus a code-dependent second character (< in ASCII and @ in EBCDIC). RVI acknowledges the message received and alerts the sender to relinquish the line as soon as possible, so the station that has been receiving can assume control of the link. An RVI sequence is illustrated in Figure B-6. RVI does not cause the sender to immediately

Sender		Receiver	Comment	
SYN SYN ENQ	$\longrightarrow$		Line bid	**Figure B-5** BISYNC TTD
	$\longleftarrow$	SYN SYN ACK0	Positive response	
SYN SYN STX ENQ	$\longrightarrow$		TTD	
	$\longleftarrow$	SYN SYN NAK	Response to TDD	
(within 2 seconds)			Avoid time-out	
SYN SYN STX ENQ	$\longrightarrow$		TTD	
	$\longleftarrow$	SYN SYN NAK	Response to TDD	
SYN SYN STX text ETB BCC	$\longrightarrow$		Data	
	$\longleftarrow$	SYN SYN ACK1	Acknowledgment	

Sender		Receiver	Comment	
SYN SYN ENQ	$\longrightarrow$		Line bid	**Figure B-6** BISYNC RVI
	$\longleftarrow$	SYN SYN ACK0	Positive response	
SYN SYN STX text ETB BCC	$\longrightarrow$		Data	
	$\longleftarrow$	SYN SYN RVI	Reverse interrupt	
SYN SYN STX text ETX BCC	$\longrightarrow$		Empty buffer	
	$\longleftarrow$	SYN SYN ACK1	Acknowledgment	
SYN SYN EOT	$\longrightarrow$		Transmit end	
	$\longleftarrow$	SYN SYN ENQ	Line bid	
SYN SYN ACK0	$\longrightarrow$		Positive response	
	$\longleftarrow$	SYN SYN STX text ETB BCC	Priority message	

discontinue transmission; rather, the sender continues transmitting until its buffers are empty and it is capable of receiving data.

Transparency

Transparency means that any bit sequences can be included in the text, even those that are also used as control characters. In its original use with RJE, the only BISYNC characters that needed to be transmitted were the control characters and displayable characters. As BISYNC's functions were expanded to include the transfer of binary data, transparency was added. Unfortunately, this add-on solution was inelegant. Without transparency a data byte that looks like an ETX character would prematurely terminate the message. Since the link protocol would interpret the two characters following the phony ETX as CRC, the CRC check would probably fail, and the block would be negatively acknowledged, thus causing the block to be retransmitted over and over until a retry limit was reached. The data link escape (DLE) character is employed to provide transparency, essentially inserted before any control characters. DLE STX initiates transparent mode, and DLE ETX, DLE ETB, DLE ITB, or a like sequence terminates the block. The DLE character can be used in this manner with the STX, ETB, ITB, ETX, ENQ, DLE, and SYN control characters.

This all seems straightforward, as if all that was needed was to frame the message with DLE STX and DLE ETX. Unfortunately, it is still possible to have within the text two adjacent characters that form a DLE ETX sequence, which would prematurely terminate the message. The solution to this problem is to insert DLE before each DLE in the text. Thus, what has happened is that one character has been picked to represent transparency. Since this character may also appear in the text, it has to be accommodated within the text. The text is scanned for any DLE characters; for each one found, an additional DLE is inserted. The data stream is scanned

Figure B-7   A Sample Text Message

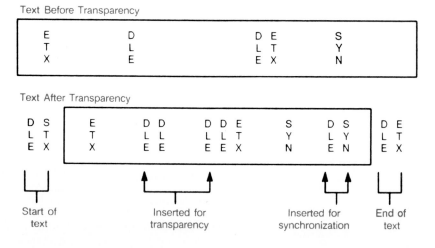

on the receiving side as well; whenever two DLE characters are encountered next to each other, one is discarded, thus ensuring that the only DLE ETX sequence is at the end of the block. The insertion of DLE will, of course, change a DLE ETX data sequence into a DLE DLE ETX sequence. DLE ETX in this case is not construed as a termination. The DLE DLE grouping indicates that DLE is for data and not control. Before and after images of a sample text message are given in Figure B-7.

Appendix C
SDLC Transmission

Synchronous Data Link Control

This appendix supplements the discussion of IBM's synchronous data link control (SDLC) protocol given in Chapter 6. You may wish to review that material prior to continuing. This SDLC discussion is focused on the control field functions and the Ns and Nr message sequencing concept. Transparency and loop configurations were briefly discussed in Chapter 6; additional information regarding these subjects can be found in the IBM reference manuals on SDLC cited in Chapter 6 (IBM, 1979). The control field provides the abilities to designate the type of the frame—unnumbered, supervisory, or informational—and to acknowledge receipt of frames.

Unnumbered Frames

Unnumbered frames are used for control functions such as resetting a station's Ns and Nr counts to zero; causing stations on switched lines to disconnect; rejecting a frame received in error; and transmitting data such as broadcast or status messages that do not need a sequence check. The general format of the unnumbered control field is given in Figure C-1. The first two bits—11—identify the frame as unnumbered. The code bits are used to identify the frame function, initialize station, reject frame, disconnect, and so on. The five bits allow for 32 different functions. The existing control functions for unnumbered frames are given in Figure C-2.

P/F Bit. The P/F (poll/final) bit, which is common to all of the control fields, is set when a station is being polled and when the final frame for a message is sent. Just as in BISYNC, messages can be broken into blocks for transmission; all but the last such block will have the P/F bit set to zero. The P/F bit also is used in loop configurations to specify optional and mandatory responses to polling.

Figure C-1 Control
Field Format:
Unnumbered Frame

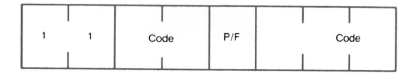

| 1 | 1 | Code | P/F | Code |

Figure C-2
Unnumbered Control
Functions

Code for **Unnumbered Control**	**Function**
UI	Identifies an information frame as unnumbered.
SNRM	Sets normal response mode. Resets Ns and Nr count fields.
DISC	Places secondary station in disconnect mode.
RD	Indicates a secondary station request to disconnect.
UA	Signals a positive acknowledgment to an SNRM, DISC, or SIM command.
RIM	Indicates a secondary station request for initialization.
SIM	Primary initializes secondary. Ns and Nr counts are set to 0.
DM	Indicates that a secondary station is in disconnect mode.
FRMR	Signals that an invalid frame has been received.
TEST	Means that a test frame has been sent to a secondary station, which will respond with a test frame.
XID	Requests an ID exchange.

Figure C-3 Control
Field Format:
Supervisory Frame

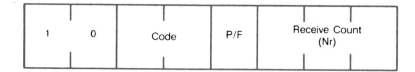

| 1 | 0 | Code | P/F | Receive Count (Nr) |

Supervisory Frames

The control field format for the supervisory frame is given in Figure C-3. The first two bits (10) designate the frame as supervisory. The P/F bit is as described above. The receive count field (explained below) is used to acknowledge receipt of frames. The code field is two bits wide and therefore can represent only four different control functions, three of which have been specified thus far. Two control functions are used to indicate whether the station is ready to receive (RR) or not ready to receive (RNR) data. The third control function (REJ) is used to reject a frame.

Information Frames

The information frame is used primarily to send data; its control field format is given in Figure C-4. Unlike the other two types of frames, only the

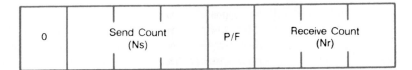

Figure C-4   Control Field Format: Information Frame

first bit (0) is used to designate the frame as informational. The P/F bit is as described above. The send count (Ns) and receive count (Nr) fields are each made up of three bits. As discussed in Chapter 6, the Ns field is used by a station to count the number of messages sent to another station. The Nr field is a count kept by a receiving station of the number of messages received from another station. Each station maintains separate Ns and Nr count fields for each station with which it communicates. When a station is initialized by the supervisor, the Ns and Nr counts are set to zero, so the Nr count becomes the message number the receiving station expects next. The first message sent is message number 0. After either count reaches 7, the next increment rolls the count over to zero, mean- ing that, at most, seven messages can be sent before an acknowledgment is necessary.

Example: How Ns and Nr Counts Are Used

This example, illustrated in Figure C-5, shows the values of the address field, the frame type, the Ns and Nr counts, and the P/F bit, in that order. The supervisor station polls the secondary stations. The supervisor uses a supervisory frame to indicate that it is ready to receive. The P/F bit is set to 1 to indicate that Station A is being polled. The Nr count is set to zero, in- dicating that the next frame expected from Station A is frame number 0. Station A has no data to send and thus responds with a supervisory frame indicating that it is ready to receive and that the next frame expected from the supervisor is frame number 0. The final bit is set to 1 in this instance to indicate that there is no data to send.

    Station B is then polled. Station B does have data to transmit and uses the information frame to do so. Four frames are required to transmit the entire message. For the first three frames the P/F bit is set to 0 to indicate

Supervisor						**Secondary Station**				
Address	Frame Type	Ns Count	Nr Count	P/F Bit		Address	Frame Type	Ns Count	Nr Count	P/F Bit
A	RR	0	0	1	⟶					
					⟵	A	RR	0	0	1
B	RR	0	0	1	⟶					
					⟵	B	I	0	0	0 data
		0	1		⟵	B	I	1	0	0 data
		0	2		⟵	B	I	2	0	0 data
		0	3		⟵	B	I	3	0	1 data
B	RR	0	4	0	⟶					
C	RR	0	0	1	⟶					

Figure C-5
Example of the Use of Ns and Nr Subfields

that more frames will follow. The last frame in the message has the P/F bit set to 1. The Ns count for Station B is incremented with each frame. The Nr count is incremented following the receipt of each frame, although the supervisor sends no acknowledgment in this case until the final frame is received. On receiving the final frame, the supervisor acknowledges receipt of all messages at once with a supervisory frame. The P/F bit is not set on this frame, since Station B is not being polled. Much of the efficiency of bit-oriented data link protocols stems from their ability to transmit multiple frames without acknowledgment and to transmit in full duplex mode. This avoids the wait times required by other protocols like BISYNC, which require that each message be acknowledged before another may be sent.

Appendix D
Packet Distribution
Networks

This appendix supplements the discussion of packet distribution networks in Chapter 10. You may wish to review that material prior to continuing. This appendix covers CCITT standards X.3, X.28, and X.25 and omits discussing standards X.75 and X.29. CCITT standards X.28, X.29, X.3, and X.25 cover the interface between data terminal equipment (DTE) and data circuit-terminating equipment (DCE) in a single packet distribution network. Standard X.75 covers the interface between two different PDNs. Standards X.28 and X.29 are quite similar: X.28 concerns the interface between the packet assembly/disassembly (PAD) and a start-stop (asynchronous) terminal; X.29 covers the same situation for a packet mode terminal (a terminal capable of performing PAD functions). In general, X.29 refers to the network-host interface; it covers the PAD-PAD interface as well. Because of the similarity between X.28 and X.29, only X.28 is discussed.

The X.3 Standard

The packet assembly/disassembly (PAD) interfaces to start-stop terminals, packet mode terminals, or other PADs.

Basic Functions of the PAD. When a PAD interfaces with a start-stop terminal, the message characters arrive at the PAD one character at a time and must be grouped together into a packet for transmission over the network. While building the buffer for the data terminal equipment (DTE), the PAD can also perform a limited amount of editing on the data, restricted to deleting characters from the buffer or deleting the buffer's entire contents. Editing is enabled by the user and is done on receiving the proper editing control signals. The PAD knows to transmit a packet whenever the packet reaches the designated packet size, a message termination character is received, or after no characters have been received for a specified amount of time. The receiving PAD must take the data from the user data field and send it one character at a time to the receiver, including framing the character with start and stop bits as necessary and adding a parity bit if required by the DTE. In addition to the handling of packet assembly/disassembly functions, the PAD is also involved in control and error functions: It is responsible for a portion of the setup and clearing of virtual calls, pacing of data to the DTE, and reacting to reset and interrupt conditions.

PAD Operations Parameters.   PAD operations are controlled by a set of PAD parameters, which in most cases the user can tailor to the operations of the particular terminal and application. The parameters of significance to business applications follow. They show the flexibility available with a PAD.

Echo.   The PAD can optionally echo a transmitted character back to the DTE. Some terminals require this feature in order to display the character on the terminal's output device.

Termination Characters.   The user can specify virtually any character as a termination character. Termination characters signal the PAD to end a message and to forward the packet to the network.

Timer Delay Interval.   Another way that a message can be terminated is via timer delay, which can be specified at values from 0 to 255, in twentieths of a second. When no characters have arrived within the delay interval, the PAD assumes the message is complete and transmits the packet. A timer delay value of 0 means there can be no delay interval in completing the message. The maximum specifiable delay is 12.75 seconds.

XON/XOFF Capability.   Some DTE equipment can announce its readiness to accept data via XON and XOFF signals. *XON* means the device is able to receive a certain number of characters, related to the device's buffer size. When the buffer is filled to a certain threshold, the device transmits the XOFF signal to the sender, which holds the sender off until the buffer is emptied below the threshold. The PAD allows this capability of the device to be enabled or disabled.

Break Signal.   The DTE can transmit a break signal to the PAD, which is a sequence of 0 bits over a designated time interval. The user can specify the action the PAD is to take on receiving such a signal: do nothing, transmit an interrupt packet to the host, reset itself, transmit a break message to the host, remove itself from the data transfer state, or discard the output to the DTE.

Padding.   On receipt of a carriage return character, some devices—especially the mechanical ones, such as printers—require a certain amount of time to move the printing mechanism to the beginning of the line. To provide sufficient time for carriage return, pad characters are sometimes inserted after the carriage return. The PAD allows from 0–7 pad characters to be transmitted to the DTE after a carriage return. Padding can also be specified to follow a line-feed character.

Line Speed.   Nineteen different speeds are available, ranging from 50 bps to 64 Kbps. Once set, the line speed may not be changed. This read-only parameter allows a host to ascertain the speed of the device with which it is communicating.

Line-Feed after Carriage Return.   The PAD can be instructed to always insert a line-feed character following a carriage return. This option provides output line-spacing for the receiving device.

Folding.   This parameter allows the length of the output to be adjusted to the device. The folding parameter can be any value from 0 to 255. A zero value means no folding is to take place; any other value represents the number of characters to transmit to the receiving device before automatically inserting the formatting characters, such as carriage return or line feed.

Editing.   The PAD can perform the limited editing functions of character deletion and line deletion. One parameter enables this capability, and there is one parameter to store each of the line and character delete codes. If the PAD is editing-enabled and receives a character that matches the character delete parameter, the last character in the edit buffer is deleted. This works just like the backspace on most terminals. Similarly, if a line delete character is received, the entire contents of the edit buffer are deleted. The edit buffer can also be displayed.

The X.28 Standard

The X.28 specifications define the manner in which a start-stop terminal interfaces with a PAD, whose functions and options have just been defined. The data terminal equipment can access a PAD via a switched or a leased connection. The speed of the connection is determined by the capability of the DTE and by the PDN administrators. The PAD expects eight-bit characters from the DTE and transmits eight-bit characters to the DTE. When looking at the characters for control purposes, the PAD looks at only the first seven bits. The eighth bit may either be parity or data; if data, then the first seven bits should not match any of the control functions, such as editing. The major portion of the X.28 standard defines the signals exchanged between DTE and PAD, including how to interrogate and alter the PAD parameters, the definition of the break signal, call establishment sequences, network user identification procedures, call clearing, and fault conditions.

The X.25 Standard

The X.25 specification defines the interface between data terminal equipment and the network for terminals operating in the packet mode, including the interface between the PAD and the network. The specification first briefly discusses the X.21 and X.21bis interfaces, the general interfaces between synchronous and asynchronous devices, respectively. That is followed by a brief discussion of the LAPB data link protocol, which is very similar to HDLC and SDLC. Frames are formatted as described for SDLC. For information regarding this portion of the X.25 recommendation, the reader is referred to the SDLC descriptions in Chapter 6 and Appendix C.

At the network level, the objective is end-to-end routing. To provide the information necessary for end-to-end routing, a portion of the data or information field is used by the PDN. The shortest message that can be transferred is three characters in length, because at least three characters of the information field are required by the PDN for routing and control. These three characters contain fields for general format identification, logical channel identification, and packet-type identification. Additional fields are defined in some packets, particularly those used for control. A representative sample of these fields is given in Figure D-1.

General Format Identification (GFI). The *general format identification* (*GFI*) is the first field of the data field of the frame. The GFI indicates the format of the remainder of the data field. The four bits of the GFI designate the sequence number modulus for the packet and also indicate whether the packet is a datagram, information packet, call setup packet,

Figure D-1 Call Request and Incoming Call Packet Format

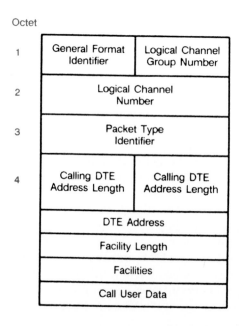

Octet		
1	General Format Identifier	Logical Channel Group Number
2	Logical Channel Number	
3	Packet Type Identifier	
4	Calling DTE Address Length	Calling DTE Address Length
	DTE Address	
	Facility Length	
	Facilities	
	Call User Data	

or control packet. The sequence number modulus operates like the Ns and Nr fields in HDLC.

Logical Channel Identification.   The *logical channel identification* field consists of two parts, the logical channel group number and the logical channel number. The group number occupies the four bits following the GFI. With four bits, 16 different channel groups can be specified. The eight bits following the channel group identification is the logical channel address. There may thus be 256 different logical addresses per channel, providing a total of 4096 different circuits or logical addresses in the network.

Packet Type.   The third octet designates the packet type, in six broad categories—call setup and clearing, data and interrupt, datagram, flow control and reset, restart, and diagnostic. Each category except diagnostic is further broken down into subtypes, such as the call setup and clearing subtypes of incoming call, call connected, clear indication, DCE clear confirmation, call request, call accepted, clear request, and DTE clear confirmation.

Information Field.   The defaulted recommended length of the information field is 128 octets, but X.25 provides for optional lengths of 16, 32, 64, 128, 256, 512, and 1024 octets. Message sequence numbers are used to account for packets. By default, the modulus for sequence numbers is 8, with 128 a suggested alternative. The sequence numbers work like those in the Ns and Nr fields of SDLC. A window size n is set that restricts a sender to transmitting at most n messages without acknowledgment. The default window size is 2 for a modulus of 8. The window size can be changed if the user has been given the option of flow control parameter negotiation, which enables the user to change the packet size, sequence number modulus, window size, and circuit speed.

Optional Parameters.   There are a number of other parameters that network administrators may optionally put under user control, such as the barring of all incoming calls. In this case, DTE will be allowed only to initiate calls. By the same token DTE can be barred from initiating calls and allowed only to receive calls. Further, a user can elect to reverse charges so the recipient of the call becomes responsible for the packets transmitted. The user might be allowed to alter the datagram queue length, which determines the number of incoming datagrams that can queue up before datagrams begin to be discarded. Thus, if queue depth is set at 16, then 16 datagrams will be allowed in the inbound queue. If 16 datagrams are waiting when another arrives, the late arrival will be discarded. Finally, the user is able to specify whether a closed or bilateral closed user group should be established. Closed user group members are allowed to communicate only with each other. In a bilateral closed user group, two DTEs that agree to communicate can do so, but communication with all other

DTEs is prohibited. Options added to these closed groups allow for incoming and outgoing communications with the rest of the user community.

Datagrams.   The X.25 specification also covers the use of datagrams. The datagram message is restricted to 128 octets. The user can elect to receive acknowledgment of datagrams in three instances—if the datagram is rejected, discarded, or accepted, result conditions that are returned to the user only when requested by the user. The user may optionally receive the capability to specify whether notification be given on nondelivery or delivery of a datagram. Datagrams are given sequence numbers, and there is an acknowledgment window that operates the same as with virtual circuits.

Appendix E
IBM's Virtual
Telecommunications Access
Method (VTAM)

The *virtual telecommunications access method* (*VTAM*) is one of a number of telecommunications access methods supported by IBM. VTAM and the telecommunications access method (TCAM) are currently the most important of the access methods because both support systems network architecture (SNA). The basic functions of VTAM include attachment of applications to terminals, routing messages between applications and terminals, providing terminal-specific access attributes, application configuration, terminal configuration, terminal definition, terminal configuration alteration, buffer management, device management, and debugging aids.

Network Configuration

A network configuration file describes the VTAM environment of communication controllers, local terminals, and SNA nodes. Two tables are maintained by VTAM to define devices—a major node table and a specific node table. The major node table contains information regarding application groups, NCPs that reside in communications controllers, local 3270 devices, switched SNA devices, and local SNA devices. Switched SNA devices are physical or logical units that can be attached to the network via switched communications links; local SNA devices are physical or logical units attached directly to the channel. A pointer from the major node table is used to link major nodes to specific nodes. The specific node table contains information about specific terminals and cluster controllers. Addresses for terminal devices are created from a combination of the major node address and the specific node table addresses. These two tables are built from the configuration file when VTAM is initialized. Applications are not defined in these tables. VTAM may be used in conjunction with a transaction control process (TCP), in which environment its functions are limited primarily to terminal interface. In the description that follows the full functions of VTAM are discussed. In the TCP environment some features may be un-utilized or not as highly utilized as in the stand-alone configuration.

Establishing Communication

Once initialized, VTAM is ready to perform its primary function of establishing communications between terminals and applications. In SNA this is referred to as a session, which is a communication between two logical devices. Sessions can be established by either the application or the terminal.

Application-Initiated Communication. Before an application can communicate with a terminal, it must first establish a connection to VTAM by invoking an OPEN macro. Via this process, VTAM creates the buffers and control blocks necessary for communication between the application and terminals. Having established a session between the application and VTAM, the application can then request attachment to a specific terminal, accomplished by a request to OPEN a destination. If the terminal is available, VTAM establishes the connection. A terminal will be unavailable if it is offline, reserved for some reason, or already attached to another application. In the latter case the request is queued, to be granted when the terminal becomes available. An application can also gain access to a terminal by having the connection privilege passed to it by an application already connected to the terminal. A terminal can be connected to only one application at a time, but one application can be attached to multiple terminals.

Terminal-Initiated Communications: The Network Solicitor. A terminal can also request connection to an application. In such a case, the terminal would have been initially defined as a monitored terminal, meaning that a special application program known as the *network solicitor* will be initially attached to the terminal and will monitor it for application connection requests. Users can either write their own network solicitor program or use one provided as part of the VTAM system. The solicitor takes inputs from the monitored terminals and passes control to the requested application if the application is willing to communicate with the terminal. When the session between the application and the terminal is finished, the terminal is passed back to the network solicitor program, which resumes monitoring the terminal. The VTAM solicitor process is illustrated in Figure E-1.

Input/Output Processing

Two types of I/O processing can be specified between an application and a terminal—record mode and basic mode. *Record mode* allows full duplex transmission, and either the application or the terminal is capable of initiat-

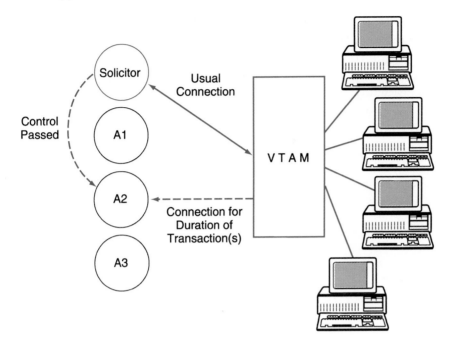

ing communication. In record mode, VTAM provides device formatting services. *Basic mode* is a half duplex transmission mode, with the application controlling the conversation: The terminal can transmit only on solicitation of information from the application. Basic mode can be used to communicate with asynchronous and binary synchronous terminals. When operating in basic mode the application is primarily responsible for device characteristics. It must insert line control characters in the text and recognize them in messages returned from the terminal.

For VTAM to communicate correctly with a terminal it must know in which of the two modes it will operate as well as terminal characteristics. For each of the operating modes, there exists a device control table containing the control routines for all types of supported devices. VTAM picks the control procedures from this list and builds a device access table for that particular terminal. The initial table with all of the routines is referred to as a *skeleton table*. The skeleton table might contain a routine common to all terminals and then several procedures tailored to a specific terminal type. VTAM then builds a terminal access table for a specific terminal by selecting the common routine and one of the specific terminal procedures.

Diagnostic and Debugging Tools

VTAM offers the user a complement of diagnostic and debugging tools, including the following.

A buffer trace logs the contents of input and output buffers, enabling the user to determine the changes made to the data by VTAM.

NCP line traces enable the user to trace one line at a time, providing information about line parameters.

Storage pool traces yield information about whether the storage pools maintained by VTAM are being used efficiently or inefficiently.

Formatted dumps can reveal all or a part of VTAM's working environment.

In addition, VTAM assists the user in handling both hardware and software errors and in attempting recovery from abnormal terminations and hardware failures.

Appendix F
IBM's Customer Information Control System (CICS)

The customer information control system (CICS) is a transaction control process (TCP) provided by IBM and is one of the most widely used TCP products. Its primary function is as an interface between terminal users on one side and application programs and database or file requests on the other. To do this, CICS manages both terminals and application processes. It runs on 370, 4331, 4341, 303x, 308x, and 309x processors under OS/VSE, OS/VS1, MVS/370, or MVS/XA operating systems.

CICS Partition

CICS occupies a large partition within an IBM mainframe computer. Part of the partition houses CICS code, message buffers, and data and part is used by the application programs that CICS manages, as depicted in Figure F-1. Unlike VTAM, in which a terminal is logged on to only one application at a time, CICS provides the linkage between applications and terminals. This means that a terminal can use multiple application processes without being attached to a specific process or being transferred from one to another. Terminals are controlled by CICS, not by the application programs. In a number of respects CICS functions like an operating system in managing its region: It starts and stops tasks, manages the memory in its partition, provides application interface to devices, and implements a priority system to determine which task will be run first.

Installation Options: Customized or Preconfigured

In installing a CICS system, the user has two basic options: customize the installation to the particular system and applications or install a system preconfigured by IBM. To customize, the user must decide which functions are required and include those code modules that support the selected

Figure F-1   CICS
Partition

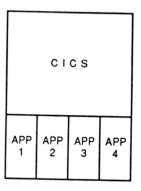

functions. The tailored system that results can provide greater economy of memory resources and efficiency of operation. The preconfigured system takes less work to install, and several preconfigured systems are available that incorporate different combinations of commonly used functions. Regardless of the initial approach, the CICS system can be tuned later to increase or decrease functionality and thus provide more efficient operations.

Intersystem Communication (ISC) and Multiregion Operation (MRO)

More than one CICS environment can be run within one system, and these different CICS environments can communicate with each other. Likewise, different nodes in a system network architecture (SNA) network can run CICS, and these CICS systems can communicate using the facilities of SNA. Thus, a terminal operating under control of one CICS system can communicate with applications or terminals under the control of another CICS system. This provides an environment for a distributed network. Communication with other nodes is referred to as *intersystem communication (ISC)* and communication between two CICS systems on one node is called *multiregion operation (MRO)*. Several CICS systems can be used in one node for separation of functions, such as separating an operational system from a development system or separating a very secure set of transactions or applications from more commonly used transactions or applications. Despite the fact that each CICS system exclusively controls terminals or applications, the databases, terminals, and applications can be shared between CICS systems via MRO or via direct access to the database.

CICS Tables

To fulfill its function of interfacing terminals and applications, CICS must have a knowledge of application processes, files, destinations, and terminals, all of which are described by tables created during the initialization process. These tables, which can be modified later to add, delete, or amend the descriptions, are created by invoking macro instructions. Just as multiple CICS systems can be generated, so, too, can multiple tables. Thus, distinct tables can be generated for production, development, and testing environments. At any given time, one CICS system will have only one set of tables for each resource—file, application, terminal, or destination. To install one CICS system, the user may be required to define up to 15 such tables, describing terminals, applications, transactions, control, system recovery, and system initialization.

Terminal Control Table.   The *terminal control table* (*TCT*) contains descriptions of terminals; a terminal can communicate with CICS only if it is described in this table. In interfacing with terminals, CICS uses the support of one of IBM's access methods, either VTAM, VTAME, BTAM, or TCAM, depending on the type of terminal being supported. For example, the 2780 and 3780 RJE terminals and most asynchronous devices are supported under BTAM, and SNA interfaces are supported under VTAM. Some terminal types—such as 3270 devices and some asynchronous devices—are supported by several access methods. The TCT contains such information as the access method interface, where error messages are displayed on the terminal, terminal type, line size, screen size, and terminal address.

Physical and Data Description Maps.   The interface between terminals and applications is via two map sets: physical maps and data description maps. A set of *physical maps* describes the screen layout for terminals, with one such map for each screen displayed on a given terminal. A set of *data description maps* represents the application's view of the data. The two map sets can be created in one of two different ways, by basic mapping support or by a screen definition facility. The *basic mapping support* (*BMS*) subsystem enables the programmer to define the screen formats and input and output data formats by use of macro commands. The online screen formatting facility known as the *screen definition facility* (*SDF/CICS*) enables the user to interactively create the screen formats and resulting maps. SDF/CICS also provides the ability to edit existing maps and test the formats online.

Because there are two maps, one terminal oriented and one application oriented, independence between the terminal and application is achieved. Thus, the terminal can be changed without a corresponding change in the application. Likewise, application changes can be made without changing the screen layout, so long as no new fields are required. In COBOL the symbolic map takes the form of a data division entry. The physical map resides in the CICS load library.

CICS Load Library Tables.   Applications written in COBOL are able to reference CICS routines by embedding CICS commands in the COBOL source. A CICS precompiler translates these commands into a format acceptable to the COBOL compiler. The same is true when PL/1 is the application language. Compiled and link-edited application programs are placed into a CICS load library.

A number of tables describing the application programs in the load library are used to associate a transaction with the application programs that will process that transaction. A transaction is identified by an identifier that is one to four characters. A transaction can be initiated from either a terminal or an application program or it can be based on a particular event or at a specified time. Usually, the terminal user enters the transaction identifier or selects it from a menu of available transactions. The tables are used to identify which program is to process a particular transaction, whether the transaction is to be audited and backed out if necessary, the estimated duration of the transaction, and if the program is to be loaded at CICS initialization time or is to reside in memory permanently.

Quasi-Reentrancy

CICS programs written in COBOL are called *quasi-reentrant*, which means they can be shared by more than one terminal at a time. Each terminal will have its own copy of data and all terminals will share the same code. At certain points in the program, reentrancy may not be allowed, since an instruction could be changed or an address modified. Thus, sharing is allowed only at specified points, such as when the process must be suspended while awaiting disk access. PL/1 programs are fully reentrant, and at any time one task can be suspended and another allowed to execute the code. Efficiency can be gained through multi-threading in CICS and through reentrancy or quasi-reentrancy in the application programs. Having multiple terminals simultaneously access one process reduces the amount of memory required for application code.

File and Database Access

CICS provides access to files and database management systems. File access to indexed sequential access method files (VSAM or ISAM) and direct access method (DAM) files can be made directly through CICS calls, whereas access to IBM's IMS, SQL/DS, and DB2 database management systems can be made through application program calls. Interfaces also exist that allow access to non-IBM database management systems.

Logical Units of Work and Sync Points

Transaction backout and journaling is provided as an option to the user. For long transactions, the user can specify synchronization points that become recovery points. The work performed between synchronization points, termed *logical units of work* (*LUW*), are units of recovery, so one transaction can have no sync points and be an LUW, whereas another transaction could define several sync points. In the latter instance, once a

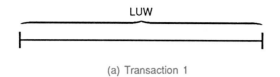

(a) Transaction 1

Figure F-2   Transactions: Sync Points and Logical Units of Work

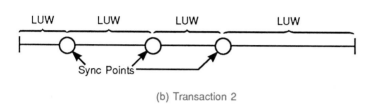

(b) Transaction 2

sync point is reached its unit of work is committed and thus will not need to be backed out in the event of a failure. This is depicted in Figure F-2.

Diagnostic and Tuning Aids

CICS provides aids for diagnosing problems and tuning the system. A command interpreter allows a user to create a CICS call, execute it, and receive a response without coding an application, thus enabling the user to interactively test a transaction or part of a transaction. An online debugging aid named the *execution diagnostic facility* (*EDF*) allows an application to be tested and permits the CICS application calls to be intercepted, examined, and changed if necessary. The response to the calls can also be trapped and modified.

An EDF allows the code to be tested and also provides for the generating of exception conditions for testing error routines. Other diagnostic aids include the gathering of statistics for system tuning and dumping of buffers, tables and the entire region or partition in which CICS resides. Statistics gathered include the number of transactions, amount of CPU time consumed by transaction, amount of paging, peak loads, number of terminal I/Os, the number of times a given application is used, and file statistics regarding reads, adds, and updates. Two utilities are available to assist in formatting and reporting these statistics—*performance analysis reporting system* (*CICSPARS*) and *service level reporter II* (*SLR*). The statistics help determine response time and use trends so that system tuning and upgrades can be effected in a timely manner.

Acronym Glossary

ABC Atanasoff-Berry computer. One of the first computers.

ACF Advanced communication function or facility. One of IBM's data communications products.

ACK Positive acknowledgment. An ASCII and EBCDIC character used for control in data communications

ACK0 Positive acknowledgment. An ASCII and EBCDIC character sequence used for control in BISYNC data communications

ACK1 Positive acknowledgment. An ASCII and EBCDIC character sequence used for control in BISYNC data communications.

ACM Association for Computing Machinery.

ACU Auto-call unit. A modem capability or separate device that provides automatic dialing for communications connections.

ADCCP Advanced data communications control procedure. An ANSI standard bit-oriented data link control. Pronounced "add-cap."

ADMD Administrative management domain. In the CCITT X.400 standard for electronic mail interchange, two types of domains are defined, public and private. The public domain is administered by a public agency such as a telephone company. The portion of the mail exchange administered by the public agency is the administrative management domain. The private domain corresponds to a corporate electronic mail system.

AlohaNet Early local area network implemented by the University of Hawaii.

AM Amplitude modulation. One method of changing the properties of a wave to represent data.

ANSI American National Standards Institute. A U.S. standards making agency.

API Application program interface. In LANs, the interface between application programs and the network software. In IBM's Netview network management system, non-IBM or IBM-compatible equipment can be interfaced to the network management facilities via Netview/PC and an application program interface. The application program interface provides the ability to capture the status of foreign equipment and take corrective action or pass the status to Netview.

ARC Attached resource computer. LAN technology originated by the Datapoint Corporation. This technology is widely used for microcomputer local area networks.

ARCnet Local area network implementation based on Datapoint's attached resource computer network.

ARPA Advanced Research Projects Agency of the U.S. Department of Defense.

ARPANET Advanced Research Projects Agency network. Early packet switching network.

ARQ Automatic request for retransmission or automatic request for repetition. When a receiving station detects an error in an incoming message, it sends a negative acknowledgment. The sending station will then automatically retransmit the message.

ASCII American standard code for information interchange. A code that uses seven or eight bits to represent characters. One of the two common computer codes. (See EBCDIC.)

Async Short for asynchronous transmission.

AT&T American Telephone and Telegraph Company. Communications provider.

ATM Automatic teller machine. An intelligent device used by financial institutions to allow users to enter transactions without the assistance of a teller.

AWG   American wire gauge. A standard that specifies the size of wires.

Baud   A measure of signaling rate on a communications link. Related to transmission speed.

Baudot   A communications code.

BCC   Block check character. Error checking character(s) appended by the sender of data and checked by the receiver.

BCD   Binary coded decimal. A computer code.

BDLC   Burroughs data link control—Burroughs Corporation. See SDLC.

BER   Bit error rate. The number of bits transmitted in error per unit of time.

BERT   Bit error rate testing. Testing a data communications line for errors by transmitting a known bit pattern and checking to see that the bit pattern is correctly received.

BISYNC   Short for binary synchronous transmission.

BIU   Bus interface unit. In a local area network, the bus interface unit provides the physical connection to the computer's I/O bus.

BMS   Basic mapping support. A CICS low-level facility that allows programmers to define terminal screen formats. See SDF.

bps   Bits per second. A measure of communications speed.

Bps   Usually bytes per second. A measure of communications speed.

BSC   Binary synchronous. A data communications protocol.

BTAM   Basic telecommunications access method. One of several IBM communications access methods.

C1 through C5   Levels of line conditioning provided by common carriers.

CAD   Computer-aided design. An application of computers in the design process. One component is computer drafting.

CAM   Computer-aided manufacturing. The use of computers to solve manufacturing problems. Includes robotic control, machine control, and process control components.

CATV   Community antenna television. CATV technology is used in some LANs.

CB radio   Citizens band radio.

CBX   Computerized branch exchange. A private branch exchange (PBX) using a computer as controller.

CCITT   Consultative Committee on International Telegraph and Telephony. An international standards organization.

CD   Carrier detect. A modem signal indicating detection of the carrier signal.

CDCDLC   Control Data Corporation data link control. See SDLC.

CICS   Customer Information Control System. IBM's terminal control program.

CICSPARS   CICS performance analysis reporting system. A CICS monitoring system.

CIU   Communications interface unit. In a local area network, the communications interface unit provides the physical connection to the transmission medium.

CMIP   Communications Management Information Protocol. A protocol for software to manage a network. See also SNMP.

CODASYL   Conference of Data Systems Language. A standards-making group.

Codec   Coder-decoder. A device for converting analog signals to digital signals for transmission over a digital communications link. On the receiving side, the codec converts digital signals back to analog signals.

CPU   Central processing unit. The central processor(s) of a computing system.

CRC   Cyclic redundancy check. A very efficient error detection method.

CRC-12   12-bit CRC.

CRC-16   16-bit CRC.

CRC-CCITT   CCITT standard CRC checking.

CRT   Cathode ray tube. A terminal that uses a cathode ray tube for display. See also VDU and VDT.

CSMA/CD   Carrier sense multiple access with collision detection. An access protocol for local area networks.

CTS   Clear to send. A signal between a modem and a controller used to initiate data transmission.

DAA   Direct access arrangement. A protective device placed between the telephone company's circuits and a subscriber's transmission devices. The DAA protects the telephone company's equipment from potential damage from the subscriber's equipment.

DATAPAC   Canadian packet switching network.

DATEX-P   West German packet switching network.

DBMS   Database management system.

DBTG Database task group. A subgroup of the CODASYL organization responsible for formulation of database standards.

DBX Digital branch exchange. A digital PBX.

DCE Data communications equipment. Communications-oriented components of a network such as telephone switching equipment, media, microwave relay stations, and so on. See DTE.

DDL Data definition language. A component of a database management system.

DDS Digital data service. A common carrier service for transmitting data in digital format.

DDX-2 Japanese packet switching network.

DEC Digital Equipment Corporation.

DES Data encryption standard. A U.S. National Bureau of Standards standard for encrypting/decrypting data.

DFS Distributed file systems. A file system capable of accessing and transferring files in a network having distributed data. The data is made accessible to nodes other than the one on which the data is located. Moreover, the access ought to be transparent to the user.

DIA Document interchange architecture. IBM approach to document exchange or transmission.

Dibits A transmission mode in which each signal conveys two bits.

DISOSS Distributed Office Support System. IBM's office automation strategy.

DLE Data link escape. An ASCII and EBCDIC character used for control in data communications.

DML Data manipulation language. A component of a database management system.

DNA Digital network architecture. Digital Equipment Corporation's network architecture.

DPSK Differential phase shift keying. See AM.

DSR Data set ready. A signal raised by a modem to indicate its local status.

DTE Data terminal or terminating equipment. Non–communications-oriented components of a data communications environment, such as computers, terminals, concentrators, and multiplexers (see DCE).

DTR Data terminal ready. A signal raised by a terminal or computer to a modem indicating the terminal's or computer's status.

EBCDIC Extended binary coded decimal interchange code. A code that uses eight bits to represent a character of information. One of the most common computer codes (see ASCII).

EDF Execution diagnostic facility. In IBM's customer information control system (CICS), a debugging facility that allows the programmer to test programs and their interface to CICS.

EDP Electronic data processing. A general term encompassing the use of computers for processing data.

EIA Electronic Industries Association. Responsible for numbers of electrical and communications standards.

ELS Level I and II Novell Corporation's Entry Level System LAN software.

E-Mail Electronic mail.

ENIAC Electronic numerical integrator and calculator. One of the first computers.

ENQ Inquiry. An ASCII and EBCDIC character used for control in data communications.

EOT End of transmission. An ASCII and EBCDIC character used to terminate transmission.

ETB End of transmission block. An ASCII and EBCDIC character used for control in data communications.

Ethernet A local area network implementation.

ETX End of text. An ASCII and EBCDIC character used for control in data communications. Signals the end of text.

EURONET European packet switching network.

Execunet An individual telephone service established by Microwave Communications, Inc.

EXPAND Tandem Computers' network architecture.

FAX Facsimile transmission.

FCC Federal Communications Commission. U.S. communications regulatory agency.

FDDI Fiber distributed data interface. An ANSI LAN standard for fiber optic LAN spanning a distance of approximately 200 kilometers and providing speeds of 100 Mbps.

FDM Frequency division multiplexing.

FDX Full duplex. A data flow technique that allows data to flow in two directions simultaneously on the communications link.

FEP Front end processor.

FIFO First-in-first-out queue management protocol.

FM Frequency modulation. See AM.

FMS File management system. A file management system provides a subset of a database management system's capabilities. An FMS provides functions such as storage allocation and file access methods for a single file.

FOX   Fiber Optic Extension. Tandem Computer's proprietary fiber optic LAN.

FSK   Frequency shift keying. See FM and AM.

Gbps   A billion bits per second.

GFI   General format identification. A control field in a packet switching message frame.

GTE   General Telephone and Electronics. A communications provider.

HC   Hyperchannel. Network System Corporation's (NSC) high-speed (50 Mbps) local area network. Used primarily to connect supercomputers, mainframes, and minicomputers.

HDLC   High-level data link control. International Standards Organization's standard for bit-oriented data link protocol.

HDX   Half duplex. A flow control technique that allows data to flow in both directions on a communication link, but in only one direction at a time.

Hz   Abbreviation for hertz. A measure of frequency. One hertz is one cycle per second.

I/O   Input/output.

IBM   International Business Machines. Computer industry leader.

IEEE   Institute of Electrical and Electronics Engineers. A professional society. Publishes documents and standards for data communications. Has undertaken to establish standards for local area networks.

IMP   Interface message processor. Node in the ARPANET.

IMS   Information management system. One of several database management systems offered by the IBM corporation.

IPX/SPX   Novell Corporation's Internetwork Packet Exchange/Sequenced Packet Exchange protocol for message exchange on a LAN.

ISAM   Index sequential access method. Database access method.

ISC   Intersystem communication. CICS ability to communicate with CICS systems on different nodes.

ISDN   Integrated services digital network. The integration of voice and data transmission (and other formats such as video and graphics images) over a digital transmission network. A network proposed by numerous common carriers.

ISO   International Standards Organization. Active in setting communications standards.

ITB   Intermediate transmission block. An ASCII and EBCDIC character used for control in data communications.

JIS   Japanese Industrial Standard. One of the JIS standards is for data codes that contain a portion of the Kanji character set and other character sets.

Kbps   A thousand bits per second.

LAN   Local area network. A network that is confined to a small geographical area. For example, the medium may be restricted to several kilometers.

LAPB   Link access procedure, balanced. Bit-oriented data link protocol standard of the CCITT.

LATA   Local access and transport areas. The region served by a regional Bell operating company (RBOC) following the divestiture of AT&T is divided into local access and transport areas. LATAs are not rigidly defined, but calls within a LATA are handled exclusively by the RBOC (the call is not handled by a long distance carrier but still may be a toll call).

LCD   Liquid crystal display. One technology for displaying data on a terminal and other devices. Used primarily in portable devices.

LDDI   Local distributed data interfaces. An ANSI proposal for high-speed LAN standard.

LED   Light-emitting diode. One source of light for fiber optics.

LIFO   Last-in-first-out queue management protocol.

LLC layer   In the IEEE LAN standards, the data link layer is divided into two sublayers, the logical link control (LLC) and media access control (MAC). The LLC layer forms the interface between the higher layers and the MAC layer. Thus, higher layers do not need to know about the details of the MAC protocol.

LRC   Longitudinal redundancy check. An error checking technique used in communications primarily in conjunction with vertical redundancy check (VRC).

LU   Logical unit. A component of IBM's systems network architecture (see SNA).

LU 6.2   An SNA logical unit type representing a program-to-program session.

LUW   Logical units of work. CICS units of recovery.

MAC layer   In the IEEE LAN standards, the data link layer is divided into two sublayers, the logical link control (LLC) and media access control (MAC). The MAC layer protocol implements the token passing or CSMA/CD protocol.

MAN Metropolitan area network. The subject of the IEEE 802.6 standard. Similar in nature to the FDDI LAN specification.

MAP Manufacturing automation protocol. A LAN for manufacturing environments.

MARK I Early computer.

MAU Multi-station access unit. In an IBM token ring LAN, a MAU is used to interconnect workstations.

Mbps A million bits per second.

MCI Microwave Communications, Inc. U.S. communications provider.

MCS Message control system. See TCP.

MIB Management information base. See SNMP.

MIPS Million instructions per second. One of a number of measures of CPU performance.

MNP Microcomputer network protocols. A set of modem protocols providing for data compression and error checking, such as MNP Level 4 and MNP Level 5.

Modem Modulator-demodulator. A device that changes digital signals to analog signals for transmitting data over telephone circuits. Also used for some fiber optic transmission (digital fiber optics do not require a modem) and any transmission mode requiring a change from one form of signal to another.

MRO Multiregion operation. The ability of two CICS systems on one node to communicate with each other.

MTA Message transfer agent. In the CCITT X.400 standard for electronic mail interchange, a message transfer agent provides the interface between the sending and receiving mail agents.

MTBF Mean time between failure. For equipment, the average amount of time it is expected to operate without a failure.

MTTR Mean time to repair. The average amount of time required to repair a broken piece of equipment and restore it to service.

MUX A multiplexer or multiplexing.

NAK Negative acknowledgment. An ASCII and EBCDIC character used for control in data communications.

NASA National Aeronautics and Space Administration. U.S. space agency.

NAU Network addressable unit. A component of IBM's systems network architecture (SNA).

NBS National Bureau of Standards. A U.S. standards sanctioning agency.

NCP Network control program. A data communications program that helps manage a communications network. Specifically, a program that runs in IBM's 37xx line of communications controllers.

NETBIOS Network basic input/output system. The low-level network interface for IBM and compatible microcomputers.

NFS Network file system. A distributed file system developed by Sun Microsystems. Sun Microsystems placed the network file system specifications in the public domain to allow computer and software vendors to create products that are able to communicate over a distributed network.

NIC A network interface card. An NIC is used as the hardware interface to a LAN.

NMS Network management system. See SNMP.

NPA Network performance analyzer. A component of IBM's systems network architecture (SNA).

NPDA Network problem determination aid. A component of IBM's systems network architecture (SNA).

Nr Number received. Control field in HDLC frame.

Ns Number sent. Control field in HDLC frame.

OA Office automation.

OCA Open communications architecture. The publishing of network interface specifications to allow easier implementation of multiple vendor networks.

OCR Optical character recognition. A data input technique that uses optics to read characters in a special font.

OEM Original equipment manufacturer.

OS Operating system.

OS/2 Operating system for IBM and IBM-compatible microcomputers. OS/2 extended version contains LAN management capabilities and data communications interfaces.

OSI Reference model for open systems interconnection. A seven-layered set of functions for transmitting data from one user to another. Specified by the ISO to facilitate interconnection of networks.

P/F Poll/final bit. Control field in HDLC frame.

PAD Packet assembly/disassembly. A function in a packet switching network that breaks messages into packets and reassembles packets when received into messages.

PAM Phase amplitude modulation. See AM.

PARS A data link protocol used in airline reservations systems.

PBX   Private branch exchange. A private telephone exchange, such as the telephone exchange for a company.

PC   Personal computer.

PCM   Pulse code modulation. One method used in digital data transmission.

PDN   Packet distribution network or public data network. A (usually) public data network where messages are divided into packets of a predefined size and routed to their destination.

PIN   A personal identification number. A PIN is used for user authentication. For example, ATM users must identify themselves with a PIN.

PM   Phase modulation. See AM.

POP   A point of presence in the U.S. public telephone network. A point of presence is a point at which a transfer is made from a local telephone company to the long-distance carrier.

POS   Point-of-sale. A retailing application using intelligent terminals (POS terminals) to manage inventory, transfer funds from purchaser to merchant account, verify credit, and so on.

PRMD   Private management domain. In the CCITT X.400 standard for electronic mail interchange, two types of domains are defined, public and private. The public domain is administered by a public agency, such as a telephone company. The portion of the mail exchange administered by the public agency is the administrative management domain. The private domain corresponds to a corporate electronic mail system.

PSE   Packet switching equipment. A node in a packet switching network.

PSK   Phase shift keying. See AM.

PTT   Postal, telephone, and telegraph. In some countries, the PTTs are responsible for providing telecommunications facilities.

PU   Physical unit. A component of IBM's systems network architecture (see SNA).

PUCP   Physical unit control point. In IBM's systems network architecture (SNA) a physical unit control point resides in nodes that do not contain a systems services control point (SSCP). The PUCP is responsible for connecting and disconnecting the node from the network.

PVC   Permanent virtual circuit. Circuit type in a packet switching network.

QAM   Quadrature amplitude modulation. See AM.

RAM   Random access memory.

RBOC   Regional Bell operating company. The AT&T divestiture resulted in the formation of RBOCs and a separate AT&T company. An RBOC is responsible for local telephone services within a region of the U.S.

RD   Receive data. The modem connection over which data is received.

REJ   Reject. An HDLC supervisory frame.

RFI   Request for information. A document issued to vendors to obtain technical information about their products and services.

RFP   Request for proposal. A document issued to vendors as an invitation for them to propose a solution to a problem.

RFQ   Request for quotation. See RFP.

RFS   Remote file systems. File systems that allow file location and access over networks. See DFS.

RJE   Remote job entry. Batch input/output capability over communications lines.

RNR   Not ready to receive. An HDLC supervisory frame.

RR   Ready to receive. An HDLC supervisory frame.

RS-232-C   An EIA standard for pin connections in cables used in serial data transmission.

RTS   Request to send. A signal raised by a processor or terminal to initiate data transfer.

RVI   Reverse interrupt. An ASCII and EBCDIC character sequence used for control in BISYNC data communications.

SABRE   Semi-Automatic Business Research Environment. Joint effort between IBM and American Airlines for online transaction processing— airline reservations.

SAGE   Semi-Automatic Ground Environment. Early U.S. military communications network for radar early warning.

SBT   Six-bit transcode. A six-bit computer code developed by IBM primarily for RJE.

SDF   Screen definition facility. A CICS capability that allows users to efficiently generate terminal screen formats.

SDLC   Synchronous data link control. IBM's bit-oriented data link protocol.

SFT   Novell Corporation's system fault-tolerant software for LANs.

SLR   Service level reporter. CICS monitoring system.

SMB   Server message block protocol. A distributed file system developed by IBM for microcomputer networks.

SMI Structure of management information. See SNMP.

SNA Systems network architecture. IBM's architecture for network implementation.

SNADS SNA distribution services. IBM's SNA delivery system. Allows users to send messages/documents using delayed delivery. A store and forward capability.

SNMP Simple Network Management Protocol. SNMP provides a guideline for creating network management software products. SNMP has four key components: the SNMP protocol, structure of management information (SMI), management information base (MIB), and the network management system (NMS).

SOH Start of header. An ASCII and EBCDIC character used for control in data communications.

Spooler A software system that collects printer output (typically on disk) and prints the data and schedules the data for printing. *Spool* is an acronym for simultaneous peripheral operation online.

SPX Novell Corporation's Sequenced Packet Exchange protocol for message exchange on a LAN. See IPX/SPX.

SQL Structured query language. A relational database language developed by IBM and later standardized by the American National Standards Institute (ANSI). SQL was once called SEQUEL by IBM and is pronounced "sequel."

SSCP Systems services control point. A component of IBM's systems network architecture (SNA).

stat mux Statistical time division multiplexer.

STDM Statistical time division multiplexing.

STE Signaling terminal equipment. Node used to provide an interface between two different packet switching networks.

STX Start of text. An ASCII and EBCDIC special character used as a data communications control character in some protocols.

SVC Switched virtual circuit. Circuit type in a packet switching network.

SYN An ASCII and EBCDIC character used for data communications control. Often used to establish synchronization between a sender and receiver.

T1 through T4 High-speed data transmission circuits from a common carrier.

TCAM Telecommunications access method. One of several IBM communications access methods.

TCP Transaction (or terminal) control process. A software system that controls the flow of messages between terminals and application programs, in addition to other functions.

TCP/IP Transmission control procedure/internet protocol, a file transfer protocol for LANs developed by the U.S. Department of Defense. Used for internet file transfers.

TCT Terminal control table. CICS table that contains descriptions of terminals controlled by CICS.

TD Transmitted data. The modem connection on which data is transmitted.

TDM Time division multiplexing.

TELENET A public packet switching network developed by General Telephone and Electronics.

TOP Technical-office-automation-oriented LAN.

TP Teleprocessing. Frequently used in conjunction with other terms, for example, *TP monitor*.

TRANSPAC French packet switching network.

TSAP The transport layer uses an address called a transport service access point to uniquely identify session entities.

TTD Temporary text delay. An ASCII and EBCDIC character sequence used for control in BISYNC data communications.

TTY Teletypewriter. Used to describe a terminal that mirrors the capability of a teletypewriter device. A dumb terminal.

TYMNET A public packet switching network.

UA User agent. In the CCITT X.400 standard for electronic mail interchange, a user agent allows a user to compose a mail message, provides a recipient address, and receives messages on behalf of a user.

UART Universal asynchronous receiver/transmitter.

UDLC Universal data link control. Sperry-Univac's bit-oriented data link protocol.

UPC Universal products code. A bar code used to uniquely identify products. This code is read by a variety of sensors. The UPC is used to input product information.

USASCII See ASCII.

V.nn A prefix for CCITT standards. For example, V.24 is a standard for serial transmission.

VAN Value-added network. See PDN.

VDT Video display terminal. See VDU.

VDU Video display unit. A terminal that uses a technique such as a cathode ray tube, liquid crystal display, and so on to represent data.

VRC   Vertical redundancy check. An error checking technique. Also known as parity checking.

VSAM   Virtual index sequential access method. An IBM database access method.

VTAM   Virtual telecommunications access method. One of several IBM communications access methods.

WACK   Wait for positive acknowledgment. An ASCII and EBCDIC character sequence used for control in BISYNC data communications.

WAN   Wide area network. A network that covers a wide geographical area (as contrasted with a local area network).

WATS   Wide area telecommunications or telephone service. An inbound or outbound telephone service that allows long-distance telephone service. In the U.S. the inbound service is associated with the 800 area code toll-free numbers.

X.nn   A prefix for CCITT standards. For example, X.25 is a packet switching standard.

Xn.dd   A prefix for ANSI data communications standards.

XOFF   A convention used between transmitter and receiver to signal readiness to receive data and pace the data flow between sender and receiver. For example, if a printer's buffer is filled and it is unable to correctly accept more data, the printer will send an XOFF signal to the transmitter to temporarily halt the flow of data. Data flow continues when the printer sends an XON signal to the transmitter.

XON   A convention used between transmitter and receiver to signal readiness to receive data. When a device such as a printer has emptied its buffer and is ready to receive more data from a transmitter, it sends an XON signal to the transmitter.

Key Terms Glossary

access method   A software subsystem that provides input and output services as interface between an application and its associated devices. It eliminates device dependencies for an application programmer.

ACK0 and ACK1   Positive acknowledgments in IBM's binary synchronous protocol.

acknowledgment, negative (NAK)   When a station receives a message and detects a transmission error, the receiver indicates that the message was not successfully received by returning a negative acknowledgment to the sender.

acknowledgment, positive (ACK)   When a station receives a message with no detected transmission errors, the message is assumed to be error free and the receiver returns a positive acknowledgment to the sender.

acoustic coupler   An acoustic coupler converts digital signals to analog and analog to digital. It is used mostly in switched communications and uses the telephone handset to pass data between a terminal or computer and the acoustic coupler.

advanced communication function (ACF)   Software support for IBM's telecommunications using SNA.

Advanced Data Communications Control Procedure (ADCCP)   An ANSI standard bit-oriented data link protocol. See high-level data link control.

aggregate data rate   The amount of information that can be transmitted per unit of time.

AlohaNet   An early local area network implemented by the University of Hawaii.

American standard code for information interchange (ASCII)   A code that uses seven or eight bits to represent characters. One of two common computer codes.

amplitude modulation (AM)   One of the three main ways of modifying a signal. It changes the amplitude of the generated wave. In data communications it is used in conjunction with phase modulation to provide high data transmission rates.

analog   Refers to measurable physical quantities, which in data communications take the form of voltage and variations in the properties of waves. Data is represented in analog form by varying the amplitude, frequency, and/or phase of a wave or by changing current on a line.

application layer   One of the layers of the International Standards Organization's open systems interconnection standard. The functions of this layer are application-dependent.

ARPANET   The first implementation of a packet distribution network, sponsored by the U.S. Advanced Research Projects Agency. Connects over 100 research organizations.

asynchronous transmission (Async)   The oldest and one of the most common data link protocols. Each character is transmitted individually with its own error detection scheme, usually a parity bit. The sender and receiver are not synchronized with each other.

attenuation   A weakening of a signal as a result of distance and characteristics of the medium.

authentication   The second step in the security measure of identification/authentication in which the user verifies that he or she is the identified user. A password is one form of authentication.

auto-call unit (ACU)   Used to place a telephone call automatically, without manual intervention.

automatic request for retransmission (ARQ)   The most common error correction mechanism. In asynchronous transmission, individual characters are retransmitted, whereas in synchronous transmission, one or more blocks may need to be retransmitted.

availability A system is available when all components a user needs to satisfy the request are operable.

backward channel See reverse channel.

bandwidth The difference between the minimum and maximum frequencies allowed. Bandwidth is a measure of the amount of data that can be transmitted per unit of time. The greater the bandwidth, the higher the possible data transmission rate.

baseband transmission Sends the data along the channel by means of voltage fluctuations. The entire bandwidth of the cable is used to carry data.

basic terminal access method (BTAM) One of IBM's data communications access methods.

baud rate A measure of the number of discrete signals that can be observed per unit of time.

Baudot code A data code derived from the telegraph industry. Its primary use is with telegraph lines or equipment originally designed for telegraphy. Represents data using five bits per character.

binary coded decimal (BCD) A coding scheme for the storage of data in digital computers. The code may either be four-bit or six-bit.

binary synchronous communications protocol (BSC or BISYNC) A transmission protocol introduced by IBM as the data link protocol for remote job entry. It later became a de facto standard for many types of data transmission, particularly between two computers. Data is transmitted a block at a time, and the sender and receiver need to be in time with each other. Specific control characters are used to indicate beginning of text, end of text, start of header, and so on.

bit A binary digit, either 0 or 1.

bit error rate The number of bits in error on a data communications per unit of time.

bit error rate testing (BERT) Testing a data communications line for errors by transmitting a known bit pattern and checking to see that the bit pattern is correctly received.

bit rate One method of measuring data transmission speed—bits per second.

block A contiguous group of bits or bytes. Often messages are broken into blocks of a specific size for transmission over a data communications line.

block check character (BCC) In the error detection methods of longitudinal redundancy check (LRC) or cyclic redundancy check (CRC), an error detection character or characters, called the BCC, is appended to a block of transmitted characters, typically at the end of the block.

breakout box A diagnostic tool that checks signals being transmitted and to change the leads on which the signal is transmitted. A breakout box may also have features allowing cable testing and generation of bit test patterns.

bridge An interconnection between like networks, for example, Ethernet to Ethernet.

broadband transmission A form of data transmission where data is carried on high-frequency carrier waves; the carrying capacity of the medium is divided into a number of subchannels, such as video, low-speed data, high-speed data, voice, and so on, allowing the medium to satisfy several communication needs.

broadcast A technology that sends signals to multiple stations at once. Satellite is one example of a broadcast technology.

buffer A temporary data storage area. In data communications data is received into a system buffer and then transferred to an application program or onto the communications link.

bulletin board See electronic bulletin board.

burst errors A grouping of errors typically caused by one source such as impulse noise.

bus A communications medium for transmitting data or power. A local area network topology.

call-back unit A security device for switched connections. It receives a call, verifies the user, severs the connection, and calls the user back.

carrier sense multiple access with collision detection (CSMA/CD) An access protocol used primarily in local area networks.

carrier signal A carrier wave is established between a sender and receiver. Upon detection of this signal by the receiver, the sender modulates the wave to allow it to carry data.

Carterphone (or Carterfone) decision A U.S. case regarding attaching devices to a telephone company's network.

cathode ray tube (CRT)   A terminal using an electron gun to bombard a phosphor-coated screen to form data images. The technology is like that of television.

central office   The local telephone company office to which a subscriber is connected. Also called an end office or Class 5 switching office.

central processing unit (CPU)   The processing components of a computer. The components of the CPU are control, arithmetic logic unit, and memory.

Centrex   A telephone company service that provides PBX capabilities to a company. With the Centrex service, the PBX equipment is located on the telephone company's premises.

chain   In database management systems, a technique used by network model database systems to establish record relationships.

channel   A data communications path. Frequently applied to high-speed data paths.

checksum   A technique used to check for errors in data. The sending application generates the checksum from the data being transmitted. The receiving application computes the checksum and compares it to the value computed and sent by the sending station.

cipher text   Encrypted data.

circuit   Either the medium connecting two communicating devices or a path between a sender and receiver where there may be one or more intermediary nodes. The exact meaning depends on the context.

circuit switching   A method of establishing a communications link between a sender and receiver on demand. The circuit is maintained for the duration of the session and is removed when sender and receiver disconnect.

Class 1 telephone switching office   See regional center.

Class 2 telephone switching office   See sectional center.

Class 3 telephone switching office   See primary center.

Class 4 telephone switching office   See toll office.

Class 5 telephone switching office   See end office.

clear to send (CTS)   A signal between a modem and a controller used to initiate data transmission.

cluster controller   A hardware device that controls several terminals. Commonly associated with the IBM 3270 family of terminals.

coaxial cable   A transmission medium consisting of one or two central data transmission wires surrounded by an insulating layer, a shielding layer, and an outer jacket. Coaxial cable has a high data-carrying capacity and low error rates.

code independence   The ability to successfully transmit data regardless of the data code, such as ASCII, EBCDIC, and so on.

codec   Short for coder-decoder. A device that converts analog signals to digital for transmission over a digital transmission link. On the receiving side, the codec translates the digital signal back to an analog signal. A codec can be used to interface analog telephone sets to digital circuits.

common carrier   A public utility that provides public transmission media, such as the telephone companies and satellite companies.

communications controller   Responsible for the direct interface to a communication line. It places data on the line and receives it, checks for errors, and manages the protocol.

computerized branch exchange (CBX)   A private branch exchange (PBX) using a computer as controller.

concentrator   A communications component (usually a computer) that concentrates a number of communications lines onto a fewer number of lines. Typically a concentrator is located in a remote location relative to the host computer(s) to which it is attached. The concentrator combines the data from several terminals or computers for transmission to the host(s). A concentrator is used to economize on communications line costs.

conditioning   A service provided by telephone companies for leased lines. It reduces the amount of noise on a line, providing lower error rates and increased speed.

Consultative Committee on International Telegraph and Telephony (CCITT)   An international standards organization.

CCITT V.10 and V.11   Electrical interfaces for data transmission.

CCITT V.24   A functional interface similar to RS-232-C.

CCITT V.25   A specification for establishing and terminating sessions with an auto-call unit.

CCITT V.28   A specification for electrical interface similar to that of RS-232-C.

CCITT V.35   A standard for data transmission at speeds up to 48,000 bits per second using a 34-pin connection.

contention   A convention whereby devices obtain control of a communications link. In contention mode, devices compete for control of the line by either transmitting directly on an idle line or by issuing a request for line control.

contention control   A convention used to determine which stations may transmit, the conditions under which transmission of data is allowed, and the pacing of data transmission.

control   Signals that are exchanged between a sender and receiver to establish, maintain, and terminate connections, communications, and the flow of data.

control characters   Characters that are used to control a communications link. Examples include start of text (STX) and end of text (EOT or ETX) characters.

conversational mode   A mode of communication between a sender and receiver in which the receiver prompts the sender for each piece of data. Contrasted with block mode, where a user is asked to enter a large block of data at one time.

crosstalk   When the signals from one channel distort or interfere with the signals of a different channel.

current loop   A transmission technique that uses changes in current flow to represent data. Does not require a modem and operates at speeds up to 19.2K bits per second without modems.

Customer Information Control System (CICS)   A TCP provided by IBM. Its primary function is as an interface between terminal users on one side and application programs or the database on the other.

cyclic redundancy check (CRC)   An error detection algorithm that uses a polynomial function to generate the block check characters. A very efficient error detection method.

data communications   The transmission of data to and from computers and components of computer systems.

data communications equipment (DCE)   Refers to modems, media, and media-support facilities such as telephone switching equipment, microwave relay stations, and transponders.

data compression   Data compression is used to reduce the number of characters or bits in a message. A common form is repeating character compression where long strings of repeating characters are replaced by the repeating group and the repeat count. Compressing data allows fewer characters to be transmitted and improves line efficiency, increasing the effective aggregate data rate.

data encryption standard (DES)   A U.S. National Bureau of Standards encryption standard. Also adopted by the International Standards Organization.

data independence   The ability to make changes in the physical storage of data without requiring changes in the applications that use the data.

data link layer   One of the layers of the International Standards Organization's open systems interconnection standard. The data link layer governs the establishment and control of the communication link.

data link protocols   Conventions that govern the flow of data between a sending and receiving station.

data set   A data set, also known as a modem, is a device used to translate from digital format to analog format and back to digital format. Used to transmit digital data over analog links such as telephone lines.

data terminal equipment (DTE)   Includes terminals, computers, concentrators, and multiplexers.

datagram   One type of connection option for a PDN. The message fits into the data field of one packet. There is less accountability for packet delivery than for other connection types.

DATAPAC   A Canadian packet distribution network.

dataphone digital service (DDS)   A digital communication service provided by the telephone companies. DDS provides communication speeds up to 56 Kbps.

DATEX-P   A West German packet distribution network.

deadlock   A state that exists when two or more processes are unable to proceed. It occurs when two or more transactions have locked a resource and request resources that other involved processes already have locked.

dedicated line   See leased line.

dial or dial-up line   See switched connection.

dibit   A transmission mode in which each signal conveys two bits of data.

digital branch exchange (DBX)   A private branch exchange that transmits data in digital format.

digital network architecture (DNA)   The architecture for building networks controlled by Digital Equipment Corporation's systems.

digital transmission   A transmission mode where data are represented by binary digits rather than an analog signal.

distortion   The change of transmitted signals resulting from noise. Distortion can result in transmission errors.

distributed processing   Refers to the geographical distribution of hardware, software, processing, and data.

domain   In IBM's SNA the network components managed by a systems services control point.

downloading   The act of transferring programs or data from a host processor to a workstation, typically a microcomputer.

echo   The reflection or reversal of the signal being transmitted. Also used to define a transmission convention where the receiver of data sends the data back to the sender to assist in error detection.

echo suppressor   A device that allows a transmitted signal to pass in one direction only, thus minimizing the echo effect.

electronic bulletin board   A software system that allows users to "post" electronic messages. Electronic bulletin boards are frequently accessed by a switched telephone connection and serve as a clearing house for software and hardware exchange and as a medium for information exchange.

electronic switching   Circuit switching equipment that makes connection electronically rather than mechanically. Electronic switching equipment is generally more error free than mechanical switches.

emulator   A diagnostic tool that enables the user to check for adherence to a specific protocol. A hardware or software system that mimics the operation of another system.

encryption equipment   Equipment that allows transmitted data to be scrambled at the sending location and reconstructed at the receiving end. Encryption is also used when storing information, for example, before writing data to a database. Encryption equipment encrypts the data before writing and decrypts it after reading.

end of transmission (EOT)   An ASCII and EBCDIC character used to terminate transmission in binary synchronous transmission. The point at which a sender has no more data to send and either relinquishes the link or becomes a receiver.

end office   A telephone company office to which a subscriber is connected. See also central office.

envelope delay distortion   Data transmission distortions that occur when signals of different frequencies are transmitted at a nonuniform speed over one medium.

equalization   See conditioning.

ergonomics   The study of how people physically adjust to their work environment. Used to define equipment and environments that are less stressful to their users.

error   All transmission media are subject to signal distortion, which can produce errors in the data received.

error burst   See burst errors.

Ethernet   A local area network implementation using CSMA/CD protocol on a bus. The IEEE 802.3 standard is based on Ethernet. One of the popular local area network implementations.

EURONET   A European packet distribution network.

extended binary coded decimal interchange code (EBCDIC)   A data code that uses eight bits to represent a character of information. One of the most common computer codes.

fiber optic   A transmission medium providing very high data rates and low errors. One or more glass or plastic fibers are woven together to form the core of the cable. This core is surrounded by a glass or plastic layer called the cladding. The cladding in turn is covered with plastic or other material for protection. The cable requires a light source, with laser and light-emitting diodes being those most commonly used.

flag   In bit-oriented protocols the bit pattern used to signal the beginning and ending of the data.

flow control   The pacing of data between a sender and receiver. Three flow control techniques are simplex, half duplex, and full duplex.

forward error correction   An error detection/ correction technique that allows some errors to be corrected by the receiving device.

frame A transmission packet. A term used to describe a transmission block in bit-oriented protocols.

frequency modulation (FM) One method of changing the characteristics of a signal to represent data. The frequency of the carrier signal is changed. Often used by lower speed modems.

frequency shift keying A form of frequency modulation.

front end processor (FEP) Systems placed at the host end of communications circuits, much like a concentrator is used at the remote end. The FEP is intended to take over much of the line management work from the host.

full duplex Data can be transmitted over a link in both directions simultaneously.

function keys Additional keys on some terminals, which transmit specific character sequences to the host.

gateway The interface between two different networks.

Gaussian noise See white noise.

geosynchronous orbit A satellite orbit in which the satellite is stationary with respect to the earth: The satellite is always positioned over the same location.

group address A device address that is recognized by a group of devices. With a message sent with a group address, all devices in the group receive the message.

guardbands Frequency separation that helps to avoid one signal's interfering with another.

half duplex transmission The data travels in both directions over a link, but in only one direction at a time.

Hamming codes One type of error correcting codes. An error detecting scheme that allows the receiving station not only to detect errors but also to correct some of them.

handshake An exchange between two stations while establishing connection. The handshake exchange is used to identify stations and establish the dialogue rules for the connection.

hertz The term used to denote frequency; one hertz is one cycle per second.

hierarchical network A network topology in which the nodes are arranged hierarchically.

high-level data link control (HDLC) A positional synchronous protocol that operates in full duplex or half duplex modes in both point-to-

point and multi-point configurations. Data is transmitted in fixed-format frames consisting of start flag, address, control information, block check character (CRC), an end-of-frame flag. HDLC is an International Standards Organization standard similar to IBM's SDLC.

host A processor that provides support to terminals or other processors.

Hyperchannel (HC) A local area network that transmits data at 50 million bits per second.

impulse noise A noise characterized by signal "spikes." In telephone circuits it can be caused by switching equipment or by lightning strikes and in other situations by transient electrical impulses such as those occurring on a shop floor. A common cause of transmission errors.

interleaving In time division multiplexing, either characters or bits are alternated on the communications medium. Alternating bits is called bit interleaving and alternating characters is called byte or character interleaving.

intermodulation noise A special form of crosstalk, which is the result of two or more signals combining to produce a distorted signal.

interrupt characters A set of characters that terminate a message or cause an interruption in transmission to perform a special action, such as a backspace.

isochronous A seldom used data link protocol with characteristics of both asynchronous and synchronous protocols. In isochronous transmission, data is transmitted a character at a time but there is always a time interval between characters. The time interval corresponds to integral number of character transmissions: Characters can be thought of as having transmission start times.

Kermit A program for transferring files from one node to another.

latency On disk drives the average time required for the data being read to revolve under the read/write heads.

leased lines Lines leased from common carriers. Lines are leased when the connection time between locations is long enough to cover the cost of leasing or if speeds higher than those available with switched lines must be attained.

limited distance modem See modem, short haul.

line driver A device that receives a signal on a line, amplifies the signal, and then forwards the signal to the next data communications or data terminal equipment. See also repeater.

line monitor, analog   An instrument that measures and displays the analog signals on the communications circuit or on the data communications side of the modem, enabling the user to check for noise and proper modulation.

line monitor, digital   Diagnostic equipment attached to a communications circuit so the bit patterns being transmitted over the link can be captured and displayed to detect transmission or protocol violations.

line protocol   A data link protocol. The line protocol may also include flow control.

link   The circuit established between two adjacent nodes, with no intervening nodes.

link access procedure, balanced (LAPB)   A bit-synchronous protocol similar to high-level data link control. LAPB is the protocol specified for X.25 networks.

local area network (LAN)   A communications network in which all of the components are located within several kilometers of each other and that uses high transmission speeds, generally one million bits per second or higher.

local loop   The connection between a telephone subscriber's telephone and the telephone company's end office.

logging   Writing data to a log file, typically for recovery purposes. Log files may also be used for auditing network activity. Items logged for recovery include transactions and before- and after-images of database records.

logical unit (LU)   In IBM's SNA, a unit that represents a system user. Sessions exist between LUs or an LU and the SSCP. Several types of LUs have been defined.

longitudinal redundancy check (LRC)   An error checking technique in which a block check character is appended to a block of transmitted characters, typically at the end of the block. The block check character checks parity on a row of bits.

mark   In data transmission, the equivalent of a 1 bit.

mean time between failure (MTBF)   A measure of the average amount of time a given component may be expected to operate before failing.

mean time to repair (MTTR)   The average time required to fix a failed component.

medium   In data communications, the carrier of data signals, such as wires, coaxial cables, fiber optics, and so on.

message control system (MCS)   See transaction control process.

message switch   A technique that routes messages to their correct destination, possibly using different paths for a given destination. Contrast with circuit switching. Also, a computer that examines messages and routes them to a processor.

microwave   A method of transmitting data using high-frequency radio waves. It requires a line of sight between sending and receiving stations. Capable of high data rates.

modem   A device that translates digital signals to analog signals at the sending end and analog signals back to digital signals at the receiving end.

modem, short haul   Allows transmission up to approximately 20 miles at varying speeds.

modem, turnaround time   The time required for a modem to make the transition from sender to receiver on half duplex links. It includes the time for the old sender to drop the carrier signal, for the new sender to recognize that the carrier signal has been dropped, and for the new sender to raise the carrier signal that must be detected by the new receiver.

modem eliminator   A device that allows data transmission over short distances without a modem. Provides for signal timing as well as data transmission.

modulation   A synonym for modification. In data transmission, changing the characteristics of a carrier signal to represent data.

multiple-point connection   A configuration in which multiple terminals share the same communications channel.

multiplexing (MUX)   A method of data transmission in which several devices are allowed to share a single link.

frequency   The bandwidth is divided into several subbands, each of which is assigned to one device.

inverse   A form of multiplexing where a high-speed communications link is divided over multiple lower speed channels.

statistical time division   Time division multiplexing variation. Time slots are not dedicated to a specific device, allowing more effective use of the medium. If only one device is sending/receiving, the link is devoted to that device. Provides very effective use of the communications link.

time division   Each device is given a time slot during which it can send/receive data. The time slot is used even if the device is not sending/receiving data.

multi-threading   A technique that allows multiple operations to be processed concurrently.

negative acknowledgment (NAK)   The mechanism used to notify a sender that the transmitted message was not successfully received.

Netview   IBM's network management system for SNA networks.

Netview/PC   IBM's network management system for non-SNA components, such as token networks, PBX systems, and other vendor components.

network   Two or more computers connected via a communications medium, together with all communications, hardware, and software components. Alternatively, a host processor, together with its attached terminals, workstations, and communications equipment such as transmission media, modems, and so on.

network, ring   A network configuration commonly used to implement local area networks. The medium forms a loop to which workstations are attached. Generally the access protocol is token passing.

network addressable unit (NAU)   In IBM's SNA, any device that has a network address, such as logical units and physical units.

network control program (NCP)   A program that resides in an IBM communications controller.

network layer   One of the layers of the International Standards Organization's open systems interconnection standard. The network layer is responsible for end-to-end message routing.

nodes   Processors in a network, either local area or wide area.

noise   Disruptions to data transmission that can result in errors in the data being transmitted. There are several types of noise, such as impulse, white, echo, and so on.

noncontinuous carrier   A carrier signal is modulated to represent data. A noncontinuous carrier is one that is raised when sending data and is not present when data is not being transmitted.

null modem   See modem eliminator.

number received (Nr)   In bit-synchronous transmission such as HDLC, a field on the transmission frame and on the receiver's system used to represent the frame sequence number the receiving station expects to receive next.

number sent (Ns)   In bit-synchronous transmission such as HDLC, a field on the transmission frame and on the sender's system used to represent the frame sequence number being transmitted.

octet   A group of eight bits. Used in bit-synchronous protocols. Data, regardless of its code, is treated as octets.

online   A terminal is said to be online when it is connected to the CPU and is capable of sending or receiving data.

online applications, types of

batch   Typically large data transfers in two directions.

data entry   Applications that consist of lengthy inputs with short responses.

distributed   Applications where the data or the processing or both are distributed among a number of processing units.

inquiry/response   Applications in which inputs generally have only a few characters and output responses have many.

interactive   Applications characterized by relatively short inputs and outputs.

sensor-based   The processor receives data from sensors and if necessary acts upon it.

OSI reference model   for open systems interconnection. A seven-layered set of functions for transmitting data from one user to another. Specified by the International Standards Organization to facilitate interconnection of networks.

application layer   Functionally determined by the user.

data link layer   Responsible for establishment and control of the physical communication path.

network layer   Responsible for end-to-end routing, message routing, and accounting information.

physical layer   Specifies the electrical connections between the computer and the medium.

presentation layer   Used for data formatting such as compression and encryption.

session layer   Responsible for establishing dialogue rules between users.

transport layer   Responsible for determining address of recipient and message integrity.

overhead, data link protocol   The number of additional characters or bits that must be appended to the message to provide control, delineation of data, and error detection.

packet assembly/disassembly (PAD)   A function in a packet switching network that breaks messages into packets for transmission and reassembles packets into messages at the message's destination.

packet distribution network (PDN)   A network that divides messages into packets for transmission at their source and reassembles the packets into messages at the destination. A PDN may be public or private. Several communications companies provide this service to the public. For public networks, users make connection locally and pay based upon the number of packets transmitted. The PDN provides the circuits and message delivery facilities. Same as X.25 network.

packet switching   The transmission of messages by dividing the message into fixed length packets and then routing the packets to the recipient. Packets may be sent over different paths and arrive out of order. At the receiving end, the packets are re-ordered. Routing is determined during transmission of the packet. See also circuit switching.

packet switching equipment (PSE)   Equipment that accepts and forwards messages in a packet distribution network.

parity error   An error detection scheme in which a bit is added to each character when transmitted, to bring the total number of 1 bits in the code representation of each character up to either an even number (even parity) or an odd number (odd parity).

path   A group of links that allows a message to move from its point of origin to its destination.

permanent virtual circuit (PVC)   One of three types of connection for a packet distribution network. A PVC provides a permanent link (like a leased line) between two nodes. It is usually selected when two nodes require continual transmission.

phase jitter   A variation in the phase of a continuous signal from cycle to cycle.

phase modulation   A change in the phase of a carrier signal. Commonly used alone or in conjunction with amplitude modulation to provide high-speed transmission (4800 bits per second and higher).

phase shift keying (PSK)   A form of phase modulation.

physical layer   One of the layers of the International Standards Organization's open systems interconnection standards. The physical layer specifies the electrical connections between the transmission medium and the computing system.

physical unit (PU)   In SNA, a hardware unit. Four physical units have been defined: Type 5, host processor; Type 4, communications controller; Type 2, cluster or programmable controller; and Type 1, a terminal or controller that is not programmable.

plain text   Unencrypted data.

point-to-point connection   Terminal or processor configuration in which two and only two devices are connected by a communications link. Contrasted with multi-point and multiplexed configurations.

polar working   One method used to implement current loop transmission.

polling   A line-sharing technique. Terminals and workstations attached to the line are asked by a host system if they have data to transmit. The data sent to the workstations to ask if they have data to send is called a poll string. Each workstation must have an address. Workstations can only transmit when the host asks them to. The addresses of stations to be polled are maintained by the host in a poll list. The host is sometimes called the primary station and the workstations are called secondary stations.

hub polling   The terminals become involved in the polling process by sending the poll string to the next station on the poll list.

roll call polling   The primary station obtains a list of addresses for terminals on the line and then proceeds sequentially down the list, polling each terminal in turn.

postal, telephone, and telegraph (PTT)   A government or quasi-government agency responsible for providing telecommunications systems. A PTT is found in countries other than the United States.

presentation layer One of the layers of the International Standards Organization's open systems interconnection standard. The presentation layer addresses message formats.

primary center A telephone company Class 3 office. A primary center is one station higher than a toll center.

primary station The station designated as the supervisor in a polled configuration.

private branch exchange (PBX) Telephone switching equipment located on corporate premises and owned by the corporation. A PBX allows telephone calls within an office to be connected locally without using the telephone company's end office or transmission circuits.

private line The lines deployed and controlled by the user rather than a common carrier.

propagation delay The amount of time it takes for a signal to travel from its source to its destination.

protocol Convention used for establishing transmission rules. Protocols are used to establish rules for delineation of data, error detection, control sequences, message lengths, media access , and so on.

public lines Those lines provided by a common carrier such as a telephone company.

pulse code modulation (PCM) A method for transmitting data in digital format.

quadbit A technique in which each signal carries four bits of data. Requires 16 different signals.

quadrature amplitude modulation (QAM) A modulation technique using both phase and amplitude modulation.

read-only memory (ROM) Computer memory that may be read but not modified. Used to store programs or data not subject to change.

receiver A device or user that is the destination of a message.

recovery The act of restoring a system to operational status following a failure.

regional center A Class 1 telephone switching office.

reliability The probability that the system will continue to function over a given time period.

remote job entry (RJE) An application of data communications. Batches of data are collected at a remote site and transmitted to a host for processing. In early implementations the input was card format and the output was printer format (between the remote terminals and host processor).

request A user sends a message to the system asking for a service, such as logon, logoff, or information.

request to send (RTS) A signal between a modem and data terminal equipment for initiating data transmission.

response The answer to a request. A response can also be an error message, such as invalid password response to a logon request.

response time The amount of time required for a user to receive a reply to his or her request. Usually the elapsed time between the user typing ENTER to send the request (or the equivalent) and the return of the first character of the response.

reverse channel Allows transmission in both directions on a line that is essentially half duplex. The reverse channel generally has a lower transmission rate than the forward channel and is used to acknowledge receipt of data. Reverse channels help reduce the need for modem turnaround.

routing An algorithm used to determine how to move a message from its source to its destination. Several algorithms are used.

adaptive A routing algorithm that evaluates the existing paths and chooses the one that will provide the best path for a message. Routes may change due to congestion and path failures.

broadcast Routing in which the message is broadcast to all stations. Only the stations to which the message is addressed accept it.

centralized One node in the network is charged with the responsibility of determining the path between nodes in the network. It determines the routing tables and distributes them to each other node.

distributed Each node calculates its own routing table based on status information periodically received from other nodes.

static A form of routing in which one particular path between two nodes is always used.

virtual There is no permanently established path; instead, each node consults its routing table to determine which node should next receive the message.

weighted   When multiple paths exist, each is given a weight according to perceived utilization. A random number is generated to determine which of the available paths to use based upon their weights.

RS-232-C standard   An Electronic Industries Association (EIA) standard for asynchronous transmission.

RS-366 standard   An Electronic Industries Association (EIA) standard for automatic call unit interface.

RS-449 standard   An Electronic Industries Association (EIA) standard that improves on the capabilities of RS-232-C.

secondary station   In a multi-point terminal network only one station is designated as the primary station (supervisor) and the others are secondary stations. Secondary stations may only transmit data when the primary station gives permission.

sectional center   In the telephone network, a Class 2 telephone switching center.

security   Security is a delaying tactic. Physical security is intended to deny access to a facility. Transmission and data security are intended to restrict access to authorized users., Typical security measures include identification and authentication (passwords), data encryption, user profiles, and so on. Security does not prevent unauthorized access to a system but simply makes it more difficult.

seek time, disk   In disk accessing, the time it takes to move the read/write heads to the proper cylinder.

select   In a multi-drop terminal configuration, stations are polled to determine if they have data to send and selected to determine if the terminals are ready to receive data.

sender   The initiator or transmitter of a message.

server   The routine, process, or node that provides a common service for one or more other entities. In one configuration for online transaction processing, application programs act as servers for users' requests. This is called a requester server environment.

session   The dialogue between two system users.

session layer   One of the layers of the International Standards Organization's open systems interconnection standard. The session layer is responsible for establishing a dialogue between applications.

short-haul modem   See modem, short haul.

simplex transmission   A mode of data transmission in which data may flow in only one direction. One station is always a sender and another is always a receiver over a simplex link.

six-bit transcode (SBT)   An IBM six-bit data code developed for use in remote job entry.

space   Asynchronous transmission term for a 0 bit.

star network   A network topology using a central system to which all other nodes are connected. All data is transmitted to or through the central system.

start bit   In asynchronous transmission the line state is changed from one state to another to indicate that a bit is about to arrive. The change in line state represents one bit and is called the start bit. The start bit is a 0 bit, also known as a space.

start-stop protocol   See asynchronous transmission.

status   The operational state of the computing system. A status message may be transmitted to all or selected system users.

stop bit   In asynchronous transmission, after the start bit, character bits, and optional parity bit are transmitted, a stop bit is sent to end the character. This bit is called a stop bit and is a 1 bit, also known as a mark.

store and forward   When transmitting data between two nodes, the messages are logged at intermediate nodes, which then forward them to the next node.

switched connection   A communications link established when one station dials a telephone number to connect to the other station. A switched connection uses voice circuits. The circuit exists for the duration of the session.

switched virtual circuit (SVC)   One of three types of circuits in a packet distribution network. When a session is required between two users, an end-to-end circuit is determined and allocated for the duration of the session. Similar to a switched connection.

synchronous   A transmission protocol where the sender and receiver are synchronized. Data is generally transmitted in blocks, rather than a character at a time as in asynchronous transmission.

synchronous data link control (SDLC)   A positional synchronous protocol that operates in full duplex or half duplex modes in both point-to-point and multi-point configurations. Data is transmitted in fixed-format frames consisting of start flag, address, control information, block check character (CRC), and end-of-frame flag. SDLC is an IBM protocol similar to HDLC.

Systems Network Architecture (SNA)   IBM's architecture for building a computer network. Encompasses hardware and software components, establishing sessions between users, and capabilities like office and message/file distribution services.

Systems Network Architecture Distribution Services (SNADS)   An SNA facility that provides asynchronous distribution of documents throughout the network.

systems services control point (SSCP)   In IBM's SNA, the process that controls a domain. It is responsible for initiating network components, establishing sessions, and maintaining unit status.

telecommunications   The transmission of data by electromagnetic systems. Includes telephone, telegraphy, video, computer data transmission, and so on.

telecommunications access method (TCAM)   One of IBM's telecommunications access methods.

telecommuting   A term applied to workers using data communications links between home and office to do their work. This allows them to work at home using terminals or workstations to obtain and submit their work.

Telenet   A public data network offered by General Telephone and Electronics Corporation.

teleprocessing monitor (TP monitor)   See transaction control process.

teletypewriter (TTY)   A terminal originally used in telegraphy. TTYs are also used as terminals in data communications networks. The term *TTY* has become generic for a class of dumb asynchronous terminals.

terminal   An input and/or output device that may be connected to a local or remote computer, called a host computer.

   dumb   Passively serves for input and/or output but does no local processing. Generally, it has no data buffer and operates in asynchronous mode.

   intelligent   Characterized by microcomputers. They can participate in the data-processing requirements of the system by assuming some of the processing functions required of the host for terminals that are not intelligent.

   smart   More actively involved in the network than dumb terminals. In general they have memory to store one or more pages of data to be received or transmitted, provide the ability to protect fields, are controllable from the host processor, operate in synchronous mode, and allow page mode operations.

testing

   functional   Done at the program and subprogram levels, to assure that the logic is correct.

   integrated   Involves the integration of programs into a system to ensure that different modules fit together. Sometimes referred to as systems testing.

   stress   Involves testing the system under load conditions to ensure that performance parameters are met.

   system   Same as integrated testing.

throughput   The amount of work performed by a system per unit of time.

time-out interval   A period of time allowed for an event to occur. If the event does not happen, the time-out expires and the process initiating the event is notified.

toll office   In the telephone network, a toll center is a Class 4 switching office.

transaction   A user-specified group of processing activities that are either entirely completed or, if not completed, leave the database and processing system in a consistent state.

transaction control process (TCP)   A process that receives inputs from terminals and routes them to the proper application processes. TCPs also may edit input data, format data to and from a terminal, log messages, and provide terminal job sequencing. Examples include IBM's CICS and Tandem's Pathway. Also called a teleprocessing monitor or message control system.

transaction rate   The number of transactions submitted or processed per unit of time. To be meaningful it must also include a description of the amount of work accomplished by the transaction. For example, processing ten transactions per second is meaningful only when the transaction activity is defined.

transfer time   In disk accessing, the amount of time required for the data to be moved from the disk to the processor's memory. In data communications, the amount of time required for a message to move from the sender to the receiver.

transparency   The ability to send any bit string as data in a message. The data bits will not be interpreted as control characters.

transponder   In satellite communications, a transponder receives the transmission from Earth (uplink), amplifies the signal, changes frequency, and retransmits the data to a receiving Earth station (downlink).

transport layer   One of the layers of the International Standards Organization's open systems interconnection standard. The transport layer is responsible for generating the end user's address and for the integrity of the receipt of message blocks.

tribits   A method of modulation that allows three bits to be represented by each signal. See dibits and quadbits.

value-added network   Same as packet distribution network (PDN).

vertical redundancy check (VRC)   The same as parity error checking. For each character transmitted an additional bit, the parity bit, is attached to help detect errors. The bit is chosen so that the number of 1 bits is even (even parity) or odd (odd parity).

virtual telecommunications access method (VTAM)   One of IBM's telecommunications access methods.

wait for positive acknowledgment (WACK)   A character used both to positively acknowledge receipt of a block and also to tell the sending station to wait before transmitting further.

white noise   One source of data communication errors. It results from the normal movements of electrons and is present in all transmission media at temperatures above absolute zero.

workstation   A term applied to microcomputers or personal productivity devices.

X.3   A CCITT standard for packet assembly/disassembly (PAD) in a packet distribution network.

X.25   A CCITT interface specification for data terminal and data circuit termination equipment in a packet distribution network.

X.28   A CCITT interface for asynchronous terminal interface to a PAD in a packet distribution network.

X.29   A CCITT interface for exchange of data and control information between PADs or a PAD and a terminal having PAD capabilities in a packet distribution network.

X.75   A CCITT recommendation for an interface between two packet distribution networks.

XOFF   A status signal used to control the flow of data to a terminal. The XOFF signal is raised when the terminal does not want the host to send more data.

XON   A status signal used to control the flow of data to a terminal. The XON signal is raised when the terminal wants the host to send more data.

Index